A Love Affair with Southern Cooking

ALSO BY JEAN ANDERSON

*The Doubleday Cookbook** (with Elaine Hanna)
The Family Circle Cookbook (with the food editors of *Family Circle*)
*Half a Can of Tomato Paste and Other Culinary Dilemmas*** (with Ruth Buchan)
The New Doubleday Cookbook (with Elaine Hanna)
*The Food of Portugal****
The New German Cookbook (with Hedy Würz)
The American Century Cookbook
The Good Morning America Cut the Calories Cookbook (co-edited with Sara Moulton)
Dinners in a Dish or a Dash
*Process This!*****
Quick Loaves

* Winner, R. T. French Tastemaker Award, Best Basic Cookbook of the Year (1975)
and Best Cookbook of the Year Overall (1975)
**Winner, Seagram/International Association of Culinary Professionals Award,
Best Specialty Cookbook of the Year (1980)
*** Winner, Seagram/International Association of Culinary Professionals Award,
Best Foreign Cookbook of the Year (1986)
**** Winner, James Beard Cookbook Awards, Best Cookbook, Tools & Techniques
Category (2003)

A Love Affair
with Southern Cooking

Recipes and Recollections

Jean Anderson

WM
WILLIAM MORROW
An Imprint of HarperCollinsPublishers

Grateful acknowledgment is made for permission to reprint:

Algonquin Books of Chapel Hill: Honeysuckle Sorbet from *Seasoned in the South* by Bill Smith. Copyright © 2005 by Bill Smith.

Allen W. Mead, M.D.: Crab Cups, Hominy Soufflé, and Shrimp Aspic from *Please Kiss the Cook* by Anne S. Mead. Copyright © 1964 by Anne S. Mead.

Beaumont Inn: General Robert E. Lee Cake from *Beaumont Inn Special Recipes*, compiled by Mary Elizabeth Dedman and Thomas Curry Dedman, Jr. Copyright © 1983 by The Beaumont Inn, Harrodsburg, KY.

Pleasant Hill Press: Chicken Hash and Indian Griddle Cakes from *We Make You Kindly Welcome* by Elizabeth C. Kremer. Copyright © 1970 by Pleasant Hill Press, Harrodsburg, KY. Also Glazed Lemon Tea Bread and Bourbon Balls from *Welcome Back to Pleasant Hill* by Elizabeth C. Kremer. Copyright © 1977 by Pleasant Hill Press, Harrodsburg, KY.

University of North Carolina Press: Sweet Slaw from *Mama Dip's Family Cookbook* by Mildred Council. Copyright © 2005 by Mildred Council. Sweet Potato Salad from *Not Afraid of Flavor: Recipes from Magnolia Grill* by Ben and Karen Barker. Copyright © 2000 by Ben and Karen Barker. Mrs. Lee's Cake (heirloom version) from *The Robert E. Lee Family Cooking and Housekeeping Book* by Anne C. Zimmer. Copyright © 1997 by the University of North Carolina Press.

I should also like to thank Condé Nast Publications, Inc., for permission to use the following recipes originally published in *Gourmet* in feature articles of mine about the South: Bananas Foster Cheesecake, Black-Eyed Pea Hummus, Broiled Oysters with Roasted Pecan Pesto, Bronzed Shrimp Creole, Creole Sauce, Corn Custards with Carrot Vinaigrette, Creamy Tasso Grits, Fried Okra and Crawfish Salad with Basil Vinaigrette, Shrimp Rémoulade on Fried Green Tomatoes, and Spiced Blackberry and Cornmeal Cobbler.

Thanks, too, to *Bon Appétit* for permission to reprint the following recipes, which appeared over the years in articles I have written: Baked Virginia Ham, Black-Eyed Pea Soup with Greens and Ham, Bourbon Custard, Lisa Ruffin Harrison's Herbed Crab Salad and Fresh Herb Mayonnaise, Maria Harrison's Batter Bread, Meri Major's Crab Soup, Nannie Hall Davis's "French" Pudding, Old-Fashioned Virginia Gingerbread with Brown Sugar Sauce, Peanut Bisque, and Sweet Potato Biscuits.

Gratitude goes, in addition, to *More* magazine for permission to reprint Beaufort Quail Jambalaya.

Finally, I'd like to add that a number of recipes in this book appeared in different form in southern food articles that I've written over the years for *Family Circle* and *Food & Wine*. All rights have reverted to me as author; still I'd like to acknowledge the magazines in which my articles originally appeared.

HarperCollins books may be purchased for educational, business, or sales promotional use. For information please write: Special Markets Department, HarperCollins Publishers, 10 East 53rd Street, New York, NY 10022.

FIRST EDITION

Designed by Lorie Pagnozzi

Library of Congress Cataloging-in-Publication Data

Anderson, Jean.
  A love affair with southern cooking: recipes and recollections / Jean Anderson.
     p. cm.
  ISBN: 978-0-06-076178-3
  ISBN-10: 0-06-076178-4
    1. Cookery, American—Southern style.

TX715.2.S68 A53 2007
641'.5975—dc22

             2006053079

07 08 09 10 11 WBC/QW 10 9 8 7 6 5 4 3 2 1

 For the Southerners,
past and present,
who have enriched my life

CONTENTS

Acknowledgments

I should like to thank, first and foremost, my good friend and colleague Joanne Lamb Hayes not only for telling me about the foods of her Maryland childhood but also for lending a hand with the recipe testing and development. Few food people are more professional, more creative, or more dedicated.

In addition, I'd like to thank my two nieces, Linda and Kim Anderson, for sharing recipes from the "southern side of their family." My gratitude, too, to Betsy Thomas and Georgia Downard, who double-checked a number of the recipes; also to Debbie Moose and Clyde Satterwhite, who assisted with sidebar research.

Down the years as I've traveled the South on article assignment, friends, acquaintances, colleagues—even strangers—have taught me about the dishes popular in their particular corners of the South and served them forth with hearty helpings of history plus snippets of gossip, legend, and lore. Many of them have graciously put treasured family recipes into my hands, many of them printed here for the first time.

I am indebted to one and all: Bea Armstrong; Anne Lewis Anderson; Janet L. Appel, Director, Shirley Plantation; Dorothy Bailey; Marcelle Bienvenue; Donna Brazile; Jennifer S. Broadwater, Shaker Village of Pleasant Hill, Kentucky; Rose Ellwood Bryan; Mrs. Pegram A. Bryant; Ruth Current; Chuck Dedman, Beaumont Inn, Harrodsburg, Kentucky; "Miz Nannie Grace" Dishman; Nancy Blackard Dobbins; Judith London Evans; Damon Lee Fowler; Mrs. Franklin (I wish I could remember the first name of this early Raleigh neighbor who taught me so much).

Deepest thanks, too, to Dr. and Mrs. William C. Friday; Jean Todd Freeman; Laura Frost; Pauline Gordon; "Miss Tootie" Guirard; Mr. and Mrs. James G. Harrison; Lisa Ruffin Harrison, Evelynton Plantation; Mr. and Mrs. Malcolm Jamieson, Berkeley Plantation; Sally Belk King; Elizabeth C. Kremer; Jane Kronsberg; Lorna Langley; Linn Lesesne; Meri Major, Belle Air Plantation; Betsy Marsh; Eleanor Haywood Mason; Garnet McCollum; Dr. and Mrs. Allen W. Mead; Amy Moore; Helen Moore; Mrs. Carey Mumford, Sr.; Nancy Ijames Myers; Virginia

Mumford Nance; Moreton Neal; Madeline Nevill; Chan Patterson; Nancy Mumford Pencsak; David Perry; Fleming Pfann; Annie Pool; "Miz Suzie" Rankin; Maria Harrison Reuge; Rick Robinson; Tom Robinson; Mary Frances Schinhan; Mary Sheppard; Mary Seymour; Florence Gray Soltys; Elizabeth Hedgecock Sparks; Kim Sunée; Pauline Thompson; Payne Tyler, Sherwood Forest Plantation, Virginia; Janet Trent; Kathy Underhill; Jeanne Appleton Voltz; Cile Freeman Waite; Lillian Waldron; Lois Watkins; Virginia Wilson; Lenora Yates; and not least, those gifted North Carolina Home Demonstration Club cooks from Manteo to Murphy.

Further, I'd like to thank these singular southern chefs for ongoing inspiration: Ben and Karen Barker of Magnolia Grill, Durham, North Carolina, Robert Carter, Peninsula Grill, Charleston; Mildred Council, Mama Dip's Country Kitchen, Chapel Hill; Marcel Desaulniers, The Trellis, Williamsburg, Virginia; John Fleer, Blackberry Farm, Walland, Tennessee; Scott Howell, Nana's and Q Shack, Durham, North Carolina; Patrick O'Connell, The Inn at Little Washington, Washington, Virginia; Louis Osteen, Louis's at Pawley's, Pawley's Island, South Carolina; Paul Prudhomme, K-Paul's Louisiana Kitchen, New Orleans; Walter Royal, Angus Barn, Raleigh; Bill Smith, Crook's Corner, Chapel Hill; Brian Stapleton, The Carolina Inn, Chapel Hill; Robert Stehling, Hominy Grill, Charleston; Frank Stitt, Highlands Bar and Grill, Birmingham; Elizabeth Terry and Kelly Yambour, Elizabeth on 37th, Savannah; plus two who left us too soon: Bill Neal, Crook's Corner, Chapel Hill, and Jamie Shannon, Commander's Palace, New Orleans.

No acknowledgments would be complete without thanking food writer Jim Villas and his mother, Martha Pearl Villas, for so many good southern "reads" and recipes; also cookbook author Damon Lee Fowler of Savannah and Suzanne Williamson of Beaufort, South Carolina, who taught me to make quail jambalaya one brisk December evening and also introduced me to my "dream" southern writer, Pat Conroy (Suzanne developed the recipes for *The Pat Conroy Cookbook*).

Other cookbook authors and writers about southern food must also be named because they have inspired and educated me over the years: Brett Anderson (no relation); the late R. W. "Johnny" Apple (southerner by marriage); Roy Blount, Jr.; Rick Bragg; Marion Brown; Joseph E. Dabney; John Egerton; John T. Edge; Marcie Cohen Ferris; Donna Florio; Bob Garner; Karen Hess; Sally Belk King; Ronni Lundy; Debbie Moose; Bill Neal; Frances Gray Patton (whose short stories so often featured food); Marjorie Kinnan Rawlings; Julia Reed; Dori Sanders; Elizabeth Hedgecock Sparks; John Martin Taylor; and Fred Thompson.

I'm indebted to Elizabeth Sims of the Biltmore Estate in Asheville for introducing me to the prize-winning Biltmore wines; to Dave Tomsky, formerly of the Grove Park Inn, his wife, Nan, and Tex Harrison, all of Asheville, for providing an insider's view of their city; and to Sue Johnson-Langdon, executive director of the North Carolina SweetPotato Commission, for a mountain of information of the state's top crop. I would also be remiss if I didn't holler "thanks" to John M. Williams, who kept fresh Georgia pecans coming for recipe testing, and Belinda Ellis, of White Lily Flour, who sent me not only a detailed history of this Tennessee miller but also bags of flour to ensure that the cakes and biscuits coming out of my test kitchen oven were as light as they should be.

Thanks go, too, to Sara Moulton, best friend and colleague for more than twenty-five years, who agreed to write the foreword to this book. I take credit for introducing Sara to my home state of North Carolina and she's returned many times.

Penultimate thanks to David Black, my agent and anchor, who found a home for this book; and two Harper editors: first Susan Friedland, who liked my different take on southern cooking enough to buy the book, and second, Hugh Van Dusen, for his editorial wisdom and guidance throughout.

Finally, I must thank *Bon Appétit*, *Gourmet*, and *More* magazines for granting permission for me to reprint the southern recipes that first appeared there in feature articles I'd written.

Foreword
by Sara Moulton

I hardly knew a thing about southern cuisine until I started working with Jean Anderson—although I'd known Jean herself for years. In fact, getting to know her was a New York thing. She had an apartment in the same building as my parents, the building overlooking Gramercy Park in which I grew up. She also had a bunch of New York jobs—freelancing for all the major food and travel magazines.

But it wasn't until I was out of cooking school myself, with half a dozen years of restaurant experience under my belt, that I began to get an idea of just how much culinary range Jean possessed. Between the time I stopped working in restaurants and began working at *Gourmet*, I apprenticed myself to Jean. I traveled with her to Portugal, Brazil, and Holland, helping to *shlep* her camera equipment (Jean's a great photographer, too) and tasting and discussing a new world's worth of food.

Jean's southern roots remained fuzzy to me until about ten years ago, when she left New York after forty-one years and returned to the Raleigh/Durham/Chapel Hill area where she grew up. I've visited her there four times, and every time I go it becomes the Full Immersion North Carolina Food Orgy. All three of the Best Triangle Restaurants in Durham. Pulled pork at the A&M Grill in Mebane. Deep-fried turkey in Sanford. Stacked pies at Mama Dip's. The Gingerbread House Contest in Asheville. Not to mention country ham in fresh-baked biscuits for breakfast at Jean's place. I eat like an electric pig (as Jean herself likes to say), and then I take the recipes back up north with me. I've told the world about them on my Food Network shows, prepared them to beguile my lunch guests at *Gourmet*, and served them up to the delight of my family at home. But finally I'm just a tourist below the Mason-Dixon Line. My friend Jean, a southern girl returned to her roots, knows southern cuisine from the ground up. Like all of the rest of her twenty-odd cookbooks, *A Love Affair with Southern Cooking* is distinguished by superb scholarship and recipes that deliver deep-dish authenticity and big flavor in equal measure.

It's also great reading, juicy with a lifetime's worth of personal reminiscences and Southern lore, all of it smart as a fresh coat of paint and much of it very funny. Jean tells me the book is a labor of love. We're all the richer for her willingness to share that love.

Introduction

I fell in love with southern cooking at the age of five. And a piece of brown sugar pie was all it took.

I'd just begun first grade at Fred A. Olds Elementary School in Raleigh, North Carolina, where I was born, and had chosen that pie over all the other desserts in the school cafeteria. The look of it fascinated me: a barely set filling that was crackly brown on top and the color of comb honey underneath.

That day I ate dessert first, pushing aside my pork chops and collards. I had never tasted anything so luxurious. It was like toffee softened on a sunny windowsill and it salved my budding sweet tooth. From that day on, I ate brown sugar pie as often as possible, sometimes taking two pieces instead of one.

Back then, there were good African American cooks in public school kitchens preparing everything fresh every day: southern fried chicken, smothered pork chops, greens or beans simmered with side meat, banana pudding, and of course that ambrosial brown sugar pie. All of it was new to me—the start of a culinary adventure that continues to this day.

But let me back up a bit. Why, you may wonder, did it take me five years to discover southern cooking if I'd been born in Raleigh? There's an easy answer.

Both of my parents were Yankees, Midwesterners to be exact; my mother came from Illinois, my father, Ohio. Not even my older brother could claim to be a Tar Heel; he was born in Vienna while my father was teaching there. I am the first person on either side of my family to be born south of the Mason-Dixon line—a distinction I am proud of.

To be honest, I think the fact that my parents *weren't southern* is the very reason why I've been absorbed with southern food (indeed with all things southern) since the age of five. I also believe that it gives me a different approach to it: I've always been more student than insider.

From the very beginning, every bite of something southern—of Sally Lunn, for example, of hush puppies or hoppin' John—was a new experience for me, something exciting, something special. I loved the funny recipe names and adored hearing the stories behind them (my mother's pot roast and gooseberry pie were never dished up with anecdotes).

Mother was a good cook—but a *midwestern* cook. So we ate the Illinois dishes her mother had taught her, along with a few New England recipes she'd picked up while at Wellesley and a few more from her young married years in Austria. I remember roast lamb in particular, a meat none of my southern friends would touch; baked ham (a pink packing-house ham, never Smithfield or country ham); parsnips or rutabaga boiled and mashed like potatoes (she had to order these specially back then); Boston brown bread (never corn bread and rarely biscuits); roasted or fricasseed chicken (never southern fried). I also remember eating beef heart and tongue, even rabbit fricasseed like chicken.

The things my school chums' mothers cooked always seemed much more appealing, exotic even. So I'd go home with them after school every chance I got, hoping that I'd be invited to stay for dinner; I often was. There might be crispy fried chicken or stuffed pork chops, sweet slaw, yellow squash pudding, fresh-baked biscuits, and—cross fingers—sweet potato pudding or pecan pie for dessert.

All through grade school and high school I reveled in the southern cooking I was served at the homes of friends; at parties given by Daddy's colleagues at North Carolina State College; at the S & W Cafeteria, where we went every Christmas Eve; and, yes, in the public school cafeterias. There was no prefabbed food back then, no vending machines coughing up cookies and colas.

Early on I began collecting southern recipes, and my mother was happy for me to try them as long as I "left the kitchen spic and span." Occasionally I would cook a complete southern dinner, and there were no complaints. My mother,

however, remained a strictly midwestern cook except for Country Captain, her dinner party staple; watermelon rind pickles; and two or three other southern recipes friends and neighbors had given her.

Sent north for college, I hurried south after graduation and went to work for the North Carolina Agricultural Extension Service, first as an assistant home agent in Iredell County about halfway between Raleigh and the Great Smokies, then nine months later as woman's editor in the Raleigh office. That job kept me on the road covering 4-H and home demonstration club functions from one end of the state to the other— from "Manteo to Murphy" (ocean to mountains).

Talk about food! There were mountains of it always—at club meetings and picnics, at pig pickin's and fish fries, at country fairs and cook-offs, many of which I was drafted to judge. In Iredell County, August was picnic month with a home demonstration club feast every night and sometimes two. It was here that I first tasted spectacular batter-fried chicken, pulled pork (barbecue), and biscuits so light they nearly levitated. Here, too, that I became acquainted with Jerusalem artichoke pickles, Japanese fruitcake, and wild persimmon pudding, all of which seemed to be accompanied by a colorful story.

These country women were born cooks and their club picnics were potluck affairs with everyone bringing strut-their-stuff recipes. It didn't take me long to discover whose fried chicken was the best, whose corn pudding, whose coconut cake.

A few years later I became a New York magazine editor (first at *The Ladies' Home Journal*, then at *Venture: The Traveler's World*, and finally at *Family Circle*), and I was often sent south to interview a good home cook or hot new chef and told to bring their best recipes back to be tested and published. My editors, most of them New Yorkers, considered me southern, and I must say that at the time my accent was as thick as sourwood honey.

Later, as a freelance food and travel writer contributing regularly to *Bon Appétit*, *Family Circle*, *Food & Wine*, and *Gourmet*, I spent even more time down south, researching and writing major features in nearly every state: Alabama, Florida, Georgia, Kentucky, Louisiana, Maryland, Mississippi, North and South Carolina, Tennessee, Virginia. I was in hog heaven.

I interviewed cooks homespun and haute, I ate in barbecue joints and crab shacks as well as at hallowed regional restaurants. I learned to milk cows and goats, to surf-cast for rockfish and drum, to gather wild persimmons and ramps. I was threatened once by a swarm of honey bees and another time—even scarier—by hundreds of stampeding turkeys.

I toured a herring cannery, catfish and crawfish farms, I slogged through cane fields and rice paddies, and I picked-my-own at peach and pecan orchards. I even went crabbing with a Chesapeake Bay waterman and floated about the Atchafalaya Swamp in a Cajun pirogue (canoe).

There were headier tours, too: at McCormick's spicy headquarters in Baltimore; the Maker's Mark Distillery in Loretto, Kentucky; the 200-year-old Winkler Bakery in Old Salem, North Carolina; and the eye-tearing Tabasco plant at Avery Island, Louisiana.

Over the years, I've received valuable one-on-one cooking lessons and I'll forever be grateful to the Southerners who showed me the light: the Virginia farm woman who taught me to bake a proper batter bread, the Cajun who demonstrated the right way to make a roux, the South Carolina plantation cook who revealed her secret fail-safe method of cooking rice. But there were many others who passed along their culinary expertise as well as their place-of-pride recipes. You'll read about them in the pages that follow.

For this is as much culinary memoir, indeed culinary love letter, as cookbook. It is not—*repeat not*—"the definitive southern cookbook." Nor was it ever intended to be.

I simply want to share the experiences—the amusing, the unique—that I've had in forty-something years of crisscrossing the South, specifically Alabama, the two Carolinas, Florida, Georgia, Kentucky, Louisiana, Maryland, Mississippi, Tennessee, and Virginia. For these eleven southern states are the ones where I've spent the most time.

I want to introduce you to the characters I've met along the way as well as to the friends I've made. My aim, moreover, is to pass along the South's rich culinary history, the gossipy stories Southerners love to tell, the snippets of folklore, and not least the precious insight I've gained by watching Southerners cook—in the mid South and Deep South, on seashore and mountaintop.

My passion for southern cooking shows no sign of cooling, and it's this passion that I'm eager to share along with a life's worth of recipes and recollections.

—Jean Anderson
Chapel Hill, North Carolina

The city of the world where you can

eat and drink the most and suffer the least.

—William Makepeace Thackeray, on New Orleans

How to Use This Book

First, please read this section carefully. The information given here includes basics that will assist you as you cook.

- Before beginning any recipe in this book, read it—twice, if necessary—so that you know exactly what you are to do. Also check to see that you have all necessary ingredients and equipment.
- Before you begin cooking, measure all recipe ingredients and do as much advance prep as possible (peeling, slicing, chunking, and so forth) so that you don't have to pause mid-recipe.
- Do not use one ingredient in place of another unless a recipe suggests substitutions.
- Pan sizes and shapes are essential to a recipe's success, so never substitute one pan for another unless alternates are specified.

Note: *For baking, I recommend that you use light-colored pans (preferably aluminum). Dark pans as well as those lined with dark nonstick coatings tend to overbrown breads, cakes, cookies, and pie crusts.*

- If a recipe tells you to "cool" something, let it come to room temperature.
- If a recipe directs you to "chill" something, refrigerate it or set it in an ice bath until uniformly cold.
- Always preheat an oven for 20 minutes, a broiler for 15 minutes.

Unless specified to the contrary

- Eggs are large.
- Butter is old-fashioned, unsalted stick butter. Use nothing else in the recipes in this book unless substitutes are given.
- Lard is rendered hog fat, *not* vegetable shortening. Many southern butchers, groceries, and supermarkets routinely carry it. Elsewhere, Hispanic groceries would be the place to look. When I lived in New York, my neighborhood Food Emporium (a high-end A & P) carried the Armour brand of lard.
- Cornmeal is usually stone-ground (see Sources, page 401). If granular supermarket cornmeal is intended, recipes will specify that.

- Rice may be "converted" (Uncle Ben's) or long-grain (Carolina). Recipes will specify which one to use for best results.
- Flour is all-purpose flour—a good balance of soft and hard wheats—*unless* a soft southern flour is called for.

Note: *Always sift flour before you measure it even if the label says "presifted," because flour compacts in transit and storage. To measure: Spoon the sifted flour lightly into a dry cup measure (these are the nested cups in 1-cup, ½-cup, ⅓-cup, and ¼-cup sizes), then level off the surface with the edge of a small, thin-blade spatula. Breads (especially biscuits), cakes, and pastries made with unsifted flour will never be as flaky or feathery as those made with sifted flour.*

- Sour cream is measured tightly packed in a dry measuring cup unless recipes direct otherwise. Here's how to do it: Scoop up a tablespoon of sour cream, drop it into the dry measure (see Flour, above, for a description of these measuring cups), then, using the bowl of the spoon, pack it in; repeat until the cup is full, then level off the top with the broad side of a small thin-blade spatula.

Note: *Mayonnaise, lard, and vegetable shortening are measured the same way, and jam and peanut butter often are as well. Recipes are specific about how each should be measured.*

- Light and dark brown sugars are measured tightly packed in a dry measuring cup unless a recipe directs otherwise.
- Molasses, honey, corn syrup, and other sticky liquids will slide out of measuring cups and spoons more easily if these have been well spritzed with nonstick cooking spray.

- All citrus juices (lemon, lime, orange, and grapefruit) are freshly squeezed. The one exception: Key lime juice. The bottled may be used if fresh Key limes are unavailable. (See Sources, page 401.)
- Vanilla is pure vanilla extract, never imitation. Ditto almond, orange, lemon, and rum extracts. I find artificially flavored extracts unpleasantly perfume-y. They can ruin a good cake.
- Freshly grated Parmesan cheese is *Parmigiano-Reggiano* if you can afford it. Otherwise, use a Wisconsin or Argentine Parmesan and grate it yourself. Thirty seconds or so in the food processor and the job is done.
- Black pepper is freshly ground.
- Salt is uniodized table salt because it's best for baked goods. You can of course substitute coarse or kosher salt in soups, salads, sides, and main dishes but increase amounts as needed to taste.

About Pork and Chicken

- **Pork:** Today's lean pork has had so much flavor and succulence bred out of it that I now use only a "boutique" brand like Niman Ranch. I suggest that you do the same when preparing the pork recipes in this book. You'll be happier with the results.
- **Chicken:** Chicken breasts have grown so large that a friend of mine said they'd "feed a family of four." I call them D cups. If you're roasting a chicken, the size of the breast doesn't matter. But it definitely does if you're frying chicken. I find that frying-size chickens (about 3 pounds) are now a special order.

How to Use This Book

Here's a tip: *If your supermarket or butcher has no fryers, go to the rotisserie department and sweet-talk the man in charge into selling you a raw rotisserie chicken weighing 2½ to 3 pounds. If he won't disjoint it for you, perhaps the butcher will. That's what I was forced to do when testing the fried chicken recipes in this book.*

About Pasteurized Eggs

Many old southern recipes call for raw eggs or ones that are not sufficiently cooked to destroy the salmonella bacteria that may (or may not) be present. It's said that only one in 10,000 eggs may be infected; still, using raw eggs is rather like playing Russian roulette. I'd rather be safe than sorry. So whenever I think it advisable to use pasteurized eggs in a particular recipe, I say so. Fortunately, you can now buy pasteurized eggs at some supermarkets and specialty groceries (Davidson is the brand my markets carry). Pasteurized eggs can be used in place of raw eggs in any recipe; their whites are slightly cloudy and take longer to whip to stiff peaks than raw egg whites. Otherwise, I see no difference between the two. If pasteurized eggs are unavailable, I'd suggest buying eggs from a small local source, perhaps some trusted vendor at your farmer's market.

As for Meringues

The time it takes to brown a meringue-topped pie may not render it safe, so use pasteurized egg whites or consider one of these other options: pasteurized egg whites sold in both powdered form (Just Whites) and in liquid (the Whole Foods grocery chain now stocks little cartons of liquid pasteurized whites). You might also consider using a meringue powder (stocked by some specialty food shops and most bakery supply houses); I personally find the flavor a bit artificial, but adding a few drops of pure vanilla extract will help erase it. If none of these options is available to you, use only eggs from a local source that you trust implicitly.

Note: *The American Egg Board recently worked out a recipe for a fully cooked meringue made with unpasteurized eggs. I haven't the space to reprint it here, but you will find the recipe posted on their website: //www.aeb.org/Recipes/EggClassics/SOFTPIE MERINGUE.htm.*

About Pie Crusts

If you still make your own pastry, good for you. Many people are too busy to do so today and I occasionally plead guilty myself. Some frozen pie crusts are excellent; find a brand that you like and stick with it.

Note: *If you use a frozen pie shell, choose a deep-dish one and recrimp the crust to make a high, fluted edge. This will minimize spillovers, which so often happen with pies. Recrimping is easy: Simply move around the edge of the crust making a zigzag pattern by pinching the dough between the thumb of one hand and the index finger and thumb of the other. Takes less than a minute. Also, before you fill the pie shell, set it—still in its flimsy aluminum tin—inside a standard 9-inch pie pan; this is for added support.*

To avoid spillovers, I slide the pie onto a heavy-duty rimmed baking sheet, preheated along with the oven to ensure that the bottom crust will be as crisp as possible.

Tip: *Also now available at many supermarkets: unroll-and-use pastry circles; look for them near the refrigerated biscuits. I find these especially good for pies larger or smaller than 9 inches—the diameter of most frozen pie shells. These pastry circles are also the ones to use when you're making a two-crust pie.*

Note: *If you are using a frozen or other prepared pie crust and a recipe calls for a fully baked pie shell, bake according to package directions.*

❀

I grew up eating well—cheese grits, homemade biscuits smothered in butter, home-cured ham, red-eye gravy—and that was just breakfast.

—*OPRAH WINFREY*

❀

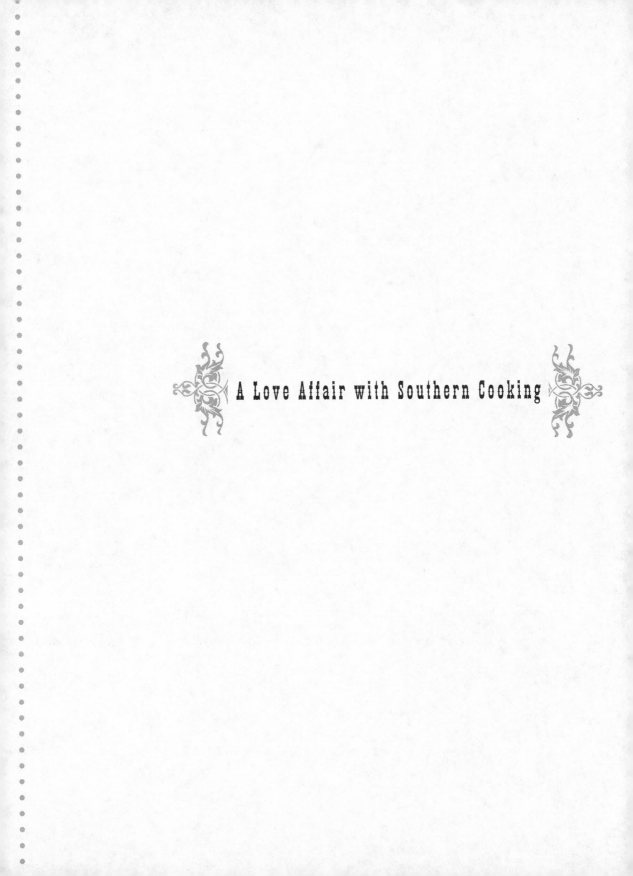

A Love Affair with Southern Cooking

A glass of wine and a bit of mutton are always ready, and such as will be content to partake of them are always welcome.

—George Washington

Appetizers and Snacks

I grew up in a southern college town where teas and open houses were the preferred way to entertain, and, being a "faculty brat," I was subjected to plenty of them. Whenever my mother was the hostess, my job was to keep the platters brimming with cheese daisies, tea sandwiches, and such.

My mother was big in clubs—the American Association of University Women (AAUW), the State College Woman's Club, the Book Exchange, the Sewing Circle—and the meetings, it seemed to me, were mostly recipe swaps. The majority of members were southern, so the recipes Mother added to her card files over the years were also southern. I have that card file today, and to riffle through it is to remember not only the recipes but also those good southern cooks who gave them to my mother.

Several of them are printed here for the first time.

The only time I remember anything alcoholic being served (except at the Carolina Country Club) was at Christmastime, when bourbon was slipped into eggnog. Most of the South was dry or semidry back then; only in New Orleans, Charleston, and parts of Florida could you buy a mixed drink.

In the North Carolina counties considered "wet," there were state-run ABC (Alcoholic Beverage Control) stores where you could buy the hard stuff. Restaurants, however, were forbidden to serve cocktails until late in the twentieth century. Incredible as it may seem, the receptionist at East Tennessee's posh Inn at Blackberry Farm told me to "bring my own" if I wanted a cocktail before dinner—in 1997! The county was still dry just ten years ago.

Throughout my childhood, the faithful preached the "evils of drink" except for "whiskey-palians" who—horrors!—drank *wine* at communion. Not so the more evangelistic denominations who preferred Welch's grape juice (and whose congregations included many a fine bootlegger).

When I was old enough to drink, the BYO (Bring Your Own) party was fashionable, but the booze had to be hidden in a brown bag in both car and restaurant. We'd order setups, sneak our brown-bagged bottles from underneath the table, then add as much bourbon, Jack Daniel's, or Southern Comfort as we wanted.

Does this explain why southern appetizers run to rib-sticking meats, cheeses, and eggs? I've always thought so; they helped "line the stomach" and sop up the booze. With no opened liquor allowed in cars, people would polish off their bottles before driving back home.

Today mixed drinks can be bought in nearly every southern town, but the Southerner's fondness for substantial appetizers persists.

What follow are such perennial favorites as barbecued meatballs, pickled shrimp, candied bacon, and boiled peanuts plus some of the truly innovative new appetizers I've enjoyed on recent travels about the South.

❧

Burn off your infested cotton! Plant Peanuts!

—GEORGE WASHINGTON CARVER

❧

BROILED OYSTERS WITH TOASTED PECAN PESTO

MAKES 4 SERVINGS

A few years ago *Gourmet* magazine sent me south to profile "Little-Known Louisiana." I'd visited New Orleans several times, also parts of Cajun Country, but I'd never spent time in the central and northern parishes (counties). Driving over from Mississippi, I entered the Felicianas or "English Louisiana." First stop: St. Francisville, high on a bluff above the great river with antebellum mansions scattered about. At The Myrtles, said to be America's "most haunted house," I encountered no ghosts. But I did discover a fine little restaurant called Kean's Carriage House. Among chef Tyler Kean's spins on southern cooking was this imaginative appetizer.

Coarse or kosher salt for anchoring the
oyster shells

¼ cup lightly toasted pecans
(10 to 12 minutes in a 350° F. oven)

2 small garlic cloves

3 cups firmly packed fresh basil leaves

2½ tablespoons coarse dry bread crumbs

2½ tablespoons freshly grated Parmesan

2½ tablespoons water

2 teaspoons fresh lemon juice

2½ tablespoons butter, at room temperature

2½ tablespoons fruity olive oil

16 oysters on the half shell

2 tablespoons finely julienned fresh basil leaves (optional garnish)

1. Preheat the broiler. Spread enough coarse salt in a large shallow roasting pan for a layer about 1/2 inch thick; set aside.
2. Whiz the pecans, garlic, basil leaves, bread crumbs, Parmesan, water, and lemon juice in a food processor or an electric blender at high speed until reduced to paste. Add the butter and olive oil and churn until smooth. Set the pecan pesto aside.
3. Carefully remove the oysters from their shells and reserve. Wash and dry the shells, then bed in the pan of salt.
4. Return the oysters to their shells, set in the broiler 3 inches from the heat, and broil for 4 minutes. Remove the pan from the broiler and spoon the reserved pesto over the oysters, dividing the total amount evenly. Return to the broiler and broil for 4 to 5 minutes or until bubbling and lightly browned.
5. Arrange four oysters on each of four heated small plates; garnish, if you like, with a little of the julienned basil, and serve hot as a first course.

PICKLED OYSTERS

MAKES 6 TO 8 SERVINGS
. . . .

Pickled oysters are a cocktail favorite wherever oysters are fresh, plump, and flavorful, meaning most of the South. The hostesses I know like to mound them in small crystal bowls, top them off with a little of the pickling liquid, and pass with toothpicks so that guests can "go spear-fishing." Though the red serranos add color, I suggest sprigging the bowl with fresh dill umbels or sprigs of Italian parsley. Come to think of it, small fennel umbels would also be attractive and appropriate. **Note:** *Because cooking clouds the oyster liquid, I pour it through a coffee filter–lined sieve directly onto the oysters and spices. Makes for a prettier presentation at serving time.*

2 dozen shucked oysters of uniform size (not too large) in their liquid (about I quart or 2 pounds)

Two 1¾-inch red serrano peppers, stemmed and cut crosswise into thin slices

4 whole allspice

4 blades mace

½ cup cider vinegar

I tablespoon sugar

I teaspoon salt, or to taste

I to 3 small fresh dill or fennel umbels or sprigs of Italian parsley (garnish)

1. Place the oysters and their liquid in a large nonreactive pan and set over moderately high heat just until the liquid begins to bubble. The minute the oysters' skirts ruffle, adjust the heat so the liquid bubbles gently, and simmer 1 minute longer.
2. Using a slotted spoon, scoop up the oysters, rinse, then place in a small, deep, heatproof, nonreactive bowl or crock along with the serranos, allspice, and mace. Set aside.
3. Add the vinegar, sugar, and salt to the oyster liquid, bring to a boil over moderately high

heat, reduce the heat so the mixture bubbles gently, and simmer uncovered for 1 minute. Line a sieve with a coffee filter and set it directly over the bowl of oysters; pour in the hot pickling liquid. Once the liquid has drained through, cool the oysters for 30 minutes, then cover and refrigerate for at least 24 hours.

4. To serve, lift the oysters, serrano slices, and spices to a small glass or crystal bowl using a slotted spoon, and top with 1 cup of the pickling liquid. Garnish with dill umbels and pass with cocktails.

COCA-COLA

"Gimme a dope." To Southerners of a certain age, "dope" is still synonymous with Coke.

It's no secret that the original Coca-Cola syrup, concocted in 1886 by Atlanta pharmacist John Pemberton, did contain cocaine. Marketed as a "nerve tonic," it was just what Southerners needed during the Civil War's agonizing aftermath.

Enter Atlanta businessman Asa Candler, who'd suffered from migraines since childhood. When a friend suggested that he try Coca-Cola, he headed to Jacob's Pharmacy, where it was served at five cents a glass. The soda jerk spooned an ounce or so of Pemberton's dark, secret syrup into a glass, then fizzed it with carbonated water.

Candler downed that first glass of Coca-Cola in 1888, emerged pain-free, and quickly wrote his brother of the amazing cure. In no time, Candler bought the recipe for Pemberton's elixir (a blend of sugar, aromatic oils [cinnamon, citrus, and coriander], vanilla, and lime juice plus cocaine, and caffeine extracted from African kola nuts). By 1891 he owned the company, and by 1895 he'd opened syrup plants in Chicago, Dallas, and Los Angeles.

Convinced of Coca-Cola's efficacy, Candler described it as "a medical preparation of great value which the best physicians unhesitatingly endorse for mental and physical exhaustion."

He aimed to have Coca-Cola served at every American soda fountain. Early on he sent a barrel of his syrup to a friend in Vicksburg, Mississippi, who, instead of fizzing it in a glass at his soda fountain, bottled it. At first Candler didn't object, but when others followed suit, he balked; bottlers were reaping huge profits. Unfortunately, he had no legal grounds to stop them.

Around the turn of the century, Coca-Cola began getting bad press because of the cocaine it contained. There were reports of people becoming addicted, of people "going funny" after drinking Coca-Cola (some soda jerks were known to double or triple the usual dose of syrup).

In 1901, or perhaps early 1902, Candler decided to remove cocaine from the Coca-Cola formula, which only he and a trusted colleague knew how to mix. He even asked a New Jersey laboratory to "de-cocaine-ize" coca leaves for him.

With Coke so successful, copycat colas began flooding the market. Candler's next move was to make Coca-Cola America's

A Love Affair with Southern Cooking

bold-face brand. No problem. He supplied every pharmacy with Coca-Cola glasses, Coca-Cola clocks, Coca-Cola calendars. He turned country barns into Coca-Cola billboards. He handed out coupons for free Coca-Cola. Then in 1916, the Root Glass Company of Terre Haute, Indiana, created the most distinctive Coca-Cola item of all: a wasp-waisted green bottle so unique a blind man could recognize it.

Soon after World War One,

Georgia banker Ernest Woodruff and a consortium of New York moneymen bought Candler out for $25 million. But it was Woodruff's son Robert, workaholic company boss for nearly sixty years, who made Coca-Cola a global colossus. A shrewd marketer, Woodruff promised every American in uniform during World War Two "a bottle of Coca-Cola for five cents wherever he is and whatever it costs the company." At General Dwight Eisenhower's request, Woodruff

opened bottling plants on major fronts (sixty-four in all) and supplied "soldier-technicians" to keep the Coke flowing. Needless to add, millions of vets came home with a thirst for it.

By the time Woodruff died in 1985, Coke had flown in a space shuttle. But more important, it had soared to number one in the world. To document this long, colorful climb to the top, the company opened the World of Coca-Cola in 1990 in—where else?—Atlanta.

❧

The banquet succeeded: the ribs and choicest fat pieces of the bullocks, excellently well barbecued, were brought into the apartment of the public square, constructed and appointed for feasting; bowls and kettles of stewed flesh and broth were brought in for the next course, and with it a very singular dish, the traders call it tripe soup . . . The dish is greatly esteemed by the Indians.

—**WILLIAM BARTRAM**, TRAVELS OF WILLIAM BARTRAM, DESCRIBING A BARBECUE IN THE ALACHUA INDIAN TOWN OF CUSCOWILLA, FLORIDA, 1773

❧

SHRIMP-STUFFED CHERRY TOMATOES

MAKES ABOUT 6 DOZEN

These popular hors d'oeuvre are easy, attractive, and accommodating because they can be made several hours ahead of time and refrigerated until serving time. It's best to use cherry tomatoes the size of a Ping-Pong ball; smaller ones are difficult to stuff, larger ones messy to eat. **Note:** *The best implement to use for hollowing out cherry tomatoes is a melon baller no more than three-fourths of an inch in diameter. The easiest way to fill them is to squirt the shrimp mixture through a pastry bag; no metal tip is needed because the opening at the bottom of the bag is just* right. **Tip:** *If you have a food processor, chunk the cheese, shrimp, and scallions and whiz in a food processor along with all remaining ingredients for about a minute or until smooth, scraping the work bowl at half-time.*

4 pints cherry tomatoes of uniform size, washed and patted dry

One 8-ounce package light cream cheese (Neufchâtel), at room temperature

6 ounces shelled and deveined cooked shrimp, finely chopped (see Tip above)

2 large scallions, trimmed and finely chopped (white part only)

2 tablespoons mayonnaise (use "light," if you like)

1½ tablespoons finely snipped fresh dill

2 teaspoons prepared horseradish

2 teaspoons fresh lemon juice

¼ teaspoon salt, or to taste

¼ teaspoon black pepper, or to taste

1. Using a sharp knife, slice ¼ inch off the stem end of each tomato, then remove a sliver from the bottom so that the tomato will stand straight without wobbling. Using a small melon baller no more than ¾ inch across or the smallest spoon of a measuring spoon set, scoop out the cherry tomatoes, leaving walls about ⅛ inch thick. Discard what you've scooped out; it's mostly seeds and water. Stand the cherry tomatoes upside down on a baking sheet lined with several thicknesses of paper toweling.

2. While the tomatoes drain, combine all filling ingredients in a small bowl, beating until smooth. Taste for salt and pepper and adjust as needed. **Note:** *If you have a food processor, mix the filling as directed in the Tip given above.*

3. Fold the top of a medium-size plastic pastry bag down about halfway, then spoon the filling into the bag. Smooth the top of the pastry bag back into place, then twist to seal and force the filling to the bottom. Turn the cherry tomatoes right side up.

4. Squirt the shrimp filling directly into the hollowed-out cherry tomatoes, swirling it up on top. Transfer the tomatoes to a second large baking sheet freshly lined with paper toweling, and set uncovered in the refrigerator until ready to serve.

5. Pass the shrimp-stuffed cherry tomatoes with cocktails or set out on a party buffet.

PICKLED SHRIMP

MAKES 16 SERVINGS

Shrimp grow fat and sweet in warm southern waters and this way of preparing them dates back to the days when there was no refrigeration: The acid in the vinegar kept the shrimp from spoiling as fast as they otherwise would. Nowadays, pickled shrimp are a picnic and party staple. **Note:** *Once drained, they keep well in the refrigerator for two to three days.*

4 pounds large raw shrimp in the shell

6 quarts boiling water mixed with 1 tablespoon salt

6 large silverskin or small yellow onions,
thinly sliced

24 whole allspice

24 peppercorns

30 whole cloves

6 large whole bay leaves

1 small lemon, thinly sliced

6 blades mace (optional)

6 cups cider vinegar mixed with
2 cups cold water

1. Cook the shrimp in the boiling salted water for 3 to 4 minutes or until bright pink. Drain, rinse in cool water, then shell and devein.
2. Layer the shrimp and onions in a 1-gallon glass jar, sprinkling with allspice, peppercorns, and cloves as you go and tucking in, here and there, the bay leaves, lemon slices, and, if desired, the blades of mace.
3. Pour in the vinegar mixture, cover, and refrigerate for 3 to 4 hours.
4. Drain the shrimp well, discard the bay leaves and whole spices, and serve cold as an hors d'oeuvre. Good, too, as a main course.

❧

Through there came a smell of garlic and cloves and red peppers, a blast of hot cloud escaped from a cauldron they could see now on a stove . . . At Baba's they were boiling shrimp.

—EUDORA WELTY, *NO PLACE FOR YOU,
MY LOVE*

❧

TIME LINE:
the people
and events that
shaped
Southern
Cuisine

1513	Ponce de León explores "the island" of Florida.
1514	The Spanish Crown empowers Ponce de León to colonize Florida.
1520	Spaniards explore the Gulf of Mexico shore as far west as Texas and the Atlantic coast as far north as the Carolinas.
1524	Florentine navigator Giovanni da Verrazano finds grapes growing in North Carolina's Cape Fear Valley. "Many vines growing naturally there that without doubt would yield excellent wines," he notes in his log.

LANCE SNACK FOODS

First came roasted peanuts in packets just right for one (1913), then the Peanut Bar (1914), then peanut butter "sandwich crackers" (1916), then my favorite, Toastchee Crackers (1938), two little Cheddar crackers sandwiched together with peanut butter. We called them "cheese nabs."

Like a lot of Southerners, I grew up on Lance snacks. But for years I never realized that they were made in Charlotte, some 150 miles west of my hometown of Raleigh. They still are.

It all began back in 1913 when Philip Lance, faced with a windfall of roasted peanuts, decided to sell them in single-serving packets. An innovative idea. Barely a year later, a GI from nearby Fort Greene gave Lance and his son-in-law and partner Salem Van Every a recipe for peanut brittle. They turned it into the Peanut Bar—a best-seller more than ninety years later.

The peanut butter sandwich cracker (another first) was created by Lance's wife and daughter in 1916 and my beloved "cheese nab" came along twenty-two years later. Shortly after World War Two, Lance began supplying restaurants with individually wrapped packets of soda crackers and before long was dispensing them via vending machine as well. But mainly down south.

In 1996 Lance's "cheese nabs" zoomed into orbit aboard the space shuttle *Columbia*. And the very next year Lance snacks (now a variety of cookies and cakes as well as the original peanuts, peanut bars, and sandwich crackers) vaulted out of the South and landed as far afield as Aruba, China, the Dominican Republic, Puerto Rico, England, Jamaica, and Western Europe.

Hardly peanuts.

SHRIMP RÉMOULADE ON FRIED GREEN TOMATOES

MAKES 6 SERVINGS

In downtown St. Francisville, Louisiana, there's a slightly spooky Victorian house set in a grove of live oaks that's both inn and restaurant. I didn't stay at the St. Francisville Inn, but I did eat there more than once. The dish I remember most is this shrimp-and-fried-green-tomato appetizer. St. Francisville, by the way, may have more buildings on the National Register of Historic Places than any town of similar size: some 140 if you count the outlying plantations. **Note:** *If the rémoulade is to mellow, make it a day ahead. Leftover sauce can be refrigerated and used another day to dress cold fish or shellfish.*

Rémoulade Sauce

½ cup Creole mustard

¼ cup vegetable oil

1½ tablespoons red wine vinegar

1 tablespoon finely minced scallion

1 tablespoon finely diced celery

1 tablespoon finely diced
green bell pepper

1 tablespoon finely chopped Italian parsley

1½ teaspoons sweet paprika

1 teaspoon Worcestershire sauce

½ teaspoon hot red pepper sauce

½ teaspoon salt

¼ teaspoon white pepper

⅛ teaspoon ground hot red pepper
(cayenne)

Shrimp

2 quarts water mixed with 1 teaspoon salt

6 jumbo shrimp, shelled and deveined

1 recipe Fried Green Tomatoes (page 220)

1. For the rémoulade sauce: Whisk all ingredients together in a small nonreactive bowl until creamy; cover and refrigerate overnight.
2. When ready to prepare the shrimp, bring the salted water to a boil in a large heavy saucepan over moderate heat. Add the shrimp, and simmer uncovered for 4 to 5 minutes or just until pink. Drain well and reserve while you prepare the fried green tomatoes as the recipe directs.
3. To serve, divide the fried green tomatoes among six heated small plates, each time fanning them into a circle. Center a shrimp on each circle of tomatoes and top with about 1 tablespoon of the sauce.

SHRIMP PASTE

MAKES ABOUT 3 CUPS

Called "potted shrimp" in England, this old-fashioned spread has been popular down south from Colonial times onward. No surprise here; America's finest shrimp come from warm southern waters, especially those lapping the Gulf Coast. In days past, this was a slow, tedious recipe—the shrimp had to be pounded to a paste in a mortar and pestle—but today's food processors make short shrift of that. How do you serve shrimp paste? Spread on cocktail melbas or stuffed into bite-size chunks of celery or hollowed-out cherry tomatoes. At fancy southern parties, I've even seen it mounded into snow peas or sugar snaps. **Note:** *Because of the saltiness of the anchovy paste and shrimp, this recipe is not likely to need salt. But taste before serving.*

1 pound shelled and deveined cooked
shrimp, halved if large

2 medium scallions, trimmed and
cut into 1-inch chunks (white part only)

3 tablespoons fresh lemon juice

2 tablespoons anchovy paste

¼ to ½ teaspoon hot red pepper sauce
(depending on how hot you like things)

¼ teaspoon black pepper

¼ teaspoon ground allspice

½ cup (1 stick) butter, at room temperature

1. Pulse the shrimp and scallions in a food processor until finely chopped.

2. Add all remaining ingredients and churn for 30 to 60 seconds or until smooth, scraping the work bowl at half-time. Taste for salt and add, if needed.

3. Pack the shrimp paste into a small bowl, cover with plastic food wrap, and refrigerate for several hours before serving.

APPETIZER SALAD OF FRIED OKRA AND CRAWFISH WITH BASIL VINAIGRETTE

MAKES 4 SERVINGS

. . . .

Here's another amazing "starter" that I enjoyed on a swing through "Little-Known Louisiana" several years ago while on assignment for *Gourmet*. Proof that Louisiana's best chefs aren't all in New Orleans, it was the specialty of Catahoula's, a country grocery-turned-restaurant in the historic town of Grand Coteau barely fifteen minutes north of Lafayette. Owner-photographer John Slaughter told me that he'd named the restaurant for the spotted, blue-eyed hound that is the state dog of Louisiana, and his portraits of them line the restaurant walls. At the time of my visit, Chef Daniel Landry was manning the Catahoula's kitchen and creating so many inspired dishes that I returned to the restaurant more than once. Catahoula's is still there but Landry, alas, has moved on. **Note:** *Landry smoked fresh sweet corn for this appetizer salad, but grilled corn works equally well. All you need to do is shuck the ears, set them 4 inches from glowing coals, and grill for about*

20 minutes, turning often. Cool the corn before cutting the kernels from the cobs. Landry's recipe also calls for pickled okra; many southern supermarkets sell it, but if unavailable, see Sources (page 401). Note, too, that shrimp may be substituted for crawfish. **Tip:** *Make the vinaigrette first and whisk vigorously just before using; save any leftover vinaigrette to dress salads another day.*

Basil Vinaigrette

1 medium garlic clove

2 tablespoons cider vinegar

1½ tablespoons finely chopped fresh basil leaves

1½ tablespoons Dijon mustard

1 teaspoon black pepper

½ teaspoon salt

1¼ cups fruity olive oil

Salad

Kernels from 2 medium ears grilled sweet corn (see Note at left)

1 medium sun-ripened tomato, peeled, cored, seeded, and cut into small dice

1 large egg

½ cup milk

1 teaspoon salt

1 teaspoon black pepper

2 cups unsifted all-purpose flour

2 cups fine dry bread crumbs

20 pickled okra pods (see Note above)

12 ounces crawfish tails or medium shrimp,
shelled and deveined

Vegetable oil for deep-fat frying
(about 4 cups)

1½ cups coarsely grated pepper Jack cheese
(about 6 ounces)

8 ounces mesclun
(mixed baby salad greens)

1. For the basil vinaigrette: Churn all ingredients except the olive oil for 20 to 30 seconds in a food processor or electric blender at high speed until smooth. With the motor running, drizzle in the olive oil and continue processing until thick and creamy; set aside (but be sure to buzz or whisk the vinaigrette just before using).

2. For the salad: Place the corn and tomato in a large nonreactive bowl and set aside.

3. Whisk the egg and milk until frothy in a small bowl with ½ teaspoon each of the salt and pepper; set aside.

4. Combine the flour with ¼ teaspoon each of the remaining salt and pepper in a pie pan and set aside. Next, combine the bread crumbs with the last of the salt and pepper in a second pie pan and set aside also.

5. Dredge each okra pod in the seasoned flour, then dip into the egg mixture, then coat with the bread crumbs, shaking off the excess and arranging on a wire rack. Dredge and bread the crawfish tails the same way and arrange on the rack. Air-dry both the okra and craw-fish tails on the wire rack for 10 to 15 minutes; this helps the breading stick.

6. Meanwhile, pour the vegetable oil into a large deep saucepan until 2 inches deep; insert a deep-fat thermometer, and set over moderately high heat.

7. When the oil reaches 375° F., deep-fry the okra in two batches, allowing 1 to 2 minutes for each to brown and lifting to paper toweling to drain. Deep-fry and drain the crawfish tails the same way. As you deep-fry, keep the temperature of the oil as near to 375° F. as possible so that the okra and crawfish tails brown nicely without becoming greasy.

8. To finish the salad, add the cheese, mesclun, and ⅔ cup of the vinaigrette to the reserved corn and tomatoes and toss well. Taste, and add a bit more vinaigrette, if needed.

9. Divide the corn and tomato mixture among four salad plates, top each portion with fried okra and crawfish, and serve as the first course of an elegant meal.

CRAB CUPS

MAKES 4 TO 4½ DOZEN
. . . .

My good friend Anne Mead, who grew up in Dillon, South Carolina, always served these at cocktail parties. For many years we lived in the same Gramercy Park apartment building and, like so many other Southerners who'd left the South, we were soon best of friends. Anne was a wonderful cook; she even published a little cook-book called *Please Kiss the Cook*, from which this recipe is adapted. I sometimes add a little finely snipped fresh dill or chopped tarragon to the crab mixture—my innovation, not Anne's. **Note:** *The bread to use for making the toast cups is thin-sliced, firm-textured white bread (sometimes called home-*

*style bread). A one-pound loaf contains 27 slices (not counting the "heels") and if the slices are not mis-shapen and you space your cuts carefully, you should be able to get two small rounds from each slice. That would be 54 rounds, total—about right for this amount of filling. The toast cups can be made a week in advance and stored in an airtight container. **Tip:** It's easier to get two rounds per slice if you roll the slices lightly with a rolling pin—just enough to stretch them without mashing the bread.*

One 1-pound loaf thin-sliced, firm-textured white bread, crusts removed (see Note on page 11)

1 pound fresh lump crabmeat, bits of shell and cartilage removed

2 cups finely diced celery (about 3 large ribs)

2 large hard-cooked eggs, finely chopped

1 small yellow onion, finely chopped

1 cup firmly packed mayonnaise (use "light," if you like)

1 tablespoon finely snipped fresh dill or moderately finely chopped fresh tarragon (optional)

½ teaspoon salt, or to taste

¼ teaspoon black pepper, or to taste

Paprika (optional garnish)

1. Preheat the oven to 300° F.
2. Using a 1 7/8- to 2-inch round cutter, cut 2 rounds from each slice of bread. Press the bread rounds gently into ungreased mini muffin pan cups measuring no more than 2 inches across the top. The bread will only half-fill the muffin cups, but shape it as best you can into shallow cups. Don't worry about ragged edges; the filling will hide them. **Note:** *Buzz the trimmings to crumbs in a blender or food processor, place in a large plastic zipper bag, and store in the freezer to use later for meat loaves and casserole toppings.*

3. Toast the bread cups on the middle oven shelf for about 20 minutes or until crisp and golden. Cool to room temperature, then remove from the muffin pans.
4. For the filling, lightly fork together the crab-meat, celery, hard-cooked eggs, onion, mayonnaise, dill (if desired), salt, and pepper. Taste for seasoning and adjust the salt and pepper as needed. Cover and refrigerate for 2 to 3 hours. Fork again just before using.
5. To fill the toast cups, scoop the crab mixture up by generous teaspoonfuls. **Note:** *I use a small spring-loaded ice cream scoop that measures 1⅛ inches across the top—a time-saver because each scoop is exactly the right amount of filling for each toast cup.*
6. Blush the tops of the crab cups with paprika, if you like; arrange on a colorful platter and serve as an accompaniment to cocktails.

CATFISH CAKES

MAKES 16 BITE-SIZE CAKES

. . . .

This recipe comes from my good friend and colleague Joanne Lamb Hayes, who grew up in Maryland. She says these are a snap, especially if you buzz everything up in a food processor. Shaped into bite-size "burgers," these are perfect cocktail fare. **Note:** *Check the ingredient list of*

*your seafood seasoning; if it contains no salt, add
about ¼ teaspoon salt to the fish mixture.*

I pound skinned catfish fillets,
cut into I-inch pieces

4 medium scallions, trimmed and
cut into I-inch pieces
(include some green tops)

½ teaspoon seafood seasoning

¼ teaspoon salt, if needed (see Note above)

1½ tablespoons vegetable oil

Tartar sauce (optional)

1. Place the catfish, scallions, seasoning, and salt, if needed, in a food processor fitted with the metal chopping blade. Pulse 8 to 10 times or until coarsely chopped.
2. Remove the catfish mixture from the food processor and shape into 16 small cakes of equal size.
3. Heat the oil in a large, heavy skillet over moderately high heat for about 1 minute or until ripples appear in the oil on the skillet bottom. Ease in the catfish cakes and cook for about 5 minutes or until well browned on one side. Turn and brown the flip sides for 3 to 5 minutes or until cooked through.
4. Serve hot, accompanied, if you like, with your favorite tartar sauce for dipping.

❧

*When prepared by an honest craftsman,
catfish becomes a noble dish...*

—A. J. McCLANE, *THE ENCYCLOPEDIA OF FISH
COOKERY*

❧

1539 Leaving his Havana base, Hernando de Soto begins extensive exploration of today's Southeast. He introduces hogs to Florida, which over time make their way north to Georgia, the Carolinas, and Virginia.

1565 The Spanish settle St. Augustine and hold it for 256 years. The foods they grew, the foods they cooked still season Florida pots.

English Captain John Hawkins reports that large quantities of muscadine wine are being made in the Spanish settlements in Florida.

1571 Franciscans introduce peaches to Georgia's offshore Cumberland and St. Simon's islands.

1579 The growing of citrus fruits is now well established around St. Augustine, Florida.

1584 Sir Walter Raleigh sends scouts to Roanoke Island (off the North Carolina mainland). One of them, Arthur Barlowe, describes the native hospitality thus: "Euery daye a brase or two of fatt Buckes, Conies [rabbits], Hares, Fishe . . . fruites, Melon, Walnuts, Gourdes, Pease." He also found the Indian corn "very white, faire, and well tasted."

PEPSI-COLA

Pepsi-Cola has the somewhat dubious distinction of having launched the singing commercial. Yes, today's 24-7 assault of inane radio and TV jingles began back in 1940 with

Pepsi-Cola hits the spot.
Twelve full ounces, that's a lot.
Twice as much for a nickel,
   too.
Pepsi-Cola is the drink for you.
Nickel, nickel, nickel, nickel,

Et cetera. Thanks, Pepsi.

The Pepsi saga began in 1893 when Caleb Bradham, a young pharmacist in New Bern, North Carolina, mixed carbonated water, sugar, vanilla, rare oils, pepsin, and kola nuts into something called "Brad's Drink."

Because his fizzy beverage was meant to ease dyspepsia, Bradham gave it a new name five years later: Pepsi-Cola.

Since then, Pepsi has shown itself to be a remarkable survivor. Bankruptcies in 1923 and 1931 were mere blips in a long-range success story.

In 1934, Pepsi began selling 12-ounce bottles for the same nickel that competitors were charging for just six ounces. Sales soared in a country beset by the Great Depression.

In 1962, the slogan "Come Alive with the Pepsi Generation" appeared in Taiwan as "Pepsi Will Bring Your Ancestors Back from the Dead." (Something was lost in translation here.)

In 1964, Diet Pepsi debuted, grabbing market share from Coke's recently introduced TaB.

In 1984, Michael Jackson's hair caught fire in a pyrotechnic malfunction while he was filming a Pepsi commercial. He suffered second-degree burns.

In 1989, Pepsi quickly backed out of a promotional deal with Madonna after one of her controversial videos featured burning crosses.

And in 1996, Pepsi offered as a joke a Harrier Jump Jet for seven million "Pepsi Points." Points were a dime, making the jet cost $700,000 instead of its $33.8 million true value. When one man actually bought enough points and tried to collect, a court ruled that it was "obviously a joke." To Pepsi's everlasting relief.

Today, Coca-Cola may hold a greater share of the soft drink market, but for millions, only Pepsi "hits the spot."

BARBECUED MEATBALLS

MAKES 4 TO 4½ DOZEN

As long as I can remember, barbecued meatballs have been a cocktail specialty among the southern hostesses I know. Properly made, they're peppery (but not too peppery), sweet (but not too sweet), and sour (not too sour). Just like good barbecue. Recipes vary significantly from cook to cook but this one, my own, has just the right balance of flavors, I think. Apart from shaping the meat mixture into small balls, this recipe couldn't be easier. The best part is that you can make the meatballs well ahead of time and freeze them—either cooked or raw.

Or you can make them—start to finish—a day in advance and refrigerate until ready to serve. I reheat them by microwave; 15 minutes at 50-percent power is about right unless you have one of the new high-wattage microwaves. If so, reheat the meatballs in their sauce in 5-minute increments at 50-percent power until steaming. **Note:** *Some hostesses serve barbecued meatballs in silver or tin-lined copper chafing dishes. I just mound them in an attractive bowl—no matter if they cool to room temperature.*

Meatballs

1 pound ground beef chuck

½ pound bulk sausage meat

1 cup moderately fine soft white bread crumbs (2 slices firm-textured white bread)

1 medium yellow onion, finely chopped

1 large garlic clove, finely chopped

2 tablespoons tomato ketchup

1 tablespoon Dijon mustard

1 large egg, well beaten

1 teaspoon salt

½ teaspoon hot red pepper sauce

2 tablespoons vegetable oil (for cooking the meatballs)

Sauce

Two 8-ounce cans tomato sauce

3 tablespoons light brown sugar

1½ tablespoons cider vinegar, or to taste

1 tablespoon Dijon mustard

1 large garlic clove, finely chopped

½ teaspoon salt, or to taste

¼ to ½ teaspoon hot red pepper sauce (depending on how "hot" you like things)

1. For the meatballs: Place all but the vegetable oil in a large bowl and, using your hands, mix thoroughly. Shape into 1- to 1¼-inch balls, arrange on a foil-lined large, rimmed baking sheet, and set uncovered in the refrigerator. Chill for 3 to 4 hours. This is to firm up the meatballs so they're easier to cook.

2. When ready to proceed, heat the vegetable oil in a large, heavy skillet over moderately high heat for 2 minutes or until ripples appear in the oil on the skillet bottom. Add half the meatballs and cook, shaking the skillet often, for 3 to 5 minutes or until uniformly brown. Using a slotted spoon, transfer the browned meatballs to a large, shallow pan and reserve. Brown the remaining meatballs the same way and add to the first batch.

3. For the sauce: Drain all drippings from the skillet, add all sauce ingredients, and whisk to combine. Set over moderate heat and bring to a boil, whisking often. Taste the sauce for vinegar and salt and adjust as needed.

4. Return the browned meatballs to the skillet, pushing them down into the sauce. Adjust the heat so the sauce bubbles gently, cover, and cook for 20 minutes, stirring once or twice, or just until the meatballs are cooked through.

5. Transfer all to a large chafing dish or attractive heatproof bowl and serve with cocktails. Put out a container of party toothpicks and colorful cocktail napkins.

NATCHITOCHES MEAT PIES

Natchitoches (pronounced NACK-uh-tish) in northwestern Louisiana is famous for two things: *Steel Magnolias*, which was filmed there in 1988, and spicy meat pies that predate the Civil War. The latter are what drew me to Nachitoches while on assignment for *Gourmet*, but the former was the talk of this nearly-300-year-old town. To orient myself, I hopped a tour bus only to learn that sites of historic significance mattered less than the various movie venues, less even than the homes rented to accommodate the stars during the shoot. So what I heard was "In the movie, this was Shelby's home (the Julia Roberts character)." . . . "This is the church where Shelby's wedding was filmed." . . . "This is where Julia Roberts lived while making the movie." . . . "This is where Dolly Parton stayed . . . Sally Field . . . Shirley MacLaine . . ." (Since my visit nearly ten years ago, I trust that Natchitoches's long and colorful history has regained pride of place.) To taste the town's famous meat pies, I headed straight to Lasyone's Meat Pie Kitchen on Second Street (yes, some of the movie folk did stop by). Here I learned that fried meat pies were originally out-the-backdoor or street food sold by the few who knew how to make them. I won't pretend they're easy. The local recipes I picked up were vague and faulty: too much flour in the filling, too much lard in the pastry. Even with major adjustments the pastry was so short the pies fell apart when fried in deep fat. What to do? Abandon tradition and bake the pies instead. They are equally delicious and a tad less caloric.

Pastry

2 cups sifted all-purpose flour

½ teaspoon baking powder

½ teaspoon salt

½ cup firmly packed lard or vegetable shortening

3 tablespoons cold milk beaten with 1 large egg

Filling

¼ pound ground beef chuck

¼ pound ground pork

2 medium scallions, trimmed and coarsely chopped (include some green tops)

¼ teaspoon salt

¼ teaspoon black pepper

⅛ to ¼ teaspoon ground hot red pepper (cayenne)

⅛ teaspoon ground allspice

1 teaspoon all-purpose flour

¼ cup water

1. For the pastry: Whisk the flour, baking powder, and salt together in a large mixing bowl. Add the lard and using a pastry blender, cut in until the texture of coarse meal. Quickly fork in the milk-egg mixture and as soon as the pastry holds together, shape into a ball. Place on a large sheet of plastic food wrap, flatten, then wrap and refrigerate until ready to proceed.

2. For the filling: Cook the beef, pork, scallions, salt, black and red pepper, and allspice in a medium-size heavy skillet over moderate heat, breaking up the clumps of meat, for about 5 minutes or until no traces of pink remain. Sprinkle in the flour, then, stirring all the while, add the water. Cook, stirring now and then, for about 5 minutes or until lightly thickened and no raw floury taste remains. Cool to room temperature.

3. Preheat the oven to 375° F. Remove the pastry from the refrigerator and roll as thin as pie crust on a lightly floured pastry cloth. Cut into rounds with a 2¾- to 3-inch biscuit cutter, then drop 1½ to 2 teaspoons of the filling onto the lower half of each round, leaving a margin of at least ¼ inch. Reroll the scraps and cut additional circles. Moisten the edges of the pastry circles all around, fold in half to enclose the filling, and crimp the edges firmly with the tines of a fork to seal. Also prick the top of each round with the fork to allow steam to escape.

4. Arrange the rounds about 2 inches apart on an ungreased large baking sheet, slide onto the middle oven shelf, and bake for 12 to 15 minutes or until the edges are brown.

5. Serve hot with cocktails.

Variation

Main-Dish Meat Pies: Prepare the pastry and filling according to the recipe. After rolling the pastry as directed in Step 3, cut into 4½-inch rounds using a pan lid as a template. **Note:** *Some cooks use an empty coffee can as a cutter and if you have one that's about 4½ inches in diameter, by all means use it. Reroll the scraps and cut additional rounds. Divide the meat filling evenly among the pastry rounds, spooning it onto the lower half of each. Fold, seal, and bake the pies as directed. Makes 8 servings.*

HEAVENLY CHICKEN LIVER MOUSSE

MAKES 10 TO 12 SERVINGS

Chicken livers have long been popular down south—perhaps because chicken farming is big business. Most old-timey southern cooks simply dredge chicken livers lightly in flour (or, better yet, in self-rising flour, which gives them a supremely crisp coating), and fry them. But Scott Howell, chef-proprietor of Nana's, a classy restaurant in Durham, North Carolina, has turned them into an ethereal mousse. This is my adaptation of the restaurant recipe, which appeared a few years ago in my *Food & Wine* profile of Howell.

There are a couple of caveats: First, all ingredients must be at room temperature, otherwise the mousse may separate. Second, the softened butter must be added one tablespoon at a time with the food processor running. After four tablespoons have been added, I stop the machine for a few seconds. Any unincorporated bits of butter will rise to the top and I pulse these in before adding any more butter. Finally, I bake the mousse in an ovenproof glass loaf pan or ring mold or an enameled metal terrine, all of which transmit heat slowly and ensure even cooking. With a metal container, the mousse tends to overcook on the outside and undercook in the center.

1½ cups heavy cream, at room temperature

4 tablespoons bacon drippings or butter (drippings add nice smoky flavor)

6 medium scallions, trimmed and cut into 1-inch chunks (use white part only)

One ½-inch cube fresh ginger, peeled

½ teaspoon brined green peppercorns, drained well

¼ teaspoon ground allspice

¼ teaspoon freshly grated nutmeg

1 pound chicken livers, halved at the natural separation, trimmed of fat and connective tissue, and brought to room temperature (see headnote)

1½ teaspoons salt

8 egg yolks, at room temperature

3 tablespoons sweet Madeira wine (Malmsey or Bual)

1 cup (2 sticks) butter, cut into pats (use the wrapper markings) and brought to room temperature

1. Preheat the oven to 275° F. Lightly butter a 6-cup ovenproof glass ring mold, an 8½ × 4½ × 2¾-inch ovenproof glass loaf pan, or a 6-cup enameled cast-iron or glazed earthenware terrine; set aside.

2. Pour ½ cup of the cream into a very small, heavy saucepan or butter warmer and set over lowest heat. Also, melt the bacon drippings in a small, heavy skillet over low heat.

3. Meanwhile, coarsely chop the scallions, ginger, and peppercorns with the allspice and nutmeg by churning 3 to 5 seconds in a food processor. Add to the skillet and sauté, stirring occasionally, for 5 minutes or until limp. Cool to room temperature.

4. Return the scallion mixture to the processor (no need to wash the blade or bowl); add the chicken livers, salt, egg yolks, and wine; and purée by churning 30 seconds. Scrape the work bowl.

5. With the motor running, drop 4 tablespoons of the butter down the feed tube one by one, making sure each one is incorporated before adding the next. Stop the machine, wait a few seconds, then open the work bowl. If any flecks of butter have risen to the top, pulse these in completely. Add the remaining butter exactly the same way, pausing after each 4 tablespoons to pulse in any flecks that float to the top. **Note:** *Have patience. If you rush things, the mixture will separate and the only way to bring it back together is to pulse in 1 to 2 tablespoons of the warm cream. Keep it handy.*

6. Force the liver mixture through a fine sieve set over a large mixing bowl. **Tip:** *I find the bowl of a ladle the best implement to use—just move it around and around the sieve.* Add the cream, including the warmed cream, and stir until no streaks of white remain.

7. Pour into the prepared container, set in a large roasting pan, and slide onto the middle oven shelf. Carefully pour enough boiling water into the pan to come halfway up the sides of the container in which you're baking the liver mousse.

8. Bake uncovered until pale golden on top and a cake tester comes out clean when inserted midway between the center and the rim— about 1 hour and 10 minutes.

9. Lift the mousse from the hot-water bath, set upright on a wire rack, and cool to room temperature. This is important. If you cover and refrigerate the mousse while it's warm, drops of water will condense and discolor the surface.

10. Cover the mousse with plastic food wrap, overwrap in aluminum foil, and refrigerate for at least 12 hours.

11. To unmold, dip a thin-blade spatula in hot water and loosen the mousse around the edge (the center tube, too, if you used a ring mold). You'll have to keep dipping the spatula in hot water as you move it around the edge of the mold. Now stand the pan or mold in about an inch of hot water for 10 seconds. Lift out of the water, place a platter on top, then invert, shaking lightly. If the mousse refuses to budge, dip again in hot water. Once unmolded, you can smooth any rough areas with the spatula.

12. Put out a basket of homemade melbas and serve the chicken liver mousse with cocktails. Or slice and serve at the start of an elegant meal, garnishing each plate with a few gherkins and a little mesclun that has been tossed in a tart vinaigrette.

❧

I have lived temperately, eating little animal food, and that . . . as a condiment for vegetables, which constitute my principal diet.

—THOMAS JEFFERSON

❧

CANDIED BACON

MAKES ABOUT 2 DOZEN PIECES

Few southern appetizers are easier or more crowd-pleasing than these crisp, caramelized slices of bacon. Before you dismiss sugar and pork as an unhealthful and unlikely combination, give this appetizer a try. Its flavor reminds me of the sugar-crusted hams of Easter. **Note:** *I use nitrite-free bacon for this recipe and do not pack the brown sugar into the measuring cup.* Much of the bacon fat drains off during the long, slow baking as indeed does most of the sugar. And wasn't it only a year or so ago that foodies were touting lard (and bacon) as "the new health foods"?

¾ cup light brown sugar, not packed

2 teaspoons dry mustard

½ teaspoon black pepper

1 pound thickly sliced, hickory-smoked bacon, each slice halved crosswise

1. Preheat the oven to 325° F. Lay a large baking rack (preferably one with a cross-hatch grid) on top of an ungreased 15½ × 10½ × 1-inch jelly roll pan. Spritz the rack well with nonstick cooking spray and set aside.

2. Combine the brown sugar, mustard, and pepper in a pie pan, whisking out all lumps. Dredge each piece of bacon on both sides in the sugar mixture until thickly coated.

3. Arrange the bacon on the rack, preferably not touching, and sprinkle generously with the remaining sugar mixture.

4. Slide the pan onto the middle oven rack and bake uncovered for 50 to 60 minutes or until the bacon is richly browned and crisp. No need to turn the bacon as it bakes.
5. Cool the candied bacon to room temperature and serve with cocktails.

SAUSAGE-STUFFED MUSHROOM CAPS

MAKES 2 DOZEN

Some years ago I spent ten days driving up and down the James River in Virginia visiting the historic plantation houses located there. Although I marveled at their architecture and museum-caliber antiques, my main mission was to research the recipes—past and present—served in those homes. My good friend Maria Harrison Reuge, descended from an old Virginia family, supplied the entrée I needed, so I came home with a notebook full of plantation recipes. One of my favorites is this appetizer from Meri Major, of Belle Air Plantation, who treated me to lunch one day and proved why she was considered one of the best cooks in Tidewater Virginia. "I just grew up watching every kind of thing being cooked," Meri told me. "Just about every part of the pig, wild turkey, every type of game, every type of seafood. I always had a natural affinity for cooking and was forever under foot in the kitchen." For this snappy hors d'oeuvre, which she calls "just so simple," Meri would use a peppery Virginia sausage. But any spicy bulk sausage will do. If only mild sausage is available, Meri suggests adding "a couple of dashes of cayenne pepper to the beaten eggs." **Tip:** *To keep the stuffed mushrooms hot while they're being served, bake them in a 9- or 10-inch quiche dish attractive enough to come to the party. That's what Meri does.* "And put out plenty of pretty forked toothpicks," *she adds.*

24 medium-size mushrooms, wiped clean with a damp cloth

½ pound spicy bulk sausage meat

1 small garlic clove, finely minced

1 tablespoon finely minced scallion or finely snipped fresh chives

1 small egg, well beaten

⅔ cup soft white bread crumbs or ⅓ cup fine dry bread crumbs

½ teaspoon soy sauce

1. Preheat the oven to 350° F.
2. Stem the mushrooms. Set the caps aside and coarsely chop the stems.
3. Cook the sausage, mushroom stems, garlic, and scallion in a medium-size skillet for 5 to 8 minutes over moderately low heat, breaking up any large sausage lumps, until the meat is lightly browned. Remove from the heat, cool for 15 minutes, then mix in the egg, bread crumbs, and soy sauce.
4. Mound the sausage mixture in the mushroom caps, then arrange in an ungreased 9- or 10-inch quiche dish or ovenproof 9 × 9 × 2-inch baking dish.
5. Bake on the middle oven shelf for 10 to 12 minutes or until bubbling and browned. Serve hot with cocktails.

INDIVIDUAL CORN CUSTARDS WITH CARROT VINAIGRETTE

MAKES 6 SERVINGS

High above Waynesville, North Carolina, with its back to the Great Smoky Mountains National Park and a full frontal view of Cold Mountain, stands the Swag, an elegantly rustic inn owned by Dr. Daniel P. Matthews and his wife, Deener. The massive wooden beams in the two-story living-dining room came from an old country church, altogether appropriate given the fact that for seventeen years Dan Matthews was the rector of Trinity Parish near Ground Zero in Lower Manhattan. Breakfasts at the Swag are bountiful and so, too, the dinners. During my stay there several years ago, these delicate corn custards were served at the start of a superb lamb dinner.

Corn Custards

1 cup heavy cream

2 large eggs

½ teaspoon salt

¼ teaspoon black pepper

⅛ teaspoon freshly grated nutmeg

⅔ cup fresh sweet corn kernels
(you'll need about 1 large ear)

Carrot Vinaigrette

½ cup coarsely chopped carrot
(you'll need about 1 medium carrot)

3 tablespoons white wine vinegar

½ cup plus 2 tablespoons vegetable oil

1 tablespoon finely chopped Italian parsley

Garnish

1 medium radicchio, trimmed and
thinly sliced

1. Preheat the oven to 350° F. Spritz six ⅓-cup ramekins or custard cups with nonstick cooking spray and set aside.

2. For the corn custards: Whisk the cream, eggs, salt, pepper, and nutmeg until thoroughly blended. Divide the corn among the six ramekins, then ladle in the custard mixture, again dividing evenly. Dampen a dish towel, fold, and smooth over the bottom of a large shallow baking pan. Stand the ramekins, not touching, on the towel.

3. Slide the pan of custards onto the middle oven shelf and pour enough boiling water into the baking pan to come a third of the way up the ramekins. Bake the custards uncovered for 20 to 30 minutes or just until set. Lift the custards to a wire rack and cool for 10 minutes.

4. While the custards bake, prepare the carrot vinaigrette: Cook the carrot in a small saucepan in just enough water to cover for about 10 minutes or until very tender. Drain well and pat dry on paper toweling. Purée the carrot with the vinegar in a mini food processor or an electric blender, then with the motor running, drizzle in the oil. Continue churning until the mixture emulsifies. Fold in the parsley.

5. When ready to serve, gently loosen each custard around the edge with a knife and invert on a salad plate. Wreathe with the sliced radicchio and top each portion with 1½ to 2 tablespoons of the vinaigrette.

FAVORITE DEVILED EGGS

MAKES 4 TO 6 SERVINGS

. . . .

Some say that deviled eggs were invented down south. I wouldn't go that far, but I do know they're far too popular to be confined to picnics. I've seen sophisticated southern hostesses pass platters of deviled eggs with cocktails and watched guests scarf them down. Of course, every Southerner has a pet recipe for deviled eggs and this one is mine; it couldn't be easier. **Note:** *Here's how I hard-cook eggs: Place the eggs in a large heavy saucepan and add enough cold water to cover them by two inches. Bring to a boil over moderately high heat, set off the heat, cover, and let the eggs stand for 15 minutes. Drain the eggs at once, then quick-chill in ice water.*

6 hard-cooked extra-large eggs
(see Note above)

¼ cup mayonnaise-relish sandwich spread

1 tablespoon Dijon mustard

2 teaspoons finely grated yellow onion

¼ teaspoon black pepper

Paprika (optional)

1. Peel the eggs, halve lengthwise, then "pop" the yolks into a small bowl and mash well with a fork. Add the sandwich spread, mustard, onion, and pepper and whisk until blended.
2. Stuff the egg whites with the yolk mixture, mounding it up nicely. Cover the eggs loosely with plastic food wrap and chill for several hours.
3. When ready to serve, arrange the deviled eggs on a colorful round platter and, if you like, blush the top of each with a little paprika.

TO MAKE ROSE PETAL WINE

Gather 1 pint fragrant pink rose petals. Cover with 1 gallon boiling water and let stand 24 hours. Squeeze dry. Discard petals. Add 1 dissolved yeast cake or package and 3 pounds sugar. Stir. Leave in a stone crock at least 6 weeks. Strain and bottle tight.
—Miss Sarah M. Nooe, Iredell County, North Carolina

It was a good meal they had together on that night . . . fried chicken . . . mashed rootabeggars, collard greens, and hot, pale golden sweet potatoes. Miss Amelia ate slowly and with the relish of a farm hand.

—CARSON McCULLERS, *THE BALLAD OF THE SAD CAFÉ*

JACK DANIEL'S TENNESSEE WHISKEY

Jasper Newton "Jack" Daniel learned to make whiskey from a Lynchburg, Tennessee, "preacherman" and went on to lift spirits in his own way. With its black label and distinctive square bottle, Jack Daniel's Old No.7 Brand Old Time Tennessee Sour Mash Whiskey—simply "jack black" to its legion of fans—is immediately recognizable in appearance and taste. This ain't no bourbon.

Licensed in 1866, Jack Daniel's is the oldest registered distillery in the country—a National Historic Site. And its oh-so-smooth, amber-hued whiskey is still made by the method Daniel perfected. Distillers blend corn, rye, and barley malt with spring water from a nearby limestone cave (it contains no iron to affect the whiskey's flavor). The resulting mash is cooked and allowed to ferment, jump-started by yeast from a previous batch—thus "sour mash."

Next step: distillation. The sour mash goes into 100-foot copper stills, then into charred oak barrels to age and acquire its amber color. What makes Jack Daniel's such a mellow whiskey is the ten-day process that follows: filtering through ten feet of sugar maple charcoal.

No one knows why Daniel named his whiskey Old No. 7. Take the distillery tour and you'll get a different theory from every guide.

Today, you can order a Jack Daniel's in more than 130 countries. But you can't buy a round in Lynchburg, Tennessee. The town that "jack black" built has been dry since Prohibition.

1585–87 With Elizabeth I's blessing, Raleigh organized an English settlement on Roanoke Island. Within a few years, it vanishes, and the fate of the "Lost Colony" still puzzles historians and archaeologists.

1607 The English found a colony at Jamestown, Virginia, under the leadership of Captain John Smith. Awed by the local bounty, he writes, "neither better fish, more plentie, nor more varitie had any of us ever seen in any place."

1609 The English colonists at Jamestown produce wine from native grapes but are disappointed with the results.

1611 Viticulturists arrive from England to help the colonists produce wines good enough to export. They fail.

1612 Realizing that Virginia's true gold is tobacco, John Rolfe begins growing bright leaf.

1614 John Rolfe marries Pocahontas and secures peace for the young Virginia colony—at least for a few years.

1616 George Yeardley, deputy governor of the Virginia colony, erects America's first windmill, imports a herd of cattle, learns to fertilize the soil, and urges the colonists to grow tobacco.

WATERCRESS-STUFFED EGGS

MAKES 4 TO 6 SERVINGS

· ·

These colorful hors d'oeuvre often show up on southern tea tables and buffets. They're also passed with cocktails.

6 hard-cooked extra-large eggs

⅔ cup finely minced tender young watercress leaves

3 medium scallions, trimmed and finely chopped (include some green tops)

3 tablespoons mayonnaise (use "light," if you like)

1 tablespoon minced parsley

1 teaspoon Dijon mustard

1 teaspoon fresh lemon juice

¼ teaspoon salt, or to taste

¼ teaspoon black pepper, or to taste

⅛ teaspoon hot red pepper sauce, or to taste

1. Peel the eggs, halve lengthwise, then "pop" the yolks into a small bowl and mash well with a fork. Add all remaining ingredients and beat with a fork until blended. Taste for salt, black pepper, and hot pepper sauce and adjust as needed.

2. Stuff the egg whites with the watercress mixture, mounding it up nicely. Cover the eggs loosely with plastic food wrap and chill for several hours.

3. When ready to serve, arrange the stuffed eggs on a colorful round platter.

CHEESE DAISIES

MAKES 4 TO 4½ DOZEN

· ·

During my growing-up years, cheese daisies appeared front and center on nearly every Raleigh buffet table, and my mother made them to perfection. Back then, faculty wives were constantly swapping recipes and this one came from a Southerner whose name, I'm sorry to say, I've forgotten. I still have Mother's smudged file card on which the recipe is recorded in the straight-up-and-down script I know so well. On the flip side, Mother noted that if the dough is too cold, "it will be too crumbly to put through a cookie press." To which I'd add, it needs to be malleable—about the consistency of Play-Doh. **Note:** *For best results, grate the cheese yourself. I use a food processor fitted with the fine shredding disk and the job is done in seconds.*

1½ cups unsifted all-purpose flour

1 teaspoon salt

½ teaspoon paprika

¼ to ½ teaspoon ground hot red pepper (cayenne), depending on how "hot" you like things

¾ cup (1½ sticks) cold butter

2 cups loosely packed, finely grated sharp Cheddar cheese (about 5 ounces)

1. Preheat the oven to 350° F. Sift the flour, salt, paprika, and cayenne together onto a piece of wax paper and set aside.

2. Cream the butter and cheese in an electric mixer at moderate speed for 2 to 3 minutes or until light. By hand, stir in the sifted dry ingredients, mixing just until the ingredients come together forming a dough about the consistency of pie pastry. Don't overmix.

3. Press the dough through a cookie gun fitted with the "daisy" or "flower" disk onto ungreased baking sheets, spacing the daisies about 2 inches apart.

4. Bake on the middle oven shelf for 10 to 12 minutes or just until the daisies feel firm. They should not brown.

5. Transfer at once to wire racks to cool. Layer the daisies between sheets of wax paper in an airtight tin, cover, and store in a cool spot until ready to serve. Or, if you prefer, label, date, and store in the freezer (the cheese daisies will remain "fresh" for 3 to 4 months).

Variation

Cheese Straws: Prepare the dough as directed, then, using a cookie gun fitted with the star tip, pipe the dough onto ungreased baking sheets in strips about 2½ inches long. Bake, cool, and store as directed. Makes 4 to 4½ dozen.

❧

We eat our supper (cold biscuits, bacon, blackberry jam) and discuss tomorrow.

—TRUMAN CAPOTE,
A CHRISTMAS MEMORY

❧

BENNE BISCUITS

MAKES ABOUT 4½ DOZEN
. . . .

To the Africans who brought them to the South Carolina Lowcountry, sesame seeds, or *benne*, as they're called, are a symbol of good luck. Today, few Lowcountry parties are complete without a plate of benne biscuits either split and buttered while warm or cooled, halved, and sandwiched together with shavings of Smithfield ham. This particular recipe is adapted from one given to me many years ago by Mary Sheppard, the gifted plantation cook at Middleton Place near Charleston. **Note:** *To toast sesame seeds, spread in an ungreased pie pan, then set on the middle shelf of a preheated 275° F. oven for 8 to 10 minutes or just until the color of pale amber. Stir the benne frequently as they toast so that they brown evenly; cool before using.*

2 cups sifted all-purpose flour

2 teaspoons baking powder

½ teaspoon baking soda

1 teaspoon salt

½ teaspoon ground hot red pepper (cayenne)

⅓ cup firmly packed lard or vegetable shortening

1 tablespoon butter

½ cup lightly toasted benne or sesame seeds (see Note above)

¾ cup buttermilk

1. Preheat the oven to 425° F.
2. Combine the flour, baking powder, soda, salt, and cayenne in a large mixing bowl, then, using a pastry blender or two knives, cut in the lard and butter until the texture of coarse meal. Add the benne, toss well, then make a well in the middle of the dry ingredients.
3. Pour in the buttermilk and fork briskly just until the mixture comes together, forming a soft dough. Turn onto a lightly floured surface, knead lightly 8 to 10 times, then, using a lightly floured rolling pin, roll to a thickness of about ½ inch.
4. Cut into 1-inch rounds using a floured small biscuit cutter (or even a bottle cap), and space about 1½ inches apart on ungreased baking sheets.
5. Bake in the lower third of the oven for 15 to 20 minutes or until lightly browned.
6. Split, butter while hot, and serve warm. Or, if you prefer, cool to room temperature, split, and fill with the thinnest slivers of Smithfield ham. Pass with cocktails or set out on a party buffet.

SHIRT TAIL PIES

MAKES 6

Not very sweet, these Appalachian apple turnovers are more snack than dessert and because they travel well, they've been a lunch-pail staple for years. In parts of the Blue Ridge and Smokies they're called "fried pies," but I prefer "Shirt Tail"; it's a perfect description of how the crimped edges ripple in the hot fat. Many country people still grow and dry their own apples; the rest of us can find dried apples at the nearest supermarket.

Filling

2 cups dried apples

2 cups water

⅓ cup sugar

¼ teaspoon ground cinnamon

⅛ teaspoon ground ginger

⅛ teaspoon freshly grated nutmeg

Pastry

2¼ cups sifted all-purpose flour

½ teaspoon salt

⅓ cup firmly packed lard or vegetable shortening

½ cup ice water (about)

For Deep-Fat Frying

2 quarts vegetable oil (about)

1. For the filling: Bring the apples and water to a boil in a large, heavy nonreactive saucepan over moderate heat. Adjust the heat so the water barely ripples, cover, and simmer for about 1 hour or until the apples are soft. Uncover, reduce the heat to its lowest point, and simmer until all water has evaporated. Mix in the sugar, cinnamon, ginger, and nutmeg and cool to room temperature.
2. Meanwhile, prepare the pastry: Combine the flour and salt in a large mixing bowl, then,

using a pastry blender, cut in the lard until the texture of coarse meal. Add the ice water slowly, forking all the while, just until the pastry holds together.

3. Roll the pastry slightly thinner than pie crust on a lightly floured surface, then cut into rounds using a 6-inch saucer as a template. Gather and reroll the scraps; you should have six pastry rounds.

4. Scoop about 1/3 cup of the apple mixture into the center of each round, moisten the edges all around with water, then fold over. Pinch the edges to seal, crimp with the tines of a fork, then prick one side of each pie several times to allow steam to escape.

5. Pour the oil to a depth of 1 1/2 to 2 inches in a deep-fat fryer or large, deep skillet; insert a deep-fat thermometer and set over moderately high heat.

6. When the fat reaches 375° F., ease in one pie and fry for 4 to 5 minutes, turning as needed so that both sides brown evenly. Lift to paper toweling to drain. Fry and drain the remaining pies the same way.

7. Serve warm or at room temperature. They're delicious either way.

CILE'S CUCUMBER TEA SANDWICHES

MAKES 26 TO 28 SMALL SANDWICHES

· ·

Not so long ago when I drove to Hattiesburg, Mississippi, to visit Jean Todd Freeman, with whom I'd worked at *The Ladies' Home Journal* in New York, she and her sister Cile Freeman

1618 Chief Powhatan dies and his successor vows to rid Virginia of the English.

1619 On December 4, America's first Thanksgiving is observed at Berkeley Plantation (in what later became Virginia) on the banks of the James River by 38 men from Berkeley Parish, England. The plantation's three-story red-brick Georgian mansion, built in 1726 and now open to the public, was the birthplace of President William Henry Harrison.

The "brides' ship" brings 90 young women to Virginia. They are the first females to set foot in the new colony. That same year, 20 Africans arrive aboard a Dutch ship as indentured servants, not as slaves.

1621 America's first grist mill is built in Jamestown, Virginia.

1624 Only 1,218 colonists remain of the 8,500 sent to the Virginia colony. Some returned to England but the majority died of disease or starvation or were killed by the natives.

Still determined to produce fine wines in their Virginia colony, the English dispatch a French wine specialist to Jamestown. He, too, fails.

Waite gave a little party for me and among the finger foods they served were these superb cucumber sandwiches. I couldn't get enough of them, so when I began the appetizer chapter for this book, I knew that Cile's cucumber sandwiches were a "must." Here's the recipe she e-mailed me—with a few minor changes. **Note:** *Cile grates the cucumbers and onion by hand, but I pulse them in the food processor until about the texture of lentils: 4 to 5 pulses, then a good scraping of the work bowl, then another 4 to 5 pulses. That's all it takes. Cile also tells me that if the cucumber seeds are coarse or large, she removes them before she grates the cucumbers. Not necessary if you use the food processor. Left full-size, these cu-* *cumber sandwiches can be served as a light lunch or supper.*

2 medium cucumbers (about 1 pound), peeled and moderately finely grated (see Note at left)

1 small yellow onion, finely chopped or grated

1½ teaspoons salt

⅔ cup firmly packed mayonnaise (use "light," if you like)

¼ teaspoon black pepper

One 1-pound loaf thinly sliced, firm-textured white bread, crusts removed

---

LITTLE DEBBIE SNACK CAKES

"Is there a real little Debbie?"

According to the Little Debbie website, that's the number one frequently asked question. And the answer?

Yes, that curly-headed moppet in the broad-brimmed straw hat is indeed real. She's the granddaughter of McKee Foods founder O. D. McKee of Collegedale, Tennessee.

Back in 1960 when McKee's first snack cake—the Oatmeal

Creme Pie—was ready for sale in family-pack cartons (an American first), he needed a catchy name. Packaging supplier Bob Mosher suggested using the name of a family member. And that got McKee to thinking. He loved the snapshot of his little granddaughter in her favorite straw hat. Exactly the image McKee wanted. So Little Debbie, then just four, became the company icon.

Those first Little Debbie Oatmeal Creme Pies sailed off the shelves in 1960 at forty-nine cents a carton—more than fourteen million of them in less than a

year. Since then, the variety of snack cakes has increased seventy-five-fold with Swiss Cake Rolls the current favorite, Nutty Bars Wafer Bars placing second, and the original Oatmeal Creme Pies not far behind. Prices are up, too, but not enough to dent sales wherever Little Debbies are sold: in all fifty states, Canada, Mexico, and Puerto Rico plus U.S. military bases around the world.

Line up the 133 billion-plus Little Debbie Snack Cakes that have sold since 1960 and they'd stretch to the moon and back four times.

Talk about taking the cake!

1. Line a mesh colander or large fine sieve with a clean, dry dish towel; add the cucumbers, onion, and salt; toss well; then let drain for about 1 hour. Bundle the cucumber mixture in the towel, then wring as dry as possible.

2. Place the cucumber mixture in a small bowl and blend in ⅓ cup of the mayonnaise along with the pepper.

3. Using the remaining ⅓ cup mayonnaise, lightly spread half of the bread slices. Spread the remaining slices with the cucumber mixture, then sandwich the two together, pressing down lightly.

4. With a sharp knife, halve each sandwich on the diagonal so that you have two small triangular sandwiches.

5. Arrange on a colorful plate and pass with cocktails.

CHEERWINE

Salisbury, a small town in North Carolina's rolling Piedmont, has a few claims to fame. George Washington passed through in 1791, Andrew Jackson came to study law, and a notorious Confederate prison was located here. But many would say that Salisbury's greatest distinction is that it's the birthplace of Cheerwine.

It all began in 1917 in the basement of a wholesale grocery store owned by L. D. Peeler near the railroad tracks. Peeler and a group of investors had bought out a Kentucky beverage company and founded the Carolina Beverage Corporation.

A salesman from St. Louis passed through town that year and sold Peeler the recipe for a wild cherry flavoring. He blended it with nine other flavors and presto: Cheerwine, a fizzy soft drink the color of Burgundy wine.

Although somewhat extravagantly called "the Nectar of the Tar Heels," Cheerwine remained a Salisbury secret for many years. Drive a few miles in any direction and nobody had even heard of it. As late as the mid-1940s a young Salisburian traveled to Raleigh to join the Marines. Sitting down to lunch at a drugstore counter, he ordered a sandwich and a Cheerwine.

"Sir," sniffed the counterman, "we don't sell wine in drugstores."

Fifty years later, a Salisburian whose brother lived in Birmingham, Alabama, was assured that he was welcome to visit as long as he brought a few six-packs of Cheerwine.

Today, Cheerwine's website tells the story of an expanding empire. The drink is now available in thirteen states, mostly southern, but there are a few outposts as far west as Texas.

What's more, two years ago Cheerwine announced an agreement with a Norwegian firm to bottle the drink in Oslo. And there have even been feelers from Russia and Africa.

The drink itself is not the only product offered by Cheerwine's makers. There is Diet Cheerwine, of course, and a sherbet called Cheerwine Swirl. The website offers recipes for Cheerwine cake, Cheerwine pie, even a Cheerwine barbecue sauce.

For Cheerwine, the future looks, well, cheerful. Yesterday: a grocery-store basement. Today: the Solid South. Tomorrow: the world?

WATERCRESS FINGER SANDWICHES

MAKES 26 TO 28 SMALL SANDWICHES

· ·

"Finger sandwich" is just another way of saying "tea sandwich," meaning that the sandwiches are dainty enough to be picked up with the fingers and eaten in one or two bites. Like cucumber sandwiches, these are tea party staples; rare is the southern hostess who doesn't serve them. **Note:** *Because of the saltiness of the cream cheese, the filling is not likely to need additional salt, but taste to make sure.* **Tip:** *So that the filling isn't watery, pat the watercress leaves as dry as possible on paper toweling before mincing.*

One 8-ounce package "light" cream cheese (Neufchâtel), at room temperature

⅔ cup finely minced tender young watercress leaves (see Tip above)

1 large scallion, trimmed and finely minced (include some green tops)

1 tablespoon mayonnaise (about)

1 teaspoon finely snipped fresh dill

¼ teaspoon black pepper

¼ teaspoon hot red pepper sauce

One 1-pound loaf thinly sliced, firm-textured white bread, crusts removed

1. Place the cream cheese in a medium-size bowl; add the watercress, scallion, mayonnaise, dill, black pepper, and hot pepper sauce, and cream until smooth. If the mixture seems stiff, beat in an additional tablespoon or so of mayonnaise. Taste for salt and add, as needed. **Note:** *The filling can be made a day ahead of time, covered, and refrigerated. Let stand at room temperature for about 30 minutes or until soft enough to spread.*

2. Spread half the slices of bread with the watercress mixture, then top with the remaining slices, pressing down lightly.

3. With a sharp knife, halve each sandwich on the diagonal so that you have two small triangular sandwiches.

4. Arrange on a colorful plate and set out on a buffet or tea table. Or pass with cocktails.

LITTLE TOMATO TRIANGLES

MAKES ABOUT 3 DOZEN SMALL OR 6 DOZEN BITE-SIZE SANDWICHES

· ·

One blistering summer night when I stopped by Crook's Corner, a favorite Chapel Hill restaurant, chef Bill Smith sent out a plate of bite-size tomato sandwiches as an appetizer—the best I've ever eaten. Bill made them especially for us because one of his staff had brought in some tomatoes from her own garden. There are five ingredients only: bread, tomatoes, mayonnaise, salt, and pepper. I now make these dandy little sandwiches whenever I find plum tomatoes full of flavor. They're the best variety for this recipe because they have firmer flesh and fewer seeds. I quarter each tomato lengthwise, scoop out the seeds, then slice each quarter into long strips ⅛ to ¼ inch wide and cut the strips crosswise into fine dice. **Note:**

Southerners insist upon Duke's mayo (page 230), but any good commercial brand will do. **Tips:** *Much to my surprise, these sandwiches can be made several hours ahead of time—something I learned after shoving a plate of leftovers into the fridge. I'd layered the sandwiches between sheets of paper toweling, then draped the lot with plastic wrap. And here's another plus: These sandwiches slice more cleanly when cold, so make the diagonal cuts (Step 3) after their stay in the fridge.*

4 firm-ripe plum tomatoes
(about 1 pound), cored and finely diced
but not peeled (see headnote)

1 teaspoon salt

½ cup firmly packed mayonnaise

¼ teaspoon black pepper

One 1-pound loaf firm-textured
white sandwich bread (18 slices, not
counting "heels"), crusts removed

1. Place the tomatoes in a large fine sieve, sprinkle with the salt, and let stand for 1 hour, shaking the sieve now and then to extract as much juice as possible. Pat the tomatoes dry on paper toweling, transfer to a small nonreactive bowl, and mix in 2 tablespoons of the mayonnaise and the pepper.

2. Using the remaining mayonnaise, skim-coat each slice of bread, then spread the tomato mixture over half of the slices. Place the remaining slices on top, mayonnaise sides down, and press firmly. **Note:** *You can prepare the sandwiches up to this point several hours or even a day ahead of time (see Tips above).*

1634 Twenty-eight-year-old Lord Baltimore founds the Maryland colony, bringing with him several hundred English men and women. En route, they pause in the Virginia colony long enough to provision themselves with hogs, cows, and poultry.

1672 King Charles II sends a group of wealthy British citizens to establish a colony in South Carolina. They call it Charles Towne.

1684–85 Captain John Thurber arrives in the port of Charles Towne from Madagascar, bringing with him a bag of rice. He gives it to Dr. Henry Woodward, who plants it and gets a good crop.

1691 Given permission to pay taxes with rice instead of money, South Carolina colonists plant vast fields of it and within a few decades, rice has become a major Lowcountry crop.

1698 Under Louis XIV, the French colonize Louisiana near the mouth of the Mississippi. Their presence helped to shape Louisiana cuisine.

1700 South Carolina rice planters harvest more rice than there are ships to export it. Still, 300 tons of Lowcountry rice is shipped to England and 30 more to the West Indies.

3. Using a freshly sharpened knife, halve each tomato sandwich on the diagonal so that you have two fairly small triangles. Then, if you're going for bite-size sandwiches, halve each triangle; I don't recommend this unless the sandwiches are cold because the tomato filling will ooze out.

4. Arrange the tomato sandwiches on a colorful plate and serve with cocktails. Or set out on a tea or coffee buffet.

Variation

Herbed Tomato Triangles: Prepare the tomato mixture as directed through Step 1, then mix in 1 tablespoon moderately finely chopped fresh basil or tarragon or 1 tablespoon finely snipped fresh dill or chives. **Tip:** *Don't make these herbed sandwiches ahead of time. The acid in the tomatoes will "brown" the fresh herbs.*

ARTICHOKE SQUARES

MAKES ABOUT 5 DOZEN

. . . .

I have no idea where this recipe originated, but I do know that it began surfacing in community cookbooks all over the South some thirty years ago and became a cocktail party staple faster than you can whistle *Dixie*. Artichoke squares are easy to make, they're cheap, and they feed a crowd. But that's not the only reason they caught the public fancy. Southerners have always been fond of artichokes—both the Jerusalem (see Jerusalem Artichoke Pickle Relish, page 361) and the globe or French artichokes used here. **Note:** *Oil-marinated artichokes*

(or hearts) are what you need because you'll use some of the oil to cook the scallions, garlic, and herbs. This recipe needs no salt because of the saltiness of the artichokes and the cheese.

Three 4-ounce jars oil-marinated artichoke hearts, drained and 2 tablespoons oil reserved

4 large scallions, trimmed and finely chopped (include some green tops)

1 large garlic clove, finely chopped

½ teaspoon crumbled dried leaf marjoram

¼ teaspoon crumbled dried leaf thyme

4 large eggs, beaten until frothy with ¼ teaspoon hot red pepper sauce

¼ cup unseasoned fine dry bread crumbs

2 tablespoons coarsely chopped parsley

2 cups coarsely shredded sharp Cheddar cheese (about 8 ounces)

1. Preheat the oven to 350° F. Spritz an 8 × 8 × 2-inch baking dish or nonreactive pan with nonstick cooking spray and set aside.

2. Chop the drained artichokes fine and place in a large mixing bowl. Heat the 2 tablespoons reserved artichoke oil in a small, heavy skillet over moderate heat for 1 minute; add the scallions and stir-fry for 2 minutes or until beginning to color. Add the garlic, marjoram, and thyme and cook, stirring often, for 3 to 4 minutes or until the scallions are limp and golden. Set off the heat and cool for 5 minutes.

3. Meanwhile, mix the beaten eggs, bread crumbs, and parsley into the chopped arti-

chokes. Fold in the shredded cheese, then the cooled scallion mixture. Pour into the baking dish, spreading to the corners.

4. Slide onto the middle oven shelf and bake uncovered for about 30 minutes or until lightly browned and set like custard. Transfer to a wire rack and cool for 15 minutes.

5. Cut into 1-inch squares and serve warm or at room temperature.

PIMIENTO CHEESE

MAKES ABOUT 4 CUPS

. . . .

"The peanut butter of my childhood," is how novelist Reynolds Price describes this beloved southern sandwich spread. I remember pimiento cheese sandwiches (or "pimento," as Southerners often spell it) being on the menu almost every day at the Fred A. Olds Elementary School in West Raleigh, also at Needham Broughton High School where I attended grades eight through twelve. I also recall vats of freshly made pimiento cheese at one mom-and-pop grocery, which could be scooped out by the pint or quart. Today, most southern supermarkets sell little tubs of pimiento cheese, locally (or at least regionally) made. Some of them are quite acceptable but none is as good as homemade. All the years that I lived in New York City, I never encountered pimiento cheese outside my own apartment. I made it often using this, my favorite recipe. And not just for sandwiches, either. Sometimes I'd stuff it into celery as I'd seen my mother's southern friends do for their sewing circle or book club meetings. I even served it as a dip for crudités, which impressed my New York friends so much they asked for the recipe. As Reynolds Price also says (he, by the way, was a few grades behind me at Needham Broughton High School), "I seldom met a non-Southerner who knew what it [pimiento cheese] was, though they take to it on contact." **Tip:** *The fastest way to grate an onion is on a Microplane grater.*

I pound very sharp, bright orange Cheddar cheese, coarsely shredded

¾ cup firmly packed mayonnaise-style salad dressing (or, for a little spicier pimiento cheese, ¾ cup mayonnaise-relish sandwich spread or a half-and-half mix of the two)

Three 2-ounce jars diced pimientos, well drained (reserve liquid)

2 tablespoons finely grated yellow onion (see Tip above)

2 tablespoons ketchup

2 tablespoons reserved pimiento liquid (about)

1½ tablespoons milk or half-and-half

1 tablespoon prepared spicy brown mustard

½ teaspoon hot red pepper sauce

¼ teaspoon black pepper

1. Place all ingredients in the large bowl of an electric mixer and beat at moderate speed for about 30 seconds or just until well blended. The mixture should be lumpy. If the pimiento cheese seems too stiff to spread easily, add a little additional reserved pimiento liquid, table-

spoon by tablespoon, until about the consistency of cream-style cottage cheese.

2. Transfer the pimiento cheese to a medium-size nonreactive bowl, press plastic food wrap flat on top, then allow to season in the refrigerator overnight.

3. Use as a sandwich spread or as a stuffing for snow pea pods, bite-size chunks of celery, or hollowed-out cucumber, or serve as a dip for crudités. Stored tightly covered in the coldest part of the refrigerator, pimiento cheese will keep for 5 to 7 days. **Note:** *You can prepare pimiento cheese entirely by food processor if you have a sturdy model with an 11- to 14-cup work bowl. Pulse the cheese through the medium shredding disk, then tip onto a large piece of wax paper. Remove the shredding disk and insert the metal chopping blade. Next drop a 1-inch chunk of yellow onion into the work bowl and chop very fine. Add half the shredded cheese, all the other ingredients, then the remaining shredded cheese. Pulse just until the consistency of cream-style cottage cheese, pausing several times to scrape the work bowl. That's all there is to it.*

HAM SALAD SPREAD

MAKES ABOUT 1½ CUPS
. . . .

Southerners, I've found, are partial to meat salads and sandwich spreads and I count myself among them. I use this particular spread not only to fill sandwiches large and small but also as a stuffing for hollowed-out cherry tomatoes, snow pea pods, and bite-size cucumber "boats." **Note:** *Because of the saltiness of the ham and the*

mustard, this recipe is not likely to need additional salt. But taste before serving and adjust as needed.

½ **pound finely ground fully cooked smoked ham**

⅓ **cup finely chopped yellow onion**

¼ **cup firmly packed mayonnaise-relish sandwich spread**

1 tablespoon Dijon mustard

2 tablespoons milk (about)

⅛ **to** ¼ **teaspoon ground hot red pepper (cayenne), depending on how "hot" you like things**

1. Combine all ingredients in a small nonreactive bowl, cover, and refrigerate for several hours or overnight.

2. When almost ready to serve, let the ham salad stand at room temperature for 30 minutes. If the mixture seems dry, add another tablespoon or two of milk.

3. Use as a spread for open-face tea sandwiches or full-size luncheon sandwiches.

❖

The South of every country is different, and the south of every South even more so.

—EUGENE WALTER, *MILKING THE MOON, A SOUTHERNER'S STORY OF LIFE ON THIS PLANET*

❖

HERBED EGG SALAD

MAKES ABOUT 2½ CUPS

Like the ham salad in the previous recipe, egg salad is quintessential comfort food for the Southerners I know. They will pile it into sandwiches, scoop it into hollowed-out tomatoes, mound it on a bed of greens, even eat it straight out of the refrigerator. It was my Mississippi friend Jean Todd Freeman who began adding freshly snipped chives and dill (or tarragon) to an otherwise fairly bland mix. She'd lived in Philadelphia, then New York, and as fiction editor of *The Ladies' Home Journal* had spent many luncheons not only wining and wooing literary agents in fancy restaurants but also picking up a few culinary tricks. Although fiction was Jean's metier, she was a "food natural" who instinctively knew what went with what. In all the years that I knew her, Jean perpetuated this little myth that she couldn't cook. I knew better. **Note:** *For directions on the easy way to hard-cook eggs, see the headnote for Favorite Deviled Eggs, page 22.*

12 large hard-cooked eggs, shelled and finely chopped

½ cup firmly packed mayonnaise

⅓ cup moderately finely chopped parsley

⅓ cup finely snipped fresh dill (or, if you prefer, ¼ cup finely chopped fresh tarragon)

¼ cup finely snipped fresh chives

2 large scallions, trimmed and finely chopped (white part only)

1 small celery rib, trimmed and cut into fine dice

1 teaspoon salt, or to taste

¼ teaspoon black pepper, or to taste

2 tablespoons milk or half-and-half (about)

1. Combine all ingredients in a medium-size non-reactive bowl. If the mixture seems dry, add another tablespoon or two of milk. Taste for salt and pepper and adjust as needed. Cover and refrigerate for several hours or overnight.
2. When ready to use, let stand at room temperature for 30 minutes, then use as a spread for open-face tea sandwiches or full-size luncheon sandwiches.

Variation

Old South Egg Salad: Omit the parsley, dill, and chives and add 1 tablespoon prepared yellow mustard; substitute ½ cup mayonnaise-relish sandwich spread for the mayonnaise and ¼ cup finely grated yellow onion for the scallions. Otherwise, prepare the recipe as directed.

BLACK-EYED PEA HUMMUS

MAKES ABOUT 1 CUP

Not so long ago I wrote an article for *Gourmet* on the Smokies and among the imaginative new southern dishes that I discovered while prowling the Tennessee and North Carolina high ground was this garlicky black-eyed pea hummus. It was the creation of Robert Carter, then the chef at the Richmond Hill Inn's Arbor Grille in Asheville. Offered as an appetizer, it came with fried green tomatoes, quartered and crisp enough to serve as dippers. A winning combination. If you don't want to bother about frying green tomatoes, serve this hummus with sesame crackers. Asheville's Arbor Grille is closed and Robert Carter now wears the toque at the Peninsula Grill in Charleston, South Carolina (see his Black-Eyed Pea Soup with Greens and Ham, page 71). **Note:** *To toast cumin seeds, swirl in a small dry skillet over moderate heat for about a minute or until fragrant; cool before using.* **Tip:** *If you make this hummus a day or two ahead of time, it will taste even better. About an hour before serving, take the hummus from the refrigerator and allow to come to room temperature.*

3 slices lean, smoky bacon, cut crosswise into strips ½ inch wide

1 cup frozen black-eyed peas, cooked and drained by package directions

½ cup firmly packed fresh cilantro leaves

¼ cup well-stirred tahini (sesame seed paste)

¼ cup water

3 large whole garlic cloves

½ teaspoon lightly toasted cumin seeds (see Note above), pulverized or finely ground in an electric coffee grinder

½ teaspoon salt, or to taste

¼ teaspoon white pepper, or to taste

½ teaspoon ground hot red pepper (cayenne), or to taste

1 recipe Fried Green Tomatoes (page 220) or sesame crackers

1. Cook the bacon in a small, heavy skillet over moderate heat, stirring often, for 8 to 10 minutes or until crisp; drain on paper toweling.
2. Pulse the black-eyed peas in a food processor until coarsely chopped. Add the drained bacon,

cilantro, tahini, water, garlic, cumin seeds, salt, white pepper, and cayenne, and churn for about a minute or until smooth. Taste for salt, white pepper, and cayenne and adjust as needed.
3. Serve as a cocktail dip with crisply fried green tomatoes, which have been quartered, or with sesame crackers.

WHITE BARBECUE SAUCE

MAKES ABOUT 1½ CUPS

Even though I grew up in the South, I had never heard of—let alone tasted—white barbecue sauce until a little over five years ago when *Gourmet* sent me south to write about the Smokies. First stop: The Inn at Blackberry Farm near Walland, Tennessee. I arrived shortly before dusk just as a huge buffet was being set up around the pool. Exactly what I needed after a bumpy flight from LaGuardia to Charlotte, a change of plane, an even bumpier hop over the Smokies to Knoxville, then a forty-five-minute last lap over winding roads. On the buffet was a platter of crisp raw vegetables and alongside it a dip the consistency of sour cream. One taste told me that this wasn't any dip I knew. "It's white barbecue sauce," chef John Fleer told me. I've subsequently learned that few Southerners beyond northern Alabama know white barbecue sauce. It's a staple there, however, used to dress or marinate everything from chicken to fish. According to Chris Lilly of Big Bob Gibson Bar-B-Q in Decatur, Alabama, white barbecue sauce was created by Big Bob himself back in 1925. Today, white barbecue sauce is as popular a table sauce in northern Alabama as ketchup is elsewhere. Every cook has a pet recipe for it: Some like it thick, others, thin; some keep it simple (nothing more than mayo, vinegar, salt, and pepper), others prefer to gussy it up. The recipe that follows—my own take on this Alabama classic—is only moderately gussied up. I like white barbecue sauce as a dip for crunchy raw vegetables but some Alabamians put out a basket of pretzels. I also often serve white barbecue sauce with cocktail shrimp in place of the proverbial red glop.

1 cup mayonnaise (use "light," if you like)

2½ tablespoons cider or white wine vinegar (purists insist upon distilled white vinegar but I find that too harsh)

1 tablespoon water (more if you prefer a thinner sauce)

1 medium garlic clove, finely minced

2 teaspoons Creole or Dijon mustard

2 teaspoons prepared horseradish

1 teaspoon coarsely ground black pepper, or to taste

1 teaspoon sugar

½ teaspoon salt, or to taste

1. Combine all ingredients in a small nonreactive bowl, whisking until smooth. Taste for salt and pepper and adjust as needed. Also, if you prefer a thinner sauce, whisk in an extra tablespoon or two of water.
2. Transfer the sauce to a 1-pint jar, screw the lid down tight, and store in the refrigerator. Stored thus, white barbecue sauce will keep for 5 to 7 days.
3. Serve as a dip for crisp raw vegetables, as a cocktail sauce for cold shrimp or other shellfish, or as a sauce for grilled or fried chicken or fish.

1704 With dowries from Louis XIV, 25 beautiful young French women sail into Mobile Bay. Hand-picked to marry marines at the French Royal Colony at Fort Louis de la Mobile, they give birth to the first generation of Alabama "first families," who later gain fame for the tables they set.

1705 Robert Beverley's *History of the Present State of Virginia* is published and describes the local bounty—from fish and shellfish to deer, and "wild turkeys of a incridible Bigness . . ."

1708 The first African slaves arrive in Louisiana.

1710 Rations grow so scarce in the Louisiana colony that to obtain food, the men are permitted to live among the local tribes. It's a move that will impact Louisiana cuisine.

1711 America's first carnival (Mardi Gras) takes place in Mobile, Alabama.

1712 The huge Carolina colony is split and soon the simple suppers of North Carolina's hard-scrabble farmers contrast sharply with the feasts of South Carolina's planter aristocracy.

1714 The French settle at Natchitoches; it is Louisiana's first permanent settlement west of the Mississippi.

MARYLAND HOT CRAB DIP

One of the joys of traveling Maryland's Eastern Shore is the chance to feast on blue crabs right out of the Chesapeake— and not only on whole steamed crab but also on freshly picked crabmeat prepared a hundred ways. Many Eastern Shore inns offer hot crab dip as an appetizer, some of them classic, others contemporary. This one, developed by the Maryland Department of Agriculture's Seafood Marketing Program, is fairly traditional. I picked it up while exploring crab country and have tweaked it to add my own touch. **Note:** *Though crackers are usually served with hot crab dip, I prefer raw, bite-size florets of broccoli or cauliflower, even crisp spears of Belgian endive.* **Tip:** *Given the stratospheric cost of lump crabmeat these days, I use "special"—less expensive flakes of body meat. Cheaper still is the brownish "claw meat." Either is a good choice for this dip because the crab will only be blended with the other ingredients.*

One 8-ounce package light cream cheese (Neufchâtel), at room temperature

½ cup firmly packed sour cream (use "light," if you like)

2 tablespoons mayonnaise-relish sandwich spread

1 tablespoon finely minced scallion

1 tablespoon fresh lemon juice

1 teaspoon Dijon mustard

1 teaspoon Worcestershire sauce

¼ teaspoon hot red pepper sauce

¼ teaspoon crushed garlic

¼ cup coarsely grated sharp Cheddar cheese

1 tablespoon milk (about)

8 ounces cooked crabmeat, picked over for bits of shell and cartilage (see Tip at left)

1. Preheat the oven to 325° F. Spritz a 1-quart casserole with nonstick cooking spray and set aside.
2. Beat the cream cheese with the sour cream, sandwich spread, scallion, lemon juice, mustard, Worcestershire sauce, red pepper sauce, garlic, and 2 tablespoons of the grated Cheddar in a medium-size mixing bowl until well combined. Whisk in 1 tablespoon milk or just enough to make the mixture creamy. Fold in the crabmeat.
3. Scoop the crab mixture into the casserole, spreading to the edge, and scatter the remaining grated Cheddar evenly on top.
4. Slide onto the middle oven shelf and bake uncovered for 25 to 30 minutes or until bubbling and tipped with brown.
5. Serve hot as a dip for crackers or bite-size chunks of raw vegetable (see Note at left).

❁

Only a Southerner knows that asking for "sweet milk" means you don't want buttermilk.

—ANONYMOUS

❁

ARTICHOKE DIP

MAKES ABOUT 3 CUPS

A riffle through any southern cookbook—especially a club or community fund-raiser—will turn up scores of artichoke recipes. Not Jerusalem artichokes, although these are plenty popular, but French globe artichokes. Did this passion for them begin in New Orleans and spread outward? Or did the aristocratic youths sent abroad to study before the Civil War come home with an appetite for artichokes? While in France, Italy, and elsewhere they would have encountered them prepared a dozen different ways. We do know that Thomas Jefferson grew artichokes at Monticello, even rare red globe artichokes. Whatever the reason, artichokes are a southern staple and this dip—superb with chips, crackers, or crudités—is a cocktail perennial. **Note:** *To pack sour cream or mayonnaise into a measure, scoop up by tablespoonfuls, packing each into one of the nested cups designed for dry ingredients, and level off with the broad side of a thin-blade spatula.*

Two 10-ounce jars marinated artichoke hearts, drained as dry as possible

4 medium scallions, trimmed and cut into 1-inch chunks (white part only)

1 small whole garlic clove

1 cup firmly packed sour cream (use "light," if you like) (see Note above)

½ cup firmly packed mayonnaise (use "light," if you like)

½ teaspoon salt (about)

½ teaspoon hot red pepper sauce (about)

1. Place all ingredients in an electric blender or food processor and whiz for 10 to 15 seconds or until fairly smooth. Taste for salt and hot pepper sauce and adjust as needed.
2. Scoop into a small nonreactive bowl, cover, and refrigerate for several hours.
3. Remove the dip from the refrigerator and allow to stand at room temperature for about 30 minutes before serving.

❖

Martha fixed lunch for Zelma and me that day. . . . She made us biscuits and fried white bacon, and served her best preserves. She had baked sweet potatoes still hot in the wood range and when we left she gave us a paper sack of them to carry with us.

—**MARJORIE KINNAN RAWLINGS,**

CROSS CREEK

❖

TO MAKE SASSAFRAS TEA

Wash the roots, cut in 2- to 3-inch pieces, place in a deep pan, cover with cold water, and boil for about 12 to 15 minutes. Drain and serve hot. Add lemon or sugar, if desired.

"The tea is a delicate pink and is delicious as a cold beverage."

—Mrs. I. K. Day, Iredell County, North Carolina

DEVILED VIDALIA DIP

MAKES ABOUT 2½ CUPS

I'm so fond of Georgia's sweet Vidalia onions that I decided to make a dip of them. On the first try I caramelized two pounds of Vidalias and even with my insatiable sweet tooth, found the dip more dessert than appetizer. By substituting sharper yellow onions for half the Vidalias, I came up with a dip that reminds me of the *agrodolce* (sweet-sour) onions I've enjoyed in Italy. I also think that using a dozen scallions (white part only) in place of one of the yellow onions would be equally delicious. I like this dip best with melba rounds, salty crackers, and peppery radishes, although it's good, too, with raw cauliflower or broccoli florets. **Note:** *When I call for something to be "firmly packed," spoon it into a dry cup measure, packing as you go, then level off the top with the broad side of a small thin-blade spatula.*

3 tablespoons butter

1 very large Vidalia onion
(about 1 pound), coarsely chopped

2 medium yellow onions
(about 1 pound), coarsely chopped
(see headnote)

1 tablespoon cider vinegar or
balsamic vinegar

1 cup firmly packed sour cream
(use "light," if you like)

¼ cup firmly packed Dijon mustard

½ teaspoon salt, or to taste

½ teaspoon black pepper, or to taste

½ teaspoon hot red pepper sauce, or to taste

1. Melt the butter in a large, heavy skillet over moderate heat. Add the Vidalia and yellow onions and cook uncovered, stirring now and then, for about 1 hour or until the color of pale caramel. Do not rush the caramelization by raising the burner heat; you risk burning the onions. Toward the end of cooking, stir the onions every few minutes.
2. Mix in the vinegar and cook and stir for about 1 minute or until it evaporates.
3. Remove the skillet from the heat and mix in all remaining ingredients. Taste for salt, black pepper, and hot pepper sauce and adjust as needed.
4. Serve warm or at room temperature as a cocktail dip.

PEPPERED PECANS

MAKES ABOUT 3 CUPS

These party-perfect pecans (or one of their countless variations) have long been popular down south. Some hostesses make double or triple batches and store the nuts in airtight containers as insurance against drop-in guests. **Note:** *The nuts you use should be absolutely fresh (see Sources, page 401) because no amount of seasoning can mask the rankness of rancid nuts.* **Tip:** *Here's a dish- and time-saver: Place the butter and garlic in a two-quart ovenproof glass measuring cup and microwave for about three minutes on LOW or until the butter melts. Let stand in* *the microwave for 5 minutes. Fish out the garlic, whisk in the Worcestershire and hot pepper sauces, add the pecans, and stir until nicely coated. How hard is that?*

3 tablespoons butter (see Tip at left)

2 large garlic cloves, slivered lengthwise

2 teaspoons Worcestershire sauce

1½ to 2½ teaspoons hot red pepper sauce (depending on how "hot" you like things)

3 cups pecan halves (see Note at left)

½ teaspoon salt

1. Preheat the oven to 350° F.
2. Place the butter and garlic in a small saucepan and set over low heat for 2 to 3 minutes or just until the butter melts; remove from the heat and let stand for 5 minutes. Fish out and discard the garlic, add the Worcestershire and hot pepper sauces, and whisk until blended.
3. Place the pecans in a large mixing bowl, drizzle with the melted butter mixture, and toss until nicely coated. Or, if you prefer, follow the directions given in the Tip.
4. Spread the pecans on an ungreased baking sheet and bake on the middle oven shelf, stirring often, for about 15 minutes or until nicely toasted. Watch carefully; nuts burn easily. Remove the nuts from the oven, sprinkle evenly with the salt, and toss well.
5. Spread the nuts on paper toweling, cool to room temperature, then store in airtight containers. Serve with cocktails.

PLANTERS PEANUTS

Two Italian immigrants took one of the South's classic foods and turned it into a business with a dapper logo known around the world.

Everyone knows Mr. Peanut, but few know the story of Amedeo Obici and Mario Peruzzi, the men who built Planters Peanuts. Obici came to America around 1887; only eleven and speaking no English, he arrived with the address of his Pennsylvania uncle pinned to his lapel.

Within nine years, Obici had built his own peanut roaster and started a street vendor business in Wilkes-Barre; by 1906, he had founded Planters with fellow Italian immigrant Peruzzi.

Obici hit upon a process for roasting peanuts in oil, then blanching them to eliminate the hulls and shells. At a time when such things were typically sold in bulk in country stores, Obici packaged his roasted peanuts in small bags bearing the company logo.

Now owned by Kraft Foods, Planters took off after the introduction of the debonair Mr. Peanut in 1916—the inspiration of a fourteen-year-old Virginia boy who'd entered the company's trademark contest. By then, Planters had relocated to Suffolk, Virginia, to be nearer its peanut suppliers and to eliminate costly middlemen. Obici and his wife bought a 260-acre Virginia estate and built an Italian villa there; Peruzzi married Obici's sister.

The sporty Mr. Peanut was everywhere, from the bright lights of Broadway to the pages of *The Saturday Evening Post*. In 1997, he made his debut in the Macy's Thanksgiving Day Parade, and today he travels in style in the yellow Planters Nut Mobile.

ROQUEFORT PECANS

A southern favorite for as long as I can remember, this recipe couldn't be easier. Use new-crop pecans only—the plumpest halves you can find. **Note:** *When toasting the nuts, spread them in a single layer in an ungreased large, rimmed baking sheet; stir well at half-time, and again spread in a single layer. Watch the nuts carefully as they toast: They burn easily.*

One-half 4-ounce package light cream cheese (Neufchâtel), at room temperature

4 ounces Roquefort, Gorgonzola, or other sharp blue cheese, crumbled

1 teaspoon finely grated yellow onion

¼ teaspoon hot red pepper sauce

4 cups (about 1 pound) perfect pecan halves, lightly toasted (10 to 12 minutes in a 350° F. oven and cooled to room temperature; see Note above)

1. Whisk the cream cheese, Roquefort, onion, and hot pepper sauce together until creamy. Cover and refrigerate for several hours.
2. When ready to proceed, "butter" the flat side of each pecan half with the cheese mixture, then sandwich the halves together two by two. **Note:** *These pecans should be served as soon as possible, so draft several helpers to help you sandwich them together.*
3. Pass with cocktails or put out on a tea table.

BOILED PEANUTS

Strangely, I never tasted boiled peanuts when I was growing up in North Carolina although goodness knows, I'd seen plenty of BOILED P-NUT signs at backcountry roadside stands. The truth is, I ate my first boiled peanut in New York while I was a food editor at *The Ladies' Home Journal.* Two doors down from my office sat Jean Todd Freeman, the fiction editor, whose mother down in Hattiesburg, Mississippi, kept her well supplied with boiled peanuts. A can of them always sat on Jean's desk. Knowing I was a "Tar Heel born and bred," Jean offered me a handful one day. When I admitted that I'd never eaten a boiled peanut, she was stunned, and then set about making a convert of me. Now that I've learned to boil peanuts, I must say that these are definitely better than the canned variety, which tend to be mushy. Properly cooked, boiled peanuts should be al dente. Although old-timers use only salt to season, some modern southern cooks also add four- or five- star anise or green cardamom pods to the pot. **Note:** *For sources of green (raw) peanuts and boiled peanuts (see Sources, page 401).*

1 pound green (raw) peanuts in the shell, washed well (see Note)

4 quarts (1 gallon) cold water

⅓ to ½ cup salt (depending upon how salty you like things)

1. Place all ingredients in a large, heavy pot and bring to a boil over high heat.

2. Adjust the heat so the water bubbles gently, cover, and simmer for 40 minutes. Set off the heat and let the peanuts steep in the hot water for 40 minutes.
3. Drain the peanuts well, shell, discard the skins, then pat dry on paper toweling.
4. Serve as a snack.

SLOW-ROASTED PEANUTS

MAKES 1 POUND
· ·

I've always wondered if we call these "peanuts" because they're legumes—like peas. So *pea-nut* or *peanut*, as we now spell it, makes sense. This is one of the easiest ways I know to pre-pare them and also one of the most delicious. But you must be picky about the pan in which you roast peanuts. I use a standard 13 × 9 × 2-inch aluminum pan (no nonstick coating) and find it just right. I once made the mistake of us-ing a dark pan and the nuts browned too fast and unevenly, at that. **Note:** *Though peanuts run to calories (166 per ounce), they are a significant source of protein, niacin, phosphorus, and potassium. Moreover, their fat is mostly monounsaturated.* **Tip:** *For best results, use plump, sweet Virginia Runner peanuts for this recipe (see Sources, page 401).*

I pound shelled and blanched raw peanuts
(see Tip above)

I tablespoon peanut oil or olive oil

¼ teaspoon salt, or to taste

1716 The French establish a fort along the Mississippi at what is now Natchez. The town grows rich on cotton and within 100 years only New York has more millionaires.

Virginia colonists begin moving west from the Tidewater lowlands and settling in the soil-rich Shenandoah Valley.

1717 The English and French import African slaves into "Spanish America" (Florida plus parts of Alabama, Mississippi, and Louisiana).

1718 The French build a rudimentary settlement near the mouth of the Mississippi and name it for the Duc d'Orléans, the Regent of France.

Germans begin settling in Louisiana southwest of Lake Ponchartrain (today's St. Charles Parish).

1720s South Carolina rice planters experience their first big boom; it lasts nearly 20 years.

1722 New Orleans becomes the capital of the Louisiana territory.

1728 William Byrd II and his assistants survey the North Carolina–Virginia line from Currituck Inlet some 240 miles westward. His notes on native American flora and fauna will prove to be invaluable.

1. Preheat the oven to 300° F.
2. Spread the peanuts in an ungreased 13 × 9 × 2-inch baking pan (uncoated, bright aluminum is best) and drizzle with the oil. Toss well, then spread the peanuts once again so that they are one layer deep and reach to the corners of the pan.
3. Slide the pan onto the middle oven shelf—crosswise—and roast the peanuts uncovered for 50 to 60 minutes, stirring several times, or until the color of pale caramel.
4. Take from the oven, sprinkle with the salt, and toss well; taste and adjust the salt as needed.
5. Drain the peanuts on several thicknesses of paper toweling, then cool to room temperature before serving. Good as a snack, good with cocktails.

❈

I remember the political rallies in the woods of Yazoo County . . . where Senator Bilbo and the others were of secondary importance to the barbecue and buttered yams and the biscuits dipped in molasses and the corn-on-the-cob, steamier and richer even than the perfervid rhetoric.

—WILLIE MORRIS,

TERRAINS OF THE HEART

❈

Soups, Muddles, and Chowders

From the fifteenth century on, Europeans exploring the New World—first the Spaniards, then the English and French—all remarked upon its bounty—and on the abundance of fish and shellfish in particular. With the Atlantic Ocean and the Gulf of Mexico pounding much of the South, turning the Lowcountry into a vast marine gumbo and making a peninsula out of Florida, it's hardly surprising that seafood soups figure prominently among the regional classics.

In *Two Hundred Years of Charleston Cooking* (1930) I find recipes for Crab Soup, Shrimp Soup, Fish Chowder, Gumbo with Crabs or Shrimp, Oyster Soup, and Oyster Stew with Mace. Mary Randolph's *Virginia House-wife* (1824) also gives us Catfish Soup, and early New Orleans cookbooks offer plenty of court bouillons and gumbos.

Two vegetable soups are quintessentially southern, too: groundnut (peanut), said to be George Washington's favorite, and okra. Both show up in Sarah Rutledge's *Carolina Housewife* (1847), and Mrs. Samuel G. Stoney's *Carolina Rice Cook Book* (1901) offers five different okra soups plus a crawfish (or shrimp) bisque. A facsimile of Stoney's book appears in Karen Hess's *The Carolina Rice Kitchen* (1992).

The muddles—the fish and shellfish stews of the Outer Banks and Lowcountry—were so commonplace that I believe they were passed down by word of mouth from father to son and mother to daughter. At least I've found no recipes for them printed before the twentieth century and even the ones I did find appear mainly in local cookbooks.

Approximately half of the recipes in this chapter call for fish or shellfish, among them what I call the Big Four: She-Crab Soup, Frogmore Stew, Pinebark Stew, and Rock Muddle. For me, the recipe origins are as colorful as their names; the headnotes tell their stories.

BLUE CRAB SOUP

MAKES 4 TO 6 SERVINGS

. . . .

Anyone living along the Chesapeake Bay or its tidal reaches knows that blue crabs are a singular delicacy. Just such a person is Meri Major, of Belle Air Plantation, whom I interviewed some time ago while on assignment for *Bon Appétit* magazine. I was researching a piece on the James River plantations of Virginia, the families who live there, and the regional recipes they serve. Wherever I went, I kept hearing about a wonderful cook named Meri Major, so I looked her up, then drove over for lunch one day. I wasn't disappointed. Meri served this delicate crab soup which, unlike so many other blue crab recipes, tastes mostly of crab. "I don't like it when excellent food is ruined by masking it with some other flavor," Meri explained. "This is especially true of seafood and most especially true of crab. That's why I've never made a crab cake." Meri told me that the Virginia way to eat this soup is to mash the lemon and egg garnish with the soup spoon at the outset so their flavors are released. I find this a perfect main dish for a small party luncheon. It needs only a fresh green vegetable or tossed salad to accompany, though I sometimes substitute thickly sliced heirloom tomatoes lightly drizzled with fruity

olive oil. **Note:** *If blue crab is unavailable, substitute Dungeness or even frozen snow crab. But don't expect the flavor to be the same.*

4 tablespoons (½ stick) butter

1 cup finely minced celery
(include a few leaves)

¼ teaspoon freshly ground white pepper,
or to taste

⅛ teaspoon freshly grated nutmeg

3 tablespoons all-purpose flour

6 cups (1½ quarts) milk (about)

2 cups (1 pint) heavy cream (about)

¼ teaspoon Worcestershire sauce, or to taste

⅛ teaspoon hot red pepper sauce, or to taste

1 pound lump crabmeat, picked over for bits
of shell and cartilage

4 tablespoons cream sherry

½ teaspoon salt, or to taste

2 medium lemons, *very* thinly sliced
and seeded (Meri uses only the
center portion of thin-skinned lemons)

3 large hard-cooked eggs, shelled and
thinly sliced (Meri slices only the center
portion of each egg and chops the ends;
these also go into the soup)

1 tablespoon finely chopped fresh parsley or
chervil (garnish)

1. Melt the butter in a large, heavy saucepan over moderately low heat. Add the celery, pepper, and nutmeg and cook, stirring occasionally, for about 10 minutes or until the celery is soft.

2. Blend in the flour and cook and stir for 2 minutes. Gradually whisk in the milk, then cook and stir for about 5 minutes or until the soup thickens slightly. Do not let the soup boil or it may curdle.

3. Add the cream and cook, stirring now and then, for 10 minutes or until the flavors mellow. Mix in the Worcestershire and hot pepper sauce. **Note:** *You can prepare the recipe up to this point a day or two in advance. Simply cover and refrigerate until ready to proceed.* **Tip:** *If you cool the soup, then smooth a sheet of plastic food wrap flat over the surface so no "skin" will form on top.*

4. When ready to proceed, gently fold the crabmeat into the soup using a large spoon; do not stir. Bring just to a simmer over moderately low heat; this will take about 10 minutes. Fold in the sherry and salt, taste for seasoning, and adjust the salt, pepper, Worcestershire, and hot pepper sauce as needed. Also thin with a little additional milk or cream, if you like.

5. To serve, place 2 slices each of lemon and hard-cooked egg in each of four to six heated large, broad-rimmed soup bowls; add the chopped hard-cooked egg, dividing the total amount evenly; then ladle in the soup. Garnish each portion with a light scattering of the chopped parsley. **Note:** *This soup is equally delicious cold. Simply transfer to a nonreactive bowl, cover, and refrigerate for several hours. Serve as directed in Step 5. Make sure the soup bowls are good and cold.*

1729 Baltimore is founded and soon swells with German immigrants.

1730 Germans, Scotch-Irish, Quakers, and Welsh Baptists who'd first settled in Pennsylvania begin funneling down the Blue Ridge into the Shenandoah Valley of Virginia. They bring with them their own religion, their own culture, and, not least, their own way of cooking.

1733 James Oglethorpe sails into the mouth of the Savannah River, establishes a new British colony, and names it Georgia after King George II. Oglethorpe also lays out the town plan for Savannah, incorporating a very British series of parks.

1734 German Protestants begin settling in the Georgia colony.

1735 The Georgia colony bans the import of slaves, rum, and other "ruinous spirits."

1737 With carriages and masked horsemen, New Orleans celebrates Carnival.

Natural History of Virginia by William Byrd II is published and describes in detail the fruits and vegetables growing in the Virginia colony, among them such European delicacies as artichokes, asparagus, and cauliflower.

TEXAS PETE HOT SAUCE

Never mind the lasso-twirling cowboy on the label. Never mind the "howdy pod'ner" tone of the website (www.texaspete.com). This hot sauce has nothing to do with Texas.

The story of Texas Pete begins in Winston-Salem, North Carolina, back in 1929 with sixteen-year-old Thad W. Garner. Just out of high school, Garner was college-bound when opportunity knocked. The Dixie Pig Barbecue Stand just down the road was up for sale, a chance, Garner thought, to make a little money.

So he plunked down $300—half the college money he'd earned driving school buses and delivering newspapers. The Dixie Pig was his, but more important, so was the recipe for its signature barbecue sauce, a blend so delicious it would launch a multimillion-dollar business.

Like that original barbecue sauce, Texas Pete Hot Sauce is "all about FLAVOR, not BURN . . . just the right blend of spices—not too hot, not too mild—to lasso the flavor of all your favorite dishes." It registers a fairly temperate 1,000 on the Scoville heat scale, as compared to two-and-a-half times that, minimum, for the more torrid Tabasco sauces.

Although 12-ounce shaker bottles of Texas Pete Hot Sauce are tabletop staples across the South, it is only one of the sauces the T. W. Garner Food Company produces today. Others include Buffalo wing sauce, honey mustard, seafood cocktail sauce, chili sauce, a meaty chili starter called Chili No Beans, and, of course, the barbecue sauce that set a teenager on the road to riches more than seventy-five years ago.

SHE-CRAB SOUP

MAKES 4 SERVINGS

Apparently this Charleston classic was created between 1908 and 1912. I find no mention of it in early South Carolina cookbooks: *A Colonial Plantation Cookbook: The Receipt Book of Harriott Pinckney Horry* (1770); Sarah Rutledge's *Carolina Housewife* (1847); or *Mrs. Hill's Southern Practical Cookery and Receipt Book* (1872). Nor does it appear in Mrs. Samuel G. Stoney's *Carolina Rice Cook Book* (1901), even though the original She-Crab Soup is said to have been thickened with rice. "Judging from the pasty versions served in most restaurants you would think its major ingredient is flour," writes Lowcountry culinary sleuth John Martin Taylor in *Hoppin' John's Lowcountry Cooking*. Taylor (a.k.a. Hoppin' John) believes that She-Crab soup descends from the rice-thickened Partan Bree, a crab soup popular in Scotland. Still, the She-Crab Soup in Blanche S. Rhett's *Two Hundred Years of Charleston Cooking* (1930), created by her butler William Deas ("one of the best cooks in the world") and believed to be the original, contains no rice. It is thickened with a small amount of flour. Rhett's husband, R. Goodwyn Rhett, was the mayor of Charleston soon after the turn of the twentieth century and during his term, President William Howard Taft visited the Rhetts' Broad Street home several times (it is now the John Rutledge House Inn). One evening, the Rhetts asked Deas to dress up his crab soup; he did, adding the orange roe to enrich the color and flavor. From that evening onward, She-Crab Soup has been "quintessentially Charleston." Charlestonians consider she-crabs sweeter and finer in every way. Taylor maintains that in the Lowcountry it is not illegal to take "sooks" (mated she-crabs) on hand-lines or to dip them up as long as they are at least five inches across the back. She-Crab Soup is a winter delicacy here because that's when the females are full of roe. Unfortunately, most of us living beyond the Lowcountry aren't likely to find she-crabs or live crabs, period, in the dead of winter and must settle for lump or backfin—scarcely a hardship. Needless to add, there are many versions of She-Crab Soup, three alone in that landmark Junior League cookbook, *Charleston Receipts* (1950). The recipe that follows is one that I've evolved over time—ever since I first tasted this delicacy in a Charleston restaurant. I now order She-Crab Soup whenever I visit Charleston, Beaufort, Pawleys Island, or any other Lowcountry locale.

DUNCAN HINES (1880–1959)

He was a traveling salesman, Kentucky-born, endlessly on the road, and forced to grab meals wherever he could. Hines found some of those meals so superb that in 1935 he and his wife, Florence, compiled a list of 167 favorite restaurants and gave it to friends and colleagues at Christmas along with this note:

"I am passing this information on to you, hoping that it may yield enjoyment and delectation, should you find yourself in the vicinity of one of these 'harbors of refreshment' as you travel hither and yon."

A year later, Hines published *Adventures in Good Eating: A Guide to the Best Restaurants along America's Highways*, a brisk seller because car-loving Americans welcomed this voice of experience. Soon RECOMMENDED BY DUNCAN HINES signs appeared in the top-rated restaurants, and travelers sought them out. They trusted Hines and his palate; he never accepted payoffs.

Now a respected restaurant critic, Hines traveled more widely than ever not only to update his dining guide each year but also to research his weekly column syndicated in 100 newspapers. Eventually there was a Duncan Hines hotel guide, even a few cookbooks.

Impressed, a businessman in Raleigh, North Carolina, named Roy Park realized that the Duncan Hines name, synonymous with quality, could sell a lot of food products, and the two men became partners in 1948. First off the assembly line in 1950: Duncan Hines Vanilla Ice Cream.

Six years later Procter & Gamble bought the brand and loaded supermarket shelves with Duncan Hines cake mixes as does the present brand owner, Pinnacle Foods of New Jersey.

Few fans of Duncan Hines cake mixes know who the man was. And his guides, long out of print, are forgotten—except by the people of Bowling Green, Kentucky, who stage a Duncan Hines Festival every August to honor this native son.

that serves it. **Note:** *According to Louis Osteen, chef-proprietor of Louis's at Pawleys as well as the author of* Louis Osteen's Charleston Cuisine, *"Frozen crab roe, from what Charlestonians call 'she-crabs,' is often available in fish markets." I've never seen it and thus do what others have done for years: Substitute coarsely sieved or crumbled hard-cooked egg yolks. They add the necessary richness.*

2 tablespoons butter

1 small yellow onion, finely chopped

1 small celery rib, trimmed and finely chopped

3 tablespoons all-purpose flour

4 cups (1 quart) milk

1 cup heavy cream

½ teaspoon salt, or to taste

¼ teaspoon black pepper, or to taste

½ pound lump or backfin crabmeat, bits of shell and cartilage removed

½ cup crab roe or 2 large hard-cooked egg yolks, coarsely sieved or crumbled (see Note above)

2 tablespoons Amontillado sherry, or to taste

1 tablespoon Worcestershire sauce

1. Melt the butter in a medium-size, heavy, non-reactive saucepan over moderate heat. Add the onion and celery and cook, stirring occasionally, for about 5 minutes or until soft but not brown.
2. Add the flour and stir until the vegetables are evenly coated. Gradually mix in the milk, cream, salt, and pepper. Bring just to a boil, stirring constantly, then adjust the heat so the mixture barely simmers and cook, uncovered, for 10 minutes, stirring occasionally.
3. Add the crabmeat, roe (if using hard-cooked yolks, add to the bowls just before serving), sherry, and Worcestershire sauce. Bring to a simmer over low heat and cook for about 5 minutes or until the flavors meld, stirring as little as possible. Taste for sherry, salt, and pepper and adjust as needed.
4. Divide the soup among four heated soup bowls (top with hard-cooked yolks, if using) and serve.

CHESAPEAKE CRAB CHOWDER

MAKES 8 SERVINGS

A most unusual soup that begins with slow-simmering veal bones, onions, celery, potatoes, carrots, and bell pepper and ends with a last-minute addition of snowy lumps of crabmeat. I'm ashamed to say that I've forgotten the name of the funky little café in the Fell's Point section of Baltimore where I enjoyed this soup more than twenty-five years ago; perhaps it no longer exists. But I have not forgotten the soup I ordered there one blustery day. This is my approximation of it. **Note:** *Because this soup must chill overnight, begin it the day before you intend to serve it.*

4 tablespoons (½ stick) butter

2 large yellow onions, coarsely chopped

3 medium celery ribs, coarsely chopped (include a few leaves)

2 medium carrots, peeled and coarsely chopped

1 small green bell pepper, cored, seeded, and
coarsely chopped

1 large whole bay leaf

½ teaspoon dried leaf thyme, crumbled

¼ teaspoon black pepper, or to taste

¼ teaspoon ground hot red pepper
(cayenne), or to taste

1 pound veal or beef knuckle bones

4 medium redskin potatoes, peeled and cut
into ½-inch dice

3½ cups beef stock or broth

3 cups water

⅓ cup medium pearl barley

One 15- or 16-ounce can crushed tomatoes
with their liquid

½ teaspoon salt, or to taste

1 pound lump crabmeat, picked over for bits
of shell and cartilage

¼ cup freshly chopped parsley

1. Melt the butter in a large, heavy kettle over
moderate heat. Add the onions, celery, carrots, and bell pepper and cook, stirring now
and then, for 10 to 12 minutes or until lightly
browned. Add the bay leaf, thyme, and black
and cayenne pepper, and cook and stir for 2
to 3 minutes.

2. Add the veal knuckle bones and potatoes, and
cook and stir for 3 minutes. Pour in the beef
stock and 2 cups of the water. Bring to a boil,
then adjust the heat so that the liquid barely
bubbles, cover, and simmer for 1 hour.

3. Add the barley and the remaining 1 cup water,
cover, and simmer 2 hours more or until the
flavors mellow and marry.

4. Discard the bones and bay leaf, then mix in
the tomatoes and salt. Cool the soup to room
temperature, cover, and refrigerate overnight.

5. When ready to proceed, skim off any fat that
has congealed on top of the soup. Set the soup
over low heat and as soon as it steams, add
the crabmeat and parsley. Heat for 3 to 5 minutes only, stirring as little as possible so that the
lumps of crabmeat remain intact. Taste for salt
and pepper and adjust as needed.

6. Ladle into heated soup bowls and serve as the
main course of a casual lunch or supper.

SHRIMP SOUP

MAKES 6 SERVINGS

In the South Carolina Lowcountry, where this
soup has been popular since plantation days,
cooks insist that it cannot be made without the
tiny local "crick" shrimp. It can, of course, but
soup made with brinier ocean shrimp will never
have the same sweet delicacy. **Note:** *This recipe
calls for finely ground cooked shrimp—a snap with a
food processor. Ten quick pulses should do the job.
You can also processor-chop the onion and celery in
tandem before you "grind" the shrimp.*

3 tablespoons butter

1 small yellow onion, finely chopped

1 small celery rib, trimmed and finely chopped

12 ounces shelled and deveined cooked shrimp (preferably Lowcountry creek shrimp), finely ground (see Note on page 51)

¼ teaspoon black pepper

3½ cups milk

½ cup milk blended with 3 tablespoons all-purpose flour (slurry)

1 cup heavy cream

2 tablespoons Amontillado sherry or medium-dry Madeira (Sercial), or to taste

½ teaspoon salt, or to taste

1. Melt the butter in a large, heavy nonreactive pan over low heat, mix in the onion and celery, then cover and cook for 10 to 15 minutes or until very soft.
2. Add the shrimp and pepper, stir well, then cook uncovered for about 5 minutes, stirring often. Add the milk, then while stirring vigorously, add the slurry in a slow, steady stream. Continue to cook, stirring constantly, for 3 to 5 minutes or until lightly thickened.
3. Mix in the cream, reduce the heat to its lowest point, and cook uncovered, stirring now and then, for 15 to 20 minutes or until the flavors meld. If necessary to keep the soup from boiling, slide a diffuser underneath the pan; if the soup should boil, it may curdle. Season to taste with sherry and salt, then heat 2 to 3 minutes more.
4. Ladle into large heated soup bowls and serve.
   Note: *I also like this soup well chilled.*

TABASCO SAUCE

Tabasco sales were slow to match the heat of the sauce itself. Edmund McIlhenny shipped his first batch in 1869—not as reported in 350 recycled cologne bottles but in 658 pristine new ones. There were few takers, however, until a New York wholesaler began distributing the sauce.

Legend has it that a Mexican-American war veteran who'd picked up some fiery peppers in the Mexican state of Tabasco gave a few to McIlhenny. "Not true," says Dr. Shane K. Bernard, McIlhenny historian and curator involved with the new company museum in New Orleans. The truth? No one knows how McIlhenny obtained those peppers. What is known is that he harvested his first crop in 1868 at his Avery Island plantation 140 miles west of New Orleans.

Another myth: McIlhenny's "secret" pepper sauce recipe came from competitor Colonel Maunsel White. Having been published several times, White's recipe, which called for boiling hot peppers, was hardly "secret." McIlhenny fermented his tabascos, blended them into a sauce with vinegar and Avery Island salt, then aged it in oaken barrels. He patented his sauce in 1870, but only in 1912 did the McIlhenny family win sole ownership of the Tabasco trademark.

I visited Avery Island not so long ago and was surprised to learn that it isn't an island. It's a salt dome and nature preserve of primeval beauty. I toured the Tabasco plant, too, eyes tearing.

There was only one Tabasco sauce then. Today there are six that climb the Scoville heat scale from tepid (Tabasco Green Pepper Sauce compounded of jalapeños) to explosive (Habanero). The original Tabasco brand Pepper Sauce ranks somewhere in the middle.

LITTLE BAY OYSTER STEW

One summer at our cottage on an inlet of Chesapeake Bay I made a deadly (well, almost) discovery. I was allergic to oysters. Here we were in the land of Chincoteagues and I couldn't touch them. Old Farmer Johnson, the caretaker for our little cottage, taught my mother the Virginia way to make oyster stew. Everyone says it's delicious.

1 pint freshly shucked oysters, drained and their liquor reserved

Oyster liquor plus enough cold water to total 1 cup

4 cups (1 quart) milk or 2 cups each milk and half-and-half

¼ cup (½ stick) butter, cut into pats

¼ teaspoon salt, or to taste

¼ teaspoon black pepper, or to taste

1 cup coarsely crushed soda crackers

1. Place the oysters and the oyster liquor mixture in a large, heavy, nonreactive saucepan, set over low heat, and cook for 2 to 3 minutes or just until the oyster skirts ruffle.
2. Add the milk, butter, salt, and pepper and without stirring, slowly bring to a simmer. Do not allow the stew to boil or it will curdle. Add the crackers, again without stirring, set the pan at the back of the stove—off direct heat—and let the stew stand uncovered for 20 minutes. Taste for salt and pepper and adjust as needed.
3. Ladle the oyster stew into heated soup plates and serve at the start of a full-course dinner or as the main course of a light lunch or supper.

1741 South Carolina's rice crop begins to fail, intermittent wars block shipping lanes (the War of Austrian Succession, the French and Indian War), and rice planters suffer a 25-year depression.

1742 Eliza Smith's *Compleat Housewife* is published in Williamsburg, Virginia. But the author and recipes are English.

1745 Founded only 27 years earlier, New Orleans already has six cabarets.

1747 The British gain control of the Caribbean.

1750 The discovery of the Cumberland Gap, a natural pass through the Appalachians, encourages southern colonists to push westward beyond the mountains.

Of America's 280,000 slaves, nearly 60 percent work plantations along the Maryland-Virginia "tobacco coast."

1751 Jesuit priests bring sugarcane to Louisiana, but the first successful crop isn't harvested until 44 years later. It fetches $12,000—a fortune in its time.

Local laws allow New Orleans's six taverns to sell wine and spirits—but not to soldiers, Africans, or Native Americans.

HATTERAS CLAM CHOWDER

Every state within the sound of the surf has a clam chowder, and this one, plumped with potatoes, carrots, and celery, belongs to North Carolina's Outer Banks. It's a good basic chowder—an easy one, too. Some Banker cooks use a half-and-half mix of oysters and clams in their chowders, but I prefer this one. **Note: *If you're unable to buy shucked clams, my Chapel Hill fishmonger, Tom Robinson, suggests that you buy clams in the shell and freeze them; this makes them easier to shuck. You may also get a little more clam juice. Robinson, who makes mid-weekly trips to the coast with his refrigerated truck, is open only at week's end, ensuring that his seafood is fresh, fresh, fresh.***

I pint shucked clams, drained and liquid reserved (about 4 dozen clams)

4 ounces salt pork, finely diced

I large yellow onion, coarsely chopped

2 large celery ribs, trimmed and moderately finely diced

4 small carrots, peeled, halved lengthwise, then each half cut into ¼-inch slices

3 medium red-skin potatoes, peeled and cut into ½-inch dice (about 1¼ pounds)

Reserved clam liquid plus enough bottled clam juice (about 2½ cups) to total 3 cups

2 cups water

2 large whole bay leaves, preferably fresh

¾ teaspoon salt, or to taste

½ teaspoon black pepper, or to taste

¼ teaspoon hot red pepper sauce, or to taste

1. Pick over the clams, discarding any bits of shell. Coarsely chop the clams and reserve.

2. Brown the salt pork lightly in a large, deep, heavy saucepan over moderate heat for 12 to 15 minutes or until most of the fat renders out and only crisp brown bits remain. Scoop the browned bits to paper toweling and reserve.

3. Add the onion, celery, and carrots to the drippings and sauté, stirring often, over moderate heat for 5 to 8 minutes or until limp and golden.

4. Add the potatoes, clam liquid, water, bay leaves, salt, pepper, and hot red pepper sauce. Bring to a boil, then adjust the heat so the mixture barely bubbles and cook uncovered for about 15 minutes or until the potatoes are tender.

5. Add the reserved salt pork, the clams and any accumulated juices, and simmer uncovered for about 5 minutes or just until the clams are done; do not boil or you will toughen them. Taste the chowder for salt, pepper, and hot pepper sauce and adjust as needed. Also remove and discard the bay leaves.

6. Ladle the chowder into heated soup bowls and serve with crackers or Hush Puppies (page 257).

PINE BARK STEW

MAKES 6 SERVINGS

. . . .

On a visit to Florence, South Carolina, in 1909, President William Howard Taft was served a bowl of Pine Bark Stew "and pronounced it good." So says the *WPA South Carolina Guide* (a Depression project launched to assist down-on-their-luck writers, artists, and photographers). In describing the stew, the *Guide* points out that it "contains no pine bark, but is a highly seasoned concoction of fish in tomato sauce." Stories abound as to the origin of this fish muddle, or more specifically, to the origin of its unusual name. I favor the one involving Revolutionary War commander Francis Marion ("the Swamp Fox"), whose troops holed up in the South Carolina Lowcountry and harassed the Redcoats with relentless raids. Marion's militia is said to have caught the makings of this stew in creeks and inlets, cooked it over campfires, and served it in bowls improvised of pine bark. I've seen bark peeled from pine saplings just the way cork is stripped from oaks in Portugal, and it seems entirely plausible that these canoe-shaped slabs could serve as soup bowls. Some food historians say "piffle," insisting that pine bark was used to fuel the fire over which the stew simmered. Others suggest that the stew's pine-bark color gave rise to its name. That seems unlikely because this stew is rosy. I like to think that a bit of resinous bark slipped into the stew by accident improved its flavor and from then on became an integral ingredient. As you might suspect, there are countless versions of Pine Bark Stew. One in my possession calls for

1752 — George Washington inherits Mount Vernon and sets about improving the farm.

1753 — Because many Louisianans can't afford French brandy, the regimental adjutant allows the sale of tafia, a cheap faux brandy made from sugarcane.

The Moravians, Protestant missionaries (German-speaking but originally from the Czech province of Moravia), travel south from Bethlehem, Pennsylvania, and begin settling in the North Carolina Piedmont. They call their community Bethabara ("house of passage") because they intend it to be merely a way station. Much of it still stands near Winston-Salem. Their contributions to local cooking can be tasted today.

1755 — The British begin a ten-year deportation of the French-speaking Acadians from Nova Scotia, shipping them to the American colonies. Denied entry, hundreds are returned to France or sent to England.

1756 — Baltimore establishes trade with the British West Indies that will last 100 years. Chief exports: barrel staves, beans, bread, corn, ham, iron, peas, and tobacco. Major imports: rum, slaves, and sugar.

bream, bacon, onions, a full bottle of ketchup, a little vinegar for tartness, some sugar to temper the tartness, ground cloves, and cinnamon, plus peppers both red and black. The ketchup put me off of that recipe. This one seems more authentic. **Note:** *If you use catfish, make sure that they are home-grown; so many of the catfish now coming to market are from South Vietnam's polluted Mekong Delta.*

6 ounces salt pork or slab bacon, cut into fine dice

1 large yellow onion, coarsely chopped

2 large all-purpose potatoes, peeled and cut into 1-inch cubes

2 large whole bay leaves, preferably fresh

1 teaspoon salt, or to taste

¼ teaspoon black pepper, or to taste

¼ teaspoon ground hot red pepper (cayenne), or to taste

6 bream, bass, catfish, or brook trout fillets (about 2 pounds) (see Note above)

3 cups boiling water

2 medium-large firm-ripe tomatoes, peeled, cored, seeded, and coarsely chopped or 1½ cups canned crushed tomatoes

1. Cook the salt pork in a large, heavy kettle over moderately high heat for 8 to 10 minutes or until crisp and brown; using a slotted spoon, scoop to paper toweling and reserve.
2. Add the onion to the kettle drippings and cook, stirring often, for about 5 minutes or until limp and lightly browned. Add the pota-

toes, cover, reduce the heat to moderately low, and "sweat" for about 10 minutes or until the potatoes are beginning to soften.
3. Mix in the bay leaves, salt, and two peppers, then lay the fish on top of the potato-onion mixture. Pour in the boiling water, then the tomatoes, and bring to a boil. Adjust the heat so the stew bubbles gently, cover, and cook for about 10 minutes or until the fish barely flakes. Taste the stew for salt, black and red pepper, and adjust as needed; discard the bay leaves. **Note:** *Southerners cook pine bark stew for 30 minutes or more, but I'm not fond of falling-apart fish.*
4. Using a slotted spatula, place a fish fillet in each of six heated soup bowls. Ladle the kettle mixture on top, sprinkle each portion with some of the reserved salt pork, and serve with Iron Skillet Corn Bread (page 254) or Hush Puppies (page 257).

Although [Mary Randolph] and her husband were both of the Virginia elite, they suffered financial problems . . . and ultimately opened a boarding house. If it were not for these reverses, she might never have written a cookbook at all. Or, if she had, it might have focused on a richer, more patrician cuisine.

—JOHN THORNE, SIMPLE COOKING (ON MARY RANDOLPH'S THE VIRGINIA HOUSE-WIFE, THE FIRST SOUTHERN COOKBOOK)

ROCK MUDDLE

MAKES 4 TO 6 SERVINGS

. . . .

Captain John Smith, nosing the *Susan Constant* into Chesapeake Bay in 1607, was awed by the schools of striped bass. After settling at Jamestown, he noted, "The Basse is an excellent Fish, both fresh and salte . . . There are such multitudes that I have seene stopped close in the river adjoining to my house with a sande at one tyde so many as will loade a ship of 100 tonnes." To Bankers (those living on the Atlantic's southern barrier islands), a striped bass is better known as a rock or rockfish. In his *Encyclopedia of Fish Cookery*, A. J. McClane writes, "The striped bass is an anadromous fish like the salmon, a saltwater inhabitant dependent upon fresh water rivers for its reproduction." He goes on to say that the striped bass is especially common between Cape Cod and South Carolina. On North Carolina's Outer Banks, the most popular way to prepare rock is in a muddle—what New Englanders would call a chowder. It's a humble dish beloved by fishermen, who sometimes boil it up right on the beach. Rock Muddle is so closely associated with the North Carolina coast that *The North Carolina Guide*, first published during the Great Depression by the WPA and now updated, includes it in its section on Food and Drink. "Fish muddles," the *Guide* begins, "are popular in the coastal plain, particularly when the rock are running in the Roanoke. A muddle," it continues, "is a stew made of various kinds of fish seasoned with fried fat meat, onions, potatoes, and pepper. At least it starts off

1764 The first Acadians arrive in Louisiana and settle in the bayous west of New Orleans. By harvesting the gifts of land and sea and preparing them the French way, they create the spicy, gutsy cooking called Cajun.

1765 Raising longhorns, a breed introduced years earlier by the Spaniards, the newly arrived Acadians build vacheries (cattle ranches) west of New Orleans.

1766 Now a town of 3,000, New Orleans is a melting pot of French, Canadians, Germans, Swiss, Creoles, Mulattos, Africans, and Native Americans, not to mention Spaniards arriving by the boatload.

After a 25-year decline, rice production rebounds in the South Carolina Lowcountry and prices remain high until the Revolution.

The Moravians begin building their commercial hub in central North Carolina near their earlier settlement of Bethabara; Salem, they call it. Now painstakingly restored and part of present-day Winston-Salem, this eighteenth-century Moravian town is a living museum offering tours and a variety of demonstrations. Old Salem's biggest attraction, however, may be the 200-year-old Winkler Bakery, which sells Moravian sugar cake, love feast buns, and peppery ginger cookies.

that way." Needless to add, recipes vary significantly. Some call for tomatoes, others don't. Some begin by rendering salt pork, others by "trying out" bacon. Newer recipes are often spiked with ketchup and/or Worcestershire sauce, but I prefer this old-fashioned muddle devoid of heavy seasoning.

4 ounces slab bacon or salt pork, cut into
¼-inch dice

1 large yellow onion, coarsely chopped

3 medium-size all-purpose potatoes,
peeled and cut into ½-inch dice

4 cups water (about)

1 teaspoon salt, or to taste

½ teaspoon black pepper, or to taste

4 pounds rockfish (striped bass), dressed,
skinned, and cut into 1½- to 2-inch chunks

1. Fry the bacon in a large nonreactive kettle over moderate heat for 12 to 15 minutes or until all drippings cook out and only browned bits remain. Scoop the bacon to paper toweling and reserve.

2. Add the onion to the drippings, raise the heat to moderately high, and cook, stirring often, for about 10 minutes or until limp and touched with brown. Add the potatoes, water, salt, and pepper; bring to a boil, then adjust the heat so the liquid bubbles gently. Cover and cook for 10 to 15 minutes or until the potatoes are nearly tender.

3. Add the fish, cover, and simmer for about 10 minutes or until the fish almost flakes at the touch of a fork; it will break apart as it cooks.

If the mixture seems thick, thin with a little additional water. Taste for salt and pepper and adjust as needed.

4. Ladle into heated soup bowls, scatter a little of the reserved bacon over each portion, and serve with soda crackers, biscuits, or corn bread.

REDFISH COURT BOUILLON

MAKES 8 SERVINGS

To classically trained chefs, a court bouillon is an aromatic broth used to cook fish, shellfish, assorted meats, and vegetables. My copy of *The New Larousse Gastronomique* offers nineteen different recipes for court bouillon but none remotely similar to the redfish court bouillon so popular in Mississippi and Louisiana. The recipe here is fairly typical although I've halved the amount of bacon drippings. Cajuns, particularly fond of court bouillon, cook it half the day to intensify the flavors. I've shortened the time and I still find this version plenty flavorful. **Note:** *If you use catfish, make sure that they are home-grown; so many of the catfish now coming to market are from South Vietnam's polluted Mekong Delta. If redfish, red snapper, and catfish are all unavailable, try tilapia. It works well here.*

3 tablespoons bacon drippings
or vegetable oil

1 large yellow onion, coarsely chopped

1 large green bell pepper, cored, seeded,
and coarsely chopped

2 large celery ribs, trimmed and
coarsely chopped

6 large scallions, trimmed and thinly sliced
(include some green tops)

1 cup coarsely chopped Italian parsley

2 large garlic cloves, finely chopped

2 large whole bay leaves, preferably fresh

Two 8-ounce bottles clam juice

One 8-ounce can tomato sauce

1 cup water

1 cup dry white or red wine

1 tablespoon Worcestershire sauce

1 teaspoon salt, or to taste

½ teaspoon black pepper, or to taste

⅛ teaspoon ground hot red pepper
(cayenne), or to taste

2½ pounds redfish, red snapper, or
catfish fillets (see Note at left)

1½ cups converted rice, cooked by package
directions

1. Put the bacon drippings in a large, heavy kettle over moderate heat and mix in the onion, bell pepper, celery, and scallions. Reduce the heat to low and cook uncovered, stirring now and then, for about 20 minutes or until the vegetables are very soft.

2. Stir in the parsley, garlic, and bay leaves and cook uncovered for 10 minutes or until the garlic is golden but not brown.

3. Mix in all remaining ingredients except for the fish and rice, bring to a boil, then adjust the heat so the mixture bubbles gently. Cover and cook for 1 hour or until the flavors mellow. Remove and discard the bay leaves. Taste for salt, black pepper, and cayenne, and adjust as needed.

4. Lay the fish on top of the kettle mixture, cover, and cook for 10 to 15 minutes or just until the fish almost flakes at the touch of a fork.

5. To serve, divide the rice among eight large heated soup bowls, lay the fish on top, again dividing the total amount evenly, then ladle in the kettle liquid.

FROGMORE STEW

MAKES 8 SERVINGS

I'd heard of Frogmore Stew for years but didn't taste it until I made it myself. I picked the recipe up a few years ago while in the South Carolina Lowcountry on article assignment for *More* magazine. My subject: Suzanne Williamson of Beaufort, who with husband, Peter Pollak, had just restored a small Palladian manor built when George Washington was president. When I asked Suzanne if she was familiar with Frogmore Stew, she nodded. "It comes from Lady Island just over the bridge." Others, among them John Martin Taylor, respected Lowcountry culinary historian and author of *Hoppin' John's Lowcountry Cooking*, insist that Frogmore Stew originated on St. Helena Island. I drove the length of Lady Island as well as adjoining St. Helena Island but found no Frogmore, although my map clearly showed it. Turns out it's only undergone a name change; Frogmore is now St. Helena. Frogmore not only had once been an important crossroads linking the Sea Island plantations and Beaufort but also had been headquarters for a bustling terrapin and caviar business. According to *Full Moon, High Tide*, a cookbook published by the Beaufort Academy, it took its name from "an ancestral English country estate." Whatever the origin of Frogmore, the namesake stew remains a Lowcountry staple. More shrimp and sausage boil than stew, it's bubbled up in outdoor cauldrons and served on plank-and-sawhorse tables spread with newspapers. There are many versions, some of them gussied up with potatoes, bell peppers, and tomatoes. But the simplest suits me best. This one is downsized for home kitchens.

4 quarts (1 gallon) cold water

4 medium yellow onions, quartered lengthwise

2 tablespoons Old Bay Seasoning or crab boil

1 teaspoon salt

½ teaspoon hot red pepper flakes, or to taste

1 pound kielbasa, dry-cured chorizo, or other spicy link sausage, cut into 1-inch chunks

6 medium ears sweet corn, shucked, stripped of silks, and cut into 2-inch chunks

3 pounds medium-large shrimp in the shell (about 20 per pound)

One 12-ounce can lager beer

1. Pour the water into a 4-gallon Dutch oven or stockpot. Add the onions, Old Bay seasoning, salt, and pepper flakes and bring to a boil over high heat.

2. Add the sausage and boil uncovered for 5 minutes; add the corn and boil 5 minutes more. Finally, add the shrimp and the beer. Adjust the heat so the liquid bubbles gently, and boil uncovered for about 5 minutes or just until the shrimp turn bright pink. Taste for red pepper and add more, if needed. Frogmore Stew should be moderately "hot."

3. Using a slotted spoon or mesh skimmer, ladle into large soup plates, making sure that everyone gets plenty of corn, sausage, shrimp, and onion. Spoon a little of the cooking liquid over each portion, if you like (discard the rest or save to use in soup later). Serve with crusty chunks of bread, coleslaw, and ice-cold beer.

❧

To the present day I retain a nostalgic hunger for these cockcrow repasts of ham and fried chicken, fried pork chops, fried catfish, fried squirrel (in season), fried eggs, hominy grits with gravy, black-eyed peas, collards with collard liquor and cornbread to mush it in, biscuits, pound cake, pancakes and molasses, honey in the comb, homemade jams and jellies, sweet milk, buttermilk, coffee chicory-flavored and hot as Hades.

—*TRUMAN CAPOTE,* THE THANKSGIVING VISITOR

❧

CAJUN SHRIMP OR CRAWFISH GUMBO

MAKES 6 TO 8 SERVINGS

Cajuns, I'm told, serve gumbo at least once a week: gumbo z'herbes, perhaps (a green gumbo made with collards and spinach), chicken gumbo, shrimp or crawfish gumbo. This particular recipe is adapted from one given to me by Miss Tootie Guirard, a lively Cajun lady from St. Martinville, Louisiana, whom I profiled some years ago for *Family Circle*. I spent about ten days with Miss Tootie and she was emphatic about the proper way to prepare gumbo. "Don't rush your roux," she warned at the outset. "It must brown very slowly in a heavy pot." She works her roux for at least thirty minutes until it is as red, as brown as iron rust. She also thickens her gumbo with okra, not gumbo filé (powdered dried sassafras leaves). "I'd never use both," she said. And one final caution: "Never cook okra in an iron pot because it will turn black." **Tip:** *This gumbo is a great make-ahead and thus is ideal for a dinner party. Cool it, then refrigerate until about twenty minutes before serving. Reheat slowly in an uncovered Dutch oven. According to Miss*

1767 The Mason-Dixon Line is drawn as far west as the Appalachians.

Defying George III's ban on exploration west of the Appalachians, Daniel Boone pushes westward into Kentucky.

Commercial sugar production begins at New Smyrna, Florida, but fails nine years later.

1768 The British Crown appropriates Cherokee lands in the Carolinas and Virginia as well as the Iroquois country between the Tennessee and Ohio rivers.

1769 Virginia colonists begin relocating to Tennessee and Kentucky.

The Virginia Assembly names French viticulturist Andrew Estave "state winemaker," but like his predecessors, he fails to produce a palatable Virginia wine.

1771 George Washington builds a grist-mill at Mount Vernon and grows rich on the superfine flour he ships as far afield as the West Indies.

Tootie, shrimp and crawfish should never cook in a covered pan because they will disintegrate.

Okra Thickener

¼ cup lard, ham or bacon drippings

I pound tender young okra, stemmed and sliced as thin as possible

One 8-ounce can tomato sauce

Roux

3 tablespoons lard

⅓ cup unsifted all-purpose flour

Gumbo

2 large yellow onions, finely chopped

I large green bell pepper, cored, seeded, and finely chopped

3 large celery ribs, trimmed and finely diced

I large garlic clove, minced

10 cups (2½ quarts) cold water

2 teaspoons salt, or to taste

¼ to ½ teaspoon ground hot red pepper (cayenne), depending on how "hot" you like things

¼ teaspoon black pepper

1½ pounds medium-size raw shrimp (or crawfish) in the shell

4 quarts (1 gallon) boiling water mixed with 1 tablespoon salt

¼ cup thinly sliced green scallion tops

¼ cup coarsely chopped Italian parsley

2½ cups converted rice, cooked by package directions

1. For the okra thickener: Melt the lard in a large, heavy, nonreactive Dutch oven (I favor enameled cast iron) over moderately high heat. Add the okra and brown lightly for 10 to 12 minutes, stirring often and scraping any slices that stick to the spoon or the sides of the Dutch oven back into the lard. Reduce the heat to low and cook the okra uncovered, stirring often, for 30 minutes. This is hard work because okra is so sticky, but persist.

2. Add the tomato sauce and cook uncovered, stirring occasionally, for 2 hours or until the okra mixture is very dry and comes together in a ball. If it threatens to burn at any point, slide a diffuser underneath the pot. Also reduce the heat to its lowest point.

3. While the okra cooks, prepare the roux: Melt the lard in a second large, heavy, nonreactive kettle over moderately high heat. Blend in the flour, reduce the heat to low, and work and stir the roux for about 30 minutes or until it is a rich rust-brown.

4. For the gumbo: Mix the onions, bell pepper, celery, and garlic into the roux; turn the heat off; and as soon as the sizzling stops, cover and let stand for 15 minutes. Add 4 cups of the cold water to the roux, set over moderate heat, and stir for 3 to 5 minutes or until thickened. Add the remaining cold water, adjust the heat so the liquid bubbles gently, then simmer uncovered for 30 to 40 minutes or

until reduced by about half. Mix in the okra thickener, salt, cayenne, and black pepper and simmer uncovered over low heat, stirring occasionally, for 1 hour.

5. Meanwhile, boil the shrimp in their shells for 1 minute exactly in the boiling salted water. Drain, rinse, shell, and devein. Halve any shrimp that are large.

6. When the gumbo has cooked for 1 hour, add the shrimp and cook uncovered for 10 minutes. Stir in the scallion tops and parsley. Taste for salt and adjust as needed.

7. To serve, mound about a cup of the rice in the middle of six to eight heated jumbo-size soup plates and ladle the gumbo on top.

❀

All the land we traveled over this day, and the day before, that is to say from the river Irvin to Sable Creek . . . thirty thousand acres at least, lying altogether, as fertile as the lands were said to be about Babylon, which yielded, if Herodotus tells us right, an increase of no less than two or three hundred for one.

—**WILLIAM BYRD II,** 1728; NOTED WHILE SURVEYING THE VIRGINIA— NORTH CAROLINA LINE

❀

1773 Young Virginia lawyer Thomas Jefferson plants a variety of European vegetables in his garden at Monticello near Charlottesville: French green beans, Italian broccoli, and German kale, among others. Believing that fine wines can be produced in Virginia, Jefferson also gives 2,000 acres of land to Philip Mazzei, who agrees that native American grapes can be made into fine wine. The American Revolution intervenes and Mazzei's wine project ends.

1774 Desperate flour shortages in New Orleans lead to dangerous adulteration.

On October 24, ten months after the Boston Tea Party, 51 ladies stage one of their own in the North Carolina town of Edenton: "We, the Ladys of Edenton, do hereby solemnly engage not to conform to the Pernicious Custom of Drinking Tea." They further resolve not to "promote ye wear of any manufacturer from England until such time that all acts which tend to enslave our Native country shall be repealed." A Colonial teapot mounted on a Revolutionary War cannon now marks the spot of the Edenton Tea Party.

COOPERATIVE EXTENSION SERVICE

Only weeks out of college, I became an assistant home demonstration agent in Iredell County, North Carolina. Right away there were three strikes against me:

1. I'd grown up in Raleigh (as exotic to some of the farm people back then as Paris was to me) and I was clueless about the 4-H Clubs with which I'd soon work.

2. I'd gone to a Yankee school (Cornell), not W.C. (Woman's College in Greensboro) like most of the other home agents. And, finally . . .

3. I knew nothing about the Cooperative Extension Service, which had just hired me, other than that the U.S. Department of Agriculture, the state of North Carolina, and Iredell County all contributed to my paycheck.

My immediate boss, the home demonstration agent, worked mainly with home demonstration club women; the other assistant agent and I divvied up the 4-H responsibilities.

The job of all Cooperative Extension agents was to help the family at the end of the road help themselves to a better life. That meant making the farm profitable, feeding the family both economically and well, and beautifying one's self and one's home.

I soon began to understand what the Cooperative Extension Service (originally the *Agricultural* Extension Service) was all about. *Cooperation* was key: between the land-grant colleges and the U.S. Department of Agriculture, between the county agents and the specialists at the land-grant colleges, between the county agents and farm families. And needless to add, between the farm and home agents—not only in their own counties but often in neighboring counties as well.

The extension movement began in 1862 when Abraham Lincoln signed the Morrill Act, creating a network of land-grant colleges. Their mission was to teach agriculture and mechanical arts which, by extension, would help farm families increase their income and quality of life.

Only with Woodrow Wilson's signing of the Smith-Lever Act in 1914, however, did the Agricultural Extension Service officially become the educational arm of the U.S. Department of Agriculture. Soon there were Extension agents in more than forty states, women as well as men. Farm boys and girls rushed to join the 4-H Club, pushing its membership to half a million by the summer of 1918. Today there are upwards of nine million 4-H'ers, along with such celebrated alums as Dolly Parton, Reba McIntyre, and Alan Shepard. Even Roy Rogers had belonged.

Nowhere, I think, has the Extension Service been more valuable than in the South. Devastated by the Civil War, its planter aristocracy had collapsed and its hardscrabble farmers, planting cotton and/or tobacco year after year, were ruining the land.

Then along came a beetle barely bigger than a grain of rice. An interloper from Mexico, the boll weevil began chomping its way across the South at the turn of the twentieth century, and by the 1920s, it had killed King Cotton.

Thanks to the Extension Service, down-and-out farmers began to revitalize their land via crop rotation. Farm agents also taught them the wisdom of diversification. Home agents showed the farmers' wives and daughters better ways to prepare and preserve food—indeed, how to bring a little glamour into their lives and homes.

My few years with the Cooperative Extension Service taught me many valuable lessons and instilled a profound respect for the South's "salt-of-the-earth." I have never lost that respect.

HAM, OKRA, AND TOMATO SOUP

MAKES 6 SERVINGS

Having grown up in Ohio, my father probably never tasted okra until he moved to Raleigh to teach at North Carolina State College, and it was *"yecchhh!"* at first bite. As a child, I remember his saying, "When I'm elected president, no farmer will be allowed to grow okra." He was joking, of course. Still, the only times I ever encountered okra were in school cafeterias, at the homes of friends, and at the old S & W in downtown Raleigh where Daddy took us on special occasions. To be honest, I wasn't crazy about okra either. But my two thoroughly southern nieces, Linda and Kim, have taught me to appreciate it.

1 small ham hock (about 1 pound)

6 cups (1½ quarts) cold water

2 large whole bay leaves, preferably fresh

2 tablespoons bacon drippings

1 large yellow onion, coarsely chopped

1 cup diced ham (from the hock, plus additional ham if needed to round out the measure)

1 tablespoon sugar

1 pound baby okra, stemmed and moderately finely chopped

One 14.5-ounce can crushed tomatoes, with all liquid

1½ teaspoons salt, or to taste

¼ teaspoon black pepper, or to taste

1. Place the ham hock, water, and bay leaves in a large nonreactive saucepan and bring to a boil over high heat. Adjust the heat so the water barely trembles, cover, and cook until the meat practically falls from the bone, about 1 hour.

2. Remove the ham hock from the pan; strip off and dice the meat. Discard the bay leaves. Reserve 4 cups (1 quart) of the ham broth for the soup. Save the rest for cooking beans or greens another day.

3. Heat the bacon drippings for 1 minute in the saucepan over moderately high heat. Add the onion and cook for 2 to 3 minutes or until

golden. Mix in the ham and sugar and cook for 2 minutes. Add the okra and cook 3 to 4 minutes longer, stirring often.

4. Pour in the reserved ham broth, then add the tomatoes, salt, and pepper. Cover and simmer for 20 minutes, stirring occasionally.

5. Taste for salt and pepper, adjust as needed, then ladle into heated soup bowls and serve with freshly baked corn bread.

CLEAN-UP-THE-GARDEN VEGETABLE SOUP

MAKES 6 SERVINGS

. . . .

I had barely begun my job as assistant home demonstration agent in Iredell County, North Carolina, when I was sent to the northern end of the county to persuade a country woman to reinstate her teenage son and daughter in the 4-H Club. Fresh out of Cornell and never having spent much time with country folk, I was startled to find that her home was a four-room cabin with daylight streaking through walls, ceiling, and floor. In the kitchen I came upon Mrs. Farmer, a blowsy, red-faced woman, making soup mix from garden gleanings. Chickens pecked up the spills and shoats (young pigs) snoozed beside the stove. Mrs. Farmer's opening shot: "Are you a lipper or a dipper?" I had no idea what she meant. "Your snuff," she continued. "What do you do with it? I'll bet you're one of them dainty l'il things what daubs it around with a toothpick"—her definition of a "dipper." She, a "lipper" and proud of it, pulled out her lower lip and upended a can of Tube

Rose directly into it. I was unprepared for the tirade that followed. Under no circumstances would she permit her children to rejoin the 4-H Club because "it was draggin' them through the flames of hell . . .'lowed them to dance!" Which she pronounced *dayntz*. Clearly we had no common ground; in fact we could barely communicate. In defense of Mrs. Farmer, however, I will say that she made one terrific soup mix and canned gallons of it "for good winter eatin'." It's the basis for this vegetable soup—but no garden needed. I buy the makings at my local farmer's market.

3 tablespoons bacon drippings or vegetable oil

1 large yellow onion, coarsely chopped

1 medium celery rib, trimmed and thinly sliced (include some leaves)

1 medium carrot, trimmed and thinly sliced

¼ cup coarsely chopped parsley

½ teaspoon dried leaf thyme, crumbled

1 large whole bay leaf, preferably fresh

4 cups (1 quart) chicken stock or broth

3 large dead-ripe tomatoes, cored, peeled, and coarsely chopped (reserve juice) or 2 cups canned crushed tomatoes, with their liquid

1½ cups fresh whole-kernel sweet corn or if unavailable, solidly frozen whole-kernel corn

1 tablespoon sugar

1 teaspoon salt, or to taste

½ teaspoon black pepper, or to taste

8 ounces tender young okra pods, stemmed and sliced ½ inch thick or if unavailable, solidly frozen sliced okra

1. Heat the drippings in a large, nonreactive soup kettle over moderately high heat for 1 minute. Add the onion, celery, and carrot and cook, stirring now and then, for 10 to 12 minutes or until limp and lightly browned.

2. Mix in the parsley, thyme, and bay leaf and cook and stir 1 to 2 minutes more. Add the chicken stock, tomatoes and their juice, the corn, sugar, salt, and pepper. Bring to a boil, then adjust the heat so the soup bubbles gently. Cover and cook, stirring occasionally, for about 1½ hours or until the vegetables are tender and the flavors well blended.

3. Add the okra, cover, and simmer 10 to 15 minutes longer or just until tender. Discard the bay leaf. Taste for salt and pepper and adjust as needed.

4. Ladle into heated soup plates and serve with fresh-baked biscuits or corn bread.

VIDALIA ONION SOUP WITH SMOKY BACON

MAKES 4 SERVINGS

The inspiration for this elegant onion soup is one that I enjoyed some while back at the Carolina Crossroads Restaurant in Chapel Hill's historic Carolina Inn. Chef Brian Stapleton here is one of some half dozen gifted chefs bringing sophisticated cuisine to the Raleigh-Durham–Chapel Hill triangle, an area once known for food that "did

not soar." Thanks to the international corporations now doing business in the Research Triangle Park, a vast rural swatch anchored by these three university towns, this is a region of increasingly cosmopolitan and demanding tastes.

4 slices richly smoked bacon, snipped crosswise at ¼-inch intervals

2 large Vidalia onions, coarsely chopped (about 1½ pounds)

2 large garlic cloves, finely minced

⅔ cup dry white wine (such as riesling, chardonnay, or pinot grigio)

Five 3-inch sprigs of lemon thyme tied in cheesecloth with 2 large bay leaves (preferably fresh)

1 medium all-purpose potato, peeled and finely diced (6 to 8 ounces)

4 cups (1 quart) chicken stock or broth

½ teaspoon salt, or to taste

⅛ teaspoon ground hot red pepper (cayenne), or to taste

1 cup light cream or half-and-half

¼ cup finely snipped fresh chives or garlic chives

1. Fry the bacon in a large, heavy soup kettle over moderate heat for about 10 minutes or until the drippings cook out and only crisp brown bits remain. Scoop the bacon onto paper toweling and reserve.

2. Add the onions to the kettle drippings and sauté for 8 to 10 minutes or until limp and lightly browned. Mix in the garlic and sauté for

1 to 2 minutes more. Add the wine and cheesecloth bag of herbs, reduce the heat to low, cover, and simmer for 10 minutes.

3. Add the potato, chicken stock, salt, and cayenne and bring to a boil. Adjust the heat so the stock bubbles gently, then cook uncovered for 15 to 20 minutes or until the potatoes are mushy. Set the soup off the heat and cool for 20 minutes. Remove and discard the cheesecloth bag.

4. Purée the soup in small batches in a food processor or electric blender at high speed, transferring each batch to a large cheesecloth-lined sieve set over a large bowl. Once the soup is strained, discard the solids. Also rinse and dry the soup kettle.

5. Return the soup to the kettle and smooth in the cream. Set uncovered over moderately high heat for about 5 minutes or just until the soup steams. Do not allow the soup to boil or it may curdle. Taste for salt and cayenne and adjust as needed.

6. Ladle into heated soup bowls, and scatter the reserved bacon and chives over each portion. Or, if you prefer, chill the soup well and serve cold, again garnishing with the bacon and chives.

CREAMY MIRLITON SOUP

MAKES 6 SERVINGS
. . . .

Also called chayotes, vegetable pears, or custard marrows, mirlitons are particularly popular in the Deep South where they are grown commercially. Their delicate, faintly sweet flavor reminds me of cymlings (pattypan squash), to which they're related. Southerners know countless ways to prepare mirlitons, among them this silky soup. Make it a day ahead, then serve hot or cold.

3 tablespoons butter

2 medium-large mirlitons (about 1½ pounds), quartered, peeled, pitted, then each quarter thinly sliced

1 large Vidalia onion (about ¾ pound), halved, peeled, then each half thinly sliced

1 medium celery rib, trimmed and thinly sliced

3 large parsley branches

1 large whole bay leaf, preferably fresh

3 cups chicken broth

½ teaspoon salt, or to taste

¼ teaspoon black pepper, or to taste

1 cup half-and-half

¼ cup buttermilk

2 tablespoons finely snipped fresh chives

1. Melt the butter in a large, heavy saucepan over moderately high heat; add the mirlitons, onion, celery, parsley, and bay leaf and stir-fry for 2 minutes. Reduce the heat to moderately low, cover, and cook, stirring occasionally, for 20 minutes or until the vegetables are golden.

2. Add the broth, salt, and pepper and bring to a boil over high heat. Adjust the heat so the soup bubbles gently, cover, and cook for 50 to 55 minutes or until the vegetables are soft.

3. Pour all into a large fine sieve set over a large heatproof bowl; discard the parsley and bay

leaf. Purée the solids in a food processor or electric blender at high speed.

4. Combine the puréed vegetables with the soup liquid, then mix in the half-and-half and buttermilk. Taste for salt and pepper and adjust as needed. Cover and chill overnight.

5. Either serve cold, garnishing each portion with the snipped chives, or reheat just until the mixture steams; do not boil or the soup may curdle. Ladle into heated soup bowls and sprinkle each portion with the chives.

Variations

Yellow Squash Soup: Prepare the soup as directed but substitute 1½ pounds thinly sliced yellow squash for mirlitons and 8 finely chopped large scallions for the Vidalia onion; also add ¼ teaspoon finely chopped fresh (or crumbled dry) rosemary. In Step 2, cook only until the vegetables are soft—15 to 20 minutes—then proceed as directed. Serve hot or cold, garnishing each portion with a small sprig of rosemary instead of freshly snipped chives.

Cool Cucumber Soup: Prepare the mirliton soup as directed, substituting 1½ pounds peeled, seeded, thinly sliced cucumbers for mirlitons and 8 finely chopped large scallions for the Vidalia onion. Omit the bay leaf and use 3 large dill sprigs in place of the parsley. In Step 2, cook only until the vegetables are soft—15 to 20 minutes—then proceed as directed. Finally, increase the amount of buttermilk to ½ cup. Serve cold and garnish each portion with freshly snipped dill instead of chives.

1775 After years of "taxation without representation," the American colonies rise up against England and the American Revolution begins.

George Washington plants "Mississippi nuts" (pecans) at Mount Vernon.

Using the Cumberland Pass, Daniel Boone and 30 axemen hack through 208 miles of forest between Kingsport, Tennessee, and the Kentucky River, clearing a "Wilderness Trail" for Kentucky-bound colonists.

1776 The American colonies declare their independence from England but the Revolutionary War continues for seven more years.

Many in New Orleans sicken and die from eating spoiled flour.

1778 Louisville is founded and named in honor of Louis XVI. Thanks to its location on the Ohio River, it becomes a major port for goods and passengers steamboating down the Mississippi. Within 50 years, Louisville is Kentucky's largest city; it still is.

1779 Thomas Jefferson imports pecan trees from Louisiana and plants groves of them at Monticello.

COOL FLORIDA AVOCADO SOUP

MAKES 4 TO 6 SERVINGS

. . . .

When I was a teenager, my mother, father, and I piled into our pea-green Mercury and headed to Florida, where my older brother was working as an intern in an architectural firm. I was excited to be heading south (a first, since our relatives all lived in the Midwest), thrilled, too, to be adding three new states to my list. Still under the spell of *Gone With the Wind*, I yearned to see Tara-like plantations and fields of cotton. From Raleigh, it took us a day and a half to reach Florida; there were no Interstates then and the speed limit was only fifty-five on the open road. We lunched in Charleston, South Carolina, still sleepy, still poor, then drove on to Savannah for the night. Arriving just as shafts of downing sun filtered through tatters of Spanish moss, I thought Savannah the most romantic city I'd ever seen. It was down-at-heel then, even slightly decadent. By noon the next day we were in the land of oranges. What impressed me even more, however, were the avocado trees; every Florida yard seemed to have one. Back home, avocados were a "special order," still my father the botanist made sure that my brother and I met them early on—sliced thin and drizzled with a not-too-tart vinaigrette. I never dreamed that avocados could be prepared any other way until I tasted a cool, ever-so-lightly curried soup on that first trip to Florida. This is my attempt to re-create that soup from those long-ago flavor memories. **Note:** *Bright green Florida avocados are much larger than the dark-skinned Hass and Fuertes of California, yet they are more delicate and lower in calories. Indigenous to and cultivated in Latin America for more than 7,000 years, avocados were introduced to Florida in 1833 by horticulturist Henry Perrine. Only at the turn of the twentieth century, however, did they become a commercial crop.*

3 tablespoons butter

1 medium yellow onion, finely chopped

1 medium celery rib, trimmed and finely chopped

1 small garlic clove, finely chopped

2 tablespoons all-purpose flour

1 teaspoon curry powder

1 teaspoon salt, or to taste

¼ teaspoon freshly grated nutmeg

⅛ teaspoon ground hot red pepper (cayenne), or to taste

2 cups chicken broth

1 large ripe Florida avocado (about 1½ pounds)

2 tablespoons fresh lemon juice

2 cups half-and-half or light cream

1. Melt the butter in a large, heavy saucepan over moderate heat. Add the onion and celery and sauté, stirring often, for about 10 minutes or until limp and golden. Add the garlic and cook 1 minute longer.

2. Blend in the flour, curry powder, salt, nutmeg, and cayenne and mellow for 1 to 2 minutes over moderate heat. Whisk in the chicken broth, then cook, stirring constantly, for about 3 minutes or until lightly thickened. Turn the

heat to its lowest point, set the pan lid on askew, and allow the soup to mellow while you prepare the avocado.

3. Halve and pit the avocado, then scoop the flesh into the work bowl of a food processor or into an electric blender cup. Sprinkle with the lemon juice and purée until smooth. Transfer to a large nonreactive bowl and set aside.

4. Ladle about 1 cup each of the soup and cream into the processor work bowl or blender cup, pulse once or twice, then buzz until smooth; add to the avocado purée. Repeat with the remaining soup and cream, add to the avocado purée, and whisk well to combine. Taste for salt and cayenne and adjust as needed.

5. Cover the soup and chill for several hours or overnight before serving. Serve as is, or to be fancy, float a few cubes of firm-ripe avocado or thin slices of lemon in each portion.

BLACK-EYED PEA SOUP WITH GREENS AND HAM

MAKES 6 SERVINGS

For several years I've followed the career of Robert Carter, now chef at the Peninsula Grill in Charleston. To my mind, he is not only South Carolina's most creative chef but also one of the South's top talents. I first encountered Carter in the late 1990s at the Richmond Hill Inn in Asheville, North Carolina, and was so smitten with his new take on southern food that I featured him in the Smoky Mountains article I was writing for *Gourmet*. To my delight, I bumped into Carter again a few years later, this time while on assignment in Charleston for *Bon Appétit*. His food was better than ever and as proof, I offer this amazing Peninsula Grill soup. **Note:** *The recipe calls for fresh black-eyed peas and I don't mind telling you that they are the very devil to shuck. Fortunately, many farmer's market vendors have already done the job for you. If fresh black-eyed peas are unavailable, substitute the frozen.* **Tip:** *This soup can be made a day or two ahead of time; indeed its flavor will be richer after a stay in the fridge. Once the soup is done, cool to room temperature, then cover and refrigerate until ready to serve. A quick re-heating is all that's needed.*

1 cup freshly shelled black-eyed peas (see Note above)

8 ounces mustard greens, torn into bite-size pieces (8 cups firmly packed)

8 ounces collards, torn into bite-size pieces (6 cups firmly packed)

2 tablespoons bacon drippings or olive oil

½ cup finely diced ham (preferably country ham)

1 large yellow onion, coarsely chopped

3 medium carrots, peeled and coarsely chopped

2 medium celery ribs, coarsely chopped

1 large garlic clove, finely minced

8 cups (2 quarts) chicken broth

1 large whole bay leaf, preferably fresh

1 teaspoon salt, or to taste

½ teaspoon black pepper, or to taste

1. Place the black-eyed peas in a large, heavy saucepan and add enough cold water to cover them by 3 inches. Bring to a boil, cover, then set off the heat and let stand for 2 hours.

2. Drain the peas and return to the pan. Once again, add enough cold water to cover them by 3 inches. This time, boil the peas uncovered for about 30 minutes or until tender (frozen black-eyed peas will take slightly less time). Drain well and set aside.

3. Half fill a large kettle with cold water and bring to a boil over moderate heat. Add the mustard greens and collards and boil uncovered for 5 minutes. Drain the greens and plunge into ice water to set the color.

4. In the same large kettle, heat the bacon drippings over moderately high heat for 1 minute. Add the ham and brown for 3 to 5 minutes. Reduce the heat to moderate, add the onion, carrots, celery, and garlic and sauté for 8 to 10 minutes or until limp.

5. Add the broth, bay leaf, salt, pepper, and the reserved black-eyed peas and greens, and bring to a boil. Adjust the heat so the mixture simmers gently and cook uncovered for 15 minutes or until the flavors meld. Discard the bay leaf; also taste for salt and pepper and adjust as needed.

6. Ladle into heated soup bowls and serve with chunks of fresh-baked corn bread.

❧

Everybody has the right to think whose food is the most gorgeous, and I nominate Georgia's.

—OGDEN NASH

❧

GALLEGOS HOUSE BEEF, BEAN, AND CABBAGE SOUP

MAKES 6 SERVINGS

Florida cooking owes much of its flamboyance to the Spaniards who settled there long before Jamestown, long before Plymouth. I took my first taste of Spanish Florida in St. Augustine, founded in 1565 by Don Pedro Menéndez de Avilés. Still in my teens and touring the Sunshine State with my parents, I entered St. Augustine's historic quarter, then slipped inside the Gallegos House just beyond the old town gates. A simple flat-roofed, two-room structure, it was a dark, cool haven from the down-beating sun. But it was a lesson in history, too, a way to portray the life of a Spanish Colonial family in the early 1700s. My favorite room in this museum house was the kitchen, where costumed women scurried about preparing old Spanish recipes. This peppery soup, a Gallegos House specialty back then, originated, the busy cooks told me, in Galicia on the northwest coast of Spain. **Note:** *Around Ybor City, Tampa's old Cuban but now multiethnic quarter, collards are often used in place of cabbage.*

1 cup dried garbanzo beans (chickpeas), washed and sorted

8 cups (2 quarts) cold water

¼ cup olive oil

1 pound boneless beef chuck, cut into ½-inch cubes

1 large Spanish onion, coarsely chopped

2 large garlic cloves, finely minced

1 large green bell pepper, cored, seeded, and coarsely chopped

½ to 1 teaspoon hot red pepper flakes (depending on how "hot" you like things)

2 teaspoons salt, or to taste

¼ teaspoon crushed cumin seeds

1 small cabbage (about 2 pounds), quartered, cored, and thinly sliced OR 2 pounds collards, trimmed, heavy veins removed, and leaves thinly sliced (see Note at left)

1. Soak the beans overnight in 2 cups of the cold water; drain and reserve.
2. Heat the olive oil in a large, heavy soup kettle over moderately high heat for 2 minutes or until ripples appear on the pan bottom.
3. Add the beef and brown, stirring often, for about 5 minutes. Reduce the heat to moderate, add the onion, garlic, bell pepper, and red pepper flakes, and cook, stirring now and then, for 8 to 10 minutes or until lightly browned.
4. Add the beans, the remaining 6 cups of water, the salt, and cumin, and bring to a boil. Adjust the heat so the mixture bubbles gently, cover, and simmer for about 1½ hours or until the beef and beans are both very tender.
5. Add the cabbage, pushing down into the liquid, cover, and cook for 15 to 20 minutes or until the cabbage is crisp-tender. Stir the soup well, taste for salt, and adjust as needed.
6. To serve, ladle into heated soup bowls and accompany with crusty chunks of bread.

1782 Baltimore's Lexington Market opens in a pasture. Still in the same location and busier than ever, the market now sprawls over two city-center blocks and is the place to go for live blue crabs, artisanal breads, homemade sausages, and farm-fresh produce.

1783 England declares an end to the hostilities with America; two months later, Congress proclaims the Revolutionary War officially over.

1784 A market comes to Fell's Point, now part of Baltimore. Still going strong, the Broadway Market sells fresh seafood, meats, fruits, vegetables, and breads.

1787 Maryland abolishes the importation of slaves.

Jonathan Lucas builds a water-powered rice mill, which streamlines rice production in the South Carolina Lowcountry.

1789 Revolutionary War general and Virginia gentleman farmer George Washington is unanimously elected America's first president; he serves for two terms.

FLORIDA BLACK BEAN SOUP

MAKES 6 SERVINGS

· ·

Right out of Columbia Journalism School, I shared the top floor of a Greenwich Village brownstone with two other recent graduates. But only one of them—the girl from Tampa—is relevant here. She talked incessantly about Ybor City (the Cuban quarter) and the marvelous black bean soup served there. She even tried to make it herself—with unsavory results. When an article assignment sent me to Tampa, I tried several different versions of the famous black bean soup, scribbling notes as I sampled.

1 pound dried black beans, washed and sorted but not soaked

12 cups (3 quarts) cold water

3 tablespoons vegetable oil, olive oil, bacon, ham, or pork drippings

1 large Spanish onion, coarsely chopped

3 large garlic cloves, minced

One 14.5-ounce can diced tomatoes, drained

2 large whole bay leaves, preferably fresh

2 teaspoons salt, or to taste

1 teaspoon dried leaf oregano, crumbled

1 teaspoon dried leaf thyme, crumbled

¼ teaspoon hot red pepper flakes

¼ teaspoon black pepper

½ cup dry sherry

¼ cup coarsely chopped Italian parsley

2 hard-cooked eggs, peeled, the whites coarsely chopped and the yolks sieved

1. Bring the beans and water to a boil in a large, heavy, nonreactive kettle over high heat. Adjust the heat so the water bubbles gently, cover, and simmer for about 1½ hours or until the beans are nearly tender.

2. Meanwhile, heat the oil for 1 minute in a large, heavy, nonreactive skillet over moderately high heat. Add the onion and garlic and stir-fry for 10 to 12 minutes or until limp and lightly browned. Mix in the tomatoes, bay leaves, salt, oregano, thyme, red pepper flakes, and black pepper, then set off the heat.

3. When the beans are almost tender, stir in the skillet mixture, cover, and simmer for 1½ to 2 hours, stirring now and then, or until the beans are mushy; remove and discard the bay leaves. Cool the soup for 20 minutes, then purée in small batches in the food processor or in an electric blender at high speed.

4. As each batch is puréed, pour into a clean large, nonreactive kettle. Add the sherry, then set over low heat for 10 to 15 minutes, stirring often, or just until the mixture steams. Taste for salt and adjust as needed.

5. To serve, ladle into heated large soup plates, then sprinkle with the parsley, chopped egg whites, and sieved yolks, dividing the amounts as evenly as possible.

❀

The corn is full of kernels and the colonels are full of corn.

—OLD KENTUCKY SAYING

❀

TIDEWATER PEANUT SOUP

MAKES 6 SERVINGS

Peanut soup, it's said, was one of George Washington's favorites, not surprising given the fact that Mount Vernon was in Tidewater Virginia—"peanut country." These underground legumes grow equally well in Tidewater North Carolina, so peanut soup has long been a specialty there, too. In the old days, cooks would shell the peanuts, roast them, mash them to paste, then simmer them into soup. This modern version takes advantage of peanut butter; use your favorite brand.

2 tablespoons butter or bacon drippings (I prefer the latter)

1 large yellow onion, coarsely chopped

1 large celery rib, trimmed and coarsely chopped

1 large ripe tomato, peeled, cored, and coarsely chopped, or ½ cup tomato sauce

½ teaspoon crumbled leaf thyme

½ teaspoon freshly grated nutmeg or ¼ teaspoon ground nutmeg

½ teaspoon salt, or to taste

¼ teaspoon black pepper, or to taste

¼ teaspoon ground hot red pepper (cayenne)

2½ cups chicken broth

1 cup firmly packed creamy-style peanut butter

¾ cup milk

¾ cup half-and-half

2 tablespoons medium-dry sherry, tawny port, or verdelho Madeira

1790s Sugar and cotton replace tobacco and indigo as Louisiana's top crops.

Between a fourth and a third of the whites now living in Virginia are German-speaking.

On a swing through South Carolina, President George Washington tours the rice plantations of George Town and Charles Town. His diary includes this entry: ". . . we were recd. under a salute of cannon & by a company of infantry handsomely uniformed." He also writes of being "introduced to upwards of 50 ladies" at a tea party given in his honor.

1791 The French Market, today a lively indoor-outdoor sprawl of eateries, shops, and farm stands covering several city blocks, first opens in New Orleans. It is America's oldest public market. Located here is the famous Café du Monde.

1792 New Orleans bakers are fined for short-weighting loaves of bread, and barrels of spoiled flour are dumped into the Mississippi.

George Town, South Carolina, a major rice-growing area, builds a tide-operated rice mill that both increases the efficiency and reduces the cost of rice production. With George Town planters growing rich, doctors, lawyers, and other professionals abandon their careers to prospect in "white gold."

¾ cup firmly packed sour cream beaten until smooth with ¼ cup milk (topping)

2 tablespoons finely snipped fresh chives (garnish)

1. Melt the butter in a large, heavy, nonreactive saucepan over moderately high heat. Add the onion and celery and cook for 6 to 8 minutes, stirring occasionally, until lightly browned.

2. Add the tomato, thyme, nutmeg, salt, black pepper, and cayenne; reduce the heat to moderate and cook and stir for 1 to 2 minutes. Mix in the broth and peanut butter and cook

---

PEANUTS

Where did peanuts originate? Some say Bolivia, others Peru, and still others Brazil. When in doubt about the life history of plants, I turn to a source I trust: *Economic Botany* (1952) by Harvard professor Albert Hill.

"The peanut," Hill writes, "is a native of South America but was early carried to the Old World tropics by the Portuguese explorers and is now grown extensively in India, East and West Africa, China, and Indonesia."

"Portuguese" is the clue here. Following the lead of Prince Henry the Navigator, explorer Pedro Alvarez Cabral claimed Brazil for Portugal in 1500, which suggests that peanuts may be indigenous to that equatorial country. However, jars of them have also been found in the Incan graves of Peru. Were peanuts carried from Brazil to Peru? Or vice versa? Or did they grow in both places simultaneously?

Most culinary historians agree, however, that African slaves, believing peanuts to possess souls, brought them to Virginia from the Congo. *Nguba*, they called them (now Anglicized into "goober"). Slaves planted peanuts throughout the South, in the beginning for their own use. Virginia's first commercial crop was harvested as silage in Sussex County in the 1840s, North Carolina's some thirty years earlier around Wilmington.

During the Civil War, the Blues and Grays both subsisted upon peanuts. The Yanks developed a taste for the curious groundnuts that had to be dug and carried some of them home. Soon after, cries of "Hot Roasted Peanuts" rang through the stands of P. T. Barnum's circuses.

Only in the early twentieth century, however, did peanuts became a major cash crop. The boll weevil had killed King Cotton, farms lay fallow, and down-and-out southern farmers were desperate. The peanut was their salvation. And George Washington Carver of Alabama's Tuskegee Institute was their savior (see page 323). He devoted his life to proving the value and versatility of this lowly legume. For despite common belief, the peanut is more *pea* than *nut*.

Today, four types of peanuts are grown: Runners (54 percent of them are churned into peanut butter) . . . Virginias (plump and sweet, the roaster's choice) . . . Spanish (small "snacking" nuts also commonly used in candy) . . . and Valencias (little redskins roasted in the shell).

Peanut trivia abounds: Two presidents grew peanuts (Thomas Jefferson and Jimmy Carter, who still owns a Georgia peanut farm); astronaut Alan Shepard carried a peanut to the moon; and a good *schmear* of peanut butter on the lips of Mr. Ed is what kept everybody's favorite TV horse talking back in the 1960s.

uncovered for 10 minutes. Set off the heat and cool for 15 minutes.

3. Purée the mixture in two batches in a food processor or electric blender until smooth. Return to the saucepan, add the milk and half-and-half, set over moderate heat, and bring just to serving temperature, stirring often. Remove from the heat, stir in the sherry, then taste for salt and pepper and adjust as needed.

4. Serve hot, topping each portion with a drift of the sour cream mixture and a scattering of chives. Or, if you prefer, chill well and serve cold.

LIGHTLY CURRIED PEANUT BISQUE

MAKES 6 SERVINGS

· ·

Completely different from the peanut soup that precedes, this one is the creation of Lisa Ruffin Harrison, a gifted home cook whom I interviewed back in the 1980s for a *Bon Appétit* article on James River plantations. I photographed at Evelynton, where Lisa grew up. "This soup is a kind of African variation on the Virginia original," Lisa says. "It should have a blend of spicy ethnic flavors and I prefer it with a good dose of cayenne," she adds, explaining that she loves to update old southern recipes. "The walnuts take the candy-bar sweetness out of the peanuts." So do pecans, which Lisa says she now prefers to walnuts.

3 tablespoons butter

2 medium celery ribs, trimmed and coarsely chopped

I large yellow onion, coarsely chopped

I teaspoon curry powder

½ teaspoon ground cumin

⅛ teaspoon ground coriander

⅛ teaspoon ground turmeric

⅛ teaspoon ground hot red pepper (cayenne)

⅛ teaspoon black pepper

¾ cup firmly packed chunky or creamy peanut butter

5 cups rich chicken stock or broth

½ cup coarsely chopped pecans or walnuts

½ cup heavy cream

½ teaspoon salt, or to taste

Garnishes

½ teaspoon sweet paprika

¼ cup coarsely chopped roasted unsalted peanuts

2 tablespoons finely snipped fresh chives

6 tablespoons mango chutney (optional)

1. Melt the butter in a large, heavy saucepan over moderate heat. Add the celery and onion and sauté for 8 to 10 minutes or until limp and golden. Blend in the curry powder, cumin, coriander, turmeric, cayenne, and black pepper, then cook and stir 1 minute more.

2. Add the peanut butter, then gradually mix in the chicken stock. Bring to a boil, adjust the heat so the soup bubbles gently, and simmer uncovered, stirring now and then, for 20 minutes or until the flavors "marry." Add the pecans and cook, stirring occasionally, for 2 minutes more. Remove the soup from the heat and cool for 10 minutes.

3. Purée the soup by churning in batches in the food processor or in an electric blender at high speed. It will still be lumpy. **Note: *For a silky soup, force through a fine sieve.***

4. Return the soup to the pan, add the cream and salt, set over moderate heat, and bring to a simmer. Taste for salt and adjust as needed. Or, if you prefer, refrigerate the soup for up to two days. When ready to serve, reheat the soup or serve cold.

5. Ladle into heated (or chilled) soup plates, and sprinkle each portion with paprika, peanuts, and chives. Then, if you like, top with the mango chutney.

ROYAL SWEET POTATO SOUP

MAKES 6 SERVINGS

"Royal" doesn't refer to "royalty" but to Alabama-born Walter Royal, one of the South's most dedicated chefs. Barely out of graduate school, Royal headed to North Carolina's Fearrington House near Chapel Hill to work with his idol, Edna Lewis. He later became sous chef at Ben and Karen Barker's Magnolia Grill in Durham, and he is now executive chef at the Angus Barn, an immensely popular restaurant near Raleigh. Royal likes to improvise with what the South grows best, in this case sweet potatoes. For the North Carolina SweetPotato Commission, he created a soup that's both silky and savory. No sugar and spice here—nor in my adaptation below.

3 slices hickory-smoked bacon, cut crosswise into strips ½ inch wide

2½ pounds sweet potatoes, peeled and diced

1 medium Granny Smith apple, peeled, cored, and coarsely chopped

1 medium yellow onion, coarsely chopped

1 large carrot, peeled and coarsely chopped

1 medium celery rib, trimmed and coarsely chopped (include a few leaves)

1 large shallot, finely chopped

1 large garlic clove, finely chopped

½ teaspoon dried leaf basil, crumbled

½ teaspoon dried leaf oregano, crumbled

¼ teaspoon dried leaf thyme, crumbled

⅓ cup unsifted all-purpose flour

8 cups (2 quarts) rich chicken stock or broth

1½ teaspoons salt, or to taste

½ teaspoon black pepper, or to taste

¼ teaspoon hot red pepper sauce, or to taste

1 cup heavy cream

Garnishes

Sour cream or crème fraîche

Reserved cooked bacon

6 sprigs of fresh lemon thyme

1. Fry the bacon in a large, heavy soup kettle over moderate heat for 10 to 12 minutes or until the drippings cook out and only crisp brown bits remain. Scoop the bacon to paper toweling and reserve.

2. Add the sweet potatoes, apple, onion, carrot, celery, shallot, and garlic to the kettle and sauté in the drippings for 8 to 10 minutes over moderate heat or until golden. Blend in the basil, oregano, thyme, and flour and cook and stir for 2 to 3 minutes.

3. Add the chicken stock slowly, stirring all the while, then mix in the salt, pepper, and hot pepper sauce. Continue stirring until the mixture boils, turn the heat to low, and simmer uncovered, stirring now and then, for about 20 minutes or until the vegetables are soft. Set off the heat and cool for 20 minutes, stirring often.

4. Purée the soup mixture in batches in the food processor, then return to the kettle. Add the cream and bring slowly to serving temperature. Taste for salt, pepper, and hot pepper sauce and adjust as needed.

5. To serve, ladle into heated soup plates, and garnish each portion with a dollop of sour cream, a scattering of the reserved bacon, and a sprig of lemon thyme. Or, if you prefer, chill well and serve cold, thinning the soup, if needed, with a little cold milk or broth.

1793 Louisiana Governor Francisco Luis Carondelet begins closing bars and taverns.

1796 Because of meager harvests, Louisiana bans the export of corn, flour, and rice.

The Newsom family develops a recipe for smoke-curing hams on their Virginia farm. The family later moves to Kentucky and today Colonel Bill Newsom's Aged Kentucky Country Hams are cured according to that 1796 recipe. (See Sources, page 401.)

1797 George Washington builds a distillery beside his prosperous grist mill at Mount Vernon and in the first year makes $7,500 on 11,000 gallons of whiskey—a fortune in those days.

1798 To improve city lighting, New Orleans butchers and bakers agree to pay a "chimney tax." At the same time, local bakers manipulate the price of flour.

1799 French botanist François André Michaux plants tea in the South Carolina Lowcountry near Charleston on what is now Middleton Place Plantation.

If anything could be called the national dish of the South,
perhaps barbecue, even more so than
fried chicken, would be it.

Damon Lee Fowler, *Classical Southern Cooking*

Main Dishes:
Meat, Fish, Fowl,
and More

Leaf through almost any early southern cookbook and you'll discover an extraordinary variety of meat, fish, and fowl as well as some unexpectedly sophisticated recipes.

In Mary Randolph's *Virginia House-wife* (1824), I find sweetbreads, saddle of mutton, black sausage, and goose. Game bird, rabbit, and venison recipes abound in Lettice Bryan's *Kentucky Housewife* (1839); she even offers a few ways to prepare beef cheeks. A glance, moreover, at Sarah Rutledge's *Carolina Housewife* (1847) turns up turtle, terrapin, and mullet roes in addition to more familiar fare. Not even Mrs. Dull's *Southern Cooking* (1928) neglects calf's brains, sweetbreads, goose, duck, rabbit, or possum.

Why, then, have so many of these fallen from favor for the home cook? Times

change, tastes change. The Civil War killed the planter aristocracy and now the self-sufficient family farm is "going with the wind," thanks to our increasingly ravenous agro-business. Supermarkets proliferate, driving the mom-and-pop grocery and family butcher out of business; stricter hunting and fishing laws, not to mention better protection of endangered species, make wild game and fish less readily available. Finally, the big food companies have wooed and won home cooks with a staggering array of convenience foods. I find this particularly dismaying down south because Southerners have always taken pride in their distinctly regional cuisine. Old family recipes were cherished and preserved from generation to generation.

So what do southern supermarkets sell today? Sealed-in-plastic hamburger, steaks, and roasts precut half a continent away; packaged poultry parts; canned or frozen seafood. Most southern meat departments, furthermore, are devoted to pork: chops, ribs, roasts, country ham slices as well as big pink packing-house hams, side meat, salt pork, bacon, and fresh-daily local sausages—hot or sagey links, patties, or one-pound blocks. Anything else is a "special order" and good luck with that. Fortunately, farmer's markets, food co-ops, and specialty groceries are beginning to fill the void in many parts of the South.

The scent of sausage frying spins me back to my childhood. Not to my mother's kitchen but to, of all places, the local car pool. I was a little girl during World War Two and to save on gas, neighbors took turns driving four or five of us kids to school, one of whom always smelled of freshly fried sausage. We got a good whiff the instant she slipped into the car.

Sausage for breakfast sounded wonderful compared to the oatmeal, orange juice, and rich Jersey milk I downed every morning (along with a tablespoon of mint-flavored cod liver oil).

My midwestern mother never fried sausage or chicken or pork chops or any of the other things Southerners automatically dropped into hot fat. She was a good meat-and-potatoes cook but the meats she chose confounded my southern friends: leg of lamb, breast of veal, rabbit, beef heart and tongue, calf's liver. There were husky goulashes, pot roasts, even Wiener schnitzel,

which I adored because it tasted like fried chicken.

Although Mother occasionally baked a ham, I don't remember her ever cooking fresh pork. To be honest, I don't know whether it was rationed during World War Two or not (I was too young to pay much attention). I do remember, however, that roast beef and steaks were strictly rationed and reserved for special occasions. Also that beef heart and tongue, and rabbit required few of the precious "red points" in my mother's ration book. Perhaps none at all. And with chickens in the backyard, we never ran out of meat or eggs.

For Mother, chicken was something to stuff and roast like turkey, something to stew, fricassee, or bubble into a massive pot of Country Captain (a southern recipe obtained from a friend). Still, chicken never hit the skillet in Mother's kitchen, much as I begged her to fry it.

For that reason, I loved going home from school with chums; *their* mothers might be frying chicken for supper and I might be asked to stay.

As for fish, Mother made a mean oyster stew (which I couldn't eat—I'm allergic to oysters), a fairly classic salmon loaf, and tuna salad. But boiled crabs were my favorite. Using pieces of string tied to safety pins threaded with bacon, my brother and I would catch crabs right in front of our summer cottage on Chesapeake Bay. Mother would drop them into a huge cauldron of sea water bubbling on the old wood stove—

just like the local salt who had taught her the Virginia way to cook live-and-kicking blue crabs.

Most of what Mother prepared, however, came out of her Illinois background, her college days at Wellesley, or her early married years in Vienna, where my father had been teaching. Exotic stuff in our devoutly southern neighborhood. The kids liked to make fun of the "Yankee" food my family ate and I didn't like that. Today I'm proud that my mother had the courage to be "different."

Back then, however, I yearned for the pork chops, fried chicken, barbecue, and sausages my friends' mothers served. They were more to my liking and in many ways still are, thus I've spent a lifetime learning to cook them as Southerners seem almost genetically programmed to do.

I have no idea why I've always been so in love with southern food. If I were Shirley MacLaine, I'd swear that I'd been southern in an earlier life.

So what you'll find in this chapter are hefty helpings of the old-fashioned southern meat, fish, and fowl dishes I adored as a child along with imaginative improvisations by some of the New South's best young chefs. Dig in.

❧

Brunswick stew is what happens when small mammals carrying ears of corn fall into barbecue pits.

—ROY BLOUNT, JR.

❧

1800 With the price and quality of bread fluctuating wildly, Louisiana creates two grades— premium and common—and fixes the price of each.

Virginians, still determined to make good wine, begin hybridizing American and European grapes: the New World varieties for hardiness, the European for finesse. (See Southern Wines, page 121.)

Wave after wave of Virginians abandon their worn-out farms and seek fertile ground in Tennessee, Kentucky, and Ohio. But they take Virginia culture and cuisine with them.

1802 President Thomas Jefferson serves home-cranked ice cream at the White House.

1803 With the Louisiana Purchase, French-Spanish Louisiana falls into American hands and its spicy flavors begin to enrich the culinary melting pot.

The population of New Orleans is now predominantly French Creole (50 percent) and Spanish (25 percent). Both influence Louisiana cooking.

1805 Members of the Shaker religious sect arrive in central Kentucky and begin converting local citizens to their celibate way of life. They will influence Kentucky cooking.

83

APPLE AND BOURBON-BASTED PORK LOIN

MAKES 6 SERVINGS
. . . .

To keep pork roasts moist, Southerners baste them with everything from orange juice to Coca-Cola. Bourbon is an old favorite; so is apple juice or cider and I've combined the two here. With pork leaner than ever, keeping it moist is doubly difficult. It helps, I find, to use more artisanal pork such as that produced by Niman Ranch and to roast it at a high temperature for a short period of time so the heat sears the outside of the meat and seals in the juices. Finally, roasting pork to a lower internal temperature (145° to 150° F.) makes it more succulent. Although tinged with pink, this pork is perfectly safe to eat; the microbes that cause trichinosis are killed at 140° F. Indeed trichinosis, prevalent when hogs were slopped with kitchen scraps, is a thing of the past. Still, if like many Southerners you prefer well-done pork, give the roast another 15 to 20 minutes in the oven. **Note:** *It's important that the pork loin be wrapped in a thin layer of fat—this, too, increases the roast's succulence.*

One 2¾- to 3-pound boned and rolled pork loin (see Note above)

½ teaspoon black pepper

1 cup apple juice (I use an organic Gravenstein juice that has deep apple flavor)

¼ cup bourbon

2 tablespoons spicy brown mustard

1¾ cups chicken broth

½ cup half-and-half

5 tablespoons all-purpose flour

½ teaspoon salt, or to taste

1. Preheat the oven to 425° F. Rub the pork well with the pepper and place in a medium-size shallow roasting pan.

2. Whisk the apple juice, bourbon, and mustard until smooth, then brush generously all over the pork roast. Let stand at room temperature for 30 minutes.

3. Brush the pork again with the bourbon mixture and roast uncovered on the middle oven rack for about 45 minutes or until an instant-read meat thermometer, thrust into the center, registers 145° to 150° F. As the pork roasts, baste generously every 10 minutes with the bourbon mixture (this keeps the drippings from charring on the pan bottom). Transfer the finished roast to a heated platter and let stand while you prepare the gravy.

4. Pour the remaining bourbon mixture (you should have ½ to ⅔ cup) into the roasting pan, set over moderate heat, and deglaze the pan by scraping up the browned bits.

5. Pour the deglazing liquid into a small saucepan and boil uncovered over high heat for about 2 minutes, stirring often, until as thick and dark as molasses. Stir in 1¼ cups of the chicken broth and the half-and-half. Quickly blend the remaining ½ cup of broth with the flour and salt, add to the pan, and cook, stirring constantly, for 3 to 5 minutes or until the gravy thickens and no raw floury taste lingers.

6. To serve, slice the pork about ½ inch thick and top each portion with plenty of gravy. Accompany with boiled rice or mashed potatoes and smother these with gravy, too.

SPICY GRILLED PORK TENDERLOIN

MAKES 4 TO 6 SERVINGS

I hesitate to call this "barbecue" although some people might. It's unlike any barbecue I've eaten; still it's a popular way to prepare pork tenderloin down south. **Note:** *If you have no gas or charcoal grill, roast the tenderloins in the oven following the directions below.*

2 large whole garlic cloves

4 large scallions, trimmed and chunked (white part only)

¾ cup pineapple juice

½ cup cider vinegar

One 8-ounce can tomato sauce

2 tablespoons tomato ketchup

2 tablespoons molasses (not too dark)

2 tablespoons Dijon mustard

1 tablespoon packed light brown sugar

1 teaspoon Worcestershire sauce

½ to 1 teaspoon hot red pepper sauce (depending on how "hot" you like things)

Two 1-pound pork tenderloins

2 tablespoons cold butter, diced

1. Whiz the garlic, scallions, pineapple juice, and vinegar in an electric blender at high speed until smooth. Pour into a jumbo-size plastic zipper bag, add all remaining ingredients except the pork and butter, seal, and shake well to combine.

1806 With Carnival getting out of hand, the Louisiana governor bans masked balls and parades.

1808 The U.S. Constitution outlaws the slave trade.

1810 President Madison annexes West Florida, which includes Florida west of the Appalachicola River and parts of Alabama and Mississippi and Louisiana east of the Mississippi.

1813 A proper market goes up near the levee in New Orleans with flagstone floors and slate roofs. Popular items: calas (hot rice cakes), Texas beef at 12½ cents a pound, *pain patate* (cold sweet potato pie), ground sassafras (filé powder) for gumbo, bay laurel, plantains, newspapers, and lottery tickets.

1815 The Shakers begin building Pleasant Hill, their settlement in the Kentucky bluegrass. By the 1850s, there are some 600 Shakers at Pleasant Hill occupying 250 buildings and working 2,800 acres of land. They become famous for their seeds, their produce, their furniture, their architecture, and their food.

BARBECUE

Arguably the best barbecue in the state, perhaps the South, maybe the world.
—**Morgan Murphy**, *Southern Living*, on Big Bob Gibson Bar-B-Q, Decatur, Alabama

Of course, every southern state believes its barbecue to be "the best in the world" and as a Tar Heel, I devoutly make that claim for North Carolina.

Fellow Tar Heel, fellow cookbook author, and good friend James Villas agrees: "Generally, I'm so prejudiced about NC 'cue that I don't even seriously consider the stuff in other states—except the resolutely superior dry-rubbed ribs in Memphis."

Even in North Carolina there are two factions: easterners insist that their peppery, smoky, vinegary pit-cooked whole hogs beat the Lexington or western-style shoulders swabbed with a thicker sauce containing—dare I say it?—a smidge of tomato. Whether eastern-style or west-ern, "pulled pork" is what most Tar Heels prefer—smoky bits of meat, plucked from the bones and served with sweet slaw and hush puppies straight from the deep-fat fryer. I do admit, how-ever, to hankering for an occa-sional plate of ribs.

As a rule, the farther south you travel, the thicker, the redder the barbecue sauce, and some South Carolina pit masters add a bit of mustard. Once again Villas agrees: "You're probably right about sauces getting thicker and more tomatoey the farther south you go . . . Georgia really piles on the tomatoes."

I seek out barbecue wherever I travel and am pleased to say that some of it has been superb. Particularly memorable was a plate of chopped barbecue I ate some years ago in the western Kentucky town of Cadiz. It had the perfectly balanced sweet-sour, smoky pit-cooked taste I associate with North Carolina's best. Blindfolded, I don't think I could have distinguished it from the revered pulled pork of Lexington, North Carolina.

Every Tar Heel has a favorite barbecue joint and will pit its 'cue against all others: Lexington Number One in Lexington, Stamey's in Greensboro, Short Sugar's in Reidsville, Melton's in Rocky Mount, Parker's in Wilson, Flip's in Wilmington, Wilber's or Scott's in Goldsboro, Skylight in Ayden. To which I'd add the A & M in Mebane and Scott Howell's Q Shack—the new go-to place in Durham. **Note:** *'Cue connoisseurs eagerly await the reopening of Ed Mitchell's in Wilson, shuttered by legal prob-lems several years ago. To them, its Eastern-style, pit-barbecued whole hogs are incomparable.*

Unique among barbecue joints, Q Shack serves six styles of barbecue—North Carolina pulled pork; Texas chile-rubbed beef brisket; mesquite-smoked chicken, turkey, or beef sausage; and St. Louis–cut pork ribs—all of them prepared fresh every day and all of them "tender as a mother's love."

Talk about eating high on the hog.

2. Add the pork tenderloins to the bag and re-seal. Refrigerate overnight, turning the bag from time to time so the pork marinates evenly.

3. When ready to proceed, pour 1/3 cup of the marinade into a measuring cup and reserve. Pour the balance into a heavy, nonreactive saucepan and set aside. Preheat the grill to moderate heat (375° F.). **Note: If you have no grill, preheat the oven to 400° F.**

4. Grill the tenderloins with the lid up, turning and brushing now and then with the reserved 1/3 cup marinade, for 25 to 30 minutes or until an instant-read thermometer, thrust into the center of a tenderloin, reads 150° F. **Note: If you have no grill, roast the tenderloins on a rack in a shallow roasting pan on the middle oven shelf for about 35 minutes or to an internal tempera-ture of 150° F., turning and brushing or basting occasionally.**

5. Meanwhile, bring the pan of marinade to a boil over moderately high heat, reduce the heat to its lowest point, set the lid on the pan askew, and keep the sauce warm while the tenderloins grill.

6. Transfer the tenderloins to a carving board, tent with foil, and let stand for 5 minutes. Add any leftover basting marinade to that in the saucepan and simmer uncovered while the tenderloins rest. Just before serving, add the diced butter to the hot marinade bit by bit and whisk until smooth.

7. To serve, slice the tenderloins 1/2 inch thick, slightly on the bias. Fan out on heated dinner plates and top each portion with some of the hot marinade.

1818 Peanuts are grown commercially for the first time in North Carolina in the sandy flats around Wilmington.

Kentucky stages its first agricultural fair at Lexington.

1820 Napoleon's nephew, Prince Charles Louis Napoleon Achille Murat, flees Bourbon France and buys a townhouse in New Orleans and a sugar plantation near Baton Rouge. An enthusiastic cook, he concocts an alligator tail soup and a turkey buzzard stew.

1820s Baltimore surpasses Philadelphia as the country's busiest flour-milling center.

Agricultural reformer Edmund Ruffin begins publishing results of experiments on his Virginia farm. To salvage depleted soil, he recommends crop rotation, good drainage, proper plowing, and the use of fertilizer. Many heed his call and within 30 years, Ruffin is both commissioner and president of the Virginia State Agricultural Society.

1821 The U.S. buys Spanish Florida, which includes parts of Alabama, Mississippi, and Louisiana, for $5 million.

SMOTHERED PORK CHOPS

MAKES 4 SERVINGS

Because today's leaner pork tends to toughen and dry as it cooks, many beloved southern dishes have suffered. One solution is to use meat from hogs that haven't been put on low-cal diets. This updated recipe is an excellent way to ensure pork's succulence. The original says to cook the chops for an hour after they're browned—a sure bet for dry, rubbery pork. I've slashed the cooking time by two thirds, and yes, the pork chops *are* done. Moreover, they're supremely juicy and tender.

½ cup unsifted all-purpose flour

1½ teaspoons salt, or to taste

½ teaspoon black pepper, or to taste

½ teaspoon dried leaf thyme, crumbled

½ teaspoon rubbed sage

Four 1-inch-thick center-cut,
bone-in pork chops (2 to 2¼ pounds)

3 tablespoons vegetable oil

1 large yellow onion, halved lengthwise, then
each half cut crosswise into thin slices

1½ cups chicken broth or water
(I prefer broth)

1½ cups converted rice, cooked by
package directions

1. Combine the flour, salt, pepper, thyme, and sage in a pie plate, then dredge each chop well on both sides. Reserve the dredging flour.

2. Heat the oil in a large, heavy skillet over high heat for 2 minutes or until ripples appear on the skillet bottom. Add the chops and brown for 4 to 5 minutes, turn, and brown the flip sides for about 3 minutes. Lift to a plate and reserve.

3. Reduce the burner heat to moderate, add the onion to the skillet, and cook, stirring now and then, for 3 to 5 minutes or until limp and golden. Blend in 3 tablespoons of the dredging flour, add the broth, and cook, stirring constantly, for 3 to 5 minutes or until the mixture bubbles and thickens.

4. Return the pork chops to the skillet, spooning the onion gravy on top. Reduce the heat to low, cover, and simmer for 20 to 25 minutes, turning the chops at half-time, or until an instant-read thermometer stuck into the meatiest part of a chop registers 150° F. Taste the gravy for salt and pepper and adjust as needed.

5. Divide the rice among four heated dinner plates and top each portion with a pork chop and plenty of onion gravy.

❧

I heard it said that the "architecture" of
Atlanta is recocola.

—JOHN GUNTHER, U.S.A.

❧

OSSABAW PORK

It's the pork of the past and it may be the pork of the future.

Weary of "the other white meat" from mass-produced hogs that have had the fat and flavor bred out of them, chefs are excited about the Ossabaw pork now being produced on a few boutique farms in the Carolinas, Georgia, and Virginia. Unlike supermarket pork, its succulence and flavor closely resemble that of Spain's prize Ibérico pork.

There's good reason for this. Ossabaws, small feral hogs free-ranging on Ossabaw Island (second largest of Georgia's Golden Isles), descend from the Ibéricos brought to the Southeast nearly five hundred years ago. Columbus introduced them to Hispaniola on his second voyage, in 1493, and De Soto loosed herds of them in Florida in 1539, reasoning that they would proliferate and provide meat for colonists to come.

And so they did, roaming the South and eventually intermingling with the English breeds introduced later. George Washington, a man who took pride in his hams, raised Ossabaws at Mount Vernon, allowing them to forage for acorns as did the Ibéricos of Spain (after all these years, they can again be seen in the Mount Vernon barnyard; a few have even been spotted in Williamsburg).

But the Ossabaw Island Ibéricos were isolated, thus these bristly, leggy, prick-eared, pointy-snouted, black or spotted hogs are a near DNA match. What's unique about them is that their fat is mostly monounsaturated and nearly liquid at room temperature—an anomaly food chemists are studying. Is Ossabaw fat the new olive oil? Can it, like olive oil, actually raise the levels of "good" cholesterol and lower the risk of heart disease? So far no one knows.

While praising the texture and taste of Ossabaw pork, chefs complain about the consistency of its fat. So farmers like Eliza MacLean of Cane Creek Farm in North Carolina's Piedmont are crossing Ossabaws with other breeds—with Farmer's Hybrid, for example, a cross favored by Niman Ranch, purveyor of quality meats. MacLean's aim: To firm the fat without losing that singular Ossabaw succulence and flavor.

With demands for Ossabaw pork growing, traditional hog farmers are paying attention. Unfortunately, breeding stock is so limited the American Livestock Breeds Conservancy considers the numbers "critical." Moreover, writes *New York Times* reporter Peter Kaminsky, "Slow Food USA has placed the Ossabaw on its metaphorical ark of endangered breeds that have been singled out for preservation."

Now quarantined, the feral Ossabaws cannot be taken off their Georgia island. Yet hunters are allowed to kill them because they eat the eggs of loggerhead turtles, an even more endangered species.

Mainly available to chefs at present, Ossabaw pork is beginning to show up at farmer's markets down south: bacons, chops, roasts, sausages. Everything but the squeal.

PORK CHOPS WITH PECAN AND ONION STUFFING

MAKES 6 SERVINGS

Southerners have always had a penchant for stuffing things: tomatoes large and small, bell peppers, eggplant, yellow squash, mirlitons, fish, shellfish. Pork chops too, of course. This recipe, my own, teams pork and pecans, a felicitous combination, but I often substitute peanuts (see the Variation that follows). As with the previous pork chop recipe, indeed with any pork chop recipe, choosing pork that hasn't had the succulence bred out of it is key. Otherwise, the chops will toughen and dry. **Note:** *If things are to move smoothly, prepare the stuffing first; it can wait but the pork chops can't.* **Tip:** *Toast the pecans before you chop them: Spread in a pie pan and set on the middle shelf of a 350° F. oven for 10 to 12 minutes or until fragrant. But watch carefully lest they burn.*

Stuffing

2 tablespoons vegetable oil

1 medium yellow onion, moderately coarsely chopped

1 medium celery rib, trimmed and finely diced

2 medium garlic cloves, finely chopped

1 cup finely chopped, lightly toasted pecans (see Tip above)

2 cups coarsely crumbled stale, dry, firm-textured white bread (4 slices)

$\frac{1}{3}$ cup coarsely chopped parsley

1 teaspoon poultry seasoning

$\frac{3}{4}$ teaspoon salt

$\frac{1}{4}$ teaspoon black pepper

3 to 4 tablespoons hot chicken broth (about)

Pork Chops

Six 1$\frac{3}{4}$-inch-thick, bone-in pork loin chops, 1 rib per chop (about 5 pounds)

2 tablespoons vegetable oil

1 teaspoon salt

$\frac{1}{2}$ teaspoon black pepper

$\frac{1}{2}$ cup hot chicken broth

1. Preheat the oven to 350° F.

2. For the stuffing: Heat the oil in a large, heavy skillet over moderately high heat for about 2 minutes or until ripples appear on the skillet bottom. Add the onion, celery, and garlic; reduce the heat to moderate; and cook, stirring often, for about 10 minutes or until the vegetables are limp. Mix in all remaining ingredients, adding only enough chicken broth to hold the stuffing together; it shouldn't be wet. Scoop the stuffing into a small bowl and reserve. Scrape the skillet well, then wipe with paper toweling so that you can use it to brown the chops. No point in dirtying two skillets.

3. For the pork chops: Using a small sharp knife and beginning on the outer curved edge (the one with the thin layer of fat), cut a pocket into each pork chop that's about 4 inches wide and 2½ to 3 inches deep. If you can sweet-talk your butcher into doing the job for you, so much the better. Pack the reserved stuffing into the pockets in the pork chops, dividing the total amount evenly.

4. Heat the oil in the skillet over moderately high heat for 1 minute, then brown the chops in two batches, allowing 3 to 4 minutes per side per chop. Remove from the heat, then lay the pork chops on their sides in an ungreased 13 × 9 × 2-inch baking pan. Sprinkle with the salt and pepper and pour the hot chicken broth into the pan around the chops.

5. Cover the pan snugly with foil, slide onto the middle oven shelf, and bake for about 40 minutes or until an instant-read meat thermometer, inserted halfway through a top chop, touching neither filling nor bone, registers 145° F. Remove the chops from the oven, lift off the foil, and let stand for about 10 minutes.

6. To serve, arrange the chops on a heated large platter and spoon some of the pan drippings over all.

Variation

Pork Chops with Peanut and Onion Stuffing: Prepare the recipe as directed but in the stuffing, substitute 1 cup finely chopped dry-roasted peanuts for the pecans and reduce the amount of salt to ¼ teaspoon. Taste the finished stuffing and add a little additional salt, if needed. **Note:** *The peanut stuffing has more crunch than the one made with pecans.*

1823 In Kentucky, James Crow distills bourbon whiskey from a sour mash of corn. He calls it Old Crow.

Grapes are found growing wild along North Carolina's Catawba River, a labrusca variety found suitable for making wine.

1824 Mary Randolph's cookbook, *The Virginia House-wife*, is published. It is America's first southern cookbook; earlier ones consisted mostly of English recipes. (It is now available in a facsimile edition with historical notes and commentaries by food historian Karen Hess. See Mary Randolph, page 131.)

1825 Pierre Simeon Patout plants grapes on his Louisiana plantation, then switches to sugarcane. Today Enterprise Plantation is America's oldest working sugarcane plantation.

Using seeds that were said to have come from Cuba, French nobleman Odet Philippe plants a small grove of grapefruits in Pinelas County, Florida. They are thought to be America's first grapefruits. Some historians believe that Philippe arrived here ten or more years later and that his grapefruit seeds may have come from the Bahamas or perhaps Jamaica.

SAUSAGE AND BLACK-EYED PEA ÉTOUFFÉE

MAKES 8 SERVINGS

. . . .

After an intensive round of recipe testing that left me with a fridge and freezer full of unused ingredients, I did what frugal southern cooks have done forever. I bubbled them into a "catch-all," in this case a Cajun-inspired though inauthentic étouffée. Serve as is or ladle over rice. It's good either way.

I pound pork sausage links, sliced ½ inch thick

I very large Vidalia onion (about I pound), coarsely chopped

I large green bell pepper, cored, seeded, and coarsely chopped

I bunch of scallions, trimmed and coarsely chopped (include some green tops)

2 large celery ribs, trimmed and coarsely chopped

2 large garlic cloves, finely chopped

Two 16-ounce packages solidly frozen black-eyed peas

3 cups chicken broth

2 large whole bay leaves, preferably fresh

I teaspoon salt, or to taste

½ teaspoon crumbled leaf thyme

½ teaspoon black pepper, or to taste

¼ teaspoon ground hot red pepper (cayenne), or to taste

One 14.5-ounce can diced tomatoes in tomato sauce

½ cup coarsely chopped Italian parsley

2½ cups converted rice, cooked by package directions (optional)

1. Set a large, heavy Dutch oven over moderately high heat for 1 minute, add the sausage, and cook, stirring often, for about 10 minutes or until most of the drippings cook out. Pour off the drippings, then spoon 2 tablespoons of them back into the Dutch oven.

2. Add the onion, bell pepper, scallions, celery, and garlic and cook, stirring often, over moderately high heat for 15 to 20 minutes or until limp and touched with brown.

3. Add the black-eyed peas, chicken broth, bay leaves, salt, thyme, black pepper, and cayenne and bring to a boil. Adjust the heat so the mixture bubbles gently, cover, and cook, stirring occasionally, for 45 minutes or until the peas are tender.

4. Mix in the tomatoes, cover, and simmer for 15 to 20 minutes or until the flavors mellow. Taste for salt, black pepper, and cayenne and adjust as needed. Remove and discard the bay leaves. Stir in the parsley and cook uncovered for 5 minutes more.

5. Ladle into heated soup bowls and serve or, if you prefer, scoop about ¾ cup rice into each bowl, then top with the étouffée.

❖

There's a lot of nourishment in an acre of corn.

—WILLIAM FAULKNER

❖

SOUSE MEAT

Remove the head, feet, and ears of one hog. Remove eyes and brains. Singe pig's feet, wash, and scrape. Singe, wash, and clean ears thoroughly in hot water. Cover meat with hot water and boil until meat drops from bones. Drain meat. Season with 1 tsp. each of salt, black pepper, and sage for each qt. Place meat in a bowl. When cool, souse meat will be firm. Serve with cold vinegar or dip in beaten eggs and bread crumbs and brown in hot fat.

—Mrs. J. F. Vickers, Iredell County, North Carolina

BREAKFAST CASSEROLE

MAKES 4 TO 6 SERVINGS

Sausage and eggs are as classic down south as bacon and eggs are elsewhere. This rib-sticking brunch staple combines the two with onion, sharp Cheddar, eggs, and cream. Some hostesses prepare the casserole the night before and bake it the next morning. I don't recommend that in this Age of Salmonella. **Note:** *Any grits will do for this recipe but I prefer coarse, stoneground yellow grits (see Sources, page 401).*

1 pound bulk sausage meat

1 medium yellow onion, moderately coarsely chopped

1¼ cups coarsely shredded sharp Cheddar cheese

1 cup grits, cooked by package directions but not seasoned (see Note at left)

2 tablespoons butter

2 large eggs, lightly beaten

½ cup half-and-half

½ cup milk

½ teaspoon salt

¼ teaspoon black pepper

1. Preheat the oven to 350° F. Lightly spritz an 8 × 8 × 2-inch ovenproof glass baking dish with nonstick cooking spray and set aside.

2. Cook the sausage and onion in a medium-size heavy skillet over moderately high heat, breaking up large sausage clumps, for 10 to 12 minutes or until the sausage is nicely browned. Drain on paper toweling, then spread over the bottom of the baking dish.

3. Add the cheese to the hot grits, then the butter, and stir until both melt. Mix in the eggs, half-and-half, milk, salt, and pepper, stirring until well blended.

4. Pour over the sausage in the baking dish and spread to the corners. Slide onto the middle oven shelf and bake uncovered for 35 to 40 minutes or until set like custard.

5. Remove from the oven and let stand for 10 minutes before serving.

SAWMILL GRAVY WITH CATHEAD BISCUITS

MAKES 4 SERVINGS

An old farm woman, newly come to town, lived around the corner from us in Raleigh and I used to fly over there after school to hear about life on the farm but mostly to sample Mrs. Franklin's homespun cooking. Sawmill gravy was a specialty of hers and a favorite of mine. She told me that it was a "country-folk" dish—equally good for breakfast, dinner, or supper. As for the recipe's unusual name, it's said that this gravy was first rustled up in a lumber camp: Bits of sausage left in the skillet were turned into a milk gravy thickened with flour or more likely, with cornmeal. I sometimes add chopped parsley just before serving; Mrs. Franklin would be appalled!

1 pound bulk sausage meat

4 tablespoons all-purpose flour

2½ cups milk or water

Salt as needed to taste

¼ cup coarsely chopped parsley (optional)

4 Cathead Biscuits (page 246) or
8 standard biscuits, either leftover or
freshly made, split in two

1. Place the sausage in a large, heavy skillet and break into small pieces with a spoon. Set over moderately high heat and brown for 8 to 10 minutes, continuing to break up the sausage; it should be very crumbly. If there are many drippings (not likely these days with pork so lean), scoop the browned sausage onto a plate. Pour off all drippings, then spoon 2 tablespoons of them back into the skillet. Also return the sausage to the skillet.

2. Reduce the heat to low, sprinkle the flour evenly over the sausage, and stir to mix. Add the milk and cook, stirring constantly, for 3 to 5 minutes or until thickened. Turn the heat down low and simmer the gravy, stirring now and then, for 5 minutes. Taste for salt and add as needed. Mix in the parsley, if you like—far from traditional but delicious.

3. Ladle the sawmill gravy over the split biscuits and serve.

BACON AND CARAMELIZED VIDALIA QUICHE

MAKES 6 SERVINGS

I have always been partial to quiche and thought that a perfectly delicious one could be made by teaming Georgia's sweet Vidalia onions with a good smoky bacon: two southern classics in an easy lunch or supper main dish. This has become a brunch favorite for me and for my friends, who sometimes ask when invited, "Are you doing that Vidalia quiche?" **Note:** *If the filling is to be properly creamy, you must choose a cheese that melts smoothly without "stringing," a well-aged Emmentaler, for example, or a fontina.*

5 slices richly smoked bacon, cut
crosswise into strips ¼ inch wide

2 medium Vidalia onions, halved
lengthwise, then each half thinly sliced
(1 to 1¼ pounds)

4 ounces fontina or well-aged Emmentaler
cheese, coarsely shredded (see Note at left)

One 9-inch unbaked pie shell
(see About Pie Crusts, page xxiii)

3 large eggs, lightly beaten

1 cup light cream

½ cup milk

½ teaspoon salt

¼ teaspoon black pepper

¼ teaspoon freshly grated nutmeg

1. Place a large, heavy baking sheet on a shelf in the lower third of the oven and preheat the oven to 400° F. This will help crisp the bottom of the pie shell.
2. Fry the bacon in a large, heavy skillet over moderate heat for 10 to 12 minutes or until the drippings cook out and only crisp brown bits remain. Using a slotted spoon, lift the bacon to paper toweling and reserve. Also pour off all drippings, then spoon 2 table-spoons of them back into the skillet.
3. Add the onions to the skillet drippings and sauté for 12 to 15 minutes or until limp and lightly browned. Remove the skillet from the heat and cool the onions for 10 minutes.
4. Meanwhile, scatter the reserved bacon and the cheese evenly over the bottom of the pie shell. When the onions have cooled, scoop them on top of the bacon and cheese, spread-ing to the edge of the pie shell; do not pack.

1828 Brunswick stew is created in Brunswick County, Virginia, by African American cook Jimmy Matthews while on a hunting trip with his master, Dr. Creed Haskins. That original Brunswick stew contained slow-simmered squirrels, onions, stale bread, butter, and seasonings. Today's chicken-based versions brim with corn, butter beans, and tomatoes. (See recipe, page 127.)

1830 To feed camp meeting crowds, Skilton M. Dennis begins barbecuing pigs in the little East North Carolina town of Ayden. Today his great-great-grandson, Pete Jones, carries on the family tradition at his celebrated Skylight Inn (see **1948**).

1831 Twenty-two-year-old Virginia farmer Cyrus McCormick perfects the mechanical reaper that his father had begun. It is the world's first successful "harvester."

1833 Dr. Henry Perrine begins cultivating Mexican avocados south of Miami and within a few years plants Mexican limes on Indian Key. These small, tart, yellow citrus fruits are now known as Key limes.

1834 Nancy Green, the model for the original Aunt Jemima logo, is born into slavery in Montgomery County, Kentucky.

Whisk the eggs, cream, milk, salt, pepper, and nutmeg together until smooth and pour slowly and evenly over the onions.

5. Slide the quiche onto the baking sheet in the lower third of the oven and bake for 10 minutes. Reduce the oven temperature to 325° F. and continue baking uncovered for 35 to 40 minutes or until the quiche is set like custard.

6. Remove the quiche from the oven and from the baking sheet, set on a baking rack, and cool for 25 minutes.

7. Cut into wedges and serve. This quiche needs nothing more to accompany it than a tartly dressed green salad.

BAKED VIRGINIA HAM

MAKES 12 TO 14 SERVINGS

. . . .

In Virginia, indeed over much of the South, baked ham means Smithfield ham (see box, page 98) or one of the other good regional hams, mahogany-hued and country-cured. It never means the pink packing-house hams so popular elsewhere. In "The Representative Ham," a *New Yorker* short story by North Carolina writer Frances Gray Patton, the author tells how a transplanted Yankee, in a burst of cost-cutting, served a "pink ham" at a church-supper fund-raiser. The dismay of one parishioner speaks for all: " 'We know which things are Representative . . . And my dear friends'— here her voice rose an octave—'pink ham does not represent St. Luke's Protestant Episcopal Church and, by God's grace, pink ham never shall!' " **Tip:** *Before buying a country ham, mea-sure the pot in which you intend to cook it. If the ham is too large to fit, have the butcher remove the hock. Or, if you have a hack saw, do the job yourself. It's easy.*

One 10- to 12-pound uncooked Virginia ham (see Tip at left)

1¼ cups fairly fine soft white bread crumbs

1¼ cups firmly packed light brown sugar

2 tablespoons light corn syrup

¼ teaspoon ground cloves

¾ cup (1½ sticks) butter, melted (about)

2 tablespoons whole cloves (about)

1. Place the ham in the sink, cover with warm water, then, using a stiff brush, scrub off the ash, salt, and mold (this, by the way, is harmless). You'll have to change the water several times as you scrub.

2. Rinse the ham well, then place in a large oval kettle, sawing off the hock if it won't fit into the kettle. Cover the ham with cold water and soak overnight, changing the water two or three times. Next day, scrub the ham again and rinse well. Also wash the kettle.

3. Return the ham to the kettle, cover with cold water, set over moderate heat, and bring to a simmer. Drain the ham and rinse both it and the kettle.

4. Once again, place the ham in the kettle and cover with cold water. Set over moderate heat and bring to a simmer. Adjust the heat so the water barely trembles, cover the kettle, and cook the ham for 5 to 5½ hours or until fork-tender. To minimize the ham's saltiness,

change the cooking water every hour or so. Drain the ham well and chill overnight.

5. When ready to proceed, preheat the oven to 350° F. Remove the ham rind, then trim the outer layer of fat until no more than 1/4 inch thick. If you have not sawed off the ham hock, do so now.

6. Combine the bread crumbs, brown sugar, corn syrup, and ground cloves in a large mixing bowl, then add the melted butter, mixing as you go, until the mixture holds together when pinched.

7. Pat the crumb mixture thickly and firmly over the ham, then, using a sharp knife, score in a diamond pattern, spacing the cuts about 1 1/2 inches apart. Stud the center of each diamond with a whole clove.

8. Ease the ham into a large, shallow baking pan, and bake uncovered in the lower third of the oven for 45 to 50 minutes or until the crumb crust is golden brown.

9. Remove the ham from the oven and cool to room temperature. Carve into slices as thin as onion skin and serve. **Note: *This is the ham to slip into biscuits. Bite-size "ham biscuits" are routinely served at southern teas, open houses, and cocktail parties. Always at room temperature.***

❧

I went to the Mason City Café, Home-Cooked Meals for Ladies and Gents, facing the square, and sampled the mash potatoes and fried ham and greens with pot-likker.

—*ROBERT PENN WARREN,*
ALL THE KING'S MEN

❧

1835 In Tidewater Virginia south of the James River, wheat replaces tobacco as the crop of choice.

1836 With ships docked six deep, New Orleans tops New York as America's busiest port.

1837 *The Picayune* newspaper (today *The Times–Picayune*) begins publication in New Orleans. Over time, it's praised for its coverage of local food and publishes its own cookbook.

1838 Thousands of Southern Cherokee, who'd shared their culinary and horticultural expertise with white settlers, are force-marched along "The Trail of Tears" into lands west of the Mississippi.

1839 Lettice Bryan's *Kentucky Housewife* is published. It is an early American classic because, as Bill Neal notes in his introduction to the University of South Carolina Press facsimile edition (1991), "We learn from it not just one dish or another, but what foods were available in the 1830s [and] how women cooked."

The cultivation of Key limes increases in Florida; they're also a common dooryard fruit.

SMITHFIELD HAM

Southern lawmakers know plenty about pork, and in Virginia, they've proved it. In 1926 the state legislature decreed that only country ham made from peanut-fed hogs "raised in the peanut belt of Virginia or North Carolina and cured within the town limits of Smithfield in the State of Virginia" could qualify as "Smithfield Ham." The residency and diet requirements have been dropped, but Smithfield hams must still be cured within the town limits.

Smithfield ham is almost as old as Virginia itself. Pigs arrived in Jamestown with the colonists in 1607. Later, when Williamsburg residents complained about swine fouling the streets, the animals were exiled to an island in the James River called, appropriately, Hog Island. As peanut farming grew, farmers discovered that hogs loosed in the fields after harvest would devour the leftovers. Peanuts imparted a special flavor to the meat, which could be salted and smoked for long storage, even in hot climates.

The earliest recorded sale of Smithfield hams was in 1779, and by 1783 business was booming. Queen Victoria, we're told, was so fond of Smithfield hams that she had a standing order for them: six every week. The world's oldest Smithfield ham is on display in, of all places, England's Isle of Wight County Museum. It was cured in 1902, one year after Queen Victoria's death.

Now, that's a squeal.

Heirloom Recipe

CURING HAMS

When first cut, put on saltpeter, and let stand 24 hours; rub this in, in hock and meat side. Then rub in salt and brown sugar. Pack in box, with hocks inside. Leave packed six weeks. Take up and wash. Rub borax in well and let this dry; then put on molasses, thick with black pepper. Let dry. Hang up and smoke. Hang for at least a year, preferably two years.

—*The Church Mouse Cook Book*, compiled by the Women of St. Paul's Episcopal Church, Ivy, Virginia, 1964

MARYLAND STUFFED HAM

MAKES 6 TO 8 SERVINGS

This is an old, old Maryland recipe that I tasted for the first time while on an article assignment on the Eastern Shore. Before the food processor, the stuffing must have been tedious to prepare because there were so many ingredients to chop: spinach, parsley, watercress, scallions. I now commit them all to the machine and let it do the work. This is an unusually colorful way to prepare ham; its rose-red and green hues make it a Christmas favorite. Good accompaniments:

sweet potatoes prepared any which way, Green Beans with Browned Butter and Pecans (page 183), and James River Corn Pudding (page 192).

4 ounces tender young spinach, trimmed of coarse stems, washed well, and patted dry on

paper toweling

1 cup loosely packed curly parsley leaves

¼ cup loosely packed tender young watercress leaves

4 medium scallions, trimmed and chunked (include some green tops)

¼ teaspoon black pepper

One 6- to 7-pound fully cooked, shank-end half ham

1½ cups dry white wine (for basting)

1. Preheat the oven to 325° F.
2. Finely chop the spinach in two batches by whizzing in a food processor for 10 seconds. As each batch is chopped, empty into a large bowl. Add the parsley, watercress, scallions, and pepper to the processor bowl and churn 10 to 12 seconds until finely chopped. Add to the spinach and toss well to combine.
3. Cut away and discard any tough rind on the ham, then trim the outer covering of fat until it is no more then ¼ inch thick. Using a sharp paring knife, make deep X-shaped cuts over the surface of the ham (each prong of the X should be about 1½ inches long), spacing the Xs about 1½ inches apart.
4. Set the ham on a counter covered with wax paper, then, using a teaspoon or your fingers, pack the spinach mixture firmly into each cut.

This is messy business. Once the ham is completely stuffed, wipe its surface with dampened paper toweling to remove any spatters or spills of filling.

5. Place the ham in an ungreased large shallow roasting pan and slide onto the middle oven shelf. Bake uncovered for 2½ hours or until lightly browned, basting every half hour with the wine.
6. Remove the ham from the oven and let stand for 30 minutes before carving.

COUNTRY HAM AND RED-EYE GRAVY

MAKES 4 SERVINGS

. . . .

I didn't taste country ham or red-eye gravy until the summer that I was ten. My family and I were driving north to visit my Ohio grandmother and after overnighting at a tourist court in the Virginia Blue Ridge, we stopped at a little mom-and-pop café-cum-gas-station for breakfast. This was my first true southern country breakfast and I was thrilled. Not so my mother, father, and brother, all of whom thought the country ham too salty and too tough. And what was it with the coffee gravy? When I asked my parents why the red-eye gravy had such a funny name, they hadn't a clue. Nor to this day have I found a surefire answer. Some say that when the ham is done and the skillet deglazed, the browned bits floating to the top resemble red eyes. I personally favor a theory suggested by John Egerton in *Southern Food: At Home, on the Road, in History* (1987). Apocryphal or not, it credits Andrew Jackson with inadvertently coming up with the name. To quote Egerton: "[Jackson] reportedly instructed a whiskey-drinking cook of his to bring him some ham with gravy 'as red as your eyes'."

Although the Southerners I know all make their red-eye with black coffee, Egerton prefers water, explaining that if the country ham is properly cured and properly smoked, the gravy doesn't need coffee to boost its flavor. He has a point. Still, for me the best red-eye does contain black coffee and that's the recipe I give here. **Note:** *Many southern supermarkets sell prepackaged "Country Ham Wafer Thins," slices of salt-cured, hickory-smoked country ham about six inches long, two and a half inches wide, and a fourth of an inch thick. Each weighs just shy of an ounce and two slices per person is about right.* **Tip:** *Most country ham is fat enough to lubricate the skillet; if not, heat a little vegetable oil or bacon drippings in the skillet before adding the ham.*

I tablespoon vegetable oil or bacon drippings (see Tip above)

8 thin slices country ham (about 8 ounces) (see Note above)

½ cup warm black coffee

1. If the ham is lean, heat the vegetable oil in a large, heavy skillet over moderately high heat for about a minute before adding the ham. If not, add the ham directly to the hot skillet. Cook the ham for about 2 minutes on each side or until richly browned; transfer to paper toweling to drain.
2. Pour the coffee into the skillet and simmer for about 2 minutes, scraping up the browned

bits on the skillet bottom. Do not allow to boil; the gravy will turn bitter.
3. To serve, arrange the country ham on heated plates and accompany with grits and/or freshly baked biscuits. Pass the red-eye gravy separately. Some Southerners spoon the red-eye over their grits (and/or biscuits), some ladle it over their ham, and some slosh it over everything. There's no right or wrong.

MUSTARD-GLAZED HAM LOAF

MAKES 6 TO 8 SERVINGS

Meat loaves, especially ham loaves, have always been popular below the Mason-Dixon because they're versatile, they're filling, and they offer every opportunity to recycle leftovers. This one of mine is equally good hot or cold. It is delicious "straight up," but I like it even better topped with the Sour Cream–Dill Sauce that follows. **Note:** *Though supermarkets now sell ground raw pork, it's sometimes impossible to buy ground ham, but that's not a problem if you own a food processor. Cut the ham into 1-inch cubes, removing excess fat and connective tissue as you go, then pulse in batches until moderately finely ground. If you have no processor, I'm afraid you'll have to feed the ham through a meat grinder.*

I pound moderately finely ground smoked ham

¾ pound moderately finely ground pork

1½ cups soft white bread crumbs, coarsely crumbled stale corn bread, or leftover cooked rice

¾ cup fresh orange juice or chicken broth
or a combination of the two

½ cup mustard pickle relish

1 medium yellow onion, finely chopped

2 large eggs

¼ cup coarsely chopped parsley

½ teaspoon salt

¼ teaspoon ground cinnamon

¼ teaspoon ground ginger

¼ teaspoon black pepper

½ cup orange marmalade blended with
2 tablespoons prepared
yellow mustard (glaze)

1. Preheat the oven to 375° F. Coat a 9 × 5 × 3-inch loaf pan with nonstick cooking spray and set aside.
2. Place all ingredients except the last (the glaze) in a large bowl and mix thoroughly, using your hands. Scoop into the pan, packing firmly and mounding slightly in the center.
3. Bake in the lower third of the oven for 40 minutes. Spread the glaze on top, reduce the oven temperature to 350° F., and bake 15 to 20 minutes longer or until nicely browned and an instant-read meat thermometer thrust into the middle of the loaf registers 165° F.
4. Let the ham loaf rest for 20 minutes in the upright pan on a wire rack, then loosen around the edge with a thin-blade spatula and ease onto a heated platter.
5. Turn right side up, slice, and serve. Or if you prefer, chill well and serve cold.

1840 Antoine's opens in New Orleans, first as a boardinghouse, but soon as an elegant restaurant. It remains open today.

More than 200 riverboats now ply the Mississippi, some of them luxury liners serving fine cuisine.

Captain Samuel F. Flood finds pecans floating at sea and his wife plants them on their property in St. Marys, Georgia. Those trees bore heavily over the years and their nuts and shoots were distributed all over the South.

1840s Peanuts become a commercial crop in Virginia.

In addition to her household duties, the southern farmer's wife tends the kitchen garden, the chicken coop, and dairy; churns the butter; smokes the meat; and bakes the bread.

1846 The son of a French planter and a slave, Paris-educated engineer-inventor Norbert Rillieux patents his new time-saving, cost-saving, and risk-saving method of refining sugar in New Orleans.

SOUR CREAM-DILL SAUCE

MAKES ABOUT 1 CUP

. . . .

¾ cup sour cream

¼ cup finely snipped fresh dill

2 tablespoons mayonnaise
(use "light," if you like)

1 tablespoon Dijon mustard

1 tablespoon well-drained small capers

1 tablespoon milk or as needed to thin to the
consistency of medium white sauce

1. Whisk all ingredients together in a small, non-reactive bowl.
2. Transfer to a sauceboat and serve with the Mustard-Glazed Ham Loaf that precedes. Or serve as an accompaniment to boiled or baked ham.

TENNESSEE COUNTRY HAM
AND HOMINY HASH

MAKES 4 SERVINGS

. . . .

Blackberry Farm, one of America's most luxurious country inns, is about a half-hour drive east of Knoxville, Tennessee, just where the Smokies rise out of the foothills. Its gifted chef is John Fleer, a graduate of the Culinary Institute of America, who has developed what he calls "Foothills Cuisine" to showcase the local bounty. Among his signature dishes is this rib-sticking hash, which I enjoyed while there. **Note:** *The hom-*

iny you want for this recipe is "big" or whole hominy, not cooked grits, which some Southerners also call hominy. **Tip:** *If country ham is unavailable in small amounts where you live (it often is outside of the South), substitute domestic prosciutto or failing that, Italian prosciutto. Both work well in this recipe. You'll need one slice about ¼ inch thick (approximately four ounces).*

3 tablespoons butter

3 medium potatoes, peeled, diced, and
blanched in hot water (about 1 pound)

1 medium yellow onion, coarsely chopped

1 small green bell pepper, cored, seeded,
and diced

1 small celery rib, trimmed and diced

1 tablespoon minced fresh jalapeño pepper

¾ cup finely diced country ham
(see Tip above)

2 cups drained, cooked hominy or one
One 15-ounce can whole hominy, drained
(see Note above)

Salt and black pepper, to taste

1 tablespoon finely snipped fresh chives

1. Melt the butter in a large, heavy skillet over moderately high heat and when it froths, add the potatoes and fry for 8 to 10 minutes or until crisp and brown.
2. Add the onion, bell pepper, celery, jalapeño, and ham and fry, stirring often, for about 5 minutes or until the vegetables are tender.
3. Mix in the hominy, season to taste with salt and pepper, then heat about 5 minutes more. Sprinkle with the fresh chives and serve for breakfast or brunch.

GRILLADES AND GRITS

MAKES 6 SERVINGS

. . . .

To be honest, I can't remember exactly when or where I first tasted grillades. Louisiana to be sure, but I don't think New Orleans because I've spent more time prowling the countryside than in the Big Easy. I didn't expect my small-town North Carolina butcher to know what I was cooking the first time I ordered two pounds of top round sliced ½ inch thick. But quick as anything, he said, "You makin' grillades?" I've taken a few liberties with what most folks would consider to be the New Orleans classic. For another layer of flavor, I like to add a little white wine, also a bit of oregano. **Note:** *Top round is exceptionally lean and unless handled with TLC will be tough. In restaurants, grillades are often scaloppine-thin, but I've had better luck keeping them tender if they are ½ inch thick. Here's another good preventive: Once the browned grillades go into the sauce, keep the heat low and keep the pan covered; too much heat will surely toughen them.* **Tip:** *If you prefer not to use bacon drippings in this recipe (they do add flavor), use ¼ cup of vegetable oil instead of two tablespoons each of drippings and oil.*

¾ cup unsifted all-purpose flour

1¼ teaspoons salt

½ teaspoon black pepper

2 pounds beef top round, sliced ½ inch thick and each slice cut crosswise into thirds

2 tablespoons bacon drippings (see Tip above)

2 tablespoons vegetable oil

1 large yellow onion, coarsely chopped

12 large scallions (about 2 bunches), trimmed and coarsely chopped (include as many green tops as possible; also reserve 3 tablespoons chopped scallions for a garnish)

1 small green bell pepper, cored, seeded, and moderately coarsely chopped

1 large celery rib, trimmed and finely chopped

3 large garlic cloves, finely chopped

2 large whole bay leaves, preferably fresh

1 teaspoon dried leaf thyme, crumbled

½ teaspoon dried leaf oregano, crumbled

¼ teaspoon ground hot red pepper (cayenne), or to taste

2 tablespoons dredging mixture (reserved from above)

1½ tablespoons tomato paste

½ cup dry white wine

1 cup beef broth

One 14.5-ounce can diced tomatoes, with their liquid

¼ cup coarsely chopped Italian parsley

1 cup grits, cooked by package directions (preferably stone-ground grits)

3 tablespoons coarsely chopped scallions to garnish (reserved from chopped scallions above)

1. Shake the flour, salt, and black pepper in a large plastic zipper bag to combine. Now dredge the beef by shaking a few pieces at a

time in the dredging mixture; tap off the excess. Reserve 2 tablespoons of the dredging mixture to thicken the sauce.

2. Heat the bacon drippings and oil in a deep, heavy skillet large enough to hold all the grillades in a single layer over high heat for 1 to 1½ minutes or until ripples appear on the skillet bottom. (I use a 14-inch, 2-inch-deep sauté pan.)

3. Brown the grillades in the hot fat in three batches over high heat, allowing about 1 minute per side per batch. As the meat browns, lift to a shallow roasting pan and reserve.

4. Add the onion, scallions, bell pepper, and celery to the skillet; reduce the heat to moderately high; and cook, stirring now and then, for 10 to 12 minutes or until limp and lightly browned. Mix in the garlic, bay leaves, thyme, oregano, and cayenne and cook, stirring often, for 2 minutes.

5. Sprinkle the reserved dredging mixture evenly into the skillet and cook, stirring, for 1 minute. Blend in the tomato paste and cook and stir 1 minute more. Add the wine and boil uncovered for about 30 seconds or until slightly reduced. Add the broth and the tomatoes and their liquid and cook, stirring constantly, for 2 to 3 minutes or until lightly thickened.

6. Return the browned beef to the skillet, arranging in one layer, and cover with the sauce. Adjust the heat so the sauce barely bubbles, cover the skillet, and cook for 5 minutes. Turn the beef in the sauce, cover the skillet again, and cook 5 minutes longer or just until the grillades are tender.

7. Transfer the grillades to a heated platter, cover loosely, and keep warm. Simmer the sauce uncovered for about 5 minutes or until the consistency of gravy. Remove and discard the bay leaves, then taste the sauce for salt and cayenne and adjust as needed.

8. Stir the parsley into the sauce, return the grillades to the skillet, and heat for no more than 30 seconds.

9. Ladle all over the grits, sprinkle with the 3 tablespoons reserved chopped scallions, and serve.

BEEF AND MIRLITON CASSEROLE

MAKES 6 SERVINGS

Wherever mirlitons grow (principally in Louisiana and Florida), these pear-shaped, white-fleshed, pale green vegetables (kin both to cucumbers and summer squash) are also called vegetable pears, christophenes, custard marrows, and chayotes. As far back as the sixteenth century, Spanish explorer Francisco Hernandez found them growing in Mexico (they're believed to be native to Guatemala) and entered this observation in his journal: "This Aztec chayoti is like a hedgehog . . . The fruit is eaten cooked and is sold in markets everywhere." In the Deep South, cooks prepare mirlitons in countless ways and among the best, I think, is this casserole. **Note:** *Mirlitons (often marketed as "chayotes") are becoming more widely available beyond the South; many specialty groceries and some supermarkets now stock them. Look for them in late fall and winter.*

1½ tablespoons bacon drippings
or vegetable oil

2 medium-large mirlitons (about
1½ pounds), quartered lengthwise,
peeled, pitted, and cut into ½-inch dice

1 pound ground beef chuck

1 large yellow onion, coarsely chopped

1 small green bell pepper, cored, seeded, and
finely diced

1 large garlic clove, finely chopped

One 4.5-ounce can chopped green chilies,
well drained

1 teaspoon salt

¼ teaspoon black pepper

2 cups coarsely crumbled stale, firm-
textured white bread (about 4 slices)

2 cups coarsely shredded
sharp Cheddar cheese

1. Lightly spritz a shallow 2-quart casserole with nonstick cooking spray and set aside.

2. Heat the bacon drippings in a large, heavy skillet over moderately high heat for 1 minute. Add the mirlitons and stir-fry for about 2 minutes or until golden. Reduce the heat to low, cover the skillet, and cook the mirlitons, stirring now and then, for about 25 minutes or until nearly tender. Toward the end of cooking, preheat the oven to 350° F. Using a slotted spoon, transfer the mirlitons to a large plate and reserve.

3. Raise the heat underneath the skillet to moderately high, add the ground beef, and cook, breaking up the clumps, for 3 to 4 minutes or until no traces of pink linger. Mix in the onion, bell pepper, and garlic and cook, stirring often, for about 10 minutes or until limp. Mix in the chilies, salt, and black pepper and cook and stir for about 1 minute. Return the mirlitons and any accumulated juices to the skillet and stir well to mix.

4. Set the skillet off the heat and mix in the crumbled bread, then the shredded cheese. Scoop all into the casserole, spreading to the edge.

5. Slide onto the middle oven shelf and bake uncovered for 25 to 30 minutes or until bubbling and tipped with brown.

6. Serve at once as the main dish of a casual lunch or supper. Sliced red-ripe tomatoes are the perfect accompaniment and all you need to round out the meal.

ROASTED RACK OF LAMB WITH FIELD PEA RELISH

MAKES 4 SERVINGS

No one in the Raleigh neighborhood of my childhood would eat lamb, and my friends were startled to learn that my mother often broiled lamb chops or roasted a leg of lamb. One night a school chum who had come home with me after school stayed for dinner. Enjoying the meal, she turned to compliment my mother: "Miz Anderson, that was the best steak I ever ate." Mother smiled, then added, "I'm glad you liked those little steaks, Bettie Lou. But actually they were lamb chops!" My friend gagged. "But we *never* eat lamb! We *hate* lamb!" That was the first time lamb had passed Bettie Lou's lips and I suspect that it was the last. Old habits die hard down south. This peculiar prejudice appears to be a "class" thing; certainly it has nothing to do with the range wars out west. The South's better-educated, more aristocratic families have always eaten lamb, indeed since Colonial days. Only the hardscrabble folk and those descended from them eschew it. Fortunately, Walter Royal, a gifted southern chef whom I once profiled for *Food & Wine*, appreciates the merits of lamb and does it proud with a peppery field pea relish. The recipes here are adapted from those that accompanied my article.

4 large garlic cloves, finely minced

1 tablespoon minced fresh rosemary or
1 teaspoon dried leaf rosemary, crumbled

½ teaspoon coarse or kosher salt

½ teaspoon hot paprika

¼ teaspoon hot red pepper flakes, crushed

¼ teaspoon black pepper

One 8-rib rack of lamb
(about 3 pounds; have the butcher
"french" the rib ends)

1 tablespoon fruity olive oil

Field Pea Relish (page 108)

1. Combine the garlic, rosemary, salt, paprika, crushed pepper flakes, and black pepper in a small bowl, then rub all over the lamb. Cover and marinate in the refrigerator for at least 4 hours or better yet, overnight.

2. Remove the lamb from the refrigerator and let stand at room temperature for 30 minutes. Meanwhile, preheat the oven to 350° F.

3. Heat the olive oil in a large, heavy skillet over moderately high heat for 1 minute. Place the lamb in the skillet fat side down, and sear for about 2 minutes. Turn, browning the meaty ends of lamb, allowing 2 to 3 minutes for each.

4. Transfer the lamb to an ungreased large shallow roasting pan, standing it on its rib ends so the fat side is up. Roast uncovered on the middle oven shelf for 20 to 25 minutes or until an instant-read thermometer, inserted in the meatiest part of the lamb, not touching bone, registers 130° F. **Note:** *The lamb will be rare; for medium-rare, roast 5 minutes longer or until the thermometer reaches 135° F. to 140° F. But roast no further, please.*

5. Remove the lamb from the oven and let stand at room temperature for 10 minutes to allow the juices to settle.

6. Carve the lamb by cutting down between the ribs. Allow two chops per person and spoon a generous portion of the field pea relish alongside.

❈

The North seldom tries to fry chicken
and this is well; the art cannot be learned
north of the line of Mason and Dixon.

—MARK TWAIN

❈

Heirloom Recipe

SPICED ROUND OF BEEF, FOR CHRISTMAS

Several of the early fund-raiser cookbooks in my collection contain recipes for Spiced Beef, a Christmas classic in many parts of the South. This one is fairly representative.

15 pounds off the round of beef, with the bone in
¼ cup saltpeter
⅓ box kitchen salt (Morton's)
1 small can ground cinnamon
1 small can ground cloves
1 quart black molasses
1 small can ground allspice

Combine the saltpeter, salt, spices, and molasses, and rub into the beef. Tie beef around with strips of gauze bandage, to hold it in shape. Place in large enamel roaster, cover, and keep in refrigerator (or, if no room, keep on cold porch) one day for each pound. Turn meat daily and baste it several times a day with the mixture and the beef juice which collects. When ready to cook, add enough water to cover, and simmer very slowly for 3 hours; let cool in the water. Trim, then tie fresh gauze strips around it. Serve sliced paper-thin, with eggnog and crackers.

—*The Church Mouse Cook Book*,
compiled by the Women of St. Paul's Episcopal Church, Ivy, Virginia, 1964

Recipe contributed by Mrs. Robert T. Phillips, Greenville, South Carolina

1847 Desperate to cool his feverish patients, an Apalachicola doctor named John Gorrie invents a primitive ice-maker—a forerunner of kitchen iceboxes.

The Carolina Housewife, a collection mainly of Lowcountry recipes and household remedies by Sarah Rutledge, is published. Like Mary Randolph's *Virginia House-wife* (1824) and Lettice Bryan's *Kentucky Housewife* (1839), it has been reprinted in a facsimile edition (see Bibliography).

Unable to mass-produce his mechanical reaper on the family's Virginia farm, Cyrus McCormick relocates to Chicago. Soon after, his two brothers join his new company.

A Louisiana slave named Antoine masters the art of grafting and cultivating pecan trees, a breakthrough that enables farmers to grow this all-American nut on a commercial scale.

1848 South Carolina commercial tea production is no longer confined to the Lowcountry. Dr. Junius Smith harvests significant quantities of it at Golden Grove Plantation near Greenville.

FIELD PEA RELISH

. . . .

Although Walter Royal created this colorful side dish to accompany his Roasted Rack of Lamb (page 105), I also like it with roast pork and baked ham. **Note:** *Black-eyed peas are the most readily available field pea; that's why I call for them here.*

½ cup peanut or corn oil

2 medium red bell peppers, cored, seeded, and finely chopped

2 medium celery ribs, trimmed and finely chopped

1 medium yellow onion, finely chopped

1 large garlic clove, finely chopped

One 1¼-pound smoked ham hock

One 16-ounce package solidly frozen black-eyed peas (see Note above)

1 teaspoon salt, or to taste

½ teaspoon hot paprika

¼ teaspoon hot red pepper flakes, or to taste, crushed

¼ teaspoon black pepper, or to taste

1 large whole bay leaf, preferably fresh

2½ cups rich chicken stock or broth

⅓ cup cider vinegar

3 tablespoons coarsely chopped Italian parsley

2 teaspoons finely chopped fresh thyme or ½ teaspoon dried leaf thyme, crumbled

1. Heat 2 tablespoons of the oil in a large, heavy saucepan over moderately high heat for 1 minute. Add the bell peppers, celery, and onion and stir-fry for about 5 minutes or until limp. Add the garlic and cook and stir for 1 minute.

2. Add the ham hock, black-eyed peas, salt, paprika, crushed pepper flakes, black pepper, and bay leaf, and cook and stir for 1 minute. Add the stock and bring to a boil. Adjust the heat so the mixture bubbles gently, then simmer uncovered for 15 to 20 minutes or until the peas are tender. Drain, reserving the cooking liquid. Discard the bay leaf.

3. Cut the meat from the ham hock into small pieces, add to the peas, and set aside.

4. Meanwhile, boil the reserved cooking liquid over high heat in an uncovered nonreactive saucepan for about 20 minutes or until reduced to ¼ cup. Add the vinegar, parsley, and thyme, then whisk in the remaining peanut oil. Pour over the black-eyed pea mixture and toss well. Taste for salt, red pepper flakes, and black pepper, and adjust as needed.

5. Serve warm or at room temperature as an accompaniment to roast lamb, roast pork, or baked ham. Good, too, with roast turkey or chicken.

❀

Fried chicken is perhaps Georgia's best known dish, but field peas come a close second and a delicately flavored little white pea we call lady peas.

—*CARSON McCULLERS,* ON HER GEORGIA CHILDHOOD

❀

LIVER MUSH

Cut into medium pieces one hog hashlet (liver, lights, and heart) and 1½ lbs. fat meat (from hog's head). Cover with water and cook until tender. When cooled, put through meat chopper. Place the ground meat back into broth in which it was cooked. Season with salt and sage to taste. Let boil and add cornmeal a little at a time, stirring constantly. When the mixture turns loose from the sides of the pot it is ready to take up and pack into pans. Slice and fry to serve.

—Mrs. Mack Oliver, Iredell County, North Carolina

ROAST VENISON WITH JUNIPER-CURRANT SAUCE

MAKES 6 SERVINGS

Although white-tailed deer overrun the South (they graze my lawn at dawn and dusk), and although hunters go after them in season with gun or bow and arrow, wild venison is a rarity unless you bag it yourself or befriend someone who does. The venison available to chefs and home cooks is ranch-raised, tender of flesh and delicate of flavor. This recipe, one I enjoyed some years ago in the Barbadoes Room of the elegantly restored Mills House in Charleston, was given to me by Chef Lindner there. I've tweaked it over the years to make it less daunting for hobby cooks. **Note:** *Begin the recipe a day ahead because the venison must marinate for 24 hours; the sauce, too, is begun in advance.* **Tip:** *Because venison is exceptionally lean, ask your butcher to pique it (insert short, thin strips of larding fat over the surface).*

One 5- to 6-pound rack of venison, piqued
(see Tip above)

4 cups (1 quart) milk

1 teaspoon salt

½ teaspoon black pepper

1 cup water

Juniper-Currant Sauce

2 tablespoons bacon drippings

4 medium carrots, peeled and thinly sliced

2 medium yellow onions, coarsely chopped

1 small celery rib, trimmed and thinly sliced
(include some leaves)

1 tablespoon juniper berries

2 large whole bay leaves (preferably fresh)

½ cup dry red wine

¼ cup water

5 cups chicken stock or broth

6 black peppercorns, crushed

½ cup firmly packed red currant jelly

2 tablespoons heavy cream

Venison pan drippings

½ teaspoon salt, or to taste

3 tablespoons flour blended with
¼ cup cold water

Optional Garnishes

Pickled Peaches (page 375) or
Bourbon'd Peaches (page 376)

Watercress

1. Place the venison in a large nonreactive bowl, pour in the milk, cover, and refrigerate for 24 hours.

2. Meanwhile, begin the sauce: Heat the bacon drippings in a large, heavy saucepan over moderately high heat for 1 minute; add the carrots, onions, celery, juniper berries, and bay leaves and sauté, stirring now and then, for 10 to 12 minutes or until lightly browned.

3. Pour in the wine and water and simmer, uncovered, for 5 minutes. Add the chicken stock and peppercorns, bring to a boil, then adjust the heat so the mixture bubbles gently. Simmer uncovered for 1 hour.

4. Smooth in the currant jelly and simmer uncovered for 15 minutes or until the sauce reduces slightly. Strain the sauce through a large fine sieve, discarding the solids. Pour the sauce into a medium-size nonreactive bowl, cover, and refrigerate.

5. When ready to proceed, preheat the oven to 450° F. Lift the venison from the milk (it should be discarded), then rub the meat generously with the salt and pepper.

6. Stand the venison on its rib ends in a large shallow roasting pan and roast uncovered on the middle oven shelf for 15 minutes. Add the 1 cup water and continue roasting, basting often with the pan drippings. Allow 20 to 25 minutes for rare venison, 35 for medium rare; further roasting will toughen the meat. Remove the venison from the oven and let stand for 15 minutes.

7. Meanwhile, finish the sauce: Bring the chilled sauce to a simmer in a medium-size nonreactive pan, then blend in the cream, venison pan drippings (plus any browned bits), and salt to taste. Quickly whisk a little of the hot sauce into the flour-water paste, stir back into the pan, and cook, stirring constantly, for 3 to 5 minutes until thickened and smooth.

8. To serve, arrange the venison on a large heated platter and garnish, if you like, with pickled or bourbon'd peaches and ruffs of watercress. Pour the sauce into a heated gravy boat and pass separately.

CRISPY BATTER-FRIED CHICKEN

MAKES 4 SERVINGS

Mark Twain was right: "The North seldom tries to fry chicken and this is well; the art cannot be learned north of the line of Mason and Dixon." Even south of the Mason-Dixon, few cooks can agree on the best way to fry chicken. Some say that an initial milk (or buttermilk) bath is essential to make the bird succulent. Others insist that salting the bird is more effective because it closes the pores and seals in the juices. Some Southerners salt and pepper the chicken before "battering" it. Others mix the seasonings into the batter, sometimes adding a pinch of paprika to enrich the color. Some cooks shallow-fry the chicken in a big iron skillet; others prefer to deep-fry (to trim cooking time and keep the orders coming, many fast-food restaurants now pressure-fry). Even the skillet school of frying is divided: Some cooks cover the skillet part of the time to keep the bird moist; others don't. And some even add a little water toward the end of cooking, again to make the bird juicy. Finally, gravy is a must in many parts of the South; it goes over the biscuits, not the chicken. Elsewhere, the chicken is fried, drained, and served as is. No gravy or, horrors, sauce of any kind. This recipe and the two that follow will produce exceptionally good fried chicken. I don't think anyone will quarrel with that. **Note:** *It's essential that you choose a small chicken for deep-fat frying—about 2½ pounds but definitely no more than 2¾. Heftier chickens will overbrown before they're done inside (170° F. on an instant-read thermometer) and may need half an hour or more in the oven—a sure-fire recipe for tough, dry chicken. Even small chickens tend to be bosomy these days, so if the breasts seem oversize, halve them crosswise so the chicken will cook evenly.* **Tip:** *If self-rising flour is unavailable (beyond the South, it's rarely a supermarket staple), use all-purpose flour and increase the baking powder and salt each to 2 teaspoons.*

One 2½- to 2¾-pound broiler-fryer, cut up
for frying (see Note above)

1½ cups buttermilk or milk

Vegetable oil for deep-fat frying
(you'll need about 6 cups or 1½ quarts)

1 cup unsifted all-purpose flour for dredging

Batter

1½ cups sifted self-rising flour
(see Tip at left)

¾ teaspoon salt

½ teaspoon baking powder

½ teaspoon black pepper

¾ cup milk

2 large eggs

1 tablespoon vegetable oil

1. Arrange the pieces of chicken one layer deep in a large, shallow nonreactive baking pan. Pour the buttermilk evenly over all, then turn the chicken in the buttermilk so it's evenly coated. Cover with foil and let stand at room temperature for 30 minutes. After 15 minutes, pour the oil into a deep-fat fryer or large deep kettle, insert a deep-fat thermometer, and set uncovered over moderately high heat; it may take 30 minutes for the oil to reach the proper temperature (360° F.). Place the dredging flour in a pie pan and set aside.

2. When the temperature of the oil reaches 325° F., prepare the batter: Whisk the self-rising flour, salt, baking powder, and pepper together in a small bowl and make a well in the middle of the dry ingredients. Combine the milk, eggs, and oil in a 1-quart spouted measure or second small bowl, whisking until frothy. Pour into the well in the dry ingredients and whisk just until the batter is smooth. The batter will be thick.

3. Remove the chicken from the buttermilk and pat dry on paper toweling. Next, roll in the dredging flour, shaking off the excess. Dip each piece of

chicken into the batter, letting the excess drain off, then place on a large rack set over foil (to catch the drips). Let the batter-coated chicken stand until the oil reaches 360° F. This standing makes the batter stick to the chicken.

4. Preheat the oven to 300° F. Spritz a baking sheet lightly with nonstick cooking spray and set aside.

5. As soon as the oil reaches 360° F., ease in the four largest pieces of chicken—they will sputter wildly and the temperature of the oil will plummet to around 350° F. Fry the chicken for 8 to 10 minutes or until richly browned. Keep raising and lowering the burner heat as needed to maintain the temperature of the oil between 350° F. and 360° F.

6. Drain the browned chicken on paper toweling, then transfer to the spritzed baking sheet and set uncovered on the middle oven shelf. This not only keeps the chicken warm but also finishes the cooking, if necessary. (The internal temperature of the chicken should be 170° F. Be careful to insert the quick-read thermometer into the meatiest part of the chicken; it should not touch bone.)

7. Deep-fry the remaining chicken in batches the same way, doing the larger pieces first; drain and set in the oven. Even the small last-batch pieces need 1 to 2 minutes in the oven.

8. Serve hot with coleslaw, potato salad, and biscuits. Or, if you prefer, serve at room temperature.

❧

The best apple is taken by the pig.

—OLD NORTH CAROLINA SAYING

❧

FRIED CHICKEN WITH GRAVY

MAKES 4 SERVINGS

This recipe was given to me nearly thirty years ago by Garnet McCollum, a North Carolina farm woman I profiled for *Family Circle* magazine. In that article, I featured about a dozen favorite family recipes, among them her superb fried chicken. I cannot improve upon it. Once salted, this chicken is refrigerated overnight, so you must begin the recipe a day ahead. **Note:** *Back when I interviewed Mrs. McCollum, chicken breasts weren't D cup in size. Now that they are, I suggest that you halve each breast crosswise so that the chicken cooks more evenly.*

One 3- to 3½-pound broiler-fryer, cut up for frying (see Note above)

2 teaspoons salt

¼ teaspoon black pepper

¾ cup unsifted all-purpose flour

Vegetable oil for frying or lard, if you can get it (Mrs. McCollum used lard)

1 tablespoon water

Gravy

4 tablespoons skillet drippings

⅓ cup unsifted all-purpose flour

2 cups water or milk, if you prefer milk gravy (the McCollums don't)

½ teaspoon salt, or to taste

⅛ teaspoon black pepper, or to taste

1. Arrange the pieces of chicken, not touching and one layer deep, in a shallow baking dish or nonreactive pan. Sprinkle with the salt, cover, and refrigerate overnight.

2. When ready to fry the chicken, drain off all accumulated juices and pat the chicken dry on several thicknesses of paper toweling. Sprinkle the chicken with the pepper, then dredge by shaking a few pieces at a time in the flour in a plastic zipper bag. As you remove the chicken from the dredging flour, shake off the excess flour.

3. Pour the oil into a large iron skillet until about an inch deep, set over moderate heat, and as soon as steam begins to rise from the oil, add the pieces of chicken, skin side down. Fry slowly for 30 minutes, keeping the heat at moderate or moderately low so that the chicken doesn't overbrown; turn and fry 30 minutes more. Add the 1 tablespoon water (the oil will spit and sputter), cover the skillet, and let stand until the spitting stops.

4. Remove the chicken to several thicknesses of paper toweling to drain, arranging so the pieces don't touch one another. Also lay a sheet of paper toweling on top.

5. For the gravy: Pour the oil and drippings from the skillet, then spoon 4 tablespoons of them back into the skillet. Blend in the flour, and cook and stir over moderately low heat for about 5 minutes or until a nice rich brown. Whisk in the water, salt, and pepper, then cook, whisking constantly, for about 5 minutes or until thickened, smooth, and no raw starch taste lingers. Taste for salt and pepper and adjust as needed. Pour the gravy into a heated gravy boat.

6. Pile the chicken onto a heated platter and serve. Pass the gravy along with a basket of fresh-baked biscuits.

1850s The single most prosperous decade for South Carolina rice planters. Many netted $30,000 a year and up—way up—while the average citizen earned just $1,200.

Bavarian Elizabeth Kettering sails to New Orleans for her brother's wedding, marries a French Market butcher, and opens a little breakfast café. Later widowed, she marries Hypolite Bégué, renames her little café Bégué's Restaurant, and, according to one theory, creates New Orleans's famous po'boy sandwich late in the nineteenth century.

1851 Cyrus McCormick's "Virginia Reaper" not only revolutionizes the harvesting of grain but also wins a gold medal at the Crystal Palace Exhibition in London.

1852 John Burnside, soon to be nicknamed "The Sugar Prince of Louisiana," begins buying sugar plantations, amasses more than 12,000 acres of cane fields, and employs more than 2,200 slaves. But he is also the first to hire free African Americans.

1853 To foster economic reform and counter its reputation for archaic agriculture methods, North Carolina stages a state fair in Raleigh. On display: cutting-edge farm equipment.

COLONEL HARLAND SANDERS (1890–1980) AND KENTUCKY FRIED CHICKEN

The quintessential "late bloomer," Harland Sanders was nearly fifty when he perfected his famous fried-chicken recipe and was a Golden Ager of sixty-two when he began franchising it. Available today in more than eighty countries and territories, his "finger lickin' good" Kentucky Fried Chicken is one of the world's best-selling fast foods.

After years of bouncing from job to job (farmhand, streetcar conductor, soldier, insurance salesman, steamboat ferry operator, railroad fireman, paralegal), Sanders came home to Corbin, Kentucky, and started the business that would make him both millionaire and celebrity. In the front room of a gas station, no less.

Here, in 1930, Sanders began serving weary travelers the southern dishes he'd learned to cook as a child. People loved his food—especially that fried chicken—and kept coming back for more. To accommodate his increasing number of fans, Sanders moved his tiny café into a motel across the street.

Among those early Sanders Café fans was fellow Kentuckian Duncan Hines, who recommended the place in his *Adventures in Good Eating*. That rave in the 1939 edition of the American motorist's bible put Sanders's little Corbin, Kentucky, restaurant on the map.

Yet barely a dozen years later Sanders was out of business. In the 1950s, the government hurled a new interstate right past Corbin. With customers dwindling, Sanders closed his café, auctioned off its equipment, and, after settling his accounts, was reduced to living on his meager monthly Social Security check.

Still believing in his fried chicken with its secret seasoning blend of eleven herbs and spices, Sanders took to the road in 1952. Crisscrossing the country, he called on restaurant owners and fried batches of chicken golden, crisp, and tender for them to taste. Dozens were impressed enough to cut a deal: Sanders would share his secret recipe and frying technique if they'd pay him a nickel for every order sold.

By 1964, there were more than 600 Kentucky Fried Chicken franchises. That same year Harland Sanders sold his stake in KFC for $2 million, but he remained its spokesman until he died in 1980 at the age of ninety. Of course he will live forever as its grinning "Kentucky Colonel" icon.

FRANK PERDUE (1920-2005)

A shy only child born the year his father began raising chickens on a small Maryland farm, beak-nosed, raspy-voiced Frank Perdue emerged in the 1970s as America's unlikeliest TV pitchman. "It takes a tough man to raise a tender chicken," he twanged, making Perdue the country's first brand-name chicken. By the '90s, he'd built a multi-billion-dollar business.

In the beginning, Perdue's father raised chickens for eggs, not eating, but he switched to the lucrative broiler business in the 1940s, first wholesale, then retail some twenty years later.

As innovative as he was entrepreneurial, Frank Perdue added marigold petals to chicken feed to give his broilers the golden skin customers preferred. He singed off the wing hairs they hated. He cross-bred Cornish with White Plymouth Rocks to give his broilers plumper breasts. He packed his chickens in ice instead of freezing them. He worked eighteen to twenty hours a day, often sleeping at the office. Frank Perdue believed in his chickens and so did millions of Americans.

With Perdue staying on as chairman of the executive committee, look-alike son Jim took over Perdue Farms, Inc., in 1991. Before long, his "What? Me-obsessed-with-chicken?" commercials were all over the tube. And as amusing as his dad's.

When Frank Perdue died in 2005 at the age of eighty-four, his Maryland-based company was employing almost 20,000 people and grossing $2.8 billion a year. Hardly chicken feed.

1856 Gail Borden patents his process for sweetened condensed milk, which he'd developed two years earlier. Although he did so in the North, his sweetened condensed milk had a greater impact in the Deep South, where fresh milk spoiled in a matter of hours.

1859 Cubans are imported to roll cigars in the factories springing up around Tampa, Florida, and their black bean soups and saffron-hued *arroz con pollo* quickly spice up the local cuisine.

1861 The opening shot of the Civil War is fired at Fort Sumter, South Carolina. The war will free the slaves and end the South's planter aristocracy. To this day, Southerners prefer to call it "The War Between the States," "The War for Southern Independence," or, even more euphemistically, "The Late Unpleasantness."

1862 The Café du Monde opens for business in the French Market of New Orleans. It is still there and its beignets and dark coffee-with-chicory are as popular as ever.

SUPER-CRUNCHY FRIED CHICKEN

MAKES 4 SERVINGS

. . . .

If you've ever wondered what gives fried chicken a super-crunchy crust, I've three words for you: self-rising flour. It contains baking powder and when the chicken is dipped into buttermilk, then into self-rising flour, the acid in the milk reacts with the baking powder: You can see it fizz. Then when the chicken goes into 360° F. fat, it fizzes further still. Talking one night with Bill Smith, the chef at Crook's Corner in Chapel Hill, I learned a couple of his secrets. He fries his chicken in a Dutch oven in just enough oil to float the pieces, and once they begin to brown, he reduces the heat and covers the pot. That way he knows the chicken won't burn by the time it's done. Only during the last few minutes does the lid come off. I use a five-inch-deep, enameled cast-iron Dutch oven twelve inches across—just big enough to accommodate all of the chicken at once. Its lid can be set on askew, leaving room for a deep-fat thermometer. Because this chicken is salted, then refrigerated for at least 12 hours, you must begin the recipe a day ahead of time. **Note:** *After finding no chickens weighing less than four pounds at my grocery, I fussed at the butcher. "Go to the take-out section," he said. "They may let you have a raw rotisserie chicken. They're under three pounds." I did. And they did—something to try the next time you can't find a small fryer.*

One 2½- to 2¾-pound broiler-fryer, cut up for frying (see Note at left)

1½ teaspoons salt

Vegetable oil for deep-fat frying (you'll need about 8 cups or 2 quarts)

1½ cups buttermilk

1½ cups unsifted self-rising flour

2 teaspoons sweet paprika

½ teaspoon black pepper

1. Arrange the pieces of chicken one layer deep in a large, shallow, nonreactive pan and sprinkle with half the salt. Turn the chicken and sprinkle the flip sides with the remaining salt. Cover and refrigerate for at least 12 hours but for no more than 24.

2. When ready to fry the chicken, pour the oil into a large, heavy Dutch oven at least 5 inches deep and 12 inches in diameter. Insert a deep-fat thermometer and set over moderately high heat. Let the oil heat slowly; it may take 35 to 45 minutes for the oil to reach the proper frying temperature of 360° F.

3. When the oil reaches 330° to 340° F., pour the buttermilk into a small bowl, then combine the flour, paprika, and pepper in a pie pan.

4. Dip each piece of chicken into the buttermilk, then roll in the flour mixture until thickly coated. Arrange the chicken pieces on a foil-lined tray so that they don't touch.

5. As soon as the oil reaches 360° F., ease in the chicken breasts and thighs, then the drumsticks, wings, and backs, arranging so the pieces don't touch or barely touch. The oil will sputter and its temperature will plummet to

around 300° F. Not a problem. The initial searing will have sealed the crust.

6. Slide the lid onto the Dutch oven, leaving enough room at the edge for the deep-fat thermometer. Continue frying the chicken, raising and lowering the burner heat to keep the temperature of the oil between 290° F. and 300° F.

7. After about 10 minutes, lift out a chicken wing and insert an instant-read thermometer in the meatiest part, not touching bone. If it reads 170° F., the wing is done. Remove the other wing, also the backs, and drain on several thicknesses of paper toweling.

8. After 15 minutes, test the chicken thighs the same way and if done, drain on paper toweling. After 18 to 20 minutes, the breasts should be done, but test to make sure.

9. Cool the chicken about 20 minutes on the paper toweling, then serve warm. Or, if you prefer, cool to room temperature before serving.

BARBECUED CHICKEN

MAKES 4 SERVINGS

. . . .

Strictly speaking, this isn't barbecue. It's chicken baked under bastings of spicy tomato sauce. Throughout the South, however, it's called barbecued chicken or oven-barbecued chicken and it's as delicious as it is easy. As recipes go, this one's modern—mid to late twentieth century. **Note:** *If the chicken breasts are unusually large, as they so often are these days, halve them crosswise.*

1863

Said to be the year that a French chef serving Kentucky general Henry Hunt Morgan creates a meaty vegetable stew for his Confederate troops. He calls it "burgoo." Some food historians disagree and call the story completely apocryphal. (See Kentucky Burgoo, page 128.)

Richmond, Virginia, publisher West & Johnston brings out the *Confederate Receipt Book: A Compilation of Over One Hundred Receipts, Adapted to the Times.* Among the helpful tips it offers southern women during the Civil War and subsequent Reconstruction are ways to preserve meat without salt and a way to brew acorns into coffee.

Outraged by the soaring price of flour, the women of Richmond, Virginia, stage a "bread riot." Covering the protest, a local paper calls them "prostitutes, professional thieves, Irish, Yankee hags."

Virginia is partitioned, its 50 western counties becoming West Virginia. Unlike Virginia, it is pro-Union.

To keep from starving during the prolonged and savage Battle of Vicksburg, the townspeople devour a field of black-eyed peas originally planted as cattle fodder.

One 3- to 3½-pound broiler-fryer,
cut up for frying (see Note on page 117)

2 tablespoons butter or vegetable oil

1 small yellow onion, finely chopped

¾ cup tomato ketchup

¼ cup cider vinegar

1 tablespoon firmly packed light brown sugar

¼ to ½ teaspoon hot red pepper sauce
(depending on how "hot" you like things)

1. Preheat the oven to 375° F.
2. Arrange the pieces of chicken skin side up on a rack in a large, shallow roasting pan so that they do not touch one another. Slide onto the middle oven shelf and bake uncovered for 30 minutes.
3. Meanwhile, melt the butter in a small, heavy saucepan over moderate heat, add the onion, and sauté for about 5 minutes or until golden. Mix in all remaining ingredients, bring to a boil, then reduce the heat and simmer uncovered for 5 minutes or until the flavors mellow.
4. Remove the chicken from the oven, turn the pieces skin side down, and baste with about half of the hot tomato sauce. Return to the oven and bake for 15 minutes. Turn the pieces skin side up, baste with the remaining sauce, and bake 15 minutes more.
5. Raise the oven temperature to 425° F. and bake the chicken for 10 minutes or until tipped with brown.
6. Serve at once with coleslaw and, if you like, with potato salad as well.

PECAN-CRUSTED OVEN-FRIED CHICKEN

MAKES 6 SERVINGS

. . . .

Judging from my collection of southern community cookbooks, this recipe seems to have surfaced in the early 1960s because that's when variations of pecan-crusted chicken began popping up in their pages. I suspect (but can't prove) that this recipe evolved from one that I helped create back when I was an assistant food editor at *The Ladies' Home Journal* in New York. We called it Chicken Imperial and it consisted of a mix of soft white bread crumbs, grated Parmesan, minced parsley, crushed garlic, salt, and pepper that was patted onto butter-dipped chicken. **Note:** *The fastest way to grind the pecans is in a food processor, but to keep them from reducing to paste, alternately churn and pulse until the nuts are about the texture of kosher salt. Forty years ago when pecan-crusted chicken first became popular, cooks would have used commercially grated Parmesan cheese. I find it both sawdusty and salty, so I use only freshly grated Italian Parmigiano-Reggiano now that it's widely available. I urge you to do the same.* **Tip:** *Easier on the purse and better than prepackaged Parmesan: Wisconsin or Argentinian Parmesan. Buy it by the chunk and grate it yourself.*

One 3½- to 4-pound broiler-fryer, cut up
for frying (if the breasts are overly large as
so many are these days, halve each crosswise)

1 cup (2 sticks) butter

1 large garlic clove, thinly slivered

1½ cups finely ground pecans
(see Note and Tip at left)

1 cup fine dry bread crumbs (unflavored)

¾ cup freshly grated Parmesan cheese
(see Note above)

1 teaspoon crumbled dried leaf thyme

¾ teaspoon salt

½ teaspoon black pepper

1. Preheat the oven to 350° F. Wash the chicken parts in cool water, pat dry on paper toweling, and set aside.

2. Place the butter and slivered garlic in a small, heavy saucepan and set over low heat until the butter melts. **Tip: *I often melt the butter in a 2-quart ovenproof glass measure in the microwave oven: 6 to 8 minutes on* DEFROST *should do it. Then I add the garlic.***

3. Combine the ground pecans, bread crumbs, grated Parmesan, thyme, salt, and pepper in a shallow roasting pan (not too large). Dip each piece of chicken into the melted garlic butter, then coat thickly with the pecan mixture and arrange in a large shallow roasting pan so that the pieces do not touch one another. Drizzle any remaining garlic butter over the chicken.

4. Slide uncovered onto the middle oven rack and oven-fry for 1 to 1¼ hours or until richly browned and no traces of pink remain in the chicken. As the chicken cooks, baste occasionally with the pan drippings.

5. Serve hot or at room temperature. I even like this chicken straight out of the refrigerator. Accompany with a tossed salad of crisp greens or, to be authentically southern, with Sweet Slaw (page 229).

1867 Mardi Gras revelry resumes after the Civil War. The Krewe of Comus celebrates with an Epicurus Parade. Krewe members wear papier-mâché costumes depicting such delicacies as oysters on the half shell, a leg of lamb, and a bottle of sherry.

1869 The first batch of Tabasco sauce is shipped from Avery Island, Louisiana. The sauce is patented a year later and over time, it becomes a kitchen staple (see box, page 52).

1870s Russians, Ukrainians, Lithuanians, and Poles emigrate to English-Irish-German-African Baltimore, settle into "ethnic" neighborhoods, and stir the local melting pot culturally and culinarily.

Caribbean-bound Clipper ships leave Baltimore harbor laden with Western Maryland coal and return with coffee, bananas, and pineapple, all now much in demand.

1872 Georgia socialite Annabella P. Hill publishes a cookbook. Called *Mrs. Hill's Southern Practical Cookery and Receipt Book*, it is based on her *New Cook Book* (1867) and helps those new to housekeeping. (A facsimile edition with observations and explanations by Savannah-based food historian and cookbook author Damon Lee Fowler is now available.)

JTF'S CHICKEN AND ARTICHOKE CASSEROLE

MAKES 6 SERVINGS

. . . .

For years the fiction editor of *The Ladies' Home Journal*, my best friend, Jean Todd Freeman, like so many southern women of a certain age and social standing, insisted that she couldn't cook. Not true. JTF, as we called her because that's the way she signed her memos, was in fact an excellent cook and this particular recipe was her dinner-party staple. We lived around the corner from one another in New York's West Village; traveled about Europe together; then after Jean returned home to Hattiesburg, Mississippi, shunpiked through the Deep South. Jean was the perfect traveling companion—witty, easygoing, deeply knowledgeable about her corner of the South, and eager to share bits of gossip, legend, and lore (always the storyteller). She introduced me to New Orleans years ago in addition to points north and west; and later to Jackson, Vicksburg, Natchez, and Hattiesburg, Mississippi, as well as to the Mississippi and Alabama gulf coasts, and the Florida Panhandle. Jean was the insider, I the tourist, and she made each jaunt memorable. **Note:** *If the chicken breasts are unduly large, halve them crosswise so that all pieces of chicken will be done at the same time.*

¾ cup unsifted all-purpose flour

1½ teaspoons sweet paprika

1¼ teaspoons salt

¾ teaspoon black pepper

One 3½- to 4-pound broiler-fryer, cut up for frying

2 tablespoons butter

2 tablespoons vegetable oil

1 pound medium mushrooms, stemmed, wiped clean, and sliced about ¼ inch thick

1 cup chicken broth

¼ cup dry vermouth or dry white wine or if using canned artichoke hearts, dry sherry or port

Three 4-ounce jars marinated artichoke hearts, well drained, or one 14-ounce can artichoke hearts, well drained and halved if large

2½ cups converted or long-grain rice, cooked by package directions

1. Preheat the oven to 375° F.
2. Shake the flour, paprika, salt, and pepper in a large plastic zipper bag to combine. Now dredge the chicken by shaking a few pieces at a time in the dredging mixture; tap off the excess. Reserve 3 tablespoons of the dredging mixture; you'll use it to thicken the sauce.
3. Heat the butter and vegetable oil in a large, heavy skillet over moderately high heat for about 2 minutes or until ripples appear on the skillet bottom. Add the chicken in batches, placing skin side down. Brown for 3 to 4 minutes on the first side, 2 to 3 on the flip side—you want a crisp golden crust. As the chicken browns, lift to several thicknesses of paper toweling to drain.
4. Pour all drippings from the skillet, then spoon 2 tablespoons of them back in. Reduce the

SOUTHERN WINES

. . . very sandie and low towards the waters side, but so full of grapes as the very beating and surge of the Sea overflowed them . . . their smell of sweetness filled the air as if they were in the midst of some delicate garden.
—*Arthur Barlowe, 1584*

Less famous than Sir Walter Raleigh, for whom he was scouting New World sites for the English to colonize, Barlowe had landed on North Carolina's Roanoke Island. The grapes he described were sweet-as-honey scuppernongs. "Good for wine," the English noted, though no records exist to prove that the Roanoke colonists actually made it. That original scuppernong vine—the Mother Vine—still grows on Roanoke Island, misshapen now and gnarled with age.

As a little girl, I remember people sipping Virginia Dare Wine (named for the first English child born in Roanoke's doomed "Lost Colony"). It was a Kool-Aid–sweet scuppernong wine and among our Raleigh friends who imbibed (many didn't), it was immensely popular. Even then I thought it was awful.

The South didn't begin making grown-up wines in earnest until after World War Two, and Virginia led the way. "Remember," the Virginia Wineries Association brags, "we made wine in Virginia in 1608, so while North Carolina may be first in flight, Virginia is first in wine!"

Maybe so. But that first scuppernong wine was so "foxy" the Jamestown colonists who made it declared it undrinkable. Ever after Virginians tried in vain to make good table wines.

A connoisseur of fine wines and an early believer in Virginia's ability to produce them, Thomas Jefferson spent thirty years trying to turn the native grapes he'd planted at Monticello into wines as palatable as those he'd enjoyed in France and Italy. But even with the help of an Italian vintner, he failed.

Today vineyards thrive in Virginia and North Carolina, particularly in the Yadkin and Roanoke river valleys, in the Shenandoah, and on the lower slopes of the Smokies and Blue Ridge. Gold-medal wines are coming out of hills once known for moonshine—cabernets, chardonnays, rieslings, viogniers, zinfandels, and more. Georgia, Tennessee, Kentucky, and Maryland are in the wine business, too, though not as aggressively or lucratively as Virginia and North Carolina.

There are even Deep South wines, mainly the dessert-sweet scuppernongs and muscadines Southerners like to sip—all of them finer by far than that first Jamestown vintage.

---

heat under the skillet to moderate, add the mushrooms, and sauté, scraping up the browned bits on the skillet bottom, for 8 to 10 minutes or until the mushrooms release their juices and these evaporate.

5. Sprinkle the 3 tablespoons reserved dredging mixture over the mushrooms and stir well. Add the chicken broth and cook, stirring constantly, for 2 to 3 minutes or until thickened. Add the vermouth and simmer uncovered for

2 minutes or just long enough for flavors to meld.

6. Arrange the browned chicken skin side up in an ungreased shallow 4-quart casserole or baking dish. Tuck the artichokes in here and there, then pour the hot mushroom sauce evenly over all, lifting the occasional piece of chicken so that it runs underneath. Cover the casserole snugly with foil.

7. Slide onto the middle oven shelf and bake for 40 minutes. Remove the foil and bake uncovered for 20 minutes more or until the chicken is done.

8. To serve, bed the rice on a large heated platter, then arrange the chicken and artichokes on top, and pour the mushroom gravy over all. Or do as JTF always did: Serve at table directly from the casserole and spoon the rice alongside. As she said, "Fewer dishes to wash."

COUNTRY CAPTAIN

MAKES 10 TO 12 SERVINGS

. . . .

Whenever my mother gave a dinner party, this was the recipe she chose because it served an army and could be made ahead of time and frozen. If memory serves, she got the recipe from Elizabeth Harrelson, the elegant southern lady who was married to Colonel Harrelson, for many years the chancellor at North Carolina State. Where did Country Captain originate? There are many theories, the most widely accepted being that during the late eighteenth or early nineteenth century, a sea captain making a port of call at Savannah traded the recipe for this mild chicken curry for a free night's lodging in town. Though Country Captain has long been a southern favorite, it did not become well known elsewhere until the 1930s, when President Franklin Delano Roosevelt, receiving physical therapy in Warm Springs, Georgia, was served Country Captain by a local hostess. The dish quickly became a Roosevelt favorite, word of it spread, and thus FDR inadvertently put Country Captain on the culinary map of America. Today cutting-edge chefs offer their own versions of it, but for me, none is better than the one I grew up with. My mother always used an old hen that had gone off laying to make Country Captain, but they are hard to come by these days unless you raise your own chickens. **Note:** *To toast slivered almonds, spread the nuts in a pie tin, set uncovered in a preheated 350° F. oven, and leave until the color of pale caramel—8 to 10 minutes; stir the nuts occasionally as they toast.*

One 6- to 6½-pound ready-to-cook roasting chicken or, if you can get it, an old hen, stripped of as much fat as possible (freeze the giblets to use another time)

4 cups water

4 tablespoons fat (skimmed from the kettle liquid) or 4 tablespoons bacon drippings or vegetable oil

3 large green bell peppers, cored, seeded, and coarsely chopped

3 large yellow onions, peeled and coarsely chopped

½ cup coarsely chopped parsley

1½ teaspoons curry powder (or more to taste)

1 teaspoon dried leaf thyme, crumbled

½ teaspoon black pepper

⅛ teaspoon ground hot red pepper (cayenne)

⅛ teaspoon ground cloves

Three 14.5-ounce cans crushed tomatoes, with their liquid

3 cups kettle liquid (in which chicken steamed)

2 teaspoons salt

½ teaspoon Worcestershire sauce

1 cup dried currants

3½ cups converted rice, cooked by package directions

1½ cups lightly toasted slivered almonds (see Note at left)

1. Place the chicken on a rack in a large, heavy kettle and pour in the water. Bring to a simmer, adjust the heat so that the water bubbles gently, cover, and steam the chicken for 1½ to 2 hours or until the leg moves easily in the hip joint.

2. Remove the chicken from the kettle; also pour the kettle liquid into a medium-size heatproof bowl, cover, and refrigerate until ready to proceed. Cool the chicken until easy to handle, then remove the meat from the bones, discard the skin, and cut the light and dark meat into 2- to 3-inch pieces. Refrigerate until ready to use.

3. Spoon the 4 tablespoons fat into the kettle (if there is insufficient fat, round out the measure

1874 Georgia establishes a state Department of Agriculture. It is America's first.

The Old Absinthe House opens in New Orleans, nicknamed "Little Paris" because here, as in the French capital, absinthe was widely drunk. Until it was banned in 1912, this green wormwood liqueur was integral to such classic New Orleans cocktails as the Sazerac.

1875 Georgia farmer Samuel Rumph develops the Elberta peach, a hybrid, which thrives on his Macon County farm and ships well because it is slow to bruise.

1877 Lafcadio Hearn, a young writer of Irish-Greek parentage, arrives in New Orleans from Ohio and begins writing about the local food, folk remedies, and superstitions. By the time he leaves ten years later, Hearn is considered the most insightful interpreter of Creole culture.

1880 Commander's Palace Restaurant opens in New Orleans's elegant Garden District.

1881 Atlanta hosts a World's Fair. Though called the International Cotton Exposition, there are 1,013 exhibits from 33 states and six foreign countries. Returning to the city he'd torched less than 20 years earlier, General William Tecumseh Sherman is impressed by the New Atlanta.

with bacon drippings or vegetable oil). Heat 1 minute over moderate heat, add the bell peppers, onions, parsley, curry powder, thyme, black pepper, cayenne, and cloves and cook, stirring now and then, until the peppers and onions are nicely softened but not brown—12 to 15 minutes.

4. Add the tomatoes, 3 cups of the reserved kettle liquid, the salt, and the Worcestershire sauce, and simmer uncovered for 50 to 60 minutes, stirring occasionally, until the flavors meld.

5. Add the reserved chicken and dried currants and simmer uncovered 30 to 35 minutes longer until the flavors mellow and the currants plump. Taste for salt and pepper and adjust as needed. Also add another 1/2 to 1 cup of the kettle liquid if the Country Captain seems thick and dry (it should not be soupy; there should be still enough liquid to soak down into the rice).

6. To serve, bed the rice on a heated, very large, deep platter, ladle the Country Captain on top, and scatter with almonds. Or, if you prefer, plate each portion separately.

INGLIS FLETCHER'S COUNTRY CAPTAIN

MAKES 8 SERVINGS

. . . .

Altogether different from the Country Captain that precedes, this one, attributed to bestselling historical novelist Inglis Fletcher, contains chicken breasts only. These are browned in a skillet, then baked in a lightly curried tomato sauce. Known as "Carolina's Chronicler," Illinois-born Inglis Fletcher settled near Edenton, North Carolina, and wrote a twelve-volume series of novels spanning some 200 years (1585 to 1789) of Tidewater Carolina history. At her most prolific between 1942 and 1964 but now largely forgotten, Fletcher deserves to be rediscovered because she was a stickler for accuracy. It's said that she spent one year researching each novel and a second year writing it. The recipe here is adapted from one that appeared in *Pass the Plate*, a fundraiser published by the Churchwomen and Friends of Christ Episcopal Church in New Bern.

1/2 cup unsifted all-purpose flour

1 teaspoon salt

1/2 teaspoon black pepper

4 whole chicken breasts, halved (3 1/2 to 4 pounds)

4 tablespoons vegetable oil

2 medium yellow onions, coarsely chopped

1 medium green bell pepper, cored, seeded, and coarsely chopped

1 medium red bell pepper, cored, seeded, and coarsely chopped

1 large garlic clove, finely chopped

4 teaspoons curry powder

One 28-ounce can whole tomatoes with their liquid (do not use tomatoes packed in sauce)

1/2 cup dried currants

1/3 cup coarsely chopped parsley

1/2 teaspoon crumbled leaf thyme

1/2 teaspoon ground mace

2 cups long-grain rice, cooked by package directions

A Love Affair with Southern Cooking

¾ cup lightly toasted slivered almonds
(8 to 10 minutes in a 350° F. oven)

1. Preheat the oven to 275° F.
2. Combine the flour, ½ teaspoon of the salt, and the pepper in a large plastic zipper bag, then dredge the chicken breasts, two at a time, by shaking in the seasoned flour.
3. Heat 3 tablespoons of the oil in a very large, heavy skillet over moderately high heat for 2 minutes, then arrange the chicken breasts skin side down in the skillet and brown 6 to 8 minutes on each side. Transfer to paper toweling to drain.
4. Spoon the remaining 1 tablespoon oil into the skillet and set over moderate heat for 1 minute. Add the onions, green and red bell peppers, garlic, and curry powder and sauté for about 10 minutes or until limp and golden, stirring often; do not brown. Add the tomatoes and their liquid, the currants, parsley, thyme, mace, and remaining ½ teaspoon salt, and simmer uncovered for 5 minutes, breaking up large clumps of tomato.
5. Arrange the chicken breasts one layer deep in an ungreased shallow 3-quart casserole, spoon the hot skillet mixture over all, and cover with aluminum foil.
6. Bake the casserole on the middle oven shelf for 45 to 50 minutes or until the chicken is fork-tender.
7. To serve, bed the rice on a heated large, deep platter, arrange the chicken on top, pour the tomato sauce over and around the chicken, then sprinkle with the toasted almonds.

1882 Tennessee traveling salesman Joel Cheek perfects a fragrant new coffee blend. Ten years later it's known as Maxwell House, taking the name of the Nashville hotel where it's served. (See box, page 317.)

J. Allen Smith and his partner J. A. Walker acquire the down-and-out Knoxville City Mills and in that Tennessee town begin grinding the soft winter wheat flours southern cooks favor.

An open-air farmer's market comes to downtown Roanoke. It is Virginia's first and it is still there.

1883 A Southern Exposition is held in Louisville to showcase the best of the "New South." Lighting the after-dark events are 4,600 Edison electric lights (Thomas Edison had once lived in Louisville). The fair is so popular it reopens every year for the next four years.

1884–85 A World's Fair comes to New Orleans. Though called the World Cotton Centennial, many of the agricultural and horticultural exhibits have nothing to do with cotton.

CHICKEN JAMBALAYA

MAKES 6 SERVINGS

. . . .

I've spent considerable time in Louisiana, most of it in Cajun Country west of New Orleans or in the lesser-known parishes to the north and west. Driving over one spring from Hattiesburg, Mississippi, I paused for several days in St. Francisville. Once called the town "two miles long and two yards wide," St. Francisville is blessed with a remarkable number of historic landmarks and outlying plantations, among them Oakley, where John J. Audubon lived and worked in 1821. Located in "British Louisiana," St. Francisville fronts the Mississippi—the dividing line between the Anglo parishes lying east of the great river and "French Louisiana" to the south and west. This is not to say that the cooking of "British Louisiana" is bland; this jambalaya easily proves otherwise. It's adapted from a recipe that appears in *Plantation Country*, a fund-raiser published by the Women's Service League of St. Francisville. As for the origin of the word *jambalaya*, see The Language of Southern Food (page 394).

3 to 4 tablespoons vegetable oil

One 3¼- to 3½-pound broiler-fryer,
cut up for frying

¾ teaspoon salt, or to taste

½ teaspoon black pepper, or to taste

6 ounces andouille sausage or chorizo, diced

1 large yellow onion, coarsely chopped

2 large celery ribs, coarsely chopped

1 large green bell pepper, cored, seeded,
and coarsely chopped

1½ cups converted rice

2½ to 3 cups chicken stock or broth (about)

1. Heat 2 tablespoons of the oil in a large, heavy kettle over moderately high heat for 2 minutes or until ripples appear on the kettle bottom. Brown the chicken in two or three batches, allowing 3 to 5 minutes per batch, seasoning with salt and pepper as the pieces brown, and adding another tablespoon of oil if needed. Drain the browned chicken on paper toweling.

2. Add the remaining oil to the kettle along with the andouille and brown for 2 to 3 minutes. Add the onion, celery, and bell pepper and sauté for about 5 minutes or until limp and golden.

3. Mix in the rice, then return the chicken to the kettle and push down into the rice mixture. Add 2½ cups of the chicken stock and bring to a boil over moderately high heat. Adjust the heat so the stock bubbles gently, cover, and cook for 25 to 35 minutes, stirring frequently, or until the chicken is tender and the rice has absorbed all the liquid. **Note:** *If the jambalaya seems dry before the chicken is done, add a little additional chicken stock.* Taste for salt and pepper and adjust as needed.

4. Dish up and serve with a tartly dressed salad of crisp greens.

A Southerner talks music.

—**MARK TWAIN,** *LIFE ON THE MISSISSIPPI*

FAMILY REUNION BRUNSWICK STEW

MAKES 20 TO 25 SERVINGS

. . . .

Some years ago when I was interviewing the granddaughter-in-law of one of our Virginia presidents, she served a clear chicken broth strewn with strips of white meat, dots of tomato, and crescents of celery. Hearing me praise her "lovely chicken soup," she snorted. "Chicken soup! Chicken soup! This is Brunswick stew!" It was unlike any Brunswick stew I'd ever eaten, and I said so. "Well," she replied. "*You're* from North Carolina. *You* make it with *potatoes*." Plus onions, plus baby butter beans, plus sweet corn, plus . . . plus . . . To be honest, the stew-masters of Brunswick County, where this "Virginia ambrosia" originated back in 1828, would never have recognized my hostess's anemic version. The original was a porridge-y muddle of squirrels, onions, and stale bread concocted by "Uncle" Jimmy Matthews, a camp cook in service to Dr. Creed Haskins of the Virginia Legislature. A hundred and sixty years later, the State General Assembly immortalized the event by proclaiming Brunswick County, Virginia, "the original home of Brunswick Stew." But they get an argument from Georgians who point to the twenty-gallon iron pot just outside their town of Brunswick; its plaque declares that America's first Brunswick stew was cooked in that pot in 1898. There are other dissenters as well—mainly food anthropologists who believe that southern Indian tribes were stewing squirrels, corn, and beans long before the White Man stepped ashore. Today, many a southern cook's most cherished recipe is the dog-eared one for Brunswick stew served at family reunions. This one comes from my Virginia stepmother's aunt, Annie Pool. Its secret, Aunt Annie once confided, is that it contains beef as well as chicken, also that "the corn is picked, shucked, and added at the very end."

One 6- to 7-pound stewing hen or capon, with neck and giblets

One 6-pound beef chuck or rump roast

12 cups (3 quarts) cold water

6 large yellow onions, coarsely chopped

18 medium all-purpose potatoes, peeled and cubed

6 cups (3 pints) freshly shelled or frozen baby lima beans (do not thaw)

6 cups (3 pints) canned tomatoes, preferably home-canned

Kernels from 12 large ears sweet corn or 6 cups (3 pints) frozen whole-kernel corn (do not thaw)

$\frac{1}{4}$ cup sugar

6 tablespoons ($\frac{3}{4}$ stick) butter

1 tablespoon salt, or to taste

$\frac{1}{2}$ teaspoon black pepper, or to taste

1. Simmer the hen, neck, giblets, and beef in the water in a covered large soup kettle over moderately low heat for about 1 1/2 hours or until the hen and beef are both tender.
2. Lift the beef, hen, neck, and giblets from the kettle and cool until easy to handle. Using

your fingers, strip the meat from the hen in bite-size pieces and reserve. Cut the beef into 1½-inch chunks and reserve; mince the giblets and reserve. Discard the neck.

3. Skim the fat from the broth and discard. Add the onions, potatoes, and limas to the kettle, cover, and simmer over moderate heat for 30 minutes or until not quite tender.

4. Return all meat to the kettle, add the tomatoes, and simmer uncovered for 20 minutes. Add the corn, sugar, and butter, and simmer uncovered, stirring now and then, for 20 minutes. Season to taste with salt and pepper, then simmer uncovered 10 minutes more or just long enough for the flavors to mellow.

5. Ladle into heated soup bowls and accompany with Iron Skillet Corn Bread (page 254).

KENTUCKY BURGOO

MAKES 12 SERVINGS

"There is no point in cooking country ham and burgoo to serve just six," Charles Patteson advises the Derby Day host in *Charles Patteson's Kentucky Cooking* (1988). "Start with the mandatory mint juleps," he continues. "Burgoo, which is midway between a hearty soup and a stew, succeeds the juleps in the guests' cups as a first course." I hadn't known that. Nor had I known that it's traditional for burgoo to be scooped into silver mint julep cups at the annual Kentucky Colonels' Barbecue the day after the Derby. In *Kentucky's Best* (1998), Linda Allison-Lewis writes that burgoo must "simmer for twenty-four hours prior to being served,"

then confides that burgoo chefs used to listen for the splatter of the "mysterious ingredient"—the ingredient that fused all flavors—being added "sometime in the dark of night." Legend has it that that ingredient was a black snake that fell out of a tree into the first batch of burgoo.

Historians doubt that but most do agree that burgoo was created during the Civil War by Gus Jaubert, a French chef serving Confederate general John Hunt Morgan. At war's end, Jaubert settled in Lexington, Kentucky, began making burgoo on a massive scale, and soon gained fame as "the burgoo king." On his death, according to Ronni Lundi, author of *Shuck Beans, Stack Cakes, and Honest Fried Chicken* (1991), Lexington cook J. T. Looney "inherited both Jaubert's pot and his title." While traveling about the Bluegrass State some years ago to research my *Grass Roots Cookbook*, I ate burgoo every chance I got. I also learned more about this Kentucky classic. Jaubert's original recipe apparently contained blackbirds. Unable to say "blackbird stew" not only because French was his first language but also because he had a hairlip, Jaubert pronounced it "burgoo." Or so I was told. Elsewhere I learned that those early burgoos contained mostly squirrels plus whatever vegetables came to hand. I daresay that there are hundreds of different recipes for Kentucky burgoo today. This downsized version of the burgoo served for years at the Pete Light Springs Restaurant in Cadiz, Kentucky, was given to me by Lois Watkins, whom I profiled in my book. "This burgoo is the best in the world," she said as she handed me the scribbled recipe. I won't quarrel with that.

1 whole chicken breast (2 halves)

1 chicken thigh

1 chicken liver

1½ pounds boneless pork shoulder

6 cups (1½ quarts) cold water

½ pound dried Great Northern beans,
washed, sorted, and soaked overnight in
2 cups cold water

2 large yellow onions, finely chopped

4 cups (1 quart) canned tomatoes (preferably
home-canned), with their liquid

4 cups (1 quart) canned whole-kernel corn
(preferably home-canned), well drained

4 cups (1 quart) canned green peas
(preferably home-canned), well drained

2 teaspoons salt, or to taste

½ teaspoon black pepper, or to taste

4 tablespoons (½ stick) butter

1. Place the chicken breast, thigh, and liver, the pork, and the cold water in a heavy, nonreactive 4-gallon kettle; set over moderately high heat and bring to a boil. Adjust the heat so the water bubbles gently, cover, and simmer for 30 minutes. Remove and refrigerate all pieces of chicken. Cover the kettle again and simmer the pork about 1½ hours longer or until very tender.

2. Remove the skin and bones from the chicken, cut the meat into 1-inch chunks, then pulse quickly in a food processor until the texture of coarsely ground meat (in the old days, the chicken was fed through a meat grinder).

When the pork is tender, cut into 1-inch chunks, then pulse just as you did the chicken. Also pulse the chicken liver.

3. Return the chicken, liver, and pork to the kettle, add the beans and their soaking water, the onions, tomatoes and their liquid, the corn, and peas. Cover and simmer for 1 hour.

4. Add the salt, pepper, and butter, reduce the heat to its lowest point, and simmer the burgoo uncovered for 3½ to 4 hours, stirring occasionally, or until as thick as chili. **Note: *If at any time the burgoo threatens to stick to the bottom of the kettle, slide a heat diffuser underneath.***

5. Taste the burgoo for salt and pepper, adjust as needed, then ladle into heated soup bowls, and serve with "Hot'ns" (page 244) or Hush Puppies (page 257).

STEWED CHICKEN

MAKES 5½ TO 6 CUPS MEAT (2¼ TO 2½
POUNDS) AND 1½ TO 2 QUARTS STOCK

Early southern cookbooks often include directions for stewing a hen because from Colonial days right up until the mid-twentieth century, many families—townspeople as well as farmers— kept a few chickens for eggs and for eating. My own family did back during World War Two, when red meat was rationed. Even though I was a little girl then, I remember dodging the feisty Leghorns as I gathered eggs. Once a hen stopped laying, Mother, following the lead of a country-come-to-town neighbor, stewed it; the meat could be used in endless ways. Because several of the southern classics in these pages call for cooked chicken, I thought that a good recipe for stewed chicken might be welcome. **Note:** *Over-the-hill hens are hard to find these days but plump roasters can be substituted.* **Tip:** *If the bird is to be tender, you must start it in cold water and never let it boil.*

One 4½- to 5-pound roasting chicken, giblets removed and excess fat discarded

1 large yellow onion, quartered

2 large celery ribs, trimmed and cut into 1-inch chunks (include some leaves)

2 large carrots, peeled and cut into 1-inch chunks

2 large whole bay leaves, preferably fresh

2 teaspoons salt

1 teaspoon black peppercorns

1. Place the chicken, giblets, and all remaining ingredients in a large stockpot and add enough cold water to cover the chicken by about 2 inches. Set over moderate heat and slowly bring to a simmer; this may take as long as an hour. Adjust the heat so the water barely bubbles, then simmer the chicken uncovered for about 1 hour or until an instant-read thermometer, thrust into the meaty inner thigh, not touching bone, registers 170° F.

2. Carefully lift the chicken from the pot and set in a large shallow roasting pan; cool until easy to handle.

3. Meanwhile, boil the stock uncovered for an hour or more over moderate heat or until reduced by one third to one half. Strain through a large fine sieve lined with cheesecloth; discard all solids.

4. Boil the strained stock uncovered in a large, heavy saucepan over moderate heat for 30 to 40 minutes or until reduced to 6 to 8 cups (1½ to 2 quarts). Cool, then pour into 1-pint preserving jars, leaving ½ inch of headroom at the top. Screw the lids down tight, and refrigerate or freeze, dating and labeling each jar. **Note:** *Use the refrigerated stock within one week, the frozen stock within three months.*

5. Using your hands, remove the chicken skin and discard. Strip the meat from the bones in smallish pieces and divide among two or three shallow plastic food containers. Cover and refrigerate or freeze, dating and labeling each container. **Note:** *Use the chilled chicken meat within two or three days, the frozen within three months.* **Note:** *Sometimes instead of stewing a chicken, I'll roast it untrussed and uncovered for about an hour at 400° F. or until an instant-read thermometer, thrust into the meaty inner thigh, not touching bone, reads 170° F. When the chicken is cool enough to handle, I strip the meat from the bones just as I do for stewed chicken and if not using straightaway, either refrigerate or freeze the meat to use later. This is a faster method but it leaves me without any chicken stock.*

❧

One man said it took the hair right off his chest, another one said it put the hair on his chest.

—ANDRE PRINCE JEFFRIES ON THE HOT CHICKEN SERVED AT PRINCE'S HOT CHICKEN SHACK IN NASHVILLE, TENNESSEE

❧

MARY RANDOLPH (1762-1828)

"The most influential American cookbook of the nineteenth century." That's how culinary historian Karen Hess describes Mary Randolph's *Virginia House-wife* (1824) in her historical notes to the facsimile edition (University of South Carolina Press, 1984).

She adds, moreover, that "a case may be made for considering it to be the earliest full-blown American cookbook."

That an "FFV" (First Family of Virginia aristocrat with ties to both George Washington and Thomas Jefferson) would write a cookbook is surprising. That she would pen what some consider "the finest cookbook ever to come out of the American kitchen" is unprecedented.

Before *The Virginia House-wife*, American women used English cookery books filled with fussy recipes. Mary Randolph was the first to recognize the emerging American cuisine and to publish such simple Virginia classics as broiled shad, turnip greens boiled with bacon, batter bread, and sweet potato pudding.

She believed that the quality of the cooking was more important than the quantity of dishes sent out of the kitchen. "Profusion is not elegance," she wrote.

The first of Thomas and Ann Cary Randolph's thirteen children, Mary Randolph was born in 1762 at Ampthill, the Chesterfield County plantation of her maternal grandparents. Though hers was a life of privilege, she learned early on that being mistress of a large plantation meant managing household finances, supervising the servants, and knowing how to preserve food safely (it's said that Mary Randolph invented the icebox). It also meant mastering the intricacies of food preparation as well as the art of elegant entertaining. No small job.

At the age of eighteen, Mary Randolph married David Meade Randolph, her first cousin once removed, becoming mistress of Presque Isle, a 750-acre plantation in Chesterfield County, Virginia. Presque Isle was an unhealthy place to raise a family, it turned out, because much of it was swampy.

Relocating to Richmond, the Randolphs built a grand red brick house. "Moldavia," as they called it, soon became the social center of the city's Federalist power elite, thanks in part to Mary's gifts as cook and hostess.

In 1802, President Jefferson, at odds with the Federalists, fired Mary's husband (his own cousin) as U.S. Marshal (a post bestowed by George Washington). Financial reversals followed, and the Randolphs were forced to sell Moldavia and downsize. Undeterred, Mary opened a boardinghouse and soon made her table the talk of the town.

Only after the Randolphs moved to Washington to spend their declining years with their son William Beverley did Mary begin her benchmark cookbook. She declares her mission in the preface: "The difficulties I encountered when I first entered on the duties of a house-keeping life, from the want of books sufficiently clear and concise to impart knowledge to a Tyro, compelled me to study the subject, and by actual experiment to reduce everything in the culinary line, to proper weights and measures."

Unfortunately, Mary Randolph died four years after her book was published and never lived to see its astounding success.

MRS. ANDERSON'S THIRTY-TWO-POUND HENS

During World War Two, we kept chickens in the backyard and it was my job to feed them, water them, and gather eggs.

When the hens "went broody" and stopped laying, Mother began to sell them as stewing hens. An old farm woman, who lived down the road, asked me one day about the hens (I couldn't have been more than eight).

"How much does them hens of your mama's weigh?" I hadn't a clue.

They were big birds, every bit as big as my Scottie. Skippy, I knew, weighed thirty-two pounds, so I told the woman, "About thirty-two pounds."

She called my mother straightaway: "Miz Anderson, I surely would like to buy one of them thirty-two-pound hens!"

My mother roared. "Gracious sakes, Jean! Don't you know that chickens are mostly feathers?" What my mother's hens did weigh was ten pounds, a mighty hefty bird in anyone's coop.

So dull he couldn't cut butter with a knife.

—OLD SOUTHERN SAYING

CHICKEN AND DUMPLINGS

MAKES 6 SERVINGS

My Yankee mother's dumplings were always soft and fluffy—the dumplings she dropped into chicken stew, the dumplings she cooked with garden peas and cream. The reason, of course, was that she made them out of biscuit dough. The first time I ordered chicken and dumplings down south, I was surprised to see that the dumplings were noodle-flat and slick. I have since queried countless southern friends about the dumplings their mothers made and nearly all say that the dumplings they knew as a child were flat. Certainly the dumpling recipes I've found in my collection of southern community cookbooks are of the noodle variety. Some are heavily seasoned, usually with bacon drippings and poultry seasoning. Others are perfectly plain and these, I think, are better because they complement rather than overpower the chicken. **Note:** *For this recipe, you'll need 5 to 5½ cups of slightly-larger-than-bite-size pieces of cooked chicken and 8 cups (2 quarts) of chicken stock (see Stewed Chicken, page 129).*

2 cups sifted all-purpose flour

1 teaspoon baking powder

1½ teaspoons salt, or to taste

⅓ cup firmly packed lard or vegetable shortening

⅓ cup milk (about)

8 cups (2 quarts) chicken stock or broth

1 chicken bouillon cube, if needed to boost the flavor of the stock

½ teaspoon black pepper, or to taste

½ teaspoon rubbed sage

½ teaspoon dried leaf thyme, crumbled

5 to 5½ cups slightly-larger-than-bite-size pieces of cooked chicken meat (see Note at left)

¼ cup coarsely chopped parsley

1. Combine the flour, baking powder, and ½ teaspoon of the salt in a large bowl. Using a pastry blender, cut in the lard until the texture of coarse meal. Whisking hard with a fork, drizzle in just enough milk to form a soft but manageable dough. Scoop onto a lightly floured surface, shape into a ball, cover, and let rest for about 10 minutes.

2. Meanwhile, place the chicken stock, bouillon cube, if needed, the remaining 1 teaspoon salt, the pepper, sage, and thyme in a large Dutch oven or stockpot and set over low heat.

3. Roll the dumpling dough as thin as pie crust on a lightly floured surface, and cut into 1½-inch squares. Gather any scraps, reroll, and cut.

4. Add the chicken to the Dutch oven, bring quickly to a boil, then ease in the dumplings, a few at a time. Adjust the heat so the stock barely bubbles, cover, and simmer for 25 to 30 minutes or until the dumplings are done, stirring gently now and then.

5. Add the parsley, taste for salt and pepper, and adjust as needed. Ladle into heated soup bowls and serve.

1885 J. Allen Smith of Knoxville, Tennessee, develops a premium finely ground, triple-sifted flour and within ten years brand-names it White Lily (his wife's name is Lillie). Even today, many Southerners swear that they can't make decent biscuits without White Lily. (See White Lily Flour, page 246.)

F. F. Hansell of New Orleans publishes Lafcadio Hearn's *La Cuisine Creole: A Collection of Culinary Recipes from Leading Chefs and Noted Creole Housewives, Who Have Made New Orleans Famous for Its Cuisine.* He defines Creole cooking as a "blending of the characteristics of the American, French, Spanish, Italian, West Indian, and Mexican." Hearn is the first to write a Creole cookbook.

1886 Atlanta pharmacist John Pemberton concocts a nonalcoholic dark brown syrup as a nerve tonic. At Jacob's drugstore nearby, it is mixed with carbonated water and sold as a revivifying beverage: Coca-Cola. (See box, page 4.)

1887–88 C. F. Sauer, a 21-year-old Richmond, Virginia, pharmacist, decides to bottle the flavorings and extracts that cooks need and sell them at prices they can afford.

CHICKEN BOG

MAKES 8 SERVINGS

. . . .

In *The Carolina Rice Kitchen: The African Connection* (1992), food historian Karen Hess suggests that chicken bog may have descended from *la soupe courte* of Provence, "an ancient festival dish, calling for mutton, *petit salé* or other cured pork, onions, aromatics, saffron, and rice." It is, she continues, "not a soup but a very thick stew or a rather wet pilau." Her theory is that with the deletion of saffron and substitution of chicken for mutton, a new dish emerged. "Several sources," Hess writes, "including Amelia Wallace Vernon, formerly of Florence County, South Carolina, have described what sounds like a similar dish using chicken instead of the mutton of Provence; it is called *chicken bog* and is made outdoors in wash tubs to serve large crowds." A particular favorite on the lower reaches of the Pee Dee River, chicken bog is not only "fixed right regular" in school cafeterias but also served at countless family reunions, church suppers, and political fund-raisers. There's even an annual Bog-Off in the little town of Loris, South Carolina, just thirty minutes northwest of Myrtle Beach. There are dozens of recipes for chicken bog, some of them strangely complicated; the point of the dish is that it's an easy way to feed an army. As for the recipe's unusual name, some say that "bog" comes from the fact that rice is grown in bogs, others that the chicken is "bogged down" in the rice, and still others that the dish is just a "soggy, boggy mess." **Note:** *Some modern cooks shortcut chicken bog by using chicken parts and canned broth. The recipe here is fairly classic.*

1 tablespoon vegetable oil

1 pound spicy country sausage links or chorizo, sliced ½ inch thick

1 large yellow onion, coarsely chopped

1 large green bell pepper, cored, seeded, and coarsely chopped

2½ cups converted rice

6 cups rich chicken stock or broth

5 cups large-ish chunks of cooked chicken plus the coarsely chopped cooked giblets (see Stewed Chicken, page 129)

1 teaspoon salt, or to taste

½ teaspoon black pepper, or to taste

1. Heat the oil in a large Dutch oven over moderately high heat for 2 minutes. Add the sausage and cook for 5 minutes or until nicely browned. Using a slotted spoon, lift the browned sausage to a plate and reserve.

2. Add the onion and bell pepper to the sausage drippings and stir-fry for 8 to 10 minutes or until limp and lightly browned.

3. Add the rice and cook and stir for 1 minute. Add the chicken stock, chicken, giblets, reserved sausage, salt, and pepper. Bring to a boil, then reduce the heat so the mixture bubbles gently, cover, and cook for 20 minutes, stirring often, or just until the rice is tender. If the bog seems soupy, cook, uncovered, for 5 to 10 minutes more. It should be about the consistency of a soft risotto. Taste for salt and pepper and adjust as needed.

4. Ladle into big soup bowls, and serve with butter beans, red-ripe tomatoes, and Jerusalem Artichoke Pickle Relish (page 361).

CHICKEN PIE

. . . .

Breathes there a southern cook who doesn't have a pet recipe for chicken pie? My own favorite is my attempt to re-create the chicken pie served at the Salem Tavern in Old Salem, a restored Moravian village in Winston-Salem, North Carolina. I order it whenever I lunch there. Unlike so many chicken pies, this one contains no carrots, no peas—just chicken and well-seasoned gravy. **Note:** *I find the chicken more succulent if I roast it, strip the meat from the carcass while the bird is still warm, and make the pie straightaway (it takes a 4½- to 5-pound chicken and 1 to 1¼ hours in a 400° F. oven). If you'd prefer to use Stewed Chicken, follow the recipe on page 129. Needless to add, turkey can be substituted for chicken; it's a splendid way to use up the big bird.*

4 tablespoons (½ stick) butter

1 medium yellow onion, finely chopped

1 medium celery rib, trimmed, halved lengthwise, then each half thinly sliced

6 tablespoons all-purpose flour

1 teaspoon salt

½ teaspoon rubbed sage

¼ teaspoon dried leaf thyme, crumbled

¼ teaspoon black pepper

2½ cups hot chicken broth

5½ to 6 cups bite-size pieces cooked chicken or turkey (see Note above)

Pastry for a 9-inch, 2-crust pie (see About Pie Crusts, page xxi)

1. Place a heavy-duty baking sheet on the middle oven shelf and preheat the oven to 425° F. **Note:** *Setting the unbaked pie on a hot baking sheet cooks the bottom crust faster and reduces the risk of its becoming soggy.*

2. Melt the butter in a large, heavy skillet over moderate heat, add the onion and celery, and cook, stirring often, for 6 to 8 minutes or until limp and lightly browned.

3. Blend in the flour, salt, sage, thyme, and pepper, then, whisking hard, pour in the hot broth. Cook, whisking all the while, for about 5 minutes or until thickened. Set the skillet off the heat, cool for 15 minutes, then fold in the chicken.

4. Scoop the chicken mixture into an unbaked 9-inch pie shell, then ease the top crust into place. Trim the crust so it overhangs the pie about one inch all round, then roll the top and bottom crusts under so that they rest upon the rim. Crimp to seal, making a high fluted edge, and cut decorative steam vents in the top crust.

5. Slide the pie onto the preheated baking sheet and bake for 30 to 35 minutes or until richly browned.

6. Cool the pie for 20 minutes, then, using a sharp serrated knife, cut into wedges and serve.

❋

Slow as molasses in January.

—*OLD SOUTHERN SAYING*

❋

BAKED WILD DUCK

Parboil duck for five minutes with small piece celery and small sliced onion. Drain; rub inside and out with salt and pepper and pinch ground ginger. Place inside duck a half of small onion, piece of apple studded with cloves, and a small white potato. Bake 20 minutes at 450 degrees uncovered; reduce heat to 350 degrees and bake covered 15 to 20 minutes per pound. Baste with equal parts melted butter, hot water and red wine or orange juice.

—*Roanoke Island Cook Book*, compiled by members and friends of the Manteo Woman's Club, Manteo, North Carolina

Recipe contributed by Mrs. Woodie Fearing

BAKED CHICKEN SALAD

MAKES 6 SERVINGS

I have no idea what southern cook decided to bake a chicken salad, but it was an inspired idea and variations on the theme now appear in scores of community cookbooks. I remember my first taste of baked chicken salad at a home demonstration club potluck luncheon in the North Carolina mountain town of Boone. I complimented the woman who'd made it on her "chicken casserole" only to be abruptly corrected: "Chicken casserole, you call it? This ain't no casserole! This is baked chicken salad!" And so it was—all the makings of chicken salad bubbling underneath a crunchy crumb crust. Here's my version of that old Watauga County recipe with a bit of garlic added. "Land sakes!" I can hear that feisty farm woman saying. "Garlic!" Back then, few good southern cooks ever used garlic—even garlic powder or salt. How things have changed! **Note:** *This recipe is also an excellent way to recycle turkey leftovers.*

3 tablespoons bacon drippings or vegetable oil

1 large yellow onion, moderately coarsely chopped

2 large celery ribs, trimmed and moderately coarsely chopped

1 medium garlic clove, finely chopped

3 tablespoons all-purpose flour

One 12-ounce can evaporated milk (use "light," if you like)

1 cup chicken broth

⅓ cup firmly packed mayonnaise-relish sandwich spread

4 cups bite-size pieces cooked chicken or turkey

⅓ cup coarsely chopped parsley

One 4-ounce jar diced pimientos, well drained

1 teaspoon salt, or to taste

½ teaspoon black pepper, or to taste

1½ cups moderately fine soft bread crumbs tossed with 1½ tablespoons butter, melted

1. Preheat the oven to 350° F. Spritz a shallow 2-quart casserole with nonstick cooking spray and set aside.
2. Heat the drippings in a large, heavy skillet over moderately high heat for 1 minute, add the onion, celery, and garlic, and cook, stirring often, for 10 to 12 minutes or until lightly browned. Blend in the flour and cook and stir for about 1 minute.
3. Add the evaporated milk and broth and cook, stirring constantly, for 3 to 5 minutes or until the mixture boils and thickens. Set off the heat and mix in the sandwich spread, then the chicken, parsley, pimientos, salt, and pepper.
4. Scoop into the casserole, spreading to the edge, then scatter the buttered crumbs evenly over all.
5. Slide onto the middle oven shelf and bake uncovered for about 30 minutes or until bubbling and tipped with brown.
6. Serve at once as the main course of a casual lunch or supper. Or do as that Watauga County farm woman did and make it your contribution to a potluck supper.

❈

Miss Sadie sniffed. "Fried chicken in the daytime is too heavy if you've got work to do. Why not chicken salad?"

—JAN KARON, *A LIGHT IN THE WINDOW*

❈

1888 Henry Ramos, a New Orleans bartender, creates a new cocktail, the Gin Fizz. It later becomes a favorite of Louisiana senator Huey Long, who introduces it to Washington, D.C., society as the Ramos Gin Fizz.

Atlanta businessman Asa G. Candler buys the Coca-Cola syrup recipe, which, he claims, has cured him of migraines. He also begins to buy the company.

Dr. Charles Shepard founds Pinehurst Tea Plantation in Summerville, South Carolina. Located near the original Michaux tea farm, its principal crop is Oolong and it remains so until Shepard's death in 1915.

1889 Twenty-five-year-old Willoughby McCormick begins making flavoring extracts and fruit syrups in the basement of his Baltimore house and sells them door to door. (See McCormick's Spices, page 186.)

1890 Thanks to the flour mills and factories of Chattanooga, Knoxville, Nashville, and Memphis, manufacturing adds more to Tennessee's economy than agriculture. This is a first.

1891 After buying the Coca-Cola Company bit by bit, Asa G. Candler finally owns it.

PRESSED CHICKEN

. . . .

Early on, I had the good fortune to work with Ruth Current, the charismatic state leader of the North Carolina Federation of Home Demonstration Clubs. "Miz Ruth," as I called her, grew up on a farm in Rowan County, and even though she traveled the world, she was at heart a southern country cook. Miz Ruth and I often traveled together, she to speak at conventions, I to cover them for the local media. On those long road trips, Miz Ruth talked about the colorful characters she'd met in her early years as an extension worker. That was back in the 1930s when the Agricultural Extension Service, still in its infancy, aimed to help the family at the end of the road climb out of poverty. Sometimes, Miz Ruth told me, she'd drive to the end of the road only to be met by a farmer with a mule. She'd climb aboard for a last-lap canter to a log cabin "so far back in them hills you had to keep wipin' at the shadows." Two of my favorite southern recipes are Miz Ruth's—this Pressed Chicken and the Chicken Mayonnaise that follows. I once asked Miz Ruth why the recipe was called Pressed Chicken. She thought that it dated back to the days when women made their own gelatin. These were not altogether reliable, so gelatin mixtures were often weighted or pressed into molds so that they were less apt to disintegrate when unmolded. **Note:** *Miz Ruth's Pressed Chicken calls for two packets of gelatin but preferring a softer gel, I use half that amount. For slightly stiffer Pressed Chicken, use one envelope plus one tea-*spoon. **Tip:** *I heat the chicken broth in a 2-quart ovenproof glass measuring cup by microwaving 5 to 8 minutes on* HIGH. *I then scoop in the gelatin, and when it dissolves, I mix in the seasonings and chill until syrupy. Still using the same measuring cup, I fold in the chicken, eggs, and celery. Saves on dishwashing.*

1 envelope unflavored gelatin (see Note at left)

¼ cup cold water

2 cups boiling chicken broth or rich stock (see Tip above)

2 tablespoons finely grated yellow onion

1 tablespoon fresh lemon juice

1 teaspoon salt, or to taste

¼ teaspoon ground hot red pepper (cayenne), or to taste

¼ teaspoon dry mustard

3 cups finely chopped cooked chicken

4 large hard-cooked eggs, shelled and finely chopped

2 medium celery ribs, trimmed and finely diced

6 large lettuce leaves

Mayonnaise

1. Lightly coat an 8 × 8 × 2-inch baking dish or nonreactive pan with nonstick cooking spray and set aside.

2. Soften the gelatin in the cold water for 5 minutes. Pour the boiling chicken broth into a large heatproof bowl (see Tip above), and add the gelatin. When it dissolves, mix in the onion, lemon juice, salt, cayenne, and mustard. Taste for salt and cayenne and adjust.

3. Set uncovered in the refrigerator for about an hour or until syrupy. Fold in the chicken, eggs, and celery, then pour into the baking dish, spreading to the corners.

4. Set uncovered in the refrigerator and chill overnight or until firm enough to cut.

5. To serve, cut the Pressed Chicken into squares and bed each on a lettuce leaf on a dinner plate. Top each portion with a generous dollop of mayonnaise. Good accompaniments: Crisp-tender asparagus spears or green beans and thickly sliced red-ripe tomatoes.

❀

Until a child was grown he saw only the wings, back, and Pope's noses of chicken while he watched the grown folks eat the breasts, legs, and such.

—CARSON McCULLERS, ON HER GEORGIA CHILDHOOD

❀

❀

The Turkey is certainly one of the most delightful presents which the New World has made to the Old.

—ANTHELME BRILLAT-SAVARIN

❀

1892 Asa G. Candler incorporates Coca-Cola and over time earns millions as its president.

Down-Easter L. W. Rogers, recently relocated to Atlanta to make his fortune, opens his first grocery, then rapidly expands throughout Georgia and South Carolina. By 1936, there are more than 400 Rogers groceries. Fifty-five years later, and already merged with the popular Virginia-based Pender chain, Rogers renames its groceries. They become Colonial Stores.

1893 Pharmacist Caleb Bradham of New Bern, North Carolina, concocts a fizzy digestif out of pepsin, kola nuts, sugar, vanilla, rare oils, and carbonated water. He calls it "Brad's Drink."

1895 Asa Candler now has three plants across the country producing the secret Coca-Cola syrup, one each in Chicago, Dallas, and Los Angeles.

1896 Booker T. Washington hires agronomist George Washington Carver to teach and conduct research at Alabama's Tuskegee Institute. (See box, page 323.)

CHICKEN MAYONNAISE

· ·

The recipe for this cool molded chicken salad, like the Pressed Chicken that precedes, came from Ruth Current, with whom I worked shortly after graduating from college. It, too, calls for two envelopes of gelatin and once again I've halved the amount. For slightly stiffer Chicken Mayonnaise, use one envelope plus one teaspoon of gelatin. I've changed Miz Ruth's recipe in another way, too: I've toasted the almonds because I like them better than raw almonds. My method of making Chicken Mayonnaise, however, is the same as for Pressed Chicken because I'm forever seeking ways to minimize kitchen time and clutter. See the Note and Tip on page 138.

1 envelope unflavored gelatin (see headnote)

¼ cup cold water

2 cups boiling chicken broth or rich stock

2 tablespoons finely grated yellow onion

1½ tablespoons fresh lemon juice

½ teaspoon salt

¼ teaspoon black pepper

½ cup firmly packed mayonnaise
(use "light," if you like)

½ cup firmly packed mayonnaise-relish
sandwich spread

2½ cups finely diced cooked chicken

½ cup coarsely chopped, lightly toasted
slivered almonds (8 to 10 minutes
in a 350° F. oven)

2 large hard-cooked eggs, peeled
and finely diced

2 medium celery ribs, trimmed
and finely diced

1 cup solidly frozen tiny green peas

6 lettuce leaves or 1 head radicchio, cored
and sliced about ½ inch thick

1. Lightly coat an 8 × 8 × 2-inch baking dish or nonreactive pan with nonstick cooking spray and set aside.
2. Soften the gelatin in the cold water for 5 minutes. Pour the boiling chicken broth into a large heatproof bowl (see Note and Tip, page 138), and add the gelatin. As soon as it dissolves, mix in the onion, lemon juice, salt, and pepper.
3. Set uncovered in the refrigerator for about an hour or until syrupy. Blend in the mayonnaise and sandwich spread, whisking until smooth. Fold in the chicken, almonds, eggs, celery, and frozen peas, then pour into the baking dish and spread to the corners.
4. Set uncovered in the refrigerator and chill overnight or until firm enough to cut.
5. To serve, cut the Chicken Mayonnaise into squares and bed each on a lettuce leaf or nest in the sliced radicchio. The perfect accompaniment: thickly sliced red-ripe tomatoes.

Variations

Turkey Mayonnaise: Prepare the recipe as directed, substituting cooked turkey for chicken.

Ham Mayonnaise: Prepare Steps 1 and 2 of Chicken Mayonnaise, increasing the amount of gelatin to 4 teaspoons. In Step 3, increase the mayonnaise to ⅔ cup and substitute 3 tablespoons each dill pickle relish and sweet pickle relish for the sandwich spread. Also add 1 tablespoon each Dijon mustard, well-drained small capers, and freshly snipped dill. Finally, use 3 cups finely diced fully cooked ham instead of the 2½ cups chicken and omit the almonds. Finish Step 3, folding in the hard-cooked eggs, celery, and frozen peas, then proceed as the recipe directs. Good with grilled yellow squash and bell peppers.

TRUSTEES' HOUSE TURKEY HASH ON INDIAN GRIDDLE CAKES

MAKES 6 SERVINGS

Here's my adaptation of a delicious hash that I've enjoyed at Shaker Village of Pleasant Hill. With thirty-four painstakingly restored buildings, this come-to-life nineteenth-century Shaker community in the Kentucky Bluegrass is to my mind one of America's most interesting museum villages. Certainly it's one of the few where you can spend the night. Or sit down to a groaning board of old Shaker recipes. Many of those served in the Trustees' Office Dining Room appear in two paperback cookbooks by Elizabeth C. Kremer, who for years managed the dining room. I have both books: *We Make You Kindly Welcome* (1970) and *Welcome Back to Pleasant Hill: More Recipes from the Trustees' House* (1977). A chicken version of this hash appears in the first. But because we're all confronted with turkey leftovers at least once a year, I think that a turkey hash makes sense.

Turkey Hash

3 tablespoons butter

1 medium yellow onion, moderately coarsely chopped

1 small celery rib, trimmed and finely diced

4 tablespoons all-purpose flour

¾ teaspoon salt

¼ teaspoon black pepper

⅛ teaspoon ground hot red pepper (cayenne)

⅛ teaspoon freshly grated nutmeg

2 cups turkey or chicken broth

3½ cups diced cooked turkey

Griddle Cakes

1 cup unsifted stone-ground cornmeal (white or yellow)

½ cup sifted all-purpose flour

2 tablespoons raw or granulated sugar

½ teaspoon baking powder

½ teaspoon baking soda

¼ teaspoon salt

⅛ teaspoon black pepper

1 cup buttermilk

1 large egg, lightly beaten

2 tablespoons vegetable oil, melted butter, or lard

3 to 5 tablespoons milk

1. For the hash: Melt the butter in a large, heavy skillet over moderate heat and when it froths, add the onion and celery, and stir-fry for 5 to 6 minutes or until limp and golden.

2. Blend in the flour, salt, two peppers, and nutmeg, then add the turkey broth gradually, stirring all the while. Continue cooking and stirring for 3 to 5 minutes or until the mixture thickens.

3. Mix in the turkey, turn the heat to its lowest point, partially cover the skillet, and allow the hash to mellow while you prepare the griddle cakes.

4. For the griddle cakes: Combine the cornmeal, flour, sugar, baking powder, baking soda, salt, and pepper in a large bowl and make a well in the center. Whisk the buttermilk, egg, and oil together in a spouted 1- or 2-quart measure, then pour into the well in the dry ingredients and whisk briskly to form a smooth batter. Add the milk, tablespoon by tablespoon, until the batter is the consistency of a thin white sauce.

5. Lightly oil a griddle or large, heavy skillet and set it over moderate heat for 1 1/2 to 2 minutes until the oil almost—but not quite—smokes.

6. Using a 1/4-cup measure, drop the batter onto the griddle, spacing the cakes about 2 inches apart. Reduce the heat to moderately low and as soon as bubbles appear on the surface of the griddle cakes, turn and brown the flip sides for 1 to 2 minutes. As the griddle cakes brown, transfer to heated dinner plates, allowing 3 to 4 per person.

7. Ladle the turkey hash over the griddle cakes and serve.

THE FIRST THANKSGIVING

If you think the first Thanksgiving took place in Massachusetts in 1620, think again.

That distinction belongs to Berkeley Plantation on the James River. Here, on December 4, 1619, Captain John Woodlief, a former Jamestown colonist, came ashore with thirty-seven new English settlers to develop the Berkeley Hundred, an 8,000-acre site named for its sponsor, Sir Richard Berkeley. Asking the settlers to kneel, Woodlief began reading Berkeley's proclamation:

"Wee ordaine that the day of our ships arrival at the place assigned for plantacon in the land of Virginia shall be yearly and perpetually kept holy as a day of thanksgiving to Almighty God."

This, insist members of the Virginia First Thanksgiving Festival, Inc., which reenacts the event every November at Berkeley Plantation, was the first Thanksgiving. No Indians and probably no food, although bacon, peas, cornmeal cakes, and cinnamon water have been mentioned.

The irony here is that for 300 years nobody remembered—let alone celebrated—that first Thanksgiving. Then one day in 1931, Berkeley Company documents surfaced in, of all places, the New York Public Library, among them a record of the 1619 ceremony.

In 1958 a group of determined believers formed the Virginia First Thanksgiving Festival, Inc., "to gain appropriate recognition for Virginia's documented claim to the first official Thanksgiving in America." And then in 1962 came a *mea culpa* from President John F. Kennedy via his special assistant Arthur M. Schlesinger, Jr.

"You are quite right," he wrote, corroborating the Virginia Festival's claim, "and I can only plead an unconquerable New England bias."

HOT BROWN

. . . .

I'd heard about Louisville's famous Hot Brown, a broiled open-face turkey sandwich in a bubbling cheese sauce, long before I tasted it. I wasn't disappointed. Over the years I've enjoyed variations on the theme here and there, some of them made with chicken, some accompanied by sautéed mushrooms, but to my mind none matches the original. Here's the back story: In the roaring '20s, Louisville's swanky Brown Hotel threw dinner dances. Hundreds came, danced till the wee hours, then retreated to the hotel dining room to feast on ham and eggs. One night in 1923 chef Fred Schmidt decided to dish up something different: He layered toast and sliced turkey in single-portion gratin pans, covered them with mornay sauce (a white sauce with cheese added), ran them under the broiler, and crowned them with a crisscross of bacon. To Louisvillians that original Hot Brown is the one and only; the hotel still serves it. Although the recipe is simple, it's more suited to chefs than to home cooks, who rarely have stacks of single-serving gratin pans. I use pie tins for my Hot Browns. They're functional but lack the glamour of copper gratins. **Note:** *Whatever you use for this recipe must be flameproof, able to take intense broiler heat; that eliminates glass and ceramic baking dishes that are merely ovenproof.* **Caution:** *Because the cheese sauce may not reach 160° F., the temperature deemed safe for eggs in this age of salmonella, I use a pasteurized egg and urge you to do the same (see About Pasteurized Eggs, page xxi).*

8 slices toast, trimmed of crusts (use firm-textured or home-style bread)

Eight ¼-inch-thick slices cooked turkey (or chicken), cut to fit the toast (I favor breast meat)

4 tablespoons (½ stick) butter

6 tablespoons all-purpose flour

2½ cups milk

1 large pasteurized egg, well beaten (see Caution at left)

⅓ cup plus 2 tablespoons freshly grated Parmesan cheese

¼ cup softly whipped cream (optional)

1 teaspoon salt, or to taste

¼ teaspoon black pepper, or to taste

8 slices crisply cooked bacon

1. Preheat the broiler. Arrange 2 slices of toast side by side in each of four single-serving metal gratin pans (or four 8-inch metal pie pans attractive enough to appear at the dinner table). Top each piece of toast with a slice of turkey and set aside while you prepare the sauce.

2. Melt the butter in a heavy medium-size saucepan over moderate heat, then blend in the flour. Add the milk and cook, whisking constantly, for 3 to 5 minutes or until thickened and smooth.

3. Blend a little of the hot sauce into the beaten egg, stir back into the pan, and cook and stir 1 minute more. Under no circumstances allow

the sauce to boil; it will curdle. Off heat, mix in the ⅓ cup grated Parmesan and when it melts, fold in the whipped cream, if desired. Finally, season to taste with the salt and pepper.

4. Ladle the cheese sauce over the sandwiches, dividing the total amount evenly. Sprinkle with the remaining 2 tablespoons grated Parmesan, again dividing evenly.

5. Slide the pans into the broiler, setting them 4 to 5 inches from the heat, and broil for 2 to 3 minutes or until bubbly and flecked with brown.

6. Crisscross 2 slices of bacon over each portion and serve.

TURKEY PURLOO

MAKES 6 SERVINGS

. . . .

Purloo is the Lowcountry word for *pilau* or *pilaf* and since plantation days when rice was king, purloos have been a popular way to recycle leftovers—especially turkey and chicken. Actually, this isn't a true purloo because the creamed turkey and mushrooms are ladled over cooked rice, not cooked with it. No matter; it's a popular South Carolina dish.

3 tablespoons butter

½ pound small mushrooms, wiped clean and quartered

1 small yellow onion, coarsely chopped

⅓ cup roast turkey (or chicken) drippings, bacon drippings, or vegetable oil

7 tablespoons all-purpose flour

2 cups chicken broth or water

3½ cups bite-size chunks cooked turkey (or chicken)

1 teaspoon salt, or to taste

¼ teaspoon black pepper, or to taste

2 tablespoons moderately coarsely chopped parsley

2 cups long-grain rice, cooked by package directions

1. Melt the butter in a large, heavy skillet over moderate heat; add the mushrooms and onion and sauté, stirring often, for 5 to 8 minutes or until the mushrooms release their juices and these evaporate. Set off the heat and reserve.

2. Blend the drippings and flour in a large, heavy saucepan, set over moderately low heat, and cook, stirring all the while, for 5 to 10 minutes or until a rich rust-brown. Add the broth and cook, whisking constantly, for about 3 minutes or until thickened and smooth.

3. Add the reserved mushroom mixture, the turkey, salt, and pepper; adjust the heat so the sauce barely bubbles, and simmer uncovered, stirring now and then, for 15 minutes or until the flavors mellow. Taste for salt and pepper and adjust as needed. Stir in the parsley.

4. To serve, bed the hot cooked rice on a heated platter and ladle the turkey mixture on top.

TO ROAST A 'POSSUM

. . . first catch the 'possum. Dress it and soak it in salt water for 12 hrs, then wash and parboil it in salt water until tender. Have ready some sliced sweet potatoes which have been boiled until done in clear water. Lay 'possum out flat in roasting pan, put slices of sweet potatoes all around it, add pepper and sufficient stock. Bake in quick oven until a nice brown. Serve on a platter using potatoes and parsley for garnishing.

—Mrs. W. T. Tatum, Iredell County, North Carolina

BEAUFORT QUAIL JAMBALAYA

MAKES 6 SERVINGS

North and South Carolina both have coastal towns named Beaufort. Tar Heels pronounce it *BEAU-fort* the French way, but in South Carolina it's *BU-fort*. For beauty and historical significance, South Carolina's Beaufort wins hands down. It's a mini Charleston with street after street of magnificent antebellum homes. Suzanne Williamson, whom *More* dispatched me to profile one Christmas, lives in one of them with her husband, Peter Pollak. No one

---

1897 Nashville builds an exact replica of the Parthenon for its Tennessee Centennial Exposition, a world's fair on a grand scale with pavilions from as far afield as Egypt. The Parthenon still stands in this "Athens of the South."

1898 Georgia bubbles up its own Brunswick stew. A plaque on a 25-gallon iron pot just outside Brunswick, Georgia, marks both the spot and the vessel in which it was cooked.

By changing the name of the fizzy stomach tonic he created in 1893 to Pepsi-Cola, druggist Caleb Bradham fixes Pepsi's official birth date at 1898 (see box, page 14).

1899 Antoine's owner Jules Alciatore creates an oyster dish so rich he calls it Oysters Rockefeller. The exact recipe is known only to Antoine's.

Benjamin Thomas and Joseph Whitehead of Chattanooga, Tennessee, persuade Atlanta Coca-Cola owner Asa Candler to let them bottle his popular new fountain drink.

Richard L. Lindsey names his Nashville, Tennessee, mill's finest flour for his three-year-old daughter, Martha White. Southerners who pride themselves on their flaky biscuits and feathery cakes still insist upon soft white flours like Martha White. (See Martha White Flour, page 324.)

loves to entertain more than Suzanne and no one does it with greater style and grace. Her secret? Check out *Entertaining for Dummies*, which she coauthored with Linda Smith. For *More*'s Christmas feature, Suzanne served this quail jambalaya in her candlelit ballroom. Among the guests was novelist Pat Conroy, who came early to kibitz in the kitchen with Suzanne; at the time, she was developing recipes for *The Pat Conroy Cookbook* (2004). **Note:** *You can substitute three halved Cornish hens for the quail, but they must be small—no more than a pound and a half apiece.*

3 tablespoons olive oil

Twelve 4-ounce quail, cleaned, dressed, and split lengthwise (see Note above)

¼ teaspoon salt

¼ teaspoon ground hot red pepper (cayenne)

2 medium yellow onions, moderately finely chopped

1 large red bell pepper, cored, seeded, and moderately finely chopped

1 large green bell pepper, cored, seeded, and moderately finely chopped

4 large garlic cloves, minced

3 cups boiling chicken broth

1½ cups converted rice

2 large whole bay leaves

1 pound fully cooked chorizo or Spanish-style sausage, thinly sliced

¾ cup canned plum tomatoes, drained and finely chopped

1. Preheat the oven to 375° F. Lightly coat a large, shallow roasting pan (preferably one attractive enough to appear at the dining table) with nonstick cooking spray and set aside.

2. Heat half the olive oil in a large, heavy skillet over moderately high heat, add half the quail, and brown 2 minutes on each side; transfer to the roasting pan. Brown the remaining quail in the remaining oil the same way and add to the pan. Sprinkle the birds with the salt and cayenne pepper and roast uncovered on the middle oven shelf for 15 minutes.

3. Meanwhile, sauté the onions, red and green bell peppers, and garlic in the skillet drippings, stirring often, for about 5 minutes or until limp. Add 1 cup of the hot broth and cook 1 to 2 minutes, scraping up any browned bits on the skillet bottom.

4. Remove the birds from the oven, transfer to a large tray, and set aside. Pour the skillet mixture into the roasting pan, add the rice and remaining hot broth, and tuck in the bay leaves.

5. Cover snugly with foil, slide onto the middle oven rack, and bake for 15 minutes or until the rice is al dente. Remove the foil cover, discard the bay leaves, and stir well.

6. Fold the chorizo and tomatoes into the rice mixture, then arrange the quail on top, skin sides up. Cover with the foil and bake for 15 minutes or until the rice is tender and the quail are done.

7. Serve at table right from the roasting pan. Or, if you prefer, divide the jambalaya among six heated dinner plates.

CATFISH

The catfish is a plenty good enough fish for anyone.
—Mark Twain

When I was a little girl, we'd pile into the family Ford on Sunday afternoons and jounce along unpaved back roads raising clouds of red dust. We'd tunnel through thickets of pine, cross fields of broomstraw, and clatter over wooden bridges, most of them one-lane and some of them covered.

I liked the bridges best because there were always people down below fishing in water as red as iron rust—men, women, children, blacks, whites. Most wore overalls and poke bonnets or straw hats. And most used homemade poles made of bamboo.

"They're after catfish," my mother explained, adding that she didn't like them because they tasted like mud (around here they're still called "mudcats"). Back then you had to catch your own catfish, befriend someone who did, or do without.

Fast-forward fifty years. The other night at Crook's Corner in Chapel Hill I feasted on catfish fingers as delicate as Dover sole. Lightly jacketed in batter, they were flash-fried just until the flesh, lean and white neath a crisp coating, parted at the touch of a fork. Of course this catfish hadn't been yanked from a muddy river. It had been farm-raised.

Today 94 percent of all U.S. Farm-Raised Catfish comes from the South, principally Alabama, Arkansas, Louisiana, and Mississippi, and each year adds more than $4 billion to the coffers of each.

These catfish swim in environmentally controlled, eco-friendly ponds. To fill them, water is pumped from deep underground, passing through filtering alluvial aquifers en route. Fed high-protein pellets compounded of soybean meal (plus a little corn and rice), these catfish reach "harvest size"—1½ pounds—within 18 to 24 months.

Once inspected by the federal Department of Commerce, U.S. Farm-Raised Catfish are processed and packaged in less than half an hour, making them about as fresh as any fish you can buy. They're also one of the most versatile: Bake them, broil them, fry them, grill them, steam them. Finally, they are nutritious; high in top-quality protein but low in calories and saturated fat, farm-raised catfish are also a moderate source of the omega-3 fatty acids believed to lower blood pressure and along with it the risk of heart disease.

All of which explains why U.S. Farm-Raised Catfish are now the fourth most popular fish in America. Mark Twain would be pleased.

SOUTHERN-FRIED CATFISH

MAKES 4 SERVINGS

I never tasted catfish until I was grown because my Yankee mother turned up her nose at them. To fill this gap in my culinary education, my Mississippi friend Jean Todd Freeman took me to a fish shack near Hattiesburg and treated me to a plate of fried catfish. Mother was wrong. These catfish tasted nothing like mud. They were farm-raised, Jean explained, then added, "what with Mississippi being the unofficial catfish capital of the world." Not quite true, but

Mississippi is nonetheless a major producer of top-quality catfish. **Note:** *Make sure the catfish you use are U.S. Farm-Raised; many sold here now come from South Vietnam's polluted Mekong Delta.*

Four 6-ounce catfish fillets (see Note above)

1 cup buttermilk

¼ cup unsifted self-rising flour

¼ cup unsifted stone-ground yellow cornmeal

¼ teaspoon salt

⅛ teaspoon black pepper

⅛ teaspoon ground hot red pepper (cayenne)

2 tablespoons vegetable oil

2 tablespoons bacon drippings

1. Arrange the catfish fillets one layer deep in a large, shallow nonreactive baking pan. Pour the buttermilk evenly over the catfish, cover, and refrigerate for several hours, turning the catfish in the buttermilk at half-time.

2. When ready to proceed, combine the flour, cornmeal, salt, black pepper, and cayenne in a pie plate. Lift the catfish fillets from the buttermilk, shaking off the excess, then dredge well on both sides in the flour mixture. Again shake off the excess.

3. Heat 1 tablespoon each oil and bacon drippings in a heavy 12-inch skillet over moderately high heat for about a minute or until ripples begin to appear on the skillet bottom. Ease in the catfish and fry 4 to 5 minutes on each side or until golden brown, adding the remaining oil and bacon drippings when you turn the fillets.

4. Drain the browned catfish on paper toweling, then serve hot with Hush Puppies (page 257) and Sweet Slaw (page 229).

BAKED BLUEFISH OR RED SNAPPER

MAKES 6 SERVINGS

"The blues are running" is a call heard up and down the East Coast and no louder, perhaps, than along North Carolina's Outer Banks. Our Raleigh next-door neighbors, the Skaales, took me to Nag's Head for a week of fishing; then only sixteen, I had never held a fishing pole. It was early autumn, the time when bluefish head south from Long Island Sound and points north. The Skaales's daughter Betty Anne, two years older than I and already an old hand at pier fishing and surf casting, couldn't wait for me to discover the joys of bluefishing. Only this time we went out in a boat and I got sick. From then on, it was pier fishing for me. That week with the Skaales was my introduction to bluefish, which had a much stronger taste than the haddock my mother always cooked. Betty Anne's parents were no more southern than my own parents; Eleanor hailed from Boston, Art from Berkeley. If memory serves, Eleanor baked that first batch of bluefish in cream with a few chopped onions: very New England, and delicious despite my earlier bout of seasickness. On subsequent trips to the OBX (Outer Banks), I learned how locals like to prepare whole bluefish—and this recipe with onion, bell pepper, and tomatoes may be the best. Boning a whole baked bluefish, however, isn't as neat as peeling a potato, so I've substituted fillets. **Note:** *Choose a baking dish attractive enough to go from oven to table; no point in trying to transfer fragile baked fish to a heated platter.*

2 pounds bluefish or red snapper fillets

2 tablespoons bacon drippings, butter, or vegetable oil

1 small yellow onion, coarsely chopped

1 small green bell pepper, cored, seeded, and coarsely chopped

1 small celery rib, trimmed and finely diced

1 small garlic clove, finely chopped

1 large whole bay leaf

1 teaspoon dried leaf basil, crumbled

1 tablespoon all-purpose flour

One 14.5-ounce can diced tomatoes with their liquid

1 tablespoon tomato ketchup

½ teaspoon salt, or to taste

¼ teaspoon black pepper, or to taste

¼ teaspoon hot red pepper sauce, or to taste

¼ cup coarsely chopped parsley

1. Preheat the oven to 375° F. Divide the bluefish fillets into 6 pieces of equal size and set aside.
2. Heat the drippings in a large, heavy skillet over moderately high heat for about 1 minute or until ripples appear on the skillet bottom. Add the onion, bell pepper, celery, garlic, bay leaf, and basil and cook for 5 to 8 minutes, stirring often, or until limp and lightly browned.

3. Sprinkle the flour evenly over the mixture and cook and stir for about a minute. Add the tomatoes and their liquid, the ketchup, salt, pepper, and red pepper sauce and cook, stirring constantly, for about 3 minutes or until the mixture thickens and boils. Taste the sauce for salt, pepper, and red pepper sauce and adjust as needed. Discard the bay leaf.
4. Spread half the sauce over the bottom of an ungreased 13 × 9 × 2-inch baking dish, arrange the fish in the sauce, then cover with the remaining sauce.
5. Slide onto the middle oven shelf and bake uncovered for 20 to 25 minutes or until the fish almost flakes at the touch of a fork.
6. Sprinkle the parsley evenly over all and serve directly from the baking dish. Accompany with fluffy boiled rice and a crisp green salad.

Heirloom Recipe

SUN-DRIED HERRING

Clean and fillet fish without separating fish. Pepper heavily and salt as for frying. Pin to clothesline and dry out in the late evening, overnight and until noon the next day. Keep under refrigeration or freeze. These fish may either be broiled or pan fried.

—*Roanoke Island Cook Book*, compiled by members and friends of the Manteo Woman's Club, Manteo, North Carolina

Recipe contributed by Mrs. Grizell Fearing

HERRING RUNS ON THE ROANOKE

"Do you know about the Cypress Grill near Jamesville?" David Perry, editor-in-chief of the University of North Carolina Press, e-mailed me when he heard I was writing a southern cookbook. "It's only open during the annual herring run and serves herring right out of the Roanoke River, a practice that has been going on since Colonial times."

I'd read about Cypress Grill in *Gourmet, The Smithsonian,* and elsewhere. But until recently, I'd never made the two-hour drive east from Chapel Hill to feast on herring right out of the latte-colored Roanoke, which eddies seaward less than 100 feet from the Grill's front door.

A friend and I drove down early one Saturday in late March to beat the lunch crowd and arrived an hour before the place opened. No problem. We sat at a picnic table, watched speedboats zip up and down the river, and talked to seventy-three-year-old Leslie Gardner, who's owned

Cypress Grill for more than thirty years (it opened in 1936 as a clubhouse for local fishermen).

"Those ain't commercial fishermen," Gardner said, indicating two men laying a herring drift (net) from a flat-bottomed metal skiff midriver. "Ain't no commercial fishing on the Roanoke nowadays." With the Roanoke's herring supplies depleted, North Carolina banned commercial fishing on the river in 1995. Even sport fishermen are allowed only a dozen herring a day.

The herring now served at Cypress Grill, a weathered clapboard shack open only from mid-January till May, now comes from the Chowan River, "over Edenton way." A government placard posted inside the Grill's front door lists the restrictions on herring fishing, and just beyond it, there's an anti-moratorium petition for diners to sign. Plenty do.

Fish shacks once lined the Roanoke's south bank around Jamesville. Today Cypress Grill is the only one where you can fill up on batter-fried herring, flounder, oysters, clams, shrimp, sweet slaw, hush puppies, your choice of homemade pie (chocolate, lemon meringue, coconut, or

pecan), plus all the iced tea you can drink.

The front room is the place to eat. We snared the window booth where we could not only see the river action but also survey the room: tables draped with blue-and-white-checked oilcloth, a wall-to-wall photo gallery chronicling the glory days of Jamesville's herring industry, Cypress Grill T-shirts for sale tacked to a lattice room divider, a three-generation family (toddler to granny) bowing their heads to say grace.

We ordered the herring, of course. But we had no idea how to eat it. Each fish was about six inches long and fried to a crisp—"cremated," the locals call it. Amused, the waitress came over to help. "Do you mind if I touch your food?" I shook my head. She parted the fish down the middle with her hands, cautioned me to avoid the backbone, then told me to eat the rest, bones and all. "They're fried hard," she explained. I bit into a piece as crunchy as a potato chip.

Once again the waitress intervened. "It's better if you sprinkle it with vinegar. And this," she added, sliding a chile-stuffed bottle of vinegar across the table, "is the Jamesville way." Some folks, she said, like barbecue sauce on their herring, others prefer Texas Pete. I stuck with plain vinegar. It did improve the flavor of the herring just as it does that of slow-cooked collards.

Cypress Grill's hush puppies, unlike the crispy brown ones I knew, were chewy and yellow and tasted of stone-ground cornmeal—no sugar, no onion. I liked them, but better still was the sweet slaw that accompanied my mountainous platter of fried herring, flounder, and shrimp.

When it came to dessert, I succumbed to the chocolate pie (dark and delicious!) and my friend to the coconut (an excruciatingly sweet chess pie with a crunch of coconut on top).

And what did our herring feast cost? Less than twenty-five dollars!

SKILLET TROUT WITH PARSLEY-PECAN PESTO

MAKES 4 SERVINGS

Trout swim the quicksilver streams of the Great Smokies and Blue Ridge and I love them fresh-caught, dredged in stone-ground cornmeal, and fried the southern way. Still I aimed for something a little more unusual by churning pecans, a key southern crop, into a sauce. It's a good combo.

Parsley-Pecan Pesto

1⅓ cups firmly packed Italian parsley leaves

½ cup freshly grated Parmesan cheese

⅓ cup very lightly toasted pecans (5 to 7 minutes in a 350° F. oven)

1 large garlic clove, peeled

⅓ cup fruity olive oil

Trout

½ cup stone-ground cornmeal

½ teaspoon salt

¼ teaspoon black pepper

¼ teaspoon ground hot red pepper (cayenne)

Four 6-ounce trout fillets

2 to 4 tablespoons vegetable oil

1. For the pesto: Churn the parsley, Parmesan, pecans, and garlic in a food processor for about 30 seconds or until very finely chopped. With the motor running, drizzle the olive oil down the feed tube and continue processing for 15 to 20 seconds until well blended, scraping the work bowl with a rubber spatula at half-time.

2. For the trout: Mix the cornmeal, salt, black pepper, and cayenne in a pie plate, then dredge the trout fillets well on both sides in the mixture. Shake off the excess.

3. Heat 2 tablespoons of the oil in a heavy 12-inch skillet over moderately high heat for 1 to 1½ minutes or until ripples appear on the skillet bottom. Ease in the trout fillets and fry 4 to 5 minutes on each side or until golden brown, adding more oil if needed.

4. Spoon ⅓ cup of the pesto over the trout fillets, dividing evenly. Cover and cook 1 to 2 minutes more or just until the pesto is heated through.

5. Arrange the trout on four heated dinner plates and serve. Pass the remaining pesto separately.

CHARCOAL-GRILLED SHAD ROE WITH TOMATO-MINT SALSA

MAKES 6 SERVINGS

Along the James River they say that "when the shadbush blooms," the spring run of shad begins. These annual runs begin farther south, usually in December in North Florida, then move up the coast, reaching the Carolinas, Virginia, and Maryland by early March if the winter has not been unduly harsh. For Lisa Ruffin Harrison of Evelynton Plantation on the James, shad roe is a supreme delicacy. She grills it, then tops it with a salsa of her own invention, proving that good home cooks are often as imaginative as three-star chefs. "The garden-fresh flavors of the tomatoes and herbs are a wonderful pairing with the rich flavor of the shad roe," Lisa says. "A good departure from the traditional bacon accompaniment." **Note:** *Like most creative cooks, Lisa continues to rework and refine her recipes. The salsa, for example, which she's simplified. "The*

tomato-mint salsa can also be raw," she recently e-mailed me, "and is particularly delicious with a milder onion like Vidalia." As for the shad roe, she had this to say: "I've found that grilling the shad roe is still a bit tricky. The roe is really hard to keep from splitting open." She adds that the last time she grilled shad roe, she "had better luck painting it with olive oil" than brushing with lemon juice and spreading with mayonnaise. She does still salt and pepper the roe, however, and she cooks it in a fish basket. "It needs babysitting," she cautions, "and should be held above the grill to avoid 'exploding' from direct heat. Five minutes per side is enough. Once off the grill, sprinkle the roe generously with the lemon juice." Lisa admits that she often now sautés the roe in a skillet, prepping it the same way and browning over moderate heat for 3 to 4 minutes per side. It's only fair, I think, to offer Lisa's updated method as well as her original recipe (below), which appeared in Bon Appétit *in the late 1980s. It's delicious.*

Tomato-Mint Salsa

1 small yellow onion, finely chopped

1 medium garlic clove, finely chopped

1 tablespoon olive oil

4 large ripe tomatoes, peeled, cored, seeded, and coarsely chopped

1 small cucumber, peeled, seeded, and cut into fine dice

3 tablespoons coarsely chopped fresh mint

3 tablespoons coarsely chopped fresh basil

2 tablespoons coarsely chopped Italian parsley

½ teaspoon salt

⅛ teaspoon black pepper

Shad Roe

6 pairs fresh shad roe

Juice of 2 large lemons

½ cup mayonnaise (about)

2 large limes, cut into thin wedges

3 to 5 sprigs of fresh mint or basil

1. Build a charcoal fire and let the coals burn until white-hot.

2. Meanwhile, begin the salsa: Sauté the onion and garlic in the oil in a medium-size heavy skillet over moderate heat for 3 to 5 minutes or until golden. Add 3 of the tomatoes and simmer, uncovered, for 8 to 10 minutes until all juices have evaporated. Set off the heat and cool to room temperature. Mix in the remaining tomato and the cucumber and set aside.

3. For the shad roe: Brush the roe liberally with the lemon juice, then sprinkle any remaining lemon juice over them and let stand for 10 minutes. Spread the mayonnaise on both sides of each pair of roe—this is to keep them from sticking to the grill or fish basket.

4. Lower the grill so it's 2 inches above the white-hot coals. Place the roe in a fish basket or directly on the grill and sear quickly on both sides. Raise the grill so it's 6 inches above the coals and grill the roe for 5 to 8 minutes on each side or until heated through.

5. Quickly finish the salsa by mixing in the mint, basil, parsley, salt, and pepper.

6. Arrange the roe on a large heated platter, ladle the salsa artfully on top, then garnish with the lime wedges and mint sprigs. Serve at once.

1900 North Carolina native David Pender opens a grocery in Norfolk, Virginia. Offering the finest fresh produce, meat, fish, and fowl, and a delivery service, the David Pender Grocery prospers. By 1926, there are 244 Penders in Virginia and North Carolina.

1901 Nineteen-year-old Tennessean Howell Campbell opens the Standard Candy Company in Nashville. At first he makes only hard candies, but 11 years later he creates America's first not-just-chocolate candy bar (see **1912**).

The *Picayune Creole Cookbook* is published in New Orleans and quickly becomes a classic. Many editions later, it is still in print.

1901–1902 To publicize its local bounty and attract international trade to its port, Charleston, South Carolina, stages a six-month exposition with Teddy Roosevelt on hand for President's Day.

The Chattanooga Bakery, later to become famous for its MoonPie, is founded.

Cocaine is removed from Coca-Cola syrup.

Heirloom Recipe

This more-than-200-year-old recipe shows how dramatically fish cookery has changed since Colonial days. It's reprinted here just as it appeared in *From North Carolina Kitchens: Favorite Recipes Old and New*, an uncopyrighted collection published in the early 1950s by the North Carolina Federation of Home Demonstration Clubs.

BAKED SHAD (1780)

Place in a large pan and cover with water. Put in oven, let simmer from 4 to 6 hours in wood stove. Stuffing for a 6-pound shad, take 2 pounds butter, 10 eggs, 2 quarts bread crumbs toasted, salt and pepper. Mix this up together then stuff shad. Then with needle and thread sew up. If the fish should get too hot, place a cloth over the top.

—Lincoln County, North Carolina

BRONZED SHRIMP CREOLE

MAKES 4 SERVINGS

Although New Orleans restaurants grab most of the press, I've dined very well in lesser-known Louisiana, which I prowled several years ago while researching a food and travel article for *Gourmet*. I remember in particular this signature shrimp dish from Lafayette's Café Vermillionville. It's a long-winded recipe, to be sure, but it's well worth the time and effort. **Note:** *Clarified butter is melted butter from which the froth and milk solids have been skimmed. Its flavor is pure sunshine.* **Tip:** *Choreography is everything here. Because the Creole Sauce must simmer for three quarters of an hour, it's best to make it a day ahead of time.*

½ cup long-grain brown rice

½ cup long-grain white rice

1½ cups (3 sticks) butter, clarified (see Note above)

4 garlic cloves, finely chopped

1 tablespoon fresh lemon juice

1 tablespoon onion flakes

1 tablespoon Worcestershire sauce

2 teaspoons salt

1 teaspoon hot red pepper sauce

1 teaspoon sweet paprika

¾ teaspoon dried leaf basil, crumbled

¾ teaspoon dried leaf thyme, crumbled

⅛ teaspoon white pepper

24 large shrimp (about 1 pound), shelled and deveined

3 cups Creole Sauce (recipe follows; see Tip above)

1 pound medium shrimp, shelled, deveined, and cut into ½-inch pieces

4 medium scallions, trimmed and thinly sliced (garnish)

1. Cook the brown rice, then the white rice by package directions; set both aside.

2. Meanwhile, combine the clarified butter, garlic, lemon juice, onion flakes, Worcestershire sauce, salt, hot red pepper sauce, paprika, basil, thyme, and white pepper in a large non-reactive bowl. Add the large shrimp, toss well, and set aside to marinate.

3. Place the Creole Sauce in a medium-size saucepan, add the shrimp pieces, and simmer uncovered, stirring occasionally, for 2 to 3 minutes or until the shrimp are cooked through. Remove from the heat and keep warm.

4. Fluff the brown rice, then the white rice. Lightly oil a ½-cup ramekin; fill one side of it with brown rice and the other side with white rice. Pack firmly, then invert in the middle of a heated dinner plate. Repeat three times and set the four plates aside.

5. Heat a well-seasoned large iron skillet over moderately high heat for 1½ to 2 minutes or until very hot. Lift six of the large shrimp from the marinade, letting the excess drain off. Add to the skillet and "bronze" by sautéing 1 to 1½ minutes on each side or just until done; transfer to a large heated plate. Bronze the remaining shrimp in batches the same way and add to the plate.

6. When ready to serve, spoon ¾ cup of the Creole Sauce–shrimp mixture around the hillock of rice on each dinner plate, arrange six of the bronzed shrimp artfully on top, then garnish with a scattering of the sliced scallions.

CREOLE SAUCE

MAKES ABOUT 4 CUPS

This recipe is integral to the Bronzed Shrimp Creole, which precedes, and should be made a day ahead of time. It's also good ladled over broiled fish, shellfish, or chicken. You can even use it to braise pork chops. **Tip:** *Wear rubber gloves when handling the jalapeño pepper.*

4 slices lean, smoky bacon, cut crosswise into strips ½ inch wide

1 medium yellow onion, finely diced

1 medium green bell pepper, cored, seeded, and finely diced

½ small red bell pepper, cored, seeded, and finely diced

3 medium celery ribs, finely diced

2 large garlic cloves, finely chopped

½ pickled jalapeño, stemmed, seeded, and finely chopped

One 28-ounce can tomatoes in purée

1¼ cups tomato juice

2 tablespoons sugar

½ chicken bouillon cube

1 teaspoon dried minced garlic

½ teaspoon dried leaf oregano, crumbled

½ teaspoon salt, or to taste

¼ teaspoon ground hot red pepper (cayenne), or to taste

5 tablespoons butter

1. Cook the bacon in a large, heavy nonreactive saucepan over moderate heat, stirring often, for about 10 minutes or until crisp.

2. Add the onion, green and red bell peppers, celery, chopped garlic, and jalapeño; reduce the heat to moderately low and cook, stirring often, for 8 to 10 minutes or until the vegetables are limp. Add all remaining ingredients except the butter, adjust the heat so the mixture bubbles gently, cover, and simmer for 40 to 45 minutes or until the sauce is thick and the flavors have mellowed.

3. Add the butter and when it melts, stir well to combine. Taste for salt and cayenne and adjust as needed. The sauce is now ready to use.

CHARLESTON SHRIMP PIE

MAKES 4 TO 6 SERVINGS

. . . .

The first time I stayed at the elegantly rebuilt and furnished Mills House in Charleston some thirty years ago, I spied this dish on the breakfast buffet, spooned up a good portion, then went back for seconds. Now, whenever I visit Charleston, I look for shrimp pie—a casserole despite its name. Four versions of it appear in Blanche S. Rhett's *Two Hundred Years of Charleston Cooking* (1930), some of them gussied up with bell pepper and tomatoes, others heavily laced with wine. Although Mrs. Rhett says that shrimp pie is a Charleston Sunday supper favorite, it's the perfect entrée for a casual brunch, lunch, or supper any day of the week. The recipe here is one that I've developed over the years, fine-tuning after each subsequent visit to Charleston.

2 tablespoons butter

4 medium scallions, trimmed and coarsely chopped (include some green tops)

¼ teaspoon freshly grated nutmeg

⅛ teaspoon ground hot red pepper (cayenne)

⅛ teaspoon black pepper

2½ cups moderately coarse soft white bread crumbs (5 slices firm-textured bread)

1¾ cups half-and-half

2 large eggs, beaten until frothy with ½ teaspoon salt

3 tablespoons dry sherry

1 pound shelled and deveined cooked shrimp, coarsely chopped

1. Preheat the oven to 350° F. Butter a 6-cup casserole well and set aside.

2. Melt the butter in a small, heavy skillet over moderate heat. Add the scallions, nutmeg, and both peppers, and cook uncovered, stirring occasionally, for about 5 minutes or until limp and golden. Set off the heat and cool to room temperature.

3. Meanwhile, soak the bread crumbs in the cream in a large mixing bowl for 15 minutes, then, using a large wooden spoon, beat hard until as smooth as paste. Mix in the cooled scallion mixture along with the eggs, sherry, and shrimp.

4. Spoon into the casserole, slide onto the middle oven shelf, and bake uncovered for 40 to 45 minutes or until lightly puffed and tipped with brown.

5. Serve at once, accompanied, if you like, with a tartly dressed green salad.

A Love Affair with Southern Cooking

SHRIMP-STUFFED MIRLITONS

MAKES 4 SERVINGS

. . . .

Flip through almost any Deep South cookbook—particularly a club or church fund-raiser—and you're likely to find a recipe for mirlitons (chayotes or vegetable pears) stuffed with a spicy shrimp mixture. Southerners love stuffing vegetables and what better than these pale green, pear-shaped relatives of summer squash? Unlike squash, mirlitons have one large seed—a slim almond-shaped one the color of ivory. Scooping it out leaves hollows just begging to be filled.

2 medium-large mirlitons (about
1½ pounds), scrubbed but not peeled

3 tablespoons butter

6 large scallions, trimmed and thinly sliced
(include some green tops)

1 small celery rib, trimmed and finely diced

8 ounces shelled and deveined cooked
shrimp, coarsely chopped

2 tablespoons finely chopped Italian parsley

¾ teaspoon salt, or to taste

¼ teaspoon black pepper, or to taste

¼ teaspoon hot red pepper sauce, or to taste

¾ cup moderately fine soft bread crumbs
tossed with 1 tablespoon melted butter

½ cup coarsely shredded mild Cheddar
cheese

1. Place the mirlitons in a large, heavy saucepan, add just enough cold water to cover them, and bring to a boil over high heat. Adjust the heat so the water bubbles gently, set the lid on askew, and cook for 50 to 60 minutes or until a fork will pierce the mirlitons easily.

2. Meanwhile, melt 2 tablespoons of the butter in a medium-size heavy skillet over moderately high heat, add the scallions and celery, and cook, stirring often, for 4 to 5 minutes or until golden. Add the remaining tablespoon of butter and when it melts, add the shrimp, parsley, salt, black pepper, and red pepper sauce, and cook and stir for 2 to 3 minutes. Set off the heat and reserve.

3. Preheat the oven to 350° F. Drain the mirlitons well, and when cool enough to handle, halve lengthwise. Using a tablespoon, remove the seeds, then scoop out the flesh, leaving shells about ⅜ inch thick. Mash or purée the mirliton flesh and stir into the shrimp mixture. Next mix in ½ cup of the buttered bread crumbs, then the cheese. Taste for salt, black pepper, and red pepper sauce and adjust as needed.

4. Mound the shrimp mixture in the mirliton shells, dividing the total amount evenly. Top with the remaining ¼ cup buttered crumbs, again dividing evenly. Place the stuffed mirlitons, not touching, in an ungreased 13 × 9 × 2-inch baking pan.

5. Slide onto the middle oven shelf and bake uncovered for 25 to 30 minutes or until lightly browned.

6. Serve at once as the main course of a light lunch or supper.

KIM'S SHRIMP AND CRAB CAKES

MAKES 4 SERVINGS

. . . .

Kim is my brother Bob's daughter and she's a whiz of a southern cook because she descends, on her mother's side, from an extended family of accomplished North Carolina cooks. She makes old family recipes often (see Aunt Bertie's Crispy Cornmeal Pancakes, page 260), but she's an innovator, too, improvising with whatever attracts her at the farmer's market and fish market. This recipe of Kim's is a winner, especially when served with the tart Tarragon-Mustard Sauce (recipe follows) that her older sister, Linda, created especially for it.

8 ounces raw medium shrimp, shelled, deveined, and cut into ¼-inch dice

8 ounces finely flaked backfin crabmeat, bits of shell and cartilage removed

¼ cup firmly packed mayonnaise (use "light," if you like)

1 large egg, lightly beaten

3 medium scallions, trimmed and very thinly sliced (include some green tops)

1 large celery rib, trimmed and finely diced

½ medium red bell pepper, cored, seeded, and finely diced

¼ cup fine dry bread crumbs

½ teaspoon salt

¼ teaspoon black pepper

¼ teaspoon hot red pepper sauce

½ cup unsifted stone-ground yellow cornmeal (for dredging)

¼ cup olive oil or 2 tablespoons each olive oil and butter (for frying)

Tarragon-Mustard Sauce (recipe follows)

1. Place the shrimp and crab in a medium-size nonreactive bowl and fork briskly to mix. Fork in the mayonnaise, then the egg. Add the scallions, celery, and bell pepper and mix well. Finally, blend in the bread crumbs, salt, black pepper, and red pepper sauce.

2. Shape the mixture into eight "burgers," each about 3 inches across and 1 inch thick. Dredge well on both sides in the cornmeal and set aside.

3. Heat the oil in a large, heavy skillet for about 2 minutes over moderate heat, then add half the crab cakes. Reduce the heat to moderate and cook for 3 to 4 minutes on each side or until the crab cakes are golden brown; drain on paper toweling. Cook and drain the remaining crab cakes the same way.

4. Serve hot with Tarragon-Mustard Sauce.

❧

We could always find something to prepare for dinner by fishing in the Mississippi River, Lake Ponchartrain . . . catfish, trout, croakers, crawfish, or plain old shrimp—my mother would just batter it up and fry it inside the old black skillet.

—DONNA L. BRAZILE, *COOKING WITH GREASE: STIRRING THE POTS IN AMERICAN POLITICS*

❧

TARRAGON-MUSTARD SAUCE

MAKES ABOUT 1 CUP

. . . .

Although my older niece, Linda, created this sauce for her sister's shrimp and crab cakes (which precede), it's equally delicious with grilled or fried fish or shellfish. An avid gardener with beds of fresh herbs just beyond her kitchen door, Linda sometimes substitutes fresh lemon thyme or oregano for tarragon and finely snipped chives for scallions. I myself have been known to use coarsely chopped cilantro or finely snipped dill in place of the tarragon. **Note:** *This sauce will taste even better if you make it several hours ahead of time and refrigerate until ready to serve.*

½ cup firmly packed mayonnaise
(use "light," if you like)

½ cup firmly packed low-fat plain yogurt

1 tablespoon Dijon mustard

1 medium scallion, trimmed and finely
chopped (include some green tops)

2 tablespoons coarsely chopped parsley

1 tablespoon coarsely chopped fresh tarragon
or 1 teaspoon crumbled dried leaf tarragon

½ teaspoon finely grated lemon zest

½ teaspoon tomato ketchup, or to taste

½ teaspoon hot red pepper sauce, or to taste

1. Whisk the mayonnaise, yogurt, and mustard together until smooth and creamy, then mix in all remaining ingredients. Taste for ketchup

---

1904 A deadly fungus, present on Asian chestnut trees imported into the U.S., is detected on American chestnuts at the Bronx Zoo. It spreads with heartbreaking speed, decimating the chestnut forests of the Southern Appalachians and blighting trees as far west as Ohio.

1905 Paper-shell pecans are introduced to Georgia and that state soon leads the nation in pecan production.

Galatoire's opens in New Orleans. Still at its Bourbon Street location, the restaurant continues to serve the dishes that made it famous: shrimp rémoulade, crab maison, Creole gumbo, and pompano with sautéed crabmeat, among others.

Columbus, Georgia, pharmacist Claud A. Hatcher creates a new soft drink and sells it in his father's grocery. Called Chero-Cola, it is the forerunner of Royal Crown Cola. (See Royal Crown Cola, page 312.)

Vincent Taormina, a Sicilian immigrant living in New Orleans, begins importing Italian delicacies and that small business later morphs into Progresso Foods.

and hot red pepper sauce, and adjust as needed. The ketchup is to mellow the tartness of the yogurt, not to add sweetness.

2. Cover the sauce and refrigerate for several hours or even overnight.

3. Let the sauce stand at room temperature for about 30 minutes before serving.

SHRIMP 'N' GRITS

MAKES 4 SERVINGS

. . . .

Just after the Civil War (or "late unpleasantness," as some Southerners still call it), shrimp 'n' grits was simple Charleston breakfast food—nothing more than shrimp, grits, and salt. So says Moreton Neal in introducing her late husband Bill Neal's 1980s spin on the post–Civil War original. Moreton includes his deliciously updated recipe in *Remembering Bill Neal* (2004), her lively memoir of the couple's college days at Duke, their travels about France, and their early struggles in the restaurant business. For many years the pioneering chef at Crook's Corner in Chapel Hill, Bill Neal elevated Lowcountry shrimp 'n' grits from humble to haute (*New York Times* food editor Craig Claiborne called him "a genius at the stove"). Indeed, Neal gave shrimp 'n' grits such star status that nearly every southern chef now offers some version of it. Neal's own creation remains a signature dish at Crook's Corner and if you're ever in town, I urge you to try it. The recipe that follows has been given yet another spin: my own.

Grits

2½ cups water mixed with ½ teaspoon salt (salted water)

⅔ cup quick-cooking grits

1½ cups coarsely shredded sharp Cheddar cheese (about 6 ounces)

¼ cup freshly grated Parmesan cheese

1 medium garlic clove, crushed

¼ cup light cream

1 tablespoon butter

⅛ teaspoon ground hot red pepper (cayenne)

Shrimp

4 thick slices hickory-smoked bacon, cut crosswise into strips ½ inch wide

2 tablespoons corn oil or vegetable oil

1 pound raw medium-large shrimp, shelled and deveined

½ pound small mushrooms, stems discarded, caps wiped clean and thinly sliced

8 large scallions, trimmed and thinly sliced (include some green tops)

1 large garlic clove, finely chopped

1 tablespoon fresh lemon juice

½ teaspoon salt, or to taste

¼ teaspoon black pepper, or to taste

¼ teaspoon hot red pepper sauce, or to taste

¼ cup coarsely chopped parsley

1. For the grits: Bring the salted water to a boil in a medium-size heavy saucepan over high heat. Slowly add the grits, whisking all the while. When the mixture returns to a boil, reduce the heat to moderately low and cook uncovered, whisking often, for 8 to 10 minutes or until thick.

2. Meanwhile, begin the shrimp: Fry the bacon in a large, heavy skillet over moderate heat for about 10 minutes or until the drippings cook out and only crisp brown bits remain. Using a slotted spoon, lift the bacon to paper toweling and reserve.

3. Add the corn oil to the skillet drippings and heat for 1 minute. Add the shrimp, distributing evenly, and cook for 2 to 3 minutes over moderate heat or just until they begin to turn pink.

4. While the shrimp cook, mix the two cheeses and the garlic into the grits along with all remaining ingredients. Cook 1 to 2 minutes, whisking now and then, or just until the cheese melts. Set the grits off the heat, cover, and keep warm, whisking occasionally, while you finish the shrimp.

5. Stir the shrimp well, add the mushrooms, and cook, stirring often, for about 5 minutes or until they release their juices and these evaporate. Add the scallions and garlic, cook and stir for 3 to 4 minutes, then mix in all remaining ingredients. Taste for salt, black pepper, and hot pepper sauce and adjust as needed.

6. To serve, puddle the grits on each of four heated dinner plates and scoop the shrimp mixture on top, dividing the total amount evenly. Finally, scatter some of the reserved bacon over each portion.

TENNESSEE BARBECUE SHRIMP

MAKES 6 SERVINGS

"I love this recipe!" says my friend Janet Trent, a textile designer and weaver who lives in the old family farmhouse a few miles outside Sanford, North Carolina, with her husband and two young daughters. "This is the closest I can get to a really tasty dish that was served at 12th & Porter restaurant in Nashville, Tennessee," says Janet, who finds it perfect for her occasional catering gigs. "Jody Faison was the chef and proprietor of this place and also of Faison's, an upscale restaurant in the Hillsboro Village section of Nashville," she adds. "I combined a few different recipe versions to come up with this one—a real treat!" When I first looked at Janet's recipe, I thought it contained so many herbs and spices that their flavors would conflict with one another. Not so. Janet's right. This is a "real treat!" Easy, too, because the shrimp are baked and served in their shells. **Tip:** *I melt the butter in a 1-quart ovenproof glass measure in the microwave—about 5 minutes on DEFROST (30-percent power)—then whisk in all of the seasonings.*

1½ pounds large shrimp in the shell

6 tablespoons (¾ stick) butter, melted (see Tip above)

3 tablespoons fresh lemon juice

2 tablespoons olive oil

½ teaspoon Worcestershire sauce

½ teaspoon black pepper

1 large garlic clove, finely minced

1 large bay leaf, crumbled

¾ teaspoon crumbled dried
leaf rosemary

½ teaspoon salt

¼ teaspoon crumbled dried leaf basil

¼ teaspoon crumbled dried leaf oregano

¼ teaspoon ground hot red
pepper (cayenne)

¼ teaspoon freshly grated nutmeg

¼ teaspoon sweet paprika

¼ teaspoon hot red pepper sauce

1. Wash the shrimp well in cool water, drain well, pat dry on paper toweling, and spread in a large, shallow, nonreactive baking pan (I use a 13 × 9 × 2-inch ovenproof glass baking dish).

2. Mix all remaining ingredients, pour over the shrimp, toss well, then cover and marinate in the refrigerator for several hours or better yet, overnight. About 20 minutes before you're ready to bake the shrimp, preheat the oven to 325° F.

3. Toss the shrimp well in the marinade, slide the pan onto the middle oven shelf, and bake uncovered for 10 minutes. Toss the shrimp well again in the marinade and bake 5 to 10 minutes longer or just until the shrimp are pink and cooked through—don't overcook or the shrimp will be tough.

4. Serve the unshelled shrimp hot or at room temperature with crusty French or Italian bread to sop up the marinade and with a bowl

to catch the shrimp shells. **Note:** *If you shell and devein the cooked shrimp, they can be served as an appetizer: Simply spear them on toothpicks and put the marinade out as a dip.*

CURRIED SHRIMP AND CHICKEN

MAKES 6 TO 8 SERVINGS

Here's a southern classic reinvented by Elizabeth Terry, for years the creative force behind Elizabeth on 37th, by some accounts Savannah's finest restaurant. With the help of husband Michael, who abandoned law to lend a hand, Terry opened Elizabeth back in 1981. Eleven years later, she'd made *Food & Wine*'s list of America's Top 25 Restaurants—a first, surely, for a self-taught chef. Craig Claiborne, the powerful *New York Times* food columnist, came, ate, and raved in private and in print. I myself was so impressed by Elizabeth's magic that I wrote about her twice: for *Food & Wine* back in the late '80s, and then again just a few years ago for *More* magazine. The recipe below is adapted from one that accompanied my *Food & Wine* article (a different version appears in Terry's cookbook, *Savannah Seasons: Food and Stories from Elizabeth on 37th*, with whimsical art by Elizabeth's older daughter, Alexis). Both recipes are new spins on Country Captain and both are brilliant; for me, however, my adaptation is easier. After twenty years behind the stove, Terry has left the kitchen, moved to California, and become a potter. Here, too, she is a virtuoso.

1 cup converted rice

1 tablespoon curry powder

2 teaspoons finely minced fresh ginger

1½ teaspoons finely grated orange zest

1½ teaspoons salt

¼ teaspoon ground hot red pepper (cayenne)

2 cups cold water

1½ pounds boneless, skinless chicken
breasts, cut crosswise and on the bias into
strips 1½ inches wide

¼ teaspoon black pepper

2 medium Granny Smith apples
(about ¾ pound), cored and cut into
½-inch dice (do not peel)

1 medium yellow onion, moderately
coarsely chopped

1 medium green bell pepper, cored, seeded,
and moderately coarsely chopped

One 14-ounce can plum tomatoes,
drained well and coarsely chopped

2½ tablespoons dried currants plumped
in 2 tablespoons hot water

2 large garlic cloves, finely minced

¾ cup rich chicken broth or stock

1½ pounds medium shrimp, shelled and
deveined

½ cup lightly toasted coarsely chopped pecans
(about 10 minutes in a 350° F. oven)

1. Preheat the oven to 400° F. Lightly coat a shallow 2½-quart flameproof casserole with non-stick cooking spray and set aside.

2. Combine the rice, curry powder, ginger, orange zest, half the salt, and the cayenne in a medium-size saucepan. Add the water, bring to a boil over high heat, adjust the heat so the mixture bubbles gently, and cook uncovered for 20 minutes until the rice is al dente.

3. Arrange the chicken one layer deep in the casserole and sprinkle with the black pepper and remaining salt. Layer the apples on top, then the onion, bell pepper, tomatoes, currants and their soaking liquid, and garlic. Pour the chicken broth evenly over all, scoop the rice on top, and spread so all ingredients underneath are covered.

4. Cover the casserole snugly with aluminum foil and set over moderate heat for about 5 minutes or until the mixture begins to boil. Slide the casserole onto the middle oven shelf and bake for 15 to 20 minutes or until the chicken is done.

5. Stir the casserole ingredients well, arrange the shrimp on top, cover, and bake 5 to 7 minutes or just until the shrimp are pink.

6. Remove the casserole from the oven and let stand, still covered, at room temperature for 15 minutes.

7. Stir well, scatter with the pecans, and serve.

Tartar sauce can lift a simple fried catfish to the realms of ecstasy, turn a fried oyster into an emperor's feast, or ennoble a fried shrimp into knighthood.

—*PAT CONROY, THE PAT CONROY COOKBOOK: RECIPES OF MY LIFE*

EASTERN SHORE CRAB CAKES

Every Southerner within the sound of the surf has a favorite crab cake recipe. This is my own because the crab cakes are as light as sea foam (not enough bread to weight them down) and they taste like crab instead of green peppers and onion and celery. As a Chesapeake waterman's wife once told me, "I like to taste the crab!"

I pound lump or backfin crabmeat,
picked over for bits of shell and cartilage,
and flaked

2 tablespoons minced parsley

2 tablespoons finely grated yellow onion

2 slices firm-textured white bread,
torn into bits and soaked in ⅓ cup milk
(don't squeeze out the milk)

I teaspoon Dijon mustard

½ teaspoon salt

¼ teaspoon black pepper

⅛ teaspoon hot red pepper sauce

2 tablespoons vegetable oil

I to 2 tablespoons butter

1. Place all ingredients except the oil and butter in a large bowl and mix lightly with a fork.

2. Shape into 8 crab cakes 1 inch thick, patting each firmly so it holds together. Cover with wax paper, and refrigerate for at least 1 hour. This chilling helps keep the fragile crab cakes from falling apart as you brown them.

3. Heat the vegetable oil and 1 tablespoon of the butter in a very large, heavy skillet over high heat until sizzling. Ease in the crab cakes, allowing plenty of space between them, and brown 4 to 5 minutes on a side, adding the additional 1 tablespoon butter, if needed. Handle gently; these crab cakes are unusually delicate.

4. Serve hot—no tartar sauce needed.

CHESAPEAKE CRAB BOIL

Waterfront fish houses up and down the Chesapeake provide moorings for boats as well as parking for cars. Most serve crab a dozen different ways but a universal favorite is the simplest: live hard-shells boiled (or steamed) in cauldrons with plenty of seasoning served on tables spread with newspaper. Bibs are "standard issue" as are little wooden mallets and metal crackers to deal with the claws. **Note:** *For this recipe you'll need a large, deep, nonreactive kettle with a rack and a tight-fitting lid—the kind used for clambakes and boiled lobster.*

2 cups beer

I cup white (distilled) vinegar

¼ cup Old Bay or other spicy
seafood seasoning

¼ cup salt

1½ dozen live-and-kicking blue crabs

I cup (2 sticks) butter, melted

1. Combine the beer, vinegar, seafood seasoning, and salt in a medium-size nonreactive bowl and set aside.

2. Place a rack in the bottom of a large, deep, nonreactive kettle. Pile half the crabs on the rack and pour in half the beer mixture. Add the remaining crabs and beer mixture.

3. Set over moderately high heat and bring to a boil. Adjust the heat so the liquid bubbles gently, cover tight, and steam the crabs for 20 to 25 minutes or until they are bright red.

4. Serve at once with melted butter and plenty of napkins. And don't forget to put out a large bowl to catch the crab shells.

Heirloom Recipe

An Outer Banks recipe as it appeared in *From North Carolina Kitchens: Favorite Recipes Old and New*, a fifty-year-old public-domain collection from the state's Home Demonstration Clubs.

HATTERAS-STYLE DRUM FISH

The drum, or channel bass, is perhaps the best-liked fish among the people of Hatteras Island, who have a wide variety to choose from. It was formerly sided, salted, dried, and stacked up, and was available at all times, to be soaked out and cooked. Thrifty housewives now pressure-can enough for their own needs. It is cooked, fresh, by many methods, but the following is a traditional style.

One side of drum, about a foot and a half, with head and tail removed, boiled in water with plenty of salt and pepper, until tender. This should be lifted out in two or three pieces and placed on a platter, to be mixed at the table. Boil and mash 8 medium potatoes, salted. Have ½ pound fat salt pork cut into tiny pieces and fried crisp. Place them in a small dish and pour some of the hot grease in a small pitcher. Mince a medium sized onion and place in small dish.

As in a tossed salad, half the pleasure of eating it is in watching the mixing. So it is with the ritual of mixing Hatteras-Style Drum Fish. The novice has to be shown the first time, but can hold his own with the second and third helpings.

On each serving plate, place a heap of mashed potatoes, a large "hunk" of fish, a spoonful (more or less) of cracklins and onions. Mix thoroughly, season with the drippings and more salt and pepper, if desired.

Some like it mixed in the kitchen and brought to the table ready to eat, perhaps garnished with hard-boiled eggs, parsley, etc., but all agree that it's wonderful food, especially when served with plenty of corn bread (not the sweet variety), coffee, pickles, and a crisp raw vegetable. Serves six hungry people.

—Mrs. Rebecca Burrus, Dare County, North Carolina

RIVER ROAD DEVILED CRAB

On Route SC 61, the Ashley River Road linking Charleston with the antebellum plantations some dozen miles northwest, there used to be a little fish house called Captain Buddy's that served the most delicious deviled crab. On recent visits, I've looked in vain for Captain Buddy's; it seems to have disappeared in Charleston's modern sprawl. Fortunately, I got the deviled crab recipe years ago.

4 tablespoons (½ stick) butter

½ cup finely chopped celery

½ cup finely chopped green or red bell pepper

2 large scallions, finely chopped (include some green tops)

1 pound lump or backfin crabmeat, picked over for bits of shell and cartilage, and flaked

2 hard-cooked eggs, finely chopped

½ cup mayonnaise (measure firmly packed)

6 tablespoons moderately fine soda cracker crumbs

1 tablespoon finely minced parsley

½ teaspoon salt

¼ teaspoon black pepper

¼ teaspoon hot red pepper sauce

1 to 2 tablespoons milk, if needed to thin the crab mixture (it should be moist, about the consistency of crab salad)

1. Preheat the oven to 350° F. Coat four large scallop or blue crab shells with nonstick cooking spray and set aside.

2. Melt the butter in a medium-size heavy skillet over moderate heat; add the celery, bell pepper, and scallions, and sauté for 3 to 5 minutes or until limp, stirring often. Tip into a large mixing bowl, add all remaining ingredients, and toss lightly to mix.

3. Divide the crab mixture among the scallop shells and set on an ungreased baking sheet. Slide onto the middle oven shelf and bake uncovered for 30 to 35 minutes or until tipped with brown.

4. Serve at once. The traditional accompaniments are Hush Puppies (page 257) and a creamy coleslaw (see Sweet Slaw, page 229).

INNER HARBOR CRAB IMPERIAL

If America has a Blue Crab Capital, it is surely Baltimore. Its Inner Harbor, once a fetid backwater of rotting piers and tumbledown warehouses, is today a lively tourist attraction with restaurants serving blue crabs every which way. I'm partial to them all but if forced to choose a favorite, I'd pick this 100-plus-year-old Baltimore classic first served at Thompson's Sea Girt House. I'm not alone. It's said that "crab cakes are to Crab Imperial as meatloaf is to prime ribs." **Note:** *You can prepare this recipe through Step 3 a couple of hours ahead of time. Scoop the crab mixture into the gratin dish, cover* *with foil, and refrigerate. When ready to bake, remove the foil, sprinkle with the paprika, and bake uncovered for 20 to 25 minutes or until bubbly and browned.*

4 tablespoons (½ stick) butter

1 small yellow onion, finely chopped

2 tablespoons all-purpose flour

⅛ teaspoon white pepper

⅛ teaspoon ground hot red pepper (cayenne)

⅛ teaspoon freshly grated nutmeg

1 cup half-and-half

2 tablespoons Amontillado sherry

½ cup mayonnaise (measure firmly packed)

2 tablespoons fresh lemon juice

½ teaspoon salt

1 pound lump crabmeat, picked over for bits
of shell and cartilage, then flaked

Sweet paprika

1. Preheat the oven to 450° F. Spritz a 5- to 6-cup gratin dish with nonstick cooking spray and set aside.
2. Melt 2 tablespoons of the butter in a small, heavy saucepan over moderate heat, add the onion, and cook, stirring often, for 5 to 8 minutes until lightly browned. Blend in the flour, both peppers, and nutmeg, and cook and stir for 1 minute. Add the half-and-half and sherry and cook, stirring constantly, for 3 to 5 minutes until thickened and smooth. Remove from the heat and blend in the mayonnaise, lemon juice, and salt; set aside.

1906 William Emerson Brock, a traveling salesman for the R. J. Reynolds Tobacco Company of Winston-Salem, North Carolina, buys Chattanooga's Trigg Candy Company. Three years later, he reincorporates it as the Brock Candy Company and builds it into one of America's premier confectioners.

Young Italian immigrant Amedeo Obici, who had been selling his roasted peanuts from a horse-drawn cart in Wilkes-Barre, Pennsylvania, founds Planters with fellow immigrant Mario Peruzzi. In less than ten years, they relocate to the Virginia peanut country. (See Planters Peanuts, page 41.)

Owen Wister's romantic novel *Lady Baltimore*, set in Charleston, South Carolina, is published and popularizes Lady Baltimore cake. (See recipe, page 326.)

To accommodate the growing community of Italians in New Orleans's French Quarter, Salvatore Lupo creates the muffaletta sandwich at his Central Grocery. It's a round loaf stuffed with Italian salami, ham, cheese, and olives.

When soil depletion and hurricanes destroy the pineapple crop in the Florida Keys, growers switch to Key limes.

3. Melt the remaining 2 tablespoons butter in a large, heavy skillet over moderate heat. Add the crab and warm for 1 minute, taking care not to break up the lumps. Gently fold the reserved cream sauce into the crab.

4. Scoop all into the gratin dish, blush the top with paprika, slide onto the middle oven shelf, and bake uncovered for about 15 minutes or until bubbling and tipped with brown.

5. Serve at once, accompanied, if you like, with fluffy boiled rice.

CRABMEAT NORFOLK

MAKES 4 SERVINGS

No one is quite sure who created this elegant but easy crab dish or how it got its name. For years, Crabmeat Norfolk was the specialty of the old, original O'Donnell's Restaurant in downtown Washington, D.C., and to this day, it's a signature dish at O'Donnell's Seafood Restaurant in Gaithersburg, Maryland. This restaurant claims that Tom O'Donnell created Crabmeat Norfolk (or at least the Norfolk style of cooking shellfish) back in 1922 while cruising the Chesapeake; he'd pick the meat from fresh-caught crabs and sauté it quickly in butter. On the other hand, Craig Claiborne, for years the food columnist of *The New York Times*, credits W. O. Snowden of Norfolk's late, lamented Snowden and Mason Restaurant for creating the recipe in 1924. Snowden's butter-bathed lumps of crab delicately spiked with vinegar is the version most widely accepted today. It was baked, Claiborne wrote, "in a Norfolk alumi-num pan," a sort of gratin that was manufactured in Norfolk at the time. Hence the name Crabmeat Norfolk. The recipe here approximates the original. To accompany it I like fluffy boiled rice and a salad of crisp greens or, even better, fresh asparagus drizzled with olive oil, then roasted for 10 to 12 minutes in a 400° F. oven.

1 pound lump crabmeat, picked over for bits of shell and cartilage, then flaked

1½ tablespoons white wine vinegar or tarragon vinegar

¼ teaspoon salt

¼ teaspoon hot red pepper sauce

¼ teaspoon Worcestershire sauce

5 tablespoons cold butter, cut into small dice

1. Preheat the oven to 375° F.

2. Place the crab in a medium-size mixing bowl; add the vinegar, salt, hot pepper sauce, and Worcestershire sauce, and toss lightly. Transfer to an ungreased, nonreactive 1-quart gratin dish and dot evenly with the butter.

3. Slide onto the middle oven shelf and bake uncovered for 15 to 20 minutes or until bubbly.

4. Serve at once.

❉

Harder than a landlord's heart.

—**DAMON RUNYON,** *ON THE TOUGHNESS OF FLORIDA STONE CRAB SHELLS*

❉

CRISPY SOFT-SHELLS

MAKES 4 SERVINGS

. . . .

"It usually comes in the third or fourth week of May, with a full waning moon," William W. Warner writes in his Pulitzer Prize–winning *Beautiful Swimmers: Watermen, Crabs and the Chesapeake Bay* (1976). "Not hundreds, but thousands of peelers will be taken by the best scrappers. The first run of soft crabs, as it is always called, has begun." When I was a little girl spending a chunk of every summer at our Chesapeake Bay cottage, an old waterman told me that a soft-shell is merely a crab that has shed its hard shell. "Only way for 'em to grow," he explained. I wasn't aware until years later that soft-shells were a singular delicacy. In New York we cheered the spring arrival of soft-shells, then plunged into a summer of feasting, sometimes at home but more often at restaurants where these fragile creatures were treated with respect. Today, "piling on" seems to be the mantra of trendy chefs: piling on of sauces, piling on of seasonings, piling on of garnishes and accoutrements. Too bad. I've yet to see anyone improve on fresh soft-shells bounced in and out of a hot skillet. And I think most Southerners would agree.

8 fresh soft-shell crabs, cleaned and dressed

½ cup unsifted all-purpose flour

¼ cup unsifted stone-ground cornmeal

1 teaspoon salt

½ teaspoon black pepper

2 to 4 tablespoons vegetable oil

2 tablespoons butter

2 large lemons, quartered lengthwise

1. Wash the crabs under cool running water and pat dry on paper toweling. Combine the flour, cornmeal, salt, and pepper in a pie pan, then dredge the soft-shells in the mixture on both sides, shaking off the excess.

2. Heat 2 tablespoons of the oil and 1 tablespoon of the butter in a large, heavy skillet over high heat for about 2 minutes or until almost smoking.

3. Add half the crabs and cook 3 to 5 minutes on each side or until crisply browned. Lift to paper toweling to drain. Brown the rest of the crabs the same way, adding the remaining butter, and if needed, another 1 to 2 tablespoons vegetable oil.

4. Serve hot with wedges of lemon.

HERBED CRAB SALAD

MAKES 4 SERVINGS

. . . .

Here's another original from Lisa Ruffin Harrison of Evelynton Plantation on the James (see her Charcoal-Grilled Shad Roe, page 152). "There's no better summer lunch in this world," she says, "than this crab salad served in tomatoes fresh from the garden." For hors d'oeuvre, Lisa sometimes stuffs the crab salad into cherry tomatoes; there's enough here for six dozen. The only crabmeat to use is "backfin lump," Lisa says. The challenge is to keep the lumps intact as you pick over the crab, removing bits of shell and cartilage, then mix in the herb mayonnaise.

4 large sun-ripened tomatoes

½ teaspoon salt

1 pound lump crabmeat

2 tablespoons fresh lemon juice

⅛ teaspoon ground hot red pepper (cayenne)

⅛ teaspoon black pepper

4 to 5 tablespoons Fresh Herb Mayonnaise
(recipe follows)

2 to 3 tablespoons finely snipped
fresh chives

1. Cut ¼ inch off the top of each tomato, then scoop out the pulp, leaving tomato shells ½ inch thick. Sprinkle the insides of the tomatoes with the salt, then drain upside down on paper toweling for 20 minutes. Save the tomato tops and pulp for salad another day.

2. Place the crabmeat in a large nonreactive bowl and sprinkle with 1 tablespoon of the lemon juice. Carefully fork the crabmeat apart, removing bits of shell and cartilage. In a separate large nonreactive bowl, combine the remaining lemon juice, the cayenne, and black pepper with 4 tablespoons of the mayonnaise.

3. Add the crab and turn it in the dressing just enough to mix without breaking up the lumps. If the salad seems dry, gently mix in the remaining tablespoon of mayonnaise.

4. Scoop into the tomatoes, scatter the chives on top, and serve as the main course of a light luncheon.

FRESH HERB MAYONNAISE

MAKES ABOUT 2 CUPS

This quick mayonnaise is delicious with chicken, turkey, and shrimp salad as well as with the crab salad that precedes. It was created by Lisa Ruffin Harrison of Evelynton Plantation, who grows her own herbs. **Note:** *Because this mayonnaise calls for raw eggs, use the pasteurized here (see About Pasteurized Eggs, page xxi).* **Update:** *A busy working mother like many women today, Lisa has simplified this recipe, which originally appeared in Bon Appétit back in the late 1980s. That was shortly before she married. "If you don't feel like making a mayonnaise, which these days I find I never have time for," she recently e-mailed me, "just use a good mayo like Duke's, our fabulous local brand. Without Duke's I'd use Hellmann's but no sweet varieties—heaven forbid!" That means omitting the eggs and the oil below and blending a good commercial mayonnaise with the remaining recipe ingredients. And how much mayonnaise would that be? My suggestion—not Lisa's—would be to start with 1 cup because this is a good dressing to have on hand. If the flavors seem strong, blend in another half cup or so. Lisa's homemade mayonnaise, after all, makes two cups.*

2 large pasteurized eggs (see Note above)

2 tablespoons Dijon mustard

1 tablespoon fresh lemon juice

3 tablespoons coarsely chopped fresh basil

3 tablespoons coarsely snipped fresh dill

2 tablespoons coarsely chopped
Italian parsley

⅛ teaspoon ground hot red pepper
(cayenne)

⅛ teaspoon black pepper

⅛ teaspoon salt

1 cup vegetable oil

1. Blend the eggs, mustard, lemon juice, basil, dill, parsley, cayenne, black pepper, and salt in a food processor for about 1 minute or until reduced to a paste.
2. With the motor running, slowly drizzle the oil down the feed tube, then continue processing until the mayonnaise is thick.
3. Transfer the mayonnaise to a small nonreactive bowl, cover, and store in the refrigerator for up to three days.

RICK'S CRISPY FRIED OYSTERS

MAKES 4 SERVINGS

There used to be a classy little Chapel Hill restaurant called Mondo Bistro, but chef Rick Robinson closed the doors, abandoned the stove, and became a realtor. Luckily, I got Rick's recipe for fried oysters when I profiled him for *Food & Wine* back in the 1990s. Mondo Bistro bedded the oysters on a tart tarragon-scented arugula salad and added a wreath of leek-pancetta ragout—a tad fussy for home cooks. I serve Rick's oysters solo—to raves, I might add.

Note: *To give the oysters extra crunch, use high-gluten bread flour for dredging.*

1907

While touring Nashville, Tennessee, President Theodore Roosevelt pauses for a cup of coffee at the famous Maxwell House Hotel. "Good to the last drop," says old Rough 'n' Ready, creating the slogan still attached to that coffee today. (See Maxwell House Coffee, page 317.)

Just three years after Syrian immigrant Abe Doumar improvised the first ice cream cone at the St. Louis World's Fair, he sets up shop at Norfolk, Virginia's Ocean View Amusement Park. Using the four-waffle iron he invented, Doumar sells 23,000 cones in a single day. Those hand-crafted waffle cones are still served at Doumar's in downtown Norfolk.

Turnbull Bakeries of Chattanooga begins manufacturing sugar cones.

The Peanut Depot fires up its roasters on warehouse row in Birmingham, Alabama. It has been roasting peanuts ever since—for grocery stores, sports arenas, and tourists' noses to the source.

In top hat and tails, President Theodore Roosevelt sails into Norfolk, Virginia, to open the Jamestown Exposition in nearby Hampton Roads. Other VIPs at the six-month world's fair commemorating the 300th anniversary of America's birth: Mark Twain, Booker T. Washington, William Randolph Hearst, and Samuel Gompers.

Vegetable oil for deep-fat frying

1½ cups unsifted bread flour or unbleached all-purpose flour (see Note on page 171)

½ cup unsifted yellow cornmeal

½ teaspoon salt, or to taste

¼ teaspoon black pepper, or to taste

⅛ teaspoon ground hot red pepper (cayenne), or to taste

24 medium oysters, shucked and drained well

1. Pour the oil into a large, deep skillet to a depth of ½ inch and set over moderate heat.

2. Meanwhile, combine the flour, cornmeal, salt, black pepper, and cayenne in a large pie pan. Taste and adjust the seasonings as needed; the mixture should be piquant.

3. As the oil in the skillet approaches 360° F. on a deep-fat thermometer, dredge the oysters in the flour mixture and let stand until the oil reaches 375° F.

4. Fry the oysters in three or four batches, allowing about 1 minute per side for them to crisp and brown; transfer to paper toweling to drain.

5. Serve hot and resist the temptation to put out tartar sauce. Rick's oysters don't need it. No cocktail sauce, either.

❁

I love to dip my oysters in a bath of hot butter, but other Lowcountry people . . . eat their oysters as God made them, savoring that giddy, briny essence of the Lowcountry as it comes from its shell.

—PAT CONROY, OYSTER ROASTS, GOURMET

❁

TIDEWATER SCALLOPED OYSTERS

MAKES 4 TO 6 SERVINGS

Thanks to the abundance of fish and shellfish in Virginia's rivers, inlets, and bays, the colonists at Jamestown, America's first permanent English settlement (1607), managed to survive. Noting the marine bounty, Captain John Smith wrote that his boats could scarcely navigate the lower reaches of the Chesapeake because the fish "were lying so thicke with their heads above the water." Shellfish, too, were plentiful. Early on oysters were simply eaten raw or roasted over campfires, but later, when women were imported to the young colony, cooking began in earnest. The dishes they prepared were English and none more so than scalloped oysters. This modern version, as elegant as it is easy, depends upon absolutely fresh oysters—preferably the Chincoteagues of Virginia.

1 quart freshly shucked oysters, drained

¾ cup oyster liquor

½ cup (1 stick) butter, cut into pats

2 tablespoons finely minced yellow onion

2 tablespoons finely minced green bell pepper

2 tablespoons all-purpose flour

1 teaspoon salt

¼ teaspoon black pepper

⅛ teaspoon ground hot red pepper (cayenne)

1 tablespoon fresh lemon juice

1¼ cups fine soda cracker crumbs

1. Preheat the oven to 375° F. Butter a 1½-quart casserole well and set aside.

2. Pick over the oysters carefully to remove any bits of shell, then place in a heavy, medium-size nonreactive saucepan along with the oyster liquor. Set over low heat and warm 3 to 4 minutes or just until the oysters ruffle.

3. Meanwhile, melt the butter in a small skillet over moderate heat, add the onion and bell pepper, and sauté for 3 to 5 minutes, stirring often, until limp. Blend in the flour, salt, black pepper, cayenne, lemon juice, and 1 cup of the cracker crumbs, then stir in the oysters and their liquor.

4. Turn all into the casserole and scatter the remaining ¼ cup cracker crumbs on top. Slide onto the middle oven shelf and bake uncovered for 20 to 25 minutes or until bubbling and lightly browned.

5. Serve at once. Good with roasted red-skin potatoes, buttered broccoli, asparagus, green peas, or beans.

BLACK-EYED PEA CAKES WITH TOMATO SALSA

MAKES 4 SERVINGS

. . . .

On a swing through Charleston in the late 1980s, my mission was to check out the new restaurants for *Food & Wine* as part of a Lowcountry feature I'd been assigned to write. At the time, the hot new restaurant was Carolina's (it's still there and still popular). I ordered these black-eyed pea cakes, one of the signature appetizers. They were rich enough to serve as the main course of a light lunch or supper and that's how I prefer them today. **Note: *You can prepare the recipe here—my adaptation of the original—through Step 3 as much as a day ahead of time.***

1 cup dried black-eyed peas, washed and sorted but not soaked

One ½-pound smoked ham hock

5 cups chicken broth

1 tablespoon butter

¼ cup minced red onion

2 large garlic cloves, minced

2 tablespoons minced red bell pepper

1 medium jalapeño pepper, stemmed, seeded, and minced

1 large egg yolk

½ cup soft white bread crumbs (about)

½ teaspoon hot red pepper sauce

2 tablespoons coarsely chopped fresh coriander

½ teaspoon ground cumin

¼ teaspoon black pepper

½ cup yellow cornmeal (for dredging)

¼ cup vegetable oil (for frying)

Tomato Salsa (recipe follows)

1. Cook the black-eyed peas and ham hock in the chicken broth in a covered large, heavy saucepan over moderately low heat for 1 to 1¼ hours or until the peas are soft. Drain into a large fine sieve, reserving the ham hock and broth for soup another day. Transfer the peas

to a large mixing bowl and cool to room temperature.

2. Meanwhile, melt the butter in a small, heavy skillet over moderately low heat; add the onion, garlic, bell pepper, and jalapeño, and stir-fry for 4 to 5 minutes or until limp. Add to the peas and cool.

3. Mix in the egg yolk along with the bread crumbs, hot pepper sauce, coriander, cumin, and black pepper, then mash with a potato masher. If too soft to shape, mix in a few more bread crumbs. Set uncovered in the refrigerator and let stand for at least 1 hour.

4. When ready to proceed, shape the mixture into 12 small patties measuring about 2½ inches in diameter and ½ inch thick. Dredge in the cornmeal, shaking off any excess.

5. Heat the oil in a large, heavy skillet over high heat for 1½ to 2 minutes or until ripples appear on the skillet bottom. Add half of the patties and brown 1 to 1½ minutes on each side; drain on paper toweling. Brown and drain the remaining patties the same way.

6. To serve, ladle a little of the Tomato Salsa on each of four luncheon plates, then arrange the black-eyed pea cakes artfully on top.

❋

My mother or grandma would prepare a big pot of red beans and rice every Monday (laundry day), along with ham hocks, smoked sausages, garlic, onions and bell peppers.

—DONNA L. BRAZILE, *COOKING WITH GREASE: STIRRING THE POTS IN AMERICAN POLITICS*

❋

❋

He likes Chevrolets and black-eyed peas, but he's sure complex inside.

—MRS. ERSKINE CALDWELL ON HER SOUTHERN NOVELIST HUSBAND

❋

TOMATO SALSA

MAKES ABOUT 2½ CUPS

. . . .

This good all-purpose salsa is my adaptation of one served at Carolina's Restaurant in Charleston, which appeared in an article I wrote some years ago for *Food & Wine*. Use it to sauce Black-Eyed Pea Cakes (recipe precedes) or in any recipe that calls for salsa. **Note:** *Prepare the recipe a day ahead of time, if you like. Scoop the salsa into a nonreactive container, cover with plastic food wrap, and store in the refrigerator.*

1 pound firm-ripe tomatoes (about 3 medium), peeled, seeded, and coarsely chopped

¼ cup finely diced red onion

2 medium scallions, trimmed and thinly sliced (include some green tops)

1 medium garlic clove, finely minced

1 small jalapeño pepper, stemmed, seeded, and minced

2 tablespoons coarsely chopped fresh coriander

¾ teaspoon ground cumin

½ teaspoon salt

½ teaspoon black pepper

2 tablespoons olive oil

1 tablespoon cider or red wine vinegar

1. Combine all ingredients in a large nonreactive bowl. Cover and refrigerate.
2. When ready to serve, pour off all liquid, then let stand at room temperature for about 30 minutes.

RED BEANS AND RICE

MAKES 6 TO 8 SERVINGS

In Louisiana, Mardi Gras means nonstop revelry that begins the weekend before Ash Wednesday and climaxes on Mardi Gras (Fat Tuesday) itself. As one Cajun told me some years ago when I was on assignment in St. Martinville, "You don't have time to cook on Mardi Gras—you're having too much fun. But at the same time," she added, "you need something substantial to eat. That's why red beans and rice are a Mardi Gras tradition. The beans can be cooked ahead of time." **Tip:** *I've discovered that the rice can also be prepared in advance: Cook it in an uncovered pan for about 20 minutes or until all the water is absorbed; the rice will be al dente. Fluff gently with a fork and cool uncovered for one hour. Spoon the rice into a plastic zipper bag and store in the refrigerator or freezer. To reheat, scoop the rice into a large fine sieve, fork lightly to separate the grains, and set over a large saucepan containing*

1908 Prohibition comes to Mississippi.

1910 Knoxville, Tennessee, stages the Appalachian Exposition with agricultural and industrial exhibits. Two pavilions salute the achievements of women and African Americans.

The Shaker settlement at Pleasant Hill, Kentucky, closes.

1911 Alabama peanut researcher George Washington Carver hosts a nine-course "peanut luncheon" at Tuskegee Institute. Among the VIP guests: Booker T. Washington.

1912 Nashville confectioner Howell Campbell creates the GooGoo Cluster, America's first multiple-ingredient candy bar. His winning combo: milk chocolate, peanuts, caramel, and marshmallow shaped into a patty.

about two inches of boiling water. Tent the rice with foil and steam for 3 to 5 minutes or just until hot. Fork again lightly and serve.

I pound dried red kidney beans, washed and sorted

8 cups (2 quarts) cold water

2 large yellow onions, coarsely chopped

I large green bell pepper, cored, seeded, and coarsely chopped

2 large celery ribs, trimmed and finely diced (include a few leaves)

4 ounces tasso (spicy cold-smoked pork) or good country ham, finely diced

2 teaspoons salt, or to taste

¼ teaspoon ground hot red pepper (cayenne), or to taste

¼ teaspoon black pepper, or to taste

Tops of 3 large scallions, thinly sliced (green part only)

¼ cup coarsely chopped Italian parsley

2½ cups rice, cooked by package directions (see Tip on page 175)

1. Soak the beans in the water overnight in a large, heavy kettle.
2. The next day, add the onions, bell pepper, celery, tasso, salt, cayenne, and black pepper to the undrained beans and bring to a boil over high heat. Adjust the heat so that the water bubbles gently, cover, and simmer for 1 hour. Uncover, reduce the heat to its lowest point, and continue simmering for 2½ to 3 hours, stirring occasionally, until the beans are soft and the mixture is as thick as chili. **Note:** *The recipe can be prepared up to this point several days ahead of time; cover and refrigerate. About 20 minutes before serving, reheat slowly, stirring frequently, then proceed as the recipe directs.*
3. Mix in the scallion tops and parsley and simmer uncovered 10 to 15 minutes more or until the flavors mellow. Taste for salt, cayenne, and black pepper and adjust as needed.
4. To serve, scoop the red beans and rice into separate heated bowls and let everyone help himself, first to the rice, then to the red beans: They should be ladled on top of the rice.

❈

I was a great cook so I would cook for people's parties and I'd earn $50 here and there by making platters, gumbo, beans and rice.

—DONNA L. BRAZILE, COOKING WITH GREASE: STIRRING THE POTS IN AMERICAN POLITICS

❈

❈

"Oh, Mr. Martin," I said . . . "I never had pork in my life." And why wouldn't it be good? It had fed on biddy-mash and skimmed milk and fluffy-ruffle petunias.

—MARJORIE KINNAN RAWLINGS, CROSS CREEK

❈

A Love Affair with Southern Cooking

Sides and Salads

My brother never did take to southern food the way I did, especially when it came to vegetables. Complaining that everything was cooked with fatback or salt pork, he preferred the butter-and-cream—seasoned vegetables of our Illinois mother.

Bob was completely happy eating parsnips, rutabaga, turnips, and such. And although I did like my mother's asparagus (which my schoolmates called "sparrow grass"), her cauliflower, her green peas with dumplings, and her spinach with nutmeg and sour cream, I never looked forward to broccoli, Brussels sprout, or parsnip days. My father disliked parsnips as much as I, so Mother usually made them for my brother whenever my father was away on business.

I don't remember my mother ever cooking corn except on the cob, I don't remember her doing anything with yellow squash other than boiling and buttering it, I don't recall her cooking collards, certainly never okra, grits, or black-eyed peas. And rarely rice for that matter. When it came to starch, Mother preferred Irish potatoes. She may have baked sweet potatoes a time or two, but she never improvised upon them as Southerners often do.

The only southern sides my mother truly relished were what she called "congealed salads" made with Jell-O. Her southern friends and neighbors were forever giving her new recipes for them (a couple of the best are included at the end of this chapter).

This is not to suggest that my mother was a lousy cook. It's just that she was a New England—educated Midwesterner who was accustomed to cooking vegetables most of my school chums had never heard of, let alone eaten. Then, too, my father-the-botanist would occasionally bring home some "exotic" to broaden our palates. I remember avocados, in particular (a fruit, yes, but one treated like a vegetable). Daddy halved it at the dinner table with great ceremony, twisted out the seed, then scooped some of the buttery flesh onto our plates and told us to spoon a little of my mother's oil and vinegar dressing on top. I wasn't impressed—then. I also remember celery root, which my mother shredded like cabbage and dressed like slaw, and a Hubbard squash that Daddy split with an axe. Mother baked biggish chunks with brown sugar and butter. All are commonplace today but in the Raleigh of my youth, they were unknown.

I always liked to go home from school with southern friends whose mothers might serve a mess o' greens for dinner, or fry up some yellow squash, or make a big batch of sweet slaw. To me these seemed more exotic than the vegetables we ate at home.

Over the years as I've traveled about the South, I've added many more southern vegetables to my repertoire: cymlings (patty-pans), mirlitons, salsify, turnip greens and collards, black-eyed peas, pole beans, and more.

Recipes and recollections follow.

❧

The only good vegetable is Tabasco Sauce.

—*P. J. O'ROURKE*, THE BACHELOR HOME COMPANION

❧

NANA'S LIMA BEANS

MAKES 4 SERVINGS

There were only two girls in my neighborhood when I was growing up: Virginia and Nancy Mumford. Though both were a little younger than I, we had many things in common, not least of which was our fondness for the way their mother, Cleone Mumford, prepared butter beans or "limas" as the Mumfords called them. Nancy (now Nancy Mumford Pencsak) recently self-published a collection of favorite family recipes, *Footsteps in the Kitchen*, and there among the side dishes is Mrs. Mumford's lima bean recipe. "Nana was famous for these," says Nancy. Her older sister, Virginia Mumford Nance, adds, "My children would rather have had another bowl of lima beans for dessert than anything else. I'd often catch them making an after-dinner raid on the leftovers and the lima beans would go first. Perhaps the greatest compliment my children gave me was the time they said, 'Mom, these are almost as good as Nana's!'"

¼ cup diced ham or better yet, country ham (about 2 ounces)

1 teaspoon corn oil

4 cups water

3 cups shelled baby butter beans or one 16-ounce package solidly frozen baby lima beans

3 tablespoons "pot likker" (cooking water from the beans)

A Love Affair with Southern Cooking

**3 tablespoons all-purpose flour
blended with ⅓ cup cold water (thickener)**

1 tablespoon butter

1 teaspoon salt

¼ teaspoon black pepper

Pinch of sugar

1. Sauté the ham in the oil in a large, heavy saucepan over moderate heat 2 to 3 minutes, stirring often, until lightly browned. Add the water and bring to a boil.
2. Add the limas, breaking up large clumps if you're using frozen beans, and return to the boil. Adjust the heat so the water bubbles gently, cover, and cook for 20 to 25 minutes or until the beans are very tender.
3. Whisk the "pot likker" from the beans into the thickener, add to the limas, and cook and stir for 2 to 3 minutes or until lightly thickened. Mix in the butter, salt, pepper, and sugar and cook and stir 2 to 3 minutes longer until no raw floury taste lingers.
4. Ladle the limas and thickened "pot likker" into heated bowls and serve as an accompaniment to baked ham, fried chicken, or roast pork, turkey, or chicken.

❀

*And now, perhaps just for our diet's healthy
balance, a spoonful or two of those lima beans,
as gay as April and as sweet as butter,
a tomato slice or two, a speared forkful
of those thin-sliced cucumbers . . .*

—THOMAS WOLFE, *OF TIME AND THE RIVER*

❀

1913   Alcoa builds a factory to manufacture aluminum "tins" for canned foods just outside Maryville on the banks of the Little Tennessee River.

Relocating from Pennsylvania, Planters builds its first processing plant in Suffolk, Virginia, and soon becomes America's largest processor of nuts.

Faced with a 500-pound surplus of raw peanuts, Philip L. Lance roasts them, packs them in serving-size paper bags, and sells them in downtown Charlotte, North Carolina, thereby launching one of America's most successful snack food companies.

1914   Agronomist George Washington Carver, publishing the results of his peanut research at Alabama's Tuskegee Institute, proves how nutritious the lowly legume is.

After receiving a peanut brittle recipe from a soldier at Camp Greene near Charlotte, North Carolina, Philip L. Lance and his partner, Salem Van Every, create the Peanut Bar. It remains one of Lance's most popular snack foods.

COUNTRY-STYLE SNAP BEANS

MAKES 4 TO 6 SERVINGS

. . . .

My brother, Bob, used to make fun of the way Southerners cooked vegetables. "Turnip greens with fatback," he'd say. "Collards with fatback, black-eyed peas with fatback, green beans with fatback." He preferred the Brussels sprouts, Swiss chard, and parsnips that our Illinois mother cooked but I, on the other hand, loved the meaty flavor of southern greens and snap beans. I never got them at home but did at the home of Mrs. Franklin, a country-come-to-town woman who lived around the corner. I'd no sooner get home from school than I'd dash over to Mrs. Franklin's to see what was left over from lunch. Usually there were snap beans prepared this way and corn pone for "sopping up the pot likker." She served the leftovers at room temperature and I thought they were marvelous. **Note:** *Because of the saltiness of the fatback, these beans may need no additional salt. But taste before serving and adjust as needed.*

2 pounds snap (green) beans, washed, tipped, and snapped in two

4½ cups cold water

4 ounces fatback, rinsed well to remove excess salt, then quartered

½ teaspoon freshly ground black pepper

Salt, if needed to taste

1. Place the beans, water, fatback, and pepper in a large, heavy saucepan and bring to a boil over high heat. Adjust the heat so the water barely bubbles, cover, and cook for 45 minutes to 1 hour or until the beans are very tender. Taste for salt and season as needed.

2. Ladle the beans into small bowls and serve as an accompaniment to fried chicken or fish, roast chicken or pork, or baked ham. And don't forget to put out a plate of corn bread, fresh from the oven.

SNAP BEANS WITH MUSTARD AND COUNTRY HAM

MAKES 4 SERVINGS

. . . .

To many Southerners, green beans are "snap beans" because they "snap" when you break them. This recipe, my own, combines three southern favorites: green beans, mustard, and country ham. I like these beans best with roast turkey, grilled or roast chicken. But they're equally delicious with pork chops or roast pork. Some southern supermarkets sell biscuit slices, slim rounds of country ham ready to cook and slip into biscuits. Others sell country ham by the piece or the pound. If not available in your area, see Sources (page 401). **Note:** *Because of the saltiness of the ham, the mustard, and the broth, these beans are unlikely to need additional salt. But taste before serving and adjust as needed.*

1 tablespoon butter, bacon drippings, or vegetable oil

3 ounces uncooked country ham, finely diced

6 medium scallions, trimmed and coarsely chopped (include some green tops)

1 pound tender young green beans, tipped and snapped in two if large

1½ cups chicken broth

2 tablespoons all-purpose flour blended with 2 tablespoons cold water (thickener)

2 teaspoons prepared yellow mustard

¼ teaspoon black pepper, or to taste

1. Melt the butter in a large, heavy saucepan over moderate heat, add the ham and scallions, and cook, stirring now and then, for 5 to 8 minutes or until lightly browned.
2. Add the beans and broth and bring to a boil. Adjust the heat so the broth bubbles gently, cover, and cook for 12 to 15 minutes or until the beans are crisp-tender.
3. Meanwhile, combine the thickener and the mustard and set aside. As soon as the beans are done, whisk a little of the hot broth into the mustard mixture, stir back into the pan, add the pepper, and cook, stirring constantly, for 3 minutes or until the broth thickens. Continue cooking uncovered, stirring occasionally, for 3 to 5 minutes or until the sauce has the consistency of a glaze.
4. Taste the beans for salt and pepper, adjust as needed, and serve straightaway.

❧

While an eon, as someone has observed, may be two people and a ham, a fruitcake is forever.

—RUSSELL BAKER

❧

1915 The world's first Negro Exposition is held in Richmond, Virginia. In addition to showcasing the fine art, folk art, and homely skills of American Negroes, its purpose is to prove that cordial relations exist between southern African Americans and Whites.

Coca-Cola's unique green glass hobble-skirt bottle, hand-blown at the Root Glass Company in Terre Haute, Indiana, is patented. It debuts a year later and becomes a soft-drink icon.

Florida's commercial shrimping industry is launched at Fernandina Beach.

1916 The state of Virginia declares prohibition, the few wineries that survived the Civil War close, and moonshining flourishes. By 1950, only 15 acres of Virginia soil are devoted to grapes—table grapes.

Clarence Saunders opens a Piggly Wiggly in Memphis, Tennessee. It is America's first self-service supermarket and stocks more than 600 different items. Today there are 600 Piggly Wigglies, most of them in the South.

Mr. Peanut, based on a teenager's drawing, debuts in Suffolk, Virginia, and with top hat, monocle, cane, and white spats, soon becomes the Planters icon.

THOMAS JEFFERSON (1743-1826)

He was the principal author of the Declaration of Independence, and he was the third president of the United States, elected for two terms.

But Thomas Jefferson was much, much more: architect, attorney, philosopher, scholar, gardener, gourmet. The last two may be the least known but they are the most relevant here.

"The greatest service which can be rendered by any country is to add a useful plant to its culture," Thomas Jefferson once wrote.

He turned Monticello, his beloved Virginia plantation, into a kind of horticultural experiment station and for nearly twenty years painstakingly recorded his observations, successes, and failures in his Garden Kalendar [sic].

Jefferson grew 250 different vegetable varieties in his garden: the beans and salsify Lewis and Clark had brought back from the West, broccoli and squashes imported from Italy, peppers obtained from Mexico, as well as such exotics or "new" vegetables as cauliflower, tomatoes, eggplant, sea kale, red celery, and red globe artichokes. Always partial to salads, Jefferson planted an assortment of unusual greens, among them corn salad, endives, nasturtiums, and radicchio. And when his olive trees succumbed, he planted sesame and pressed the seeds into oil—excellent for salad dressings, he noted.

"I am curious to select one or two of the best species or variety of every garden vegetable and to reject all others from the garden to avoid the dangers of mixing or degeneracy," Jefferson wrote. Which explains why he grew twenty varieties of beans at Monticello and fifteen of English peas (his favorite).

He was equally experimental with fruit. Between 1769 and 1814, Monticello historians tell us, Jefferson planted 1,031 fruit trees in his South Orchard, a vast horseshoe-shaped plot embracing two vineyards and berry squares. Growing here: 38 varieties of peach, 27 of plum, 18 apple, 14 cherry, 12 pear, seven almond, six apricot, and one quince.

To Jefferson, a plant's ornamental potential was also important. He made an arbor of scarlet runner beans; juxtaposed rows of green, purple, and white broccoli and even of purple and white eggplant. Sesame or okra framed his tomato beds, and cherry trees lined the "long, grass walk" to filter the downpouring summer sun.

Try as he would, however, Jefferson failed to produce an acceptable table wine at Monticello. While minister to France, he'd toured vineyards there and in northern Italy as well. He even brought an Italian vintner to Monticello but he, too, was unsuccessful (see Southern Wines, page 121).

Jefferson's contributions to the American table do not end with the fruits and vegetables he introduced. He was the first to serve ice cream (his hand-written recipe for vanilla ice cream still exists). The first, too, to acquaint us with macaroni. Indeed, Jefferson was so fond of pasta he sketched the design of a pasta machine and later imported one from Italy. It's said that today's ubiquitous mac 'n' cheese descends from one that Jefferson served at the White House.

Thomas Jefferson may even have been the father of the vegetarian movement. "I have lived temperately," he wrote, "eating little animal food, and that . . . as a condiment for vegetables, which constitute my principal diet."

Is that why he lived to be eighty-three?

GREEN BEANS WITH BROWNED BUTTER AND PECANS

MAKES 4 SERVINGS

Fairly new as southern recipes go, this one's more popular with the younger generation than the boiled-to-death beans of their grandmother's day. Because they cook quickly in a minimum of water, these beans retain most of their nutrients. They complement every kind of red meat, also fish and fowl. **Note:** *It may take half an hour for the butter to brown, so begin there. If you try to rush things by revving up the burner heat, you'll burn the butter in no time.*

4 tablespoons (½ stick) butter

1 cup water mixed with 1 teaspoon salt

1 pound tender young green beans,
tipped and snapped in two if large

¼ teaspoon black pepper, or to taste

½ cup lightly toasted coarsely chopped pecans
(8 to 10 minutes in a 350° F. oven)

1. Place the butter in a small, heavy saucepan and set over low heat for 25 to 30 minutes, swirling the pan often, until a rich topaz brown (see Note above).

2. Meanwhile, bring the salted water to a boil in a large, heavy saucepan over moderately high heat. Add the beans and return to the boil. Adjust the heat so the water ripples gently, cover, and simmer for 12 to 15 minutes or just until the beans are crisp-tender. Watch carefully and if the beans threaten to boil dry, add a bit more water.

3. When the beans are done, drain well, return to the pan, add the pepper, and shake over moderate heat to drive off excess moisture. Add the nuts and browned butter, toss well, and heat for 1 to 2 minutes. Taste for salt and pepper and adjust as needed.

4. Transfer to a heated vegetable dish and serve.

BLACK-EYED PEAS WITH SMOKED HAM HOCK

MAKES 6 SERVINGS

On New Year's Day, Southerners feast upon black-eyed peas (for good luck), collard greens (for prosperity), and hog jowl or other cut of pork (for robust health). It's an old and convivial custom. Being the daughter of Midwesterners, I joined the festivities only after I was allowed to drive the family car. I'd meet friends at the Sir Walter Hotel in downtown Raleigh for the ritual New Year's meal. It may not have improved my health, luck, or fortune, but it did make me feel truly southern. It still does. **Note:** *Now that hog jowl is hard to come by, many Southerners substitute fatback or side meat. Others prefer a ham hock because of the smokiness it imparts.*

One 16-ounce bag dried black-eyed peas,
washed and sorted but not soaked

One 10- to 12-ounce smoked ham hock

6 cups cold water (about)

1½ teaspoons salt

½ teaspoon freshly ground black pepper

1. Place the black-eyed peas and ham hock in a large, heavy saucepan, then add just enough cold water to cover by 1 1/2 inches. Stir in the salt and pepper, set over moderately high heat, and bring to a boil.

2. Adjust the heat so that the water bubbles gently, set the pan lid on askew (to minimize "boilovers"), and simmer, stirring occasionally, for 40 to 45 minutes or until the beans are soft, almost all the water has boiled away, and the mixture has a porridge-y consistency. **Note: *If at any point the beans threaten to boil dry as they cook, add a little additional cold water.***

3. Drain off any excess cooking water (there should be little, if any), then remove the ham hock, strip off the meat (there won't be much), and cut into small pieces. Stir the meat back into the black-eyed peas.

4. Serve hot with roast pork, Classic Collards (page 189), and corn bread fresh from the oven.

LITTLE HAVANA BLACK BEANS AND RICE

MAKES 6 SERVINGS

Some years ago a Columbia J-School classmate who was working in Miami took me to "Little Havana," the city's Cuban quarter, and to an authentic restaurant there. We ordered everything from fried plantains to *menudo* (tripe) to Cuban bread to black beans prepared this way. Florida cooking has always had a Spanish accent, first because Spaniards discovered and colonized it, second because waves of Cubans arrived—originally to Tampa in 1886 to make cigars, then to Miami in a massive mid-twentieth-century migration to escape the Castro regime.

I pound dried black beans,
washed and sorted

6 cups water

3 tablespoons olive oil

I large yellow onion, coarsely chopped

I small green bell pepper, cored, seeded,
and coarsely chopped

I small red bell pepper, cored, seeded,
and coarsely chopped

I large garlic clove, minced

I large whole bay leaf, preferably fresh

I teaspoon dried leaf oregano, crumbled

1/2 teaspoon dried leaf thyme, crumbled

1/2 teaspoon ground cumin

1 1/2 teaspoons salt, or to taste

1/4 teaspoon hot red pepper flakes,
or to taste, crushed

2 1/2 cups converted rice, cooked by
package directions

1. Place the beans in a large, heavy kettle, add just enough cold water to cover them by 1 inch, and soak overnight.

2. Next day, drain the beans well, rinse, and return to the kettle. Add the 6 cups water and bring to a boil over high heat. Reduce the heat until the water bubbles gently and cook uncovered for 1 to 1 1/2 hours until the beans

are tender. If the mixture seems "soupy," scoop up 1 cup of the beans, mash, and return to the kettle. Keep the beans warm over lowest heat while you proceed with the recipe.

3. Pour the oil into a large, heavy skillet and set over moderately high heat for 2 minutes or until ripples appear on the pan bottom. Add the onion, bell peppers, garlic, bay leaf, oregano, thyme, cumin, salt, and crushed red pepper flakes, and sauté, stirring often, for about 10 minutes or until limp and golden.

4. Stir the skillet mixture into the beans, cover, and cook over low heat, stirring occasionally, for 15 to 20 minutes or just until the flavors marry. Discard the bay leaf. Taste for salt and red pepper and adjust as needed.

5. To serve, divide the rice among six heated dinner plates and ladle the beans on top.

❁

I viewed with pleasure this gentleman's exemplary improvements in agriculture; particularly in the growth of rice, and in his machines for shelling that valuable grain . . .

—**WILLIAM BARTRAM,** *TRAVELS OF WILLIAM BARTRAM,* ON A VISIT IN 1773 TO THE HONORABLE H. ANDREWS, ESQUIRE, OF CHARLESTON, SOUTH CAROLINA

❁

1916 Philip Lance's wife and daughter begin sandwiching Lance crackers together with peanut butter and the "sandwich cracker" soon joins the Lance snack food line.

1917 Earl Mitchell, Sr., a salesman traveling about the South for the Chattanooga Bakery, has the idea for the MoonPie. It was the sort of cheap, rib-sticking snack folks craved. (See MoonPie, page 308.)

Using her own homemade mayonnaise, Eugenia Duke of Greenville, South Carolina, makes sandwiches for GIs at nearby Fort Sevier. Her mayo is so good a local grocer takes a few jars, demand grows, and before long Duke's mayonnaise is number one throughout the South. (See Eugenia Duke, page 230.)

H. C. Newsom sells a few of his aged country hams at his store in Princeton, Kentucky—hams smoke-cured according to a 121-year-old family recipe. Today those hams, the highly prized Col. Bill Newsom's Aged Kentucky Country Hams, are produced the age-old way by H. C. Newsom's granddaughter, Nancy Newsom Mahaffey, aka "The Ham Lady."

George E. Hutchens of High Point, North Carolina, opens the first of 52 Food Worlds, a popular North Carolina–Virginia grocery chain. In 1984, Food World is acquired by NC's upscale Harris Teeter supermarkets.

McCORMICK'S SPICES

Most of us just find old high school annuals in our cellars. But Willoughby M. McCormick found a spice empire. It all began in Baltimore in 1889 when twenty-five-year-old McCormick began mixing root beer, flavorings, and syrups in his basement and selling them door to door under the Bee Brand and Silver Medal labels. He had a staff of three at the time—two girls and a boy—and an optimistic motto: "Make the Best—Someone Will Buy It." Just in case the "best" someone needed wasn't flavorings, McCormick also made Iron Glue ("Sticks to Everything but the Buyer") and Uncle Sam's Nerve and Bone Liniment ("For Man or Beast"). In 1896, McCormick bought the F. G. Emmett Spice Company of Philadelphia and moved its equipment to Baltimore. He added mustard and tea to his line, and in 1910 he became one of the first to package tea in gauze pouches, making "southern nectar" faster and easier to brew. McCormick's grew with the world of food. It went bicoastal in 1947 by acquiring Schilling & Company of San Francisco (a coffee, spice, and extract house), and formed McCormick de Mexico, S.A. Over time, it established itself in Asia, Canada, France, and Germany, and also developed spice blends to meet growing interest in Asian and Southwestern cuisines. Today Old Bay Seasoning, TV Time popcorn, Zatarain's foods, and Golden Dipt seafood products, among others, all belong to McCormick's, the global giant that began in a Baltimore basement.

BARBECUED BEANS

MAKES 6 SERVINGS

You might call these the southern "Boston-Baked." Many barbecue joints offer them as a side for pulled pork or ribs. But I like them as a main course with hefty helpings of sweet slaw. **Note:** *An old-fashioned bean pot is best for baking the beans, but if you have none, choose a deep casserole with a snugly fitting lid. Like many casseroles, these beans will be more flavorful if baked one day and served the next. Take them from the fridge and let stand at room temperature for half an hour, then reheat by setting in a 350° F. oven for about 30 minutes.*

I pound dried navy or pea beans, washed and sorted

2 large yellow onions, moderately finely chopped

2 large garlic cloves, minced

3 tablespoons bacon, ham, or pork drippings

¾ cup tomato ketchup

½ cup cider vinegar

⅓ cup firmly packed light brown sugar

2 tablespoons prepared spicy brown mustard

2 teaspoons salt

½ teaspoon black pepper

¼ teaspoon ground hot red pepper (cayenne)

5 cups boiling water (about)

A Love Affair with Southern Cooking

1. Place the beans in a large, heavy kettle, add just enough cold water to cover them by 1 inch, and soak overnight.

2. When ready to proceed, preheat the oven to 350° F. Drain the beans well, rinse, and place in an ungreased 3-quart bean pot or deep casserole. Mix in all remaining ingredients.

3. Lay a small sheet of aluminum foil (not heavy-duty) over the top of the bean pot, then press the lid into place. It's important that the pot be completely sealed.

4. Bake the beans in the lower third of the oven for 4 to 5 hours or until tender. **Note: Check the pot after 3 hours and if it seems to be cooking dry, add a little additional boiling water. Reseal the bean pot and continue baking.**

5. Serve as an accompaniment to pulled pork, barbecued ribs, roast pork, pork chops, baked ham, grilled hot dogs, or chicken. Or make these beans the main course of a casual supper for family and friends.

SCALLOPED CABBAGE

MAKES 8 SERVINGS

Time and again, I find recipes for creamed or scalloped vegetables in early southern cookbooks. Running throughout the vegetable chapter of Sarah Rutledge's *Carolina Housewife* (1847) is this directive: "Make a good sauce, with a pint of milk, butter, flour, and salt; put [the vegetable] in, let it have a boil up, and serve." Elsewhere, creamed vegetables are taken a step further: They're put into a casserole, topped with crumbs, and baked—an excellent way to cook cabbage. This recipe is especially good with baked ham (a buffet favorite) or roast pork, turkey, or chicken. **Note:** *You can prepare Scalloped Cabbage ahead of time through Step 5; cover and refrigerate until about an hour before serving. When baking, increase the oven time by 10 to 15 minutes.*

5 tablespoons butter

I medium yellow onion, halved lengthwise and each half thinly sliced

I large cabbage (about 3 pounds), trimmed, quartered, cored, and each quarter sliced $\frac{1}{2}$ inch thick (remove overly coarse leaf veins)

$1\frac{1}{2}$ cups chicken broth

5 tablespoons all-purpose flour

$\frac{1}{4}$ teaspoon freshly grated nutmeg

I cup half-and-half or milk

$\frac{1}{4}$ cup freshly grated Parmesan cheese

I teaspoon salt, or to taste

$\frac{1}{4}$ teaspoon black pepper, or to taste

2 cups soft white bread crumbs tossed with $2\frac{1}{2}$ tablespoons butter, melted (topping)

1. Melt 2 tablespoons of the butter in a large Dutch oven over moderate heat, add the onion, and sauté for 3 to 4 minutes or until limp and lightly browned.

2. Add the cabbage, turning until lightly glazed; pour in $\frac{1}{2}$ cup of the chicken broth and adjust the heat so the mixture bubbles lightly.

3. Cover and cook the cabbage for about 40 minutes or until crisp-tender, stirring occasionally and bringing the bottom pieces up on top.

Using tongs or a slotted spoon, transfer the cabbage to an ungreased 13 × 9 × 2-inch baking dish. Preheat the oven to 350° F.

4. With high heat under the Dutch oven, boil the cooking liquid for 2 minutes or until reduced by about half. Turn the heat to moderately low, add the remaining 3 tablespoons of butter, and when it melts, blend in the flour and nutmeg. Whisking constantly, add the remaining cup of broth and the half-and-half and cook for 3 to 5 minutes or until thickened. **Note:** *At first the mixture will lump, but if you whisk hard, it will smooth out.* Add the cheese, salt, and pepper, and whisk until the cheese melts. Taste for salt and pepper and adjust as needed.

5. Pour the hot sauce evenly over the cabbage in the baking dish, stir gently to incorporate, then scatter the topping evenly over all.

6. Slide onto the middle oven shelf and bake uncovered for 35 to 40 minutes or until bubbling and nicely browned.

7. Serve at once as an accompaniment to baked ham or roast pork, turkey, or chicken.

SKILLET CABBAGE WITH BACON

MAKES 4 TO 6 SERVINGS

. . . .

Cabbage has always gotten a bad rap but it's the cook, not the cabbage, that's usually at fault. Too often cabbage is cooked to death, turning bitter and smelling up the house. This quick and easy recipe proves that cabbage can be delicious. It's based on my memory of the skillet cabbage served in my grammar school cafeteria. This was *pre* prefab food; lunches were prepared fresh every day by good home cooks. Today's schoolchildren should be so lucky.

6 slices hickory-smoked bacon, cut crosswise into strips ½ inch wide

One small cabbage (2 to 2¼ pounds), quartered, cored, and each quarter sliced 1 inch thick

⅓ cup chicken broth or water

1 teaspoon salt, or to taste

¼ teaspoon black pepper, or to taste

1. Fry the bacon in a large, heavy skillet over moderate heat for 10 to 12 minutes or until the drippings cook out and only crisp brown bits remain. Scoop the bacon onto paper toweling and reserve. Pour off the drippings, then return 2 tablespoons of them to the skillet.

2. Add the cabbage, turn in the drippings for 2 to 3 minutes until nicely glazed, then add the broth, salt, and pepper. Cover and cook over moderate heat, stirring occasionally and separating the pieces of cabbage, for 10 to 12 minutes or until crisp-tender.

3. Return the reserved bacon to the skillet, toss the cabbage well, then taste for salt and pepper and adjust as needed.

4. Serve hot with baked ham, ham loaf, or roast pork, turkey, or chicken.

CLASSIC COLLARDS (OR TURNIP GREENS)

MAKES 4 TO 6 SERVINGS

The first time I ever ate collards—in the Fred A. Olds Elementary School cafeteria in Raleigh, North Carolina—they were prepared exactly this way. So were turnip greens, which were served on alternate days. Choose tender young collards if you can find them; they won't need a full hour to cook, perhaps only 30 or 40 minutes. Traditionalists, however, like their greens "well done." **Tip:** *I find collards easier to wash if I trim and slice them first. I also find the rinse water clinging to the leaves almost enough to cook them, although die-hard Southerners prefer a kettle full of water.* **Note:** *Because of the saltiness of the fatback, these greens are not likely to need additional salt.*

3 large bunches (about 2 pounds) collards or turnip greens, trimmed of coarse stems

4 ounces fatback, rinsed well to remove excess salt, then quartered

¼ teaspoon black pepper

1 to 1½ cups water, if needed

1. Remove the coarse central veins from the collard leaves, then stack 4 or 5 leaves together and slice crosswise at 1-inch intervals. When all of the greens have been prepared, wash them well in several changes of cool water.
2. Pile the greens in a large nonreactive kettle, add the fatback and pepper, cover, and cook over moderate heat 15 minutes. Stir and if the greens seem dry, add 1 cup of the water. Cover again and cook 15 minutes more. Stir and if most of the water has evaporated, add the final ½ cup. **Note:** *Young collards and turnip greens may be done after 30 minutes.*
3. If the greens are not good and soft, cover again and cook 15 to 30 minutes longer.
4. Serve in soup bowls with plenty of "pot likker." Accompany with fresh-baked corn bread and a cruet of cider vinegar to drizzle over the greens.

NEW SOUTHERN COLLARDS (OR TURNIP GREENS)

MAKES 4 TO 6 SERVINGS

Many young Southerners are abandoning the recipes of their mothers and grandmothers and cooking old favorites in new and innovative ways. These collards stir-fried in olive oil with no stinting on garlic prove the point.

3 large bunches (about 2 pounds) collards or turnip greens, trimmed of coarse stems

3 tablespoons olive oil

6 large scallions, trimmed and thinly sliced (include some green tops)

3 large garlic cloves, finely chopped

¼ teaspoon black pepper

Salt to taste

1. Remove the coarse central veins from the collard leaves, then stack 4 or 5 leaves together

and slice crosswise at 1-inch intervals. When all of the greens have been prepared, wash them well in the sink in several changes of cool water. Spin the collards as dry as possible in a salad spinner, then pat dry on paper toweling. Set aside.

2. Heat the olive oil in a very large, deep skillet over moderately high heat for 2 minutes. Add the scallions and garlic and stir-fry for about 5 minutes or until limp and golden.

3. Add the collards and pepper and stir-fry 5 minutes or until the leaves glisten and begin to wilt. Cover and steam 10 to 15 minutes or just until crisp-tender. Mix in salt to taste.

4. Serve hot with roast chicken or pork or broiled chicken. Good, too, with baked ham.

CASSEROLE OF CREAMED COLLARDS WITH PARMESAN CRUMBS

MAKES 6 SERVINGS
. . . .

Having lived in New York most of my adult life, I worried that coming home to North Carolina would land me in a gastronomic desert. Hardly! Several Manhattan-caliber chefs are stirring things up in the Raleigh-Durham-Chapel Hill Triangle where I now live. One of the most gifted is Scott Howell, chef-owner of Nana's in Durham. A graduate of the Culinary Institute of America who worked with David Bouley in New York as well as at Jams and two San Domenicos (on Central Park South and in Imola, Italy), Howell puts sophisticated spins on his Tennessee grand-

mother's home cooking (Nana's is named for her). Not so long ago, I profiled Howell for *Food & Wine* and among the featured recipes was this unusual casserole of collards. What follows is my downsize family version.

I cup water

4 slices hickory-smoked bacon, cut crosswise into strips $\frac{1}{4}$ inch wide

4 pounds collards, washed and sorted, then tough leaf veins and stems removed

I large yellow onion, coarsely chopped

I cup heavy cream

$\frac{3}{4}$ teaspoon salt, or to taste

$\frac{1}{4}$ teaspoon black pepper, or to taste

I large egg lightly beaten with I large egg yolk

Topping

$\frac{1}{3}$ cup coarse, dry unseasoned bread crumbs

3 tablespoons freshly grated Parmesan cheese

$\frac{1}{2}$ tablespoon minced fresh Italian parsley

$\frac{1}{2}$ teaspoon minced fresh sage or $\frac{1}{4}$ teaspoon rubbed sage

I small garlic clove, minced

2 teaspoons fruity olive oil

1. Bring the water and the bacon to a boil in a large, heavy, nonreactive saucepan over moderately high heat. Add the collards, a handful at a time, stirring each batch until wilted before adding the next. When the water

returns to a boil, add the onion, cover, and simmer for 40 to 45 minutes or until the collards are very tender.

2. Meanwhile, prepare the topping: Pulse all ingredients briskly in a food processor until uniformly crumbly; set aside.

3. Drain the collard mixture in a large fine sieve and cool until easy to handle. Meanwhile, preheat the oven to 350° F. Also butter a shallow 2-quart flameproof casserole; set aside.

4. Press the collard mixture fairly dry in the sieve, then coarsely chop and place in a large bowl. Mix in the cream, salt, pepper, and beaten egg.

5. Scoop into the casserole, spreading to the edge, and cover snugly with foil. Slide onto the middle oven shelf and bake for 30 minutes. Remove the foil, scatter the reserved topping over the collards, then return to the oven and bake uncovered about 20 minutes longer or until golden. Meanwhile, preheat the broiler.

6. For the finishing touch, set the casserole in the broiler 10 inches from the heat and broil for 1 to 2 minutes or until tipped with brown.

7. Serve at once with baked ham or roast pork, turkey, or chicken.

❖

Only a Southerner knows how many collards
or how much turnip salad it takes
to make "a mess o' greens."

—ANONYMOUS

❖

1918 With the founding of the Albany District Pecan Exchange, Albany, Georgia, becomes "The Pecan Capital of the World."

Lee and Otis Mathis plant 500 acres of pecan trees near Paxton, Florida, making their grove the state's largest. They also develop the Eliot pecan—the sweetest and meatiest.

Arnaud's opens in New Orleans and gains fame for its French 75 cocktail (a potent mix of gin, Cointreau, champagne, and lemon juice named for a 75-mm French army gun).

To create national awareness for its roasted Virginia peanuts, Planters takes an ad in *The Saturday Evening Post.*

1919 The first loaves of bread come from the ovens of the Flowers Bakery in Thomasville, Georgia. Within 25 years, Flowers is baking the famous Sunbeam brand bread. Soft and as white as a magnolia blossom, it is just what Southerners love.

Prohibition begins and no southern city is more affected than New Orleans. Soon thousands of good citizens are brewing spirits at home and frequenting speakeasies where "a wink will get them a drink."

JAMES RIVER CORN PUDDING

. . . .

This recipe was given to me many years ago by James G. Harrison of Coggins Point Farm on the south side of the James River about halfway between Richmond and Williamsburg, Virginia. "People try to make a dessert of corn pudding," Mr. Harrison told me then. "You should never put sugar in corn pudding!" His wife, Maria, would prepare this recipe only when corn was young and sweet because its flavor depends on absolutely fresh corn.

2 tablespoons butter

2 tablespoons all-purpose flour

2 cups milk

2 large eggs, beaten until frothy

2 cups fresh whole-kernel sweet corn (4 small to medium ears)

½ teaspoon salt

¼ teaspoon black pepper

1. Preheat the oven to 400° F. Butter a 1½-quart casserole well and set aside.

2. Melt the butter in a medium-size saucepan over moderate heat, blend in the flour, then add the milk and cook, whisking constantly, for about 5 minutes or until thickened and smooth. Blend about 1 cup of the hot sauce into the eggs, stir back into the pan, and cook and stir 1 minute—do not

boil. Set off the heat and mix in the corn, salt, and pepper.

3. Pour the corn mixture into the casserole, set in a large shallow baking pan, and slide onto the middle oven rack. Pour enough hot water into the pan to come halfway up the sides of the casserole.

4. Bake the pudding uncovered for 40 to 45 minutes or until set like custard. Cool for 10 minutes, then serve as a vegetable. It's delicious with roast or fried chicken, also with Baked Virginia Ham (page 96).

MAQUE CHOUX

. . . .

The best time to make this Cajun classic is when sweet corn and tomatoes are in season, and the fresher the better. However, I make it off-season using canned tomatoes and flash-frozen corn, which is often sweeter than what I buy at my farmer's market. People often ask me what *maque choux* means. I wish that I had an easy answer. Some say that the word is American Indian and that it refers to the corn, pepper, and tomato stew they passed along to the Cajuns. On the other hand, John Folse writes in his *Encyclopedia of Cajun and Creole Cuisine* that *maque choux* derives from the Creole word for corn (*maque*) and the French word for cabbage (*choux*). Early Louisianans apparently did make *maque choux* with cabbage. Today chicken and shrimp are likelier additions, particularly among the Cajuns. I personally prefer this vegetable version.

4 tablespoons bacon drippings

1 large yellow onion, coarsely chopped

1 medium green bell pepper, cored,
seeded, and coarsely chopped

1 large garlic clove, finely chopped

4 cups fresh or solidly frozen
sweet corn kernels

½ cup water

3 large ripe tomatoes, peeled, cored,
and chopped or one 14.5-ounce can diced
tomatoes in sauce

½ teaspoon salt, or to taste

¼ teaspoon black pepper, or to taste

¼ teaspoon ground hot red pepper
(cayenne), or to taste

1. Heat the drippings in a large, heavy nonreactive skillet over moderately high heat for 1 minute. Add the onion and bell pepper and cook, stirring often, for 5 minutes. Add the garlic and cook and stir 3 to 5 minutes more or until limp and lightly browned.

2. Add the corn and water, stirring until the mixture boils. Adjust the heat so the liquid bubbles gently, cover, and cook for 10 to 15 minutes or until the corn no longer tastes raw.

3. Mix in all remaining ingredients and cook uncovered, stirring often, for 10 minutes or until the flavors mellow. Taste for salt, black pepper, and cayenne and adjust as needed.

4. Ladle into a heated vegetable dish and serve as an accompaniment to roast chicken or turkey, roast pork, or baked ham. Good, too, with boiled or grilled shrimp.

BUTTERMILK CORN CAKES

MAKES 4 SERVINGS

These are popular in many parts of the South both as breakfast food and as a potato substitute. If served at the start of the day, they're accompanied by sausage, country ham, or bacon and topped with sorghum molasses or maple syrup. If served as a lunch or dinner "side," they're more apt to come with melted butter or gravy. **Note:** *Small corn kernels work best here; I use either canned or frozen whole-kernel sweet corn.* **Tip:** *The best implement to use for apportioning the batter is a spring-loaded ice cream scoop. Mine holds a scant one-fourth cup and it's perfect.*

1 cup sifted all-purpose flour

1 tablespoon sugar

1 teaspoon baking powder

½ teaspoon baking soda

½ teaspoon salt

¼ teaspoon black pepper

¾ cup buttermilk

1 large egg

2 tablespoons corn oil, melted butter, or
bacon drippings

1¼ cups canned or thawed, frozen
whole-kernel corn, well drained
(see Note above)

1. Spritz a griddle or large heavy skillet well with nonstick cooking spray and set aside.

2. Combine the flour, sugar, baking powder, baking soda, salt, and pepper in a large mixing bowl and make a well in the center.

3. Whisk the buttermilk, egg, and oil in a small bowl until frothy and mix in the corn. Pour into the well in the dry ingredients and stir only enough to mix; the batter should be lumpy.

4. Set the griddle over moderately high heat for about 1 minute or until a drop of the batter sizzles. Using a scant 1/4 cup of batter for each corn cake (see Tip above), drop onto the griddle, spacing the cakes about 2 inches apart and spreading each until about 4 inches in diameter (an offset spatula spritzed with nonstick cooking spray is the gadget to use here).

5. Cook the corn cakes for about 2 minutes or until bubbles appear on the surface and these begin to break. Using a pancake turner that has been lightly coated with nonstick cooking spray, turn the pancakes and brown the flip sides for 2 to 2 1/2 minutes. As the corn cakes brown, transfer them to a heated plate.

6. Serve for breakfast with maple syrup, sorghum molasses, or, if having country ham, with red-eye gravy (see page 99). Or serve in place of potatoes and pass a little bowl of melted butter or gravy (pork and chicken gravy are best) so that everyone can help themselves.

❧

To this day, my favorite meal is fried chicken, field peas, green beans cooked all day with ham, fried okra, and corn bread.

—DEBORAH NORVILLE, GEORGIA NATIVE

❧

GRITS CASSEROLE

MAKES 6 TO 8 SERVINGS

Few non-Southerners can understand the Southerner's passion for grits. And I must confess that when I first tasted grits in my grammar school cafeteria, I didn't see what all the fuss was about. The little puddle of gruel spooned onto my plate tasted like nothing at all until a classmate told me to mix in some butter, salt, and pepper. Unfortunately, boiled grits is (yes, "grits" IS singular) the introduction most of us get, usually at breakfast where it's the classic accompaniment to eggs, country ham, and red-eye gravy. However, there are dozens of other ways to prepare grits, among them this superb casserole. Serve hot as a potato substitute with baked ham or roast pork, chicken, or turkey. Or serve as the main course of a light lunch or supper accompanied by a tartly dressed green salad and perhaps some sliced heirloom tomatoes.

4 cups (1 quart) milk

1/2 cup (1 stick) butter

1 teaspoon salt

1/4 teaspoon ground hot red pepper (cayenne)

1 cup grits (not instant)

1/3 cup butter, melted

1/4 cup freshly grated Parmesan cheese

1 cup finely grated sharp Cheddar cheese

1/4 teaspoon sweet paprika

1. Butter a 9 × 9 × 2-inch baking dish well and set aside.
2. Bring the milk, butter, salt, and cayenne to a boil in a large, heavy saucepan over moderate heat. Reduce the heat slightly, then add the grits very slowly, whisking hard.
3. Reduce the heat to its lowest point and continue whisking until the mixture is thick and smooth. Cover and simmer slowly for 20 minutes, stirring now and then to keep the grits from sticking to the pan and sliding a diffuser underneath the pan, if necessary.
4. Set off the heat and beat hard with a hand electric mixer for 2 to 3 minutes. Scoop the grits into the baking dish, spreading to the corners and smoothing the top. Chill for several hours until firm.
5. When ready to proceed, preheat the oven to 350° F. Also, butter a second 9 × 9 × 2-inch baking dish well and set aside.
6. Cut the hardened grits into strips ½ inch wide, dipping your knife frequently into tepid water to keep the grits from sticking. Now divide each strip into 4 dominos of equal size.
7. Arrange the dominos in rows in the baking dish, standing them on end and at an angle, domino-style—the rows will fit snugly in the pan. Drizzle the melted butter evenly over all, sprinkle with the Parmesan, then the Cheddar, and finally the paprika.
8. Bake uncovered on the middle oven shelf for 40 to 45 minutes or until bubbling and touched with brown. Serve at once.

❧

Only a Southerner knows that grits is singular.

—ANONYMOUS

❧

1919 Sid Weaver and George Ridenhour serve barbecue from a tent they've pitched across from the county courthouse in Lexington, North Carolina; soon Jess Swicegood pitches a barbecue tent of his own. Thus begins the tradition of "Lexington" or Western North Carolina barbecue. It differs from East Carolina's vinegary 'cue in two ways: Only pork shoulder is used and the sauce is redder and sweeter thanks to the addition of a little ketchup and sometimes a bit of sugar as well. Recipes, needless to add, remain deeply secret.

Atlanta banker Ernest Woodruff assembles a consortium of New York bankers and, in what would now be called a leveraged buyout, takes over the Coca-Cola Company. The amount paid to former owner Asa G. Candler: $25 million.

1920 Chicken farmer Arthur Perdue founds Perdue Farms in Salisbury, Maryland. That same year his only son, Frank, is born.

1921 When the boll weevil decimates their cotton crops, Georgia farmers begin planting peanuts. They soon become a major crop and remain so.

After disease attacks Georgia peaches, the U.S. Department of Agriculture sets up the Peach Research Station at Fort Valley, Georgia.

CREAMY GRITS WITH TASSO

MAKES 4 TO 6 SERVINGS

This is my adaptation of a delightful side dish dreamed up by John Fleer, the gifted chef at the Inn at Blackberry Farm in the Tennessee foothills. As a matter of fact, Fleer characterizes his elegant Appalachian cooking as "Foothills Cuisine." I featured him in an article I wrote some years ago for *Gourmet* and among Fleer's recipes that accompanied the article was a somewhat different version of these grits. **Note:** *This recipe calls for two distinctly southern specialties: stone-ground grits and tasso (richly spiced, cold-smoked, cured, pickled pork or beef). Neither is widely available but both can be ordered online (see Sources, page 401).*

I tablespoon butter

4 medium scallions, trimmed and finely chopped (include some green tops)

1½ cups chicken broth

½ cup stone-ground grits, preferably white (see Note above)

½ teaspoon salt, or to taste

¼ teaspoon black pepper, or to taste

½ cup water (about)

2 ounces tasso, cut into ¼-inch dice (see Note above)

¼ cup coarsely chopped red bell pepper

¼ cup coarsely chopped green bell pepper

2 tablespoons light cream or half-and-half

1. Melt the butter in a large, heavy saucepan over moderate heat, add the scallions, and cook, stirring often, for 3 to 5 minutes or until limp. Add the broth and bring to a boil.

2. Whisking constantly, add the grits, then the salt and pepper. Adjust the heat so the broth barely bubbles and cook the grits uncovered for 35 minutes, adding ¼ cup water each time the mixture threatens to cook dry.

3. While the grits cooks, brown the tasso in a small, heavy skillet over moderate heat for 3 to 5 minutes. Add the red and green bell peppers and cook for about 3 minutes or until crisp-tender. Set off the heat and reserve.

4. When the grits mixture is thick, blend in the cream and cook, stirring often, for 3 to 5 minutes or until steaming. Fold in the reserved tasso mixture.

5. Serve hot as an accompaniment to grilled or roast chicken, turkey, or pork. Good, too, with fried catfish.

GARLICKY CHEESE GRITS

MAKES 4 SERVINGS

This is my twist on an old southern classic. I've substituted quick-cooking grits for old-fashioned, added garlic (which few southern traditionalists would ever do), and substituted cayenne pepper for black because I like its bite. This dish partners well with roast chicken and grilled shrimp but to my mind, is too rich for anything fried. It can also be served as the centerpiece of a casual lunch or supper and needs nothing more than a green salad to accompany it.

2½ cups water mixed with ½ teaspoon salt (salted water)

⅔ cup quick-cooking grits

2 cups coarsely shredded sharp Cheddar cheese (about 8 ounces)

I medium garlic clove, crushed

¼ cup light cream

I tablespoon butter

⅛ to ¼ teaspoon ground hot red pepper (cayenne), depending upon how "hot" you like things

1. Bring the salted water to a boil in a medium-size heavy saucepan over high heat. Slowly add the grits, whisking all the while.
2. When the mixture returns to a boil, reduce the heat to moderately low and cook uncovered, whisking often, for 8 to 10 minutes or until thick. Mix in the cheese and garlic along with all remaining ingredients and cook 1 to 2 minutes, whisking now and then, or just until the cheese melts.
3. Dish up and serve.

A respectable Georgia breakfast means fish roe and grits or at least eggs or maybe country sausage.

—*CARSON McCULLERS,* ON HER GEORGIA CHILDHOOD

TO MAKE LYE HOMINY THE OLD-FASHIONED WAY

Take about a gallon of corn and 4 or 5 cups of wood ashes and boil until hulls and eyes will slip off. Wash in cold water until eyes, hulls, and ashes are removed. Boil until tender. Wash again and store until ready to use.

—Mrs. Mack Oliver, Iredell County, North Carolina

HOMINY SOUFFLÉ

MAKES 6 SERVINGS

Only a Southerner can understand the subtle semantics of grits and hominy and, to be perfectly honest, some Southerners are on shaky ground here. To me, hominy was always "big hominy," whole corn kernels puffed in a lye bath (in Mexico and the Southwest, it's known as *posole*). Yet in South Carolina, especially the Lowcountry, grits becomes hominy when cooked. This explains the recipe title above. My good friend Anne Mead, who grew up in Dillon, South Carolina, used to serve this lovely soufflé for Sunday brunch with fried country ham or sausage. I called it grits soufflé until Anne corrected me. "It's *hominy* soufflé," she said. "I *cook* the grits *before* I make the soufflé." What follows is my spin on Anne's recipe; it appears in *Please Kiss the Cook*, a little collection of family favorites that she printed some years ago. **Note:** *For this recipe, I prefer coarse, stone-ground yellow grits, never quick-cooking (see Sources, page 401). There's an old-fashioned country mill one county over and that's where I head whenever I'm out of stone-ground grits or cornmeal. I buy by the gunny sack and share with friends.* **Tip:** *My method of cooking grits is unorthodox, but it works for me. Instead of whisking the grits gradually into boiling water, I whisk a slow stream of boiling water into the grits.*

¾ **cup grits (see Note above)**

½ **teaspoon black pepper**

I **cup boiling water mixed with**
¾ **teaspoon salt**

2 **cups milk or I cup each**
milk and half-and-half

2 **tablespoons butter**

I **cup coarsely grated sharp Cheddar cheese**

4 **large eggs, separated**

1. Preheat the oven to 350° F.
2. Place the grits and pepper in the top of a medium-size double boiler and whisk in the boiling salted water. Set over simmering water and cook, whisking constantly, for about 5 minutes or until thick.
3. Remove from the heat and whisk in the milk. Set the double boiler top directly over moderately low heat and cook, whisking often, for

12 to 15 minutes or until the mixture is the consistency of thin porridge.
4. Transfer the grits mixture to a large bowl, add the butter and cheese, and whisk until both melt. Beat the egg yolks lightly, blend about 1 cup of the hot grits mixture into the eggs, then stir back into the bowl.
5. Whip the egg whites to soft peaks, fold about 1 cup of the beaten whites into the grits mixture to lighten it, then fold in the remaining whites gently but thoroughly until no streaks of white or yellow remain.
6. Pour the mixture into an ungreased 2½-quart soufflé dish, slide onto the middle oven shelf, and bake for 40 to 45 minutes or until puffed, browned, and the soufflé jiggles slightly when you nudge the dish.
7. Rush the soufflé to the table and serve as an accompaniment to roast meat, fowl, or fish. Or serve as the centerpiece of a Sunday brunch accompanied by fried country ham or sausages. **Note:** *If you opt for country ham, don't forget the red-eye gravy (see page 99).*

EGGPLANT PIE

MAKES 6 TO 8 SERVINGS

This recipe comes from my friend Janet Trent's mother-in-law, Amy Moore, who grew up on a twenty-acre farm near McClellanville, South Carolina, thirty miles upcountry from Charleston (her family's lived in the area since the early 1700s). Though the farm was small, there were field crops, a kitchen garden, cows, and chickens, which meant fresh produce, fresh milk, fresh butter and eggs, fresh poultry. Amy says that her way of cooking has changed little since her childhood: She uses whatever is fresh and available, measuring by eye and preparing enough "to make the table groan." Now the wife of a physician in Charlotte, North Carolina, Amy's known for being a good cook. Janet's husband, Dargan, says that growing up, he remembers his mother making many, many eggplant pies. Janet adds that she's watched Amy make eggplant pie countless times and that she does it "just a little differently from one time to the next." Janet has tried substituting fresh celery for celery salt and adding fresh onion, too, but "for whatever reason, Amy's eggplant pie always seems to be better than mine. Play around with it," Janet suggests. "I hope you enjoy it as much as our family does." What follows is my adaptation of Amy's original recipe.

4 large eggplants (about 4½ pounds), peeled and cut into 1-inch chunks

2 tablespoons salt

2 tablespoons butter

1 medium-large yellow onion, coarsely chopped

1 teaspoon celery salt

½ teaspoon onion salt

½ teaspoon black pepper

2 slices firm-textured whole-wheat bread, toasted and torn into small pieces

2 large eggs well beaten with ¼ cup evaporated milk and 1 tablespoon Worcestershire sauce

4 cups coarsely shredded sharp Cheddar cheese (about 12 ounces)

1. Spread the eggplant chunks one layer deep on four large rimmed baking sheets, sprinkle each pan of eggplant with 1½ teaspoons of the salt, toss well, spread again, and let stand for 30 minutes (this is to rid the eggplant of most of its liquid).

2. Take the eggplant up by handfuls, squeeze out as much liquid as possible, drop into a colander, and rinse very well under cool running water; you'll have to do this in small batches. Squeeze dry again, then spread on several thicknesses of paper toweling. When all of the eggplant has been spread on paper toweling, cover with more paper toweling and press down hard to extract as much remaining moisture as possible.

3. Preheat the oven to 350° F. Coat a 13 × 9 × 2-inch heatproof baking dish with nonstick cooking spray and set aside.

4. Melt the butter in a broad-bottomed Dutch oven over moderately high heat, add the onion, and sauté, stirring often, for 5 to 7 minutes until lightly browned. Add the eggplant and sauté, stirring often, for about 10 minutes or until touched with brown.

5. Mix in the celery salt, onion salt, and pepper, reduce the heat to low, cover, and cook for 20 to 25 minutes, stirring occasionally, until the eggplant is soft. If there is excess liquid in the pot, raise the heat to high and boil uncovered for 1 to 2 minutes, stirring often.

6. Set off the heat and mix in the toast, egg mixture, and half of the cheese. Scoop into the

prepared pan, spreading to the edge, and scatter the remaining cheese evenly on top.

7. Bake uncovered on the middle oven shelf for about 30 minutes or until bubbling and brown. Let the eggplant pie stand 15 to 20 minutes at room temperature before serving.

8. Serve as an accompaniment to baked ham or roast lamb, beef, turkey, or chicken.

BAKED PECAN-STUFFED MUSHROOMS

MAKES 6 SERVINGS

Southerners have a penchant for stuffing things—pork chops, tomatoes, bell peppers; you name it. But I am particularly partial to these pecan-stuffed mushrooms. They're delicious with roast beef or pork, turkey, or chicken. **Note:** *I often put these mushrooms out as cocktail hors d'oeuvre but cool them first so they're easy to handle. This recipe makes 3½ dozen bite-size hors d'oeuvre.*

3½ dozen (about 1 pound) uniformly small mushrooms (no more than 1½ inches across)

1 cup finely chopped pecans

2 ounces (¼ cup firmly packed) cream cheese, at room temperature

¼ cup finely chopped parsley

2 tablespoons freshly grated Parmesan cheese

1 medium garlic clove, crushed

1 teaspoon finely minced fresh lemon thyme or ¼ teaspoon crumbled dried leaf thyme

½ teaspoon salt

¼ teaspoon black pepper

⅓ cup half-and-half blended with ¼ cup heavy cream

1. Preheat the oven to 350° F. Remove the mushroom stems, wipe clean, chop fine, and reserve. Also wipe the mushroom caps clean and reserve.

2. Combine all remaining ingredients except the half-and-half mixture with the chopped mushroom stems, then pack firmly into the mushroom caps, mounding as needed.

3. Arrange the mushrooms one layer deep in an ungreased 13 × 9 × 2-inch baking pan, drizzle the half-and-half mixture over all, then cover the pan with aluminum foil.

4. Slide onto the middle oven rack and bake for 40 to 45 minutes or until the mushrooms are tender, basting once or twice with the cream in the pan.

5. Remove from the oven, baste once again with the cream, and serve hot as a vegetable. Or, if you prefer, cool to room temperature and serve as an hors d'oeuvre.

❧

From the Radley chicken yard tall pecan trees shook their fruit into the schoolyard, but the nuts lay untouched by the children: Radley pecans would kill you.

—HARPER LEE, TO KILL A MOCKINGBIRD

❧

OKRA

A cousin of both cotton and hibiscus, okra is indigenous to Central Africa, probably to Ethiopia. Unfortunately no records exist to tell us exactly where it originated, no documents to note its arrival in Europe or Asia.

What is certain, however, is that okra arrived in the American South with the slave trade in the seventeenth and eighteenth centuries. Some say New Orleans was the port of entry, even that the French—not the African slaves—introduced the finger-shaped pods still known there as *gumbo* or *gombo*.

I'm more inclined to believe culinary historian Karen Hess, who writes in *The Carolina Rice Kitchen: The African Connection (1992)* : "Gumbo, or *gombo* . . . refers to the patois of the French-speaking Africans of the Diaspora, particularly in Louisiana and the French West Indies . . ."

Elsewhere in the South, particularly in the Lowcountry, where okra also appeared early on, it is called just that, its name, according to African expert Jessica B. Harris, an Anglicization of *nkruma*—the word for okra in Twi, a Ghanese dialect.

After all these years, okra has never become popular above the Mason-Dixon or west of Louisiana, perhaps because the truly tender, the truly fresh is rarely available. But down south in the Land of Okra, its popularity has never waned.

There would be no gumbos without okra (it's used to thicken as well as to flavor), no Limpin' Susan (an okra pilau), no crispy fried rounds dredged in cornmeal.

OKRA PILAU

Often called "Limpin' Susan," this Lowcountry pilaf is best when made with fresh okra no bigger than your little finger. In researching the recipe, I was startled to discover that some people call red beans and rice "Limpin' Susan," also to note that Deep South cooks often add shrimp and tomatoes to this more familiar version. This old Lowcountry dish was created, I suspect, by a good plantation cook back when Carolina rice was king for she, better than anyone else, knew how to accentuate the crisp delicacy of okra and minimize the sliminess. She may have used chopped country ham in her pilau in place of bacon—by all means follow suit if you have it. Then use 2 tablespoons bacon drippings to cook the scallions and okra.

4 slices smoky bacon, cut crosswise into strips ½ inch wide

6 large scallions, trimmed and thinly sliced (include some green tops)

1 pound baby okra, stemmed and sliced about ½ inch thick, or 2 cups solidly frozen sliced okra

1 cup converted or long-grain rice, cooked by package directions

½ teaspoon salt, or to taste

½ teaspoon black pepper, or to taste

1. Cook the bacon in a large, heavy skillet for 10 to 12 minutes over moderate heat or until the drippings cook out, leaving only crisp brown bits; drain these on paper toweling.

2. Raise the heat to high, add the scallions and okra to the drippings, and cook for 4 to 5 minutes or until lightly browned; to minimize the sliminess, stir as little as possible.

3. Mix in the rice, salt, and pepper and heat 1 to 2 minutes or until the pilau reaches serving temperature. Add the bacon, toss lightly, then taste for salt and pepper and adjust as needed.

4. Serve hot as an accompaniment to roast chicken or pork, broiled or fried fish or shellfish.

AUNT BERTIE'S OKRA CAKES

MAKES 4 TO 6 SERVINGS

Bertie was my brother's sister-in-law. And from what my nieces, Linda and Kim, tell me, she was a wonderful southern cook. They still prepare okra Aunt Bertie's way. "You have to watch as you mix in the flour and the water," Kim cautions. "And mix just till the okra slices hold together." What my father called "the mucilaginous quality of okra" and what he hated about it is the glue that does the job here. "Slime's a good thing in this recipe," Kim says. But miracle of miracles, these okra cakes emerge from the skillet as crisp as can be.

I pound tender okra pods no bigger than your little finger, washed and sliced ⅛ inch thick

3 tablespoons all-purpose flour

3 to 4 tablespoons cold water

I teaspoon salt

½ teaspoon black pepper

I cup vegetable oil (for frying)

1. Place the okra in a large nonreactive bowl and add the flour, 3 tablespoons of the water, the salt, and pepper. Beat hard until the okra mixture hangs together when taken up on a spoon. If it seems dry, beat in the remaining tablespoon water. Set aside.

2. Pour the oil into a heavy, 12-inch nonreactive skillet and set over high heat for about 3 minutes or until almost smoking.

3. Drop the okra mixture from rounded tablespoons into the hot oil, spacing well apart and cooking only 4 or 5 cakes at a time. Brown for 2 to 3 minutes on each side or until crisp, then drain on paper toweling. Fry and drain the remaining okra cakes the same way.

4. Serve hot as an accompaniment to fried or roast chicken, pork chops or roast pork, or baked ham.

NEW SOUTH OKRA

MAKES 4 SERVINGS

My father used to say, "When I am president, no farmer will be allowed to grow okra and every farmer will be forced to grow one acre of sweet corn." He was kidding, of course. But it was no joke that he detested okra, not that my equally Midwestern mother had any desire to eat it either. So I grew up down south not eating okra and it was only when my thoroughly southern nieces taught me to cook it properly that I began to appreciate it. "This is how I do it all the time," my niece Kim told me recently. Her method is so simple and is equally delicious with grilled fish, chicken, or pork. And you know what? I think that my father might have liked it this way.

3 tablespoons fruity olive oil

12 ounces tender okra pods no bigger than your little finger, washed and patted dry on paper toweling

¼ teaspoon salt

⅛ teaspoon black pepper

1. Pour the olive oil into a heavy, 12-inch nonreactive skillet and set over high heat for about 2 minutes or until almost smoking.
2. Add the okra and cook at high heat, shaking the skillet often, for about 5 minutes or until the okra are evenly and richly browned; they will "sing" and "hiss" as they cook.
3. Cover the skillet, reduce the heat to moderate, and cook the okra for 3 minutes exactly.
4. Drain the okra on paper toweling, sprinkle with salt and pepper, and serve.

❈

Black-Eyed Peas with Ham Hock . . .
Fried Okra . . . Country Corn Bread . . .
Sweet Potato Pie . . . You talk of supping
with the gods.

—JAMES DICKEY, JERICHO

❈

1922 A large sugar refinery is built in Baltimore Harbor.

1923 Mose Lischkoff and Frank Mosher turn a sack of potatoes into kettle-fried chips. The place: the basement of a Hill's grocery in Birmingham, Alabama. The end result: Golden Flake Snack Foods, one of the South's biggest and best.

With moonshining big business in the mountains of Virginia, Franklin County near Roanoke is nicknamed "the wettest place in the U.S."

Chef Fred Schmidt creates the Hot Brown, an open-face turkey sandwich, at the Brown Hotel in Louisville, Kentucky.

Ernest Woodruff's son Robert is named president of Coca-Cola; he reigns for nearly 60 years and builds the company into a global conglomerate.

1924 Bob Melton builds a barbecue restaurant on a shady bank of the Tar River in Rocky Mount, North Carolina. Today, Melton's is synonymous with the best "East Carolina 'cue," meaning a peppery, vinegary sauce. Some 30 years later, *Life* magazine crowns Bob Melton "The King of Southern Barbecue."

OKRA-TOMATO TART

MAKES 6 SERVINGS

. . . .

What others call casseroles, Southerners often call tarts—this crumb-covered casserole, to name one. It teams three perennial favorites—okra, tomatoes, and bacon, in this case drippings—but adds a whiff of curry. Following the precedent set generations earlier by Country Captain (page 122)? Perhaps. Beaufort, South Carolina, whence this recipe comes, is less than an hour north of Savannah, where Country Captain is said to have been introduced by a sea captain. The recipe here is adapted from one that appeared in a favorite community cookbook of mine, *Full Moon, High Tide: Tastes and Traditions of the Lowcountry*, published by the Beaufort Academy in 2001. I find it perfect with fried chicken, roast chicken or pork, and baked ham. It's good, too, with boiled or broiled shrimp. **Note:** *Frugal southern cooks save bacon drippings to use in recipes.*

2 tablespoons bacon drippings or butter

6 large scallions, trimmed and thinly sliced (include some green tops)

I pound baby okra, trimmed and sliced about ¼ inch thick

Two 14.5-ounce cans diced or crushed tomatoes, with their liquid

I tablespoon sugar

Salt to taste

½ teaspoon crumbled dried leaf marjoram

½ teaspoon crumbled dried leaf basil

¼ teaspoon curry powder

¼ teaspoon hot red pepper sauce

Topping

1½ cups coarse soda cracker crumbs (you'll need about 30 two-inch-square crackers)

2 tablespoons grated Parmesan cheese

3 tablespoons butter, melted

1. Preheat the oven to 375° F. Lightly spritz a shallow 2½-quart casserole with nonstick cooking spray and set aside.

2. Heat the bacon drippings in a large, heavy skillet over moderately high heat 1 minute, add the scallions, and cook and stir 1 to 2 minutes or until wilted.

3. Add the okra and cook and stir 5 to 7 minutes or just until crisp-tender. Mix in the tomatoes and their liquid, the sugar, and all seasonings, then cook and stir for about a minute or just until the mixture boils.

4. Pour into the baking dish, spreading to the edge. Quickly combine all the topping ingredients and scatter evenly over the tomato mixture.

5. Bake on the middle oven shelf for 18 to 20 minutes or until bubbly and lightly browned.

6. Serve at once as a side dish.

❦

Only a Southerner knows that red-eye gravy is breakfast food and fried green tomatoes aren't.

—ANONYMOUS

❦

OKRA AND GREEN TOMATO FRITTERS

MAKES 6 SERVINGS

This is the recipe that made an okra convert of me. My niece Kim served it one Sunday and that was it. For extra flavor, substitute 1 to 2 tablespoons bacon drippings for the oil. Kim usually does.

¼ cup sifted all-purpose flour

¼ cup stone-ground cornmeal
(preferably white)

1½ teaspoons salt

½ teaspoon black pepper

4 baby okra (about 2 ounces), stemmed
and thinly sliced (⅓ to ½ cup)

1 small green tomato (about 4 ounces),
cored and coarsely chopped

4 large scallions, trimmed and
coarsely chopped
(include some green tops)

2 large eggs, lightly beaten

3 to 4 tablespoons corn oil or 2 tablespoons
corn oil and 1 to 2 tablespoons
bacon drippings

1. Combine the flour, cornmeal, salt, and pepper in a large bowl. Place the okra, green tomato, scallions, and eggs in a 2-quart measure and mix well. Pour the okra mixture into the flour mixture and stir only enough to combine—no matter if a few floury specks show.

1925 Tom Huston of Columbus, Georgia, invents a mechanical peanut sheller, then a roasting process, all because farmers are paying for his mechanical help in peanuts, not dollars.

Idaho native W. M. Davis buys a small Miami grocery. From that humble beginning, his heirs launch the Winn-Dixie chain of southern supermarkets through a series of mergers and acquisitions. Today, with more than 1,000 stores, Winn-Dixie is one of America's largest food retailers.

1926 Columbus, Georgia, inventor Tom Huston bags his shelled and roasted peanuts in cellophane tubes, then sells them as "Tom's Toasted Peanuts." And that is the start of Tom's Foods, today a producer of more than 300 different snacks and munchies.

The Mount Olive Pickle Company is founded in Mount Olive, North Carolina, and its "dills," "bread-and-butters," and relishes are soon number one in the South. (See Mount Olive Pickles, page 362.)

A hurricane wipes out Florida's Key lime industry and they're reduced to dooryard fruit.

2. Heat 3 tablespoons of the oil in a large, heavy skillet over high heat until ripples appear on the skillet bottom.

3. Drop the fritter batter from a tablespoon into the hot oil and brown 2 to 3 minutes on a side, adding the remaining oil, if necessary.

4. Drain the fritters quickly on paper toweling and serve as an accompaniment to baked ham, roast pork, or chicken. Good, too, with chicken, shrimp, or ham salad.

GRATIN OF VIDALIA ONIONS

MAKES 6 TO 8 SERVINGS

. . . .

The sweet Vidalia onions of Georgia are immensely versatile. Here, for example, I've taken four pounds of them and prepared them as the French might prepare leeks. The Vidalias, I think, are even better. This side dish partners perfectly with roast pork or chicken, not to mention the Thanksgiving turkey. Forget the traditional creamed onions and serve this gratin instead.

4 tablespoons (½ stick) butter

4 large Vidalia onions, halved lengthwise, then each half sliced ¼ inch thick (about 4 pounds)

3 tablespoons all-purpose flour

½ teaspoon salt, or to taste

¼ teaspoon black pepper, or to taste

¼ teaspoon crumbled leaf thyme

¼ teaspoon freshly grated nutmeg

1 cup half-and-half

½ cup chicken broth

¼ cup freshly grated Parmesan cheese

Topping

1½ cups moderately coarse soft bread crumbs

3 tablespoons freshly grated Parmesan cheese

2 tablespoons butter, melted

1. Preheat the oven to 375° F. Lightly butter a 2-quart gratin dish or shallow casserole and set aside.

2. Melt 2 tablespoons of the butter in a large, heavy skillet over moderately high heat, add the onions, and sauté for 10 to 12 minutes, stirring often, until soft. Transfer to the gratin dish.

3. Melt the remaining 2 tablespoons butter in the same skillet over moderate heat; blend in the flour, salt, pepper, thyme, and nutmeg and cook, whisking constantly, for 1 minute.

4. Combine the half-and-half and chicken broth, then slowly add to the skillet, whisking all the while. Continue whisking for 3 to 5 minutes or until thickened and smooth. Blend in the Parmesan, taste for salt and pepper, and adjust as needed. Pour the sauce over the onions, spreading to the edge.

5. Quickly make the topping by tossing all ingredients together. Scatter evenly on top of the sauce and onions.

6. Bake uncovered on the middle oven shelf for 20 to 25 minutes or until bubbling and tipped with brown.

7. Serve at once.

VIDALIA ONIONS

It was a freaky year for onions in Toombs County, Georgia, back in 1931. Farmer Mose Coleman's crop had no bite; in fact his big ivory-skinned onions were so sweet they were a hard sell at $3.50 per fifty-pound bag.

Over time, Georgians developed a taste for Toombs County sweet onions and when a farmer's market opened in the town of Vidalia in the '40s, appetites increased. Pretty soon these sugary jumbos—now named after the town—could be bought at the Piggly Wiggly.

I first tasted a Vidalia in the mid '70s in New York when a colleague who'd just received a box of them served them at a dinner party. We marveled at their crispness, their juiciness, but above all their sweetness. Our hostess sent each of us home with a few to try, and soon we were introducing these unique South Georgia onions to others. And writing about them, too.

By 1977, "America's Favorite Sweet Onion" was so popular the Vidalia town fathers decided to stage a festival to celebrate the spring harvest. It erupts every April with parades and fun for all. Thirteen years later, Georgia named the Vidalia the official state vegetable.

Today, thousands of South Georgia acres are devoted to growing Vidalias; indeed they account for 13 percent of the state's vegetable cash receipts. Most supermarkets sell them in season (April to December) but they can also be ordered farm-fresh (see Sources, page 401).

1926 Virginia ferry boat captain S. Wallace Edwards begins serving sandwiches on his Jamestown-Scotland run using his family's salt-cured, hickory-smoked country ham. The demand for that ham is soon so great that Edwards devotes full time to it. Today, Edwards hams are a Virginia classic.

1927 C. F. Sauer of Richmond, Virginia, becomes America's largest producer of spices and extracts.

Chef Henry Haussner, newly arrived from Germany, opens a restaurant in Baltimore. For more than 70 years it is where locals and visitors go for fine German food.

1928 Henrietta Dull, a home economist and "The First Lady of Georgia Cooking," writes *Mrs. Dull's Southern Cooking*, the twentieth century's first comprehensive southern cookbook.

Nashville's Cheek-Neal Coffee Company is bought by the Postum Company and the name is changed to Maxwell House Products Company. A year later the company has a new name: the General Foods Corporation.

SCALLOPED OYSTER PLANT

MAKES 4 SERVINGS

. . . .

Southerners have always doted upon salsify—or "oyster plant," as they prefer to call this mellow ivory-fleshed root—because its flavor reminds them of oysters. And no more so than when scalloped (creamed) and baked under a coverlet of buttered bread crumbs (to which I've added finely ground pecans). Serve with roast beef, veal, lamb, pork, turkey, or chicken. **Note:** *Salsify discolors the instant it's cut, so waste no time getting it into the acidulated water. It also grays if cooked in aluminum, so use a nonreactive pan. Don rubber gloves before working with salsify, then pitch them out when the job's done; if you don't, your hands will be covered with a sticky substance that soap and water won't remove.*

1 pound salsify, scrubbed, trimmed, peeled, and cut into 2-inch chunks (see Note above)

2 quarts cold water mixed with 2 tablespoons fresh lemon juice (acidulated water)

4 tablespoons (½ stick) butter

3 tablespoons all-purpose flour

½ teaspoon salt, or to taste

¼ teaspoon black pepper, or to taste

¼ teaspoon freshly grated nutmeg

¾ cup half-and-half or light cream

¾ cup milk

3 tablespoons grated Parmesan cheese

Topping

1 cup fine soft bread crumbs

⅓ cup finely ground pecans

1 tablespoon grated Parmesan cheese

2 tablespoons butter, melted

1. Preheat the oven to 375° F. Also butter a shallow 1-quart baking dish or gratin pan and set aside.

2. Place the salsify in a large nonreactive bowl, add the acidulated water, and soak for 20 minutes; this is to preserve the salsify's country-cream color.

3. Meanwhile, bring 1½ quarts of lightly salted water to boil in a large nonreactive saucepan. Drain the salsify, add to the boiling water, cover, and cook for about 20 minutes or until firm-tender. Drain well and slice ⅛ inch thick.

4. Meanwhile, melt the butter in a small, heavy saucepan over moderate heat. Blend in the flour, salt, pepper, and nutmeg and cook and stir for 2 to 3 minutes. Add the half-and-half and milk and cook, stirring constantly, for 3 to 5 minutes or until thickened and smooth. Add the Parmesan cheese and stir for a minute or two or until it melts. Taste the sauce for salt and pepper and adjust as needed.

5. Combine the sauce with the salsify and turn into the baking dish. Quickly mix all topping ingredients and scatter evenly over the salsify.

6. Slide the baking dish onto the middle oven shelf and bake uncovered for 30 to 35 minutes or until bubbling and brown.

7. Serve at once as an accompaniment to any roasted meat or fowl.

SPINACH MADELEINE

MAKES 6 SERVINGS

. . . .

Little did Madeline Nevill know that the recipe she created for her Junior League fund-raiser would become a Deep South classic. The year: 1959. The place: Baton Rouge, Louisiana. The cookbook: *River Road Recipes*, of which a *New York Times* reviewer wrote: "If there were community cookbook Academy Awards, the Oscar for best performance would go hands down to *River Road Recipes*." I interviewed Madeline several years ago while writing about "Little-Known Louisiana" for *Gourmet*, never dreaming that she was the Madeline of Spinach Madeleine; the names are spelled differently. I began my trip in "English Louisiana," staying for three days at Madeline's stylish Green Springs bed-and-breakfast just north of St. Francisville. After breakfast one morning, she told me that her guests all urged her to come up with a breakfast version of Spinach Madeleine. "I tried, but nothing was as good as the original," she said, adding that that recipe was something she'd just hit upon nearly fifty years earlier. As for the disparity in the spelling of the name, the very English *Madeline* confessed that she'd chosen the French *Madeleine* "because it sounded more gourmet-ish." **Note:** *One of the key ingredients in the original recipe—a six-ounce roll of jalapeño cheese—is rarely available today, so I've reworked the recipe using current supermarket staples. I've also trimmed the fat for the calorie and cholesterol-conscious.* **Tip:** *This recipe can be prepared in advance through Step 5, covered and refrigerated until about an hour before serving. If you do so, increase the overall baking time by 10 to 15 minutes.*

Two 10-ounce packages frozen chopped spinach (no need to thaw)

2 tablespoons butter

2 tablespoons finely chopped yellow onion

1 medium garlic clove, finely chopped

2 tablespoons all-purpose flour

½ cup spinach cooking water

½ cup evaporated milk
(use fat-free, if you like)

1 teaspoon Worcestershire sauce

¾ teaspoon celery salt

¼ teaspoon salt

¼ teaspoon hot red pepper sauce

6 ounces sharp Cheddar cheese, cut into small dice

2 to 3 tablespoons well-drained canned diced jalapeño peppers (depending on how "hot" you like things)

1½ cups soft white bread crumbs tossed with 2 tablespoons butter, melted (topping)

1. Preheat the oven to 350° F. Coat a shallow 2-quart casserole with nonstick cooking spray and set aside.

2. Cook the spinach by package directions, but do not salt the cooking water and do not season the spinach. Drain in a large fine sieve set over a large bowl, then press out as much water as possible. Reserve ½ cup of the spinach cooking water, rounding out the measure, if necessary, with tap water.

3. Melt the butter in a medium-size heavy saucepan over moderate heat, add the onion and garlic, and sauté, stirring often, for 2 to 3

minutes or until limp and golden. Blend in the flour and cook and stir for about a minute.

4. Combine the spinach cooking water, evaporated milk, Worcestershire sauce, celery salt, salt, and hot pepper sauce in a large measuring cup; pour into the saucepan and cook, whisking constantly, for 3 to 5 minutes or until thickened and smooth. Add the cheese, a few pieces at a time, then the jalapeños and cook, stirring often, until the cheese melts. Do not allow the mixture to boil because the cheese may "string." Mix in the reserved spinach.

5. Scoop into the casserole, smoothing to the edge, and sprinkle the topping evenly over all.

6. Slide onto the middle oven shelf and bake uncovered for 35 to 40 minutes or until bubbly and richly browned.

7. Remove from the oven, let stand 5 minutes, then serve as an accompaniment to roast pork, turkey, or chicken. Good, too, with baked ham.

SWEET POTATOES

The New World potatoes Columbus introduced to Spain around 1500 were sweet potatoes (*Ipomoea batatas*) and by the middle of the sixteenth century, species of various hue were being grown there: red, purple, and white.

Food historians believe that the Spaniards also carried sweet potatoes to the East Indies and Philippines and that the Portuguese ferried them from there to China, India, and Malaya. The Belgians, we're told, were attempting to grow sweet potatoes by the end of the sixteenth century; so, too, herbalist John Gerard of London. Neither had much luck.

According to Albert F. Hill, for years a professor of economic botany at Harvard, "The sweet potato requires a sandy soil and a warm, moist climate." Which explains why it grows so well in the South. And why Southerners are so partial to it. For years they've been stirring sweet potatoes into everything from soups to salads to breads to pies.

As the nation's number-one producer of sweet potatoes, North Carolina stages a "Yam Festival" every October in the little town of Tabor City with parades, cook-offs, contests, and coronations. "Yam" is of course a misnomer, for true yams (genus *Dioscorea*) are wholly unrelated to the sweet potato and in fact are not very sweet.

Louisiana, another top producer of sweet potatoes, is best known for the sweet-as-candy, vermillion-fleshed Beauregard, which was developed there in 1987 and quickly became the trendy chef's darling. It still is.

In Colonial times, doctors prescribed sweet potatoes to children, believing that they could prevent measles, mumps, whooping cough, and other childhood diseases. Perhaps they were onto something. We now know that sweet potatoes are an exceptional source of beta carotene, the precursor of vitamin A, and that they also contain impressive amounts of vitamin C plus a respectable dose of vitamin E. Moreover, they are fiber-rich but fat- and cholesterol-free.

Small wonder they've been called "nature's health food."

SWEET POTATO CASSEROLE

MAKES 6 TO 8 SERVINGS

I particularly like this sweet potato casserole because it isn't candy-sweet—no marshmallows, no canned crushed pineapple, no honey, and not very much sugar. I don't boil the sweet potatoes before I mash them; I bake them so they're less watery and have better flavor. Here's how: Pierce each sweet potato with a sharp-pronged kitchen fork, set on a baking sheet, then bake on the middle oven shelf for about 1 hour at 400° F. or until you can pierce a potato easily with a fork. Cool the potatoes to room temperature, peel, then mash until light and fluffy.

3 cups firmly packed unseasoned mashed sweet potatoes (about 3 pounds) (see headnote)

½ cup firmly packed light brown sugar

½ cup fresh orange juice

4 tablespoons (½ stick) butter, melted

2 tablespoons fresh lemon juice

2 teaspoons finely grated orange zest

½ teaspoon freshly grated nutmeg or ¼ teaspoon ground nutmeg

¼ teaspoon ground cinnamon

¼ teaspoon ground ginger

¼ teaspoon salt, or to taste

¼ teaspoon black pepper, or to taste

1. Preheat the oven to 350° F. Butter a 2-quart casserole and set aside.

2. Combine all ingredients in a large mixing bowl, beating until smooth. Taste for salt and pepper and adjust as needed

3. Scoop into the casserole, spreading to the edge and roughing the surface. Bake uncovered on the middle oven shelf for about 45 minutes or until tipped with brown.

4. Serve hot as an accompaniment to roast turkey, chicken, or pork. Good, too, with pork chops.

SCALLOPED ORANGE AND WHITE POTATOES

MAKES 6 TO 8 SERVINGS

Southerners dote upon scalloped vegetables—scalloped oyster plant (salsify), scalloped tomatoes, and of course everyone's favorite, scalloped potatoes. I've added my own twist here: a mix of sweet and Irish potatoes (bakers or russets) heightened with garlic, fresh bay leaves, and lemon thyme. This is a great make-ahead, so it's ideal for a dinner party. Serve with baked ham or any roasted meat or fowl. **Note:** *Fresh edible bay leaves (bay laurel) are the ones to use here because only they have the proper lemony-gingery fragrance. Luckily, many farmer's markets sell little pots of bay laurel, as do a few specialty groceries. Just make sure what you buy is edible. Bay laurel makes an attractive house plant and all you need is a sunny spot. I keep a little bay laurel tree in the garden window over my sink and it's thriving thanks to the southern exposure. I also kept one on my New York City windowsill for years; that, too, was "south light."* **Tip:** *You can prepare this recipe through Step 3 a day ahead of time; cover with foil and refrigerate. Before* *baking, set the casserole on the counter, remove the foil, and let stand for about half an hour.*

I tablespoon bacon drippings
or vegetable oil

2 large whole garlic cloves, finely
chopped

1½ teaspoons finely chopped fresh lemon
thyme or I teaspoon dried leaf thyme,
crumbled

2 tablespoons all-purpose flour

2 cups light cream or half-and-half

I teaspoon salt

½ teaspoon black pepper

4 large fresh bay leaves, bruised
(see Note on page 211)

3 medium baking potatoes
(about 1½ pounds), peeled and
thinly sliced

I large sweet potato (about I pound),
peeled and thinly sliced

2 tablespoons butter, cut into
small dice

1. Preheat the oven to 425° F. Spritz a shallow 2-quart casserole or gratin dish with nonstick cooking spray and set aside.

2. Heat the bacon drippings in a small, heavy saucepan over moderate heat for 1 minute, add the garlic and lemon thyme, and cook, stirring often, for 3 to 5 minutes or just until the garlic softens. Blend in the flour and cook and stir 1 minute more. Whisking hard, add the cream, salt, and pepper. Drop in the bay leaves and cook, whisking constantly, for 3 to 5 minutes or until the sauce is thickened and smooth.

3. Place the baking and sweet potatoes in the casserole and toss well to mix. Pour in the hot sauce and push the bay leaves down into the potatoes, distributing them evenly. Shake the casserole gently to level the sauce and potatoes, then dot with butter (see Tip above).

4. Slide the casserole onto the middle oven shelf and bake uncovered for about 40 minutes or until the potatoes are crusty-brown on top and tender underneath.

5. Remove the casserole from the oven, discard the bay leaves, and serve.

RICE

In tropical countries rice replaces all other cereals as the staff of life . . .
—Albert F. Hill, Economic Botany (1952)

In this esteemed textbook, Harvard professor Albert Hill also noted that rice originated somewhere in Southeast Asia and that its cultivation began in the dimmest past. The Chinese were growing rice more than 4,000 years ago and there are records to prove it. Indeed, in classical Chinese, Hill pointed out, the words for *rice culture* and *agriculture* are synonymous. And in other languages "the word for *rice* and the word for *food* are identical."

How rice reached these shores is a journey both long and circuitous. From China, rice entered India before the rise of Greek civilization. It appeared in Syria and North Africa early on, too (about 1500 BC), but it wasn't grown in Europe (Italy) until 1408—forty-three years before Columbus was born.

Although Columbus introduced a number of Old World foods to the New World, rice was not one of them. Its time and place of arrival here are well documented.

Charleston Receipts (1950), to my mind the gold standard for community cookbooks because it's intensely local, devotes a special section to rice and in it tells how the grain first came to South Carolina "around 1685" aboard a ship out of Madagascar (Botanist Hill agrees that rice arrived via Madagascar but puts the date a year earlier).

The ship's captain befriended Dr. Henry Woodward, a Charles Towne pillar, and gave him "a small quantity of rice, less than a bushel." Thanks to the Lowcountry's optimal growing conditions, that rice, once planted, flourished for more than 200 years. But it was another strain introduced somewhat later that became world famous as "Carolina Gold." Or so some food historians believe.

In *The Carolina Rice Kitchen: The African Connection*, Karen Hess chronicles in painstaking detail the culinary importance of rice and traces the evolution of such southern classics as jambalaya, hoppin' John, and pilau (pronounced *purloo* or *purloe* in the Lowcountry). Most were slave dishes, created by the Africans who had been imported to plant, tend, harvest, and mill the rice grown in South Carolina, Georgia, Louisiana, and elsewhere about the Deep South.

"As one views this vast hydraulic work," David Doar writes in his description of a rice plantation in *Rice and Rice Planting in the South Carolina Low Country* (1936), "[one] is amazed to learn that all of this was accomplished in the face of seemingly insuperable difficulties by every-day planters who had as tools only the axe, the spade, and the hoe, in the hands of intractable negro men and women, but lately brought from the jungles of Africa."

Most came from West Africa's Windward Coast, where the cultivation of rice had long been known, and those in greatest demand were from the River Gambia and Gold Coast. One July day in 1785, Charleston's *Evening Gazette* reported the arrival of "a choice cargo of wind-ward and gold coast negroes, who have been accustomed to the planting of rice."

Some fifteen years earlier, Eliza Lucas Pinckney, mistress of more than one Lowcountry rice plantation, sent a bag of her best "Carolina Gold" to her sons' headmaster in England together with a note explaining that South Carolinians liked rice with their meat "in preference to bread."

The Civil War decimated the rice crop, and the subsequent freeing of slaves marked the beginning of the end. Around the turn of the twentieth century, rice was being replaced by more lucrative, less labor-intensive crops. The last crop of Carolina Gold, we're told, was harvested near Charleston in 1935.

Today Carolina Gold is staging a comeback among "boutique farmers" in the South Carolina Lowcountry. And thanks to new disease-resistant strains, long-grain rice is once again a major crop in Louisiana and Mississippi, this country's third and fourth largest producers after Arkansas and California.

In truth, much of the California rice crop is short-grain—good for risotto, maybe, but not for the fluffy boiled and steamed rices, the purloos and hoppin' Johns so essential to the southern table.

LOWCOUNTRY RED RICE

MAKES 4 TO 6 SERVINGS

You might call this a tomato pilaf; indeed it almost has the consistency of risotto even though it's made with long-grain rice, not the short-grain variety preferred for risottos. Some cooks add no onion to red rice, but I think it improves the flavor of this humble dish. If tomatoes are in season and bursting with flavor, by all means substitute two medium tomatoes (or one large) for the canned crushed tomatoes. Peel them, core them, seed them, and chop as fine as possible. Serve red rice in place of potatoes; you'll find it especially good with roast pork, chicken, or turkey. **Note:** *There's good reason to add the tomatoes at the end: Being acidic, they will toughen the rice if cooked along with it.* **Tip:** *Don't rush the browning of the bacon; if you keep the heat low and let the drippings accumulate slowly, the bacon is less likely to burn.*

5 slices smoky lean bacon, cut crosswise into strips ¼ inch wide

1 medium yellow onion, coarsely chopped

1 cup long-grain rice

2 cups chicken broth

1 cup canned crushed tomatoes (see headnote)

½ teaspoon salt, or to taste

¼ teaspoon black pepper, or to taste

1. Fry the bacon in a large, heavy saucepan over moderately low heat for about 15 minutes or until the drippings cook out and only crisp brown bits remain. Scoop the browned bits to paper toweling and reserve.

2. Add the onion to the pan, then cook and stir in the drippings for 3 to 5 minutes or until lightly browned. Add the rice, and cook and stir for about a minute until it glistens.

3. Pour in the chicken broth, bring to a boil, adjust the heat so that the liquid barely bubbles, then cover and cook for about 15 minutes or until all the liquid is absorbed and the rice is tender.

4. Mix in the crushed tomatoes, salt, and pepper, and cook uncovered for about 5 minutes or until almost all the liquid has been absorbed. Taste for salt and pepper and adjust as needed.

5. Scoop the rice into a heated serving dish, sprinkle with the reserved bacon, and serve. **Note:** *I often mix in the bacon before I dish up the rice so that its smoky-meaty flavor has a chance to permeate.*

HOPPIN' JOHN

MAKES ABOUT 6 SERVINGS

According to Karen Hess in *The Carolina Rice Kitchen: The African Connection* (1992), "Hoppin' John is one African-American dish that made it to the Big House." She adds that the appearance of this cowpea pilau in Sarah Rutledge's *Carolina Housewife* (1847) seemed to indicate "that the old slave dish had been accepted by some of the most aristocratic elements of the Lowcountry." As for the recipe's unusual name, Hess dismisses what she calls the current "pop etymology." Her own theory, developed after prodigious research, suggests that Hoppin' John descends from *bahatta k-chang*, *bahatta* being a Persian word for "cooked rice," and *k-chang* a Malay word for various legumes. Hess further believes that the recipe for Hoppin' John may have arrived in Africa via Madagascar and that it was carried there by Muslims before making its cross-continental journey to Gambia and elsewhere along the west coast of Africa, which was to become a major rice-growing region. "My construction is logical," she writes. "*Bahatta k-chang* and Hoppin' John both designate rice and peas, products indigenous to Asian and African tropics."

The recipe here was given to me many years ago by Mary Sheppard, the plantation cook at Middleton Place near Charleston. Although Mary's Hoppin' John was made with dried cowpeas, she told me that black-eyed peas are perfectly acceptable. In fact the Hoppin' John served every New Year's Day at the old Sir Walter Hotel in downtown Raleigh, North Carolina, always contained black-eyed peas. "Hoppin' John's supposed to be good luck," Mary Sheppard told me the day I interviewed her for *Family Circle*. "You eat it with green s [turnip salad or collards]. They're 'sposed to be good luck, too." **Note:** *Some people cook the rice along with the cowpeas. But Mary Sheppard always cooked the two separately and combined them just before serving.*

I cup dried cowpeas or black-eyed peas, washed and sorted but not soaked

4 ounces hickory-smoked slab bacon, cut into ½-inch dice

1928 Claud A. Hatcher changes the name of his Georgia soft drink firm from the Chero-Cola Company to the Nehi Corporation and soon Nehi beverages are sold all over the South.

C. F. Sauer of Richmond, Virginia, acquires Duke's Mayonnaise but continues using its plant in Greenville, South Carolina.

Emmett Montgomery opens a hot dog stand in Irondale, Alabama, near Birmingham. Over time, it becomes the Irondale Café and is later immortalized as the Whistlestop Café by actress-playwright Fannie Flagg in her movie *Fried Green Tomatoes*.

The U.S. Sugar Corporation opens a modern refinery in Clewiston, Florida.

1929 Brothers Benny and Clovis Martin, both former New Orleans streetcar conductors and now owners of a little French Market restaurant, make sandwiches out of leftovers for striking streetcar workers. A nickel, it's said, would buy one of these "poor boys" a hefty sandwich of beef trimmings, potatoes, and gravy (today's po'boys are usually filled with fried oysters). Although Madame Hypolite Bégué (Elizabeth Kettering) is also said to have created the po'boy in the late nineteenth century, most culinary historians credit the Martins. But there's discrepancy about the date. Some say 1922, not 1929.

2½ cups water

1 teaspoon salt, or to taste

⅛ teaspoon ground hot red pepper
(cayenne), or to taste

⅛ teaspoon black pepper, or to taste

1¼ cups long-grain rice, cooked by package
directions

1. Bring the cowpeas, bacon, and water to a boil in a large, heavy saucepan over moderate heat. Reduce the heat so the water bubbles gently, cover, and simmer for 40 to 45 minutes or just until the peas are firm-tender; drain well.

2. Season the peas with salt, cayenne, and black pepper. Add the rice and toss gently. Taste for salt, cayenne, and black pepper and adjust as needed.

3. Serve hot; this is particularly good with roast pork, braised pork chops, or baked ham.

YELLOW SQUASH PUDDING

MAKES 4 TO 6 SERVINGS

Until the late 1950s, or perhaps early '60s, there was a delightful tea room in Raleigh, North Carolina, called the Reinlyn House. Run by two elderly women (sisters, if memory serves), it was located on Hillsboro Street in a Charles Addams–style Victorian near the State Capitol. That proud old house, like so many others in Raleigh, succumbed to the wrecking ball, and although the tea room relocated to a small strip mall just off Glenwood Avenue, it didn't survive.

The one Reinlyn recipe that I've remembered all these years is the yellow squash pudding, which I've tried to duplicate here. The secret, I discovered, is slow, slow cooking so that the onions and squash actually caramelize. Despite its time on the stovetop and in the oven, this squash pudding requires very little attention. **Note:** *Before I had a food processor, I chopped the squash by hand. Now I chunk it and processor-chop in four batches, pulsing each to just the right texture. I also processor-chop the onion.*

3 tablespoons butter

1 large yellow onion, coarsely chopped

1 teaspoon crumbled dried leaf marjoram

½ teaspoon crumbled dried leaf thyme

¼ teaspoon freshly grated nutmeg

12 tender young yellow squash
(about 2½ pounds),
trimmed and coarsely chopped

¾ teaspoon salt

½ teaspoon black pepper

¾ cup soda cracker crumbs (not too fine)
mixed with 2 tablespoons melted butter
(topping)

1. Lightly butter a shallow 2-quart flameproof casserole and set aside.

2. Melt the butter in a large, heavy saucepan over moderately high heat. Add the onion, marjoram, thyme, and nutmeg; reduce the heat to moderate, and sauté for about 10 minutes, stirring now and then, until the onion is lightly browned.

3. Mix in the squash, salt, and pepper, then cover and cook for 40 to 45 minutes until the squash is very soft, stirring now and then. Toward the end of cooking, preheat the oven to 350° F. **Note:** *If the squash threatens to boil dry—not likely if you keep the heat at moderate or moderately low—add about 1/4 cup water.*

4. Scoop the squash mixture into the prepared casserole, spreading to the edge, and bake uncovered on the middle oven shelf for 30 minutes. Stir well, scatter the topping evenly over all, then bake 30 minutes longer or until the topping is touched with brown. **Note:** *If the topping is not brown enough to suit you, slide the casserole into the broiler, setting about 5 inches from the heat, and broil 1 to 2 minutes.*

5. Serve hot with fried chicken or roast pork, turkey, or chicken. Delicious, too, with baked ham.

BAKED STUFFED YELLOW SQUASH

MAKES 6 SERVINGS

. . . .

Among the vegetables Southerners love to stuff, yellow squash are at the top of the list. Some cooks like to mix sausage, ham, or hamburger into their squash stuffing, but I prefer this meatless one. **Note:** *Only straight-neck yellow squash will do here. Bypass any squash languishing at your supermarket and choose tender young ones at your farmer's market.*

3 medium straight-neck yellow squash
(1 to 1½ pounds), trimmed and scrubbed
(see Note above)

1½ cups coarse soda cracker crumbs

½ cup freshly grated Parmesan cheese

3 tablespoons finely grated yellow onion

1 tablespoon minced parsley

1 teaspoon finely chopped fresh thyme or
½ teaspoon crumbled leaf thyme

½ teaspoon salt

¼ teaspoon black pepper

¼ teaspoon freshly grated nutmeg

1 large egg, lightly beaten

1½ tablespoons butter, cut
into small dice

1. Preheat the oven to 350° F. Spritz a 13 × 9 × 2-inch baking pan with nonstick cooking spray and set aside.

2. Place the squash in a large, heavy saucepan, add enough cold water to cover by 1 inch, set over moderately high heat, and bring to a boil. Cover the pan and boil for 5 minutes. Drain the squash and when cool enough to handle, halve lengthwise, then scoop out the centers, leaving shells about 1/4 inch thick. Chop and reserve the scooped-out squash.

3. Place the crumbs, 1/4 cup of the cheese, the onion, parsley, thyme, salt, pepper, and nutmeg in a large bowl and toss well. Mix in the egg and chopped squash.

4. Stuff the crumb mixture into the squash shells, mounding it up in the middle. Dot each stuffed squash with butter, dividing the total amount evenly, then sprinkle with the remaining 1/4 cup cheese.

5. Arrange the squash, not touching, in the baking pan, and bake uncovered on the middle oven rack for 25 to 30 minutes or until tipped with brown.

6. Serve at once as an accompaniment to roast pork, turkey, or chicken. Good, too, with baked ham.

BRAISED CYMLINGS

MAKES 4 TO 6 SERVINGS

I first tasted these braised cymlings (Southerners call them "fried") at the home of a grade school chum and adored them at first bite. Known elsewhere as pattypan squash, cymlings are staging a comeback after years in eclipse. Boutique farmers, moreover, are growing them in a variety of colors—white, yellow, green-and-yellow-striped, as well as the more familiar celadon. I still like them prepared this way and find them the ideal accompaniment for roast pork, turkey, or chicken.

2 ounces salt pork or slab bacon, cut into small dice

8 small young cymlings measuring 3 to 3½ inches across (about 2¼ pounds), peeled and cut into sixths

1 small yellow onion, minced

Salt and black pepper, to taste

1. Fry the salt pork slowly in a large, heavy skillet over moderately low heat for 5 to 7 minutes or until most of the fat cooks out and only crisp brown bits remain. Spoon off most of the drippings but leave the bacon in the skillet.

2. Add the cymlings and onion, cover, and cook, turning now and then in the drippings, for 8 to 10 minutes or until tender.

3. Season with salt and pepper and serve.

SCALLOPED TOMATOES

MAKES 4 TO 6 SERVINGS

Back in the 1970s when I began writing a food series for *Family Circle* magazine called "America's Great Grass Roots Cooks," the first person I profiled was a North Carolina farm woman in Rockingham County. From my growing-up years in the Tar Heel State, I knew that I'd find there just the person to kick off the series. And so I did: Mrs. Oscar McCollum, who lived just outside the county seat of Reidsville. Of this dish she said, "This is a real old recipe. One I grew up on. I put up my own tomatoes, so I use them. But you could use store-bought."

3 cups home-canned or store-bought tomatoes with their liquid

4 tablespoons (½ stick) lightly salted butter

3 cups moderately coarse stale white bread crumbs (not dry crumbs)

3 tablespoons sugar

1 teaspoon salt

¼ teaspoon black pepper

¼ teaspoon ground allspice

1. Preheat the oven to 400° F. Butter a 9 × 9 × 2-inch baking dish and set aside.

2. Heat the tomatoes and butter in a large non-reactive saucepan over moderate heat just until the butter melts. Mix in the crumbs, sugar, salt, and pepper.

3. Turn into the prepared baking dish and sprinkle lightly with the allspice.

4. Bake uncovered on the middle oven shelf for 40 to 45 minutes or until lightly browned. Let stand at room temperature about 5 minutes before serving.

❊

Soft as butter in August.

—OLD NORTH CAROLINA SAYING

❊

❊

His wife, Regina, lived out her life here, much beloved by the Kitchen Gang, of which she was a baking, frying, slicing, dicing bonafide member.

—ANNE RICE, *BLACKWOOD FARM*

❊

1930   Planters of Suffolk, Virginia, introduces peanut cooking oil.

Time magazine profiles Tom Huston of Columbus, Georgia, as "The Farmer Boy Who Became Peanut King." He had founded Tom's Foods four years earlier.

The chestnut blight has reduced southern chestnut forests to skeletons, destroying an important source of food.

Warner Stamey, a high schooler who'd worked at Jess Swicegood's Lexington Barbecue, opens a place of his own in Shelby, North Carolina, modeling everything after Swicegood's—right down to the sawdust on the floor.

George W. Jenkins opens the first Publix grocery in Winter Haven, Florida. Today there are nearly 1,000 employee-owned Publix supermarkets scattered across the South.

1930s   The Brock Candy Company of Chattanooga creates a new Christmas favorite: chocolate-covered cherries.

Harland Sanders opens a restaurant in Corbin, Kentucky. The house specialty: fried chicken "battered" with a secret blend of herbs and spices. (See Colonel Harland Sanders, page 114.)

FRIED GREEN TOMATOES

MAKES 4 TO 6 SERVINGS

. . . .

Every southern cook has a pet recipe for fried green tomatoes and this one is an amalgam I've evolved over the years. What gives these tomatoes especially good flavor is the flour-and-cornmeal combo used to dredge them, also the addition of bacon drippings to the frying oil. Two of my favorite appetizers, Black-Eyed Pea Hummus (page 35) and Shrimp Rémoulade (page 8), call for fried green tomatoes—and you won't go wrong using this recipe. **Note:** *I find the granular yellow "supermarket" cornmeal too gritty for dredging the tomatoes, so if the stone-ground is unavailable, simply double the amount of flour below.*

6 hard green tomatoes, each measuring 2 to 2½ inches across

1 extra-large egg

1 teaspoon salt

1 teaspoon black pepper

1 cup fine dry bread crumbs

½ cup unsifted all-purpose flour

½ cup unsifted stone-ground yellow cornmeal

¼ cup vegetable oil plus 2 tablespoons bacon drippings, or 6 tablespoons vegetable oil (for frying)

1. Without coring or peeling the tomatoes, slice them ³⁄₈ inch thick; discard the end pieces and spread the slices on paper toweling while you proceed with the recipe.

2. Whisk the egg until frothy in a small bowl with ½ teaspoon each of the salt and pepper; set aside.

3. Combine the bread crumbs with another ¼ teaspoon each of the salt and pepper in a pie pan and set aside. Next, combine the flour, cornmeal, and remaining salt and pepper in a second pie pan and set aside also.

4. Dredge each tomato slice in the flour-cornmeal combo, then dip into the egg mixture, then coat with the bread crumbs, shaking off the excess. Air-dry the breaded slices on a wire rack for 15 to 20 minutes. This helps the breading stick to the tomatoes.

5. Place the oil and bacon drippings in a large, heavy iron skillet and set it over moderately high heat for about 2 minutes. When a cube of bread sizzles when dropped into the hot oil, begin frying the green tomatoes, allowing 1 to 1½ minutes for each side to brown. As the tomatoes brown, lift to paper toweling to drain.

6. Serve hot as a vegetable. Or use as other recipes direct.

❀

"That reminds me, whatever you do, Kate . . . take that fresh Lady Baltimore cake out to the house . . . And make Rachel hunt through the shelves for some more green tomato pickle."

—EUDORA WELTY, *KIN*

❀

CORN BREAD DRESSING WITH PECANS AND BACON

MAKES 12 TO 14 SERVINGS, ENOUGH TO
STUFF A 12- TO 15-POUND TURKEY

. . . .

Many corn bread dressings are made with sausage, but because those dressings tend to be greasy, I prefer a good lean bacon cooked until crisp and brown. This dressing is fairly light—not too moist, not too dry. I always bake it separately because I think this method safer. If you want to stuff the bird, do so just before you shove it into the oven. Spoon the dressing lightly into the body and neck cavities, then truss the bird. If there's extra dressing—and there usually is—bundle it in aluminum foil and bake 30 to 35 minutes at 350° F.

It's important to make the corn bread a day or two before you use it. I split it horizontally, spread it on a baking sheet, and let stand at room temperature, turning the pieces several times as they dry. I also set the slices of white bread out to dry. **Note:** *To toast the pecans, spread in a jelly-roll pan or rimmed baking sheet, then set on the middle shelf of a 350° F. oven for 10 to 12 minutes, stirring well at half-time.*

12 cups (3 quarts) ¾- to 1-inch chunks stale,
dry corn bread (Iron Skillet Corn Bread,
page 254, or your own favorite recipe;
see headnote)

6 slices stale, dry firm-textured white bread,
cut into ½-inch cubes (see headnote)

2 cups coarsely chopped toasted pecans
(see Note above)

½ cup coarsely chopped parsley

1 pound hickory-smoked bacon, each slice
cut crosswise into strips ½ inch wide

1 cup (2 sticks) butter, melted, or
1 cup bacon drippings or vegetable oil

2 very large yellow onions,
coarsely chopped

4 large celery ribs, trimmed and coarsely
chopped (include a few leaves)

1 tablespoon rubbed sage

1½ teaspoons dried leaf thyme, crumbled

6 cups chicken broth or stock

3 extra-large eggs, well beaten

1 teaspoon salt

½ teaspoon black pepper

1. Preheat the oven to 350° F. Spritz a 13 × 9 × 2-inch baking pan with nonstick cooking spray and set aside.

2. Place the two breads, pecans, and parsley in a very large mixing bowl and set aside.

3. Brown the bacon in a very large, heavy skillet over moderate heat, stirring often, for 12 to 14 minutes until all the drippings render out. Drain the bacon on paper toweling and if you intend to use the drippings in the dressing, pour them into a measuring cup. You should have about 1 cup; if not, round out the measure with melted butter or vegetable oil.

4. Heat ½ cup of the melted butter or bacon drippings in the same skillet for about 1 minute over moderately high heat. Add the onions and celery and cook, stirring often, for 10 to

12 minutes until lightly browned. Add the sage and thyme, and cook and stir for 1 to 2 minutes more.

5. Scoop the skillet mixture into the mixing bowl along with the reserved bacon and remaining melted butter or bacon drippings; toss well. Add 3 cups of the chicken broth, the eggs, salt, and pepper and toss well again.

6. Transfer the dressing to the baking pan, spreading to the edges, then drizzle the remaining 3 cups chicken broth evenly on top.

7. Cover snugly with heavy-duty foil and bake on the middle oven shelf for 25 minutes. Stir the dressing well, cover again with foil, and bake 20 minutes more or until steaming.

8. Serve hot with roast turkey, chicken, or pork and top with lots of gravy.

CHESAPEAKE OYSTER-CORN BREAD DRESSING

MAKES 10 TO 12 SERVINGS

. . . .

Some years ago when *Food & Wine* asked me to write an article on regional American turkey stuffings, I knew that this one was a "must." I'd found it in my mother's recipe file, dog-eared and double-starred. Ever meticulous about recipe sources, Mother had written "Mrs. Johnson, Whitestone, VA" in the upper right-hand corner of the card. She was the wife of the farmer who served as caretaker for our summer cottage. Located on what we called "the little bay," an inlet of the Chesapeake, our cottage was just downriver from an oyster pound. Even though I'm allergic to oysters, I did enjoy chugging up Anti-Poison Creek with my father to fetch them for my mother. The recipe below is adapted from the one that appeared in *Food & Wine*. **Note:** *As for corn bread, use any favorite recipe (not a mix because most are too sweet) as long as it's firm enough to break into chunks without disintegrating. I favor Iron Skillet Corn Bread (page 254).*

1½ pints shucked oysters with their liquor

5 cups coarsely crumbled stale, dry corn bread (see Note above)

4 cups coarsely crumbled soda crackers

4 medium celery ribs, trimmed and coarsely chopped (include a few leaves)

1 medium yellow onion, coarsely chopped

¼ cup minced fresh parsley

2 teaspoons poultry seasoning

1 teaspoon finely grated lemon zest

1 teaspoon black pepper, or to taste

½ teaspoon salt, or to taste

¾ cup (1½ sticks) butter, melted

1 tablespoon fresh lemon juice

1. Preheat the oven to 350° F. Spritz a deep 3-quart casserole with nonstick cooking spray. Also lightly coat the dull side of a large piece of aluminum foil with nonstick spray; set both aside.

2. Pour the oysters and their liquor into a large fine sieve set over a large bowl. Measure out and reserve 1 cup of the liquor; if there is insufficient oyster liquor, round out the measure with bottled clam juice or water.

A Love Affair with Southern Cooking

3. Coarsely chop the oysters, place in a large mixing bowl, then add the corn bread, soda crackers, celery, onion, parsley, poultry seasoning, lemon zest, pepper, and salt and toss well to mix. Add the melted butter, lemon juice, and 1/2 cup of the reserved oyster liquor and toss well again. Taste for salt and pepper and adjust as needed.

4. Spoon the dressing into the casserole, spreading to the edge, then drizzle the remaining 1/2 cup oyster liquor evenly on top. Place the foil on top, dull side down, and smooth tightly over the sides of the casserole.

5. Slide the casserole onto the middle oven shelf and bake for 35 to 40 minutes or until the dressing is steaming-hot.

6. Serve with roast turkey, capon, or even with roast pork.

CAJUN RICE, SAUSAGE, AND TASSO DRESSING

MAKES 10 TO 12 SERVINGS

. . . .

Here's another recipe adapted from my *Food & Wine* feature on regional American dressings. The inspiration for this one was Miss Tootie Guirard, a fine Cajun cook whom I'd interviewed some years earlier for *Family Circle*. I spent a week with Miss Tootie in St. Martinville, Louisiana, and left with a notebook full of colorful Cajun sayings and culinary wisdom. According to Miss Tootie, no Cajun cook would ever "rush a roux." It should brown slowly, ever so slowly, so that its flavor is robust but not bitter. Because of the saltiness of the sausage, tasso, and broth, this dressing is unlikely to need additional salt. But taste before serving. **Note:** *The best plan is to make this long-winded recipe a day in advance, refrigerate it, and reheat just before serving. I fluff the dressing, cover, and microwave on REHEAT (75 to 80 percent power) for 10 to 15 minutes.* **Tip:** *To save time, prepare the roux and rice mixtures simultaneously.*

Roux Mixture

2 tablespoons lard, bacon drippings, or vegetable oil

3 tablespoons all-purpose flour

1 medium yellow onion, moderately finely chopped

1 medium green bell pepper, cored, seeded, and finely diced

1 large celery rib, trimmed and finely diced

2 cups water

4 ounces bulk sausage meat

4 ounces tasso (spicy cold-smoked pork) or good country ham, finely ground

Rice Mixture

2 tablespoons lard, bacon drippings, or vegetable oil

1 large garlic clove, minced

1 small yellow onion, moderately coarsely chopped

1 large celery rib, trimmed and
finely diced

¼ to ½ teaspoon ground hot red pepper
(cayenne), depending on
how "hot" you like things

¼ teaspoon black pepper

2½ cups (1 pound) converted rice

5 cups rich chicken broth

⅓ cup thinly sliced green scallion tops

¼ cup minced Italian parsley

3 tablespoons butter

1. For the roux mixture: Melt the lard in a medium-size heavy saucepan over moderately low heat, blend in the flour, and cook, stirring often, for about 30 minutes or until as red as iron rust. If at any time the roux threatens to burn, reduce the heat to its lowest point.

2. Stir in the onion, bell pepper, and celery, and cook and stir for about 5 minutes or until limp. Add the water, bring to a boil, then reduce the heat so the mixture bubbles gently. Simmer uncovered for 40 to 45 minutes or until the roux mixture is only 1 inch deep.

3. For the rice mixture: While the roux reduces, melt the lard in a large, heavy saucepan over moderate heat. Add the garlic, onion, celery, cayenne, and black pepper and cook, stirring often, for about 5 minutes or until the vegetables are limp. Add the rice, and cook and stir for 3 minutes more.

4. Raise the burner heat to moderately high, add the broth, and as soon as it boils, reduce the heat and simmer uncovered for 15 minutes.

Stir well, cover, and cook 5 to 10 minutes more or until the rice has absorbed all the liquid.

5. When the roux is nearly done, brown the sausage and tasso in a small, heavy skillet over moderately high heat for 3 to 4 minutes, breaking up large clumps. Mix into the reduced roux and reserve.

6. Stir the scallion tops, parsley, and butter into the rice mixture, and as soon as the butter melts, fold in the reserved roux mixture.

7. Transfer the dressing to a large heated bowl and serve as an accompaniment to roast turkey or capon.

PICNIC POTATO SALAD

MAKES 8 TO 10 SERVINGS

No southern picnic, family reunion, or church supper would be complete without this simple potato salad. Often a couple of finely diced celery ribs are added to the mix and sometimes a little chopped green or red bell pepper as well. But the southern cooks I know stick to the recipe below. In the old days, all-purpose potatoes went into the salad, but I prefer the sweeter "red-skins." **Note:** *Duke's is the sandwich spread Southerners would use here. It was developed early in the twentieth century by Eugenia Duke of Greenville, South Carolina (see box, page 230).*

4 pounds large red-skin potatoes, cooked
until firm-tender, peeled, and cubed

6 large hard-cooked eggs, peeled and
coarsely chopped

1 medium yellow onion, coarsely chopped

2 cups (1 pint) mayonnaise-relish sandwich
spread (see Note at left)

3 tablespoons prepared yellow mustard
(it should be "taxicab" yellow)

2 tablespoons milk (about)

1 tablespoon cider vinegar

2 teaspoons celery seeds

1½ teaspoons salt, or to taste

½ teaspoon black pepper, or to taste

1. Place the potatoes, eggs, and onion in a very large bowl and toss gently to mix.
2. Whisk all remaining ingredients together in a small bowl or 1-quart measure, pour over the potato mixture, and toss well. If the salad seems dry, add 1 to 2 tablespoons more milk. Also taste for salt and pepper and adjust as needed.
3. Cover and refrigerate the salad 2 to 3 hours before serving.

❧

*The courthouse square was covered
with picnic parties sitting on newspapers,
washing down biscuits and syrup
with warm milk from fruit jars.
Some people were gnawing on
cold chicken and cold fried pork chops.
The more affluent chased their food
with drugstore Coca-Cola.*

—HARPER LEE, *TO KILL A MOCKINGBIRD*

❧

1930S Double Cola is formulated in Chattanooga. "Double" refers to the size of the bottle (twice that of rival colas), not to flavor, which is lighter. Double Cola remains a southern favorite, although its bottles are no longer oversize.

1931 Toombs County, Georgia, farmer Mose Coleman discovers that this year's onions are not typically, tearfully hot. They're as sweet as apples— the very first Vidalias. (See Vidalia Onions, page 207.)

1932 The Krystal Company is founded in Chattanooga and soon launches the South's first chain of fast-food restaurants. Today more than 400 Krystal restaurants serve the company's signature square oniony burgers around the clock.

Herman W. Lay, a Tennessee traveling salesman, begins selling Atlanta-made potato chips out of the trunk of his Model A Ford.

1933 The Tennessee Valley Authority (TVA) installs an electric power plant in Muscle Shoals, Alabama, and soon this backwoods booms with poultry farms.

SWEET POTATO SALAD

MAKES 8 TO 10 SERVINGS

North Carolina tops all other states when it comes to sweet potato production, so it's scarcely surprising that local chefs are constantly devising new ways to prepare them. And none, to my mind, is more inventive than Ben Barker, who with wife Karen owns Durham's award-winning Magnolia Grill. I've profiled the Barkers many times (for *Bon Appétit*, *Food & Wine*, *More*), and among the recipes that I remember with particular fondness is Ben's twenty-four-karat sweet potato salad. Although an earlier version of it appeared in a *Food & Wine* article of mine, the recipe here is adapted from the Barkers's cookbook, *Not Afraid of Flavor* (2002). I find it equally good with cold baked ham, cold roast pork, or grilled, fried, or barbecued chicken. **Note:** *Barker makes his own pepper relish but tells home cooks it's okay to use a favorite commercial brand. With its tart oil-based dressing, this salad is perfect for a picnic; it can also be made a day or two in advance but should be brought to room temperature before being served.* **Tip:** *Mix the parsley in at the last minute; if added earlier, it will discolor.*

2 pounds sweet potatoes, peeled and cut into
½-inch cubes

1 cup bottled bell pepper relish
(see Note above)

1 medium garlic clove, finely minced

2 tablespoons Dijon mustard

1 teaspoon Worcestershire sauce

1 teaspoon salt, or to taste

½ teaspoon black pepper, or to taste

¼ cup fruity olive oil

¼ cup coarsely chopped Italian parsley
(see Tip at left)

1. Boil the sweet potatoes in a large, heavy saucepan over moderate heat in just enough lightly salted water to cover for about 10 minutes or until barely tender. Drain well, quick-chill in ice water, then drain well again, and pat dry on paper toweling.
2. Combine the relish, garlic, mustard, Worcestershire sauce, salt, and pepper in a large nonreactive bowl, then add the olive oil in a slow stream, whisking vigorously all the while.
3. Add the sweet potatoes and parsley and toss gently in the dressing. Taste for salt and pepper, adjust as needed, and serve.

BLACK-EYED PEA SALAD

MAKES 4 TO 6 SERVINGS

I use frozen black-eyed peas in this popular southern salad for three reasons: They're available year-round, they taste "fresh," and they do not disintegrate as dried black-eyed peas so often do when cooked. I simmer the frozen peas no more than 15 to 17 minutes because I like them al dente. This also means that I can use less dressing because firmer black-eyed peas don't "suck it up" the way softer peas do. **Note:** *Don't rush the browning of the bacon; the fat should render slowly so that the bacon is neither blackened* *nor bitter.* **Tip:** *The easiest way to cut bacon into thin strips is to use kitchen shears and snip straight across the stacked slices.*

8 thin slices lean, hickory-smoked bacon, cut crosswise into strips ½ inch wide (see Tip above)

⅔ cup finely diced red onion (about ½ medium-small)

⅔ cup finely diced green bell pepper (about 1 small)

⅔ cup finely diced red bell pepper (about 1 small)

One 16-ounce package frozen black-eyed peas, cooked by package directions (see headnote)

Dressing

3 tablespoons corn oil or vegetable oil

2 tablespoons bacon drippings

2 tablespoons cider vinegar, or to taste

1 teaspoon salt, or to taste

½ teaspoon black pepper, or to taste

1. Brown the bacon slowly in a large, heavy skillet over moderately low heat, stirring occasionally and separating the pieces. This may take as long as 30 minutes, but you can proceed with the salad while the bacon cooks. When all of the fat has rendered out and the bacon is crisp and brown, lift to paper toweling to drain using a slotted spoon. Pour the drippings from the skillet and reserve.

2. Place the onion and bell peppers in a large heatproof bowl and toss well. Drain the cooked black-eyed peas well, then dump at once on top of the vegetable mixture in the bowl and let stand for 10 minutes. The heat of the peas wilts the vegetables slightly and mellows their flavors.

3. Meanwhile, prepare the dressing. Place all ingredients in the skillet in which you browned the bacon, set over moderately high heat, and bring to a boil, scraping any browned bits from the skillet bottom.

4. Pour the boiling dressing over the salad, toss well, and marinate at room temperature for 30 minutes. Taste for vinegar, salt, and pepper and adjust the seasonings as needed.

5. Add the reserved bacon to the salad, toss well, and serve as an accompaniment to chicken prepared any which way—broiled, grilled, fried, roasted. Good, too, with fried fish, especially catfish.

Variation

A Black-Eyed Pea Salad for Today: Prepare as directed but add 1 finely minced large garlic clove to the vegetable mixture in Step 2. In the dressing, substitute 5 tablespoons fine, fruity olive oil for the corn oil and bacon drippings; also use red wine vinegar instead of cider vinegar. Finally, in Step 5, add 1 tablespoon coarsely chopped fresh basil and/or Italian parsley along with the reserved bacon. Toss well and serve.

CORN BREAD SALAD

. . . .

I find this zesty salad perfect for a picnic because it can be made ahead of time, it travels well, it feeds an army, and people invariably like it. Use a corn bread mix if you must. Your salad will be better, however, if you take time to bake a batch of corn bread (do it several days ahead so it has time to dry). The corn bread recipe I suggest below provides just the right amount of one-inch corn bread chunks (about eight cups) and, unlike that prepared from a mix, isn't sweet. **Note:** *Frugal southern cooks have always saved bacon drippings to use as a seasoning. This salad owes its smoky-meaty flavor to them. If you have no drippings, use those created below and round out the measure with corn or vegetable oil (but don't expect the salad to be as flavorful). Better yet, make a "southernized" panzanella of the salad by substituting a fruity olive oil.*

I recipe Iron Skillet Corn Bread (page 254), baked as directed and cooled (see headnote)

8 ounces hickory-smoked bacon, cut crosswise into strips ½ inch wide

⅔ cup bacon drippings (see Note above)

⅔ cup corn, vegetable, or olive oil

⅓ cup cider vinegar, or to taste

I teaspoon salt, or to taste

½ teaspoon black pepper, or to taste

I large green bell pepper, cored, seeded, and coarsely chopped

I large red onion, coarsely chopped

4 firm-ripe Roma (Italian plum) tomatoes, cored, seeded, and diced but not peeled

⅓ cup coarsely diced, well-drained bread and butter pickles or sweet pickles

1. Preheat the oven to 350° F.
2. Halve the corn bread horizontally, then break into 1-inch chunks. Spread on two ungreased large jelly-roll pans, slide into the oven, and bake for 30 to 35 minutes, stirring occasionally, until crisp and lightly browned.
3. Meanwhile, cook the bacon in a large, heavy skillet over moderately high heat for about 10 minutes, stirring now and then, until all of the drippings render out and only crisp brown bits remain. Using a slotted spoon, scoop the bacon to paper toweling to drain.
4. Pour the drippings into a 1-quart measure, add enough additional bacon drippings to total ⅔ cup, then add the corn oil, vinegar, salt, and pepper. Return all to the skillet and set over lowest heat.
5. Place the bell pepper, onion, tomatoes, and pickles in a large heatproof bowl. As soon as the corn bread is crisp and lightly browned, remove from the oven and dump on top of the vegetables in the bowl. This will wilt them slightly and mellow their flavor.
6. Now drizzle the hot skillet mixture evenly into the bowl and toss the salad well. Taste for salt, pepper, and vinegar, adjust as needed, and toss well again.
7. Serve as an accompaniment to fried chicken, roast pork, or chicken. Good, too, with pork chops, baked ham, and hot dogs. **Note:** *If you make the salad ahead of time, let it come to room temperature before serving. Toss well and dish up.*

SWEET-SOUR COLESLAW

MAKES 6 TO 8 SERVINGS

Down south there are three basic types of coleslaw: Sweet Slaw (shredded cabbage and sometimes carrots in a sweet and creamy mayonnaise dressing; at right), Barbecue Slaw (coarsely shredded or sliced cabbage in a peppery, reddish, oil-and-vinegar dressing; page 231), and this distinctly Germanic oil-and-vinegar–dressed slaw containing onion and green bell pepper as well as cabbage. Was it introduced by German settlers funneling south from Pennsylvania and points north through the Shenandoah Valley? My research suggests so. This isn't a fancy recipe and its flavor improves on standing in the refrigerator. Because it's less likely to spoil than mayonnaise-dressed slaws, it's a good choice for a picnic.

Coleslaw

8 cups (2 quarts) finely sliced cabbage (you'll need a 2½- to 2¾-pound cabbage)

1 medium-size green bell pepper, cored, seeded, and finely chopped

1 medium-size sweet onion (Vidalia, Spanish, or Bermuda), finely chopped

Dressing

1 cup cider vinegar

¾ cup sugar

⅔ cup corn oil or vegetable oil

1 teaspoon salt

1 teaspoon dry mustard

1 teaspoon celery seeds

1. For the coleslaw: Place the cabbage, bell pepper, and onion in a large nonreactive mixing bowl. Toss well and set aside.
2. For the dressing: Combine all ingredients in a small nonreactive pan and bring to a boil over moderate heat, stirring until the sugar dissolves.
3. Pour the hot dressing over the slaw and toss well. Cool to room temperature, then cover and refrigerate until ready to serve.

SWEET SLAW

MAKES 6 TO 8 SERVINGS

To most of the country, coleslaw is crisp and sharp, but down south it's sometimes so soft and sweet it might be dessert. The best sweet slaw I ever ate is that served at Mama Dip's Kitchen in Chapel Hill, North Carolina. It's *not* overly sweet; in fact the balance of sweet and tart is exactly right. Mama Dip (Mildred Council), a six-foot-two African American well into her seventies, has written two best-selling cookbooks, *Mama's Dip's Kitchen* (1999) and *Mama Dip's Family Cookbook* (2005). This coleslaw, which I double-order every time I eat at Dip's, appears in her second cookbook—a last-minute addition after I raved on and on about it.

8 cups (2 quarts) moderately finely grated cabbage (you'll need a 2½- to 2¾-pound cabbage)

¾ cup firmly packed mayonnaise

¼ cup cider vinegar

2 tablespoons sugar

½ teaspoon salt, or to taste

1. Place the cabbage in a large nonreactive bowl. Quickly whisk together all remaining ingredients, pour over the cabbage, and mix well. At first you may think that there isn't enough dressing. There is because the cabbage will release a fair amount of liquid.

2. Let the slaw stand at room temperature for 30 minutes, mix well, then cover and refrigerate for several hours.

3. Stir the slaw well, taste for salt, and adjust as needed, then serve as an accompaniment to fried chicken, fish or shellfish, or any kind of barbecue.

EUGENIA DUKE AND THE SOUTH'S FAVORITE MAYONNAISE

When France's Duc de Richelieu routed entrenched English troops from the port of Mahón on the Mediterranean island of Minorca in 1756, the duke, something of a gourmet, ordered his chef to come up with a special sauce to commemorate the victory. The chef combined egg yolks, olive oil, and vinegar, *et voilà!* Mahonaisse. Eventually, mayonnaise.

But in 1917, Eugenia Duke of Greenville, South Carolina, created a version that many mayonnaise lovers—especially Southerners—contend beats all rival brands nine ways to Sunday.

As World War One raged in Europe, Mrs. Duke decided to do her part for the war effort by making sandwiches for doughboys training at Fort Sevier near Greenville. Spread with her homemade mayonnaise, Mrs. Duke's sandwiches soon had the soldiers lining up for more.

Before long, a Greenville drugstore began selling Mrs. Duke's sa ndwiches and then a grocery off ered to stock her bottled mayonnaise. In no time, the demand was such that Mrs. Duke gave up sandwich making to concentrate on her creamy spread.

C. F. Sauer, a condiment and spice company based in Richmond, Virginia, bought Mrs. Duke out in 1929, but her mayonnaise remains one of the Sauer mainstays.

A southern lady whose name, coincidentally, is also Eugenia, reminisced recently: "This may sound weird, but I used to love peanut butter and banana sandwiches made with Duke's. Then weight gain and cholesterol caught up with me."

When she moved from North Carolina to Florida, she couldn't find Duke's. "But Food Lion came to town," she said, "and along came Duke's."

Not one to mince words, she added: "Of course, I now have to buy the low-fat crap. But there's nothing like the real thing. And that's Duke's!"

BARBECUE SLAW

I see this reddish slaw more and more often at barbecue joints across the South and occasionally order it instead of the classic—and more caloric—mayonnaise-based Sweet Slaw, which precedes. Like Sweet-Sour Coleslaw (page 229), Barbecue Slaw is a good choice for picnics and tailgate parties.

Coleslaw

8 cups (2 quarts) finely shredded cabbage (you'll need a 2½- to 2¾-pound cabbage)

I medium-size sweet onion (Vidalia, Spanish, or Bermuda), finely chopped

Dressing

I cup cider vinegar

⅔ cup corn or vegetable oil

½ cup sugar

2 tablespoons ketchup or barbecue sauce

I teaspoon salt

½ dry teaspoon mustard

½ teaspoon sweet paprika

¼ to ½ teaspoon hot red pepper sauce, depending on how "hot" you like things

1. For the coleslaw: Place the cabbage and onion in a large nonreactive mixing bowl. Toss well and set aside.
2. For the dressing: Combine all ingredients in a small nonreactive pan and bring to a boil over moderate heat, stirring until the sugar dissolves.
3. Pour the hot dressing over the slaw and toss well. Cool to room temperature, then cover and refrigerate until ready to serve.

SMOTHERED LETTUCE

My first job right out of college was with the North Carolina Agricultural Extension Service, first as an assistant home agent in Iredell County, then, nine months later, as Woman's Editor in the Raleigh head office. In this newly created position, my job was to cover the activities of 4-H Club girls and Home Demonstration Club women for newspapers, radio, and television. I was forever on the road, sometimes driving as many as 500 miles a day. I loved it, especially the tips passed along by the state agents who'd been crisscrossing the state for years. "Whenever you're in Morehead," they'd tell me, "be sure to eat at the Sanitary Fish Market." "If you're near Hillsborough, lunch at The Colonial Inn." "If you're headed to the mountains and it's not out of the way, by all means stop at the Nu-Wray Inn in Burnsville." I did, time and again. Only thirty miles north of Asheville and now nearly 200 years old, the Nu-Wray offers a glimpse of early mountain life. It fronts the town common and still serves some of the no-nonsense country cooking that made it famous. Whenever I visited, I'd order the inn's famous smothered lettuce (some Southerners call it "wilted" lettuce). What follows is my approximation of that salad and I think it comes pretty close. I like it with almost any meat or fowl. **Note:** *Iceberg is the lettuce to use here because it adds welcome crunch. It should be coarsely chopped— easy enough if you use this method: Halve the head of lettuce from top to stem end. Lay each half cut- side down, then slice from top to bottom, spacing the cuts ½ inch apart but not separating the slices. Give each half a quarter turn and slice at right angles to the first cuts, again spacing them ½ inch apart. That's all there is to it.*

8 slices hickory-smoked bacon,
cut crosswise into strips ½ inch wide

2½ tablespoons cider vinegar

2 teaspoons sugar

¼ teaspoon salt

¼ teaspoon black pepper

8 cups (2 quarts) coarsely chopped
iceberg lettuce (you'll need about
a 1½-pound head)
(see Note above)

6 medium scallions, trimmed and thinly
sliced (include some green tops)

1. Fry the bacon in a large, heavy nonreactive skillet over moderate heat for 10 to 12 min- utes or until the drippings cook out and only crisp brown bits remain. Scoop the bacon to paper toweling and reserve.
2. Pour all drippings from the skillet and mea- sure. You'll need ¼ cup drippings and if insuf- ficient, round out the measure with corn oil or other vegetable oil. Return the drippings to the skillet; add the vinegar, sugar, salt, and pepper, and bring to a boil over moderate heat, stirring occasionally.
3. Quickly mound the lettuce and scallions in a large bowl, pour the hot dressing evenly over all, add the reserved bacon, and toss well.
4. Serve at once. This is a light, refreshing salad, so be generous with the portions.

MOLDED VEGETABLE SALAD

MAKES 8 SERVINGS

. . . .

Does anyone love a gelatin salad more than a Southerner? I doubt it. Even my Yankee mother, who moved to Raleigh, North Carolina, after marrying my equally Yankee father, became quite southern in her adoration of "congealed salads," although she took to few other things southern and in the forty years that she lived below the Mason-Dixon, always spoke with an Illinois twang. Never content to leave well enough alone, Mother was forever improvising with a molded salad recipe that she'd picked up from a neighbor, a friend, or a fellow club wom- an. Some, I have to say, were sweet enough to serve as dessert. My own favorites, however, were made with unflavored gelatin and con- tained plenty of fresh fruits or vegetables. This is one of the better molded salads that landed in my mother's recipe file. **Note:** *This salad needs no dressing; the mayonnaise is built in.*

2 envelopes unflavored gelatin

¼ cup cold water

1 cup boiling water

2 tablespoons fresh lemon juice

2 tablespoons sugar

¾ teaspoon salt

¼ teaspoon hot red pepper sauce

1 cup mayonnaise (use "light," if you like)

½ cup finely chopped yellow onion

½ cup coarsely chopped red bell pepper

½ cup coarsely chopped green bell pepper

½ cup finely diced celery

1 cup moderately coarsely
shredded cabbage

1 cup moderately coarsely
shredded carrots

1. Lightly coat a fluted, nonreactive 2½-quart mold with nonstick cooking spray and set aside.

2. Soften the gelatin in the cold water in a large heatproof bowl for 5 minutes. Add ¾ cup of the boiling water, the lemon juice, sugar, salt, and hot pepper sauce. Stir until the gelatin dissolves completely.

3. Blend the mayonnaise with the onion and remaining ¼ cup boiling water, then mix into the gelatin mixture along with all remaining ingredients.

4. Pour all into the mold and cover loosely with wax paper. Set uncovered in the refrigerator and chill for several hours or overnight until firm.

5. To unmold, dip the mold quickly into hot water, then invert on a colorful round platter. **Tip: If the platter is wet, you'll find the unmolded salad easier to center.**

6. Cut into wedges and serve as is, or if you prefer, serve on a bed of colorful mixed greens.

1933 Harriet Ross Colquitt publishes *The Savannah Cook Book*, a spiral-bound paperback brimming with "receipts for rice dishes, and for shrimp and crab concoctions which are peculiar to our locality." In his introduction, Ogden Nash rhymes, "Everybody has the right to think whose food is the most gorgeous, and I nominate Georgia's."

After nearly 20 years of pit-roasting barbecue for Goldsboro, North Carolina, businessmen, African American janitor Adam Scott turns his back porch into a small barbecue restaurant. Today a third generation operates Scott's Famous Barbecue, now located on Williams Street and still drawing crowds. North Carolina supermarkets also sell Scott's Famous Barbecue Sauce.

Prohibition ends—but not in much of the South.

1934 The "new Chero-Cola" debuts as Royal Crown Cola and is an immediate hit. In no time, the favorite fast-food southern lunch is "a MoonPie and an RC."

As a substitute for absinthe, banned by the U.S. in 1912 because of the harmful effects of the wormwood it contained, Legendre & Company of New Orleans develops a look- and taste-alike anise liqueur called Herbsaint.

SHRIMP ASPIC

MAKES 6 SERVINGS

. . . .

One of my best New York friends was fellow Southerner Anne Mead, who grew up in Dillon, South Carolina. Like me, she lived on Gramercy Park; like me, she loved to cook; and like me, she wrote a cookbook. Called *Please Kiss the Cook*, Anne's is a collection of family favorites, the recipes her doctor husband and two sons like best. Most recipes are southern (no surprise here), among them this refreshing aspic, which her mother liked to serve at bridge luncheons on sultry Dillon days. **Note:** *I heat the tomato juice by microwave in a large measuring cup in which I can also make the aspic. Saves on dishwashing.* **Tip:** *For better flavor, use fresh shrimp, not frozen or canned.*

2 envelopes unflavored gelatin

½ cup cold water

2½ cups tomato juice

1 tablespoon finely grated yellow onion
(a Microplane is the tool to use here)

1 teaspoon prepared horseradish

1 teaspoon Worcestershire sauce

½ teaspoon salt

⅛ teaspoon ground hot red pepper (cayenne)

1½ cups finely diced cooked, shelled, and deveined shrimp (about 10 ounces cooked, shelled, and deveined shrimp or 25 to 30 medium-small; see Tip above)

½ cup finely diced green bell pepper

½ cup finely diced celery

6 iceberg lettuce cups

1. Spritz a decorative, nonreactive 6-cup ring mold with nonstick cooking spray; set aside.
2. Soften the gelatin in the cold water in a small ramekin. Meanwhile, heat 1½ cups of the tomato juice in a 2-quart ovenproof glass measuring cup by microwaving for 5 minutes at 50 percent power or until steaming.
3. Scoop the softened gelatin into the hot tomato juice and whisk until dissolved. Mix in the remaining 1 cup tomato juice, the grated onion, horseradish, Worcestershire sauce, salt, and cayenne. Set uncovered in the refrigerator for 1 to 1½ hours or until the consistency of unbeaten egg white.
4. Fold in the shrimp, bell pepper, and celery and ladle into the mold. Set uncovered in the refrigerator and chill for several hours or overnight until firm.
5. When ready to serve, divide the lettuce cups among six salad plates. Unmold the aspic by dipping quickly into hot water, then inverting on a large plate. **Tip:** *If the platter is wet, you'll find the unmolded salad easier to center.*
6. Cut the aspic into six wedges and bed on the lettuce. Pass a small bowl of mayonnaise.

Variations

Shrimp Aspic with Fresh Tarragon: Prepare Shrimp Aspic as directed, but fold in 1 tablespoon finely minced fresh tarragon (or dill) along with the shrimp, bell pepper, and celery.

Crab Aspic with Fresh Herbs: Prepare Shrimp Aspic with Fresh Tarragon as directed, but substitute ½ pound lump crabmeat for the shrimp, carefully removing bits of cartilage and shell.

Basic Tomato Aspic: Prepare Step 1 of Shrimp Aspic as directed. In Step 2, increase the amount of tomato juice to 2¼ cups and the grated onion to 2 tablespoons; also add 1 tablespoon each ketchup and fresh lime (or lemon) juice, and ¼ teaspoon celery salt. Omit Step 3. Pour the aspic into a 4-cup mold that has been lightly coated with nonstick cooking spray and proceed as the recipe directs. Makes 4 servings.

MRS. B'S APRICOT CHIFFON SALAD

MAKES 6 TO 8 SERVINGS

Mrs. B was Mrs. Pegram Bryant, my first land-lady. After college, I worked for a spell in Iredell County, North Carolina, as an assistant home demonstration agent, headquartering in the county seat of Statesville. Like many small southern towns, it was a social place; family mattered. So I was lucky to land in the garage apartment of the socially prominent Bryants. Mr. B owned a local newspaper and Mrs. B descended from a distinguished Statesville family. Although Mrs. B rarely cooked, she spent hours in the kitchen supervising her maid, Dorothy. I was often asked to join the Bryants for midday Sunday dinner (the only time I drank sweet tea from silver goblets) and that's where I first tasted this apricot salad. I complimented Mrs. B on it and asked for the recipe, and she obliged. I use a large decorative ring mold instead of the little individual molds Mrs. B fancied; I turn it out on

1934 Pepsi-Cola, now available in 12-ounce bottles, still costs just a nickel—the same as six-ounce bottles of competing colas. As a result, Pepsi sales soar despite the Depression.

1935 To counter pest damage to southern pecans, the U.S. Department of Agriculture establishes two pecan research stations, one at Thomasville, Georgia, and one at Monticello, Florida.

1936 Georgia entrepreneur William Stuckey sets up a roadside stand on the New York–Miami route to sell homegrown pecans and homemade candies.

Duncan Hines, a traveling salesman from Bowling Green, Kentucky, publishes a pocket guide to the restaurants he's enjoyed on the road. He calls it *Adventures in Good Eating* and soon every motorist has to have one. (See Duncan Hines, page 49.)

With a $1,500 loan, W. T. Harris opens his first grocery in Charlotte, North Carolina. It later morphs into the giant Harris Teeter supermarket chain, one of the South's finest.

a large round platter and wreathe it with finely cut lettuce. Mrs. B never served mayonnaise with her apricot salad and neither do I. **Note:** *I've added a teaspoon of unflavored gelatin to Mrs. B's original recipe for two reasons: First, there's an enzyme in pineapple (bromelin) that weakens gelatin and second, can sizes have changed since Mrs. B gave me her recipe; instead of the 15-ounce can of apricots she called for, I've substituted two 8½-ounce cans—a larger amount. That extra teaspoon of gelatin strengthens the gel.*

Two 8½-ounce cans syrup-packed apricot halves, liquid drained and reserved

One 8-ounce can syrup-packed crushed pineapple, liquid drained and reserved

1 tablespoon fresh lemon juice

One 3-ounce package orange-flavored gelatin

1 teaspoon plain gelatin

¾ cup boiling water

¾ cup heavy cream, softly whipped

2 cups thinly sliced iceberg or romaine lettuce

1. Lightly coat a decorative, nonreactive 6-cup ring mold with nonstick cooking spray and set aside.
2. Mix the reserved apricot and pineapple liquids with the lemon juice and reserve. Pulse the apricots briskly in a food processor until finely chopped and reserve also.
3. Dissolve the two gelatins in the boiling water in a medium-size metal bowl, stirring often to make sure that there are no undissolved lumps in the bottom. Mix in the reserved fruit liquids. Set uncovered in the refrigerator for 45 to 50 minutes, stirring now and then, or until the consistency of unbeaten egg white.
4. Using a hand electric mixer or a whisk, beat the partially congealed gelatin until frothy, then fold in the reserved apricots, crushed pineapple, and whipped cream.
5. Spoon all into the ring mold, smoothing the top. Set uncovered in the refrigerator for about 2 hours, then cover loosely and let stand overnight or until firm.
6. When ready to serve, quickly dip the ring mold into hot water, loosen the salad around the edge and central tube with a small knife or thin-blade spatula, and invert on a large round platter. Wreathe the lettuce around the edge.
7. Cut into wedges and serve.

❖

The fields surrounding the towns and groves were plentifully stored with Corn, Citruels, Pumpkins, Squashes, Beans, Peas, Potatoes, Peaches, Figs, Oranges, etc.

—**WILLIAM BARTRAM,** *TRAVELS OF WILLIAM BARTRAM,* ON SEMINOLE CROPS IN FLORIDA, 1773

❖

Breads

In the Colonial South, corn breads gradually gained favor as indeed they did elsewhere about early America. Usually they were thick cornmeal-and-water pastes flattened into rounds (pones) much like those the local tribes made.

According to early eighteenth-century Virginia historian Robert Beverley, *pone* descends from the Indian word *oppone*, and in some fine homes it was chosen "over wheat bread." Often pones were baked on the blades of hoes propped up in front of the fire (hoe cakes) or simply buried in embers (ash cakes).

Yet to settlers accustomed to wheat breads, "any form of bread made with corn instead of wheat was a sad paste of despair," writes Betty Fussell in *The Story of Corn* (1992). "Sad" because corn breads, nearly impossible for the inexperienced English

colonists to leaven with yeast, remained flat and heavy.

Over time, however, good southern cooks—many of them plantation cooks—learned to add a little wheat flour to their cornmeal batters and to lighten cornmeal pastes with beaten eggs, a technique used to this day for batter bread (spoon bread). The combination of sour milk or buttermilk and soda was another effective leavener, for biscuits as well as for corn breads.

Both North and South can boast of their own regional corn breads, but there are differences: As a rule, Northerners prefer yellow cornmeal, Southerners white. Northerners also tend to sweeten their corn breads while Southerners prefer a salty tang. None of the three corn breads in Mary Randolph's *Virginia House-wife* (1824) contains a grain of sugar.

And in the nearly three dozen corn bread recipes in Sarah Rutledge's *Carolina Housewife* (1847), I find only three that call for any sweetener: Chicora Corn Bread (1 tablespoon of brown sugar to a quart of milk and "as much cornmeal as will make a thick batter"); Indian Cakes (2 tablespoons molasses to a pint of milk and "meal enough to make a thick batter"), and Corn Muffins (1 tablespoon sugar to "three pints of cornmeal . . . and a pint of blood-warm water").

What also distinguishes *The Carolina Housewife* are its thirty recipes for rice bread, among them a johnny cake made with rice—altogether appropriate for the Lowcountry, where rice plantations flourished until the Civil War. According to culinary historian Karen Hess, in "large stretches of the South, Indian pone was the more usual name for cornmeal cakes while johnny cake was customarily made of rice."

Right up until World War Two, many southern cooks baked fresh bread for breakfast, dinner, and supper—usually biscuits or corn bread. But for special occasions there might be batter bread, sweet potato rolls, or Sally Lunn. Whatever the bread, it was given place of pride at the table.

My mother, transplanted to the South several years before I was born, made superb yeast breads but her particular favorite was yeast-free Boston brown bread, which she steamed in recycled Rumford baking powder tins. The rattle of those cans in Mother's big enamel kettle is a sound I'll never forget.

I didn't share Mother's passion for Boston brown bread. What I craved were the fresh-baked biscuits and corn breads nearly everyone else in our Raleigh neighborhood ate several times of day. Of course nearly everyone else was southern born and bred.

Our round-the-corner neighbor, Mrs. Franklin, taught me how to make skillet corn bread and corn pone when I was in grammar school, explaining that for really good corn bread, I'd have to get some stone-ground meal from Lassiter's Mill clear across town. Mother indulged me although she never really cared for corn bread herself.

I didn't taste hush puppies until I was in high school, and I couldn't wait to try them at home. Ignoring Mrs. Franklin's advice, I used granular supermarket cornmeal, and the hush puppies shattered the second they hit the deep fat. I didn't perfect the recipe until years later when I was writing *The Doubleday Cookbook*.

Corn breads continued to fascinate me during my growing-up years and became a near obsession while I was at Cornell; they were practically unheard of in Upstate New York. In a surge of culinary evangelism, I made corn breads the subject of my experimental cookery thesis and got an A. I still have that thesis, snug in its brown binder, and I refer to it now and then. Even today, the information remains rock-solid.

Fortunately, stone-ground cornmeal, both white and yellow, is more widely available than it was during my childhood (see Sources, page 401). My own competence has improved, too; I now make batter bread without trepidation. Ditto crackling bread, hush puppies, and half a dozen other southern classics.

I've also developed a light touch with biscuits (thanks to Cornell food chemistry courses) and I bake them as often as I dare using lard, the southern shortening of choice. But they're off-limits whenever I'm trying to shed the pounds that recipe-testing inevitably packs on.

In the pages that follow, you'll find an authentic assortment of some of the South's best breads—everything from Wild Persimmon Bread to Sweet Potato Biscuits to yeasty, high-rising Sally Lunn to Hush Puppies and Cracklin' Bread.

Most are easy, many are quick—just what you need to complete a proper southern meal.

BLACK WALNUT BREAD

MAKES A 9 × 5 × 3-INCH LOAF

. . . .

Not so long ago whole families would head for the woods to gather black walnut windfalls; my father, brother, and I often did on crisp autumn days. Finding black walnuts was fun; shelling them and extricating the sweet nut meats wasn't, but we persisted. As I've said many times, my mother wasn't a southern cook but she was a collector of southern recipes, among them this black walnut bread. It was one of the few southern recipes that she actually made. Sometimes she'd substitute wild hickory nuts for black walnuts; there was a tall hickory tree just outside our front door. If Mother had neither black walnuts nor hickory nuts on hand,

she'd use pecans from the two pecan trees in our backyard. **Note:** *It's no longer necessary to gather your own black walnuts; you can order them online (see Sources, page 401).*

1½ cups sifted all-purpose flour

¼ cup sugar

½ teaspoon salt

½ teaspoon ground cinnamon

¼ teaspoon ground ginger

¼ teaspoon ground nutmeg

2 cups bran flakes

¾ cup coarsely chopped black walnuts, wild hickory nuts, or pecans

½ cup seedless raisins or dried currants

1 cup milk

1 large egg

3 tablespoons vegetable oil

½ cup molasses (not too dark)

1 teaspoon baking soda

1. Preheat the oven to 325° F. Coat a 9 × 5 × 3-inch loaf pan with nonstick oil-and-flour baking spray and set aside.

2. Sift the flour, sugar, salt, cinnamon, ginger, and nutmeg together into a large mixing bowl. Add the bran flakes, black walnuts, and raisins; toss 4 to 5 times to dredge the nuts and raisins, then make a well in the middle of the dry ingredients.

3. Whisk the milk, egg, and vegetable oil in a small bowl until creamy. In a separate small bowl or 2-cup measuring cup, combine the

molasses and baking soda; the mixture will fizz—proof that the soda is good and fresh. Pour the molasses mixture into the well in the dry ingredients, then add the milk mixture and stir only enough to combine. It's good if a few floury specks show; they prove that you haven't overbeaten the batter.

4. Scoop the batter into the pan, spreading to the corners, and bake on the middle oven shelf for about 1 hour or until nicely browned, springy to the touch, and a cake tester inserted in the middle of the loaf comes out clean.

5. Cool the loaf in the upright pan on a wire rack for 10 minutes, loosen around the edge with a thin-blade spatula, then turn out on the rack and cool to room temperature before slicing.

Note: *This bread freezes well. Wrap snugly in plastic food wrap, overwrap in aluminum foil, date, label, and store in a 0° F. freezer. Serve within 3 to 4 months.*

ABOUT WILD PERSIMMONS

Wild or native persimmons (*Diospyros virginiana*) thrive throughout the South. About the size of Ping-Pong balls, they are much smaller than Japanese persimmons (*Diospyros kaki*), sweeter, too, and more intensely flavored. Southerners have long prized them, but today with developers bulldozing miles of forests to build "McMansions," millions of wild persimmon trees are toppling. As a result, their honeyed fruit is more precious than ever, especially since deer, possums, and raccoons gobble them up almost as fast as they fall from the tree.

Season: It varies from area to area, but as a rule, fully ripe wild persimmons begin to drop from the tree in late September and continue to do so well into December.

Gathering: Contrary to the old wives' tale, you don't have to wait till after first frost to gather wild persimmons. If they've fallen from the tree, if they're shriveled and coppery of hue, if their caps slip right off, they're ready to eat. If not, beware. A green persimmon will turn your mouth inside out. Unfortunately, bees dote upon ripe persimmons, so keep your wits about you when picking up windfalls.

Pulping or Puréeing: First, wash the persimmons by sloshing gently up and down in a sink full of cold water, repeat several times, then scoop onto several thicknesses of paper toweling. Next, force the persimmons through a food mill or colander set over a large bowl, leaving the skins and seeds behind.

Yield: 1 quart wild persimmons makes about 2 cups pulp.

Freezing: Like apples and peaches, wild persimmons darken when exposed to the air. To prevent discoloration, mix 1/8 teaspoon powdered ascorbic acid (vitamin C) into each 1 quart persimmon pulp. Pack into 1-pint freezer containers, leaving 1/2 inch head space. Snap on the lids, date, label, and set on the freezing surface of a 0° F. freezer. Use in any recipe that calls for unsweetened persimmon pulp.

Maximum Storage Time: One year.

WILD PERSIMMON BREAD

MAKES A 9 × 5 × 3-INCH LOAF

This recipe is adapted from one created by Laura Frost, once the chef at Sleddon's in Southern Pines, North Carolina. That restaurant is gone now—but not memories of the delicious food served there. For tips on gathering and puréeing wild persimmons, see About Wild Persimmons, which precedes.

2 cups unsifted all-purpose flour

I cup sugar

2 teaspoons baking powder

½ teaspoon baking soda

I teaspoon ground cinnamon

¼ teaspoon ground nutmeg

¼ teaspoon ground mace

½ teaspoon salt

¾ cup coarsely chopped pecans, walnuts, or black walnuts

I cup wild persimmon pulp

½ cup milk

2 large eggs, lightly beaten

4 tablespoons (½ stick) butter, melted

1. Preheat the oven to 350° F. Lightly coat a 9 × 5 × 3-inch loaf pan with nonstick cooking spray and set aside.
2. Sift the flour, sugar, baking powder, baking soda, cinnamon, nutmeg, mace, and salt together into a large mixing bowl. Add the pecans, toss well, then make a well in the middle of the dry ingredients.
3. Combine the persimmon pulp, milk, eggs, and melted butter in a small bowl; pour into the well in the dry ingredients and stir only enough to combine.
4. Scoop the batter into the pan, spreading to the corners, and bake on the middle oven shelf for about 45 minutes or until nicely browned, springy to the touch, and a cake tester inserted in the middle of the loaf comes out clean.
5. Cool the loaf in the upright pan on a wire rack for 10 minutes, loosen around the edge with a thin-blade spatula, then turn out on the rack and cool to room temperature before slicing. **Note:** *This bread freezes well. Wrap snugly in plastic food wrap, overwrap in aluminum foil, date, label, and store in a 0° F. freezer. Serve within 3 to 4 months.*

MANGO-PECAN BREAD

MAKES A 9 × 5 × 3-INCH LOAF

I picked this recipe up years ago on one of my many trips to the Sunshine State and am ashamed to say that I don't remember the source. As a food and travel writer, I am forever collecting leaflets and brochures, many of which contain uncredited local recipes. In any event, this is my tested version of this unusual Florida quick bread. **Tip:** *Because mangoes— even dead-ripe mangoes—are so fibrous, the best way to mash them is to pulse in a food processor. Aim for a texture that approximates cottage cheese.*

2¼ cups sifted all-purpose flour

¾ cup raw sugar or granulated sugar

1½ teaspoons baking powder

¼ teaspoon baking soda

I teaspoon ground cinnamon

¼ teaspoon freshly grated nutmeg

¼ teaspoon salt

I cup coarsely chopped pecans or walnuts

½ cup seedless raisins

I cup coarsely mashed fresh mango
(you'll need one 14- to 16-ounce mango;
see Tip, which precedes)

2 large eggs, lightly beaten

½ cup vegetable oil

I teaspoon vanilla extract

1. Preheat the oven to 350° F. Coat a 9 × 5 × 3-inch baking pan with nonstick oil-and-flour baking spray and set aside.
2. Whisk the flour, sugar, baking powder, baking soda, cinnamon, nutmeg, and salt together in a large bowl. Add the pecans and raisins, toss well, then make a well in the middle of the dry ingredients.
3. Combine the mashed mango, eggs, oil, and vanilla in a 2-quart measure; pour into the well in the dry ingredients and mix only enough to combine. The batter should be lumpy.
4. Scoop the batter into the prepared pan, spreading to the corners, and bake in the lower third of the oven for 50 to 55 minutes or until the bread begins to pull from the sides of the pan and a cake tester inserted in the middle of the loaf comes out clean.
5. Cool the bread in the upright pan on a wire rack for 10 minutes, then loosen around the edge with a small thin-blade spatula and turn out. Cool the bread right side up to room temperature before cutting.

PECANS

The Creeks store up the last [hickory nuts] in their towns . . . They pound them to pieces, and then cast them into boiling water, which, after passing through fine strainers, preserves the most oily part of the liquid . . . [the hickory milk] is as sweet and rich as fresh cream, and it is an ingredient in most of their cookery, especially homony [sic] and corn cakes.
—**WILLIAM BARTRAM,** TRAVELS OF WILLIAM BARTRAM, ON A VISIT TO GEORGIA, 1773

The pecan is a type of hickory and it's possible that the nuts Bartram observed were actually pecans. Anyone who's tried to crack a rock-hard hickory nut and pry out the measly bits inside knows that if pecans were growing in Georgia at the time of Bartram's visit, the Creeks would surely have chosen them. One good whack shatters the shell and frees the meat.

Pecan, according to Sturtevant's Notes on Edible Plants, comes from the Indian (probably Algonquin) word pecaunes, which, I learned elsewhere, means "nuts requiring a stone to crack."

We know that tribes up and down the Mississippi were using pecans just as Bartram describes. We know, too, that as early as the 1540s Cabeza de Vaca wrote of Indians wintering on pecan meal ground from nuts gathered along the great river and its tributaries.

Having found fossilized pecans in Texas and Mexico, archaeologists believe that this is where they originated millions of years ago. As for their abundance along the Mississippi and beyond, historians suggest that nomadic tribes carried them there.

The first person to write down the Indian word *pecaunes* (misspelled *pacane)* is said to have been a ship's carpenter visiting Natchez around the turn of the eighteenth century. He was trav-eling with Pierre LeMoyne (Sieur d'Iberville), the young Canadian dispatched to complete LaSalle's star-crossed exploration of the Mississippi.

In 1775 George Washington planted what he called "Mississippi nuts" at Mount Vernon and in1779 Thomas Jefferson imported pecan trees from Louisiana for his gardens at Monticello.

Today there are more than 500 varieties of pecans, some of them named after the Indian tribes that grew them. Pecan farming is big business through-out the South but Georgia, according to the Georgia Pecan Commission, "leads the nation in pecan production." And has for more than a hundred years.

Southerners can't get enough of them. They bake pecans into breads, pies, cakes, and cookies. They freeze them into ice cream. Stir them into sides and salads. Spice them, sugar them, boil them into candy.

Recently, nutritionists have begun to recognize and appreciate the nutritional importance of pecans. They're rich in largely unsaturated oleic acid (thought to lower LDL or "bad choles-terol") and in addition, they contain phytochemicals that may (repeat *may*) help prevent heart disease as well as cancers of the colon and stomach. Pecans, moreover, are rich in vitamins B_1 and E, good sources, too, of magnesium, copper, zinc, and fiber.

Reason enough to enjoy pecans with a clear conscience.

GLAZED LEMON TEA BREAD

MAKES A 9 × 5 × 3-INCH LOAF

One of the fresh-baked breads served at Shaker Village of Pleasant Hill, Kentucky, this one is as much cake as bread: fine textured and both sweet and tart. The recipe here is adapted from one that appears in Elizabeth C. Kremer's *Welcome Back to Pleasant Hill: More Recipes from the Trustees' House* (1977). Shaker Village, if you don't know it, is an authenti-cally restored nineteenth-century Shaker village located some twenty-five miles south of Lexington. I've visited many times not only because the purity of Shaker design epitomizes the best of American architecture but also because there are daily demonstrations in everything from quilting to coopering to broom making. The best part about Shaker Village is that you can stay in one of the former residences and enjoy Shaker dishes in the Trustees' Office Dining Room. If you haven't been to Shaker Village, by all means go and take the kids. **This is a slice of American history at its best.**

I½ **cups sifted all-purpose flour**

I½ **teaspoons baking powder**

¼ **teaspoon salt**

⅓ **cup firmly packed vegetable shortening or 6 tablespoons butter**

I **cup sugar**

Finely grated zest of I large lemon

2 large eggs

½ **cup milk**

½ **cup finely chopped pecans**

Glaze

⅓ **cup sugar blended with the juice of I large lemon**

1. Preheat the oven to 350° F. Spritz a 9 × 5 × 3-inch loaf pan with nonstick cooking spray and set aside.

2. Sift the flour, baking powder, and salt together onto a piece of wax paper and set aside also.

3. Cream the shortening, sugar, and lemon zest in a large electric mixer bowl first at low speed, then at high speed for about a minute or until well blended. With the machine at medium speed, beat the eggs in one at a time.

4. At low mixer speed, add the sifted dry ingredients alternately with the milk, beginning and ending with the dry and beating after each addition only enough to combine. Fold in the pecans. Scoop the batter into the pan, smoothing the top and spreading to the corners.

5. Bake the bread in the lower third of the oven for 45 to 50 minutes or until it pulls away from

the sides of the pan and feels springy when touched.

6. Transfer the bread to a wire rack but do not remove from the pan. Pour the glaze evenly over the loaf, then cool to room temperature.

7. To serve, loosen the tea bread around the edge using a thin-blade spatula, turn out on the rack, then cut into slices about 3/8 inch thick. **Note:** *This tea bread freezes well. Wrap snugly in plastic food wrap, overwrap with aluminum foil, date, label, and store in a 0° F. freezer. Serve within 3 months.*

"HOT'NS"

MAKES ABOUT 1 DOZEN

Every Southerner knows what a "hot'n" is: a biscuit straight from the oven. The name, it's said, dates back to World War Two when southern hostesses liked to invite soldiers stationed at nearby military bases over for home-cooked Sunday dinners. One hostess, passing a basket of buttermilk biscuits, said to the Yankee lieutenant on her left, "Have a hot'n." And he, thinking that that was the name of the bread, inquired a little later, "May I have another hot'n?" The name stuck. There are dozens of biscuit recipes but this one is fairly classic. The preferred flour is soft and self-rising—White Lily, for example (see box, page 246). And the shortening of choice is lard—hog lard with sometimes a bit of butter added—because it makes for extra-flaky biscuits and also adds subtle meaty flavor. **Note:** *If self-rising flour is unavailable (it was the whole time I lived in New York), substitute all-purpose flour and add 1½ teaspoons baking powder and ½ teaspoon salt.*

2 cups unsifted self-rising flour

½ teaspoon baking soda

½ cup firmly packed lard or
vegetable shortening

1 tablespoon butter

¾ cup buttermilk

1. Preheat the oven to 425° F.
2. Place the flour and baking soda in a large mixing bowl, add the lard and butter, then, using a pastry blender or two knives, cut the fat into the dry ingredients until the texture of uncooked oatmeal.
3. Drizzle in the buttermilk, forking briskly, then continue forking just until a soft dough forms.
4. Turn onto a lightly floured surface and knead lightly 5 to 6 times. With a floured rolling pin, roll the dough out until about ¾ inch thick. Cut into rounds using a floured 2-inch biscuit cutter and space about 1½ inches apart on a large ungreased baking sheet. Gather scraps, reroll, and cut as before.
5. Bake in the lower third of the oven for 15 to 18 minutes or until puffed and lightly browned.
6. Serve at once—and no stinting on butter (or gravy).

❈

Sally went into the cupboard and took out a pottery crock of blackberry preserves, the mouth sealed with beeswax. She gave it to Ada and said, "This'll be good on your leftover biscuits."

—*CHARLES FRAZIER, COLD MOUNTAIN*

❈

1937 The first Krispy Kreme doughnuts are deep-fried and honey-glazed in Winston-Salem, North Carolina. (See Krispy Kreme Doughnuts, page 282.)

Two popular southern grocery chains—Atlanta-based Rogers and Norfolk-based Pender—merge with a combined total of more than 500 stores. Two brand new Pender-Rogers supermarkets open as "Big Stars," one in Greensboro, North Carolina, and one in Griffin, Georgia. They are the first of many.

1938 To raise funds, the Girl Scouts, founded 26 years earlier in Savannah, Georgia, begin selling cookies made by Interbake Foods of Richmond, Virginia. Earlier, they'd baked their own.

Herman Lay buys the Atlanta firm whose potato chips he'd been selling out of the trunk of his car and renames it H. W. Lay & Company. Soon Lay's Potato Chips are the South's favorite.

Lance introduces Toastchee®, two square Cheddar crackers sandwiched together with peanut butter. They're best sellers to this day.

WHITE LILY FLOUR

If it weren't for White Lily, the South would never rise again . . . we'd be eating bagels instead of biscuits.
—*Southern Cookin' with Ron Williams*, www.gritz.net

Southerners *do* eat bagels but they're not about to forsake their beloved biscuits, most of all those featherweight Angel Biscuits (page 248). These, I've heard (but can't prove), were created at White Lily headquarters in Knoxville, Tennessee—sometime in the mid twentieth century.

For nearly 125 years this company has been milling the light baking flour Southerners insist upon for flaky biscuits and cakes so light they nearly levitate. It all began back in 1882 when young Georgian J. Allen Smith settled in Knoxville ("the soft wheat belt"), then, with the aid of four local businessmen, incorporated and reactivated the derelict Knoxville City Mills.

From the outset, Smith's goal was to produce the finest flour available, and to achieve it, he built modern facilities and replaced the old grindstones with steel rollers. Seven times he rolled his wheat, and southern cooks were impressed. Not so Smith, who added multiple sift-ings and by 1896 had produced a flour so fine, so soft he named it White Lily (after his wife, Lillie).

Within six years, White Lily sales had zoomed past the million-dollar mark. Bulk-shipped in wooden barrels, the flour was now sold from Virginia to Florida. Soon flour sacks replaced the barrels, to the delight of frugal housewives, who could turn them into shirts and dresses (never mind that all of them were stamped with the White Lily logo).

Over time White Lily introduced self-rising flour and cornmeal, then an array of time-saving mixes. But none better than the light baking flour that had made White Lily an icon.

CATHEAD BISCUITS

MAKES 4 LARGE BISCUITS

"What you see there, Joe, is what we call the Cathead Biscuit, the gift of an all-knowing and benevolent God." Thus writes Joseph E. Dabney in the bread chapter of his delightful book, *Smokehouse Ham, Spoon Bread, and Scuppernong Wine* (1998). Until he sank his teeth into a cathead biscuit at Berry College near Rome, Georgia, Dabney thought that no one baked better biscuits than his Scotch-Irish South Carolina mother. They were, he writes, "so satisfyingly stout and yet so fluffy and down-home delicious—particularly when she showed me how to dip them into breakfast coffee for what she called 'coffee soakee'. " According to Dabney, southern mountain folk are particularly partial to Cathead Biscuits smothered with Sawmill Gravy (page 94). As for their unusual name, some long-ago someone said that these biscuits were as big as a cat's head—"a medium-size female," southern radio humorist Ludlow

Porch later joked to a listener who'd called in to ask about them. "They're soft and fluffy and almost fall out of your hands into your mouth," Porch added. I now realize that the giant biscuits our round-the-corner neighbor, Mrs. Franklin, made were Cathead Biscuits, although she didn't call them that. Most afternoons after school, I'd race over to Mrs. Franklin's hoping that she had at least one left from lunch that I could smother with gravy or dip into "pot likker" from the greens she'd cooked earlier. Even cold, they were wonderful. Mrs. Franklin made them with bacon drippings and that's the way I like them because of their meaty flavor. **Note:** *With three ingredients only, these biscuits couldn't be easier to make. Still, if they're to be light and fluffy, you must use a good, soft southern flour like White Lily or Martha White and handle the dough as little as possible. Because of their size, Cathead Biscuits bake at a lower-than-usual temperature and never brown like conventional biscuits.* **Tip:** *If self-rising flour is unavailable, substitute all-purpose flour and add 1 teaspoon baking powder and 1/2 teaspoon salt.*

5 tablespoons melted bacon drippings
or lard, plus more for the pan

1 1/2 cups unsifted self-rising flour
(see Note and Tip above)

2/3 cup buttermilk, at room temperature

1. Preheat the oven to 375° F. Grease a well-seasoned 8-inch iron skillet with bacon drippings or lard and set aside.
2. Place the flour in a large mixing bowl and make a well in the center. Whisk the buttermilk with 4 tablespoons of the bacon drip-pings until creamy, then pour into the well in the flour. Using a large spoon, stir just until a soft dough forms. Do not overmix.
3. Turn the dough onto a well-floured surface and knead lightly for about a minute. Shape the dough into a round 1 1/2 inches thick, quarter lengthwise, then quarter crosswise so that you have four pieces of equal size. Roll each piece of dough into a ball and place in the skillet, arranging so that they don't touch one another. Brush the tops of the biscuits with the remaining 1 tablespoon bacon drippings.
4. Slide the skillet onto the middle oven shelf and bake the biscuits for 30 to 35 minutes or until puffed and the color of pale parchment.
5. Serve hot. **Note:** *I like to spoon hot chicken or sausage gravy over Cathead Biscuits, but some Southerners butter them and spread with blackberry jam or sweet sorghum.*

RIZ BISCUITS

MAKES ABOUT 1 1/4 DOZEN BISCUITS

While researching my *American Century Cookbook* back in the 1990s, I had the devil's own time tracing Angel Biscuits (which follow) back to their source. They seemed to have surfaced thirty or forty years earlier as the South's hot new biscuit, and recipes for them began popping up everywhere. It was my good friend Jeanne Voltz who showed me the light. An editor, cookbook author, and food historian of note, Jeanne kept a library of food facts in her head. When I asked her about Angel Biscuits, she said that her Alabama family had made something called Riz Biscuits (colloquial for risen biscuits), then passed along the recipe. Like Angel Biscuits, they contain three leavenings: baking powder (in the self-rising flour), baking soda, and yeast.

2½ cups sifted all-purpose self-rising flour

2 tablespoons sugar

¼ teaspoon baking soda

⅓ cup firmly packed lard or vegetable shortening (it should be ice cold)

One ¼-ounce package active dry yeast dissolved in ¼ cup very warm water (105° to 115° F.)

⅓ to ½ cup buttermilk

2 tablespoons butter, melted

1. Whisk the flour, sugar, and baking soda together in a large mixing bowl; then, using a pastry blender, cut in the lard until the texture of small peas. Quickly fork in the yeast mixture and just enough buttermilk to make a soft but workable dough.

2. Turn onto a floured surface and knead 4 to 5 times until smooth. With a floured rolling pin, roll the dough to a thickness of ¼ inch, then cut into rounds using a floured 2½-inch biscuit cutter. Press any scraps together, roll, and cut into rounds as before.

3. Beginning with the rerolled-and-cut rounds, brush half of the total number with melted butter and space 2 inches apart on ungreased baking sheets. Top with the remaining rounds and brush with the last of the melted butter.

4. Cover with a clean, dry cloth and let rise in a warm, draft-free spot for about 45 minutes or until doubled in bulk. Toward the end of rising, preheat the oven to 375° F.

5. When the biscuits are fully risen, bake in the upper third of the oven for about 15 minutes or until nicely browned. Serve hot—no additional butter needed.

ANGEL BISCUITS

MAKES ABOUT 2½ DOZEN BISCUITS

. . . .

I remember exactly when I first encountered these celestial biscuits. It was in the early 1970s as I prowled the South in search of great grassroots cooks to feature in a new series I was writing for *Family Circle* magazine. Through county home demonstration agents, I obtained the names of the local women who'd won prizes at the county and state fairs. I then interviewed two or three of them in each area before choosing my subject. And all, it seemed, couldn't stop talking about "this fantastic new biscuit recipe" that was all the rage—something called Angel Biscuits. The local cookbooks I perused also featured Angel Biscuits, often two or three versions of them in a single volume. Later, when I began researching my *American Century Cookbook*, I vowed to learn the origin of these feathery biscuits. My friend Jeanne Voltz, for years the *Woman's Day* food editor, thought that Angel Biscuits descended from an old Alabama recipe called Riz Biscuits (see preceding recipe), which she remembered from her childhood. Helen Moore, a freelance food columnist living near Charlotte, North Carolina, told me that a home economics professor of hers at Winthrop College in South Carolina had given her the Angel Biscuits recipe back in the 1950s. "I remember her saying, 'I've got a wonderful new biscuit recipe. It's got yeast in it.' " Others I've queried insist that Angel Biscuits were created at one of the fine southern flour millers; some say at White Lily, others at Martha White (and both are old Nashville companies). In addition to the soft flour used to make them, Angel Biscuits owe their airiness to three leavenings: yeast, baking powder, and baking soda. Small wonder they're also called "bride's biscuits." They are virtually foolproof.

5 cups sifted all-purpose flour
(preferably a fine southern flour;
see headnote)

1 tablespoon baking powder

1 teaspoon baking soda

¼ cup sugar

2 teaspoons salt

1 cup firmly packed vegetable shortening or
lard or a half-and-half mixture of the two

2 cups buttermilk

One ¼-ounce package active dry yeast
dissolved in ¼ cup very warm water
(105° to 115° F.)

1. Preheat the oven to 400° F.
2. Sift the flour, baking powder, baking soda, sugar, and salt into a large mixing bowl. Using a pastry blender, cut in the shortening until the texture of coarse meal. Add the buttermilk and yeast mixture and toss briskly with a fork just until the mixture forms a soft dough.

3. Turn the dough onto a well-floured surface and with floured hands, knead lightly for about a minute. With a floured rolling pin, roll the dough out until 5/8 inch thick; then, using a well-floured 2½- to 2¾-inch cutter, cut into rounds. Place on ungreased baking sheets, spacing about 1½ inches apart. Gather scraps, reroll, and cut as before.
4. Bake in the lower third of the oven for 15 to 18 minutes or until the biscuits are nicely puffed and pale tan on top. Serve at once with plenty of butter.

SWEET POTATO BISCUITS

MAKES ABOUT 1 DOZEN BISCUITS

A while back when I was writing a food and travel story for *Bon Appétit* on the James River Plantations of Virginia, one of the charming local hostesses I interviewed was Payne Tyler of Sherwood Forest, the country estate of President John Tyler (Payne's husband, Harrison Ruffin Tyler, is a grandson). A favorite family recipe, which I've adapted from Payne's original, are these delicate sweet potato biscuits. "There's a story that goes with them," Payne told me. "I grew up at Mulberry Hill Plantation in Edgefield County, South Carolina, eighteen miles from Aiken. My best friend's grandmother—everybody called her 'Dearest'—ate breakfast every morning at ten and it was always the same: sweet potato biscuits, tea, and guava jelly. My friend Emily Ann and I liked them so much we often raced from school to Dearest's home and ate her breakfast,"

Payne continues. "She just sat there, smiled, and watched us. Never said a negative word, but I presume someone cooked another breakfast for her. Anyhow, that's how I happen to have the receipt for these sweet potato biscuits. They are marvelous with goose or duck." I also like them with roast turkey, chicken, and pork and with baked Virginia ham. **Note:** *I bake the sweet potato for this recipe instead of boiling it because it will be less watery and have richer flavor (one hour at 400° F. is about right).*

1¾ cups sifted all-purpose flour

1 tablespoon baking powder

½ teaspoon salt

¼ cup firmly packed lard or vegetable shortening

1 cup firmly packed unseasoned mashed sweet potato (about 1 large potato; see Note above)

¾ cup milk

1. Preheat the oven to 400° F.
2. Sift the flour, baking powder, and salt into a large mixing bowl; then, using a pastry blender or two knives, cut in the lard until the texture of coarse meal. Make a well in the middle of the flour mixture.
3. Combine the mashed sweet potato and milk in a small bowl, whisking until smooth; pour into the well in the flour mixture and mix briskly until the dough holds together.
4. Turn the dough out onto a well-floured surface, sprinkle a little flour over the top, and with well-floured hands, pat the dough out until ¾ inch thick (it is too soft and sticky to roll).
5. Using a well-floured 2¾-inch biscuit cutter, cut the dough into rounds and arrange on ungreased baking sheets, spacing them about 1½ inches apart. Gather the scraps of dough, pat out, and cut as before.
6. Bake the biscuits in the lower third of the oven for 25 to 30 minutes or until nicely browned.
7. Serve hot with plenty of butter.

MY FAVORITE SOUTHERN COMMUNITY COOKBOOKS

Wherever I travel, I pick up community cookbooks, and I now have a library of at least a thousand. But I am choosy about those I buy because not every church or club fund-raiser is worth its price. For me, a local cookbook must have regional flavor. A sense of time and place. And all the better if historical notes and bits of folklore accompany the recipes. Here, then, are the southern community cookbooks that measure up in my eyes, the ones I refer to again and again. **Note:** *The majority are still in print and can be ordered online; even the out-of-print can be searched on the Internet. I omit prices because these change from printing to printing.*

Bethabara Moravian Cook Book. 7th ed. Compiled by the Women's Fellowship, Bethabara

Moravian Church, Winston-Salem, NC, 1981.

Cabbage Patch Famous Kentucky Recipes. Compiled by the Cabbage Patch Circle, Louisville, 1952.

Cane River Cuisine. The Service League of Natchitoches, Louisiana, Inc., 1974.

Charleston Receipts. The Junior League of Charleston, Inc., 1950. With its strong sense of time and place, this is the gold standard by which I judge all local cookbooks.

Come On In! Recipes from The Junior League of Jackson, Mississippi. The Junior League of Jackson, Inc., 1991.

The Cooking Book. The Junior League of Louisville, Inc., 1978.

The Farmington Cookbook. A fund-raiser published to benefit Farmington, an 1810 Federal-style Kentucky home designed by Thomas Jefferson. Louisville, KY: Courier-Journal Lithographing, 1968.

Favorite Recipes of the Lower Cape Fear. Published by the Ministering Circle, Wilmington, NC. Revised edition, 1980. Better yet, the 1955 edition.

From North Carolina Kitchens: Favorite Recipes Old and New. Compiled by the North Carolina Federation of Home Demonstration Clubs, 1953. Long out of print but worth tracking down because of its mother lode of heirloom recipes and nuggets of folk wisdom.

Full Moon, High Tide: Tastes and Traditions of the Lowcountry. Compiled by the Beaufort (SC) Academy, 2001.

Gasparilla Cookbook: Favorite Florida West Coast Recipes. Compiled by The Junior League of Tampa, Inc., 1961.

Gracious Goodness! The Junior League of Macon, Georgia, Inc., 1981.

Key West Cookbook. The Woman's Club of Key West, 1949.

Maryland's Way: The Hammond-Harwood House Cook Book. Published by The Hammond-Harwood House Association, Annapolis, 1963.

Natchez: Authentic Antebellum Recipes of the Old South, 1790-1865. Compiled by Southland Graphics, Kingsport, TN, 1987.

Plantation Country. The Women's Service League, West Feliciana Parish, St. Francisville, LA, 1981.

Putting on the Grits. The Junior League of Columbia, SC, Inc., 1985.

River Road Recipes. The Junior League of Baton Rouge, Inc., 1959.

Savannah Style. The Junior League of Savannah, Inc., no date.

Toast to Tidewater: Celebrating Virginia's Finest Food & Beverages. The Junior League of Norfolk-Virginia Beach, Inc., 2004. The seafood chapter alone is worth the price of the book.

Vintage Vicksburg. The Junior Auxiliary of Vicksburg, MS, 1985.

Virginia Cookery Past and Present (including "A Manuscript Cook Book of The Lee and Washington Families" published for the first time). The Woman's Auxiliary of Olivet Episcopal Church, Franconia, VA, 1957.

BEATEN BISCUIT

Rub half a pound of butter and a little salt into 4 quarts of flour. Wet the whole with a little more than a pt. of new milk. Knead it, mold it, pound it, roll it half an inch thick, cut it, and bake in a quick oven. To do it well will require half an hour's kneading.
—From *North Carolina Kitchens, Favorite Recipes: Old and New*, 1953

CORN MUFFINS

MAKES ABOUT 1½ DOZEN MUFFINS

With the exception of biscuits, corn breads are the universal southern favorite. And the quicker the better; these classic corn muffins are ready to serve in half an hour. **Note:** *For extra flavor, use bacon drippings as the shortening. In days past, frugal southern cooks would keep a jar or old coffee tin of bacon drippings at the ready—to stir into corn breads; to dress cooked collards, turnip greens, and snap beans; even to wilt lettuce. To this day, wilted lettuce (also known as Smothered Lettuce, page 231) remains popular in much of the South.*

1½ cups unsifted stone-ground yellow cornmeal

½ cup sifted all-purpose flour

2 tablespoons sugar

1 tablespoon baking powder

¾ teaspoon salt

¼ teaspoon black pepper

1 large egg, lightly beaten

1 cup milk

3½ tablespoons melted bacon drippings or lard or, if you prefer, 3 tablespoons vegetable oil

1. Preheat the oven to 400° F. Spritz 18 muffin pan cups with nonstick cooking spray and set aside (I use three 6-muffin pans).
2. Combine the cornmeal, flour, sugar, baking powder, salt, and pepper in a large mixing bowl and make a well in the center.
3. Whisk the egg, milk, and bacon drippings together in a small bowl or 1-quart measure until creamy, pour into the well in the dry ingredients, and stir only enough to combine. The batter should be lumpy and it's best if a few floury specks show because they prove that you haven't overbeaten the batter. Overbeating is the fastest way to toughen a muffin.
4. Spoon the batter into the muffin pan cups, dividing the total amount evenly.
5. Bake in the lower third of the oven for 20 to 25 minutes or until lightly browned and springy to the touch. Serve hot with plenty of butter.

When I'm old and gray, I want to have a house by the sea . . . and a damn good kitchen to cook in.

—*AVA GARDNER*, NORTH CAROLINA NATIVE

TO MAKE CRACKLIN'S

First of all, sweet-talk your butcher into saving 1 pound of pork fat trimmings for you. Preheat the oven to 275° F. Using a very sharp knife, cut the pork fat into ¼-inch dice and spread over the bottom of a large, heavy Dutch oven (I use an enameled cast-iron pot that measures 12 inches across). Add 1½ cups boiling water, stir well, then cover the Dutch oven and set on the lowest shelf of the oven. Bake for 1 hour. Remove the lid; stir the pork fat well and again spread it over the bottom of the pot. Bake uncovered 2 to 2½ hours longer, stirring every 30 minutes, until all the fat has cooked out and only crisp brown bits remain. Scoop the brown bits to several thicknesses of paper toweling to drain, and when cool, store in an airtight plastic container until ready to use. Use as recipes direct. Makes 1 cup cracklin's. **Note:** *Thrifty Appalachian folk would save the drippings to use in cooking or to dress vegetables; I don't because of their high cholesterol content.*

"Shut your eyes and open your mouth
and I'll give you a surprise," she said.
It was not often that she made crackling bread;
she said she never had time . . . she knew
I loved crackling bread.

—**HARPER LEE,** *TO KILL A MOCKINGBIRD*

1939 — Duncan Hines lists Harland Sanders's Corbin, Kentucky, restaurant in his popular guide, *Adventures in Good Eating.*

Gustav Brunn emigrates from Germany to Baltimore, bringing with him his spice grinder and a dream: to start a spice business. His winning blend of mustard, celery, ginger, bay leaves, and cayenne—Old Bay Seasoning— pairs superbly with Chesapeake fish and shellfish.

Willis and Paul Teeter open Teeter's Food Mart in Mooresville, North Carolina. It is the first of several, which later merge with the Charlotte-based Harris supermarkets.

1940 — Pepsi launches the singing commercial by airing its bouncy "Pepsi-Cola hits the spot" on radio.

1940s — Using the milk of their Holstein cows and following the techniques of their French Trappist brothers at Port du Salut, the monks at Gethsemani Farms near Bardstown, Kentucky, begin making and selling artisanal cheeses.

1941 — Baltimore author Marian Tracy writes *Casserole Cookery*, an instant bestseller that depends heavily upon convenience foods.

RICE MUFFINS

One cup boiled rice (left over will answer), 1 cup sweet milk, 2 eggs well beaten, 5 tablespoons melted butter, ½ teaspoonful salt, 1 tablespoon sugar, 3 teaspoonfuls baking powder and 1½ cupfuls flour mixed into soft batter which will drop from a spoon. Stir after all ingredients are in, lightly but thoroughly and drop into hot buttered muffin rings.

—*Good Recipes by Athens' Housewives,*
1916–1917

IRON SKILLET CORN BREAD

MAKES AN 8-INCH ROUND LOAF

Whenever my New York friends fly south for a visit, I serve this corn bread for breakfast—straight from the oven. My good friend Sara Moulton liked it so well that she asked for the recipe, then featured it on her Food Network show *Cooking Live.* What makes this particular corn bread so special is the contrast of textures: It's crusty-brown on the outside and soft, in fact almost creamy, inside. The recipe comes from my stepmother's aunt Annie Pool, a Virginia farm woman and exceptionally gifted cook who was never fazed when several dozen members of the extended family showed up for the annual Thanksgiving feast. **Note:** *The way to enjoy*

this corn bread is to split each wedge horizontally while it's hissing-hot, tuck in a couple of pats of butter, then eat the instant they melt.

2 cups unsifted stone-ground cornmeal (preferably white)

1 tablespoon sugar

½ teaspoon salt

¼ teaspoon baking soda

⅓ cup firmly packed lard or vegetable shortening (I always use lard because it gives the corn bread better flavor)

2 large eggs, lightly beaten

2 cups buttermilk

1. Preheat the oven to 425° F.
2. Combine the cornmeal, sugar, salt, and baking soda in a large mixing bowl and make a well in the middle of the dry ingredients.
3. Place the lard in a well-seasoned 8-inch iron skillet with an ovenproof handle and set on the middle oven shelf for 2 to 3 minutes or until the lard melts completely.
4. Meanwhile, add the eggs and buttermilk to the well in the dry ingredients and stir only enough to mix. Pour in the hot melted lard and stir briskly to incorporate.
5. Pour the batter into the hot skillet and bake on the middle oven shelf for about 25 minutes or until nicely browned and a cake tester inserted midway between the center and the edge comes out clean.
6. Rush the skillet from oven to table, cut the corn bread into wedges, and serve with plenty of fresh unsalted butter.

CRACKLIN' BREAD

MAKES AN 8 × 8 × 2-INCH LOAF

Cracklin's are the crisp meaty bits left after pork fat has been rendered into lard—a delicious by-product of the annual autumn hog killings. Fortunately you needn't butcher your own hogs to obtain cracklin's today. They can be ordered (see Sources, page 401) or you can make your own from pork fat trimmings (see page 253). This simple recipe comes from the Smoky Mountains.

2 cups unsifted stone-ground cornmeal (do not use granular supermarket meal)

¾ teaspoon salt

½ teaspoon baking soda

1 cup cracklin's (see headnote)

1¾ cups sour milk or buttermilk

1. Preheat the oven to 400° F. Coat an 8 × 8 × 2-inch square pan with nonstick cooking spray and set aside.
2. Combine the cornmeal, salt, and baking soda in a large mixing bowl; add the cracklin's, toss well to mix, then make a well in the middle of the dry ingredients.
3. Pour the milk into the well in the dry ingredients and stir only enough to form a stiff dough. Scoop into the pan, spreading to the corners.
4. Bake the cracklin' bread on the middle oven shelf for 30 to 35 minutes or until lightly browned and springy to the touch.
5. Cut into squares and serve hot. No butter needed.

1943 Sema Wilkes begins her long career as a Savannah restaurateur by cooking part-time at a men's boardinghouse. Her specialty: The southern country cooking she grew up with.

Alabama agronomist George Washington Carver dies. During his years of research at Tuskegee Institute, he developed more than 300 peanut products, among them peanut cheese, peanut chili sauce, peanut mayonnaise, and several different peanut butters.

Douglas Odom and his wife, Louisa, create a secret spice blend for sausage and launch the Tennessee Pride company. Still family-owned but now manufactured in Arkansas as well as the Volunteer State, Tennessee, Pride remains one of the South's favorite sausages.

1944 Melvin Alexander buys a 93-year-old building in Baltimore's Fell's Point, and before long turns the old tavern into a crab house with the help of his in-laws, the Obryckis.

1945 California's Rosefield Packing Company opens a Skippy Peanut Butter plant in Portsmouth, Virginia.

KENTUCKY CORN LIGHT BREAD

"This is the best corn bread I ever put in my mouth," Lois Watkins of Trigg County, Kentucky, said of this old family recipe some years ago when I flew out to interview her for a *Family Circle* series I was writing on America's best country cooks. First steamed and then baked, it is incredibly light—more angel food than corn bread. I use a 2-quart steamed pudding mold to cook it, but an 8-inch tube pan works nearly as well. The trick is to grease the mold or pan well, then dust it with cornmeal. **Note:** *Use only stone-ground cornmeal for this recipe (see Sources, page 401); the granular supermarket variety won't work.*

2½ cups unsifted stone-ground cornmeal (yellow or white)

⅔ cup sifted all-purpose flour

½ cup sugar

1 teaspoon baking soda

1 teaspoon salt

2 cups buttermilk

1 large egg, lightly beaten

¼ cup lard or butter, melted

1. Grease a 2-quart steamed pudding mold or 8-inch tube pan well, then dust with cornmeal and tap out the excess. Set the pudding mold or tube pan aside.
2. Combine the cornmeal, flour, sugar, baking soda, and salt in a large mixing bowl and make a well in the center.
3. Whisk the buttermilk, egg, and melted lard in a small bowl or 1-quart measure until creamy; pour into the well in the dry ingredients and beat hard for about 1 minute.
4. Pour the batter into the prepared mold and snap on the lid (or cover the tube pan snugly with foil). Set the mold on a rack over boiling water in a deep kettle (the bottom of the mold should not touch the water), cover the kettle, and steam the bread 35 minutes. Toward the end of steaming, preheat the oven to 375° F.
5. Lift the pudding mold from the kettle and remove the lid. Slide the uncovered mold onto the middle oven shelf and bake the bread for about 35 minutes or until it is lightly browned and begins to pull from the sides of the mold.
6. Remove the mold from the oven and cool in the upright mold on a wire rack for 2 to 3 minutes; this helps keep the bread from cracking as you unmold it.
7. Using a thin-blade spatula, carefully loosen the bread around the edge and central tube, then invert on a heated round plate.
8. Cut into wedges and serve hot with plenty of butter.

MARIA HARRISON'S BATTER BREAD (SPOON BREAD)

Maria (pronounced muh-RYE-ah, the southern way) is the mother of my good friend and colleague Maria Harrison Reuge, formerly a *Gourmet* editor and now the owner, with her French chef husband, Guy, of Mirabelle, a splendid little restaurant on the North Shore of Long Island. I've eaten "high on the hog" there, as they'd say down south. When I was heading for Tidewater Virginia to research a food and travel article for *Bon Appétit* magazine, Maria opened many James River plantation doors for me. She grew up on Coggins Point Farm overlooking the James with her brother Jimmy (now married to Lisa Ruffin of Evelynton Plantation), and this "old southern receipt" is one she remembers her mother making. Batter bread, also called "spoon bread," is in fact a corn bread soufflé popular throughout the South. There are many different recipes for it, but Maria Harrison's is hands down the best I've eaten. What goes with batter bread? Just about everything: Think of it, if you like, as a potato substitute, although to tell the truth, many Southerners serve potatoes *and* batter bread at the same meal. **Note:** *If your batter bread is to be light, you must use stone-ground cornmeal (preferably white; see Sources, page 401) and cook it until very thick. The granular yellow cornmeal sold at supermarkets simply will not work.*

I tablespoon vegetable oil

2 cups cold water

I teaspoon salt

I cup stone-ground white cornmeal
(see Note above)

2 cups milk

2 large eggs, lightly beaten

1. Position the shelf in the middle of the oven and preheat to 425° F. Spoon the oil into a 2-quart soufflé dish and set on the middle oven shelf while you proceed with the recipe.

2. Bring the water and salt to a boil in a large, heavy saucepan set over moderate heat. Slowly whisk in the cornmeal and cook, stirring constantly, for about 2 minutes or until thick and pastelike.

3. Remove from the heat, add 1 cup of the milk, and beat until smooth and creamy. Next beat the eggs in, half at a time, then blend in the remaining 1 cup milk.

4. Remove the hot soufflé dish from the oven, pour in the batter, and return to the middle oven shelf. Bake for 40 to 45 minutes or until the batter bread is puffy and brown and quivers slightly when you nudge the dish.

5. Rush the batter bread to the table and serve with plenty of butter, salt, and freshly ground black pepper.

HUSH PUPPIES

MAKES 3 TO 3½ DOZEN

It was bound to happen: hush puppy mixes and hush puppy "shooters." I prefer to make mine from scratch and to drop them into the hot fat the old-fashioned way—from a rounded teaspoon—instead of from a spring-loaded "gun" that shoots the batter out in squiggles.

I'm not exactly sure where I ate my first hush puppy, probably on Chesapeake Bay. We sometimes roared across "the little bay" from our summer cottage to eat at some little fish house in Whitestone or Irvington, Virginia. Or maybe it was on one of our jaunts to the Carolina coast.

Wherever, whenever, I couldn't have been more than eight or ten. From then on, I've ordered hush puppies every chance I get—with fried fish, of course, but also with fried chicken and pulled pork (barbecue). For me the perfect hush puppy is fine-textured and light, not too sweet and with just a whiff of onion. And it must come straight from the deep-fat fryer. Any languishing on a steam table turns it leaden in seconds.

As with so many southern recipes, there's a story to explain this one's amusing name. Said to date back to the days of Reconstruction after the Civil War, these little corn bread fritters were stirred up by fish camp cooks, fried in deep fat, then tossed to quiet the hounds while their masters ate. In *Southern Food: At Home, on the Road, in History* (1987), John Egerton, an author for whom I have profound respect, writes that hush puppies originated in Florida, probably "in the general vicinity of St. Marks . . . an old fishing village on the Gulf Coast south of Tallahassee." **Note:** *You must use a floury, stone-ground cornmeal when making hush puppies. Those made with granular meal will fly apart in the hot fat.*

Vegetable oil (for deep-fat frying)

2½ cups sifted stone-ground cornmeal (preferably white)

1 tablespoon sugar

1 teaspoon salt

1 teaspoon baking soda

½ teaspoon baking powder

1¼ cups buttermilk

¼ cup finely grated yellow onion

1 large egg

1. Pour 2 inches of oil into a deep skillet, insert a deep-fat thermometer, and set over moderate heat.

2. Meanwhile, combine the cornmeal, sugar, salt, baking soda, and baking powder in a large bowl, pressing out all lumps and making a well in the middle of the dry ingredients.

3. Whisk the buttermilk, onion, and egg together in a small bowl, then pour into the well in the dry ingredients and stir briskly to mix.

4. When the oil in the skillet has reached 375° F., scoop the hush puppy batter up by rounded teaspoonfuls and ease into the oil. Fry, no more than 6 to 8 at a time, for 2 to 2½ minutes, turning as needed, until richly browned on all sides. **Note:** *Keeping the temperature of the oil as close as possible to 375° F. is key, so adjust the burner heat as needed. If the oil is too cool, the hush puppies will be greasy; if it's too hot, they will burn before they are done inside.*

5. As the hush puppies brown, lift to paper toweling with a slotted spoon. Also skim any small bits from the oil, and continue frying the hush puppies until all are done.

6. Serve hot with fried fish or shellfish, fried chicken, or pork barbecue.

❧

Lucia insisted that they have a regular hour for breakfast just like they did for other meals . . . a regular breakfast made for other regular habits.

—FLANNERY O'CONNOR, THE CROP

❧

SARAH RUTLEDGE (1782-1855)

She wasn't the first South Carolina lady to write a cookbook. Eliza Lucas Pinckney and her daughter Harriott Pinckney Horry (page 374) beat her to it with handwritten collections of family receipts and home remedies (both published posthumously in the twentieth century).

But Sarah, in 1847, was the first to publish a major cookbook—"for charitable purposes," Anna Wells Rutledge writes in her introduction to the 1979 facsimile of *The Carolina Housewife* (University of South Carolina Press). Reluctant to claim authorship, Sarah identified herself only as "A Lady of Charleston." Altogether proper back then, when, according to local etiquette, a lady's name appeared in print only three times: at birth, marriage, and death.

That tradition persisted well into the twentieth century. When I was a junior editor at *The Ladies' Home Journal* in the early 1960s, we wanted to feature Charleston's exclusive St. Cecilia Ball. Not a chance.

Like Pinckney and Horry, Sarah Rutledge belonged to the planter aristocracy; her father, Edward Rutledge, signed the Declaration of Independence; so, too, her mother's brother Arthur Middleton. She would have known and socialized with Harriott Pinckney Horry, whose brother Thomas Pinckney took young Sarah to England to be educated along with his own children.

There are more than 550 recipes in *The Carolina Housewife*, twenty-one of them from *The Receipt Book of Harriott Pinckney Horry, 1770*, according to historian Richard J. Hooker, who edited the facsimile edition of that book (University of South Carolina Press, 1984). "At least three of those," Hooker points out in his introduction to the Horry book, "were ones that Harriott had taken" from her own mother. He is quick to add, however, that some of Horry's receipts "were so changed in wording [by Rutledge] as to suggest that they might have come indirectly . . ."

It was common practice for relatives and friends to share favorite recipes just as they do today. Those that Sarah Rutledge gives us are decidedly Lowcountry. There are, for example, some twenty recipes for rice bread in *The Carolina Housewife*, even more for corn and hominy breads. Soups abound, in particular those featuring such local staples as rice, okra, benne seeds, ground-nuts (peanuts), turtle, terrapin, oysters, shrimp, and crab. There are pilaus galore, too, including that Lowcountry rice and black-eyed pea classic called Hoppin' John.

To quote directly from Sarah Rutledge's preface: "The one [cookbook] now offered is (as it professes to be) a selection from the family receipt books of friends and acquaintances, who have kindly placed their manuscripts at the disposal of the editor."

AUNT BERTIE'S CRISPY CORNMEAL PANCAKES

MAKES 4 SERVINGS

. . . .

My niece Kim has been bragging about these light-as-air "corn breads" for years and urged me to include them in this book. They come from her mother's side of the family (my brother was Kim's dad). I never met Aunt Bertie (who died at 79) but like her many sisters, she was a good southern cook. I recently drove down to Fuquay-Varina, North Carolina, where Kim shares a barn-red bungalow with her older sister, Linda, to watch her make Aunt Bertie's cornmeal pancakes; I'd never tasted them. Like Aunt Bertie, Kim's a "by guess and by gosh cook." She rarely resorts to precise measures because she instinctively knows when something's right or wrong. This time I made her use measuring cups and spoons for this old word-of-mouth recipe. Kim has improved the original by using self-rising cornmeal and her pancakes practically rise off the plate. Linda's boyfriend, Eric Eibelheuser, a transplanted New Jersey–ite now working in North Carolina, joined us the day Kim tested Aunt Bertie's cornmeal pancakes and, like the rest of us, was blown away by them. "You could make a meal out of these!" he said. Quite so. Serve them for breakfast, lunch, or supper accompanied by sourwood or tupelo honey or, if you prefer, homemade muscadine, damson, or fig preserves (pages 380, 382, and 384). **Note:** *Kim says that only a well-seasoned cast-iron skillet will do for frying the pancakes. She pours in about 1/4 inch of vegetable oil,* then sets over fairly high heat until it's "spitting-hot." Kim's skillet is small—only eight inches across—so she must cook the pancakes in three batches. In my ten-inch skillet, I can do it in two.

1/2 cup unsifted self-rising, stone-ground yellow cornmeal

1/4 cup unsifted all-purpose flour

1/2 teaspoon sugar

1/4 teaspoon salt

1/8 teaspoon black pepper

2/3 cup cold water (about)

1 1/3 cups vegetable oil (for frying)

1. Combine the cornmeal, flour, sugar, salt, and pepper in a medium-size mixing bowl, then whisk in just enough water to make a batter slightly thicker than pancake batter.

2. Pour the vegetable oil into a 10-inch cast-iron skillet and set over moderately high heat for about 2 minutes or until ripples appear on the skillet bottom.

3. Reduce the heat to moderate and fry the pancakes in two batches, dropping the batter into the skillet by rounded tablespoons, spacing them well apart, and browning 45 seconds to 1 minute on each side or until crisp and golden. Drain on paper toweling.

4. Serve the cornmeal pancakes hot with honey, jam, or preserves. No butter needed, although Aunt Bertie usually put out a plate of butter as well as a pot of honey and jars of homemade jams and preserves.

HOT DINNER ROLLS

MAKES 2 TO 2½ DOZEN ROLLS

. . . .

Florence Soltys, one of Chapel Hill's most accomplished hostesses, often serves these rolls at luncheons and dinners. The recipe, she tells me, is one that she remembers her Tennessee aunt, Rhoda Gray, making when she was a child. Florence also tells me that she descends from two old East Tennessee families: the Grays on her father's side and the Hills on her mother's. "We were hill people who settled around Cades Cove," she adds. That nineteenth-century village is now a major attraction of the Great Smoky Mountains National Park. The dairy farm where Florence spent her childhood—"not far from Gatlinburg"—is still in the Gray family. Her brother, a retired veterinarian, now runs it. **Note:** *This rich yeast dough can be shaped into cloverleaf, fan-tans, Parker House rolls, pan rolls, anything you fancy. I personally favor cloverleaf rolls.*

I cup milk

3 tablespoons butter or vegetable shortening

3 tablespoons sugar

I teaspoon salt

One ¼-ounce package active dry yeast dissolved
in ¼ cup very warm water (105° to 115° F.)

I large egg, lightly beaten

4 to 4½ cups sifted all-purpose flour

I tablespoon butter, melted

1. Heat the milk in a small, heavy saucepan for about 3 minutes over moderate heat or until it steams. Pour the milk into a large heatproof bowl and mix in the butter, sugar, and salt; cool until an instant-read thermometer registers 105° to 115° F.

2. Mix in the yeast mixture, then the egg, and finally 4 cups of the flour. Mix well by hand, adding more flour as needed until you have a soft but manageable dough; this will take about 3 minutes.

3. Shape the dough into a ball, place in a large buttered bowl, turn in the bowl so the buttered side is up, then cover with a clean, dry cloth and let rise in a warm, draft-free spot for about 1 hour or until doubled in bulk.

4. Punch the dough down, then shape into cloverleaf rolls, fan-tans, Parker House rolls, or pan rolls—whatever you fancy—placing in greased muffin pan cups or on greased baking sheets. Cover with a clean, dry cloth and let rise in a warm, draft-free spot for about 45 minutes or until doubled in bulk.

5. Toward the end of rising, preheat the oven to 375° F. Brush the rolls gently with the melted butter and bake on the middle oven shelf for 15 to 18 minutes or until lightly browned.

6. Serve hot with plenty of butter.

❀

Food—two banana cakes and a baked ham, a platter of darkly deviled eggs, new rolls—and flowers kept arriving at the back, and the kitchen filled with women . . .

—EUDORA WELTY, *THE GOLDEN APPLES*

❀

SWEET POTATO YEAST ROLLS

MAKES 2 DOZEN CLOVERLEAF ROLLS

. . . .

This recipe is adapted from one sent to me by the North Carolina SweetPotato Commission. This southern state tops all others in the production of sweet potatoes and the commission's mission is to spread the gospel of the golden tubers: their impressive nutritional value, their round-the-calendar availability, their easy-on-the-budget price, and, not least, their delicious versatility.

Two ¼-ounce packages active dry yeast

⅓ cup granulated sugar or raw sugar

½ cup very warm water (105° to 115° F.)

¾ cup very warm milk (105° to 115° F.)

⅓ cup plus 3 tablespoons butter, melted

1 cup puréed cooked sweet potato

1 teaspoon salt

1 teaspoon finely grated lemon zest

¼ teaspoon freshly grated nutmeg

5 to 5½ cups unsifted unbleached all-purpose flour

1. Spritz 24 standard-size muffin pan cups with nonstick cooking spray and set aside.

2. Combine the yeast, 1 teaspoon of the sugar, and the warm water in a small bowl, and set aside to "work" for about 5 minutes. It will bubble and froth.

3. Meanwhile, beat the remaining sugar, the milk, ⅓ cup melted butter, sweet potato purée, salt, lemon zest, and nutmeg in a large electric mixer bowl at low speed just enough to combine. When the yeast mixture is good and frothy, add and beat until smooth.

4. With the mixer at low speed, add 2 cups of the flour, then beat for 2 to 3 minutes at moderately high speed until elastic. Continue adding the flour, about ½ cup at a time, until you have a soft but manageable dough.

5. Turn the dough onto a lightly floured surface and knead vigorously for several minutes, adding only enough additional flour to keep the dough from sticking.

6. Shape the dough into a ball, place in a buttered bowl, then turn the dough in the bowl so the buttered side is up. Cover with a clean, dry cloth and set in a warm draft-free spot for about 1 hour or until the dough has doubled in bulk.

7. Punch the dough down, turn onto a lightly floured surface, and knead for about a minute. Divide the dough into 24 pieces of equal size, then from each piece, shape 3 same-size balls. Place 3 balls in each muffin pan cup and brush with the remaining melted butter.

8. Cover the rolls with a cloth and set in a warm, draft-free spot for about 30 minutes or until doubled in bulk. Toward the end of rising, preheat the oven to 375° F.

9. When the rolls are fully risen, bake in the lower third of the oven for 20 to 25 minutes or until nicely browned and hollow sounding when thumped.

10. Serve hot with plenty of fresh sweet butter.

FARMHOUSE BREAD

MAKES THREE 8 × 4 × 3-INCH LOAVES

"My Aunt Zella Gray was a marvelous cook," Florence Soltys told me when she handed me this old East Tennessee recipe. A maiden lady, Zella Gray lived near enough to the dairy farm where Florence grew up to share the loaves she baked. Now living in Chapel Hill, North Carolina, Florence still bakes Aunt Zella's bread whenever her busy schedule permits. And lucky the family and friends who get to eat it.

2¼ to 2¾ cups very warm water
(105° to 115° F.)

¼ cup sugar

Two ¼-ounce packages active dry yeast

8 cups sifted all-purpose flour, plus
more for kneading

½ cup nonfat dry milk powder

1 tablespoon salt

½ cup firmly packed vegetable shortening
or ½ cup (1 stick) butter, cut into pats

1. Place ½ cup of the warm water in a spouted 1-quart measure and mix in 1 tablespoon of the sugar and all of the yeast. Let stand in a warm spot for about 5 minutes or until frothy.
2. Meanwhile, combine 2 cups of the flour, the milk powder, salt, and remaining sugar in a large mixing bowl. Add the shortening and using a pastry blender, cut into the dry ingredients until the texture of coarse meal. Mix in the remaining flour.

1946

Krispy Kreme is registered as a trademark by the U.S. Patent Office. The company is incorporated and takes over doughnut shops in South Carolina, Tennessee, West Virginia, and elsewhere in North Carolina.

Brennan's opens on Royal Street in New Orleans's French Quarter and becomes famous for its lavish breakfast. Its signature dish: Bananas Foster.

At its tiny Plymouth plant, the Florida Foods Corporation packs 2,500 cases of fresh orange juice in ice, loads them onto freight cars, and ships them to Washington, D.C., to be served at the Hot Shoppe restaurants. And that is the start of Minute Maid.

Truett Cathy names his new ten-stool, South Atlanta café the "Dwarf Grill," never dreaming that it would become the South's popular Chick-fil-A restaurant chain.

W. T. Young Foods of Lexington, Kentucky, introduces Big Top Peanut Butter. The stemmed, pressed glass goblets in which it was packed are now collector's items.

3. Add the yeast mixture and 1¾ cups of the remaining warm water and mix well, adding more of the water as needed to make a soft but workable dough.

4. Turn the dough onto a floured surface and knead for about 5 minutes or until smooth and elastic. Shape the dough into a ball, place in a large buttered bowl, then turn the dough in the bowl so the buttered side is up.

5. Cover the dough with a clean, dry cloth and let rise in a warm, draft-free spot for about 1 hour or until doubled in bulk. Punch the dough down, cover, and again let rise until doubled in bulk—about 1 hour.

6. Punch the dough down once more, knead briefly on a lightly floured surface until satiny, then divide into three pieces of equal size. Quickly grease three 8 × 4 × 3-inch loaf pans, shape each piece of dough into a loaf, and place in the pans. Cover with a clean, dry cloth and let the loaves rise in a warm, draft-free spot for about 1 hour or until doubled in bulk. Toward the end of rising, preheat the oven to 350° F.

7. Bake the loaves on the middle oven shelf for 35 to 40 minutes or until richly browned and hollow sounding when thumped.

8. Remove the loaves from the oven. Let stand in the upright pans on wire racks for 5 minutes, then invert and turn right side up. Cool to room temperature before cutting.

❀

If you burn your bread,
it means your husband's angry.

—OLD SMOKIES SUPERSTITION

❀

SALLY LUNN

MAKES A 10-INCH TUBE LOAF

This lightest and loveliest of yeast breads, much prized in the Colonial South, is said to date back to the Jamestown Colony, specifically to 1619 when a shipload of "Virginia maides" arrived from England to keep house for the men who had settled there twelve years earlier. In *Food in England* (1954), Dorothy Hartley writes that the bread's name comes from the cry made by a buxom lass hawking buns on the streets of Bath. "Yelled in good west-country French," that cry was "Solet Lune! Soleilune! [sun and moon]." "An appropriate name," Hartley reasons, "for a round bun, flat gold on top, and flat white below." She adds that the buns were "an infernal trouble to make, taking from sunrise to sunset to 'raise'." Their tops were gilded with beaten egg yolks, and, Hartley continues, they were "split hot and embosomed in clouds of cream." I will never forget my first bite of a quite different Sally Lunn at the King's Arms in Colonial Williamsburg. I remember a waiter trundling a cart over to our table and cutting a fat wedge from a loaf that looked for all the world like angel food cake except that it was yellow. Even though I was no more than ten, I couldn't wait to find a recipe for Sally Lunn. This one is adapted from a recipe found in the Jamestown Foundation files.

One ¼-ounce package active dry yeast

¼ cup very warm water (105° to 115° F.)

⅓ cup butter, softened

⅓ cup sugar

3 large eggs, beaten until frothy

1 cup warm milk (105° to 115° F.)

4 cups sifted all-purpose flour combined
with 1 teaspoon salt

1. Butter a 10-inch tube pan well and set aside.
2. Mix the yeast into the warm water in a small bowl and set aside to soften for about 5 minutes. Meanwhile, beat the butter and sugar in a large electric mixer bowl at high speed until light and fluffy. Add the eggs and beat just enough to combine.
3. Combine the softened yeast with the warm milk, then, with the mixer at low speed, add the flour alternately with the yeast mixture, beginning and ending with the flour.
4. Remove the bowl from the mixer, cover with a clean, dry cloth, then set in a warm, draft-free spot for about 1 hour or until the dough has doubled in bulk.
5. Stir the dough down, then pour into the tube pan, spreading as evenly as possible. Again cover with a cloth and set in a warm spot to rise until doubled in bulk; this second rising will take 30 to 40 minutes. Toward the end of rising, preheat the oven to 350° F.
6. When the dough is fully risen, bake the Sally Lunn in the lower third of the oven for 45 to 50 minutes or until nicely browned and hollow sounding when thumped.
7. Remove the Sally Lunn from the oven and cool in the upright pan on a wire rack for 10 minutes. Using a thin-blade spatula, loosen the bread around the edge and around the central tube, then invert on a large round platter.
8. Cut the Sally Lunn into wedges and serve warm with fresh sweet butter.

1947

McCormick of Baltimore acquires A. Schilling & Co., a San Francisco coffee, extract, and spice house, gaining West Coast distribution for its East Coast products.

Vernon Rudolph offers Krispy Kreme franchises at $3,500 a pop and throws in ten bags of doughnut mix, vital equipment, packaging supplies, and a Chevrolet panel truck.

Reynolds Metals of Louisville, Kentucky, rolls out aluminum foil.

Italian immigrant Anthony Rossi founds a citrus shipping business in southwest Florida; over time it becomes Tropicana.

The Pender-Rogers chain of Atlanta begins renaming its self-service stores. They are now Colonial Stores. In fewer than ten years, Colonial extends its reach by absorbing the midwestern Albers and Stop and Shop chains. By 1970, there are 430 Colonial groceries in nine states.

MORAVIAN SUGAR CAKE

MAKES 12 SERVINGS
. . . .

"Cake" is a misnomer, for this is a delicate yeast bread dimpled with melted butter and brown sugar. I buy it whenever I go to Old Salem, a faithfully restored Moravian town on the south side of Winston-Salem, North Carolina. Sugar cake is still baked at the 200-year-old Winkler Bakery there, and I've watched the staff, in period dress, knead and shape the dough. Sugar cake is also served for breakfast at the nearby Brookstown Inn, an old cotton mill given new life as a luxury bed-and-breakfast.

One ¼-ounce package active dry yeast

¼ cup granulated sugar

½ cup very warm water (105° to 115° F.)

¼ cup firmly packed mashed potatoes, at room temperature

I tablespoon nonfat dry milk powder

½ teaspoon salt

½ cup (I stick) butter, melted

I large egg, at room temperature

2¼ to 2½ cups unsifted all-purpose flour

⅓ cup firmly packed light brown sugar mixed with ½ teaspoon ground cinnamon

1. Generously spritz a 15 × 10 × 1-inch jelly-roll pan with nonstick cooking spray and set aside.

2. By hand, combine the yeast, ½ teaspoon of the sugar, and ¼ cup of the warm water in a large electric mixer bowl and let stand for 5 minutes or until the yeast activates and the mixture froths.

3. Add the remaining sugar and the remaining water, the potatoes, dry milk, salt, ¼ cup of the melted butter, the egg, and ½ cup of the flour. Beat at low speed just long enough to combine, raise the mixer speed to high, and beat for about 2 minutes or until satiny. With the mixer at low speed, add 1½ cups of the remaining flour, ½ cup at a time, and continue beating after each addition to incorporate.

4. Turn the dough onto a lightly floured surface, and knead for about 2 minutes, working in the remaining ¼ to ½ cup flour until you have a soft, workable dough.

5. With well-buttered hands, pat the dough over the bottom of the jelly-roll pan, stretching and pushing to the edge and into the corners. Brush the dough with 1 tablespoon of the remaining melted butter, then set the uncovered pan in a warm, draft-free spot for about 30 minutes or until doubled in bulk. Toward the end of rising, preheat the oven to 375° F.

6. When the dough is fully risen, poke deep holes all over the surface with your fingers, scatter the brown sugar mixture evenly over all, then drizzle with the remaining butter. Again set uncovered in a warm, draft-free spot, this time for 10 to 15 minutes or until the dough has risen as high as the rim of the pan.

7. Bake the sugar cake on the middle oven shelf for 18 to 20 minutes or until lightly browned and springy-firm to the touch.

8. Remove from the oven, cool in the upright pan on a wire rack for about 20 minutes, then cut into large squares and serve.

Variation

Love Feast Buns: Among the Moravians, these puffy, faintly spicy buns are served at special Christmas and Easter services called Love Feasts. They're still baked the traditional way in the Winkler Bakery's brick ovens and when their yeasty scent comes wafting out the door, hungry customers line up on the street to buy their fill. To prepare the buns: Omit Step 1 of the Sugar Cake recipe. Follow Steps 2 and 3, adding ¼ teaspoon each ground mace and freshly grated nutmeg along with the first ½ cup flour. Proceed as directed in Step 4, then, with well-buttered hands, shape the dough into a ball, place in a well-buttered large bowl, cover with a clean, dry cloth, and allow to rise in a warm, draft-free spot for about 1 hour or until doubled in bulk. Punch the dough down, then roll to a thickness of ½ inch on a well-floured pastry cloth using a well-floured stockinette-covered rolling pin. Cut into 2½-inch rounds with a floured biscuit cutter. Knead the scraps into a ball, then roll and cut as before. Arrange the rounds on well-greased baking sheets, spacing at least 3 inches apart. Cover with a clean, dry cloth, and set in a warm, draft-free spot until doubled in bulk—about 45 minutes this time. Bake the buns in the lower third of a preheated 350° F. oven for about 15 minutes or until golden brown. Transfer to wire racks at once and brush generously with melted butter—you'll need 2 to 3 tablespoons. Makes about 1½ dozen buns (including rerolls).

1948 Kentuckian Duncan Hines, whose name is synonymous with good food, teams up with entrepreneur Roy Park to launch the Duncan Hines line of cake mixes.

Pete Jones opens a barbecue joint in Ayden, North Carolina ("The Collard Capital of the World"), pit-barbecuing whole hogs the way his family has done since the 1830s. Word spreads and soon people drive miles out of their way just to eat at Jones's Skylight Inn. In the mid-1990s, *National Geographic* will dub it "The Barbecue Capital of the World."

1949 Lou Bono fires up the pits at his new Jacksonville, Florida, barbecue restaurant and begins roasting meat low and slow over hardwood coals. He also concocts a smoky-peppery sauce to go with it. That original Bono's Pit Bar-B-Q spawned some two dozen more in Florida, Georgia, North Carolina, and Colorado.

America's first big cook-off, the National Chicken Cooking Contest, takes place on the Delmarva Peninsula (the Chesapeake's Eastern Shore). It becomes an annual event though its venue changes from year to year.

Heirloom Recipe

SALT-RISING BREAD

Try as I would, I could not make salt-rising bread, indeed couldn't even get the "starter" to fizz. My failure got me to thinking: In the old days, Southerners used unpasteurized milk and locally ground cornmeal that hadn't been irradiated. Moreover, their kitchens weren't overheated or swabbed with "antibacterials." To make salt-rising bread, there must be airborne microbes and a medium in which they can proliferate.

Because I adore salt-rising bread, I reprint a recipe for it that appeared in *From North Carolina Kitchens: Favorite Recipes Old and New*, an uncopyrighted little paperback published some fifty years ago by the North Carolina Federation of Home Demonstration Clubs:

In the evening, take a pint of milk and heat almost to the boiling point. Into this put one handful (¼ cup) each of meal and flour. Add a teaspoon of sugar, a pinch of soda, and a pinch of salt (⅛ teaspoon). Put into this seven white beans, let rise overnight in a warm place.

In the morning, take out the beans, add enough flour to make it thick, having warmed the flour and yeast. Set in a warm place to rise. After it has risen (and smells ruined—the worse it smells, the better the yeast), mix with 2 quarts of flour, 3 tablespoons of sugar, 2 tablespoons of lard, 4 teaspoons of salt, and enough warm water to make a soft sponge. Make into loaves. Keep covered in a warm place and let rise to about twice its size. Bake in a moderate oven.

The seven white beans are not a hoax, as you might think, but are to make the bread rise, not sink.

—Mrs. J. E. Gentry, Ashe County, North Carolina

PAIN PERDU (LOST BREAD)

MAKES 6 SERVINGS

Known elsewhere as French toast, this Louisiana brunch and breakfast classic deliciously recycles stale French bread. In New Orleans, I've even seen it made with brioche. The recipe here is my attempt to duplicate the Pain Perdu made to order every morning at a funky little motel near Bayou Teche; I spent a week there years ago while on article assignment in Cajun country.

¼ cup light cream or half-and-half

4 large eggs

½ cup sugar

1 teaspoon finely grated lemon zest

½ teaspoon vanilla extract

⅛ teaspoon freshly grated nutmeg

12 slices stale French bread, each measuring about 4 inches across and 1 inch thick

1 quart vegetable oil (for deep-fat frying)

Confectioners' (10 X) sugar (for dusting)

1. Beat the cream, eggs, sugar, lemon zest, vanilla, and nutmeg in a large electric mixer bowl at moderately high speed for about 2 minutes until thick and creamy.

2. Place 3 to 4 bread slices in the egg mixture, let stand for 15 seconds, then turn the slices and soak the flip sides for another 15 seconds. Transfer the dipped slices to a wax paper–lined baking sheet. Repeat until all slices are saturated with the egg mixture. Cover with foil or plastic food wrap and refrigerate for several hours.

3. When ready to proceed, pour the oil into a large, deep skillet and insert a deep-fat thermometer. Set over moderate heat and bring the oil to a temperature of 380° F. Meanwhile, preheat the oven to 250° F. Also line two baking sheets with foil and set aside.

4. When the oil reaches 380° F., ease three slices of soaked bread into the skillet and fry until a rich golden brown; this will take 1 to 2 minutes per side if you keep the temperature of the oil as close to 380° F. as possible. Drain the browned slices on paper toweling, then transfer to foil-lined baking sheets and set in the oven to keep warm. Repeat until all of the slices have been browned.

5. To serve, overlap two slices of Pain Perdu on each of six heated plates, dust with confectioners' sugar, and serve at once with heated cane syrup or maple syrup.

1949 Ed and Edie Obrycki take over the little crab house that brother-in-law Melvin Alexander had started a few years earlier in Baltimore and rename it Ed Obrycki's Olde Crab House. It is soon a local landmark.

1950 The Junior League of Charleston, South Carolina, publishes *Charleston Receipts* to raise funds for the Charleston Speech and Hearing Center. Still selling well, it is the quintessential community cookbook because its recipes and voice are distinctly local.

1950s With bananas a major New Orleans import, restaurateur Owen Brennan challenges his chef Paul Blangé to do something interesting with them. The result: Bananas Foster, named after a Brennan's regular, and to this day the restaurant's most famous recipe.

Warner Stamey begins teaching young Wayne Monk the secrets of "Lexington" North Carolina barbecue. Monk eventually buys Lexington Barbecue (originally Lexington Barbecue No. 1) and goes on to become North Carolina's most admired 'cue meister.

CALAS (RICE FRITTERS)

MAKES ABOUT 2 DOZEN

. . . .

To quote *American Cooking: Creole and Acadian* (a Time-Life Foods of the World cookbook by Peter S. Feibleman), "Before the turn of the century, the cala woman vending *'Bella cala! Tout chaud!'* ('Nice cala! Piping hot!') was a familiar sight along the streets of the French Quarter of New Orleans." The cala women, the book continues, have disappeared. But not the spicy rice fritters they sold; they're now a Sunday brunch specialty at several New Orleans restaurants. In a Raleigh *News & Observer* article, food writer Fred Thompson tells of the calas he enjoyed pre–Hurricane Katrina at the Big Easy's Old Coffee Pot Restaurant. When asked about calas, his waitress replied, "Oh, sweetie, you have now hit on sumpin' mighty good, real eating. Rice like you never had 'fore now. Better than beignets. This is the original black people's food." Sunday, it turns out, was the cooks' day off in New Orleans, so to earn a little extra money, they'd make calas, take to the streets, and sell them.

⅔ cup sifted cake flour (preferably a silky southern flour like White Lily or Martha White)

3 tablespoons granulated sugar

1 tablespoon baking powder

¾ teaspoon ground cinnamon

½ teaspoon freshly grated nutmeg or ¼ teaspoon ground nutmeg

⅛ teaspoon salt

2 large eggs lightly beaten with 1½ teaspoons vanilla extract

2 cups cooked long-grain rice, at room temperature (measure lightly packed)

Vegetable oil for deep-fat frying (2 to 2½ quarts)

Confectioners' (10X) sugar (for dusting)

1. Whisk the flour, granulated sugar, baking powder, cinnamon, nutmeg, and salt together in a large bowl. Add the egg mixture and whisk just until combined; fold in the rice. Do not overbeat or your calas will be tough. Cover loosely and let stand at room temperature for 20 minutes.

2. Meanwhile, pour the oil into a deep-fat fryer or large kettle at least 4 inches deep, insert a deep-fat thermometer, and set over high heat until the oil reaches 350° F.

3. Working with about a third of the cala mixture at a time, drop from a rounded tablespoon (or better yet a No. 24 spring-loaded ice cream scoop) into the hot oil, spacing the calas well apart. Fry for 3 to 4 minutes, turning as needed until evenly browned and keeping the oil as near to 350° F. as possible. Lift to paper toweling to drain.

4. Dust the calas with confectioners' sugar and serve warm for Sunday breakfast or brunch with drizzlings of cane syrup or maple syrup.

Desserts and Confections

Southerners have always been sweet on desserts. Is it because, prerefrigeration, some desserts were so loaded with sugar they wouldn't spoil at room temperature? Or because sugarcane was (and still is) grown in the Deep South? I suspect a bit of both.

Then, too, there's the sweet-tooth English heritage of the original Virginia and Carolina colonists. Early southern cookbooks are freighted with rich English creams, plum puddings, fruitcakes, and cheese cakes—not cheesecakes in the New York sense, but cheese-less "curds" as in the achingly sweet lemon curd ("cheese") that goes into lemon chess pie. As a culinary term the word *chess,* some suggest, may be a corruption of "cheese."

As the colonists came to appreciate New World foods and observed how simply local tribes prepared them, they began to improvise. Take sweet potatoes. Although they had been known in England as far back as the fifteenth century, few sweet potato recipes appear in English cookbooks. Nor do I find any mention of them in *Food in England* (1954), Dorothy Hartley's comprehensive survey of English cookery that begins with the Bronze Age. In early southern recipe books, however, sweet potato cakes, puddings, and pies proliferate—usually in old English recipes given a new ingredient and a new spin.

The same can be said of wild persimmon puddings; cakes and confections made with pecans instead of almonds; cinnamon-y pies with sliced green tomatoes doubling for apples; and, not least, Kentucky bourbon (corn whiskey) displacing brandy and/ or wine in various English desserts.

Introducing the 1984 facsimile edition of Mary Randolph's original *Virginia House-wife* (1824), food historian Karen Hess writes: "As important as local Indian contributions were, the transformation of Virginia cooking cannot primarily be attributed to them. It is only when we ask whose hands did the cooking that we get a satisfactory answer . . ."

Among the South's landed gentry, those hands were black, hands familiar with ground-nuts (peanuts), benne (sesame seeds), and rice, all of which arrived in the South early on and landed in a variety of sweets—particularly in South Carolina.

Unlike the Virginia colonists, many of the English who settled the South Carolina Low-country had been living in the Caribbean and brought their slaves with them. So there were French (Creole) influences in and around Charleston as well as in New Orleans, home of beignets, pralines, and king cake (a spicy ring frosted in Mardi Gras purple [for justice], green [faith], and gold [power] that is served on Twelfth Night, the day the gift-bearing Magi visited baby Jesus. A miniature baby Jesus effigy is baked into the cake, or sometimes a tiny trinket, or even a dried bean. The one who gets the hidden treasure is blessed with good luck. But he must also bring the king cake to next year's party.) The Huguenot impact on southern cooking may have been less significant, although in *The Carolina Rice Kitchen* (1992), Karen Hess traces several rice puddings back to France.

The dessert chapters in southern cookbooks both old and new often outweigh nearly every other (here, too, I'm afraid).

But then, Southerners have always prided themselves on their ice creams, puddings and pies, candies, cakes, and cookies.

And why not? We have them to thank for such American classics as Lady Baltimore Cake, Lane Cake, Robert E. Lee Cake, Japanese Fruitcake, Benne Wafers, Peanut Brittle, Key Lime Pie, and Black Bottom Pie, not to mention the whole delicious repertoire of chess pies.

You'll find them all in the following pages.

❧

So on a typical Thanksgiving . . . we'd have baked chicken, fried chicken, smothered chicken, turkey, Creole gumbo, dirty rice, white rice, collard greens, stuffed bell peppers, macaroni and cheese, cornbread, rolls, sweet potato pie, pecan pie, apple pie, muffins and cake.

—*DONNA L. BRAZILE, COOKING WITH GREASE: STIRRING THE POTS IN AMERICAN POLITICS*

❧

❧

. . . I said, "I'd be glad to. But what is a pound party?"

"Everybody brings a pound of something. Sugar, or butter, or candy, or a cake. A cake's fine. Such as that."

—*MARJORIE KINNAN RAWLINGS, CROSS CREEK*

❧

PEACH COUNTRY COBBLER

MAKES 6 TO 8 SERVINGS

From early July through mid September, farmer's markets and side-of-the-road stands offer tree-ripened peaches by the bushel. It's a precious time for southern cooks, a time of cobblers and crisps, pickles and pies, jams and preserves. If Southerners have a favorite peach, it's probably a toss-up between the white-fleshed Georgia Belle, the hardy golden Sunhigh, and the Elberta, a free-stone, honeysuckle-sweet hybrid developed in Macon County, Georgia, in 1875. **Note:** *Instead of making the topping the old-fashioned way, modern southern cooks are more apt to use a food processor. Here's how: Pulse all the dry ingredients briefly to combine; sprinkle the diced butter evenly on top and pulse until the texture of coarse meal. Drizzle the milk over all, then pulse just enough to form a soft dough: Three to four brisk zaps should do it.*

Peach Mixture

¾ cup sugar

2 tablespoons cornstarch

6 cups sliced, peeled, and pitted firm-ripe peaches (3¾ to 4 pounds)

2 tablespoons fresh lemon juice

1 tablespoon butter

Topping

1½ cups sifted all-purpose flour

2 tablespoons sugar

2 tablespoons baking powder

1 teaspoon finely grated lemon zest

½ teaspoon salt

¼ teaspoon freshly grated nutmeg

5 tablespoons ice-cold butter, diced

¾ cup milk

Optional Accompaniment

1 pint vanilla ice cream or 1 cup heavy cream, softly whipped

1. Preheat the oven to 400° F.
2. For the peach mixture: Combine the sugar and cornstarch in a large nonreactive pan, pressing out all lumps. Mix in the peaches, lemon juice, and butter, and bring to a boil over high heat. Cook and stir for 1 minute, then set off the heat.
3. For the topping: Combine the flour, sugar, baking powder, lemon zest, salt, and nutmeg in a large bowl. Add the butter and, using a pastry blender, cut in until the texture of coarse meal. Drizzle the milk over all and fork quickly just until a soft dough forms—no matter if a few floury specks show.
4. Scoop the peach mixture into an ungreased shallow 2½-quart casserole, spreading to the edge. Drop the topping by tablespoons on top, spacing evenly.
5. Bake on the middle oven shelf until bubbly and golden brown, 30 to 35 minutes.
6. Serve warm or at room temperature, topped, if you like, with vanilla ice cream or whipped cream.

SURRY COUNTY SONKER WITH MILK DIP

MAKES 12 SERVINGS

Sonkers are cobblers unique to Surry County, North Carolina, which abuts the Virginia state line just where the foothills begin their climb toward the Blue Ridge. No one I queried could tell me the origin of this unusual dessert, of the milk dip that traditionally accompanies it, or even of its name. But there are theories. Some say the name has to do with the way the sonker's made; that makes no sense to me. Others believe that it comes from the looks of the sonker: It sometimes sinks a bit on cooling. Is "sonker" by chance colloquial for "sinker?" There's no arguing, however, that sonkers have been made in Surry County as long as anyone can remember or that grans and great-grans could "stir one up in a jiffy." To celebrate the sonker, Surry County stages a festival early every October on the streets of Mount Airy (Andy Griffith's hometown and the Mayberry of his popular TV series). What goes into a sonker? Sweet potatoes are popular but so are peaches, blueberries, blackberries, and especially strawberries, a Surry County specialty.

Pastry

3 cups sifted all-purpose flour

½ teaspoon salt

I cup firmly packed cold lard or vegetable shortening

I large egg lightly beaten with 2 tablespoons cider vinegar

2 tablespoons butter, melted

3 tablespoons sugar

Filling

I cup sugar

⅓ cup unsifted all-purpose flour

I teaspoon apple pie spice or I teaspoon ground cinnamon mixed with ¼ teaspoon ground nutmeg

I cup water

½ cup (I stick) butter, melted

½ teaspoon almond extract

8 cups (2 quarts) blueberries, blackberries, strawberries, pitted dark red cherries, or peeled, pitted, and thinly sliced peaches (about 4½ pounds peaches)

Milk Dip

½ cup sugar

2 tablespoons plus I teaspoon cornstarch

3 cups milk

½ teaspoon vanilla extract

⅛ teaspoon salt

1. For the pastry: Whisk the flour and salt together in a large mixing bowl, then, using a pastry blender, cut in the lard until as fine as possible. Add the egg-vinegar mixture, then fork briskly to form a soft but workable dough. Shape into a ball, divide in half, then shape each half into a round about 1 inch thick.

Wrap in plastic food wrap and refrigerate for several hours.

2. When ready to proceed, preheat the oven to 350° F. Lightly grease a 13 × 9 × 2-inch baking pan and set aside.

3. For the filling: Combine the sugar, flour, and spice in a large mixing bowl. Whisk in the water, melted butter, and almond extract. Add the fruit and toss well to mix.

4. To assemble the sonker: Roll each half of the pastry dough on a lightly floured surface into a 13 × 9-inch rectangle. Using a sharp knife or pastry wheel, cut one pastry rectangle crosswise into 1-inch strips and the second rectangle lengthwise into 1-inch strips. Reserve five nice 13-inch strips and seven pretty 9-inch strips.

5. Press the remaining strips over the bottom of the baking pan so they cover it completely. Slide onto the middle oven shelf and bake for 12 minutes; do not brown. Remove from the oven and raise the oven temperature to 375° F.

6. Scoop the fruit mixture on top of the partially baked pastry, spreading to the corners. Top with the reserved pastry strips, crisscrossing them in a lattice design. Brush the pastry strips generously with the 2 tablespoons melted butter, then sprinkle with the 3 tablespoons sugar.

7. Return the sonker to the middle oven shelf and bake for 45 to 50 minutes or until bubbling and nicely browned.

8. Toward the end of baking, prepare the milk dip: Combine the sugar and cornstarch in a medium-size heavy saucepan, then whisk in the milk. Set over moderate heat and cook,

1952 With a new highway bypassing his Corbin, Kentucky, restaurant, Harland Sanders begins selling fried-chicken franchises to other restaurants, shares his secret recipe, and demonstrates his pressure-frying technique. His take? A nickel on every order of chicken sold.

1954 Burger King opens its first hamburger stand in Miami.

1955 Grace Grissom, a young Knoxville secretary, and her husband buy into, then take over an embryonic fast-food company making sandwich spreads. Today Mrs. Grissom's Salads (gelatin, tuna, chicken, and ham, etc.) are Tennessee supermarket staples.

Procter & Gamble buys W. T. Young Foods of Lexington, Kentucky, makers of Big Top Peanut Butter. Under the P & G label, Big Top reappears as Jif.

Joe Rogers, Sr., and Tom Forkner build their dream fast-food restaurant in Avondale Estates, an Atlanta suburb. Waffle House, they call it, and it's the first in a far-flung chain.

1956–57 C. F. Sauer of Richmond, Virginia, begins manufacturing vegetable oils, liquid salad dressings, and mustard.

whisking constantly, for about 3 minutes or until the mixture thickens. Remove from the heat and whisk in the vanilla and salt.

9. Cool the sonker for about 10 minutes (especially important if it's made with berries or peaches), then cut into large squares. Arrange on heated dessert plates, and pass the milk dip so that everyone can help himself.

Variation

Sweet Potato Sonker: Prepare the pastry as directed above. While it chills, boil 8 to 9 scrubbed, unpeeled medium-size sweet potatoes (about 3½ pounds) in a large, heavy saucepan for 20 to 25 minutes or until almost tender. Drain the potatoes, cool, then peel and slice thin (you will need 8 cups sliced potatoes). Finish the sonker as directed, substituting 1 cup apple juice for the water, ½ cup firmly packed light brown sugar for the 1 cup granulated, and 1 teaspoon vanilla extract for the ½ teaspoon almond extract. Bake as directed and serve with the milk dip.

SPICED BLACKBERRY AND CORNMEAL COBBLER

MAKES 6 TO 8 SERVINGS
. . . .

This imaginative recipe comes from chef John Fleer of The Inn at Blackberry Farm in the foothills of the Tennessee Smokies. Some years ago I spent several idyllic days there on assignment for *Gourmet* and of all the desserts I tried, this cobbler was a distinct winner. As the inn's name suggests, blackberries grow wild there (as they do over much of the South). Their flavor is more

intense than that of cultivated berries and if you can find them, by all means use wild blackberries for the cobbler. Many farmer's markets sell them in season, as do roadside vendors. Garden blackberries can of course be substituted for the wild as can dewberries, blueberries, or raspberries. **Note:** *Masa harina or tortilla flour is more widely available than ever; look for it in specialty food shops, Hispanic groceries, or in the "international section" of your supermarket.* **Tip:** *This cobbler can be made several hours ahead of time—no need to refrigerate.*

Blackberry Mixture

3 pints blackberries (see headnote)

1½ cups granulated sugar

¼ cup firmly packed light brown sugar

1½ tablespoons cornstarch

1 tablespoon dark rum or bourbon

1½ teaspoons finely grated lemon zest

1 teaspoon ground cinnamon

Topping

¾ cup unsifted all-purpose flour

¾ cup unsifted *masa harina*, preferably white (see Note above)

½ cup unsifted stone-ground yellow cornmeal

1½ teaspoons baking powder

¼ teaspoon baking soda

¼ teaspoon ground cloves

¼ teaspoon salt

5 tablespoons butter, at room temperature

¾ **cup unsifted confectioners' (10 X) sugar**

1 large egg

1 cup buttermilk

1. Preheat the oven to 400° F. Butter a shallow 3-quart baking dish (it should be no more than 2 inches deep) and set aside.

2. For the blackberry mixture: Mix all ingredients in a large nonreactive bowl; set aside.

3. For the topping: Sift the flour, *masa harina*, cornmeal, baking powder, baking soda, cloves, and salt into a large mixing bowl and set aside. Cream the butter and confectioners' sugar in a large electric mixer bowl at moderate speed for 1 to 2 minutes or until fluffy; beat in the egg. With the mixer at low speed, add the flour mixture alternately with the buttermilk, beginning and ending with the flour and beating after each addition only enough to combine.

4. Scoop the batter (it will be quite thick) into a pastry bag fitted with a ½-inch plain tip and pipe over the berries in a lattice pattern, spacing the rows 1½ inches apart.

5. Slide the cobbler onto the middle oven shelf and bake for 25 to 30 minutes or until bubbly and lightly browned.

6. Serve hot, or, if you prefer, cool the cobbler to room temperature before serving.

❧

The inside was dim, and what light did come in the little windows and the door fell in beams through an atmosphere thick with the dust of ground corn.

—CHARLES FRAZIER, *COLD MOUNTAIN*

❧

1957 Mississippi-born Craig Claiborne becomes food editor of *The New York Times* and quickly changes the way newspapers cover food.

Promising quality food at low prices, Food Town opens in Salisbury, North Carolina. Known today as Food Lion, it operates more than 1,200 supermarkets throughout the South and mid-Atlantic.

1958 Georgia-based Royal Crown Cola test-markets Diet Rite, America's first diet cola. But only in the South.

1959 The first of the Fat Boy's barbecue chain is established at Cape Canaveral.

Castro refugees swarm into Miami and soon create "Little Havana" on Southwest Eighth Street (*Calle Ocho*), an area chock-a-block with Cuban restaurants, bars, and clubs.

1960 Wilbur Hardee opens a little "walk-up" burger joint in Greenville, North Carolina. There are no tables and the menu is limited.

WILD PERSIMMON PUDDING

MAKES 4 SERVINGS

. . . .

I first tasted wild persimmon pudding when I was an assistant home demonstration agent in Iredell County, North Carolina, and I have loved it ever since. Back then, every farm woman had a pet recipe for this pudding and served it year-round even though wild persimmons were in season only from late September until Christmas. Whole families would go out and gather bushels of fallen fruit (the best indication that they were ripe and honey-sweet), prep them, and freeze the pulp (see About Wild Persimmons, page 240). This particular persimmon pudding is adapted from a recipe given to my niece Linda by her friend Laura Frost, who was the chef at Sleddon's, a "fine-dining" restaurant in Southern Pines, North Carolina— now closed, alas. **Note:** *If wild persimmons are unavailable, you can buy wild persimmon purée (see Sources, page 401). You can also substitute the big orange Japanese persimmons for the wild. But the pudding will taste different.*

I cup unsifted all-purpose flour

½ teaspoon baking soda

½ teaspoon salt

¼ teaspoon ground cinnamon

¼ teaspoon freshly grated nutmeg

⅛ teaspoon ground cloves

2 extra-large eggs

¼ cup sugar

I cup wild persimmon pulp (see headnote)

7/8 cup milk

1½ tablespoons butter, melted

Topping

I cup heavy cream, whipped to soft peaks with 2 tablespoons confectioners' (10X) sugar and I teaspoon vanilla extract (or I tablespoon Cognac)

1. Preheat the oven to 350° F. Lightly coat a 1-quart casserole with nonstick cooking spray and set aside.

2. Sift the flour, baking soda, salt, cinnamon, nutmeg, and cloves together onto a large piece of wax paper and set aside.

3. Beat the eggs and sugar in a large electric mixer bowl at moderately high speed until thick and pale yellow. Reduce the mixer speed to low and beat in the persimmon pulp and milk. Add the sifted dry ingredients and mix by hand until well blended. Finally, stir in the melted butter, mixing only enough to combine.

4. Pour the batter into the prepared casserole, spreading to the edge, then set in a baking pan and slide onto the middle oven shelf. Pour hot water into the pan to come halfway up the sides of the casserole.

5. Bake the pudding in the water bath for about 1 hour or until it pulls from the sides of the casserole.

6. Serve warm with a dollop of topping scooped over each portion.

SUGAR

The story of the Deep South's sugar industry is bittersweet. Sweet for the planters who became "white gold" millionaires, bitter for slaves forced to work in unconscionable conditions.

The root of it all? A honey-sweet, bamboolike grass native to New Guinea that moved from Old World to New via a lengthy, roundabout journey. According to Alan Davidson in *The Oxford Companion to Food*, the Greek historian Herodotus knew sugarcane in the fifth century BC, and "in 327 BC Alexander the Great sent some back to Europe from India." At about the same time (even earlier, some say), Persians were boiling and crystallizing cane sap into a coarse brown sugar much like the jaggery (palm sugar) of India.

Arab traders took sugarcane to Spain early in the eighth century and Moors taught the Spaniards how to crystallize it into sugar some three centuries later. Columbus, food historians agree, carried cuttings from the Canary Islands to Hispaniola on his second voyage there in 1493, though sugarcane didn't reach Florida for another forty-two years. It was planted in the vicinity of Cape Canaveral (*Canaveral* is Spanish for "*cane field*") but did not thrive.

By the time Florida's first commercial crop was harvested in 1767 at the New Smyrna Colony, Jesuits had already introduced sugarcane to South Louisiana. That state's first bumper crop, grown by Etienne de Bore of New Orleans in 1795, yielded 100,000 pounds of sugar.

In Lousiana, as in Florida, sugarcane proved to be a lucrative but unpredictable crop, subject to the whims of nature and susceptible to a variety of diseases. Then, too, wars decimated the fields of cane more than once down the years. Compare, for example, the 264,000 tons of sugar Louisiana produced in 1861 with the post–Civil War total of 5,971 tons. Moreover, the number of sugar plantations had shrunk from 1,200 in 1861 to a mere 175 in 1864. A catastrophic loss.

In the beginning, planters forced local Indian tribes to work the cane fields, and when they fled, slaves were imported from Africa. Indeed the sugar industry has been called "the engine that drove the slave trade." Sugarcane is one of the most labor-intensive plants on earth. Cuttings must be laid flat in trenches at specific intervals and when ripe, the cane must be cut level to the ground with machetes and crushed under spinning millstones. The runoff is collected and boiled in giant cauldrons. There were accidents every step of the way, many of them fatal.

By the middle of the nineteenth century, sugar refining was being simplified, most of all by New Orleans native Norbert Rillieux, the son of a French planter and a slave mother. After studying engineering in Paris, Rillieux invented a revolutionary new evaporating pan that would shortcut the tedious process of crystallization. It was patented in 1846.

Still, sugar remained a boom-or-bust business—and does to this day. Florida now produces about a fourth of this country's sugar and Louisiana isn't far behind at 20 percent. Recent hurricanes have taken their toll in both states and threaten to do so in the future. According to sugar producers, however, there's an even greater threat: CAFTA (the Central American Free Trade Act), which they insist will "rob" them of billions of dollars a year.

Time will tell.

GRATED SWEET POTATO-COCONUT PUDDING

MAKES 8 TO 10 SERVINGS

. . . .

The South has an intense and ongoing love affair with sweet potatoes, perhaps because they grow well in most states below the Mason-Dixon. For whatever reason, good southern cooks have been dreaming up new ways to use sweet potatoes for years. This popular pudding, now nearly seventy years old, is one of the best. **Tip:** *If you grate the sweet potatoes directly into the milk, they will not darken. If you do so, stir the milk-potato mixture into the pudding batter as directed in Step 2. If not, fold them in after the milk is added.*

½ cup granulated sugar

½ cup firmly packed light brown sugar

½ cup (1 stick) butter, at room temperature

¼ cup unsifted all-purpose flour

2 large eggs

2 teaspoons vanilla extract

½ teaspoon salt

One 12-ounce can evaporated milk, plus enough whole milk to total 2½ cups

3 cups coarsely grated raw sweet potatoes (about 1 pound or 2 medium)

1 cup freshly grated or sweetened, flaked coconut

1 cup heavy cream, whipped to soft peaks with 1 tablespoon confectioners' (10X) sugar and ½ teaspoon vanilla extract (optional topping)

1. Preheat the oven to 350° F. Spritz a 9 × 9 × 2-inch baking pan with nonstick cooking spray and set aside.

2. Mix together the granulated sugar, brown sugar, butter, flour, eggs, vanilla, and salt in a large bowl to combine. Stir in the milk mixture (including the sweet potatoes if you grated them into the milk as suggested in the Tip above). Otherwise, fold in the sweet potatoes, then the coconut.

3. Scoop the mixture into the baking pan and spread to the corners. Bake uncovered on the middle oven shelf for 50 to 55 minutes or until lightly browned and set in the center.

4. Cool the pudding in the upright pan on a wire rack for 15 to 20 minutes, then spoon up and serve. Drift each portion, if you like, with the whipped cream topping or pass it separately.

OLD KENTUCKY HOME BISCUIT PUDDING WITH BOURBON SAUCE

MAKES ABOUT 8 SERVINGS

. . . .

Thrifty southern cooks put yesterday's biscuits to good use in this "bread" pudding. And if there are leftover raisins, they might be plumped with bourbon and tossed in. That's the Kentucky way. This recipe is my approximation of a biscuit pudding I once enjoyed at Kurtz's Restaurant in Bardstown, Kentucky. I failed to ask for the recipe—stupid me. If my flavor memory hasn't failed me, I think this attempt to "crack" that recipe comes reasonably close. Even if I've missed by a mile, the pudding is delicious. **Note:** *The sauce won't cook fully; to be safe, use a pasteurized egg (see About Pasteurized Eggs, page xxi).*

Pudding

¾ cup seedless raisins or sultanas (golden raisins)

¼ cup bourbon

4 large eggs

1¼ cups sugar

1 tablespoon vanilla extract

¼ teaspoon freshly grated nutmeg

2 cups milk

2 cups light cream or half-and-half

6 stale 3-inch buttermilk biscuits, coarsely crumbled (8½ cups crumbs)

Bourbon Sauce

½ cup (1 stick) butter

¾ cup granulated sugar

¼ cup firmly packed light brown sugar

¼ teaspoon salt

⅓ cup water

1 large pasteurized egg (see Note above)

¼ cup bourbon

1. For the pudding: Plump the raisins in the bourbon for 3 to 4 hours.
2. When ready to proceed, beat the eggs, sugar, vanilla, and nutmeg in a large electric mixer bowl at high speed for about 2 minutes or until creamy. With the machine at low speed, gradually beat in the milk and cream. By hand fold in the biscuit crumbs, then the plumped raisins and any remaining bourbon. Set aside for 20 minutes.
3. Preheat the oven to 350° F. Butter a 2½-quart casserole well and set aside.
4. Stir the biscuit mixture and scoop into the casserole, spreading to the edge. Bake uncovered on the middle oven shelf for 60 to 65 minutes or until nicely browned, puffed, and set.
5. Meanwhile, prepare the bourbon sauce: Melt the butter in a small, heavy saucepan over moderate heat. Add the two sugars, the salt, and water, then cook, stirring constantly, until the sugars dissolve. Adjust the heat so the mixture bubbles gently, and cook uncovered for 5 minutes or until syrupy. Whisk the egg until frothy in a small, heatproof bowl; then, whisking all the while, drizzle in the hot syrup. Finally, mix in the bourbon.
6. When the pudding tests done, remove from the oven and cool for 10 to 15 minutes.
7. To serve, spoon the warm pudding onto dessert plates and ladle a little of the sauce over each portion.

❖

"Edna Earle! . . . Have you got a few cold biscuits I could have before supper, or a little chicken bone I could gnaw on?"

—EUDORA WELTY, *THE PONDER HEART*

❖

KRISPY KREME DOUGHNUTS

When I was growing up in Raleigh, I knew exactly when the doughnuts would come out of the fryer at the Krispy Kreme shop on North Person Street and I'd beg my mother to drive me there. Later, when I was old enough to drive, I'd go over myself and buy a big bag of honey-glazed doughnuts, still warm and as light as a dandelion puff.

In the beginning, I believed that Krispy Kreme was a small Raleigh business, but I learned a few years later that the company had been founded in Winston-Salem, about 100 miles west. It all began in 1937 when a doughnut maker named Vernon Rudolph managed to buy a New Orleans pastry chef's secret recipe for yeast-raised doughnuts. Rudolph set up shop in a little Winston-Salem storefront, made some batches of dough, cut it into rings, fried them in deep fat, then glazed them with honey. Captivated by the aroma, passersby pounded on Rudolph's door and begged to buy some of his doughnuts. Soon they were selling as fast as he could make them.

To North Carolinians, Krispy Kremes are the only doughnuts worth eating, vastly superior to the heavier sugar-dusted variety made of cake. Even after I'd moved to New York, I would make a pilgrimage to Krispy Kreme whenever I came home to visit.

Today Krispy Kremes are sold in nearly 300 stores across the country, each one capable of producing 10,000 doughnuts a day in twenty different flavors.

For me, however, the original honey-glazed Krispy Kreme remains the one and only.

KRISPY KREME BREAD PUDDING WITH JACK DANIEL'S-RAISIN SAUCE

MAKES 6 TO 8 SERVINGS

There's a popular Krispy Kreme bread pudding down south that contains both honey-glazed doughnuts and sweetened condensed milk, but as much as I love sweets, this one sets my teeth on edge. So I've come up with a version that's a tad less sinful. The only doughnuts to use are the original honey-glazed Krispy Kremes. And they should be at least two days old. **Note:** *This pudding puffs majestically as it bakes, hence the need for a 2½-quart baking dish. Rush it to the table just as you would a soufflé. If you're not in the mood for the sauce, top the pudding with fresh berries or thinly sliced fresh peaches and a trickle of milk or cream.*

2½ cups milk

3 large eggs

⅓ cup raw or granulated sugar

¼ cup Jack Daniel's Tennessee whiskey, dark rum, or brandy

½ teaspoon ground cinnamon

¼ teaspoon freshly grated nutmeg

¼ teaspoon salt

6 dry honey-glazed Krispy Kreme doughnuts, broken into 1-inch pieces (about 7 cups)

Jack Daniel's–Raisin Sauce (page 284)

1. Preheat the oven to 350° F. Thoroughly butter a 2½-quart soufflé dish or straight-sided casserole and set aside.

2. Whisk the milk, eggs, sugar, whiskey, cinnamon, nutmeg, and salt in a large bowl until well combined. Add the doughnuts, toss lightly, and let stand for 10 minutes.

3. Scoop all into the soufflé dish, spreading to the edge and smoothing the top.

4. Slide the soufflé dish onto the middle oven shelf and bake uncovered for 35 to 40 minutes or until puffed, lightly browned, and set like custard.

5. Serve at once with Jack Daniel's–Raisin Sauce.

❧

These suppers—stag affairs served by the ladies—offered the same collations, with trifling differences, month after month . . . fried chicken or chicken pie, a baked ham, four or five vegetables, cornbread and beaten biscuit and hot rolls . . . and a dessert course of a homey dish like tipsy parson, ambrosia, or Cousin Pokie's apple pudding.

—*FRANCES GRAY PATTON, THE FINER THINGS OF LIFE*

❧

❧

. . . a cousin twice removed, Harriet Parker from Flomaton, made perfect ambrosia, transparent orange slices combined with freshly ground coconut . . .

—*TRUMAN CAPOTE, THE THANKSGIVING VISITOR*

❧

1960 Harris Super Markets and Teeter's Food Mart, both of North Carolina, merge, forming the popular Harris Teeter chain. Over time, Harris Teeter is bought by a Charlotte holding company, goes public, and buys 52 Food Worlds, 52 Big Stars, and South Carolina's Bruno stores. Stretching from Virginia to Florida, there are now some 150 Harris Teeters.

Scribner's publishes Clementine Paddleford's long-awaited *How America Eats*, which devotes nearly 150 pages to southern cooking. The popular roving food editor of *This Week Magazine*, Paddleford spent 12 years researching and writing the book.

With America's increasing thirst for wine, Virginia re-enters the wine business. (See Southern Wines, page 121.)

Chattanoogan O. D. McKee creates family-pack cartons of snack cakes and names them after his four-year-old granddaughter, Debbie. Today Little Debbie Snack Cakes are an American staple.

JACK DANIEL'S-RAISIN SAUCE

MAKES ABOUT 2 CUPS

Delicious over vanilla ice cream as well as Krispy Kreme Bread Pudding (page 282).

1 cup water

½ cup Jack Daniel's Tennessee whiskey

¼ cup firmly packed light brown sugar

1½ tablespoons cornstarch

¼ teaspoon freshly grated nutmeg

⅛ teaspoon salt

½ cup seedless raisins

2 tablespoons butter

1½ tablespoons fresh lemon juice

1. Combine the water, whiskey, brown sugar, cornstarch, nutmeg, and salt in a small saucepan, whisking until smooth.
2. Add the raisins and butter and bring to a boil over moderately high heat. Reduce the heat so the liquid bubbles gently, then cook and stir for about 1 minute or until the mixture thickens.
3. Whisk in the lemon juice and serve warm with Krispy Kreme Bread Pudding.

❀

He made in an old fashion hand freezer the ice cream which Uncle Willy sold over his soda fountain.

—**WILLIAM FAULKNER,** THE TOWN

❀

HUGUENOT TORTE

MAKES 6 SERVINGS

I've always associated this apple-nut pudding with Charleston, South Carolina, because I've enjoyed it there both in private homes and in restaurants. I've made it back home, too, following the recipe in *Charleston Receipts*, a Junior League fund-raiser first published in 1950 and now past its thirtieth printing. Then along comes Lowcountry insider and culinary sleuth John Martin Taylor to burst the bubble. In *Hoppin' John's Lowcountry Cooking* (1992), Taylor "outs" the "Charleston classic" and reveals its true identity: Ozark Pudding. In other words, it is an *Arkansas* classic. Taylor explains how he researched Huguenot Torte (named for the French Protestants who settled in and around Charleston) and tracked down Evelyn Florance, who baked it for Charleston's Huguenot Tavern back in the 1940s. She admitted that her recipe, first printed in *Charleston Receipts* and later praised by Clementine Paddleford in *The New York Herald Tribune*, was indeed Ozark Pudding, tweaked and adapted. Here's another adaptation: my own.

¾ cup unsifted all-purpose flour

1½ teaspoons baking powder

Pinch of ground cinnamon

Pinch of salt

1 large egg

½ cup firmly packed light brown sugar

¼ cup granulated sugar

1 teaspoon vanilla extract

¾ cup finely chopped peeled and cored apple
(about 1 large Golden Delicious or
Rome Beauty)

¾ cup finely chopped pecans, black walnuts,
or walnuts

1 cup heavy cream, softly whipped with 2
tablespoons confectioners' (10 X) sugar and
1 teaspoon vanilla extract (topping)

1. Preheat the oven to 350° F. Coat an 8 × 8 × 2-inch baking pan with nonstick oil-and-flour baking spray and set aside.
2. Sift the flour, baking powder, cinnamon, and salt onto a piece of wax paper and set aside also.
3. Beat the egg, two sugars, and vanilla at high speed for about 2 minutes in a small electric mixer bowl or until very thick. By hand mix in the sifted dry ingredients, apples, and pecans.
4. Scoop the batter into the pan, spreading to the corners, and bake on the middle oven shelf for about 30 minutes or until crusty brown on top.
5. Remove the torte from the oven and cool in the upright pan on a wire rack for 30 minutes.
6. To serve, cut into large squares and drift each portion with some of the whipped cream topping.

❧

It's as good as a pig eating slop.

—OLD NORTH CAROLINA SAYING

❧

1960s Martha White Flour of Nashville, Tennessee, introduces Bix Mix and invites customers "to make the world's best biscuits" just by adding water.

1961 Wowed by Hardee's success, Jim Gardner and Leonard Rawls, Jr., of Rocky Mount, North Carolina, open a fancier Hardee's. Charcoal-broiled burgers cost 15 cents, cheeseburgers a nickel more. Today there are nearly 2,500 Hardees at home and abroad.

Herman Lay merges his southern snack food company with the Frito Company of Dallas, forming Frito-Lay, Inc.

With embargos on Cuban products, sugar refining booms in Florida.

1962 Diet Rite goes national and within 18 months is America's fourth best-selling cola.

Planters introduces dry-roasted peanuts, shaving calories from one of America's favorite snack foods.

1963 Coke introduces a new diet cola called TaB.

The Thomas J. Lipton Company establishes a tea research station on Wadmalaw Island near Charleston and over time proves that the South Carolina Lowcountry is an ideal habitat for high-quality black tea.

EAST TENNESSEE STACK CAKE

MAKES A 6-LAYER, 9-INCH CAKE, ABOUT 16
SERVINGS

. . . .

This old family recipe comes from my good friend Florence Gray Soltys, who grew up on a dairy farm just where the Tennessee foothills rise toward the Smokies. "The recipe was a favorite of my Aunt Rhoda Gray," Florence says. "I often add bourbon to the apple mixture and serve with whipped cream." **Note:** *Some dried apples need to be washed, usually those bought at roadside stands or farmer's markets.*

Dried Apple Filling

I pound dried apples, washed well if
necessary (see Note above)

10 cups water

I cup firmly packed light brown sugar

½ cup granulated sugar

¼ cup bourbon

½ teaspoon ground cloves

½ teaspoon ground allspice

½ teaspoon ground ginger (optional)

Pastry

6 cups sifted all-purpose flour

I teaspoon baking soda

I teaspoon salt

I cup (2 sticks) butter or
vegetable shortening

2½ cups granulated sugar

2 large eggs

½ cup buttermilk mixed with
I teaspoon vanilla extract

Topping

I cup heavy cream, whipped until stiff with 2
tablespoons confectioners' (10 X) sugar

1. For the filling: Place the dried apples in a large nonreactive saucepan, add the water, and cook uncovered for 55 to 60 minutes or until the apples are soft enough to mash and most of the liquid has been absorbed. Using a slotted spoon, scoop the apples into a large heatproof bowl and mash thoroughly. Mix in all remaining filling ingredients and cool to room temperature. **Note:** *You can make the filling several days ahead of time and refrigerate until ready to use.*

2. When ready to proceed, arrange two racks about 4 inches apart as near the middle of the oven as possible. If yours is a small oven, place one rack in the middle. Preheat the oven to 450° F.

3. For the pastry: Sift the flour, baking soda, and salt onto a piece of wax paper and set aside.

4. Cream the butter and sugar in an electric mixer briefly at low speed and then at high speed for about 2 minutes or until fluffy. Beat the eggs in one by one.

5. Add the sifted dry ingredients alternately with the buttermilk mixture, beginning and ending with the dry and beating after each addition only enough to combine.

6. Divide the dough into six equal parts, shape into balls, then place each on a sheet of parchment paper or aluminum foil and cover with a sheet of floured wax paper. Roll two balls of dough into rounds about 9 inches across. Peel off the wax paper, then flour the rim of a 9-inch round layer cake pan and using it as a "cookie cutter," cut each circle of dough into a perfect 9-inch round. Gently pat any scraps of dough into the center of the rounds; these won't show after they're baked.

7. Ease each pastry circle, parchment and all, onto a baking sheet, slide into the oven, and bake for 7 to 8 minutes or until delicately browned. Lift the baked pastry circles (still on the parchment) at once to wire racks to cool. Shape, bake, and cool four more pastry rounds the same way. **Note: If your oven is large enough to accommodate two baking sheets on each rack, so much the better. Otherwise, you will have to bake the pastry circles one or two at a time.**

8. To assemble the stack cake: Working on a large round cake plate, sandwich the six pastry rounds together with the apple filling, dividing the total amount evenly. Do not spread filling on the top layer.

9. Cover the stack cake with a domed "cake keeper" or large turned-upside-down bowl and let stand in a cool spot (not the refrigerator) for at least 12 hours before cutting.

10. To serve the stack cake, cut into wedges and top each portion with the sweetened whipped cream.

1964 After selling fried chicken franchises to more than 600 North American restaurants, Harland Sanders sells his company to a group of investors, among them future Kentucky governor John Y. Brown, Jr. Now $2 million richer, Sanders remains KFC spokesman.

The chicken breast sandwich—fried breast fillets on buttered buns—is invented at Truett Cathy's Dwarf Café in South Atlanta. The sandwich is an instant hit and becomes the specialty of Cathy's soon-to-open Chick-fil-A restaurant. Before long, Chick-fil-As proliferate throughout the South.

Holly Farms of North Wilkesboro, North Carolina, introduces Holly-Pak poultry: chicken parts sealed in chilled, quality-controlled packages.

Pepsi-Cola launches Diet Pepsi and quickly grabs market share from TaB.

1965 Sema Wilkes and her husband buy the old Savannah boardinghouse where she'd cooked for 22 years, renovate, and reopen as Mrs. Wilkes' Boarding House restaurant. Now a Savannah landmark, the dining room still packs them in for breakfast and lunch.

BANANA PUDDING

MAKES 8 SERVINGS

. . . .

Country restaurants proliferate all over the South and despite their sometimes cutesy names (Ye Olde Country Kitchen, Grannie's Pantry), most serve the good down-home cooking today's mothers and grandmothers knew as children. Many of these restaurants serve salad-bar style so that you can heap your plate, choosing from a dozen or more "mains and sides," then go back for dessert. Front and center here—nearly always—is a big pan of banana pudding. Some restaurants now cut corners by using vanilla pudding mixes and commercial whipped toppings. Others still make banana pudding the old-fashioned way. This is a good from-scratch recipe.

¾ cup sugar

⅓ cup unsifted all-purpose flour

¼ teaspoon salt

4 cups (1 quart) milk

1 cup half-and-half

3 large eggs, lightly beaten

1½ teaspoons vanilla extract

75 vanilla wafers (about ¾ of a
12-ounce box)

6 medium firm-ripe bananas
(about 2¼ pounds)

1 cup heavy cream, whipped to soft peaks with
2 tablespoons confectioners' (10 X) sugar
and ½ teaspoon vanilla extract

1. Combine the sugar, flour, and salt in a large, heavy saucepan. Whisk in the milk and half-and-half, set over moderate heat, and cook, stirring constantly, for 7 to 8 minutes or until thickened and smooth. Whisk a little of the hot mixture into the beaten eggs, stir back into the pan, and cook, stirring constantly, for about a minute or until an instant-read thermometer inserted into the mixture registers 160° F. Remove from the heat and mix in the vanilla.

2. Skim-coat the bottom of an ungreased 9 × 9 × 2-inch pan with about ½ cup of the hot pudding, then "pave" with 25 vanilla wafers, arranging the cookies side by side so that they touch one another.

3. Peel the bananas, slice ¼ inch thick, and layer a third of them on top of the vanilla wafers, again arranging side by side. Spread with a third of the remaining pudding, add another 25 vanilla wafers, then half the remaining bananas, each time arranging the same way. Spread with half the remaining pudding. Repeat the layers once more, then top with a final layer of pudding.

4. Frost the pudding with the whipped cream, set in the refrigerator, slide a small baking sheet on top, and chill for at least 1 hour before serving.

❀

Everybody knew something was bad wrong with Gaten . . . Wouldn't even eat a spoonful of Everleen's banana pudding. I could have eaten the whole thing by myself . . . They said Gaten was in L.O.V.E.

—DORI SANDERS, *CLOVER*

❀

MY DOUGHNUT STAND

The summer all the neighborhood kids had lemonade stands, I decided to sell doughnuts, mostly because I loved to watch them pop up in the deep fat and flip themselves over. I marvel now that my mother would let a ten-year-old work with 375-degree deep fat—especially since I had to stand on a step stool to see into the pot. But let me she did. My doughnuts were dreadful—leaden and greasy right out of the fryer. Eaten cold, they were a major Maalox moment. Still, deliverymen always stopped to buy a few. I made no money on the doughnut stand; in fact it bankrupted me. But the experience taught me how to plan and budget.

AMBROSIA

MAKES 4 TO 6 SERVINGS

Somewhere down the line Southerners lost their way when it came to making ambrosia. They filled it with canned crushed pineapple and, worse still, with mini marshmallows and maraschino cherries. In its purest form, ambrosia is nothing more than alternate layers of sliced oranges and freshly grated coconut. No empty calories here. In *Mrs. Hill's Southern Practical Cookery and Receipt Book* (1872), however, Annabella P. Hill includes a somewhat more elaborate version. To quote: "Ambrosia is made by placing upon a glass stand . . . alternate layers of grated cocoanut, oranges, peeled and sliced round, and a pineapple sliced thin. Begin with the oranges, and use cocoanut last, spreading between each layer sifted loaf sugar. Sweeten the cocoanut milk, and pour over." Here's the recipe I like best. **Note:** *To make pineapple fans, slice the peeled and cored fruit into thin rings, then cut each into wedges measuring about 1½ inches across at the widest point.*

4 medium navel oranges, peeled, halved lengthwise, and each half cut crosswise into thin slices

1¼ cups unsweetened grated coconut (preferably freshly grated)

2 cups freshly cut pineapple fans (optional; see Note above)

½ cup superfine sugar

⅓ cup fresh orange juice

3 large mint sprigs (garnish)

1. Layer the orange slices, grated coconut, and, if you like, the pineapple fans in a medium-size glass bowl, sprinkling each layer with the sugar.

2. Pour the orange juice evenly over all, cover, and refrigerate for several hours.

3. Remove from the refrigerator and allow to stand at room temperature for about 15 minutes. Sprig with mint and serve.

MRS. JULIA RENO PHILLIPS'S RECIPE FOR EGG CUSTARD

Over the years as I've traveled about the South, I've haunted tag sales, antiques shops, and bookstores, keeping an eye out for community cookbooks (there are now more than a thousand of them in my library). I'm partial to the typed, mimeographed collections because they're intensely local and less likely to recycle the big food company recipes that proliferate in slicker volumes. There's no putting on airs in these little pamphlets and often the quaint language of ages past surfaces as a sort of culinary time capsule. This old recipe (from *Heritage Recipes*, printed in 1971 by the Haywood County Extension Homemakers in the Great Smokies) shows what I mean.

First an incentive: When Dr. Herbert Mease rode by in his covered buggy and hollered, "Julia, can you have a custard by the time I come back?"

Then to the barn and gathered six fresh eggs, then to the spring house for some good rich milk (2 cups). Beat the eggs well (no, not with an electric beater . . . she had none), but with a fork, but well; then add about four tablespoons sugar, not too much sugar, they will be watery; then grate some nutmeg generously. Have a tin pan ready and place a good short crust; bake in oven (no thermometer), use your better judgment; now with the electric ovens, I would say 350 degrees, until done.

—Mrs. Edith Phillips Russell, Beaverdam Club

AUNT EMMA'S BOURBON CUSTARD

MAKES 8 TO 10 SERVINGS

I love Tidewater Virginia, particularly that woodsy stretch undulating along the north bank of the James River (Route 5) between Richmond and Williamsburg. There are half a dozen imposing plantations here in FFV (First Family of Virginia) country, one of which (Berkeley, built in 1726) was the birthplace of one American president (William Henry Harrison) and the ancestral home of a second (Ohio-born Benjamin Harrison). Here, too, is Sherwood Forest, the home of President John Tyler. When I was a food editor at *The Ladies' Home Journal*, I covered Tyler's granddaughter's debut. Two decades later, I returned to Sherwood Forest to interview Payne Tyler, the wife of Tyler grandson Harrison Ruffin Tyler, for a *Bon Appétit* article on James River plantation recipes. This unusual bourbon custard appeared in that article. The recipe, Payne told me, is one from her South Carolina family; she grew up at Mulberry Hill Plantation in Edgefield County near Aiken. The recipe was her Aunt Emma's. It seems that Aunt Emma's mother-in-law, Effie, could only make one thing: angel food cake, which called for a dozen egg whites. According to Payne, Aunt Emma thought that there must be a way to use up the twelve egg yolks, so she created this bourbon custard. "It's just like eating silk," Payne says.

4 cups (1 quart) heavy cream

1 cup sugar

12 jumbo egg yolks, lightly beaten

½ cup fine bourbon

1. Preheat the oven to 325° F. Butter a 2-quart casserole and set aside.

2. Bring the cream and sugar to a simmer in a large, heavy saucepan over moderate heat, stirring until the sugar dissolves.

3. Whisk 1 cup of the hot cream mixture into the beaten egg yolks, then stir back into the saucepan and cook and stir for about a minute or just until the mixture begins to thicken. Do not boil or the custard may curdle. Strain the custard into a large heatproof bowl and mix in the bourbon.

4. Pour the custard into the casserole and set in a large shallow baking pan. Slide onto the middle oven shelf, then pour enough hot water into the pan to come halfway up the sides of the casserole.

5. Bake the custard for 1 to 1¼ hours until lightly browned; the custard may not be completely set.

6. Transfer the custard to a wire rack and cool to room temperature, then cover and refrigerate for several hours or until softly set.

I know folks all have a tizzy about it, but I like a little bourbon of an evening. It helps me sleep.

—LILLIAN CARTER

BONNEY-CLABBER OR LOPPERED MILK

I reprint here an old dessert just as it appears in *From North Carolina Kitchens: Favorite Recipes Old and New*, an uncopyrighted collection of recipes from the state's Home Demonstration Club women published in the 1950s.

Set a china, or glass dish of skimmed milk away in a warm place, covered. When it turns—i.e. becomes a smooth, firm, but not tough cake, like blanc-mange—serve in the same dish. Cut out carefully with a large spoon, and put in saucers, with cream, powdered sugar, and nutmeg to taste. It is better, if set on the ice for an hour before it is brought to table. Do not let it stand until the whey separates from the curd.

Few people know how delicious this healthful and cheap dessert can be if eaten before it becomes tart and tough; with a liberal allowance of cream and sugar. There are not many jellies and creams superior to it.

—Pasquotank County, North Carolina

Only a Southerner knows that "gimme some sugar" doesn't mean "pass the sugar bowl."

—ANONYMOUS

PORT WINE JELLY

MAKES 4 TO 6 SERVINGS

This is such an old-fashioned recipe that few people bother to make it any more. And that's a shame because it's both simple and sophisticated. I first tasted wine jelly one Sunday lunch when I was no more than ten. It had been made by the wife of one of my father's Botany Department colleagues at North Carolina State College and it came to table in stemmed goblets snow-capped with whipped cream. Thinking that this was some new flavor of Jell-O, I dove in; then I made a face, put down my spoon, and refused to eat any more. My moratorium lasted until I'd acquired a taste for fine wine. I don't know where wine jellies originated—England, I suspect. But I do know that from Colonial days (when gelatin had to be made at home by boiling calves' feet) right up through the mid twentieth century, wine jellies were often served at the end of elegant southern dinners. **Note:** *Other wines can be substituted for port: a malmsey (sweet Madeira), for example, an amontillado (sherry), even a Marsala.*

2 envelopes unflavored gelatin

2 cups water

½ cup sugar

½ cinnamon stick

One 3-inch strip orange zest

One 2-inch strip lemon zest

2 cups fine fruity port such as a ruby or late-bottled vintage (see Note above)

1 cup heavy cream, whipped to soft peaks with 2 tablespoons confectioners' (10X) sugar

1. Soften the gelatin in ½ cup of the water in a medium-size, nonreactive, heatproof bowl.

2. Meanwhile, bring the remaining 1½ cups water, the sugar, cinnamon stick, and orange and lemon zests to a boil in a small, heavy, nonreactive saucepan over moderate heat, stirring occasionally. Adjust the heat so that the liquid bubbles lazily and simmer uncovered for 5 minutes. Discard the cinnamon stick and the orange and lemon zests.

3. Pour the hot liquid over the softened gelatin and stir until the gelatin dissolves completely. Cool 10 minutes, then stir in the port wine. Cool 20 minutes more, then set uncovered in the refrigerator and chill for several hours or until the wine jelly is set.

4. To serve, break the wine jelly into small pieces with a fork (they should look like garnets or rubies), then layer into stemmed goblets with the sweetened whipped cream.

❁

. . . the day started out without a fuss and the pantry shelves laid out with rows of jelly glasses . . . and white stone-china jars with blue whirligigs and words painted on them: coffee, tea, sugar, ginger, cinnamon, allspice.

—KATHERINE ANNE PORTER,
THE JILTING OF GRANNY WEATHERALL

❁

Heirloom Recipe

PIG'S FOOT JELLY

Some years ago, the Home Demonstration Club Women of Iredell County, North Carolina, where I once worked, assembled and mimeographed a collection of old country recipes. This is one of them. *My brother and sister and I were raised at the home of our grandparents, Colonel and Mrs. S. A. Sharpe. Our grandmother had been raised on the ancestral plantation, the McKee place, three miles from town. She knew and taught us many of the pioneer ways of cooking. Pig's foot jelly was one of our favorites. It was a holiday dessert served in the finest of cut glass bowls. My sister remembers that it was her duty to whip the solid jelly with a silver fork into thousands of sparkling diamonds. Before the days of gelatin, animal skin and bones were cooked or rather simmered in water to extract the jelly. The broth was strained through a sieve and allowed to cool. The solid fat was removed and the jelly rubbed over with a clean hot cloth to remove more of the particles of fat.*

The broth was reheated and strained through a cheesecloth bag that had been dipped in boiling water. Next, an egg white was beaten to a froth and the shell crumbled. The white and crumbled shell were added to the broth. It was heated and any impurities clung to the egg and were strained away. Now the jelly is ready to sweeten to taste. Wine to taste is added when the mixture is lukewarm. It is allowed to harden. Sometimes lemons were sliced into the jelly. Serve with whipped cream.

—Mrs. Katherine N. Knox, Iredell County, North Carolina

1965 To bolster the strength and stamina of University of Florida football players ("the Gators"), college physicians create a carbohydrate-electrolyte sports drink that keeps them well hydrated during practice and play. "Gatorade," they call it.

1966 Birmingham-based *Progressive Farmer* magazine becomes *Southern Living* because of migrations from country to city. First called *Southern Living Classics*, it becomes *Southern Living* after its 1985 merger with *Southern Accents*, an Atlanta magazine.

To connect with his students at Rabun County High School in the mountains of northeast Georgia, English teacher Eliot Wigginton helps them create their own magazine. They name it *Foxfire* (after a phosphorescent fungus found in local forests) and focus upon the food and folkways of the Georgia Appalachians. *Foxfire* is still published twice a year.

Mississippi finally repeals Prohibition—the last state to do so.

PEANUT BUTTER ICE CREAM WITH WARM CHOCOLATE SAUCE

MAKES 6 TO 8 SERVINGS

Shortly before Hurricane Hugo ravaged Charleston back in 1989, *Food & Wine* sent me there to write an article on the Lowcountry, which also included Beaufort, South Carolina, and Savannah, Georgia. At the time, Charleston was just emerging as a restaurant town and a new arrival that I particularly liked was Morton's on the first floor of a boutique bed-and-breakfast called the Vendue Inn. Everything I ordered was first-rate but nothing more so than this ice cream, which arrived on a plate elaborately painted with raspberry coulis, crème anglaise, and chocolate sauce. I dispense with the art work and serve the ice cream under simple ladlings of chocolate sauce. Though battered by Hugo's 135-mile-an-hour winds and swamped by tidal surges, the Vendue Inn is back and better than ever. Morton's is gone, however, replaced by a rooftop bar and restaurant with a gull's-eye view of Charleston harbor. **Note:** *Raw egg yolks go into this ice cream, so use pasteurized eggs (see About Pasteurized Eggs, page xxi).*

1 cup firmly packed creamy-style peanut butter

4 cups (1 quart) milk

8 large pasteurized egg yolks (see Note above)

¾ cup sugar

Warm Chocolate Sauce (recipe follows)

1. Place the peanut butter and milk in a medium-size heavy saucepan, set over moderately low heat, and cook, whisking constantly, for 3 to 5 minutes or until the peanut butter melts and the mixture is completely smooth. Set off the heat, cover, and keep warm.

2. Beat the egg yolks and sugar in a large electric mixer bowl at high speed for 8 to 10 minutes until the color and consistency of mayonnaise. With the mixer at low speed, slowly add the warm peanut butter mixture. Put through a fine sieve and quick-chill in an ice bath, whisking often.

3. Pour the ice cream mixture into an ice cream maker and freeze according to the manufacturer's directions.

4. Scoop the ice cream onto dessert plates and top with Warm Chocolate Sauce.

WARM CHOCOLATE SAUCE

MAKES ABOUT 2½ CUPS

Serve with the homemade Peanut Butter Ice Cream that precedes or with commercial vanilla, hazelnut, butter pecan, dulce de leche, or chocolate ice cream. **Note:** *For clarified butter, melt 1 cup (2 sticks) butter in a small, heavy saucepan over low heat, then set aside until the milk solids settle to the bottom. Strain the liquid butter through a fine sieve lined with several thicknesses of cheesecloth. Or even easier, skim the froth from the melted butter, then very slowly pour it into a measuring cup, leaving the milk solids behind.*

1 pound bittersweet chocolate,
coarsely grated

¾ cup clarified butter (see Note at left)

½ teaspoon vanilla extract

1. Place the chocolate and clarified butter in the top of a double boiler, set over simmering water, and cook over low heat, stirring often, for 3 to 4 minutes or until absolutely smooth. Set off the heat and blend in the vanilla.
2. Serve warm over ice cream. Good, too, over pound cake.

MISSISSIPPI FRESH FIG ICE CREAM

MAKES 6 SERVINGS

This recipe comes from my friend Moreton Neal, who grew up in Mississippi but now lives in Chapel Hill, North Carolina. She says that every summer when figs hung heavy on the bush, her grandmother would make this ice cream "for the family gatherings of my childhood." Later Moreton served her grandmother's fig ice cream at La Résidence, the restaurant she and former husband Bill Neal opened at Fearrington Village, then relocated to downtown Chapel Hill. The fig ice cream was so popular, she adds, "that several of our patrons asked to be called as soon as it appeared on the menu. We served it drizzled with a good ruby port." **Note:** *Moreton's grandmother mashed the figs for her ice cream, but I purée them in a food processor. If you prefer a slightly coarser texture, pulse*

1967 The National Football League names Gatorade its official sports drink.

Buddy Smothers enters the barbecue business in Knoxville, Tennessee, because he misses what he grew up on back in Alabama. Some say Buddy's Bar-B-Q, a small family chain, serves east Tennessee's best. Buddy's motto: "We cook it slow . . . but you get it fast!"

1968 The Red Lobster chain of seafood restaurants is launched in Lakeland, Florida.

Procter & Gamble begins manufacturing Pringles Potato Chips in Jackson, Tennessee. Compounded of dried potato flakes, these extruded, identically shaped chips are packed in tubular containers to keep them crisp, fresh, and intact.

With Phase One of its restoration completed, Shakertown (now Shaker Village) at Pleasant Hill, Kentucky, is open to the public. Of particular interest to visitors: the dining room and its menu of authentic Shaker recipes.

the figs only until moderately finely chopped. **Tip:** *Turn the egg whites into angel food cake; it's perfect with fresh fig ice cream.*

3 cups half-and-half

8 large egg yolks

1⅓ cups sugar

¼ teaspoon salt

1 cup heavy cream

1 tablespoon vanilla extract

3 tablespoons fresh lemon juice

2 cups puréed, peeled, dead-ripe figs
(20 to 22 medium-size)

¾ cup good ruby port

1. Pour the half-and-half into a medium-size saucepan, set over moderate heat, and bring to a simmer, stirring occasionally; this will take about 5 minutes. Moreton says that her grandmother just heated it until a "skin formed on the top." If you stir the half-and-half as it heats, it won't "skin."

2. Meanwhile, whisk the egg yolks lightly with ⅔ cup of the sugar and the salt in a medium-size heatproof bowl, then continue whisking as you slowly add the scalded half-and-half.

3. Pour back into the saucepan and cook, whisking constantly, over moderately low heat for 8 to 10 minutes or just until the custard thickens; it should coat the back of a metal spoon. Do not allow the custard to boil; it will curdle.

4. Remove the custard from the heat, mix in the heavy cream and vanilla, then quick-chill in

an ice bath for 15 to 20 minutes or until refrigerator-cold, stirring often.

5. Mix the remaining ⅔ cup sugar and the lemon juice into the puréed figs, then combine with the cooled custard.

6. Pour into an ice cream maker and freeze according to the manufacturer's directions.

7. To serve, scoop out the ice cream and spoon 2 tablespoons of the port over each portion.

BILL SMITH'S AMAZING HONEYSUCKLE SORBET

MAKES ABOUT 8 SERVINGS

I'll never forget the midsummer night friends and I were dining in the garden at Crook's Corner in Chapel Hill. Suddenly chef Bill Smith arrived at our table with a bowl of sorbet. "Let me know what you think of this," he said. "It's a new recipe I'm working on." We were blown away. Bill had captured the sensuous floral fragrance every Southerner knows so well—honeysuckle—and spun it into a silky sorbet (the recipe is in his new cookbook, *Seasoned in the South*). In his headnote Bill says that Crook's owner, Gene Hamer, had urged him to turn honeysuckle nectar into something edible. On steamy nights the heady scent of honeysuckle running amok just outside the restaurant was driving the staff nuts. Having read that Arabs in Spain and Sicily had made flower ices, Bill decided to give that a try. The trick was to capture the bouquet of the honeysuckle, not the bitterness. He succeeded. "The best flowers," Bill writes, "seem to be the wild ones with the pinkish throats, although the regular ivory-colored ones are fine." He nixes bland honeysuckle hybrids, also flowers picked by the side of the road, which have a sooty flavor. Finally, he stresses the importance of removing "all the leaves that invariably get mixed up in the flowers" lest the sorbet taste of chlorophyll. Apart from picking the honeysuckle blossoms (best done at night), Bill's recipe is hardly labor-intensive.

4 cups (1 quart) freshly picked honeysuckle blossoms (measure tightly packed but avoid bruising the flowers)

6⅔ cups cool water

2 cups sugar

½ teaspoon fresh lemon juice

A tiny pinch of ground cinnamon (Bill takes it up on the tip of a boning knife)

1. Pick over the honeysuckle blossoms carefully, removing all leaves and bits of stem. Place the flowers in a large, nonreactive bowl and pour in 5⅓ cups of the water. Place a heavy plate on top to keep the flowers submerged, and let stand on the counter overnight.

2. Next day, place the remaining 1⅓ cups water in a small, heavy saucepan and mix in the sugar. Bring to a boil over moderate heat, then boil uncovered for 3 to 5 minutes or until about the consistency of light corn syrup. Remove from the heat, add the lemon juice (to keep the syrup from crystallizing), and cool to room temperature.

3. Meanwhile, strain the honeysuckle infusion, pressing the blossoms gently to extract every drop of nectar. Mix in the cooled syrup, then the cinnamon—"just a speck," Bill cautions. "You don't want to taste it but you can tell if it's not there."

4. Pour the honeysuckle mixture into an ice cream maker and freeze according to the manufacturer's directions. **Note:** *Stored tightly covered in the freezer, this sorbet will keep for about two weeks. Soften slightly before serving.*

WATERMELON ICE

MAKES 8 SERVINGS

I dote upon watermelon as much as the next Southerner. But instead of devouring it by the slice, I churn it into this easy ice. Short of an A/C, it's a fast way to take the sizzle out of summer.

2 envelopes unflavored gelatin

½ cup cold water

One 7-pound chunk ripe watermelon

One 6-ounce can frozen pink lemonade or limeade concentrate, thawed

¼ cup light corn syrup

2 tablespoons sugar, or to taste

2 tablespoons fresh lime or lemon juice, or to taste

¼ teaspoon salt

Two to three drops red food coloring (optional)

1. Soften the gelatin in the cold water in a small heatproof bowl, set in a larger bowl of boiling water, and stir until the gelatin dissolves. Set aside.

2. Discard the watermelon seeds and rind, then cut the flesh into 1½-inch chunks. Purée in batches in a food processor or electric blender at high speed. Reserve 6 cups of the purée. Drink the rest as a "smoothie" or combine with a fresh fruit cocktail.

3. Mix the dissolved gelatin into the purée along with all remaining ingredients. Taste and add more sugar and/or lime juice, if needed.

4. Pour the watermelon mixture into an ice cream maker and freeze according to the manufacturer's directions.

5. Dish up and serve.

FROZEN FRUIT SALAD

MAKES 8 SERVINGS

No southern cookbook would be complete without at least one frozen fruit salad because they were all the rage fifty years ago. Apparently they were known even earlier; in *Fashionable Food* (1995), Sylvia Lovegren reprints a frozen fruit salad recipe that had appeared in *The Kelvinator Book of Recipes* in the late 1920s or early '30s— just when refrigerators were replacing iceboxes in homes across the South. (In some areas, Kelvinator is generic for refrigerator, as in "Honey, would you go to the Kelvinator and get me a Coke?") As for frozen fruit salads, I don't remember their being popular in my hometown of Raleigh until the '50s. Suddenly everybody was talking about them. And in competitions as fierce as any card game, bridge club hostesses were one-upping one another by creating ever more cloying frozen fruit salads. Calling them "salads" was absurd, a silly euphemism. They were dessert pure and simple although often served on iceberg lettuce—*with* the main course. This recipe is representative of the frozen fruit salads so popular in the 1950s South, also of those endlessly recycled in community cookbooks. I like the fact that it contains chopped pecans and doesn't contain canned fruit cocktail or whipped cream. Still, it's plenty rich.

One 8-ounce package cream cheese, at room temperature (use the lighter version, Neufchâtel, if you like)

One 8-ounce can crushed pineapple, with its liquid

2 tablespoons fresh lemon juice

One 6-ounce jar red maraschino cherries, drained

One 3.5-ounce jar green maraschino cherries, drained

2 cups miniature marshmallows

1 cup coarsely chopped pecans

1. Combine the cream cheese, crushed pineapple, and lemon juice in a large bowl, then fold in all remaining ingredients.

2. Scoop into a nonreactive 8 × 8 × 2-inch baking dish, spreading to the corners. Cover with aluminum foil and freeze for several hours or until firm.

3. Cut into large squares and serve.

SWEET POTATO CHEESECAKE

MAKES 10 TO 12 SERVINGS

. . . .

Southerners so love sweet potatoes that they will stir them into soups, salads, breads, puddings, cakes, even cheesecakes. There may be as many cheesecake recipes as there are cooks who make them but this one of mine "gets a gold star," as one friend put it. The variety of sweet potato that I prefer is the red-skinned Beauregard because of its brilliant orange flesh. **Note:** *For better flavor, I bake the potato instead of boiling it—one hour at 400° F. is about right. Be sure to prick the potato several times before it goes into the oven, otherwise it may explode. Cool the potato until easy to handle before peeling and puréeing—a snap in the food processor. I also buzz the gingersnaps to crumbs in the processor and chop the pecans there as well. I've even been known to mix the filling by processor, churning the first nine ingredients until smooth, pulsing the eggs in one at a time, then with the machine on, drizzling the milk down the feed tube as slowly as possible.*

Crust

2 cups fine gingersnap crumbs
(about forty 2-inch-round cookies)

1 cup pecans, very finely chopped

½ cup (1 stick) butter, melted

¼ cup raw sugar (available at most
supermarkets)

¼ teaspoon freshly grated nutmeg

Filling

Two 8-ounces packages light cream cheese
(Neufchâtel), at room temperature

1¼ cups firmly packed puréed, baked
sweet potato (about 1 very large or
1-pound sweet potato)

⅔ cup raw sugar

¼ cup firmly packed light brown sugar

1 tablespoon bourbon

¾ teaspoon ground cinnamon

¾ teaspoon ground ginger

½ teaspoon freshly grated nutmeg

¼ teaspoon salt

2 jumbo eggs

1 cup evaporated milk
(use "light," if you like)

Topping

1 cup sour cream (use "light," if you like)

¼ cup raw sugar

1 teaspoon vanilla extract

¼ cup finely chopped, lightly toasted pecans
(4 to 5 minutes in a 375° F. oven)

1. Preheat the oven to 375° F.
2. For the crust: Combine all ingredients and pat over the bottom and halfway up the sides of an ungreased 10-inch springform pan. Slide onto the middle oven shelf and bake for 8 to 10 minutes or just until the crust firms up a bit. Transfer to a wire rack to cool.

3. Meanwhile, prepare the filling: Beat the cream cheese, sweet potato, two sugars, bourbon, cinnamon, ginger, nutmeg, and salt in a large electric mixer bowl at medium speed for about 1 minute or until smooth. Beat the eggs in one by one, then with the mixer at low speed, add the milk in a thin, slow stream. Beat a few seconds longer or until smooth.

4. Rap the bowl of filling on the counter several times to expel large air bubbles, then pour into the crust and spread to the edge. Set on a large baking sheet, slide onto the middle oven shelf, and bake for 40 to 45 minutes or until the filling is set like custard.

5. Meanwhile, prepare the topping: Whisk the sour cream, sugar, and vanilla together in a small bowl, then set aside.

6. When the cheesecake tests done, remove from the oven (baking sheet and all), set on a wire rack, and cool for 10 minutes exactly. Also raise the oven temperature to 475° F.

7. Using an offset spatula, carefully spread the topping over the partially cooled filling; it should touch the crust all around. Sprinkle the toasted pecans evenly on top.

8. Return the cheesecake, still on the baking sheet, to the middle oven shelf and bake for 10 minutes—no longer.

9. Remove the cheesecake from the oven and from the baking sheet. Set on a wire rack and cool for 45 minutes, then place in the coldest part of the refrigerator and slide a large round tray on top (a pizza pan is perfect). Cool for at least 12 hours or better yet, overnight.

10. To serve, release the springform clamp and lift off the sides of the pan. Leave the cheesecake on the pan bottom and cut into slim wedges.

BANANAS FOSTER CHEESECAKE

MAKES 10 TO 12 SERVINGS

. . . .

I've breakfasted on Bananas Foster at Brennan's, the New Orleans restaurant where chef Paul Blangé created the recipe more than fifty years ago. Named for Richard Foster, a local merchant and Brennan's regular, this classic (bananas caramelized, flamed with rum, and served over vanilla ice cream) has appeared in countless cookbooks and is now all over the Web. But few know this elegant variation, which I had the good sense to order at Café Vermillionville in Lafayette while researching a Louisiana article for *Gourmet*. Bananas Foster Cheesecake is a make-ahead and about all it has in common with the Brennan's classic are bananas, butter, brown sugar, and rum.

Crust

Nine 5 × 2½-inch graham crackers

2 tablespoons granulated sugar

4 tablespoons (½ stick) butter, melted

12 to 13 ladyfingers, halved crosswise

Banana Filling

4 tablespoons (½ stick) butter

½ cup firmly packed dark brown sugar

2 tablespoons banana liqueur

2 tablespoons dark rum

½ teaspoon vanilla extract

⅛ teaspoon ground cinnamon

4 medium firm-ripe bananas, peeled, halved crosswise, then each half cut lengthwise into slices ¼ inch thick

¼ cup lightly toasted sliced almonds (about 5 minutes in a 350° F. oven)

Cream Cheese Layer

Three 8-ounce packages cream cheese, at room temperature

I cup granulated sugar

5 large eggs, lightly whisked

2 tablespoons banana liqueur

I tablespoon vanilla extract

Praline Topping

I cup (2 sticks) butter

I cup firmly packed dark brown sugar

I½ tablespoons water

I½ cups very lightly toasted pecans (5 to 8 minutes in a 350° F. oven)

1. Preheat the oven to 350° F. Butter a 10-inch springform pan well, then waterproof it by wrapping the outside with a large sheet of heavy-duty aluminum foil; set aside.
2. For the crust: Place the graham crackers and sugar in a food processor or electric blender, then grind to fine crumbs. With the motor running, drizzle in the melted butter. Press the crumb mixture firmly over the bottom of the springform pan, then stand the ladyfingers, rounded ends up and "shoulder to shoulder," around the side of the pan; press lightly into the crumbs to anchor.

1969 Dan Evins opens the first of a string of Cracker Barrel restaurants in Lebanon, Tennessee.

The Captain D's seafood chain (originally called Mr. D's) debuts in Donelson, Tennessee. Its quickly served seasonal seafood is so popular that by the turn of the twenty-first century, there are more than 550 Captain D's scattered across 22 states.

The original Long John Silver's begins serving fish and chips in Lexington, Kentucky.

1970 The U.S. Department of Agriculture relocates its Georgia peach and pecan research stations to Byron, Georgia, and establishes the USDA Southeastern Fruit and Tree Nut Research Laboratory. This new research facility not only seeks ways to control the pests and diseases attacking peaches and pecans but also those affecting Asian pears, apples, blueberries, Chinese chestnuts, nectarines, and plums, all important southern crops.

1970s Switching to European varietals, Virginia vintners begin producing cabernets, chardonnays, and rieslings. By 1982, the majority of Virginia wines are varietals.

3. For the banana filling: Place the butter and brown sugar in a large nonstick skillet, set over moderate heat, and cook, stirring often, for 5 to 8 minutes or until the butter melts and the mixture is smooth. Mix in the banana liqueur, rum, vanilla, and cinnamon and cook, whisking often, for 1 to 2 minutes or until the sugar dissolves completely.

4. Add the bananas, reduce the heat to low, and cook for 30 seconds. Turn the bananas gently and cook about 30 seconds longer or until slightly softened. Set off the heat and sprinkle in the almonds.

5. For the cream cheese layer: Beat the cream cheese and sugar in a large electric mixer bowl at high speed for about 2 minutes or until light and fluffy. Reduce the speed to low and beat in half of the eggs. Scrape the bowl well, then beat in the remaining eggs, the banana liqueur, and vanilla.

6. Scoop half of the cream cheese mixture into the graham cracker crust, smoothing to the edge, then bake uncovered on the middle oven shelf for 10 minutes. Remove from the oven and cool on a wire rack for 5 minutes.

7. Carefully spoon the banana filling over the baked layer, rearranging the bananas, if necessary, so that they do not overlap. Top with the remaining cream cheese mixture, again spreading to the edge.

8. Set the springform pan in a large shallow roasting pan and ease onto the middle oven shelf. Pour enough boiling water into the roaster to come halfway up the sides of the springform pan. Bake the cheesecake uncovered for 50 to 60 minutes or until golden on top and set in the center.

9. Transfer the cheesecake to a wire rack and cool to room temperature. Cover loosely and refrigerate for 24 hours.

10. Next day, prepare the praline topping: Place the butter and sugar in a large, heavy saucepan, set over moderate heat, and cook, stirring constantly, for 5 to 8 minutes or until the butter melts and the mixture is smooth. Add the water and stir to incorporate. Fold in the pecans and cool the topping to room temperature.

11. To serve, release the springform clamp and lift off the sides of the pan. Leave the cheesecake on the pan bottom, then cut into slim wedges and ladle some of the topping over each portion.

SWEET POTATO PIE

MAKES 6 TO 8 SERVINGS

Baked sweet potatoes, I think, make better pie than boiled sweet potatoes. For two reasons: Baked sweet potatoes are never watery, and that stint in the oven caramelizes some of their natural sugars, making for richer, deeper flavor (I give them about one hour at 400° F.). There are dozens of recipes for sweet potato pie, but this one—a merging of several different recipes that I've collected in my prowls about the South—is especially good because it's not cloyingly sweet.

2 cups firmly packed unseasoned mashed, cooked sweet potatoes (about 2 pounds)

¼ cup granulated sugar

¼ cup firmly packed light brown sugar

2 tablespoons all-purpose flour

¾ teaspoon freshly grated nutmeg or
¼ teaspoon ground nutmeg

¼ teaspoon ground cinnamon

¼ teaspoon ground ginger

¼ teaspoon salt

3 large eggs

¾ cup milk or evaporated milk
(I prefer the latter)

3 tablespoons butter, melted

1 teaspoon vanilla extract

One 9-inch unbaked pie shell
(see About Pie Crusts, page xxi)

1. Preheat the oven to 325° F. Beat the sweet potatoes, granulated sugar, brown sugar, flour, nutmeg, cinnamon, ginger, and salt in a small electric mixer bowl at low speed for about 30 seconds, then at high speed for 1 minute or until light, pausing several times to scrape the bowl.

2. With the mixer at low speed, beat in the eggs one by one. With the mixer still at low speed, add the milk, melted butter, and vanilla. Pour the filling into the pie shell.

3. Slide the pie onto a baking sheet and bake on the middle oven shelf for 1 hour and 10 minutes or until puffed, lightly browned, and a cake tester inserted halfway between the edge and the center comes out clean.

4. If you want to serve the pie warm, cool on a wire rack for 30 minutes. Or, if you prefer, cool the pie to room temperature before serving.
Note: *The filling will fall somewhat but this is as it should be.*

1972

Doubleday, attracted by *Foxfire* magazine and convinced that its homespun information would have vast appeal, publishes *The Foxfire Book: Hog Dressing, Log Cabin Building, Mountain Crafts & Foods, Planting by the Signs, Snake Lore, Hunting Tales, Faith Healing, Moon Shining.* That first *Foxfire Book* spawned 14 others.

After failing to grab the New Orleans lunch crowd with his Chicken on the Run, Al Copeland rethinks his fast-food restaurant, spices up his fried chicken, and reopens as Popeyes. It is the first restaurant in a huge chain of Popeyes.

Newly acquired by the Federal Company, the Knoxville mill built by J. Allen Smith is renamed White Lily Foods after its bestselling White Lily Flour.

Sandy Beall and four University of Tennessee fraternity brothers open the first Ruby Tuesday restaurant next door to the Knoxville campus. Their aim of serving quality food at a fair price in a casual atmosphere catches on; today there are hundreds of Ruby Tuesdays scattered across the country.

SWEET POTATO MERINGUE PIE

MAKES 6 TO 8 SERVINGS

. . . .

Tabor City, North Carolina, is "The Yam Capital of the World," so it's not surprising that the state stages its annual Yam Festival there the fourth weekend in October. "Yam" is a misnomer, for what Tabor City celebrates with parades and "yam royalty" coronations is the sweet potato harvest. North Carolina produces 40 percent of America's sweet potatoes, more than any other state, so is it any wonder that this little town and outlying areas are blessed with imaginative cooks who prepare sweet potatoes every which way? This unique sweet potato pie is one of them. What makes it unique? For starters, the filling, made altogether with granulated sugar (no brown sugar) and spiced only with nutmeg (no cinnamon, no ginger), isn't the usual custardy pumpkin-pie type; it has the silken texture of whipped sweet potatoes. And then there's that cloud of meringue on top.

2 cups firmly packed unseasoned mashed, cooked sweet potatoes (you'll need about 2 pounds of sweet potatoes)

½ cup sugar

¼ teaspoon freshly grated nutmeg

¼ teaspoon salt

3 large pasteurized egg yolks (see About Pasteurized Eggs, page xxi)

1 cup milk

2 tablespoons butter, melted

1 teaspoon vanilla extract

One 9-inch unbaked pie shell (see About Pie Crusts, page xxi)

3 large pasteurized egg whites, beaten to soft peaks with ¼ cup sugar (meringue)

1. Preheat the oven to 350° F. Beat the sweet potatoes, sugar, nutmeg, and salt in a small electric mixer bowl at moderately low speed for about 1 minute or until well blended.

2. Reduce the mixer speed to low and beat in the egg yolks one by one. With the mixer still at low speed, add the milk, melted butter, and vanilla. Pour the filling into the pie shell, smoothing to the edge.

3. Slide the pie onto the middle oven shelf and bake for 35 to 40 minutes or until a cake tester inserted halfway between the edge and the center comes out clean.

4. Remove the pie from the oven and immediately spread the meringue over the hot filling, swirling into peaks and valleys and making sure that it touches the crust all around. Return the pie to the oven and bake for 15 minutes or until the meringue is tipped with brown.

5. Set the pie on a wire rack and cool to room temperature before cutting.

TAR HEEL GREEN TOMATO PIE

MAKES 6 SERVINGS

More than a hundred years old, this unusual pie was a dessert favorite at end-of-summer picnics back when I was an assistant home demonstration agent in Iredell County, North Carolina. Always held in August (green tomato time), these feasts were—and still are—the surest way to taste southern country cooking at its best. I soon learned that if I wanted any green tomato pie, I'd better grab a slice at the outset and save it for dessert; it disappeared that fast. **Tip:** *If I'm in a rush, I'll use the commercial unroll-and-use pastry circles now sold at many supermarkets (look for them near the refrigerated biscuits) instead of making the crust from scratch. The elderly farm woman who gave me this recipe so many years ago would have loved these handy time-savers.*

8 medium-size green tomatoes
(2 to 2¼ pounds), cored and sliced
¼ inch thick but not peeled

1 tablespoon fresh lemon juice

½ cup firmly packed light brown sugar

½ cup granulated sugar

½ cup unsifted all-purpose flour

½ teaspoon salt

¼ teaspoon ground cinnamon

¼ teaspoon freshly grated nutmeg

4 tablespoons (½ stick) ice-cold butter,
cut into small dice

Pastry for a double-crust 9-inch pie
(see Tip above)

1 tablespoon light or heavy cream

1 pint vanilla ice cream (optional)

1. Slide a heavy baking sheet onto the middle oven shelf and preheat the oven to 425° F.

2. Place the tomatoes and lemon juice in a large nonreactive bowl, toss well, and set aside.

3. Combine the two sugars, flour, salt, cinnamon, and nutmeg in a second large bowl; then, using a pastry blender, cut in the butter until the texture of lentils and set aside.

4. Using your favorite recipe, make the pastry and divide in half. Roll one half on a lightly floured surface into a circle 12 inches across, then ease into a 9-inch pie pan. Pat firmly over the bottom and up the sides of the pan, letting the excess overhang the rim. **Note:** *If you prefer, substitute the commercial unroll-and-use pastry circles (see Tip at left).*

5. Layer the sliced tomatoes and crumbly sugar mixture into the pie shell, beginning with the sugar mixture and ending with the tomatoes—there should be about 4 layers of each.

6. Roll the remaining pastry into a 14-inch circle and cut into strips ½ inch wide. Lay half the strips on top of the tomatoes, spacing 1 inch apart; brush lightly with the cream. Now form a lattice top by laying the remaining pastry strips at right angles to the first, again spacing 1 inch apart and brushing with cream. Trim the bottom crust and strips so they overhang the pan 1 inch all around. Roll the two up together so they rest on the rim of the pan, then crimp in a zig-zag design. Brush with the remaining cream.

7. Set the pie on the baking sheet and bake for 20 minutes; reduce the oven temperature to

375° F. and continue baking for 35 to 45 minutes or until the pastry is richly browned and the juices are translucent and bubble thickly. What's key here is baking the pie until the flour thickens the juices that exude from the tomatoes. An underbaked pie will be soupy. **Note:** *If the crimped edge is overbrowning, cover with a strip of foil.*

8. Remove the pie from the oven. Lift off the baking sheet, set on a wire rack, and cool for several hours before cutting.

9. To serve, cut into wedges and top, if you like, with scoops of vanilla ice cream.

VINEGAR PIE

MAKES 6 TO 8 SERVINGS

In olden days when lemons were scarce, enterprising cooks would counterfeit lemon chess pie by substituting cider vinegar, which was cheap and widely available, for precious lemon juice. This recipe comes from Lillian Waldron, an old friend of my stepmother, Anne Anderson; the two grew up in Lynchburg, Virginia. Anne says that vinegar pie is one of her most requested desserts and a particular favorite of her granddaughters, Linda and Kim Anderson. **Tip:** *To catch boilovers, bake the pie on a baking sheet.*

1½ cups sugar

½ cup (1 stick) butter, melted

3 large eggs

1½ tablespoons cider vinegar

1 teaspoon vanilla extract

One 9-inch unbaked pie shell (see About Pie Crusts, page xxi)

1. Preheat the oven to 325° F.
2. Beat the sugar and melted butter in a small electric mixer bowl for about 1 minute, first at low speed, then at moderate, until well combined; scrape the bowl down at half-time.
3. With the mixer at low speed, beat in the eggs one by one and continue beating for about 30 seconds or until light. Mix in the vinegar and vanilla, and when thoroughly combined, pour the filling into the pie shell.
4. Slide the pie onto a baking sheet and bake on the middle oven shelf for about 1 hour or until puffed, nicely browned, and a cake tester inserted halfway between the edge and the center comes out clean.
5. If you want to serve the pie warm, cool on a wire rack for 30 minutes. Or, if you prefer, cool the pie to room temperature before serving. **Note:** *The filling will fall but this is as it should be. Cut the pieces small—this pie is rich.*

BUTTERMILK PIE

MAKES 6 TO 8 SERVINGS

Like Vinegar Pie, Buttermilk Pie was often baked in lieu of lemon chess pie because in the butter-churning days of old, there was always plenty of buttermilk on hand. To this day, Buttermilk Pie is beloved throughout the South. **Tip:** *To catch any boilovers, it's a good idea to set the pie on a baking sheet before you slide it into the oven.*

A Love Affair with Southern Cooking

1½ cups sugar

3 tablespoons all-purpose flour

6 tablespoons (¾ stick) butter, melted

3 large eggs

1½ cups buttermilk

1 teaspoon vanilla extract

¼ teaspoon freshly grated nutmeg (optional)

One 9-inch unbaked pie shell (see About
Pie Crusts, page xxi)

1. Preheat the oven to 325° F. Beat the sugar,
flour, and melted butter in a small electric
mixer bowl for 1 minute, beginning at low
speed, then raising to moderate so that all
ingredients are well blended. Scrape the bowl
well at half-time.

2. Reduce the mixer speed to low and beat in the
eggs one by one; continue beating for 30 seconds or until light. With the mixer still at low
speed, add the buttermilk, vanilla, and nutmeg, if using. When thoroughly combined,
pour the filling into the pie shell.

3. Slide the pie onto a baking sheet and bake on
the middle oven shelf for about 1 hour and 10
minutes or until puffed, nicely browned, and a
cake tester inserted halfway between the edge
and the center comes out clean.

4. If you want to serve the pie warm, cool on a
wire rack for 30 minutes. Or, if you prefer, cool
the pie to room temperature before serving.
Note: *The filling will fall but this is as it should be.*
Cut the pieces small—this pie is rich.

1973 Stephen Kuhnau, who'd grown
up sickly in south Louisiana,
opens a health food store in
Kenner and begins serving
"smoothies"—nutritious fruit
shakes he'd created years earlier
while jerking sodas. Before long,
Smoothie King bars are popping
up all over the U.S. and Stephen
Kuhnau has been crowned "Mr.
Smoothie King."

1974 Now fully restored, the Shaker
Village at Pleasant Hill,
Kentucky, offers rooms for
overnighters, each furnished in
the simple form-follows-function
Shaker style.

1975 Michael Barefoot opens a 500-
square-foot coffee roastery in
Chapel Hill, North Carolina, and
calls it A Southern Season. Today
it is one of America's premier
specialty food shops.

Using his grandmother's biscuit
recipe, Maurice Jennings
launches Biscuitville to serve
quality breakfasts to those in a
hurry. This Burlington, North
Carolina—based fast-food
chain now operates dozens of
restaurants in Virginia and North
Carolina.

MOONPIE

Traveling the East Tennessee mining country back in 1917, Chattanooga bakery salesman Earl Mitchell asked the miners what sort of snack they'd like. Something filling for their lunch pails is what they wanted.

"How big?" Mitchell asked.

"As big as the moon and twice as thick!" one miner replied, cupping his hands to frame a newly risen full moon.

Back at the Chattanooga bakery, Mitchell saw marshmallow-dipped graham cookies, big round ones drying in the sun. Mitchell suggested adding a second cookie, then coating the cookie sandwich with chocolate. It was done.

Ah, thought Mitchell. MoonPie. Soon after, the MoonPie began its steady march throughout the South and by the time of the Great Depression, it had become a staple.

The drink of choice to wash down a MoonPie was Royal Crown Cola, and in no time "Gimme an RC and a MoonPie" was almost a mantra.

Only a nickel for the pie and a nickel for the drink, together they were enough to hold anybody—even a hungry ten-year-old boy—till suppertime.

The first MoonPies—marshmallow-filled, chocolate-dipped cookie sandwiches—were about the size of small Frisbees (well, almost). Now, in addition to the original, they also come in such flavors as banana, strawberry, and coconut.

Today the MoonPie is celebrated in song ("Weezie and the MoonPies," to name just one) and tossed from floats into crowds of Mardi Gras revelers. There's even a World Championship MoonPie Eating Contest every year in Oneonta, Alabama.

Yvette Lance, a contest organizer, says the object is to see who can down the most MoonPies in five minutes. No drink allowed, not even an RC. The records: twelve for the big double-deckers and twenty-one for the smaller MoonPies. The winner gets a fifty-dollar Wal-Mart gift certificate and a new title: "MoonPie King of the Year."

BLACK BOTTOM PIE

MAKES 6 TO 8 SERVINGS

No one knows for sure when or where this southern classic originated. On one of the many online food sites, I read that a recipe for Black Bottom Pie had appeared in Lafcadio Hearn's *Creole Cook Book* (1885). Not true—nor does anything remotely similar. According to James Beard (*American Cookery*, 1972), the recipe began showing up in cookbooks early in the 1900s. In community cookbooks, perhaps. Yet long research for my *American Century Cookbook* (1997) turned up no mention of black bottom pie before 1940. That year both *The Woman's Home Companion Cook Book* and *The Good Housekeeping Cook Book* printed recipes for it, although only the latter called it Black Bottom Pie. *Woman's Home Companion* not only titled it Two-Tone Chocolate Rum Pie but also changed the crumb crust from gingerbread to chocolate.

Marjorie Kinnan Rawlings's *Cross Creek Cookery*, published two years later, is by most accounts the book that launched Black Bottom Pie. Combining two recipes, one obtained from an old hotel in Louisiana and another from a southern friend, Rawlings was positively lyrical about the version she'd created: "I think that this is the most delicious pie ever eaten . . . a pie so delicate, so luscious, that I hope to be propped up on my dying bed and fed a generous portion. Then I think that I should refuse outright to die . . ." For her crumb crust, Rawlings says to roll fourteen gingersnaps to fine crumbs; fourteen of today's cookies would barely dust the bottom of a pie tin.

As for the pie's name, some suggest that it derives from the Black Bottom Stomp, a New Orleans dance popular in the 1920s and '30s—about the time the pie was gaining local fame. Others insist that it comes from the color of the bottom (chocolate) layer—as black as bayou mud. Despite its unknown origin, Black Bottom Pie has remained a southern favorite for nearly seventy years. **Note:** *Because the egg whites used in the top (rum) layer are not cooked, it's best to use pasteurized eggs for this recipe.* **Tip:** *The easiest way to make chocolate curls is to run a swivel-bladed vegetable peeler over a square of room-temperature semisweet chocolate. At first the curls may break, but as the heat of your hands softens the chocolate, you'll be able to shave off lovely long curls.*

Crumb Crust

1½ cups finely crushed gingersnaps (about thirty 2-inch round cookies)

4 tablespoons (½ stick) butter, at room temperature

Bottom (Chocolate) Layer

½ cup sugar

1½ tablespoons cornstarch

4 large pasteurized egg yolks, beaten well (see About Pasteurized Eggs, page xxi)

2 cups steaming hot milk

1 teaspoon vanilla extract

Two 1-ounce squares unsweetened chocolate, broken into small pieces (I whack the still-wrapped squares with a cutlet bat, then unwrap)

Top (Rum) Layer

1 envelope unflavored gelatin, softened in 3 tablespoons cold water

2 tablespoons rum, preferably dark rum (though not traditional, bourbon is also good)

4 large pasteurized egg whites

⅛ teaspoon cream of tartar

½ cup sugar

Topping

1 cup heavy cream, beaten to fairly stiff peaks

Semisweet chocolate curls (see Tip at left)

1. For the crust: Preheat the oven to 350° F. Mix the crumbs and butter well, then pat over the bottom and up the sides of an ungreased 9-inch pie pan. **Tip:** *You'll find this easier if you butter your hands lightly before handling the crumb mixture.* Slide the crust onto the middle oven shelf and bake for 5 minutes (this is just to firm the crust up a bit; longer baking will make it too hard to cut easily). Remove the crust from the oven and cool.

2. For the bottom layer: Combine the sugar and cornstarch in a medium-size bowl, then whisk in the egg yolks. Drizzle the hot milk into the egg mixture, whisking all the while. Stir back into the pan and cook over low heat, whisking constantly, for 2 to 3 minutes or until the consistency of custard sauce. Do not boil or the filling will curdle. Scoop 1 cup of the hot filling into a small bowl (keep the rest of it hot), add the vanilla, then the chocolate, and stir until melted. Spread over the bottom of the crumb crust.

3. For the top layer: Mix the softened gelatin into the remaining hot custard and whisk until it dissolves completely; stir in the rum and cool to room temperature. Beat the egg whites

---

Heirloom Recipe

ORANGE PUDDING

Shirley Plantation, sprawled along the banks of the broad but sinuous James River, dates back to a land grant of 1613. The eleventh generation of the Hill-Carter family to call Shirley home now lives in the Great House (circa 1723), a tall, proud red brick mansion with a unique Queen Anne forecourt. It was here that Ann Hill Carter, the mother of Robert E. Lee, once lived; in 1793 she married "Light Horse Harry" Lee in the parlor. Among Shirley's eight original eighteenth-century brick buildings is the stone-floored kitchen with double hearths, bake oven, and upstairs quarters for the cooks and other domestic slaves. The house and grounds are open to the public daily; the old kitchen is also used for special programs and exhibits. The Shirley Plantation Collection (handwritten Carter family receipts and other plantation documents) is now housed at the John D. Rockefeller Jr. Research Library at Colonial Williamsburg. That's where a Shirley volunteer researcher found this old family favorite.

Set 1 pot of milk over the range in a saucepan. Mix one tablespoonful of corn starch with two tablespoonsful of cold milk and the yolks of three eggs adding four tablespoonsful of sugar and a little salt.

When the milk is hot-not-boiling stir in the mixture and let it boil stirring constantly. Peel and slice five oranges removing the seeds and lay them in a dish sprinkling each layer with sugar.

While the custard is still hot pour over the oranges. Beat the whites to a stiff froth adding two tablespoonsful of sugar and pour over the top of the custard.

Serve when quite cold.

with the cream of tartar until silvery, then, beating all the while, add the sugar gradually. **Note:** *Liquid pasteurized egg whites take longer than the raw to whip to stiff peaks—perhaps 5 minutes at highest electric mixer speed. When properly whipped, pasteurized egg whites will be the consistency of boiled icing. If using raw egg whites from a known and trusted source, beat only until the whites peak softly.*

4. Fold about a cup of the beaten whites into the cooled custard to lighten it, then fold in the remaining whites until no streaks of white or yellow remain. Scoop the rum mixture over the chocolate layer, smoothing the top and spreading so that it touches the crust all around. Chill the uncovered pie for several hours or until the filling has set.

5. For the topping: Frost the pie with the whipped cream and scatter the chocolate curls decoratively on top.

6. Chill the pie uncovered for several hours or overnight before cutting.

❀

On our parents' and grandparents' farms
we saw hogs grow fat and meaty,
and we understood why a child eating
a huge meal or taking the largest piece of pie
was called a pig.

—JEANNE VOLTZ AND ELAINE J. HARVELL,
THE COUNTRY HAM BOOK

❀

1976 — Mildred Council, a single African American mother of more than half a dozen children, opens Mama Dip's Kitchen in Chapel Hill, North Carolina, on a shoestring. Cooking what she knew best—fried chicken, sweet slaw, greens with side meat, buttermilk biscuits, pecan pie— Mama Dip was soon packing them in. Today her restaurant is a local institution and Dip herself has become a regular on local and national television.

Beatrice Foods of Chicago buys Krispy Kreme and alters the original recipe.

A Georgia peanut farmer named Jimmy Carter is elected president of the United States and during his term, Americans embrace grits and collards and all foods southern.

New Orleans–based Popeyes establishes its first franchise and within ten years has 500 fast-food restaurants specializing in spicy Cajun chicken, red beans and rice, po'boys, and other Louisiana classics.

ROYAL CROWN COLA

An RC and a MoonPie are to southern eating as Flatt and Scruggs are to southern music.

The beverage half of the duo, whose initials stand for Royal Crown, was created in 1905 by Columbus, Georgia, pharmacist Claud A. Hatcher. A new flavor in his early line of soft drinks, he called it Chero-Cola.

By 1912, ballooning sales forced Hatcher to move his soft drink operation out of his basement into larger quarters. His newly named Chero-Cola Company continued to thrive and soon Hatcher had developed the popular Nehi line of fruit-flavored sodas. Following Hatcher's death in 1933, the company reorganized and reformulated Chero-Cola. After six months of fine-tuning, it reemerged as Royal Crown.

Although many people considered RC a strictly southern beverage, by 1940 it was sold in forty-seven of the then forty-eight states. By 1954, the company was selling its drinks in cans: a first. Four years later, Royal Crown introduced America's first diet soft drink, Diet Rite. But back then it was considered a specialty dietary product and was not widely marketed.

With the arrival of the more weight-conscious 1960s, however, RC promoted Diet Rite aggressively coast to coast. The current company owners, Cadbury Schweppes, marked RC's hundredth birthday in 2005 with contests and prizes.

But you had to provide your own MoonPies.

KEY LIME PIE

MAKES 6 TO 8 SERVINGS

I've eaten Key lime pie all over Florida—in the Keys, whence it comes; in Miami; and up and down the east and west coasts. Some pies have crumb crusts (a post–World War Two innovation, I'm told), others the more classic pastry shells. Some are swirled about with meringue, others with whipped cream. Some are chiffon pies with the meringue folded into the filling, some are even frozen. My own preference is for what my friend Jeanne Voltz calls a "legal" variation: whipped cream spread over a pale ivory filling (not a drop of green food coloring) cradled in a traditional pastry crust. Still, I welcome the innovations dreamed up by another friend, Kim Sunée, food editor of *Cottage Living* magazine. Instead of slathering meringue or whipped cream over her filling, she skim-coats it with a cup of crème fraîche tempered with two tablespoons of confectioners' sugar. I find that inspired. As for the crust, Kim favors a graham cracker one but sometimes substitutes finely chopped dry-roasted macadamias for maybe a fifth of the crumbs.

Thought to have originated in Key West in the mid 1850s shortly after Gale Borden introduced sweetened condensed milk, Key lime pie owes its flavor, even its texture, to the tiny, tart yellow Key limes that once proliferated throughout the Keys. They are believed to have been introduced to Indian Key in the mid 1830s by Dr. Henry Perrine, then U.S. consul in Yucatán, who, it's said, had Mexican limes, as they're also known, shipped and planted there. Their excep-

A Love Affair with Southern Cooking

tional acidity "cooks" (thickens) the egg yolks in the filling, something the more familiar green Persian limes are too mellow to do. But as I would soon learn, genuine Key lime juice sometimes fails, too. I squeezed a dozen Key limes for the half cup of juice this recipe requires, stirred it in carefully, then continued stirring for several minutes, but my filling never really set up. So I baked the pie briefly and that solved the problem. I'm aware that that's not traditional—sacrilegious, some say. But you cannot cut a filling the consistency of mustard. **Note:** *If you are unable to find fresh Key limes, use bottled Key lime juice. Most specialty food shops sell it and you can also order it online (see Sources, page 401).*

4 large pasteurized egg yolks (see About
Pasteurized Eggs, page xxi)

Pinch of salt

One 14-ounce can sweetened condensed
milk

½ cup fresh Key lime juice
(12 to 14 Key limes; see Note above)

1 baked 9-inch pie shell (see About Pie
Crusts, page xxi)

1¼ cups heavy cream, whipped to soft peaks
with 3 tablespoons confectioners' (10 X)
sugar

1. Preheat the oven to 350° F. Whisk the egg yolks and salt until smooth, then whisk in the sweetened condensed milk. Add the lime juice slowly, whisking gently all the while, then continue whisking for about 2 minutes or until slightly thickened.

2. Pour the filling into the baked pie shell, spreading to the edge; slide onto the middle oven shelf and bake for 15 minutes or until softly set.

3. Remove the pie from the oven, set on a wire rack, and cool to room temperature.

4. Swirl the whipped cream over the filling, making sure that it touches the crust all around. Refrigerate the pie for several hours before serving.

5. To serve, cut the pie into slim wedges. Refrigerate any leftover pie.

Variation

Classic Key Lime Pie with Meringue: Prepare the recipe through Step 2. While the pie bakes, beat 3 large pasteurized egg whites to soft peaks with ⅓ cup sugar or unsifted confectioners' (10X) sugar (my preference because it makes for a more stable meringue). Swirl the meringue over the hot filling, making sure that it touches the crust all around. Return to the middle oven shelf and bake for 12 to 15 minutes or until the meringue is tipped with brown. Cool the pie before cutting. Any leftover pie should be stored in the refrigerator.

❋

*Destination: Lime Pie! . . . Down in the Keys,
where the wild limes grow, everyone uses
the little yellow-green fruit with a tang
that no other lime can boast.*

—CLEMENTINE PADDLEFORD,
HOW AMERICA EATS

❋

BROWN SUGAR PIE

. . . .

I fell in love with this pie at the age of five in, of all places, the basement cafeteria of the Fred A. Olds Elementary School in Raleigh. It was my introduction to southern cooking and the beginning of my lifelong fascination with it. I have, however, added a personal fillip: After melting the butter, I let it brown slightly.

1 pound light brown sugar

4 large eggs

¼ cup milk

2 teaspoons vanilla extract

¼ teaspoon salt

½ cup (1 stick) butter, melted (see headnote)

One 9-inch unbaked pie shell (see About Pie Crusts, page xxi)

1. Preheat the oven to 325° F.
2. Blend the brown sugar, eggs, milk, vanilla, and salt until smooth, then add the butter in a slow stream, beating all the while.
3. Pour the filling into the pie shell, slide the pie onto a baking sheet, and bake on the middle oven shelf for 50 to 60 minutes or until puffed and golden brown.
4. Transfer the pie to a wire rack and cool to room temperature before cutting. The filling will fall slightly—all chess pies do as they cool. Serve as is or top with whipped cream.

150-YEAR-OLD MOLASSES PIE

. . . .

Sorghum molasses (or "sweet sorghum," as it's also known) is most likely what cooks in rural Kentucky, the Blue Ridge, and the Smokies would have used in this pie a hundred years ago or more because nearly every family grew a patch of this grain to feed their livestock—plus a little extra for themselves. Early on, farmers learned how to press the juice from sorghum's ripe seed clusters and boil it down into a sweet, thick syrup the color of amber: "nothin' better on hot biscuits or pancakes." If you're traveling about Appalachia, you're bound to see mason jars of sorghum molasses for sale at roadside stands and in country stores. I urge you to buy a quart. Sorghum molasses is lighter, mellower, and sweeter than cane molasses and its flavor is unique. You can also order sorghum molasses online (see Sources, page 401) and, failing that, you can substitute a light, unsulfured cane molasses in this recipe and in any others that call for "sweet sorghum."

⅓ cup sugar

3 tablespoons all-purpose flour

1 teaspoon freshly grated nutmeg or ½ teaspoon ground nutmeg

¼ teaspoon salt

3 large eggs

¾ cup molasses (see headnote)

½ cup milk or evaporated milk (I prefer evaporated milk)

2 tablespoons butter, melted

1½ teaspoons vanilla extract

One 9-inch unbaked pie shell
(see About Pie Crusts, page xxi)

1. Preheat the oven to 325° F. Whisk together the sugar, flour, nutmeg, and salt in a medium-size bowl. Whisk the eggs in, one by one, then mix in the molasses, milk, melted butter, and vanilla.

2. Pour the filling into the pie shell, slide the pie onto a baking sheet, and bake on the middle oven shelf for about 1 hour or until puffed and a cake tester inserted halfway between the edge and the center comes out clean.

3. If you want to serve the pie warm, cool on a wire rack for 30 minutes. Or, if you prefer, cool the pie to room temperature before serving. **Note:** *The filling will fall somewhat but this is as it should be.* Cut the pieces small and serve as is or topped by a scoop of vanilla ice cream or a generous ladling of whipped cream.

LEMON CHESS PIE

MAKES 8 SERVINGS

. . . .

Next to brown sugar pie, this is my favorite chess pie. There are several theories as to how these pies came by their name. Some say that "chess" is a corruption of "chest," meaning that these pies were so rich they could be stored in chests at room temperature. Others offer a different explanation: It seems that long ago when a good plantation cook was asked what she was making, she replied, "Jes pie," which over time

became "chess." Still others insist that "chess" derives from "cheese," as in the English lemon "cheese" (or curd). According to food historian Karen Hess, "cheese" was spelled "chese" in seventeenth-century England. In her historical notes and commentaries for the 1984 facsimile edition of Mary Randolph's *Virginia House-wife* (1824), Hess writes: "Since the archaic spellings of cheese often had but one 'e' we have the answer to the riddle of the name of that southern favorite 'Chess Pie.' "

When I lived in New York, I baked dozens of lemon chess pies for the annual Gramercy Park fund-raiser and they sold as fast as I could unpack them. From that experience, I learned to buzz up the filling in the food processor. I even grate the lemon zest by processor. Here's how: Strip the zest from the lemons with a swivel-bladed vegetable peeler, then churn it with the sugar to just the right texture. I next pulse in the lemon juice, then the eggs one by one. Finally, I drizzle the melted butter down the feed tube with the motor running. That's all there is to it.

1½ cups sugar

Finely grated zest of 3 large lemons

Juice of 3 large lemons

5 large eggs

⅓ cup butter, melted

One 9-inch unbaked pie shell
(see About Pie Crusts, page xxi)

1. Preheat the oven to 325° F.

2. Combine the sugar, lemon zest, and lemon juice in a medium-size bowl. Beat the eggs in,

one by one, then add the butter in a slow stream, beating all the while.

3. Pour the filling into the pie shell, slide the pie onto a baking sheet, and bake on the middle oven shelf for about 45 minutes or until puffed and delicately browned.

4. Transfer the pie to a wire rack and cool to room temperature before cutting; don't fret when the filling begins to fall. This is what gives chess pies their silken texture. Cut into slim wedges and serve.

KENTUCKY CHESS PIE

MAKES 8 SERVINGS

It's said that to sample Kentucky's best chess pie, you must head for The Old Talbott Tavern in Bardstown. I did exactly that some years ago. And although I'd only eaten two or three other versions of the famous Kentucky Chess Pie, the tavern's won hands down. What follows is my stab at the tavern's secret recipe, and I think it comes pretty close. In business since 1779, the Talbott Tavern has hosted such VIPs as Abraham Lincoln, Daniel Boone, Stephen Collins Foster, John James Audubon, even the exiled King Louis Philippe of France, who settled in with his entire entourage. The second-floor murals were painted by the young royal, then later shot up by Jesse James. Those murals suffered far greater damage early in 1998 when fire ravaged the inn. Shuttered for nearly two years, the Talbott Tavern is once again open and serving the recipes that made it famous. Bardstown, if you don't know it, is where you'll find "My Old Kentucky Home" of Stephen Foster fame as well as some of Kentucky's best bourbon (it calls itself "The Bourbon Capital of the World").

1 cup granulated sugar

¾ cup firmly packed light brown sugar

1 tablespoon stone-ground cornmeal

¼ teaspoon salt

5 large eggs

⅓ cup heavy cream

1 tablespoon cider vinegar

1 tablespoon vanilla extract

½ cup (1 stick) butter, melted

One 9-inch unbaked pie shell (see About Pie Crusts, page xxi)

1. Preheat the oven to 400° F.

2. Combine the two sugars, the cornmeal, and salt in a medium-size mixing bowl, pressing out all lumps. Beat the eggs in, one by one, then blend in the cream, vinegar, and vanilla. Add the melted butter in a slow, steady stream, beating all the while.

3. Pour the filling into the pie shell, slide the pie onto a baking sheet, and bake on the middle oven shelf for 10 minutes. Lower the oven temperature to 325° F. and continue baking for 45 minutes or until puffed and the filling jiggles only slightly when you nudge the pan.

4. Transfer the pie to a wire rack and cool to room temperature before cutting. **Note:** *The filling will fall somewhat as it cools, but this is the nature of chess pies.*

MAXWELL HOUSE COFFEE

One of the advertising world's best-known slogans, "Good to the last drop!" wasn't created by an astute account executive. It was uttered by a United States president.

While visiting Nashville, Tennessee, back in 1907, President Theodore Roosevelt sipped a cup of the Maxwell House coffee, smiled, and said, "Good to the last drop!"

The Maxwell House Hotel had been serving its signature coffee since 1892 when an entrepreneur named Joel Cheek showed up with one of his prize blends, hoping to make a sale. He succeeded and soon Cheek's prize blend was so popular the hotel gave it its name.

Cheek, a farmer's son, started his career with the single silver dollar his father had given him when he turned twenty-one. "Freedom dollar," his father called it, meaning he was free to go out on his own.

By 1900, Cheek was producing the Maxwell House blend for home use. And though he didn't create its famous slogan, he believed in advertising and put plenty of money into it.

The company that eventually became General Foods bought Maxwell House in 1928. Since then, there's been no need to tell the company to wake up and smell the coffee; it not only has kept abreast of coffee trends but also has created a few.

In 1976 Maxwell House developed a special grind for automatic drip pots—a first. And today it offers flavored coffees and prepacked pods for the new single-cup brewers.

But no matter how the method of brewing coffee changes, Maxwell House remains "Good to the last drop!"

NANNIE HALL DAVIS'S "FRENCH" PUDDING PIE

MAKES 8 TO 10 SERVINGS

Like many Virginians, my friend Maria Harrison Reuge was raised on damson plum preserves. This particular recipe, given to me by her parents when I visited them at their James River farm, is a chess-type pie flavored with damson preserves (see Sources, page 401). The recipe belonged to Maria's great-grandmother and when I asked if it was French, Maria's father said, "No. In those days, whenever you thought something extra good, you'd call it French."

1 cup (2 sticks) butter,
at room temperature

1 cup sugar

4 large eggs, separated

1 cup damson plum preserves (see headnote)

One 10-inch unbaked pie shell (see About Pie Crusts, page xxi)

Brown Sugar Sauce (page 346; optional)

1. Preheat the oven to 350°F.

2. Cream the butter and sugar in a large electric mixer bowl at moderately high speed for 1 to 2 minutes until light. Beat the egg yolks in one by one, then beat in the preserves, ⅓ cup at a time. Whip the egg whites to soft peaks and fold into the preserves mixture. Pour the filling into the pie shell.

3. Slide the pie onto a baking sheet and bake in the lower third of the oven for 40 to 45 minutes or until lightly browned and the filling barely jiggles when you nudge the pan.

4. Transfer the pie to a wire rack and cool to room temperature before cutting. Serve as is or, if you like, top each portion with Brown Sugar Sauce.

JEFF DAVIS PIE

MAKES 8 SERVINGS

. . . .

Although born in Kentucky, Jefferson Davis moved to Mississippi when he was a child and grew up there. This rich-as-Croesus pie named in his honor was given to me by my good Mississippi friend, Jean Todd Freeman. The two of us worked together in New York at *The Ladies' Home Journal*, I in the food department and Jean as fiction editor. We often traveled about the Deep South on article assignment together and during those trips she taught me much of what I know about it today. Jean told me that this pie recipe is nearly 150 years old and that it had been created by a good plantation cook who admired the president of the Confederacy. I later learned that there are as many stories

about the origin of Jeff Davis pie as there are different recipes for it. Some say that the pie was actually created by a freed slave working for a Missouri merchant and that it was *his* admiration for Davis that prompted her to name her pie after him. Some Jeff Davis pies call for brown sugar instead of white; some add nuts, chopped dates and/or raisins; some are heavily spiced; some are made with evaporated milk instead of cream; and some are lavishly swirled about with meringue. I personally prefer Jean's version. A similar pie—all butter, sugar, and eggs but no milk or cream—is popular in Charleston and elsewhere about the Lowcountry. It's known as Transparent Pie because its filling, once baked, is nearly clear. Translucent would be a truer description, but a pie named "translucent" hasn't the appeal or glamour of one called "transparent."

1¾ cups sugar

1 tablespoon all-purpose flour

½ cup (1 stick) butter, at room temperature

1 cup heavy cream

2 large whole eggs

4 large eggs, separated

¼ teaspoon freshly grated nutmeg

¼ teaspoon salt

One 9-inch baked pie shell
(see About Pie Crusts, page xxi)

1. Preheat the oven to 325° F.

2. Combine 1¼ cups of the sugar, the flour, and butter in the top of a double boiler. Whisk in the

cream, 2 whole eggs, 4 egg yolks, nutmeg, and salt. Set over simmering water and cook and stir for about 10 minutes or until as thick and smooth as custard sauce. Set off the heat.

3. Beat the 4 egg whites with the remaining ½ cup sugar in a large electric mixer bowl at high speed for 2 to 3 minutes or until thick and silvery. Because of the high percentage of sugar, the whites will not whip into a meringue. Gently but thoroughly fold the beaten whites into the custard until no streaks of white or yellow remain.

4. Pour the custard into the pie shell, set the pie onto a baking sheet, and bake on the middle oven shelf for 35 to 40 minutes or until puffed and as brown as caramel.

5. Cool the pie to room temperature on a wire rack, then cover loosely with plastic food wrap and refrigerate for an hour or more until firm.

6. Cut into slim wedges and serve.

CLASSIC PECAN PIE

MAKES 8 SERVINGS

. . . .

I'd always thought that pecan pie predated "the late unpleasantness," as Southerners used to call the Civil War, or perhaps even belonged to Colonial Days. But in researching my *American Century Cookbook* (1997), I discovered to my great surprise that it became popular only in the twentieth century. Even John Egerton, a southern culinary historian and author whom I respect, says that he's found "no recipes or other bits of evidence to prove" that pecan pie existed long ago. Another food historian, Meryle Evans,

1977 The first Vidalia Onion Festival is held in—where else?—Vidalia, Georgia.

Jack Fulk and Richard Thomas open the first Bojangles' restaurant in Charlotte, North Carolina, offering fresh Cajun-style chicken and from-scratch buttermilk biscuits among other southern favorites. Today there are some 340 Bojangles' restaurants at home and abroad.

1978 Chef Alex Patout opens his first Cajun restaurant in New Iberia, Louisiana.

Catering to the increasing demand for specialty foods, Michael Barefoot moves A Southern Season to larger quarters in Chapel Hill's Eastgate Shopping Center. His well-stocked food emporium also begins attracting national attention.

Phyllis Jordan enters the coffee and tea business in New Orleans. By the turn of the twenty-first century, P. J.'s Coffee & Tea has grown from a single retail shop to a multimillion-dollar business that not only imports, roasts, and distributes fine coffees but also franchises cafés where exotic coffees and teas can be enjoyed with fresh-baked pastries.

believes that pecan pie dates only as far back as 1925 and that it was created by Karo home economists to "push product." The majority of pecan pies do contain corn syrup—either light or dark. I prefer the former. I also prefer this recipe given to me by a friendly neighbor who loved to teach "the little Yankee girl," as she called me, all about southern food. I was an eager pupil.

1⅓ cups perfect pecan halves

One 9-inch baked pie shell (see About Pie Crusts, page xxi)

1 cup firmly packed light brown sugar

1 cup light corn syrup

3 large eggs, lightly beaten

2 tablespoons lightly browned melted butter

1 tablespoon all-purpose flour

2 teaspoons vanilla extract

¼ teaspoon salt

1. Preheat the oven to 350° F. Arrange the pecans in concentric circles in the bottom of the pie shell and set aside.

2. Blend all remaining ingredients together until smooth and carefully ladle into the pie shell, trying not to dislodge the pecans. They will float to the top as the pie bakes.

3. Slide the pie onto a baking sheet and bake on the middle oven shelf for 45 to 50 minutes or until puffed and golden brown.

4. Transfer the pie to a wire rack and cool to room temperature, then cut into slim wedges. Serve as is or top with whipped cream or vanilla ice cream—"to cut the richness," Southerners say.

ALABAMA PEANUT PIE

MAKES 8 SERVINGS

Although George Washington Carver (see box, page 323) is credited with creating peanut butter, the peanut butter cookie, and numerous other peanut desserts, this particular pie may or may not be his. It's something I adapted from an anonymous recipe in an old southern community cookbook.

1 cup blanched, shelled raw peanuts

1 cup sorghum molasses or dark corn syrup

½ cup sugar

½ cup (1 stick) butter, at room temperature

3 large eggs

2 teaspoons vanilla extract

¼ teaspoon salt

¼ teaspoon freshly grated nutmeg

One 9-inch unbaked pie shell (see About Pie Crusts, page xxi)

1. Preheat the oven to 325° F.

2. Spread the peanuts in an ungreased baking pan and roast slowly until golden; this will take 15 to 18 minutes. Remove the peanuts from the oven and raise the temperature to 350° F.

3. Cool the peanuts, then grind very fine (a food processor does this in about 30 seconds). Empty the nuts into a large mixing bowl, add the molasses, sugar, butter, eggs, vanilla, salt, and nutmeg, and beat hard until smooth and creamy.

A Love Affair with Southern Cooking

4. Pour the filling into the pie shell and slide onto a baking sheet. Bake in the lower third of the oven for about 50 minutes or until puffed, nicely browned, and a cake tester inserted halfway between the edge and the center comes out clean.

5. Cool the pie to room temperature before cutting. Make the pieces small; this pie is very rich. Serve as is or top with whipped cream or, if you prefer, with scoops of vanilla or dulce de leche ice cream.

Heirloom Recipe

MRS. LEE'S CAKE

Here, just as it appears in *The Robert E. Lee Family Cooking and Housekeeping Book* written by Lee's great-granddaughter Anne Carter Zimmer (1997), is the original Robert E. Lee Cake. Here it is titled simply "Mrs. Lee's Cake."

Twelve eggs, their full weight in sugar, a half weight in flour. Bake it in pans the thickness of jelly cakes. Take two pounds of nice "A" sugar, squeeze into it the juice of 5 oranges and three lemons together with the pulp. Stir in the sugar until perfectly smooth, then spread it over the cakes as you would jelly—putting one above another till the whole of the sugar is used up.

—Mrs. Robert E. Lee

GENERAL ROBERT E. LEE ORANGE AND LEMON CAKE

MAKES ONE 9-INCH, 4-LAYER CAKE

The famous Confederate general never tasted this particular cake, for it's one of the dozens of variations of Mrs. Lee's Cake (see the Heirloom Recipe at left) that surfaced after the Civil War. This delicious but distinctly different version is the specialty of the historic Beaumont Inn in Harrodsburg, Kentucky, and has been ever since Annie Bell Goddard first baked it. That was nearly 100 years ago, soon after she and her husband bought a Greek Revival building (c. 1845) that had been a school for young ladies and turned it into an inn. As for the cake's name, there's an easy explanation for it as well as for the Lee memorabilia scattered about the inn, which Goddard descendants, the Dedmans, now run with style and grace. Annie Bell Goddard was a fan of Robert E. Lee and her cake does him proud. I ordered it for dessert when I visited the Beaumont Inn some twenty-five years ago and liked it so much that I adapted the original recipe (printed in *Beaumont Inn Special Recipes*) for a "best of the Bluegrass" food and travel article I was writing for *Family Circle*. This is my adaptation. **Note:** *When making the frosting, use the yolks of pasteurized eggs. They go in raw and though salmonella poisoning wasn't a problem in Annie Bell Goddard's day, it can be today (see About Pasteurized Eggs, page xxi).*

Cake

2 cups cake flour, sifted twice
before it is measured

1½ teaspoons baking powder

½ teaspoon cream of tartar

9 large eggs, separated

2 cups sugar, sifted six times

Finely grated zest of 1 large lemon

Juice of 1 large lemon

⅛ teaspoon salt

Frosting

Two 16-ounce boxes confectioners'
(10 X) sugar

½ cup (1 stick) butter, cut into slim pats
and softened slightly

Finely grated zest of 3 large oranges

Finely grated zest of 2 large lemons

¼ cup fresh lemon juice

3 large pasteurized egg yolks (see Note,
page 321)

3 to 4 tablespoons fresh orange juice

1. For the cake: Preheat the oven to 325° F. Grease four 9-inch layer cake pans well and set aside.
2. Sift the flour with the baking powder and cream of tartar six times and set aside.
3. Beat the egg yolks in a large electric mixer bowl at high speed for about a minute until thick. Beat the sugar in gradually, then add the lemon zest and continue beating at high speed until the color and consistency of may-

onnaise. This will take about 10 minutes. Beat in the lemon juice.

4. Sift about one fourth of the flour mixture over the yolk mixture and fold in by hand, gently but thoroughly. Repeat twice. The last of the flour mixture goes in at the end.
5. Beat the egg whites with the salt until stiff peaks form. Blend about one third of the beaten whites into the yolk mixture to lighten it, then scoop the remaining whites on top and fold in until no streaks of white or yellow show—easy does it. Using the lightest of touches, fold in the remaining flour mixture.
6. Divide the batter among the four pans and rap each lightly on the counter to expel large air bubbles.
7. Bake the cakes in the lower third of the oven for 25 to 30 minutes or until springy to the touch and a cake tester inserted halfway between the center and the rim comes out clean.
8. Invert the cakes on wire racks immediately but do not remove the pans. Instead, cool the cakes to room temperature in the upside-down pans. Lift off the pans and let the cakes stand for 1 hour before frosting.
9. For the frosting: Beat the confectioners' sugar, butter, orange and lemon zests, lemon juice, and egg yolks until smooth and silky. Begin at low mixer speed, then gradually raise it to high as the sugar is incorporated. Finally, add just enough of the orange juice to make the frosting a good spreading consistency.
10. Sandwich the four cake layers together with some of the frosting, then smooth the rest over the top and sides of the cake.
11. Cut the cake into slim wedges and serve.
    Note: *Because the frosting contains raw egg yolks, refrigerate any leftover cake.*

GEORGE WASHINGTON CARVER (1864–1943)

He's been called "The Father of Peanut Butter" but that doesn't begin to cover the contributions made by this "poor insignificant black boy," as he once described himself.

Born toward the end of the Civil War near Diamond Grove, Missouri, Carver is said to have been kidnapped along with his mother and sister by Confederate night raiders. His master, Moses Carver, paid to have them returned, but only baby George was found.

Always sickly and thus spared the toil of hardier slaves, young George was allowed to wander field and forest studying the wild plants. With the abolition of slavery, the Carvers took the child in, raised him as their own son, and encouraged his intellectual curiosity.

Earning a high school diploma was nearly impossible for a freed slave, but Carver succeeded by bouncing from school to school in Missouri and Kansas. College followed, first Simpson in Indianola, Iowa, for music and art, then Iowa State for undergraduate and graduate degrees in agricultural research. At both schools, he was the first black student.

In 1896, Booker T. Washington lured Carver to Alabama to teach and conduct research at Tuskegee Normal and Industrial Institute. He stayed until his death nearly fifty years later.

It was here that Carver's "peanut obsession" began. Determined to help farmers decimated by the boll weevil and spent land, Carver championed peanuts as a way to replenish the soil's nitrogen. He also advocated crop rotation. But old ways die hard.

That's when Carver set out to prove how lucrative peanuts could be. Over time, he developed more than 300 uses for the lowly legume—everything from peanut butter to cooking oils and candies. And these were merely the "edibles."

His 1925 extension bulletin *How to Grow the Peanut and 105 Ways of Preparing It for Human Consumption* begins, "Of all the money crops grown by Macon County farmers, perhaps there are none more promising than the peanut in its several varieties and their almost limitless possibilities." Among the booklet's 105 peanut recipes are soups, breads, pies and puddings, cakes, cookies, and candies, even ice creams.

By now Carver had become famous, dispensing advice to presidents (Calvin Coolidge and both Roosevelts) as well as to world leaders as disparate as Henry Ford, Mahatma Gandhi, and the Crown Prince of Sweden, who studied with Carver for three weeks.

In 1942, Franklin D. Roosevelt bestowed the Roosevelt Medal of Outstanding Contribution to Southern Agriculture upon Carver, and a year later he budgeted $30,000 for the George Washington Carver National Monument near Carver's Missouri birthplace. Carver half-dollars were minted between 1951 and 1954 and commemorative stamps were issued in his honor in 1948 and again in 1998.

And still the accolades come, some sixty years after George Washington Carver's death.

No, "The Father of Peanut Butter" definitely doesn't cover it.

MARTHA WHITE FLOUR

Unlike Betty Crocker, Martha White wasn't a made-up icon. She was the pretty three-year-old daughter of Richard Lindsey, Sr., who founded Nashville's Royal Flour Mill in 1899.

The Martha White logo (a picture of little Martha in a round frame) was reserved for Lindsey's finest flour. Milled of low-gluten wheat, it was the cotton-soft flour Southerners depended upon for biscuits and cakes of delicate crumb.

When Tennessean Cohen Williams sold the family farm and bought the old Royal Flour Mill in 1941, he changed the company's name to Martha White, the better to build the brand. He also created the slogan—"Goodness gracious, it's good!"—which, by 1945, was appearing on every bag of flour and cornmeal that came out of his mill.

In another canny move, Williams made Martha White the official sponsor of Nashville's Grand Ole Opry in 1948. It still is, although the company itself has since been gobbled up by a succession of conglomerates, from Pillsbury to Smucker's.

Originally available only around Nashville, and then only in the South, Martha White products (flours and cornmeals plus a roster of jiffy mixes) are now sold in supermarkets from Michigan to New Mexico. Still, it's down south that they're as hot as fresh-baked biscuits.

FRESH COCONUT CAKE

MAKES ONE 9-INCH, 3-LAYER CAKE

To use an old southern expression, "it grieves me" to see young southern cooks abandoning family heirloom recipes in favor of cake mixes. Especially since many of America's classic cakes originated down south: Lady Baltimore, Lane Cake, Japanese Fruitcake. I hesitate to add coconut cake to the list, but I will say that it's always been a southern specialty and that no one made it better than Annie Pool of Halifax County, Virginia. Her kin all call her coconut cake "the nearest thing to ambrosia." When I interviewed Annie Pool some years ago, she shared a few secrets: Only fresh coconut put through a meat grinder would do (if she'd had a food processor, she could have saved worlds of time), but even more important, Annie Pool sprinkled the water (from inside the coconut) over each cake layer before she iced it. That explains her cake's exceptional moistness. **Note:** *If you've never grappled with a fresh coconut, here's how to go about it: Before you break the coconut open, loosen the meat by rapping the shell all over with a hammer. Next, pierce two of the coconut "eyes"; drain off and reserve the coconut water. Now using the hammer, crack the coconut into manageable pieces and pry the meat from the shell. Remove the dark skin with a vegetable peeler, then rinse the coconut in cool water and pat dry on paper toweling. Finally, cut the coconut into 1-inch chunks and pulse in two-cup batches in the food processor until finely ground.*

Cake

3 cups sifted all-purpose flour

2 teaspoons baking powder

¼ teaspoon salt

1 cup (2 sticks) butter, at room temperature

2 cups sugar

4 large eggs, separated

1 cup milk

1 teaspoon vanilla extract

1 teaspoon lemon extract

Reserved coconut water (see headnote)

Icing

4 cups sugar

1⅓ cups water

3 tablespoons butter

11 cups finely ground fresh coconut (you'll need 2 to 3 coconuts) (see Note at left)

1. For the cake: Preheat the oven to 350° F. Coat three 9-inch layer cake pans with non-stick oil-and-flour baking spray and set aside.

2. Sift the flour, baking powder, and salt onto a piece of wax paper and set aside.

3. Cream the butter in a large electric mixer bowl at high speed for 2 to 3 minutes or until light and silvery, then, with the motor running, add the sugar gradually. Continue beating for 2 to 3 minutes until light and fluffy. Add the egg yolks and beat till fluffy.

4. Combine the milk, vanilla, and lemon extract. With the mixer at low speed, add the sifted dry ingredients alternately with the milk mixture, beginning and ending with the dry and beating after each addition only enough to combine. Beat the egg whites to soft peaks and fold into the batter—gently—until no streaks of white or yellow remain.

5. Divide the batter among the three pans and bake in the lower third of the oven for 35 to 40 minutes or until the layers pull from the sides of the pans and are springy to the touch.

6. Cool the cake layers in their upright pans on wire racks for 10 minutes, then loosen around the edge and turn out on the racks. Cool to room temperature.

7. For the icing: Combine the sugar and water in a medium-size heavy saucepan and insert a candy thermometer. Set over moderate heat, stir until the sugar dissolves, then cook uncovered without stirring until the syrup reaches 232° F. Remove from the heat, drop in the butter, and cool for 20 minutes.

8. Meanwhile, place 8 cups of the ground coconut in a large bowl. As soon as the syrup has cooled for 20 minutes, beat for 1 minute with a hand electric mixer at high speed. Pour the syrup over the coconut in the bowl and toss well to mix.

9. To assemble the cake: Center one layer on a large round plate. Sprinkle with ⅓ cup of the reserved coconut water, then spread with the icing—not too thick—and scatter some of the remaining ground coconut on top. Repeat with the two remaining layers, pressing each firmly into place. Cover the top and sides of the cake with the remaining icing and coconut. **Note: *Both are crumbly, but if you press them firmly into the cake, they'll stick.***

10. Let the cake stand at room temperature for 2 to 3 hours before serving. To cut the cake, use your sharpest serrated knife and a gentle seesaw motion.

LADY BALTIMORE CAKE

MAKES A 9-INCH, 3-LAYER CAKE

. . . .

While researching my *American Century Cookbook* (1997), I was surprised to discover how many versions there were of this beloved southern cake. Some were white cakes, and some were yellow like the original, a variation of the popular "lady" cake of the day, said to have been created by Alicia Rhett Mayberry of Charleston. While visiting the South Carolina town he called America's "most lovely . . . most wistful" in the early 1900s, novelist Owen Wister discovered the cake at the Women's Exchange Tea Room there. *Lady Baltimore*, he called the cake, the tea room, and his best-selling set-in-Charleston novel published in 1906. Was his *Lady Baltimore* heroine based upon Charleston belle Alicia Rhett Mayberry? Some say so. There is no denying, however, that Wister's rhapsodizing about Lady Baltimore cake sent readers scurrying for the recipe. He writes of it as early as page 17: "I should like a slice, if you please, of Lady Baltimore . . . Oh, my goodness! . . . It's all soft, and it's in layers, and it has nuts— but I can't write any more about it; my mouth waters too much!" The recipe here is updated and adapted from Alicia Rhett Mayberry's, which appears in *Two Hundred Years of Charleston Cooking* (1930), a recipe anthology assembled by Blanche S. Rhett and edited by Lettie Gay. **Note:** *Refrigerate any leftover cake.*

Cake

3½ cups sifted cake flour

4 teaspoons baking powder

½ teaspoon salt

1 cup (2 sticks) butter, at room temperature

2 cups sugar

8 large egg yolks

1¼ cups milk

1 teaspoon almond extract

4 large egg whites, beaten to soft peaks

Frosting

3 cups sugar

½ cup fresh lemon juice

¼ cup boiling water

4 large egg whites, beaten to stiff peaks

1 teaspoon vanilla extract

2 cups coarsely chopped walnuts

2 cups coarsely chopped seedless raisins

1. For the cake: Preheat the oven to 350° F. Grease and flour three 9-inch layer cake pans well, tap out the excess flour, and set aside.

2. Sift the flour, baking powder, and salt onto a piece of wax paper and set aside also.

3. Cream the butter in a large electric mixer bowl, first at low speed and then at high for 2 to 3 minutes or until light and fluffy. With the machine at moderately low speed, add the sugar gradually and continue beating for 1 to 2 minutes or until light. Add the egg yolks two at a time, beating well after each addition.

4. With the mixer at low speed, add the sifted dry ingredients in three batches, alternating with the milk, beginning and ending with the dry,

and beating after each addition only enough to combine. Stir in the almond extract.

5. Mix about 1 cup of the beaten egg whites into the cake batter to lighten it, then gently fold in the rest until no streaks of white remain. Divide the batter among the three pans and rap each sharply on the counter once or twice to expel large air bubbles.

6. Bake in the lower third of the oven for 25 to 30 minutes or until the cakes are springy to the touch and a cake tester inserted midway be-tween the center and the rim comes out clean.

7. Cool the cakes in the upright pans on wire racks for 5 minutes, then turn out on the racks and cool to room temperature.

8. Meanwhile, prepare the frosting: Combine the sugar, lemon juice, and water in a heavy 4-quart saucepan; insert a candy thermom-eter. Set over moderately high heat, stir until the sugar dissolves, then cook without stir-ring until the syrup spins a long thread (234° to 236° F.). Beating with an electric mixer at high speed, add the boiling syrup to the stiffly beaten egg whites in a thin stream, then continue beating until the frosting is stiff enough to hold its shape. Stir in the vanilla, then fold in the chopped nuts and raisins.

9. To assemble: Place one cake layer upside down on a large round platter and spread with one fourth of the frosting. Add a second layer, right side up this time, and spread with another one fourth of the frosting. Add the third and final layer, right side up, then swirl the remaining frosting over the top and sides of the cake.

10. Let stand until the frosting firms up a bit, then cut into slim wedges and serve.

1979 Chef Paul Prudhomme opens K-Paul's Cajun restaurant in New Orleans and quickly adds two new classics to our culinary repertoire: blackened redfish and Cajun popcorn.

Baltimore-based McCormick, the world's largest spice company, opens a plant in Bedford, Virginia, to produce frozen onion rings under its Golden West label.

1980 Franklin Garland plants 350 European filbert and holly oak seedlings inoculated with black Périgord truffle spores on his farm near Hillsborough, North Carolina.

Harborplace, a complex of shops, boutiques, and restaurants featuring such local specialties as fried oysters, crab imperial, and deviled crab, opens in Baltimore's Inner Harbor.

1981 Bill Neal, a self-taught cook, becomes chef at Crook's Corner in Chapel Hill, North Carolina. By reinventing the recipes he grew up with in South Carolina, Neal creates "the New Southern Cooking." Craig Claiborne calls him "a genius at the stove."

327

IDA'S HEIRLOOM FRUITCAKE

MAKES 13 POUNDS OF FRUITCAKE OR TEN 5⅝ × 3 × 2-INCH LOAVES

. . . .

Ida Friday, wife of Dr. William C. Friday, who for three decades was president of the University of North Carolina, is famous for the fruitcakes she makes, decks with pecans and glacéed fruits, and distributes among friends each Christmas. My own family always looked forward to Ida's fruitcake—dense, dark, delicious, and unlike any we'd ever eaten. The fruitcake mixture is baked in a huge roaster, stirred every 15 minutes, then packed into buttered pans; no further baking needed. When I asked Ida if I might include her recipe in this cookbook, she brought me a small loaf to sample as well as the typed recipe. She told me that the recipe comes from her Orangeburg, South Carolina, ancestors and that it's well over a hundred years old; it may even date as far back as the Civil War. Speaking of which, Ida's grandfather was four years old when Sherman's troops began their march through South Carolina torching houses. The day Yankees rode into her grandfather's yard, the little boy ran up to a dismounted soldier, hugged him around the knees, looked up, and asked, "Are you my papa?"

"No, son. But I hope he comes home safe," the Yankee replied, leaping upon his horse and leading his troops away. The boy's home was spared and his father did come home safe. **Note:** *Some of the ingredients in this archival recipe are called for by "rounded cups;" I've taken the liberty of converting these to today's more precise measurements.*

Ida told me that you need two helpers when you make this fruitcake, not only to prep the fruits and nuts but also to pack the mixture into the pans while it is still hot. "One to scoop," she said, "and two to pack." For her, making fruitcake is a two-day project. Day one is devoted to preparing the fruits and nuts, which are then covered overnight. Day two is for making and baking the fruitcakes, for decorating, and wrapping. Although Ida makes fruitcakes of different sizes and shapes, sometimes even packing the mixture into muffin pans, I find 5 5/8 × 3 × 2-inch loaves perfect for gift giving. **Tip:** *If these fruitcakes are to compact properly, the pieces of fruits and nuts must be small.*

Fruits and Nuts

7 cups shelled pecans

1 pound glacéed green cherries, each cherry quartered lengthwise (from stem to blossom end)

1 pound glacéed pineapple, cut into ½ × ¼ × ¼-inch rectangles

1 pound glacéed citron, cut into ¼-inch dice

Two 15-ounce boxes golden seedless raisins (sultanas)

One 15-ounce box dark seedless raisins

8 ounces pitted dates, cut into ¼-inch dice

8 ounces dried figs, stemmed and cut into ¼-inch dice

4 ounces glacéed lemon rind,
cut into ¼-inch dice

4 ounces glacéed orange rind,
cut into ¼-inch dice

1 cup sifted all-purpose flour
(for dredging)

Batter

3¼ cups sifted all-purpose flour

1 scant tablespoon ground cinnamon

1 scant tablespoon ground allspice

1 scant tablespoon ground nutmeg

1 teaspoon ground cloves

1 pound (4 sticks) butter, at room
temperature

2 cups sugar

12 large eggs

Decorations

5 glacéed red cherries, halved

20 small fan-shaped pieces of glacéed
pineapple

40 perfect pecan halves (saved from
the 7 cups above)

1. Preheat the oven to 350° F. Lightly butter a 15½ × 10½ × 1-inch jelly-roll pan—a bright aluminum one—and set aside. Also butter the bottom of a 20 × 14 × 10-inch turkey roaster and set aside. Finally, butter ten 5 5/8 × 3 × 2-inch loaf pans and set aside.

2. For the fruits and nuts: Reserve 40 perfect pecan halves for decorating the fruitcakes. Coarsely chop the rest, spread half of them in the jelly-roll pan, and bake on the middle oven shelf for 10 to 15 minutes, stirring once or twice, or until lightly toasted; do not over-brown. Transfer to an ungreased large roasting pan. Toast the remaining pecans the same way and add to the roasting pan.

3. Add all of the prepared fruits to the pecans and toss well using your hands. Sprinkle the dredging flour evenly over all, then again mix thoroughly with your hands. It's important that all fruits and nuts be lightly coated with flour.

4. For the batter: Sift the flour, cinnamon, all-spice, nutmeg, and cloves onto a large piece of wax paper and set aside.

5. Cream the butter in a large electric mixer bowl at medium speed for 1 to 1½ minutes or until light and fluffy. With the mixer running, add the sugar gradually, creaming all the while. Beat the eggs in one by one, then, with the mixer at low speed, add the sifted dry ingredients in three batches, beating only enough to combine. Do not overmix.

6. Scoop the batter—it's quite stiff—over the surface of the fruit and nut mixture, distributing evenly. Then, working in sections and using your hands, mix thoroughly until all fruits and nuts are well coated with the batter. Transfer the mixture to the turkey roaster, spreading to the edge.

7. Bake uncovered in the lower third of the oven for 15 minutes. Remove the pan from the oven, close the oven door, and stir the

mixture thoroughly, scooping it again and again from the edge to the center and from the bottom to the top. Repeat the process three times, baking in 15-minute increments, removing the pan from the oven, closing the door, and stirring the mixture as thoroughly as before. Total baking time: 1 hour. Stir the finished mixture well; it should be uniformly moist and crumbly.

8. Turn the oven off and pull the shelf and the turkey roaster most of the way out of the oven. Now working fast, pack the hot crumbly mixture firmly into the prepared loaf pans in layers (this is a three-person job: one scooper, two packers). Ida packs in a layer about 3/4 inch thick, then adds another and another until the pan is full. **Note:** *For packing, I use a same-size loaf pan spritzed on the outside with nonstick cooking spray and press down as hard as possible; I then tamp the mixture firmly into the corners with a tablespoon. It's essential that you pack each layer into the pan as firmly as possible; otherwise your fruitcakes may crumble when you remove them from the pans.* **Tip:** *If the fruitcake mixture becomes too dry to pack, Ida suggests drizzling in just enough wine to soften it. I used a little dry white wine (but dry sherry or port would also be good).*

9. Once all pans have been packed with fruitcake, let stand right side up for an hour or two before unmolding.

10. To unmold her fruitcakes, Ida Friday runs the pans briefly over an electric stovetop burner. Lacking her experience and afraid that I might burn the cakes, I used a simmering water bath instead—a half-filled 13 × 9 × 2-inch baking pan set over low heat. Here's my technique: Working with one pan of fruitcake at a time, let each stand for 30 seconds in the simmering water, then invert at once onto your work surface (Ida uses her marble counter, I a plastic cutting board or sheet of foil placed dull side up on the counter).

11. The instant a fruitcake is inverted, decorate the bottom while it is still warm. I center half a glacéed red cherry in each loaf, add a little glacéed pineapple fan above and below, then bracket the cherry with 4 pecan halves so that they form a large X. Of course, you can decorate the cakes any way you fancy, but keep the designs simple so that the cakes will slice easily. **Note:** *It's imperative that each nut, each piece of fruit be pressed firmly into the fruitcake; otherwise they will not stick.*

12. When the fruitcakes have cooled to room temperature, wrap snugly in plain plastic food wrap (not colored, which will obscure the decoration), pulling hard with each turn so that you compact the cakes and seal in the decorations. **Note:** *This recipe may seem complicated; in fact it isn't. Once all the fruits and nuts are prepped, Ida's fruitcake is easier than those that bake for hours in pans lined with buttered paper.*

JAPANESE FRUITCAKE

MAKES ONE 9-INCH, 4-LAYER CAKE
. . . .

It isn't Japanese, it isn't fruitcake, and it's unknown in some parts of the South. Where it is known, however—mainly the eastern Carolinas (although it was also a Carter family Christmas favorite when the former president was growing up in Plains, Georgia)—it's both classic and beloved. Recipes vary significantly. Some cooks fold crushed pineapple and/or diced maraschino cherries into their filling, some prefer a tart lemon-coconut filling, some use a spice cake batter only and skip the nuts.

When and where did Japanese Fruitcake originate? And what accounts for its unusual name? No one knows for sure. When I queried southern food historian and cookbook author Damon Lee Fowler about this, he told me that a recipe for "Japanese Cake" appears in the *Tested Recipe Cook Book* published in 1895 by the Board of Women Managers of the Cotton States and International Exposition held that same year in Atlanta. It differs from today's Japanese Fruitcake only in the details. "The contributor," Fowler continued, "is presumably an American woman (at least her husband has a western name) living in Shanghai, China." That cake contains no nuts and the filling is a cornstarch-thickened lemon-coconut one.

The two-tone version here—for me the quintessential Japanese Fruitcake—was given to me years ago by Pauline Gordon, a housing specialist with the North Carolina Agricultural Extension Service. An elderly lady when I went to work in the "state office" in Raleigh, Miss Gordon was famous for her Japanese Fruitcake, an old family recipe from Kingstree, South Carolina. Like other extension specialists, Miss Gordon traveled the state, in her case to teach Home Demonstration agents the finer points of interior decorating. As she drove, she liked to keep a wedge of Japanese fruitcake on the empty seat beside her for a handy snack. One day a yellow jacket, perched on the piece she slipped into her mouth, stung her tongue. Being an old country girl, Miss Gordon simply pulled onto the shoulder, grabbed a gob of wet clay, and rubbed it on the sting—"to draw the poison and stop the swelling." I don't know if this old home remedy worked but I do know that she lived to tell the tale. Many times.

Cake

3 cups sifted cake flour

2 teaspoons baking powder

¼ teaspoon salt

1 cup (2 sticks) butter, slightly softened

2 cups sugar

2 teaspoons vanilla extract

4 large eggs

1 cup milk

1 cup seedless raisins or dried currants
(these are actually tiny Zante raisins)

1 cup coarsely chopped pecans

2 tablespoons all-purpose flour

1 teaspoon ground cinnamon

½ teaspoon ground allspice

½ teaspoon freshly grated nutmeg

Filling

1½ cups fresh orange juice

⅓ cup fresh lemon juice

Finely grated zest of 1 large orange

Finely grated zest of 1 large lemon

2 cups sugar

¼ cup unsifted all-purpose flour

½ teaspoon salt

3 cups freshly grated coconut or
sweetened flaked coconut

1. For the cake: Preheat the oven to 350° F. Coat four 9-inch layer cake pans well with nonstick oil-and-flour baking spray and set aside.

2. Sift the cake flour, baking powder, and salt onto a piece of wax paper and set aside also.

3. Cream the butter, sugar, and vanilla in a large electric mixer bowl at moderate speed for 2 to 3 minutes or until light and fluffy. Beat the eggs in one by one, then reduce the mixer speed to low and add the sifted dry ingredients alternately with the milk, beginning and ending with the dry. Beat after each addition only enough to combine; overmixing will toughen the cake.

4. Divide the batter in half. Quickly dredge the raisins and pecans in the all-purpose flour and fold into half of the batter along with the cinnamon, allspice, and nutmeg.

5. Spoon the yellow cake batter into two of the pans, dividing the total amount evenly, then the spiced batter into the remaining two pans, again dividing evenly.

6. If possible, bake all four layers at the same time on the middle oven shelf for 20 to 25 minutes or until springy to the touch and a cake tester inserted in the middle comes out clean. Otherwise, bake the two yellow layers, then the two spice. Cool the baked layers in the upright pans on wire racks for 15 minutes, then invert on the racks and cool to room temperature.

7. Meanwhile, prepare the filling: Combine all ingredients but the coconut in a large, heavy, nonreactive saucepan, set over moderately high heat, and cook, stirring constantly, for 5 minutes or until thickened and smooth. Reduce the heat to low and simmer uncovered, stirring now and then, for 10 minutes. Add the coconut and cook, uncovered, stirring occasionally, for 20 to 25 minutes or until the consistency of marmalade.

8. To assemble the cake: Center a spice layer on a large round plate and spread generously with the filling. Top with a yellow layer, press firmly into place, and spread with more filling. Repeat—spice layer, yellow layer—each time pressing the new layer firmly into the one underneath and spreading with filling; don't be stingy. The last of the filling goes on top of the cake, not on the sides, although if some of it dribbles down the sides, so much the better. That's how I like it.

9. Let the cake stand for at least 24 hours before cutting; this gives the filling time to seep into the cake and firm up a bit.

Heirloom Recipe

In this early twentieth-century Georgia recipe pamphlet, Japanese fruitcake is called simply Japanese Cake and appears to be four layers and two cakes. The "spice" called for is probably allspice. Today's Japanese fruitcake usually consists of two plain layers and two spice layers.

JAPANESE CAKE

Seven eggs, 1 cup butter, 2 cups sugar, 3 cups flour, 2 teaspoonfuls of baking powder. Use this with the whites of 7 eggs, baking in four layers. With the yolks of the 7 eggs, use same quantity of butter, sugar, flour and baking powder, adding 1 teaspoonful each of ground spice, cloves and cinnamon and 1 box of seeded raisins; bake in 4 layers.

JAPANESE CAKE FILLING

Three cups sugar, 2 tablespoonfuls corn starch mixed with sugar (dry), 1 large cocoanut grated, juice of 3 oranges, juice and rind of 2 lemons. Mix together and pour over 1 teacup of boiling water. Cook until thick, put between layers using white and dark layers alternately.

—*Good Recipes by Athens' Housewives,*
1916–1917

1982

Elizabeth and Michael Terry open Elizabeth on 37th Street in a down-at-heel Savannah neighborhood. Elizabeth's updated renditions of old Georgia recipes are applauded by America's top food critics.

In a $22 million leveraged buy-out, a group of Krispy Kreme franchisees buys the company back from Beatrice Foods. Their first move is to reinstate Krispy Kreme's signature yeast-raised doughnut recipe.

Alabama-born and -bred Frank Stitt, after cooking in France, comes home and opens his first restaurant in Birmingham. He calls it Highlands Bar and Grill and before long his fusion of the southern country cooking of his youth with the Provençal flavors he discovered in France attracts national attention and wins hefty helpings of praise.

Knoxville, Tennessee, hosts the World's Fair with pavilions from around the world. Its theme: energy. Its symbol: the 266-foot Sunsphere with a revolving restaurant on top.

BLACKBERRY JAM CAKE WITH BROWNED BUTTER FROSTING

MAKES ONE 9-INCH, 2-LAYER CAKE

Blackberries grow wild over much of the South and from early childhood on my brother and I would head into the brambles to fill our buckets. Daddy made a competition of the picking and rewarded the owner of the first filled bucket with a dollar—a fortune in those days. My Illinois mother turned the berries into jams and jellies, pies and cobblers. But never this spicy cake; I obtained the recipe while on assignment in Kentucky several years after she died. I have since eaten similar cakes in that swath of Appalachia that meanders through Virginia, Tennessee, and North Carolina before dipping into northernmost Georgia and South Carolina. Some cooks frost their jam cakes with chocolate icing but I think this browned butter frosting is a better choice.

Cake

1½ cups sugar

1 teaspoon ground cinnamon

½ teaspoon ground ginger

½ teaspoon ground allspice

½ teaspoon freshly grated nutmeg

½ teaspoon salt

6 tablespoons (¾ stick) butter

2 large eggs

¾ cup sieved blackberry jam

1½ teaspoons baking soda

1½ cups buttermilk

2⅔ cups sifted all-purpose flour

Filling

1 cup sieved blackberry jam

Frosting

4 tablespoons (½ stick) butter, chilled

2½ cups unsifted confectioners' (10X) sugar

1 teaspoon vanilla extract

¼ teaspoon salt

3 to 5 tablespoons half-and-half, milk, or evaporated milk

1. For the cake: Preheat the oven to 350° F. Coat two 9-inch layer cake pans with nonstick oil-and-flour baking spray and set aside.

2. Combine the sugar, cinnamon, ginger, allspice, nutmeg, and salt in a large electric mixer bowl. Add the butter and beat at moderately high speed for about 2 minutes or until light and fluffy. Beat the eggs in one by one, then mix in the jam.

3. Quickly dissolve the baking soda in the buttermilk (it will fizz), then, with the mixer at low speed, add the flour alternately with the buttermilk mixture, beginning and ending with the flour. Do not overbeat or your cake will be tough.

4. Divide the batter among the two pans and bake in the lower third of the oven for 40 to 45

minutes or until the layers pull from the sides of the pans and are springy to the touch.

5. Cool the cake layers in their upright pans on wire racks for 10 minutes, then loosen around the edge and turn out on the racks. Cool to room temperature.

6. To assemble the cake, place one layer upside down on a large round plate, spread with the jam filling, and set the second layer on top, this time right side up.

7. For the frosting: Melt the butter in a small, heavy saucepan over low heat, then allow it to brown slowly for 10 to 12 minutes or until the color of amber. Pour into a ramekin and set in the freezer for a few minutes or just until the butter begins to harden.

8. Using a hand electric mixer, cream the chilled butter, the confectioners' sugar, vanilla, and salt until smooth, then beat in the half-and-half, tablespoon by tablespoon, until the frosting is a good spreading consistency. **Note: *You can make the frosting in a food processor fitted with the metal chopping blade. Simply whiz the butter, sugar, vanilla, and salt for several seconds until creamy, then pulse in the half-and-half 1 tablespoon at a time.***

9. Swirl the frosting over the top and sides of the cake, then allow to dry for at least an hour before cutting. Make the pieces small; this cake is rich. Just what Southerners like.

❧

If you drop a dish cloth while you're cooking, company will come and go hungry.

—OLD SMOKIES SUPERSTITION

❧

1983 Former Vanderbilt football hero Christie Hauck re-creates a beloved childhood cookie, then launches a Nashville empire that not only wholesales Christie Cookies to hotels and colleges across the country but also sells them locally and via mail order.

Asked by President Ronald Reagan to plan an American menu for the economic summit held in Williamsburg, Virginia, *New York Times* food writer Craig Claiborne features barbecue from Lexington, North Carolina.

Using his mother's cheesecake recipe, one oven, and one baker, 21-year-old Adam Matthews of Louisville starts a business that now sells cheesecakes all over the U.S., Canada, Caribbean, and Mexico. Its name? Adam Matthews.

1984 "Hee Haw Honey" Mackenzie Colt settles in Nashville to write songs but gets into the candy business instead. Colts Chocolates fans now include everyone from Dolly Parton to President George W. Bush.

Don Pelts realizes a lifelong dream by opening Corky's Ribs & BBQ in Memphis. With its 1950s ambience and pork shoulders pit-roasted 22 hours over hickory chips, Corky's soon becomes the talk of Tennessee. Today there are branches as far north as Illinois and as far south as Florida.

LANE CAKE

MAKES AN 8-INCH, 4-LAYER CAKE

. . . .

Open any southern community cookbook and you're likely to find Lane Cake. Or rather, one of the many versions of this popular Alabama white cake. Some are three-layer, nine-inch cakes, others a towering four layers but only eight inches across. Mainly, however, it's the frosting and the egg yolk–thickened coconut filling that vary. Most fillings also contain bourbon (or brandy), pecans, and raisins, plus a few glacéed red cherries or maraschinos. Some recipes call for frosting the cake with the filling as well as spreading it between the layers because "it's the best part of Lane Cake." In my search for authenticity, I find that the older Lane cakes include not only recipes for a rich fruity filling but also one for boiled icing. Originally called "Prize Cake" because it had won a prize at the Alabama State Fair, this classic later took the name of its creator, Emma Rylander Lane of Clayton, Alabama. Mrs. Lane published the Prize Cake receipt in her cookbook, *Some Good Things To Eat* (1898). But according to Cecily Brownstone, longtime food editor of the Associated Press and a friend of Mrs. Lane's granddaughter, that recipe was "vague in the extreme." Does this explain why there are so many different Lane cakes? The recipe here is an especially good one. Do as Southerners do and serve it at Christmastime. It's a delicious substitute for fruitcake. **Note:** *To finesse the sticky job of chopping raisins, I use dried "currants." They are actually Zante raisins, a variety so small they need no chopping.* **Tip:** *For this cake (indeed for most cakes),*

southern cooks would use one of their beloved "soft" flours such as White Lily or Martha White.

Cake

3⅓ cups sifted cake flour
(see Tip at left)

1 tablespoon baking powder

½ teaspoon salt

1 cup (2 sticks) butter (no substitute)

2 cups sugar

1 cup milk mixed with 2 teaspoons vanilla extract

6 large egg whites

⅛ teaspoon cream of tartar

Filling

8 large egg yolks

1½ cups sugar

¾ cup (1½ sticks) butter, melted

1 cup flaked coconut

1 cup moderately finely chopped pecans

¾ cup dried currants (see Note at left)

⅓ cup moderately finely chopped glacéed red cherries (optional)

¼ cup bourbon or brandy

1 teaspoon vanilla extract

Icing

2 cups sugar

½ cup water

2 tablespoons light corn syrup

2 large egg whites

¼ teaspoon salt

I teaspoon vanilla extract

1. For the cake: Preheat the oven to 350° F. Grease and flour four 8-inch layer cake pans well, tap out the excess flour, and set aside. Sift the flour, baking powder, and salt onto a piece of wax paper and set aside also.
2. Cream the butter in a large electric mixer bowl, first at low speed and then at high for 2 to 3 minutes or until light and silvery. With the machine at moderately low speed, add the sugar gradually and continue beating for 1 to 2 minutes or until fluffy.
3. With the mixer at low speed, add the sifted dry ingredients in three batches, alternating with the milk mixture and beginning and ending with the dry. Beat after each addition only enough to combine.
4. Beat the egg whites until silvery in a second large bowl with clean beaters, add the cream of tartar, then continue beating for about 3 minutes or until the whites peak softly.
5. Mix about 1 cup of the beaten whites into the cake batter to lighten it, then gently fold in the rest until no streaks of white remain. Divide the batter among the four pans, rap each sharply on the counter once or twice to expel large air bubbles, then bake in the lower third of the oven for about 25 minutes or until the cakes are springy to the touch and a cake tester inserted midway between the center and the rim comes out clean.
6. Cool the cakes in the upright pans on wire racks for 5 minutes, then turn out on the racks and cool to room temperature.

1984 Lexington, North Carolina, stages the first of its annual barbecue festivals, serving two and a half tons of barbecue to 30,000 people. Today you can quadruple those figures.

1985 *Bill Neal's Southern Cooking*—mainly a collection of the "new southern" recipes that made him and Crook's Corner, his restaurant in Chapel Hill, North Carolina, famous—is published by the University of North Carolina Press. It becomes the go-to book for young southern chefs eager to put a modern spin on regional classics.

R. J. Reynolds tobacco company, based in Winston-Salem, North Carolina, enters the food business by buying Nabisco.

Planters adds honey-roasted peanuts to its inventory.

A specially engineered can of Coca-Cola soars into space aboard a NASA shuttle. That same year, long-time company "Boss" Bob Woodruff dies.

1986 Nathalie Dupree of Social Circle, Georgia, intensifies national interest in southern food with *New Southern Cooking,* her PBS TV series and tandem cookbook.

7. Meanwhile, prepare the filling: Set the top of a double boiler on the counter and add the egg yolks and sugar. Using a hand electric mixer, beat at moderate speed for 5 minutes or until thick, then, beating all the while, drizzle in the melted butter. Set over simmering water and cook, beating constantly, for about 8 minutes or until thickened. Fold in the coconut, pecans, dried currants, glacéed cherries, if you like, bourbon, and vanilla, then cook and stir 1 minute longer. Remove from the heat and cool to room temperature.

8. To assemble: Place one cake layer upside down on a large round platter and spread with one third of the filling. Add a second layer, right side up this time, and spread with another third of the filling. Add a third layer, placing upside down, and spread with the remaining filling. Set the fourth and final layer in place, right side up. Let the cake stand while you prepare the icing.

9. For the icing: Combine the sugar, water, and corn syrup in a medium-size heavy saucepan and insert a candy thermometer. Bring to a boil over high heat, stirring until the sugar dissolves, then cook without stirring until the syrup spins a long thread (234° to 236° F.)

10. Beat the egg whites and salt with an electric mixer at high speed until soft peaks form, then, beating constantly, add the boiling syrup in a thin stream. Continue beating for 3 to 4 minutes or until the icing is stiff enough to hold its shape; stir in the vanilla. Swirl the warm icing over the top and sides of the cake and cool for at least 1 hour before cutting. **Note:** *Because the filling and the icing both contain egg, refrigerate any leftover Lane cake.*

LOUISIANA FRESH FIG CAKE

MAKES A 10-INCH BUNDT CAKE

Back-roading through Louisiana shows the Pelican State at its best: antebellum plantations approached by long allées of live oak, sleepy towns that time forgot, bald cypresses wading in the inky waters of the Atchafalaya. No surprises here. But what did surprise me were the miles and miles of sugarcane rustling in the wind, the vast pecan orchards, and, in every yard, it seemed, fig bushes bent under their burden of fruit. This dark and spicy cake puts those figs to good use along with Louisiana pecans and raw sugar. The figs that thrive in Louisiana, indeed throughout most of the South, are green figs. And they are what local cooks would use here. I've discovered, however, that black Mission figs work equally well.

2¾ cups sifted all-purpose flour

1½ teaspoons baking powder

½ teaspoon baking soda

1 teaspoon ground ginger

1 teaspoon ground cinnamon

½ teaspoon freshly grated nutmeg

½ teaspoon black pepper

¼ teaspoon salt

¾ cup (1½ sticks) butter

1¼ cups raw sugar

3 extra-large eggs

2 teaspoons vanilla extract

1 cup buttermilk

1½ cups coarsely chopped pecans

½ pound firm-ripe figs, washed, stemmed, and coarsely chopped (see headnote)

1. Preheat the oven to 350° F. Coat a 10-inch (12-cup) Bundt pan with nonstick oil-and-flour baking spray and set aside.
2. Sift the flour, baking powder, soda, ginger, cinnamon, nutmeg, pepper, and salt onto a large piece of wax paper and set aside also.
3. Cream the butter in an electric mixer at low speed for 5 minutes or until silvery and light. Add the sugar and cream at low speed for 3 minutes. Beat the eggs in one by one, then beat in the vanilla.
4. With the mixer still at low speed, add the sifted dry ingredients alternately with the buttermilk, beginning and ending with the dry. To avoid overbeating the batter, I add the dries in three batches, the buttermilk in two. By hand, fold in the pecans and figs.
5. Scoop the batter into the prepared pan, spreading to the edge. Also rap the pan sharply on the counter two or three times to level the batter.
6. Bake the cake in the lower third of the oven for about 1 hour or until it begins to pull from the sides of the pan, is nicely browned, and a cake tester inserted halfway between the rim and the center tube comes out clean.
7. Cool the cake in the upright pan on a wire rack for 15 minutes; loosen around the edge with a small, thin-blade spatula; then invert on the rack and cool to room temperature.
8. Cut into wedges and serve as is or top each portion with a scoop of vanilla ice cream or a drift of whipped cream.

1986 The Georgia State Legislature demarcates the 20-county Vidalia onion–growing area.

Peter Pan peanut butter, first manufactured in Chicago in 1928 and now owned by Conagra, relocates to Sylvester, Georgia. Today it is the only plant making Peter Pan.

Ben and Karen Barker open Magnolia Grill in Durham, North Carolina, which captures the national fancy and wins a kettle full of awards.

Obrycki's Olde Crab House moves into new Baltimore quarters with space enough for large private parties.

1987 The Southern Progress publishing corporation, now owned by Time, Inc., launches a new food and fitness magazine called *Cooking Light*. It is one of the most successful start-ups in magazine history. Among its monthly features: classic recipes (both southern and otherwise) trimmed of calories, fat, and cholesterol.

Flamers, the first of a chain of charcoal-broiled-to-order burger restaurants, opens in Jacksonville, Florida. Today Flamers' burgers can be enjoyed throughout the U.S. and as far afield as Puerto Rico, Egypt, and the Philippines.

COLD-OVEN POUND CAKE

MAKES A 10-INCH TUBE CAKE

. . . .

This recipe comes from Lenora Yates of Winston-Salem, North Carolina, the best pound cake baker I know. Now in her eighties, Lenora was my father's secretary long years ago when he was a professor of botany at North Carolina State College. She still bakes this pound cake regularly for family and friends and always has a wedge of it waiting whenever my stepmother stops by on her way to our mountain house near Boone. Starting the cake in a cold oven, Lenora believes, accounts for its fine texture. But vigorous creaming of the butter, shortening, and sugar surely helps too, as do Lenora's years of experience. **Note:** *Choose a good all-purpose flour for this recipe, not cake or "light" flour; neither has enough gluten to support the heavy batter. Also use a light-colored pan for baking this cake; the batter is so rich that a dark pan or one lined with a dark non-stick coating will cause the cake to overbrown.* **Tip:** *If the butter, shortening, and eggs are refrigerator-cold, you can cream them to supreme fluffiness.*

3 cups unsifted all-purpose flour

1 teaspoon baking powder

1 cup (2 sticks) butter (see Tip above)

½ cup vegetable shortening

3 cups sugar

6 extra-large eggs

¾ cup milk

2 teaspoons lemon extract

2 teaspoons vanilla extract

1. Butter and flour a 10-inch tube pan, tapping out the excess flour, and set aside. Sift the flour and baking powder together onto a large piece of wax paper and set aside also.

2. Cream the butter, shortening, and sugar in a large electric mixer bowl at low speed for 3 minutes, scraping the bowl at half-time, then raise the mixer speed to medium and cream 2 to 3 minutes longer or until light and fluffy.

3. With the mixer at low speed, add the eggs one by one, beating well and scraping the bowl after each addition. With the mixer still at low speed, add the sifted dry ingredients alternately with the milk, beginning and ending with the dry—four additions of the dry and three of the milk are about right. Scrape the bowl well, then beat in the lemon and vanilla extracts.

4. Scoop the batter into the prepared pan, spreading to the edge, then rap the pan several times on the counter to level the batter and release large air bubbles.

5. Place the cake in the lower third of the oven, set the thermostat at 350° F., turn the oven on, and bake the cake for 1 hour and 10 minutes to 1 hour and 20 minutes or until it begins to pull from the sides of the pan, is springy to the touch, and a cake tester inserted halfway between the rim and the central tube comes out clean.

6. Cool the cake in the upright pan on a wire rack for 20 minutes. Using a small thin-blade spatula, loosen the cake carefully around the edge and around the central tube. Invert the cake on a wire rack and cool to room temperature before cutting. Delicious as is or with sliced sweetened-to-taste fresh strawberries or peaches ladled on top.

BROWN SUGAR POUND CAKE WITH WILD HICKORY NUTS

MAKES A 10-INCH TUBE CAKE

. . . .

When I was about ten, I rescued a robin hatchling that had fallen from its nest and raised that bird to maturity. Mitzy spent the night in the tall hickory tree just outside my bedroom window and each morning would peck at my screen until I came down to greet her. In the fall, when hickory nuts rained down upon the ground, my brother and I would gather them for Mother while Mitzy perched on a branch above. Hickory nuts, our father told us, were related to pecans (he knew such things because he was a botanist). They did indeed taste like pecans although they seemed—I'm searching for the right word here—"smokier." There all similarity ends, however, because hickory nuts are hard-shelled and their meat exceedingly tedious to extract. Mother baked hickory nuts into cookies and stirred them into fudge. But she never baked this cake because I didn't obtain the recipe until after she had died. It is an old North Carolina favorite and I must say that it is heaven. **Note:** *Choose a good all-purpose flour for this recipe, not cake or "light" flour; neither has enough gluten to support the heavy batter. Also use a light-colored pan for baking this cake; the batter is so rich that a dark pan or one lined with a dark nonstick coating will cause the cake to overbrown.*

3 cups sifted all-purpose flour

½ teaspoon baking powder

¼ teaspoon salt

1¼ cups (2½ sticks) butter, slightly softened

1 pound light brown sugar

5 large eggs

1 cup milk

1 tablespoon vanilla extract

1 cup moderately finely chopped hickory nuts, black walnuts, or pecans

1. Preheat the oven to 325° F. Butter and flour a 10-inch tube pan well, then tap out the excess flour. Set the pan aside.

2. Sift the flour, baking powder, and salt together onto a piece of wax paper and set aside.

3. Cream the butter in a large electric mixer bowl at moderate speed for 1 to 2 minutes or until fluffy, then add the brown sugar gradually, beating all the while; continue beating until light. Beat the eggs in one by one.

4. Add the sifted dry ingredients alternately with the milk, beginning and ending with the dry and beating after each addition only enough to combine. Stir in the vanilla and the nuts. Pour the batter into the prepared pan, spreading to the edge.

5. Bake on the middle oven shelf for 1 hour and 20 to 25 minutes or until the cake begins to pull from the sides of the pan and the top springs back slowly when touched.

6. Cool the cake in the upright pan on a wire rack 15 minutes, then loosen around the edge and the central tube, and turn out on the wire rack. Cool completely before cutting.

BOURBON

I've been drinking "bourbon and branch" ever since I reached the age of consent but I'm ashamed to admit how little I knew about it. I certainly had no idea that Abraham Lincoln had two ties to Kentucky's best.

One: To earn money during farming's off-season, Lincoln's father worked in a bourbon distillery. Two: Throughout the Civil War, Lincoln's top general, Ulysses S. Grant, had a ready supply of Kentucky bourbon. Reminds me of the old Bob Newhart routine in which Lincoln says something like, "Find out what brand Grant drinks and send a case to each of my other generals."

The spirited story of bourbon begins shortly after the Whiskey Rebellion of 1794 when, in an effort to restore calm, the young U.S. government offered sixty acres of land west of the Alleghenies (later Kentucky) to each settler who would build a permanent home there and raise corn.

Feisty Scotch-Irish distillers from western Pennsylvania to Georgia eagerly accepted, realizing that the corn they were required to grow could replace some of the rye in the whiskey they'd been making. Moreover, fermented and distilled corn would be easier to ship and sell than the grain itself. The result? A happy marriage of Old World tradition and New World corn. In barrels stamped BOURBON (to indicate Bourbon County's various river ports), the new Kentucky distillers began shipping corn whiskey down the Ohio, then the Mississippi, to New Orleans.

Before long, bourbon was being prescribed for medicinal purposes, and to keep the quality of what he sold both high and consistent, Louisville druggist George G. Brown began selling standard-proof bourbon in sealed bottles. A milestone.

Soon there was another. In the mid nineteenth century, Scottish physician-chemist James C. Crow introduced the sour mash process, a method still used for all straight bourbons. Some of the fermented (sour) mash drained from one batch of bourbon is added to the next along with the yeast. It's a way to check bacterial growth and produce bourbon of consistently high quality.

In 1964, the U.S. Congress declared bourbon "America's Native Spirit" and decreed that only whiskey made in the United States that met certain requirements could be called bourbon. It must:

- Be made from a mash of at least 51 percent corn (often more is used) mixed with barley and another grain (usually rye but occasionally wheat).
- Be aged for at least two years in charred new oak barrels; if aged for less than four, the number of years must be stated on the bottle.
- Never contain any additive that alters the bourbon's flavor, color, or sweetness.
- Never have a final distillate of more than 160 (U.S.) proof; this must be cut to 125 proof or less before bourbon can be barreled. It is bottled later at various proofs.

Bourbon can be made anywhere in the United States, but only Kentucky is allowed to print its name on the label as place of origin.

Although the mixture of grain, type of yeast, degree of char on the barrels, aging time, even barrel location in the warehouse vary from brand to brand and account for differences in color, taste, proof, and finesse, one ingredient remains constant among Kentucky distillers: the state's natural limestone-rich water.

And this, most would agree, is what makes Kentucky bourbon America's best.

· ·

KENTUCKY BOURBON CAKE

MAKES A 10-INCH TUBE CAKE

· ·

Marion Flexner, an Alabaman by birth and a Kentuckian by adoption, tells a little-known tale in her classic *Out of Kentucky Kitchens* (1949). To quote: "This cake isn't a native Kentuckian at all, and Dame Rumor asserts with authority that a certain Frankfort matron (about 25 years ago) coaxed a famous New York maître d'hôtel to give her the recipe by crossing his palm with a lot of silver." I wonder. Savannah-based southern food historian and cookbook author Damon Lee Fowler doubts the "palm-crossed-with-silver" story and believes that Kentucky bourbon cake may descend from early southern fruitcakes, which, like this one, have a pound-cake base. The Rich Fruit Cake in Mary Randolph's *Virginia House-wife* (1824) is similar, although it contains more dried fruits and brandy instead of bourbon. Ditto several recipes in Lettice Bryan's *Kentucky Housewife* (1839). I find an even closer match in the Kentucky Cake in *The Blue Grass Cook Book* (1904) by Minnie C. Fox; egg whites are used instead of whole eggs and the nuts are lacking. In my many years in New York I never once encountered bourbon cake, and I had to travel to Kentucky to try the dense pecan-and-raisin-filled Christmas favorite that the Bluegrass State calls its own. The only liquid ingredient? Good Kentucky bourbon. **Note:** *Use a 10-inch tube pan to bake this cake, a light-colored one to discourage overbrowning; and butter and flour it well.* You'll note that the oven temperature is unusually low—250° F.—and that the cake bakes for at least 2½ hours. That explains its fine texture. Some southerners wrap the cooled cake in a bourbon-soaked cloth and let it "season" for a week or so, adding more bourbon as needed to keep the cloth moist. I find that unnecessary; the cake's plenty spirited without it. **Tip:** *If the butter is refrigerator-cold, you can cream it to uncommon fluffiness.*

4 cups sifted all-purpose flour

3 cups lightly toasted pecans, coarsely chopped (10 to 12 minutes in a 350° F. oven)

3 cups seedless raisins

1½ teaspoons freshly grated nutmeg

½ teaspoon baking soda

¼ teaspoon salt

1 pound (4 sticks) butter (no substitute) (see Tip on page 343)

1½ teaspoons vanilla extract

2 cups sugar

6 extra-large eggs, separated

¾ cup bourbon

1. Preheat the oven to 250° F. Generously butter a 10-inch tube pan, dust with flour, then tap out any excess flour and discard; set the pan aside.

2. Place ½ cup of the sifted flour in a large bowl, add the pecans and raisins, and toss well; set aside. Whisk the remaining 3½ cups flour, the nutmeg, baking soda, and salt together in a second large bowl and set aside also.

3. Cream the butter and vanilla in a large electric mixer bowl at low speed for 3 minutes, scraping the bowl often, then raise the mixer speed to medium and cream 2 to 3 minutes longer or until light and fluffy. Scrape the bowl well, set the mixer at moderately low speed, and add the sugar gradually. Raise the mixer speed to high and beat hard for 3 to 5 minutes or until fluffy and almost white, pausing several times to scrape the bowl.

4. With the mixer at low speed, add the egg yolks one by one, beating well and scraping the bowl after each addition. With the mixer still at low speed, add the sifted dry ingredients alternately with the bourbon, beginning and ending with the dry—four additions of the dry and three of bourbon are about right.

5. Using clean beaters, whip the egg whites in a separate clean bowl until soft and billowing—the stage just before soft peaks. Fold about a fourth of the beaten whites into the batter to lighten it (it's very thick), then fold in the balance—gently—until no streaks of white or yellow remain. By hand, fold in the dredged pecans and raisins and all dredging flour.

6. Scoop the batter into the pan, smooth the top, and rap once or twice on the counter sharply to release large air bubbles. **Note: *Kentucky cooks often decorate the surface of the batter with pecan halves and candied red and/or green cherries before the cake goes into the oven. A nice touch at Christmastime.***

7. Slide the cake onto the middle oven shelf and bake for 2½ to 2¾ hours or until it begins to pull from the sides of the pan, feels springy to the touch, and a cake tester inserted midway between the central tube and the edge of the pan comes out clean.

8. Cool the cake in the upright pan on a wire rack for 20 minutes. Carefully loosen around the edge and central tube with a small, thin-blade spatula and invert on a wire rack.

9. Cool the cake to room temperature, then, before cutting, invert on a round plate so the cake is right side up. This cake needs no frosting. **Note: *If you don't intend to serve the cake right away, wrap in plastic food wrap—or, if you prefer, in a bourbon-soaked cloth—and store in an airtight tin. That's the Kentucky way.***

MORAVIAN GINGERBREAD

MAKES A 13 × 9 × 2-INCH CAKE

. . . .

This recipe is a downsized family version of the gingerbread served at Salem Tavern in Old Salem, a faithfully restored eighteenth-century Moravian town in North Carolina's rolling Piedmont. What makes this gingerbread different is that the ginger is freshly chopped. I do the chopping in a food processor, a shortcut those efficiency-minded Moravians would have welcomed.

1¼ cups (2½ sticks) butter, slightly softened

2 cups sugar

3 large eggs

1 cup molasses (not too dark)

½ cup finely chopped peeled fresh ginger

1 teaspoon ground cinnamon

½ teaspoon freshly grated nutmeg

Pinch of ground cloves

1 teaspoon baking soda

1 tablespoon cider vinegar

3½ cups sifted all-purpose flour

1 cup milk

1. Preheat the oven to 375° F. Grease and flour a 13 × 9 × 2-inch baking pan well. Tap out the excess flour and set the pan aside

2. Cream the butter in a large electric mixer bowl at moderate speed about 1 minute or until fluffy. Gradually beat in the sugar. Add the eggs one by one, beating well after each addi-

tion. Now mix in the molasses, ginger, cinnamon, nutmeg, and cloves.

3. Combine the baking soda and vinegar and beat into the butter mixture. By hand add the flour alternately with the milk, beginning and ending with flour and stirring after each addition only enough to combine.

4. Spread the batter evenly in the pan and bake on the middle oven shelf for 45 to 50 minutes or until a cake tester inserted in the middle of the gingerbread comes out clean.

5. Transfer the pan of gingerbread to a wire rack and cool to room temperature before serving.

6. Cut into squares and top, if you like, with drifts of whipped cream, scoops of vanilla ice cream, or, better yet, scoops of dulce de leche ice cream.

OLD VIRGINIA GINGERBREAD

MAKES 12 SERVINGS

. . . .

This old family recipe was given to me by James Harrison of Coggins Point Farm on the south side of the James River. He was the father of my friend Maria Harrison Reuge, who, with her French husband, Guy, owns Mirabelle, a first-rate restaurant in the little Long Island town of St. James. Some years ago when I interviewed Mr. Harrison about old Virginia recipes, he told me that his father "always called this 'molasses bread' because he thought it tasted more like molasses than ginger." What's unique about this gingerbread is that it's baked in custard cups, inverted on dessert plates, then topped with Brown Sugar Sauce (recipe follows).

2 cups sifted all-purpose flour

I teaspoon ground ginger

½ teaspoon ground cinnamon

I cup molasses (not too dark)

I teaspoon baking soda

½ cup (I stick) butter,
at room temperature

I cup loosely packed light brown sugar

2 large eggs, separated

½ cup milk

1. Preheat the oven to 350° F. Spray twelve 8-ounce custard cups with nonstick cooking spray and set aside. Sift the flour, ginger, and cinnamon together onto a piece of wax paper and set aside also.

2. Combine the molasses and baking soda in a small bowl and let stand while you proceed with the recipe; it will fizz and foam. Cream the butter in a large electric mixer bowl at moderately high speed for 1 to 2 minutes or until light and fluffy. Gradually beat in the sugar, then, with the mixer running, add the egg yolks one by one.

3. By hand, fold the sifted dry ingredients in alternately with the milk, beginning and ending with the dry. Blend in the molasses-soda mixture.

4. Beat the egg whites to soft peaks, then fold into the batter until no streaks of white or brown remain; easy does it.

5. Scoop a scant ½ cup of the batter into each custard cup, then arrange the custard cups, not touching, on a large baking sheet.

6. Slide the baking sheet onto the middle oven shelf and bake the individual gingerbreads for about 25 minutes or until springy to the touch and a cake tester inserted into the middle of one comes out clean.

7. Transfer the gingerbreads to a wire rack and cool in the upright custard cups for 5 minutes. Using a small thin-blade spatula, carefully loosen each gingerbread around the edge and invert on a dessert plate.

8. Top each individual gingerbread with Brown Sugar Sauce and serve.

BROWN SUGAR SAUCE

MAKES ABOUT 1¼ CUPS

According to James Harrison, who gave me this old Virginia recipe years ago, "When properly made, the sauce will be caramel-like and very dark." He adds that although it was routinely served at his Grandmother Davis's house as a topping for Old Virginia Gingerbread, which precedes, it is equally spectacular over vanilla ice cream. Harrison remembers the sauce being put on to simmer just as the family sat down to Sunday dinner. By the time dessert was served, it was ready. If the sauce is to be silky-smooth, you must keep the burner heat at the lowest possible point, using a diffuser, if necessary. The sauce should warm just enough to dissolve all the sugar crystals, not become so hot that the eggs "scramble."

¼ cup (½ stick) butter, at room temperature

2 cups loosely packed dark brown sugar

2 large eggs

2 tablespoons hot (but not boiling) water

2 tablespoons bourbon or brandy

1. Cream the butter and sugar in a small electric mixer bowl at moderately high speed for 1 to 2 minutes or until light and smooth. With the motor running, add the eggs one by one, then continue beating for 1 minute. Beat in the hot water.

2. Transfer the sauce to the top of a double boiler and set over barely simmering water. Adjust the burner heat so that the water in the bottom of the double boiler stays below a simmer, then cook, stirring briskly every 20 minutes or so, until the sugar dissolves completely and the sauce thickens and is absolutely smooth. This may take as long as 1 1/2 hours. But be patient. If you rush things, your sauce will turn gritty and you might as well pitch it out. Only a silky sauce will do.

3. As soon as the sauce is just the right consistency, mix in the bourbon and cook 5 minutes longer, stirring occasionally.

4. Ladle warm over gingerbread or serve as an ice cream topper.

❖

Good coffee and the Protestant religion can seldom if ever be found together.

—OLD CREOLE SAYING

❖

1987 Lipton manager Mack Fleming and third-generation English tea taster Bill Hall buy the 127-acre Wadmalaw Island tea farm, found the Charleston Tea Plantation, and begin producing this country's only homegrown tea. They call it American Classic.

Lattimore M. Michael, a Cleveland, Mississippi, grocer known for the superb burgers he serves at his store, opens a restaurant called the Back Yard Burger. A year later he is selling franchises; today there are Back Yard Burgers in some 18 states.

1988 The Virginia General Assembly claims Brunswick stew as Virginia's own. According to its proclamation, a camp cook named Jimmy Matthews made squirrel stew one day for his master, Creed Haskins. The place: Brunswick County, Virginia. The year: 1828.

After closing many of its Colonial stores, financially troubled Grand Union sells its Virginia and North Carolina Big Star supermarkets to North Carolina's up-and-coming Harris Teeter chain.

1989 Fred Carl, Jr., begins manufacturing Viking gas ranges for home kitchens in Greenwood, Mississippi. They incorporate many features of heavy-duty professional ranges.

GRATED SWEET POTATO CAKE WITH COCONUT TOPPING

MAKES ONE 9 × 9 × 2-INCH CAKE

. . . .

Of all the sweet potato recipes to come out of the South, this one—similar to but better than carrot cake—may be the most delicious. I admit to having an insatiable sweet tooth, as do too many other Southerners.

Cake

2½ cups sifted all-purpose flour

3 teaspoons baking powder

1½ teaspoons ground cinnamon

1 teaspoon ground ginger

½ teaspoon freshly grated nutmeg

½ teaspoon salt

1 cup granulated sugar

¼ cup firmly packed light brown sugar

1 cup corn oil or vegetable oil

4 large eggs

1½ cups coarsely grated raw sweet potato
(about one 8-ounce potato)

¼ cup water

1 cup coarsely chopped pecans,
black walnuts, or wild hickory nuts

Topping

½ cup sugar

3 tablespoons cornstarch

¼ teaspoon salt

One 12-ounce can evaporated milk

1 cup sweetened grated or
flaked coconut

1½ teaspoons vanilla extract

1. Preheat the oven to 350° F. Coat a 9 × 9 × 2-inch baking pan with nonstick oil-and-flour baking spray and set aside.

2. For the cake: Sift the flour, baking powder, cinnamon, ginger, nutmeg, and salt onto a large piece of wax paper and set aside.

3. Beat the granulated sugar, brown sugar, and oil in a large electric mixer bowl for 1 minute at medium speed or until well combined. Beat the eggs in one by one. By hand, mix in the sifted dry ingredients, grated sweet potatoes, water, and pecans.

4. Scoop the batter into the pan, spreading to the corners, then slide onto the middle oven shelf and bake for 50 to 55 minutes or until the cake is springy to the touch, begins to pull from the sides of the pan, and a cake tester inserted in the middle comes out clean.

5. Remove the cake from the oven and cool right side up on a wire rack.

6. Meanwhile, prepare the topping: Whisk the sugar, cornstarch, and salt together in a medium-size heavy saucepan. Add the milk, set over moderate heat, and cook, whisking constantly, for 3 to 4 minutes or until the mixture becomes thick and shiny. Set off the heat and mix in the coconut and vanilla. Spread at once over the cake, then cool for 10 minutes or until the topping is firm.

7. To serve, cut the cake into rectangles, but make them small; the cake's unusually rich. **Note:** *Refrigerate any leftovers.*

ALABAMA TEA CAKES

Whenever I thumb through antiquarian southern cookbooks, I'm struck by the dearth of cookie recipes. The reason, I suspect, is that being so small and thin, cookies burned easily in unreliable ovens. Only with the arrival of thermostated ovens in the early twentieth century did cookies come into their own. There is, however, one old-fashioned cookie recipe that appears regularly in early cookbooks and that's the tea cake. I have tea cake recipes from nearly every southern state but my favorite is this one given to me years ago by Miz Susie Rankin, a wise and witty Alabama farm woman who lived near the town of Demopolis. Miz Susie kept the dough for this 100-year-old recipe in her refrigerator, and any time she "wanted to do something nice for a child," she'd pull out "a gob of dough" and bake some tea cakes.

I cup (2 sticks) butter, at
room temperature

2 cups sugar

I tablespoon freshly grated nutmeg

I½ teaspoons vanilla extract

¼ teaspoon salt

2 large eggs

I teaspoon baking soda dissolved in ½ cup
buttermilk

5½ cups sifted all-purpose flour

1. Cream the butter, sugar, nutmeg, vanilla, and salt in a large electric mixer bowl for 2 to 3 minutes or until light and fluffy. Beat in the eggs, then stir in the soda-buttermilk mixture. With the mixer at low speed, add the flour 1 cup at a time.

2. Divide the dough into four equal parts, flatten each into a large round disk on a sheet of heavy-duty aluminum foil, then wrap and refrigerate for several hours or until stiff enough to roll. Or, if you prefer, label, date, and freeze the dough to use later. In a 0° F. freezer, it will keep well for about 3 months.

3. When ready to proceed, preheat the oven to 375° F. Spritz several baking sheets with non-stick cooking spray and set aside.

4. Working with one fourth of the dough at a time, roll as thin as pie crust on a lightly floured surface. Using a floured 2¾- to 3-inch biscuit or cookie cutter, cut into rounds. Gather the scraps, reroll, and cut.

5. Space the tea cakes about 2 inches apart on the baking sheets and bake on the middle oven shelf for 8 to 10 minutes or until pale tan.

6. Transfer at once to wire racks to cool. Store the tea cakes in airtight canisters, layering them between sheets of wax paper.

GEORGIA PECAN BALLS

MAKES ABOUT 3 DOZEN

. . . .

Adapted from a recipe sent to me by the Georgia Pecan Commission, these cookies remind me of Mexican Wedding Cakes or what Virginia friends call "moldy mice." Why, I have no idea. Nor could they enlighten me. Not too sweet and easy to make, pecan balls are perfect for the holiday season. **Tip:** *To get a jump on things, bake them weeks ahead. Layered into airtight containers between sheets of wax paper and stored in the freezer, they'll taste oven-fresh when thawed.*

½ cup (1 stick) butter, at room temperature

2 tablespoons granulated sugar

1 teaspoon vanilla extract

¼ teaspoon salt

1 cup unsifted all-purpose flour

1 cup finely chopped pecans

One 1-pound box confectioners' (10X) sugar

1. Preheat the oven to 375° F.

2. By hand, combine the butter, granulated sugar, vanilla, and salt, beating until light. Work in the flour and pecans, taking care not to overmix.

3. Roll the dough into 1- to 1½-inch balls and space about 2 inches apart on ungreased baking sheets. **Note:** *If the dough is too soft to shape, chill well, then shape.*

4. Bake the pecan balls on the middle oven shelf for 18 to 20 minutes or until pale tan and irre-sistible smelling. Roll at once in the confectioners' sugar until nicely coated.

5. Cool the cookies before serving. Or, if desired, freeze and serve later (see Tip at left).

OLD SALEM SUGAR COOKIES

MAKES ABOUT 5 DOZEN

. . . .

Whenever I visit Old Salem, an eighteenth-century Moravian village come to life in Winston-Salem, North Carolina, I zip over to the 200-year-old Winkler Bakery and load up on thin-as-onion-skin ginger cookies and these old-fashioned sugar cookies—my all-time favorites. This recipe is my updated, downsized version of the old institutional one. **Note:** *Because the cookie dough must season overnight before it's rolled, begin this recipe the day before you bake the cookies.*

2 cups plus 2 tablespoons sifted all-purpose flour

½ teaspoon baking soda

½ teaspoon cream of tartar

½ teaspoon salt

½ teaspoon ground nutmeg

¾ cup (1½ sticks) butter, at room temperature

1¼ cups sugar

1 teaspoon vanilla extract

½ teaspoon lemon extract

¼ teaspoon almond extract

2 large eggs

I large egg yolk

1. Sift the flour, baking soda, cream of tartar, salt, and nutmeg together onto a piece of wax paper and set aside.

2. Cream the butter in a large electric mixer bowl at moderately high speed for about 1 minute until light and fluffy. Gradually beat in the sugar and continue beating until again light. With the motor running, add the vanilla, lemon and almond extracts, then the eggs and egg yolk. Sift in the combined dry ingredients and beat at low speed just enough to form a soft, sticky dough.

3. Shape the dough into a ball, flatten slightly, then wrap in aluminum foil and allow to season overnight in the refrigerator.

4. Next day when ready to proceed, preheat the oven to 325° F. Also grease several baking sheets and set aside.

5. Working with about one fourth of the dough at a time, roll on a well-floured pastry cloth with a well-floured stockinette-covered rolling pin to a thickness of ⅛ inch or about as thin as pie crust.

6. Cut into rounds with a well-floured 2¾- to 3-inch biscuit or cookie cutter and space the cookies about 2 inches apart on the cookie sheets. Or, if you prefer, cut into fancy shapes but note that you may end up with fewer cookies.

7. Bake the cookies in the lower third of the oven for 12 to 15 minutes or until lightly browned around the edge.

8. Transfer at once to wire racks and cool to room temperature. Layer the cooled cookies between sheets of wax paper in a large, airtight container and store in a cool, dry spot.

1990 New Orleans chef Susan Spicer launches her Bayona restaurant near the French Quarter and introduces dishes that are part Creole, part Cajun, but mostly global.

The Vidalia onion is named Georgia's official "state vegetable."

The $15 million World of Coca-Cola museum opens in Atlanta. Today, more than 3,000 tourists trek through each day to learn the story of Coke, or, as Mark Pendergrast, author of *For God, Country and Coca-Cola*, puts it, "the myth of Coca-Cola."

1991 The James Beard Foundation names Emeril Lagasse, chef-proprietor of Emeril's in New Orleans, "Best Chef in the Southeast."

1992 Franklin Garland finds the first black Périgord truffle on the acre he'd planted 12 years earlier with spore-inoculated filbert and oak seedlings on his farm near Hillsborough, North Carolina. It weighed more than two ounces.

The James Beard Foundation names Patrick O'Connell of the Inn at Little Washington in Washington, Virginia, Best Chef in the Mid-Atlantic and Mark Militello, chef-proprietor of Mark's Place in North Miami Beach, Best Chef in the Southeast.

BENNE SEEDS

What others call sesame seeds, Southerners call *benne*, especially those living in the Georgia–South Carolina Lowcountry.

An African staple and symbol of good luck, benne (from the Bantu for "sesame") arrived in the South in the seventeenth and eighteenth centuries along with slaves from West Africa, who were offloaded and sold in the ports of Charleston, Savannah, and New Orleans.

Many plantation owners encouraged slaves to grow their own food, generally allotting an acre to each family. Thus began the introduction of African foods to the southern table. "Above all," Karen Hess writes in Chapter One of *The Carolina Rice Kitchen: The African Connection*, (1992), "[slaves] grew greens, but presumably they also raised such African favorites as okra, sorghum, black-eye peas, eggplant, and benne seed . . ."

Africa, culinary historian Alan Davidson believes, is where benne seeds originated. "Wild species, with one exception, are African," he writes in *The Oxford Companion to Food*, "but there is a 'second source of diversity' in India, where sesame was introduced in very early times."

The Greek classicists were writing of sesame oils as early as the fifth century BC and an even older Egyptian clay tablet lists it in the inventory of King Nebuchadnezzar's palace.

The Lowcountry sultriness proved perfect for growing benne, an annual plant sometimes as tall as six feet. It flowers, then bears pods of a hundred seeds or more. When ripe, these split at the gentlest touch, showering seeds in every direction—a fact not lost on Scheherazade, who, in spinning tales for *One Thousand and One Nights*, gave Ali Baba the magical command "Open, Sesame" to enter the den of the Forty Thieves.

In the Lowcountry today, benne are more popular than ever. In addition to the ever-popular benne wafers and cookies, fudges and brittles, innovative young chefs are frying benne-crusted shrimp and chicken, heightening the flavor of greens with toasted sesame oil, and updating such African originals as benne soups, breads, and pilaus. Delicious!

BENNE WAFERS

MAKES ABOUT 6 DOZEN

I've always been partial to benne wafers, an easy drop cookie with a delicate caramel flavor.
Note: *To toast sesame seeds, spread in an ungreased pie pan and set on the middle shelf of a 275° F. oven for 8 to 10 minutes, stirring once or twice. Watch closely; benne burn easily.*

½ cup (1 stick) butter, at room temperature

½ cup granulated sugar

½ cup firmly packed light brown sugar

1½ teaspoons vanilla extract

1 large egg

1 cup sifted all-purpose flour

¼ teaspoon salt

½ cup lightly toasted sesame seeds
(see Note at left)

1. Preheat the oven to 350° F. Spritz two or three baking sheets with nonstick cooking spray and set aside.

2. Cream the butter, two sugars, and vanilla in a large electric mixer bowl at moderately high speed for 1 to 2 minutes or until light. With the mixer at low speed, beat in the egg, then the flour and salt. Fold in the sesame seeds.

3. Drop the dough from rounded ½ teaspoons onto baking sheets, spacing the cookies about 3 inches apart (they spread considerably as they bake).

4. Bake on the middle oven shelf for 10 to 12 minutes or until irresistible smelling and the color of caramel.

5. Remove the cookies from the oven, let stand on the baking sheets for about a minute, then transfer to wire racks to cool.

6. To store, layer the cookies between sheets of wax paper in airtight tins.

❈

"Oh, my," she exclaims, her breath smoking the windowpane. "It's fruitcake weather!"

—TRUMAN CAPOTE,
A CHRISTMAS MEMORY

❈

1993 The James Beard Foundation names Marcel Desaulniers, chef-proprietor of the Trellis restaurant in Williamsburg, Virginia, Best Chef in the Mid-Atlantic and Susan Spicer, chef-proprietor of Bayona in New Orleans, Best Chef in the Southeast.

The Atlanta Bread Company Bakery Café takes off in suburban Atlanta. Its artisanal breads—sourdough, focaccia, pumpernickel, and such—are baked fresh every day.

1994 Pillsbury buys Martha White, the 95-year-old Nashville miller known for its soft white flours—the Southerner's preference.

The James Beard Foundation names Allen Susser, chef/proprietor of Chef Allen's in Aventura, Florida, Best Chef in the Southeast.

The E. J. Brach Corporation buys Tennessee's Brock Candy Company and phases out the production of hard candies at Brock's Chattanooga plant to concentrate on fruit snacks.

TENNESSEE WHISKEY BALLS

MAKES ABOUT 5 DOZEN

. . . .

Bourbon balls are well known throughout the South and routinely show up at holiday open houses during Christmas and New Year's. These whiskey balls, however, are mellower because they are made with Jack Daniel's, a supremely smooth sour mash "sipping whiskey" that's been made in the town of Lynchburg, Tennessee, for nearly 150 years. The Jack Daniel Distillery, the first to be registered in America, is a National Historic Site that can be toured. **Note:** *To toast pecans, spread halves or large pieces on an ungreased baking sheet and set in a 325° F. oven for 10 to 12 minutes. Cool the nuts, then pulse in a food processor until as fine as cornmeal.*

3½ cups fine vanilla wafer or graham cracker crumbs

2 cups finely ground lightly toasted pecans (see Note above)

2 cups unsifted confectioners' (10 X) sugar

½ cup unsweetened cocoa powder

¼ teaspoon freshly grated nutmeg

⅓ cup light corn syrup

½ cup Jack Daniel's Tennessee Whiskey

1 cup sifted confectioners' (10 X) sugar (for dredging)

1. Knead the vanilla wafer crumbs, pecans, 2 cups unsifted confectioners' sugar, the cocoa, nutmeg, corn syrup, and whiskey in a large mixing bowl until well blended.

2. Shape into 1-inch balls, then roll in the 1 cup sifted confectioners' sugar until snowy.

3. Place the whiskey balls in airtight containers, separating the layers with wax paper. Cover and allow to season for about a week before serving.

PECAN PRALINES

MAKES ABOUT 20

. . . .

I've spent a fair amount of time poking about the Cajun Country west of New Orleans and what fascinates me there, almost as much as the crawfish farms, are the pecan orchards and sugarcane fields. Small wonder pecan pralines are a Louisiana classic. There may be as many recipes for them as there are cooks. Some like to begin by boiling pure cane syrup down until it is as dark as molasses. Others prefer brown or granulated sugar. And still others favor buttermilk over sweet milk. I've tried many different praline recipes and keep returning to this one given to me nearly twenty-five years ago by a wonderful Cajun cook named Miss Tootie Guirard of St. Martin Parish. **Tip:** *Choose a dry sunny day for making pralines. They won't firm up in rainy or humid weather.*

3 cups sugar

1½ cups milk

¼ teaspoon salt

2 tablespoons butter

2 cups coarsely chopped pecans

1. Cut 20 four-inch squares of heavy-duty aluminum foil, place dull side up, butter each well, then arrange—not touching—on baking sheets. Set aside.

2. Mix the sugar, milk, and salt well in a large, deep, very heavy pan, then drop in the butter. Insert a candy thermometer, set over moderately low heat, and bring to a boil without stirring.

3. Reduce the heat slightly and continue cooking without stirring until the candy reaches the soft ball stage—238° F. on a candy thermometer. This may take as long as an hour. If you try to rush things, your pralines will be gritty.

4. The instant the candy thermometer reaches 238° F., set the pan off the heat and stir in the pecans. Beat hard with a wooden spoon for 30 seconds, then pour the candy onto the buttered foil squares, making each praline about 3 inches across. You'll have to work fast because the candy hardens quickly.

5. Let the pralines cool for an hour, then peel off the foil and arrange in a single layer on a large platter. Or layer between sheets of wax paper in an airtight canister and store in a cool, dry spot.

❈

"Young lady, I carried you some Bigbee pecans. I thought you might not harvest their like around here."

—EUDORA WELTY,
THE OPTIMIST'S DAUGHTER

❈

FRIDAY PEANUT BRITTLE

MAKES ABOUT 1¾ POUNDS

. . . .

This recipe comes from Dr. William C. Friday, who for thirty years was president of the University of North Carolina and with whom my father worked for at least ten as first vice president. I never knew that Bill was a peanut brittle aficionado until a few years ago when I appeared on *North Carolina People*, his public television show (UNC-TV). We spent half an hour cooking recipes from my recently published *American Century Cookbook*, and afterward, Bill inquired if I'd like to see how he made peanut brittle. Of course! When I asked how he'd become famous for his peanut brittle, he said that the *Chapel Hill News* had done a Christmas story some ten years earlier on the edible gifts he and his wife make each year: Ida's fruitcake (see page 328) and his brittle.

Like the fruitcake, the brittle is an old recipe from Ida's family in Orangeburg, South Carolina. Bill and Ida are most specific about how their brittle should be made. "Only use a cast-iron frying pan," they instruct (my 12-incher is perfect because it's three inches deep and that's important). The Fridays also insist that you use a large marble slab—at least 20 inches by 30—when pouring out the brittle. And that you butter it well. "I just smear the butter around with my hand," Bill says. At the end of his neatly typed recipe, Bill included the name of his peanut supplier "because you've got to use the right kind of peanuts." He lists the A & B Milling Company of Enfield, North Carolina (aka Aunt Ruby's Peanuts; see Sources, page 401), which sells the large, pale-skinned Virginias, and that's what I ordered. Shelled, *blanched* peanuts arrived a day later; the Fridays prefer the *unblanched* because they make the brittle more flavorful. All I can say is that except for using blanched peanuts, I followed the Fridays' recipe to the letter and within 15 minutes had poured out the best peanut brittle I've ever eaten. Unlike most, theirs is more peanut than brittle.

1½ cups sugar

½ cup light corn syrup

¼ cup hot water

2¾ cups shelled unblanched (or blanched) raw peanuts (see headnote)

1¼ teaspoons baking soda

1. Butter a large marble slab well and set aside (see headnote).
2. Combine the sugar, corn syrup, and hot water in a well-seasoned deep 12-inch cast-iron frying pan, stirring until absolutely smooth.
3. Set over high heat and as soon as the mixture boils, mix in the peanuts. Cook, stirring constantly over high heat, for 7 to 8 minutes or until the nuts are chocolaty brown and the syrup is the color of caramel. **Note:** *The Fridays do not use a candy thermometer; indeed it's virtually impossible to do so, but I did take the temperature of the hot brittle mixture after 8 minutes and it was 295° F.*
4. Remove the frying pan from the heat, sprinkle the baking soda evenly over the hot brittle, and stir vigorously; the mixture will foam.

5. Pour the brittle onto the buttered marble slab and spread to a thickness of ½ inch. Let it cool for a minute or two, then loosen the brittle gently with a pancake turner so that it doesn't stick to the marble as it cools.
6. Cool the brittle to room temperature, then break into chunks. Store in an airtight container.

PULLED MINTS

MAKES ABOUT 5 DOZEN

. . . .

I'll never forget learning to make pulled mints in the kitchen of Mrs. Pegram Bryant one wintry night too many years ago to count. Mrs. B, as I called her, was a well-off, well-connected resident of Statesville, North Carolina. Nearly seventy when I met her, she had a full-time maid and yard man, both of whom lived at the back of her property. She also had a two-room garage apartment, which she allowed me to rent after an intense grilling. "Now who was your mother?" Mrs. B had begun. It was the southern way to trace bloodlines. "You wouldn't know her," I replied. "We were on the other side." I had meant in the Civil War but Mrs. B, an active member of the Colonial Dames, sputtered, "You mean that your people were Red Coats?" (In fact, some of them were.) After a walking-on-eggs start, Mrs. B and I became best of friends. I adored her outspokenness. And I loved hearing her reminisce about her youth, about the cotillions and teas and the "dainties" served there. Like other society matrons, Mrs. B rarely cooked. Her files bulged with old family receipts, however, and she had taught her maid,

Dorothy, how to prepare them. Once a year Mrs. B donned an apron and began her December ritual of making pulled mints for family and friends. Soon I was pulling the blistering taffylike strands, too, and relishing every minute. I wanted to taste the mints as soon as they cooled, but Mrs. B said, "No. We have to wait for them to cream up." That bit of magic took about a week in a tightly covered container. When I left Statesville, Mrs. B pressed the pulled mints recipe into my hand. It was, she told me, an old Allison family recipe. Mrs. B had been born an Allison and she'd been making those mints since her cotillion days. **Note:** *Choose a sunny day for making pulled mints; they won't cook up or cream up in rainy or humid weather. Dry weather is key.*

¾ **cup water**

4 **tablespoons (½ stick) butter**

2 **teaspoons cider vinegar**

2 **cups sugar**

1 **teaspoon peppermint extract**

¼ **teaspoon vanilla extract**

1 **drop yellow food coloring**

3 **drops green food coloring**

1. Place the water, butter, and vinegar in a large, heavy saucepan and insert a candy thermometer. Set over low heat and as soon as the butter melts, mix in the sugar. Heat slowly without stirring until the mixture reaches 267° F. This may take as long as 35 or 40 minutes. Meanwhile, generously butter a large baking sheet and set aside.

2. Set the candy off the heat and add the peppermint and vanilla extracts and the yellow and green food coloring. Do not stir.

3. Pour the hot candy onto the buttered baking sheet and cool until you can make a thumbprint in the surface. With lightly buttered hands, gather the candy into a ball and knead in the flavorings, food coloring, and melted butter; it won't have combined with the candy.

4. When the candy is stiff enough to pull, stretch into thin strands, then reshape into a ball. Continue pulling, twisting, and reshaping until the candy takes on a silvery sheen and becomes too stiff to pull.

5. Quickly stretch and twist into a rope about 1 inch in diameter, then, with buttered kitchen shears, snip crosswise at ½-inch intervals.

6. Wrap each mint in wax paper, place in an airtight canister, and allow to "season" for about a week. Taffy-stiff when they go into the canister, the mints will emerge at week's end as soft as butter creams.

❧

. . . three times a day she spread that enormous table with solid food, freshly baked bread, huge platters of vegetables, immoderate roasts of meat, extravagant tarts, strudels, pies— enough for twenty people.

—KATHERINE ANNE PORTER, *HOLIDAY*

❧

SUGARED AND SPICED PECANS

MAKES 6½ TO 7 CUPS

With pecans being one of the South's principal crops, southern cooks not only know dozens of ways to prepare them but also continue to dream up new recipes. Spiced pecans, as far as I know, belong to the latter half of the twentieth century, as do their countless variations. This particular recipe is my own. Serve as a snack, add to a tea table, or pass at the end of an elegant dinner. Some people like to serve spiced pecans with cocktails but I frankly find them too sweet to pair with drinks.

4 cups pecan halves

2 large egg whites, beaten until frothy with
3 tablespoons cold water

1½ cups sugar

2 teaspoons ground cinnamon

1 teaspoon ground ginger

1 teaspoon salt

½ teaspoon ground nutmeg

½ teaspoon black pepper

1. Preheat the oven to 250° F. Spritz a large rimmed baking sheet with nonstick cooking spray or, if you prefer, use a nonstick baking sheet. Set the pan aside.

2. Dip the pecans, about half of the total amount at a time, in the beaten egg whites, then place in a large sieve to drain. Meanwhile, combine all remaining ingredients and divide between two large plastic zipper bags.

3. Shake the pecans briskly in the sieve to drain off the excess beaten egg whites, then place half of them in each of the zipper bags of spiced sugar, seal, and shake well to coat.

4. Spread the pecans on the baking sheet and bake on the middle oven shelf for 15 minutes. Stir well and again spread the pecans on the baking sheet.

5. Reduce the oven temperature to 200° F. and bake the pecans 2 hours longer or until glistening and richly browned, stirring and spreading every half hour or so.

6. Remove the pecans from the oven, break apart, spread on a clean baking sheet, and let stand at room temperature for at least an hour or until crisp and dry. **Note:** *Stored in an airtight container, these spiced pecans will keep "fresh" for several weeks.*

❀

Four states claim pecan pie for their own—
Alabama, Tennessee, Mississippi,
and Georgia. I have eaten this incarnate
richness in each . . . my choice goes
to the Georgia pie.

—CLEMENTINE PADDLEFORD,
HOW AMERICA EATS

❀

Pickles and Preserves

Right up until World War Two (perhaps I should say until war's end), many southern cookbooks devoted almost as many pages to food preservation as they did to food preparation. Occasionally even more. There's good reason for this.

The South is hot six to eight months out of twelve (year-round in South Florida); therefore, conserving food safely was every cook's preoccupation before home freezers revolutionized their lives. So was "putting food by" for the family to enjoy in fallow winter months. Because the South was largely agricultural, food was "home-grown." And that meant meat and dairy as well as fruits and vegetables.

I find the scope of food conservation in *The Receipt Book of Harriott Pinckney Horry, 1770,* breathtaking. This South Carolina plantation matron teaches not only how "to keep tomatoes for winter use" but also how to extend the shelf life of butter as much as a month by adding a finely pounded blend of salt, sugar, and saltpeter: one ounce per pound of butter. There are also directions on how "to preserve small green oranges" and "dry peaches" plus something I've never heard of: "To Mango Muskmellons or Cucumbers"—basically brining and pickling with garlic, horseradish, ginger, and mustard seeds.

I'm not so sure about the "mango-ing," but Horry's walnut "catchup" and mushroom "catchup" are recipes I'd like to try. The second comes from her mother, Eliza Lucas Pinckney, as does this recipe for Mushroom Powder:

Take 4 lb. Mushrooms that have been squeez'd and dry them with a little spice [possibly allspice, nutmeg or mace, and black pepper] in the Sun or Oven, and Powder them for Made Dishes.

Note: *For more on this influential mother and daughter, see box, page 374.*

Mary Randolph (*The Virginia Housewife,* 1824) tells her readers how to cure bacon, beef, and herring. She also offers a recipe for oyster "catsup," which, she says, ". . . gives a fine flavour to white sauces, and if a glass of brandy be added, it will keep good for considerable time."

Randolph doesn't neglect the more conventional pickles, jams, and brandied fruits, nor do Lettice Bryan (*The Kentucky Housewife,* 1839) and Sarah Rutledge (*The Carolina Housewife,* 1847). All three show how to make a variety of "spirits," and Bryan, under "Domestic Liquors," shares such quaint recipes as rose brandy, raspberry cordial, and gooseberry wine.

In my few years with the North Carolina Agricultural Extension Service, my first job was to teach 4-H Club girls how to can what they had grown—usually tomatoes, cucumbers, butter beans, yellow squash, peaches, and apples. To be honest, they knew more than I.

Later, as the extension's woman's editor in the Raleigh office, I coauthored (with food preservation specialist Rose Ellwood Bryan) step-by-step pamphlets on the correct way to make jams, jellies, and so forth. I even doubled for Rose Ellwood on

UNC-TV demonstrating how to can peaches—LIVE for one solid hour with no breaks or commercials. Unfortunately, I became so rattled that I canned the pits instead of the peaches, then got the silly giggles. That ended any dreams of a television career.

Every summer when I was little, my mother flew into an orgy of watermelon-rind pickling using a recipe supplied by a southern friend (you'll find that recipe on page 378). And during World War Two, she faithfully preserved much of what my father grew in our Victory Garden: strawberries and tomatoes, for sure, but also asparagus, corn cut from the cob, and an end-of-summer soup made of garden gleanings. The jiggling gauge on the lid of Mother's big pressure canner scared me to bits because I'd heard tales of nasty explosions.

Canning and pickling fell from favor after the war, but once again, thanks to the recent proliferation of farmer's markets and the dewy produce they sell, Southerners are trying their hands at what their grandmothers had done almost on autopilot. Today's plunge into pickling and preserving, however, has little to do with necessity as it did in grandmother's day. It's mainly for fun. Or maybe to take the blue ribbon at the state fair.

Fortunately, twenty-first-century picklers and preservers can use food processors to speed the slicing, dicing, chopping, and puréeing—no matter how old the recipe. That's something those eighteenth- and nineteenth-century food conservationists would surely have welcomed.

JERUSALEM ARTICHOKE PICKLE RELISH

MAKES ABOUT 6 HALF-PINTS

When I worked as an assistant home demonstration agent in Iredell County, North Carolina, I loved to prowl the countryside and ferret out the local food specialties. Early on I discovered Dixie Dames, a small shop just outside Statesville that sold heavenly homemade pickles and relishes. If memory serves, there were two Dixie Dames (elderly sisters) and the things they sold were made from handed-down family recipes. There were Plantation Circles (watermelon rind pickles the color of celadon) and bread and butter pickles, but my own favorite was the Jerusalem Artichoke Pickle Relish. Jerusalem artichokes, which run wild all over North Carolina, are a type of sunflower in no way related to the prickly green globe artichokes. The Jerusalem part of their name is said to be a corruption of *girasole*, the Italian word for sunflower. These artichokes are faun-skinned, knobby tubers, supremely crisp, nut-sweet, and low in calories because their starch (inulin) is a form that the body cannot metabolize. Today they're sold as sunchokes and nearly every green market sells them in season (fall and winter). The recipe that follows is my attempt to reproduce that wonderful Dixie Dames Jerusalem Artichoke Pickle Relish of my youth.

2 to 2½ pounds Jerusalem artichokes, skins scraped off and the tubers coarsely chopped (you will need exactly 1 quart of prepared artichokes)

1 pint coarsely chopped cored and seeded red bell peppers (about 4 large peppers)

1 pint coarsely chopped yellow onions (about 3 large onions)

1 gallon cold water mixed with 1 cup pickling salt (brine)

1⅓ cups sugar

2½ cups cider vinegar

1½ tablespoons mustard seeds

1 tablespoon ground turmeric

1. Place the artichokes, peppers, onions, and brine in a large nonreactive kettle, cover, and soak at room temperature for 3 hours. Drain in a cheesecloth-lined colander, then bundle in cheesecloth and squeeze as dry as possible. Return to the kettle, discarding the cheesecloth.

2. Wash and rinse 6 half-pint preserving jars and their closures and submerge in a large kettle of boiling water.

3. Bring the sugar, vinegar, mustard seeds, and turmeric to a full rolling boil in a large nonreactive saucepan, then boil uncovered for 1 minute. Pour over the relish and mix well.

4. Lift the preserving jars from the boiling water one by one and pack with relish, leaving ¼ inch head space at the top. **Tip:** *To avoid spills, use a wide-mouth canning funnel.* Run a thin-blade spatula around the inside of the jar to release air bubbles; wipe the jar rim with a clean, damp cloth, then screw on the closure.

5. Process the jars for 10 minutes in a boiling water bath (212° F.). Lift from the water bath; complete the seals, if necessary, by tightening the lids, then cool to room temperature.

6. Date and label each jar, then store on a cool, dark shelf several weeks before opening.

MOUNT OLIVE PICKLES

The farmers around Mount Olive, North Carolina, found themselves in something of a pickle in 1926.

That year had been a very good one for cucumbers in the small town some sixty miles southeast of Raleigh—perhaps a bit too good. There was a glut of cucumbers on the market. What to do?

The town's Chamber of Commerce decided to go into the pickle business. A company was formed that grew, vat by vat, and eventually transformed Mount Olive into "The Pickle Capital of the South."

Today the company buys 120 million pounds of choice cucumbers and peppers from nine states as well as Mexico and India. Walk into any supermarket in the South today and you'll see arrays of Mount Olive pickles, peppers, and relishes.

The company also conducts an annual "pickle drop," an idea stemming from the reputed skills of American bombardiers during World War Two. They were so accurate, it was said, that they could drop a bomb into a pickle barrel.

This inspired Pickle Packers International in Chicago to invite people to drop pickles from a skyscraper into a barrel on the sidewalk—the winner getting a year's supply of pickles.

In 1999, the Mount Olive company, describing itself as "The Pickle and Pepper of the Millennium," decided to stage its own version of a pickle drop every New Year's Eve.

Over the years the festivities have grown and hundreds attend. A marquee mimics the Times Square event, a band plays the Pickle Polka, and the crowd sings "Auld Lang Syne" while a lighted, three-foot-long plastic pickle is dropped from a flagpole into a redwood vat at the appropriate time.

The appropriate time happens to be seven p.m., which is midnight Greenwich Mean Time. And where does all this take place? At the corner of Cucumber and Vine.

On a hot day in Virginia, I know nothing more comforting than a fine spiced pickle, brought up trout-like from the sparkling depths of the aromatic jar below the stairs of Aunt Sally's cellar.

—THOMAS JEFFERSON

CUCUMBER STICK PICKLES

MAKES ABOUT 6 PINTS

Some years ago when I was sleuthing out some of the South's best home cooks, I was told to look up Mrs. Ivan Dishman of Sugar Grove, North Carolina; that's up in the Blue Ridge not far from Boone. Better known as "Miz Nannie Grace," she was famous for her pickles and relishes and was kind enough to share several old family recipes with me. For these pickles she said she "just grabbed cucumbers out of the garden as they matured." The ones to use are the little Kirbies or pickling cucumbers, which are rarely waxed. For Mrs. Dishman's special relish, see Blue Ridge Sweet Red Pepper Relish (page 368).

22 Kirby cucumbers, each about 5 inches long (approximately 5 pounds)

3 quarts boiling water

1 quart cider vinegar

3 cups sugar

3 tablespoons pickling salt

2 teaspoons celery seeds

1 teaspoon ground turmeric

¾ teaspoon mustard seeds

1. Scrub the cucumbers well in cold water, then trim, cut into 4½-inch lengths, and quarter each piece lengthwise.
2. Place the cucumber sticks in a large, heavy kettle; add the boiling water, cover, and let stand for 4 to 5 hours.
3. When ready to proceed, wash and rinse 6 one-pint preserving jars and their closures and submerge in a large kettle of boiling water.
4. Combine the vinegar, sugar, salt, celery seeds, turmeric, and mustard seeds in a small, heavy nonreactive saucepan; bring to a boil over moderate heat then reduce the heat to low and simmer uncovered for 5 minutes.
5. Meanwhile, lift the preserving jars from the boiling water one by one and pack with the cucumber sticks, standing them on end and wedging as tightly as possible. **Note:** *For prettier jars, Mrs. Dishman rings the most attractive*

1995 Georgia pecan growers establish the Georgia Pecan Commission to promote year-round sales.

The James Beard Foundation names Elizabeth Terry, chef-proprietor of Elizabeth on 37th Street in Savannah, Georgia, Best Chef in the Southeast.

The North Carolina Pork Producers Association begins holding its annual Championship Pork Cook-Off at the Lexington Barbecue Festival. With a population just shy of 20,000, Lexington can boast more than 20 barbecue restaurants.

1996 Krispy Kreme comes to the Big Apple, opening its first doughnut shop on West 23rd Street in the city's trendy Chelsea district.

Lance Toastchee® crackers soar into space aboard the *Columbia* shuttle.

1997 Lance snack foods go global, reaching markets across the Caribbean, England, Western Europe, and China.

The James Beard Foundation names Norman Van Aken, chef-proprietor of Norman's in Coral Gables, Florida, Best Chef in the Southeast.

The Atlanta Bread Company Bakery Café, opened only four years earlier, is so successful there are now more than 160 of them operating in 24 states.

cucumber sticks around the outside, then fills the center with less-than-perfect pieces.

6. Ladle the boiling vinegar mixture into each jar, covering the cucumber sticks completely but leaving ¼ inch head space at the top. Run a thin-blade spatula around the inside of the jar to release trapped air bubbles; wipe the jar rim with a clean, damp cloth, then screw on the closure.

7. Process the jars for 10 minutes in a boiling water bath (212° F.). Lift from the water bath; complete the seals, if necessary, by tightening the lids, then cool to room temperature.

8. Date and label each jar, then store on a cool, dark shelf several weeks before opening.

Variation

Potato Salad Pickles: The only difference here is that Mrs. Dishman cuts the raw cucumber sticks into ¾-inch chunks and adds ¾ teaspoon black peppercorns to the boiling vinegar mixture. It's important that you pack the cucumber chunks into the jars as tightly as possible, otherwise they will float when the vinegar mixture is added. Process as directed above, then store in a cool, dark spot for several weeks before opening. How do you use potato salad pickles? Add them to your favorite potato salad, tasting as you go so that the amount is exactly right.

❊

The greatest service which can be rendered by any country is to add a useful plant to its culture.

—THOMAS JEFFERSON

❊

SWEET YELLOW SQUASH PICKLES

MAKES 6 TO 8 PINTS

A taste of these squash pickles whirls me back to my growing-up years in Raleigh, North Carolina. Knowing how I doted upon them, my mother would buy a pint or two whenever she spotted them at the farmer's market or some local church bazaar. When I was twelve, I tried to "crack" the recipe and made a batch of squash pickles myself. They weren't half bad, but I've perfected the recipe over the years. **Note:** *For best results, use small straight-neck squash; they slice more neatly than crooknecks. Four of them weigh about a pound.*

3 to 3½ pounds tender young straight-neck yellow squash, trimmed, scrubbed, and sliced ¼ inch thick (you will need 12 cups sliced squash)

4 to 4½ pounds silverskin onions, peeled and thinly sliced (you'll need 12 cups sliced onions)

½ cup pickling salt

6 cups (1½ quarts) crushed ice

3½ cups sugar

2 cups (1 pint) white (distilled) vinegar

2 cups (1 pint) cider vinegar

2 teaspoons mustard seeds

1¾ teaspoons celery seeds

1¾ teaspoons ground turmeric

1. Layer the sliced squash and onions in a very large nonreactive bowl, sprinkling each layer

with salt. Pile the ice on top, set the bowl in the sink, and let stand for 3 hours.

2. Drain the squash and onions, transfer to a very large colander, and rinse under the cold tap. Drain well, then, using the bowl of a ladle, press out as much liquid as possible.

3. Wash and rinse 8 one-pint preserving jars and their closures and submerge in a large kettle of boiling water.

4. Bring the sugar, white and cider vinegars, mustard and celery seeds, and turmeric to a rolling boil in a large nonreactive kettle. Add the squash and onions and, stirring gently, return to the boil.

5. Lift the preserving jars from the boiling water one by one. Pack with pickles, making sure they are submerged in the pickling liquid and leaving 1/4 inch head space at the top of the jar. **Tip:** *To avoid spills, use a wide-mouth canning funnel.* Run a thin-blade spatula around the inside of the jar to release air bubbles; wipe the jar rim with a clean, damp cloth, then screw on the closure. Repeat until all jars are filled.

6. Process the jars for 10 minutes in a boiling water bath (212° F.). Lift from the water bath; complete the seals, if necessary, by tightening the lids, then cool to room temperature.

7. Date and label each jar, then store on a cool, dark shelf several weeks before opening.

GREEN TOMATO PICKLES

MAKES 6 TO 8 PINTS

Next to watermelon rind pickles, these are probably the South's favorite because they go with almost everything: fried chicken or fish; roast pork, turkey, or chicken; or ham or chicken salad. **To make their pickles crisp, Southerners use pickling lime (see About Pickling Lime, page 366). Note:** *For best results, use tomatoes about the size of golf balls.*

I gallon small, hard green tomatoes
(about 5 pounds), cored and sliced
1/4 inch thick but not peeled

2 gallons (8 quarts) cold water, mixed with
1 1/2 cups food-grade pickling lime
(lime water; see headnote)

5 pounds sugar

4 cups (1 quart) white (distilled) vinegar

4 cups (1 quart) cider vinegar

1 teaspoon black peppercorns

1 teaspoon whole allspice

1/2 teaspoon whole cloves

1/2 teaspoon blade mace

1 cinnamon stick, broken in several places

1. Soak the tomatoes in the lime water in a large nonreactive kettle for 24 hours. Drain well, cover with cold water, and soak 4 hours longer, changing the water every hour. Drain the tomatoes, then rinse well in several changes of cold water. Also wash and rinse the kettle well.

2. Return the drained tomatoes to the kettle and add the sugar and two vinegars. Tie all the spices in cheesecloth and drop into the kettle. Bring to a boil over moderately low heat, then set off the heat, cover, and let stand 24 hours.

3. Next day, set the kettle over moderately low heat and bring the tomatoes and pickling liquid to a boil. Adjust the heat so that the mixture barely

bubbles and simmer uncovered for 45 minutes to 1 hour, stirring occasionally, or until the pickles are translucent. Discard the spice bag.

4. Meanwhile, wash and rinse 8 one-pint preserving jars and their closures and submerge in a large kettle of boiling water.

5. Lift the preserving jars from the boiling water one by one. Pack with tomatoes, making sure they are covered with the pickling liquid and leaving ¼ inch head space at the top of the jar.

Run a thin-blade spatula around the inside of the jar to release air bubbles; wipe the jar rim with a clean, damp cloth, then screw on the closure. Repeat until all the jars are filled.

6. Process the jars for 15 minutes in a boiling water bath (212° F.). Lift from the water bath; complete the seals, if necessary, by tightening the lids, then cool to room temperature.

7. Date and label each jar, then store on a cool, dark shelf several weeks before opening.

ABOUT PICKLING LIME (CALCIUM HYDROXIDE)

To crisp green tomato pickles and other favorites, southern cooks have always used pickling lime (also called slaked lime, hydrated lime, or lime hydrate). Although its safety has been questioned of late, two food safety specialists with the North Carolina Cooperative Extension Service in Raleigh (Angela M. Fraser, Ph.D., and Carolyn J. Lackey, Ph.D.) believe that food-grade pickling lime is safe if you follow their recently published guidelines.

Be sure to use lime as a soak solution only and to rinse product [food being pickled] in several changes of water before proceeding with recipe. Do not use lime purchased from lumber supply stores for food use.

To eliminate excess lime, the U.S. Department of Agriculture suggests resoaking "limed" food three times in fresh water, allowing one hour for each soak, then rinsing well afterward.

To these caveats, I'd add another: Avoid inhaling pickling lime dust.

Food-grade pickling lime can be bought at some pharmacies and at housewares stores that sell canning supplies. (Also see Sources, page 401.)

If you're still skeptical about the safety of pickling lime, substitute Ball's new Pickle Crisp (calcium chloride), using as directed. You can also crisp pickles by layering them with grape leaves (preferably scuppernong leaves) overnight in a large nonreactive kettle. The bitter tannin in grape leaves inhibits the enzymatic action that softens fruits and vegetables. Before proceeding with your recipe, remove the grape leaves and rinse the food to be pickled.

A Love Affair with Southern Cooking

FARMER'S MARKET CORN RELISH

MAKES 8 TO 10 PINTS

. . . .

This recipe was given to my mother long ago by the woman at the Raleigh farmer's market from whom she bought corn. I don't remember Mother making the relish; indeed her hand-written, card-file recipe for it is pristine. I, on the other hand, often put up a batch of relish during the all-too-short sweet-corn season. It's delicious with baked ham or roast pork, turkey, or chicken. I've even tossed it into salads, casseroles, and corn breads. **Note:** *Cut the kernels from the cob carefully and cleanly; you don't want the corn's "milk" to cloud the relish.*

16 medium ears just-picked
yellow sweet corn, shucked and
stripped of silks

4 cups (1 quart) finely diced celery
(about 1 large bunch)

2 cups (1 pint) finely diced, cored, and
seeded green bell peppers
(about 3 large)

2 cups (1 pint) finely diced, cored, and
seeded red bell peppers
(about 3 large)

1 cup moderately coarsely chopped
yellow onion
(about 1 large)

4 cups (1 quart) cider vinegar

1 cup sugar

2 tablespoons pickling salt or
coarse salt

2 teaspoons celery seeds

¼ cup unsifted all-purpose flour

2 tablespoons dry mustard

1 teaspoon ground turmeric

¼ teaspoon ground hot
red pepper (cayenne)

⅓ cup cold water

1. Boil the ears of corn uncovered in a large, heavy kettle of unsalted water for 10 minutes; drain and quick-chill in ice water. Drain well again and cut the kernels from the cobs. **Tip:** *Holding an ear at a slight angle to a cutting board, I cut straight down, freeing about 3 rows of kernels at a time. Do not scrape the cobs.* Measure out and reserve 8 cups (2 quarts) of the corn kernels (save any extra for chowder or corn bread).

2. Wash and rinse 10 one-pint preserving jars and their closures and submerge in a large kettle of boiling water.

3. Place the celery, green and red bell peppers, onion, vinegar, sugar, salt, and celery seeds in a very large nonreactive kettle. Set over high heat and bring quickly to a boil. Adjust the heat so the mixture bubbles gently and simmer uncovered for 5 minutes.

4. Meanwhile, blend the flour, mustard, turmeric, cayenne, and water in a small bowl to form a smooth paste. Whisk in a little of the hot relish liquid, then stir back into the kettle. Cook, stirring constantly, for about 3 minutes or until slightly thickened.

5. Add the 8 cups corn kernels, cover, and boil for 5 minutes, stirring occasionally.

6. Lift the preserving jars from the boiling water one by one. Ladle in the hot relish, leaving ¼ inch head space at the top of the jar. Run a thin-blade spatula around the inside of the jar to release trapped air bubbles; wipe the jar rim with a clean, damp cloth, then screw on the closure. Repeat until all jars are filled. **Tip:** *To avoid spilling or dribbling relish down the sides of the jars as you fill them, use a wide-mouth canning funnel.*

7. Process the jars for 15 minutes in a boiling water bath (212° F.). Lift from the water bath; complete the seals, if needed, by tightening the lids and cool to room temperature.

8. Date and label each jar, then store on a cool, dark shelf several weeks before opening.

BLUE RIDGE SWEET RED PEPPER RELISH

MAKES 10 TO 11 PINTS

. . . .

"My mother used to make this relish and her mother made it, too," Miz Nannie Grace Dishman of Sugar Grove, North Carolina, told me years ago when I interviewed her for a *Family Circle* article. "It's still the family favorite," she added. "We eat it on hot dogs and hamburgers but it's real good, too, on pinto beans and green beans." For years, Mrs. Dishman and her daughter Brenda put up hundreds of quarts of pickles and relishes, fruits, and vegetables, nearly all of them homegrown.

Mrs. Dishman always chopped the vegetables "real fine" for her pepper relish. "But," she continued, "if you like prettier jars, cut them right coarse."

12 large red bell peppers, cored, seeded, and moderately coarsely chopped (about 4½ pounds)

12 very small yellow onions, moderately coarsely chopped (about 2 pounds)

12 small Golden Delicious apples, cored, peeled, and moderately coarsely chopped (about 4 pounds)

3 quarts boiling water (about)

2½ cups cider vinegar

2½ cups cold water

2½ cups sugar

4 teaspoons pickling salt

1. Place the peppers, onions, and apples in a very large nonreactive kettle, add just enough of the boiling water to cover them, and let stand uncovered at room temperature for 10 minutes.

2. Meanwhile, wash and rinse 11 one-pint preserving jars and their closures and submerge in a large kettle of boiling water.

3. Combine the vinegar, cold water, sugar, and salt in a medium-size nonreactive kettle and bring to a boil over moderate heat. Reduce the heat to low, stir until the sugar dissolves completely, then simmer uncovered for 5 minutes.

4. Drain the vegetable mixture well and return to the same kettle. Pour in the hot vinegar mixture, set over moderate heat, and bring to a full rolling boil. Set off the heat.

5. Lift the preserving jars from the boiling water one by one. Ladle in the hot relish, leaving ¼ inch head space at the top of the jar. Run a thin-blade spatula around the inside of the jar to free trapped air bubbles; wipe the jar rim with a clean, damp cloth, then screw on the closure. Repeat until all the jars are filled. **Tip:** *To avoid spilling or dribbling relish down the sides of the jars as you fill them, use a wide-mouth canning funnel.*

6. Process the jars for 10 minutes in a boiling water bath (212° F.). Lift from the water bath; complete the seals, if needed, by tightening the lids, then cool to room temperature.

7. Date and label each jar, then store on a cool, dark shelf several weeks before opening.

❀

She remembered (as one remembers first the eyes of a loved person) the old blue water cooler on the back porch . . . among the round and square wooden tables always piled with snap beans, turnip greens, and onions from today's trip to Greenwood.

—EUDORA WELTY, *DELTA WEDDING*

❀

1998 A Chattanooga microbrewery (Big River Grill and Brewing Works) takes top honors for its Iron Horse stout at the World Beer Cup Competition in Rio de Janeiro. That same year its Sweet Magnolia brown ale wins a gold medal at the American Beer Festival.

The James Beard Foundation names Frank Brigsten, chef-proprietor of Brigsten's in New Orleans, Best Chef in the Southeast.

The AmRhein Wine Cellars open at Bent Mountain in the Roanoke Valley. Within five years, its Virginia-style wines fermented from estate-grown grapes have won 18 state and nine international medals for excellence. (See Southern Wines, page 121.)

1999 Haussner's German restaurant, a Baltimore institution for more than 70 years, closes. Its art collection is auctioned off—some of it at Sotheby's in New York.

GREEN TOMATO PICKLE RELISH

MAKES ABOUT 4 PINTS

Southern cooks find this spicy relish a handy way to use up the late-September glut of green tomatoes. With green tomato relish in the pantry, deviled eggs, potato salad, egg salad, and ham salad—southern favorites all—can be made in a hurry. In the old days, I used to chop all the vegetables by hand. I now use the food processor, taking care to chop everything in smallish batches (no more than two inches of vegetables in the work bowl at a time). Finally, I pulse each batch briskly until I get just the texture I want. **Note:** *If this relish is to have the proper crunch, you must use hard green tomatoes and firm cucumbers. Kirby cucumbers, the small pickling variety, are the ones to use here. They're usually unwaxed and available at most supermarkets.*

8 cups (2 quarts) cored, peeled, and coarsely chopped hard green tomatoes (2½ to 3 pounds)

1 medium-large red bell pepper, cored, seeded, and coarsely chopped

1 medium-large green bell pepper, cored, seeded, and coarsely chopped

1 large yellow onion, coarsely chopped

3 firm Kirby cucumbers, peeled, halved, seeded, and coarsely chopped (see Note above)

½ cup pickling salt

1 cup sugar

1½ cups white (distilled) vinegar

1½ cups cider vinegar

1 tablespoon mustard seeds

2 tablespoons pickling spice blend, tied in cheesecloth (spice bag)

1. Place all the vegetables in a very large nonreactive bowl, sprinkle with the salt, and toss well. Cover and let stand overnight at room temperature. Next day, drain all in a large sieve and press out as much liquid as possible. Set aside.

2. Wash and rinse 4 one-pint preserving jars and their closures and submerge in a large kettle of boiling water.

3. Meanwhile, bring the sugar, white and cider vinegars, mustard seeds, and spice bag to a boil in a large nonreactive kettle. Adjust the heat so the mixture bubbles easily and cook uncovered for 10 minutes, stirring now and then. Mix in the drained vegetables and return to a boil. Remove the spice bag.

4. Lift the preserving jars from the boiling water one by one and ladle in enough hot relish to fill the jar to within ¼ inch of the top. Run a thin-blade spatula around the inside of the jar to release air bubbles; wipe the rim with a clean, damp cloth, then screw on the closure. Repeat until all the jars are filled. **Tip:** *To avoid spilling or dribbling relish down the sides of the jars as you fill them, use a wide-mouth canning funnel.*

5. Process the jars for 10 minutes in a boiling water bath (212° F.). Lift from the water bath; complete the seals, if needed, by tightening the lids, then cool to room temperature.

6. Date and label each jar, then store on a cool, dark shelf several weeks before opening.

DILLED SNAP BEANS

MAKES ABOUT 4 PINTS

Back when I was a junior food editor at *The Ladies' Home Journal* in New York, two attractive young southern women came into our test kitchens one day bearing jars of snap beans that they'd pickled. They told us they'd used an old family recipe and hoped that we liked their "Dilly Beans" enough to write a little something about them because they aimed to market them. That was my first encounter with "Dilly Beans." Those two Southerners didn't share their family recipe—only jars of beans, which, thanks to our item about them, soon became everyone's favorite low-cal cocktail food (each bean contains about one calorie). This recipe is my own.

2 pounds straight, tender, young green beans, tipped and cut into 4-inch lengths

4 garlic cloves, halved lengthwise

Eight 4-inch sprigs of fresh dill, washed and patted dry, or 4 teaspoons dill weed

1½ cups white (distilled) vinegar

1½ cups cider vinegar

1 cup water

¼ cup sugar

2 tablespoons pickling salt

½ teaspoon crushed red pepper flakes, crushed

1. Wash and rinse 4 one-pint preserving jars and their closures and submerge in a large kettle of boiling water.

2. Remove the jars from the boiling water one by one, pack snugly with the beans, then push two garlic halves and two dill sprigs or 1 teaspoon dill weed down into each jar.

3. While packing the jars, boil the two vinegars, water, sugar, pickling salt, and red pepper flakes uncovered in a large nonreactive saucepan over moderate heat for 5 minutes. Keep hot.

4. When all the jars have been packed, ladle enough of the hot pickling liquid into each to cover the beans and come to within ¼ inch of the top. Run a thin-blade spatula around the inside of each jar to release air bubbles; wipe the rim with a clean, damp cloth, then screw on the closure.

5. Process the jars for 10 minutes in a boiling water bath (212° F.). Lift from the water bath; complete the seals, if necessary, by tightening the lids, then cool to room temperature.

6. Date and label each jar, then store on a cool, dark shelf for about a month before serving.

PICKLED OKRA

MAKES ABOUT 8 PINTS

I'm not a huge fan of okra, I must admit. But I do like them pickled the old southern way.

When choosing okra for this recipe, go for pods about the size of your little finger. Larger ones may be tough. **Note:** *To crisp their pickled okra, southern cooks use pickling lime (see About Pickling Lime, page 366).*

4 pounds small okra of uniform size, washed well

4 quarts (1 gallon) cold water,
mixed with 1½ tablespoons food-grade
pickling lime (lime water)

4 cups (1 quart) white (distilled) vinegar

4 cups (1 quart) cider vinegar

6 cups sugar

2 tablespoons mustard seeds

1 tablespoon black peppercorns

1 tablespoon ground turmeric

1½ teaspoons celery seeds

1½ teaspoons pickling salt

4 small silverskin onions, peeled, sliced
tissue-thin, and separated into rings

1. Soak the okra in the lime water in a very large nonreactive kettle for 2 hours. Drain, rinse well in several changes of cold water, and set aside. Also rinse the kettle well.

2. Wash and rinse 8 one-pint preserving jars and their closures and submerge in a large kettle of boiling water.

3. Bring the two vinegars, sugar, mustard seeds, peppercorns, turmeric, celery seeds, salt, and onions to a boil in the rinsed-out kettle over moderate heat. Add the okra and as soon as the mixture returns to the boil, cook uncovered for 1 minute exactly; no longer or the okra will soften.

4. Remove the jars from the boiling water one by one and pack snugly with the okra and onion slices. When all the jars are packed, ladle enough of the hot pickling liquid into each to cover the okra and come to within ¼ inch of the top. Run a thin-blade spatula around the inside of each jar to release air bubbles; wipe the rim with a clean, damp cloth, then screw on the closure.

5. Process the jars for 10 minutes in a boiling water bath (212° F.). Lift from the water bath; complete the seals, if necessary, by tightening the lids, then cool to room temperature.

6. Date and label each jar, then store on a cool, dark shelf for about a month before serving.

PICKLED FIGS

MAKES 4 TO 5 PINTS

There were two giant fig bushes in our backyard and my job was to pick the green-skinned figs when they were firm but ripe. From a neighbor woman, who'd just moved to town from the country, my mother learned how to pickle figs the old-fashioned southern way. I never liked fresh figs, but I do dote upon these pickled figs.

5 pounds small firm-ripe figs, washed but
not peeled or stemmed

2 quarts (½ gallon) boiling water

3 cups sugar

4 cups (1 quart) cider vinegar

4 cups (1 quart) cold water

1 tablespoon whole cloves, bruised

½ tablespoon whole allspice, bruised

1 cinnamon stick, broken in several places

One 2-inch strip lemon zest

One 3-inch strip orange zest

1. Prick each fig with a sterilized needle (this is to keep the figs from bursting in the boiling water bath), then place the figs in a large, heavy kettle. Pour in the boiling water and let cool to room temperature.
2. Meanwhile, place the sugar, vinegar, and water in a large, heavy nonreactive kettle. Tie the cloves, allspice, cinnamon, and lemon and orange zests in cheesecloth and drop into the kettle. Set over moderate heat and bring to a boil.
3. Ease the figs into the kettle, adjust the heat so that the pickling syrup barely bubbles, then simmer uncovered for about 25 minutes or until the figs are translucent. Discard the spice bag.
4. Meanwhile, wash and rinse 5 one-pint preserving jars and their closures and submerge in a large kettle of boiling water.
5. Lift the preserving jars from the boiling water one by one. Using a slotted spoon, pack the figs snugly in the jar, leaving ¼ inch head space at the top. Ladle enough boiling pickling syrup into the jar to cover the figs, again leaving ¼ inch head space. Run a thin-blade spatula around the inside of the jar to release air bubbles; wipe the jar rim with a clean, damp cloth, then screw on the closure. Repeat until all the jars are filled.
6. Process the jars for 10 minutes in a boiling water bath (212° F.). Lift from the water bath; complete the seals, if necessary, by tightening the lids, then cool to room temperature.
7. Date and label each jar, then store on a cool, dark shelf several weeks before opening.

1999

Mildred Council writes *Mama Dip's Kitchen* because Craig Claiborne liked her country cooking so much he urged her to write a cookbook. Part autobiography (with stories about growing up poor and black in Chatham County, North Carolina, during the Depression and World War Two), it has now sold more than 100,000 copies.

The James Beard Foundation names Jamie Shannon, of Commander's Palace in New Orleans, Best Chef in the Southeast.

By acquiring the Spice Hunter of San Luis Obispo, California, and its 300-product inventory, the 112-year-old C. F. Sauer spice company of Richmond, Virginia, enters the natural foods and boutique spice markets.

Now merged with A & W restaurants and with more than 1,200 eateries at home and abroad, Long John Silver's, begun 30 years earlier in Lexington, Kentucky, is America's largest chain of fast-food fish houses.

ELIZA LUCAS PINCKNEY (1722–1793) AND HARRIOTT PINCKNEY HORRY (1748–1830) LIKE MOTHER, LIKE DAUGHTER

In 1989, nearly 200 years after her death, Eliza Lucas Pinckney was enshrined in the South Carolina Business Hall of Fame.

Yet few people have any idea who she was or why she was the first woman so honored. Born of English parents in Antigua in 1722, Eliza relocated with her family to the South Carolina Lowcountry as a teenager, a move her father hoped would improve his wife's fragile health. With her father's return to Antigua seven years later, young Eliza stayed on to manage his Wappoo Creek Plantation near Charleston and supervise the running of two others. She taught two slave children to read, learned a bit of law, and, more important, experimented with seeds her father sent her from Antigua, among them indigo. Eliza had always loved "the vegetable world extremely."

Within five years, she not only had reaped a successful crop of indigo but also had developed a technique for making the valuable blue dye the English needed for their military uniforms. With demands for Carolina rice faltering, plantation owners switched to indigo and it made them rich.

At age twenty-two, Eliza married Charles Pinckney, a wealthy widower some years her senior, and she bore four children, three of whom lived: two sons (both statesmen of national stature) and daughter Harriott.

In 1768, Harriott married a prosperous French Huguenot, Daniel Horry, of Hampton Plantation on the lower Santee; within two years she had begun *The Receipt Book of Harriott Pinckney Horry, 1770*. Published 214 years later as *A Colonial Plantation Cookbook* by the University of South Carolina Press, it contains twenty-six entries from Eliza's handwritten receipt book (now at the South Carolina Historical Society in Charleston).

When her daughter was widowed, Eliza moved in with her and the two traveled up and down the East Coast, in the end to Philadelphia to find a cure for Eliza's cancer. She died there in 1793 at the age of seventy-one (George Washington was one of the pallbearers).

Always interested in food preparation and preservation, Harriott continued to travel and at one point visited Mary Randolph's boardinghouse in Richmond, Virginia, noting the "excellent fare and genteel treatment."

What impressed her most, however, was the "refrigerator" that Mary Randolph had invented, two boxes separated by firmly packed layers of powdered charcoal. Into the inner box went five pecks of ice, which kept perishables cold for twenty-four hours. Harriott sketched the contraption in detail, hoping to build one of her own back home.

Harriott Pinckney Horry's major contribution, however, is her receipt book, one of the first to set down Colonial American recipes in "scientific" detail. It's true that a few of them descend from Hannah Glasse's very English *Art of Cookery, Made Plain and Easy* (London, 1747). True, too, that some show the French influence of the Huguenots.

Still, the majority are Harriott's distinctly Lowcountry receipts, her mother's, or ones shared by friends and other relatives. Together they provide a glimpse of life among South Carolina's plantation aristocracy before and after the American Revolution.

PICKLED PEACHES

MAKES 6 TO 8 PINTS

In many parts of the South, the Thanksgiving turkey or Easter ham wouldn't be the same without pickled peaches or Bourbon'd Peaches (page 376). In the old days, southern women not only pickled their own peaches but picked them, too. Some still do. Experienced cooks know that the best varieties to pickle are small, firm-ripe clingstones: the yellow-fleshed Florida Dawn or Florida King, for example; the rosy Indian Cling; or even semi-clings like Redhaven and Springbrite. They know, too, that if pickled peaches are to be plump and full of flavor, they must stand in the pickling syrup overnight.

6 pounds small firm-ripe peaches about the size of apricots

4 quarts (1 gallon) cold water, mixed with 2 teaspoons powdered ascorbic acid (acidulated water)

4½ cups sugar

3 cups cold water

1½ cups white (distilled) vinegar

1½ cups cider vinegar

3 cinnamon sticks, broken in several places

3 large blades of mace

One 2-inch strip lemon zest

One 2-inch strip orange zest

Whole cloves (2 for each peach)

1. Blanch the peaches in batches in boiling water, allowing 30 seconds for each. Transfer at once to ice water, then slip off the skins. Submerge the peeled peaches in the acidulated water while you prepare the pickling syrup.
2. Place the sugar, water, and two vinegars in a very large nonreactive kettle. Tie the cinnamon, mace, and lemon and orange zests in cheesecloth and drop into the kettle. Set over moderately high heat and bring to a boil.
3. Meanwhile, lift the peaches from the acidulated water and stud each with 2 cloves. As soon as the pickling syrup boils, ease 6 peaches into the kettle, adjust the heat so the

mixture bubbles gently, and cook uncovered for 5 minutes. Using a slotted spoon, lift the peaches to a large heatproof bowl. Repeat until all the peaches have cooked 5 minutes.

4. Bring the pickling syrup to a rolling boil, return all of the peaches to the kettle, then set off the heat, cover, and let stand overnight.

5. The next day, wash and rinse 8 one-pint preserving jars and their closures and submerge in a large kettle of boiling water.

6. Lift the peaches from the pickling syrup with a slotted spoon and transfer to a large bowl. Set the kettle over high heat and quickly bring the pickling syrup to a full boil. Discard the spice bag.

7. Pack the peaches as attractively and tightly as possible in the hot preserving jars, filling to within ¼ inch of the top, then ladle in just enough boiling pickling syrup to cover the peaches. Run a thin-blade spatula around the inside of each jar to release air bubbles; wipe the rim with a clean, damp cloth, then screw on the closure.

8. Process the jars for 15 minutes in a boiling water bath (212° F.). Lift from the water bath; complete the seals, if necessary, by tightening the lids, then cool to room temperature.

9. Date and label each jar, then store on a cool, dark shelf for about a month before serving.

❊

The drier the season, the sweeter the peach.

—OLD SOUTHERN SAYING

❊

BOURBON'D PEACHES

MAKES 6 TO 8 PINTS

To Southerners, a peach preserved in aged bourbon or sour mash beats a brandied peach every time. As with pickled peaches, the best varieties to choose are small, firm clingstones (see headnote for Pickled Peaches, page 375). Serve Bourbon'd Peaches with baked ham or roast pork, turkey, or chicken.

6 pounds small firm-ripe peaches about the size of apricots

4 quarts (1 gallon) cold water, mixed with 1 tablespoon powdered citric acid and 1 teaspoon powdered ascorbic acid (acidulated water)

6 cups sugar

6 cups (1½ pints) cold water

3 cups syrup (from boiling the peaches)

3 cups fine aged bourbon or sour mash whiskey

1. Wash and rinse 8 one-pint preserving jars and their closures and keep submerged in boiling water.

2. Blanch the peaches in batches in a separate kettle of boiling water, allowing 30 seconds for each. Transfer at once to ice water, then slip off the skins. Submerge the peeled peaches in the acidulated water while you prepare the syrup.

3. Place the sugar and water in a very large non-reactive kettle, set over moderate heat, and

bring to a boil. Working with 6 to 8 peaches at a time, lift from the acidulated water and ease into the boiling syrup. Adjust the heat so the syrup bubbles gently, and cook the peaches uncovered for 5 minutes.

4. As the peaches finish cooking, pack into the hot jars as attractively and snugly as possible, leaving 1/4 inch head space at the top of each jar. Repeat until all the peaches have cooked 5 minutes and been packed into jars.

5. Insert a candy thermometer in the kettle of syrup and boil uncovered until the syrup reaches 220° F. Set the kettle off the heat and cool the syrup for 5 minutes.

6. Measure 3 cups of the syrup into a medium-size nonreactive saucepan and add the bourbon. Set over moderate heat and bring to a simmer—do not boil—then ladle just enough hot bourbon syrup into each jar to cover the peaches, again leaving 1/4 inch head space.

7. Run a thin-blade spatula around the inside of each jar to release air bubbles; wipe the rim with a clean, damp cloth, then screw on the closure.

8. Process the jars for 10 minutes in a boiling water bath (212° F.). Lift from the water bath; complete the seals, if necessary, by tightening the lids, then cool to room temperature.

9. Date and label each jar, then store on a cool, dark shelf for about a month before serving.

❦

Wild as a peach orchard hog.

—OLD SOUTHERN SAYING

❦

2000 Mississippi-born long-time *New York Times* food editor, columnist, and restaurant critic Craig Claiborne dies at the age of 79. A bachelor, he leaves his entire estate to the Culinary Institute of America at Hyde Park, New York.

The James Beard Foundation names Ben Barker chef-proprietor (with his wife Karen) of Magnolia Grill in Durham, North Carolina, Best Chef in the Southeast.

2001 Eliot Wigginton, long-time editor of *Foxfire* magazine, coauthors *The Foxfire Book of Appalachian Cookery* with Linda Garland Page.

The James Beard Foundation names Frank Stitt, chef-proprietor of Highlands Bar and Grill in Birmingham, Alabama, Best Chef in the Southeast.

2002 The James Beard Foundation names Anne Kearney of Peristyle in New Orleans Best Chef in the Southeast.

Now painstakingly restored, George Washington's grist mill opens at Mount Vernon.

2003 The James Beard Foundation names Karen Barker of Magnolia Grill in Durham, North Carolina, America's best pastry chef.

WATERMELON RIND PICKLES

MAKES ABOUT 8 PINTS

. . . .

One of the few southern recipes that my mid-western mother embraced is this one for water-melon rind pickles. I loved working beside her in the kitchen when it was time to make our an-nual batch: My job was to peel the watermelon rind and cut it into one-inch cubes. After I'd seen "plantation circles"—little rounds of rind—I began using my mother's smallest biscuit cut-ter. "Too much waste," she said. So I resumed cutting the rind into cubes. **Note:** *You need wa-termelon rind at least ³⁄₄ inch thick to make good pickles.*

8 pounds peeled and trimmed
³⁄₄- to 1-inch-thick watermelon rind
showing no traces of pink

1 cup pickling salt dissolved in 4 quarts
(1 gallon) cold water (brine)

5 quarts (1 gallon plus 1 quart) water

6 pounds sugar

4¹⁄₂ cups cider vinegar

4 chili pequins (tiny dried red chiles)

3 blades of mace

2 cinnamon sticks, broken in two

2 tablespoons whole allspice

1 tablespoon mustard seeds

1 tablespoon whole cloves

2 cardamom pods, bruised

2 large bay leaves, crumbled

Two 1-inch cubes fresh ginger, peeled and
coarsely chopped

1 large lemon, sliced and seeded

1. Cut the watermelon rind into 1-inch cubes, place in a very large nonreactive kettle, add the brine, cover, and let stand overnight.

2. Next day, drain the rind, rinse well, and drain again. Also rinse the kettle. Return the rind to the kettle, add 4 quarts of the water, and bring to a boil over high heat. Adjust the heat so the water bubbles gently and cook uncovered for 10 to 15 minutes or until the rind is crisp-tender. Drain well.

3. Place the sugar, vinegar, and remaining 1 quart water in the kettle and stir well. Tie all of the spices and the lemon slices in several thicknesses of cheesecloth and drop into the kettle. Bring to a boil over moderately high heat, then boil uncovered for 10 minutes.

4. Return the rind to the kettle, bring to a boil, adjust the heat so the pickling syrup bubbles gently, and cook uncovered for 15 to 20 min-utes or until the rind is translucent.

5. Meanwhile, wash and rinse 8 one-pint pre-serving jars and their closures and submerge in a large kettle of boiling water.

6. Lift the preserving jars from the boiling water one by one. Using a slotted spoon, pack the rind snugly in the jar, leaving ¹⁄₄ inch head space at the top. Ladle enough boiling pick-ling syrup into the jar to cover the rind, again leaving ¹⁄₄ inch head space. Run a thin-blade spatula around the inside of the jar to release air bubbles; wipe the jar rim with a clean,

damp cloth, then screw on the closure. Repeat until all the jars are filled.

7. Process the jars for 5 minutes in a boiling water bath (212° F.). Lift from the water bath; complete the seals, if necessary, by tightening the lids, then cool to room temperature.

8. Date and label each jar, then store on a cool, dark shelf several weeks before opening.

WILD BLACKBERRY JAM

MAKES 6 TO 8 HALF-PINTS

. . . .

When my brother and I were little, we looked forward to the first flurry of blackberry blossoms along roadsides, in fields, and in woods because there'd soon be berries to pick. Not an easy task because the brambles were full of thorns and not easily accessible. **Note:** *Wild blackberries make better jam than the cultivated because their flavor is more intense. Still, farmer's market blackberries can be substituted as can blueberries, dewberries, and raspberries.*

10 cups (2½ quarts) firm-ripe
wild blackberries

6 cups sugar

1 tablespoon fresh lemon juice

1. Wash the blackberries well in cool water and drain thoroughly. Place the berries in a large bowl and crush with a potato masher. You will need exactly 9 cups of crushed berries.

2. Place the 9 cups crushed blackberries in a large, heavy nonreactive kettle; add the sugar

and lemon juice, and stir well. Insert a candy thermometer.

3. Set the uncovered kettle over moderate heat and bring the berry mixture slowly to a boil, stirring until the sugar dissolves completely. Now cook slowly, still uncovered, stirring as needed to keep the jam from sticking to the bottom of the kettle, until the jelling point is reached (218° to 220° F.).

4. Meanwhile, wash and rinse 8 half-pint preserving jars and their closures and submerge in a large kettle of boiling water.

5. Ladle the boiling jam into the hot jars, filling each to within ¼ inch of the top. **Tip:** *To avoid spills, use a wide-mouth canning funnel.* Wipe the jar rims with a damp cloth and screw on the closures.

6. Process the jars for 15 minutes in a hot water bath (185° F.). Lift from the water bath; complete the seals, if necessary, by tightening the lids, then cool to room temperature.

7. Date and label each jar, then store on a cool, dark shelf for about a month before serving.

❀

Breakfast was on the table . . . grits,
ham and eggs, and red-eye gravy.
Grandpa had spread butter and
Aunt Everleen's homemade blackberry jelly
on hot biscuits as soon as
he took them out of the oven.

—**DORI SANDERS,** *CLOVER*

❀

MUSCADINE JAM

MAKES 6 TO 7 HALF-PINTS

. . . .

As a child, one of my greatest joys was to lie atop our next-door neighbor's grape arbor reading a good book, plucking the occasional muscadine and sucking its honeyed flesh into my mouth. What I didn't know then was that the muscadine *(Vitis rotundifolia)* and its bronze cultivar (the scuppernong) were found growing wild here by early European explorers. Discovering them along the North Carolina coast in 1584, Arthur Barlowe, one of Sir Walter Raleigh's scouts, wrote of their flourishing "on the sand and on the green soil, on the hills as on the plains . . . in all the world the like abundance is not to be found." Unlike other varieties, muscadines and scuppernongs do not bunch; indeed the grapes often seem to grow singly. They are tough-skinned, blessed with intense grape flavor, and make superlative jam (my childhood favorite for P, B, and J sandwiches). People often confuse muscadines with scuppernongs because the two can be used interchangeably, but to Southerners the black-skinned grapes are "muscadines" and the bronzy green are "scuppernongs." **Tip:** *This recipe calls for peeled muscadines—not as tedious a job as it sounds. Simply whack the grapes lightly with a cutlet bat or the broad side of a chef's knife and the flesh will pop out of the skins.*

4 pounds stemmed muscadine or scuppernong grapes

¾ cup cold water

6 cups sugar

2 tablespoons fresh lemon juice

1. Wash the grapes in a sink full of cool water and drain well. Peel the grapes (see Tip at left), then place the skins and the ¾ cup cold water in a large, heavy nonreactive kettle and the grapes in a second large, heavy nonreactive kettle, this one broad-bottomed.

2. Set the two kettles over moderate heat and bring each to a boil. Adjust the heat under the grapes so that they bubble gently; cover and simmer for 20 minutes or until the grapes are mushy. At the same time, cover the grape skins and boil 20 minutes or until they are tender. If they threaten to boil dry, add a little additional water.

3. Force the grapes through a food mill or fine sieve, extracting as much pulp and liquid as possible. Return the grape pulp to the kettle, then mix in the grape skins and any remaining water, the sugar, and lemon juice. Insert a candy thermometer.

4. Bring to a boil over moderate heat, stirring until the sugar dissolves, then cook uncovered, stirring occasionally, until the mixture reaches the jelling point (218° to 220° F.).

5. Meanwhile, wash and rinse 7 half-pint preserving jars and their closures and submerge in a large kettle of boiling water.

6. Ladle the boiling jam into the hot jars, filling each to within ¼ inch of the top. **Tip:** *To avoid spills, use a wide-mouth canning funnel.* Wipe the jar rims with a damp cloth and screw on the closures.

7. Process the jars for 10 minutes in a hot water bath (185° F.). Lift from the water bath; complete the seals, if necessary, by tightening the lids, then cool to room temperature.
8. Date and label each jar, then store on a cool, dark shelf for about a month before serving.

SPICY PEACH BUTTER

MAKES 6 TO 8 HALF-PINTS

Among some southern mountain folk, peach butter is more popular than peach jam, maybe because it seems less fussy. It's not as sweet as peach jam but is a good bit spicier, yet it's equally tasty on hot biscuits, hoecakes, and corn pones. As with peach jam, freestone Georgia Belles and Elbertas are the peach varieties to use.

6 pounds medium firm-ripe peaches, washed and drained (see headnote)

1 cup cold water

Sugar (½ cup for each 1 cup of cooked peaches)

2 tablespoons fresh lemon juice

2 teaspoons finely grated orange zest

1 teaspoon ground ginger

½ teaspoon freshly grated nutmeg

¼ teaspoon ground cloves

1. Blanch the peaches in batches in boiling water, allowing 30 seconds for each. Transfer at once to ice water, then slip off the skins. Drain the peaches well, pit, and coarsely chop.

2003 R. C. Bigelow Tea of Connecticut buys the Charleston Tea Plantation but continues to produce its famous American Classic Tea.

With North Carolina First Lady Mary Easley on hand for the festivities, A Southern Season opens its new 59,000-square-foot food emporium at Chapel Hill's University Mall. It is now larger than New York's Dean & DeLuca, to which it is often compared.

The James Beard Foundation names Anne Quatrano and Clifford Harrison of Bacchanalia in Atlanta Best Chefs in the Southeast.

2004 A mysterious blight threatens Georgia's multimillion-dollar Vidalia onion crop.

North Carolina tobacco farmers begin growing black Périgord truffles under the direction of Franklin Garland, who'd mastered the technique on his farm near Hillsborough.

The James Beard Foundation names Louis Osteen, chef-proprietor of Louis's at Pawley's on Pawley's Island, South Carolina, Best Chef in the Southeast.

Category-four hurricane Charley decimates one third of Florida's citrus groves.

2. Transfer the peaches to a large nonreactive kettle, add the 1 cup cold water, and bring to a boil over moderate heat. Adjust the heat so that the peaches simmer gently and cook uncovered for 10 to 15 minutes or until they are very soft. Measure the cooked peaches carefully and make a note of the total amount.

3. Return the peaches to the kettle, then for every 1 cup of peaches, add ½ cup sugar. Also add the lemon juice, orange zest, and three spices. Insert a candy thermometer.

4. Bring to a boil over moderate heat, stirring until the sugar dissolves, then cook uncovered, stirring occasionally, until the mixture reaches the jelling point (218° to 220° F.).

5. Meanwhile, wash and rinse 8 half-pint preserving jars and their closures and submerge in a large kettle of boiling water.

6. Ladle the boiling peach butter into the hot jars, filling each to within ¼ inch of the top. **Tip:** *To avoid spills, use a wide-mouth canning funnel.* Wipe the jar rims with a damp cloth and screw on the closures.

7. Process the jars for 10 minutes in a hot water bath (185° F.). Lift from the water bath; complete the seals, if necessary, by tightening the lids, then cool to room temperature.

8. Date and label each jar, then store on a cool, dark shelf for about a month before serving.

❀

Her hand was as light with her pastry as with her husband, and the results as happy.

—ANONYMOUS

❀

DAMSON PRESERVES

MAKES 4 TO 5 HALF-PINTS

. . . .

The damson plum (*Prunus insititia*) is believed to have been introduced into Greece by Alexander the Great, who found it growing near Damascus; into Western Europe by Crusaders returning from Jerusalem; and into the New World by the English colonists. According to *Sturtevant's Notes on Edible Plants*, the damson still grows wild throughout Europe and Asia as well as over much of the United States. Sturtevant describes the damson thus: "The fruit is globular, black or white, of an acid taste but not unpleasant, especially when mellowed by frost; it makes a good conserve." Quite so. The tiny, tart, black-skinned, golden-fleshed damsons are what Southerners prize for preserves. **Note:** *It's important that the plums not be fully ripe, for if they are, they will not contain enough natural pectin to thicken the preserves.*

3 pounds firm-ripe damson plums, halved and pitted but not peeled (you'll need 5 cups of prepared damsons)

I cup water

4 cups sugar

2 teaspoons finely grated orange zest

I teaspoon finely grated lemon zest

¼ teaspoon freshly grated nutmeg

1. Place all ingredients in a large, heavy nonreactive kettle—a broad-bottomed one is best—and insert a candy thermometer. Set over

moderately low heat and bring to a boil, stirring now and then. Adjust the heat so the mixture bubbles gently, then cook uncovered, stirring occasionally, until the mixture reaches the jelling point (218° to 220° F.).

2. Meanwhile, wash and rinse 5 half-pint preserving jars and their closures and submerge in a large kettle of boiling water.

3. Ladle the boiling preserves into the hot jars, filling each to within 1/4 inch of the top. **Tip: To avoid spills, use a wide-mouth canning funnel.** Wipe the jar rims with a damp cloth and screw on the closures.

4. Process the jars for 15 minutes in a hot water bath (185° F.). Lift from the water bath; complete the seals, if necessary, by tightening the lids, then cool to room temperature.

5. Date and label each jar, then store on a cool, dark shelf for about a month before serving.

❈

The year was 1584 . . . [English captain Arthur Barlowe] was looking for a landfall. He turned toward the perfumed sand banks [in what is now North Carolina] to discover a woven ambuscade of vines bearing golden brown fruit . . . the "mother vineyard," home of America's first grape, the scuppernong.

—CLEMENTINE PADDLEFORD,
HOW AMERICA EATS

❈

2005 Category-four hurricane Katrina, followed by category-three Rita, lashes New Orleans, closing such famous restaurants as Antoine's, Emeril's, and Commander's Palace, at least temporarily. It also savages Louisiana's sugar and shrimping industries.

Frank "It-takes-a-tough-man-to-make-a-tender-chicken" Perdue dies at the age of 84 in his home state of Maryland.

2006 By the end of March, nearly 40 percent of the Louisiana restaurants shuttered by Hurricane Katrina were up and running, most of them in New Orleans. Brennan's reopens in mid May in time for its seventieth birthday.

John Besh, executive chef of Restaurant August, wins the James Beard Award for Best Chef in the Southeast. This New Orleans restaurant suffered minimal damage from hurricanes Katrina and Rita and managed to reopen by early fall.

Planters Peanuts celebrates its hundredth birthday.

FIG PRESERVES

MAKES 8 HALF-PINTS

Whatever figs my mother didn't pickle, she would preserve, again using an old southern recipe. My favorite way to eat fig preserves was on hot buttered biscuits.

4½ pounds small firm-ripe figs, washed but not peeled or stemmed

6 cups sugar

4 cups (1 quart) water

⅔ cup fresh lemon juice

1. Prick each fig with a sterilized needle (to keep the figs from bursting) and set aside.
2. Bring the sugar, water, and lemon juice to a boil in a large, heavy, nonreactive kettle over high heat. Add the figs, adjust the heat so the liquid bubbles gently, then cook the figs uncovered for 20 to 25 minutes until translucent. Set off the heat, cover, and let the figs plump in the syrup overnight.
3. The next day, wash and rinse 8 half-pint preserving jars and their closures and submerge in a large kettle of boiling water.
4. Set the kettle of figs over moderate heat and slowly bring to a boil. Skim off the froth, then pack the figs as attractively and tightly as possible in the hot preserving jars, filling to within ¼ inch of the top. Ladle in just enough boiling syrup to cover the figs, again leaving ¼ inch head space. Run a thin-blade spatula around the inside of each jar to release air bubbles; wipe the rim with a clean, damp cloth, then screw on the closure.
5. Process the jars for 20 minutes in a hot water bath (185° F.). Lift from the water bath; complete the seals, if necessary, by tightening the lids, then cool to room temperature.
6. Date and label each jar, then store on a cool, dark shelf for about a month before serving.

SHENANDOAH APPLE-BLACKBERRY JELLY

MAKES 4 HALF-PINTS

For me one of the loveliest parts of the South is Virginia's fertile Shenandoah Valley, where apple orchards twill the foothills and wild blackberries are yours for the picking. This recipe, 100 years old or more, shows how women made jelly before commercial pectins were available in liquid or powdered form. The apples provide the pectin and produce a jelly of exquisite delicacy.

2½ medium Rhode Island Greening apples (about ¾ pound), washed and thinly sliced but not peeled or cored

1 cup water

10 cups (2½ quarts) firm-ripe wild blackberries, washed and drained

3 cups sugar (about)

1. Place the apples along with their stems, cores, and seeds in a medium-size, heavy nonreactive kettle. Add the water and bring to a boil

over moderately high heat. Adjust the heat so the mixture bubbles gently, cover, and cook for 15 minutes.

2. Add the blackberries and crush well with a potato masher; cover and boil 5 minutes more.

3. Suspend two damp jelly bags over two large heatproof bowls (or line each of two large footed colanders with four thicknesses of cheesecloth and stand in the bowls). Pour half the berry mixture into each jelly bag and let the juice drip through undisturbed. The juice extraction may take an hour or longer, so have patience. If you try to rush things by squeezing the bags, your jelly will be cloudy.

4. Meanwhile, wash and rinse 4 half-pint preserving jars and their closures and submerge in a large kettle of boiling water.

5. Measure the extracted juice carefully; you should have 4 cups. Pour the juice back into the kettle, now rinsed and dried, and for every cup of juice, add ¾ cup of sugar. Insert a candy thermometer.

6. Set over moderately low heat and bring to a boil, stirring until the sugar dissolves. Adjust the heat so the mixture bubbles gently, then cook uncovered, stirring occasionally, for about 15 minutes or until the mixture reaches the jelling point (218° to 220° F.).

7. When the jelly is done, skim off the froth, then ladle the boiling jelly into the hot jars, filling each to within ¼ inch of the top. **Tip:** *To avoid spills, use a wide-mouth canning funnel.* Wipe the jar rims with a damp cloth and screw on the closures.

8. Process the jars for 5 minutes in a boiling water bath (212° F.). Lift from the water bath; complete the seals, if necessary, by tightening the lids, then cool to room temperature.

9. Date and label each jar of jelly, then store on a cool, dark shelf for about a month before serving.

MAYHAW JELLY

MAKES ABOUT 4 HALF-PINTS

My Mississippi friend Jean Todd Freeman and I both worked at *The Ladies' Home Journal* in New York and both lived in the West Village. Jean loved to throw dinner parties and it was at one of these that I first encountered mayhaw jelly, a quivery hillock the color of a Pink Perfection camellia. North Carolina, where I grew up, is too cold for mayhaws to flourish—a variety of hawthorne that thrives in swamps farther south, loses a flurry of white blossoms in early spring, then bears tart red "berries" in late April and early May (botanically, mayhaws are closer to apples than to berries). After Jean returned to Hattiesburg, Mississippi, she always brought a jar of mayhaw jelly whenever she flew up to New York to visit. Southern women, she told me, have been making it since Civil War days. This recipe is adapted from one offered by the Georgia Cooperative Extension Service. How do you serve mayhaw jelly? With butter on straight-from-the-oven biscuits or corn bread.

1½ pounds fully ripe mayhaws

½ pound barely ripe mayhaws
(these are needed for pectin,
which is what makes jelly gel)

4 cups (1 quart) cold water

Sugar (¾ cup for each cup of mayhaw juice)

1. Place all of the mayhaws and the water in a large nonreactive saucepan, set over moderate heat, and bring to a boil, stirring occasionally. Reduce the heat so the mixture barely bubbles and simmer uncovered, stirring often, for 10 to 15 minutes or until the mayhaws are mushy. Do not boil or overcook the mayhaws because you'll destroy some of their natural pectin.

2. Mash the mayhaws with a potato masher, then pour them and all of their liquid into a jelly bag suspended over a large heatproof bowl or into a footed colander lined with several thicknesses of cheesecloth set in a large bowl. Be patient and let the juice trickle through at its own speed. If you force the juice through by pressing the mayhaws, you will cloud the jelly. When all of the juice has been extracted, measure and jot down the exact amount.

3. Return the juice to the saucepan, now rinsed out, and for every cup of juice, mix in ¾ cup of sugar. Insert a candy thermometer.

4. Set over moderately low heat and bring to a boil, stirring until the sugar dissolves. Adjust the heat so the mixture bubbles gently, then cook uncovered, stirring occasionally, for about 15 minutes or until the mixture reaches the jelling point (218° to 220° F.). You can also try this "sheeting" test to determine if the jelly is done: Take up a spoonful of the hot jelly mixture and if the drops run together, forming a solid sheet as they fall from the spoon, the jelly is ready.

5. While the jelly cooks, wash and rinse 4 half-pint preserving jars and their closures and submerge in a large kettle of boiling water.

6. When the jelly is done, skim off the froth, then ladle the boiling jelly into the hot jars, filling each to within ¼ inch of the top. **Tip:** *To avoid spills, use a wide-mouth canning funnel.* Wipe the jar rims with a damp cloth and screw on the closures.

7. Process the jars for 5 minutes in a boiling water bath (212° F.). Lift from the water bath; complete the seals, if necessary, by tightening the lids, then cool to room temperature.

8. Date and label each jar of jelly, then store on a cool, dark shelf for about a month before serving.

HOT PEPPER JELLY

MAKES 6 HALF-PINTS

Wherever I travel about the South, I'm reminded of the popularity of hot pepper jelly. It's a farmer's market staple to be sure, but I've also seen it for sale in gift shops and thrift shops, at local candy stores, even in barbecue joints and mom-and-pop cafés—little jars stacked up by the cash register. Often the jelly is the pride and joy of the owner's mother or daughter. And often it is excellent. I've bought many a jar, cradled it in my carry-on luggage, then served it with cocktails as good southern hostesses do, shimmering atop cream cheese–spread crackers or melbas. Or even easier, as "Hot Jezebel," nothing more than a large block of cream cheese liberally blobbed with hot pepper jelly. Most of my southern cookbooks, particularly the little church or club fund-raisers, include at least one recipe for hot pepper jelly, some of them flecked with diced peppers, others as clear, as sparkling as fine rosé. Some of these jellies are as hot as West Hell, others more tepid. That's what I prefer. If you have an asbestos palate, add a little hot red pepper sauce to the mix. **Note:** *Choose unwaxed peppers for this recipe; wax will affect the jelly's texture, flavor, and clarity. Your jelly will have better color if all the peppers are red; green jalapeños and serranos will redden as they ripen. Just set them on the counter for a couple of days or pop into a brown paper bag with an apple; that will hasten the ripening.* **Tip:** *Wear rubber gloves when handling hot peppers and keep your hands away from your face.*

8 large red bell peppers (about 3 pounds), stemmed, cored, seeded, and quartered

4 medium jalapeño peppers, stemmed, cored, seeded, and quartered (see Note and Tip above)

2 small serrano peppers, stemmed, cored, seeded, and quartered (see Note and Tip above)

2 medium garlic cloves, crushed

6 cups sugar

½ cup white (distilled) vinegar

2 tablespoons fresh lime juice

½ to 1 teaspoon hot red pepper sauce (if you prefer a "hotter" jelly)

Two 3-ounce pouches liquid pectin

1. Wash and rinse 6 half-pint preserving jars and their closures and submerge in a large kettle of boiling water.

2. Cut the bell peppers, jalapeños, and serranos into 1- to 1½-inch chunks and pulse in two batches in a food processor or electric blender at high speed until very finely chopped.

3. Line a large fine sieve with several layers of cheesecloth and set over a glass or ceramic bowl. Scoop in the chopped peppers, add the garlic, and press out as much juice as possible; if necessary, bundle the peppers in the cheesecloth and wring out the juice. You will need 2 cups; if there is insufficient pepper juice, round out the measure with tap water. Discard the peppers.

4. Pour the pepper juice into a deep, nonreactive 2-gallon kettle. Add the sugar, vinegar, lime juice, and, if desired, the hot pepper sauce. Bring to a boil over high heat, adjust so the mixture bubbles easily, then cook uncovered for 5 minutes, stirring now and then.

5. Mix in the liquid pectin and as soon as the mixture returns to a rolling boil, cook for 1 minute exactly.

6. Set the kettle off the heat. Quickly skim off the froth, then ladle the boiling jelly into the hot jars, filling each to within ¼ inch of the top. **Tip:** *To avoid spills, use a wide-mouth canning funnel.* Wipe the jar rims with a damp cloth and screw on the closures.

7. Process the jars for 10 minutes in a boiling water bath (212° F.). Lift from the water bath;

complete the seals, if necessary, by tightening the lids, then cool to room temperature.

8. Date and label each jar of jelly, then store on a cool, dark shelf for about a month before serving.

✿

My nephew, Lee Bailey, thought my [pepper] jelly so good and so unique that he strongly urged me—fairly forced me, in fact—to start selling it . . . Now I put up about 400 jars a week.

—**FREDDIE BAILEY,** *AUNT FREDDIE'S PANTRY*

✿

✿

When one has tasted watermelons, one knows what angels eat. It was not a southern watermelon that Eve took, we know because she repented.

—**MARK TWAIN**

✿

2007 Krispy Kreme introduces a new caramel-flavored, 100-percent whole-wheat doughnut. Coated with the original glaze, it weighs in at 180 calories—approximately 20 fewer than KK's beloved honey-dipped classic. Not much, it's true; still, this doughnut's carbs come mainly from the whole-wheat flour used to make it, meaning that they are the more nutritious complex carbs. Coming next? A trans-fat-free KK doughnut.

After years of archaeological research and careful reconstruction, a faithful replica of George Washington's distillery is up and running at Mount Vernon.

The following are defined or discussed elsewhere: Benne Seed, Calas, Catfish, Cathead Biscuits, Chicken Bog, Chicken Mayonnaise, Court Bouillon, Cracklin's, Cracklin' Bread, Cymlings, Dumplings, Groundnuts, Hominy, Hoppin' John, Hush Puppies, Jerusalem Artichokes, Key Limes, Limpin' Susan, Maque Choux, Mayhaw, Mirliton, Muddle, Muscadine, Pine Bark Stew, Pressed Chicken, Red-Eye Gravy, Rock, Sally Lunn, Sawmill Gravy, Scuppernong, She-Crab, Shirt Tail Pies, Smithfield Ham, Sonker, Spoon Bread, and Sugar Cake. See the index for page numbers.

Alligator pear: What many Southerners call the avocado because it's pear-shaped and its skin is alligator-like: pebbly, leathery, and green.

Andouille: This most beloved of Cajun sausages—smoky, peppery, and 100 percent pork—is integral to gumbos and jambalayas. It's made throughout Cajun country but La Place, Louisiana, claims to be "The Andouille Capital of the World" and stages lively festivals to prove it.

Ash cakes: The simplest of corn breads and an old Appalachian favorite: Mix enough stone-ground cornmeal with water to make a thick mush, shape into cakes a little bigger than hamburgers, ease onto the hearth, cover with white-hot ashes, and bake until done. Brush off the ashes and serve as a sop for pot likker.

Awendaw (also incorrectly spelled Owendaw): A Lowcountry spoon bread made with grits. It's named for Awendaw, a small community about halfway between Charleston and Georgetown directly north, where Indian and African cultures merged.

Baby backs: Spareribs cut from a very young pig. Q-masters I know say they're too lean and flavorless for first-class barbecued ribs.

Batter bread: The Tidewater Virginia name for "spoon bread." In some parts of the South, it also means a thin-enough-to-pour corn bread batter baked in an iron skillet. (See Maria Harrison's Batter Bread, page 256.)

Battered: Food (chicken, for example) dipped into batter before it's fried. Some old-time southern cooks also consider dredging to be "battering."

Batty cakes: A corruption of "batter cakes." These are old-fashioned pancakes or griddle cakes made with stone-ground cornmeal. Sometimes they are served for lunch or supper with butter; more often they show up at the breakfast table with butter plus sweet sorghum, honey, or molasses.

Beaten biscuits: "I can still hear the pounding of that dough out-of-doors atop an old tree trunk," Craig Claiborne writes of his Mississippi childhood in *Craig Claiborne's Southern Cooking* (1987). "That dough" was beaten biscuit dough and according to Claiborne, "it was beaten at least 200 times" until very stiff and white. Only then was it rolled thin, cut into small circles, and baked until the color of parchment. Unfortunately, beaten biscuits are seldom if ever made at home anymore; they're too labor intensive. In the old days, southern families had a faithful cook with a strong arm. Or failing that, a beaten biscuit machine: a marble slab with a double roller through which the dough was cranked again and again until it blistered. I remember beaten biscuits being a supermarket staple when I was growing up in Raleigh. They came twelve to a carton, and, I believe, they were manufactured someplace in Maryland. Accustomed to flaky buttermilk biscuits, I never liked beaten biscuits—too tough. Besides, they were always served cold. To my southern friends, however, they were the daintiest, most delicious biscuits in all creation, especially when split and filled with slivers of Smithfield ham as thin as onion skin.

Beignet: Pronounced ben-YAY, this is the New Orleans equivalent of a doughnut. Holeless and square instead of round, these pillows of deep-fried dough served with lavish dustings of confectioners' sugar have been a staple at the city's French Market for nearly 200 years. Some food historians believe that Ursuline nuns, arriving from France early in the eighteenth century, brought the recipe for beignets with them. Others credit the Cajuns for introducing beignets to Louisiana. The traditional accompaniment? Steaming mugs of café au lait, the dark Louisiana coffee with chicory mellowed with hot milk.

Biloxi bacon: Mullet, so nicknamed along the Gulf Coast because this "trash fish" supports the masses in summer while, as one local wit put it, the Yankees (or "snowbirds" seeking summer) sustain them in winter.

Boudin: A popular Louisiana sausage that may contain cooked rice as well as pork shoulder, pork liver, onions, and assorted spices. Made the traditional way, the mixture is stuffed into natural hog casings. In Cajun Country, boudins are made at *boucheries* or hog-butcherings. And sometimes grilled and served there, too.

Bouilli: Beef brisket. Creole cooks simmer it into soup, hash it for breakfast, and sometimes serve it as the main course of a family meal.

Burr artichoke: The true artichoke; what we know as the French or globe artichoke.

Busters: Crabs just beginning to molt. Cajuns, who consider busters a supreme delicacy, lift off the hard carapaces, leaving barely developed "soft shells" underneath.

Butter beans: Baby limas.

Café brûlot: Lightly sweetened dark New Orleans coffee aromatic of orange zest and cinnamon. Laced with brandy and flamed in a *brûlot* bowl, the coffee is served in demitasses.

Cajun cooking: The spicy cuisine developed by the Acadians (French deported from Nova Scotia) who settled around the Atchafalaya Swamp and bayous west of New Orleans nearly 250 years ago. Crawfish and shrimp predominate in Cajun recipes as do peppery sausages, smoky hams and bacons, and tomatoes right off the vine. But onion, garlic, and green bell pepper, a good Cajun cook once told me, are "The Holy Trinity of Cajun cooking."

Calamondins: The tiny, tart fruits of citrus trees that have become popular house plants. Sometimes called "Chinese oranges" because they're believed to have originated there, calamondins grow well in Florida. In addition to being ornamental, they make superlative marmalade.

Carolina Gold: The yellow-husked rice once grown in the South Carolina Lowcountry; it helped launch the planter aristocracy and made men rich. The Carolina brand rice sold in nearly every supermarket is not Carolina Gold; apart from name, it has little in common with the rice that had been the choice of Chinese emperors.

Cat: Catfish.

Chayote: Another name for **mirliton** (see page 68).

Cheney briar: The Lowcountry word for a nasty, invasive, sharply thorned vine known elsewhere as smilax. The baby shoots, I'm told, taste like asparagus and occasionally show up in local farmer's markets.

Chicory: The practice of roasting the fleshy root of endive and adding it to coffee dates back to eighteenth-century Europe and it may have been the French who introduced coffee with chicory to New Orleans. No one can say for sure. What is known, however, is that to stretch precious coffee during the lean Civil War years, cooks routinely added roasted chicory grounds because chicory was available and it was cheap. To this day, Louisianans prefer coffee with chicory to "everyday American," although those unaccustomed to this dark brew find it excessively bitter.

Chincoteagues: The exquisitely briny Chesapeake oysters taken off the Virginia island of Chincoteague. Some connoisseurs consider Chincoteagues to be the East Coast's finest oysters.

Chinquapins: I always thought that these tiny, buttery acorns came from an oak tree. Not so. They're the "fruit" of a variety of chestnut that grows throughout the South. There was a large chinquapin tree in our front yard when I was a child, and I loved to gather the little brown acorns and string them into necklaces. My father told me that they were edible, also that people liked to roast them just like peanuts. I never tried this, although I did munch a few raw chinquapins; to me they tasted bitter. I've subsequently learned that chinquapins were an important food among Native Americans, who pounded them into meal, pressed them into oil, boiled them into "milk," and no doubt ate them raw or roasted. Frugal mountain folk still use chinquapins much as they would wild hickory nuts or black walnuts.

Chit'lins: Chitterlings or the small intestine of a hog. Cleaned, boiled, and then fried, chit'lins are particularly popular among country folk.

Christophene: Another name for mirliton.

Clabber (also called **bonney-clabber** or **loppered milk**): Thick soured milk the consistency of yogurt. Spooned over cornmeal mush along with molasses, cane syrup, or sugar, it was (and still is) a breakfast favorite in many parts of the South but no more so than in the Louisiana bayous—Cajun Country. In North Carolina, clabber is used to make pancakes (clabber cakes); and when topped with heavy cream, sweetened with sugar, and strewn with freshly grated nutmeg, it is eaten for dessert. (See Heirloom Recipe for Bonney-Clabber, page 291.)

Coal yard: A cup of black coffee; the term was popularized early in the twentieth century, or perhaps even earlier, by New Orleans African Americans.

Collation: In New Orleans, a tea party or a coffee.

Coon: A racoon; some southern country folk still trap them and eat them.

Cooter: Believed to be a corruption of *kuta* (West African for "turtle"), a cooter is a sea turtle. Before sea turtles became an endangered species, Lowcountry cooks made a specialty of cooter soups. Today they're more apt to use terrapin (an amphibious turtle found in brackish water)—if they make turtle soup at all.

Corn pone: In its simplest form a corn pone is nothing more than a thick-enough-to-shape mixture of cornmeal, baking powder (or soda), salt, and water or buttermilk. Patted into burger-size rounds, pones are browned on a well-greased griddle, baked till done "clean through," then served with greens—to sop up the pot likker. But there are more elaborate corn pones, too. One old Outer Banks recipe from Mrs. Rebecca Burrus of Dare County—printed in *From North Carolina Kitchens: Favorite Recipes Old and New*, an uncopyrighted collection of recipes from the state's Home Demonstration Club women—is sweetened with sugar and molasses, then set to rise overnight. Too soft to shape, the batter is baked in a Dutch oven, uncovered for the first two hours, then with the lid on for another hour. Mrs. Burrus accompanied her Pone Bread recipe with the following note: "As far back as the oldest Hatteras resident can remember, pone bread has been considered a treat. It was first cooked in fireplaces, in iron pots, with hot coals on the lids, and later, in modern ovens. No camp meeting was complete without several of these, and not many Sundays passed without each home having a pone bread, cooked the day before. This bread packs well and keeps for a week or more (if well hid) . . . In the days before freezer lockers and short hunting seasons, all the thrifty islanders had a barrel of salted wild fowl, which made an excellent stew, and its gravy was enjoyed over the pone bread. Any gravy is good with it, however."

Country ham: Before refrigeration, farmers used salt to preserve their hams. Over time, they'd add assorted seasonings to the "cure" and soon each family was zealously guarding its own secret recipe. At hog killing time, they'd rub fresh hams with their secret blend, then let them stand until the salt and seasonings permeated the meat. Only then were hams hung in the smokehouse—usually over smoldering hickory coals. Known as a "dry cure," this method produces mahogany-hued hams, firm of flesh and intensely salty-smoky of flavor. The most famous (and some say the most elegant) country ham is the Smithfield (see Baked Virginia Ham and Smithfield Ham, pages 96 and 98). But there are some other mighty fine southern hams, too, among them the Edwards Hams of Surry, Virginia; A. B. Vannoy Hams of North Carolina; Benton's Smoky Mountain Country Hams of Tennessee; and Colonel Bill Newsom's Aged Kentucky Country Hams (see Sources, page 401). **Note:** *The big packing-house hams—what Southerners call "city hams" or "pink hams"—are wet-cured. That is, they are either immersed in brine or, as is more likely these days, injected with a salt solution. Many of these mass-produced hams now carry "water added" phrases on their labels.*

Coush-coush caillé (also spelled **couche-couche** and cush-cush): A crusty skillet-browned cornmeal mush and Cajun breakfast staple. In years past coush-coush was accompanied by clabbered milk, but these days it's more often served with sweet milk and sugar or cane syrup and bacon.

Cowpea: The preferred name for this big family of beans is **southernpea** (see page 398) according to Elizabeth Schneider in *Vegetables from Amaranth to Zucchini* (2001). One of the food world's most diligent researchers and careful writers, Schneider is the absolute authority on fruits and vegetables.

Crawdads: Crayfish or **crawfish** (see below).

Crawfish: Colloquial for crayfish throughout the South. Cajuns tell a charming story about the origin of crawfish: It seems that when the British began deporting the French from Acadia (Nova Scotia) some 250 years ago, lobsters swam alongside the ships. But by the time they'd reached New Orleans, they were so tired and hungry they'd turned into crawfish. Settling west of New Orleans among the bayous, the Cajuns raised crawfish cookery to high art. Today, crawfish farming is big business in Louisiana, with buckets of them being shipped far and wide. (See Sources, page 401.)

Cream peas: See **Lady peas.**

Creecy greens: A bitter wild cress of the mustard family also called winter cress (because it's a cold-weather green) and dry land cress (because it grows in meadows and along roadsides). Old-time southern cooks boil creecy greens with a piece of ham or side meat just as they would collards or turnip salad. But those less wedded to tradition pick it young and toss it into salads. Finding fresh creecy greens isn't as easy as it once was, but you can grow your own. You can also buy canned creecy greens (see Sources, page 401).

Creole cuisine: With ties to France, Spain, and the Caribbean as well as to European aristocracy, Creoles developed an elegant cuisine, a fusion of these three cultures plus additional influences from Africans and Native Americans and even from the German and Italian chefs imported to cook for wealthy Creole families. (The Germans, it's been said, introduced the art of sausage making, although the French were also well versed in *charcuterie.*) Compared to the gutsy country cooking of the Cajuns, who settled in the bayous some hundred miles west of New Orleans, Creole cooking is more refined, more sophisticated. It's the cuisine that made New Orleans famous.

Creole mustard: Sharp, spicy mustard made from brown mustard seeds that are steeped in distilled white vinegar, then coarsely ground and heightened with a little horseradish. New Orleans trenchermen like to slather it on their po' boys, but it's used in countless recipes, too.

Crick (creek) shrimp: The sweet, tiny shrimp netted in Lowcountry inlets, creeks, and rivers. Dusted with floury cornmeal and deep-fried until crisply golden, they are heaven.

Crowder pea: One of the four major groups of **southernpea** (see page 398), so named because the peas (actually beans) are crowded in the pod.

Crybabies: An edible pacifier. These spicy molasses cookies were once used to quiet crying infants and toddlers. In some areas, they still are.

Cush: Equal parts crumbled stale corn bread and biscuits fried in meat drippings with chopped onion. It's a frugal main dish, but in happier times it may be served in addition to meat.

Cushaw: A large (10- to 12-pound) green-and-white–striped crookneck squash with fibrous golden flesh. Like more familiar varieties of winter squash, cushaws are baked into pies or, sometimes, sugared, spiced, baked, and served as a vegetable. Particularly popular among Creoles and Cajuns, cushaws are believed to have been brought to the Deep South from the West Indies during the latter half of the nineteenth century.

Custard marrow: What some Southerners call mirliton (see page 68).

Diamondback: Not a rattlesnake but an amphibious southern turtle used to make soup.

Dirty rice: Rice cooked with bits of liver or chicken liver. A Louisiana favorite.

Dressing: What Southerners call stuffing, as in turkey stuffing. Of course, "dressing" also means salad dressing.

Dry land cress: See **Creecy greens**.

Étouffée: A Cajun stew (usually crawfish or shrimp) served over rice with lots of roux-thickened gravy.

Fatback (also known as **side meat** and **sowbelly**): Fat trimmed from the back of a hog, usually salt-cured. Fatback containing a streak of lean ("streaky") is often cooked along with a pot of green beans, collards, or turnip greens.

Field apricots: See **Maypops**.

Field pea: A synonym for **cowpea**; its preferred name is **southernpea** (see page 398).

Filé powder (also called **gumbo filé** and sometimes more simply, **filé**). An aromatic green-gray powder made of dried sassafras leaves—a Choctaw innovation used both to flavor and thicken stews, which Creole and Cajun cooks quickly applied to their gumbos. A Cajun cook I interviewed some years ago was adamant on one point: Filé powder is never used to thicken gumbos containing okra because okra does the job. When I told her that I'd seen many recipes containing both okra and filé powder, she sniffed, "Well, they aren't authentic!"

Geechees: Lowcountry African Americans, many of whom were isolated for years on the dot-dash string of Sea Islands below Charleston. Their contribution to

Lowcountry cooking cannot be overestimated. Also see **Gullah**.

Goobers: Peanuts.

Green corn: Corn picked before it's fully ripe. Southerners prize its slightly grassy flavor and like to grate the immature kernels and stir them into corn cakes, fritters, and puddings.

Green peanuts: Freshly dug raw peanuts. Farmer's markets sell them both in the shell and out. (See Sources, page 401.)

Grillades: Thin beef or veal steaks cut from the round, quickly browned, then simmered in a spicy tomato sauce and served with grits. A New Orleans breakfast favorite. (See recipe, page 103.)

Grits: Except in the South Carolina Lowcountry where grits (from the word *grist*) is coarsely ground dried corn, grits is ground dried hominy (yes, *grits* is singular). Supermarket grits is about the texture of polenta, but persnickety southern cooks prefer it stone-ground and coarser.

Groundnuts: Peanuts.

Ground peas: Peanuts.

Guinea squash: Another name for eggplant commonly used in the Deep South (Louisiana, Mississippi, Alabama, and Georgia).

Gullah: The patois spoken by Lowcountry African Americans (**Geechees**), who influenced Lowcountry cuisine both as plantation cooks and as home cooks. Not so long ago, you could hear Gullah on the streets of Charleston as fish and vegetable vendors made their rounds.

Gumbo: A spicy Creole-Cajun stew (or soup) and culinary melding of four cultures: African (*gumbo* derives from the Bantu *gombo*), Native American, French, and Spanish. The best-known gumbos brim with crawfish or shrimp, sausages, okra (the thickener if filé powder isn't used), tomatoes, peppers sweet and hot, onions, garlic, bay leaves, parsley, and assorted other seasonings. (See recipe, page 61.)

Gumbo filé: See **Filé powder**.

Half moons: Fried fruit turnovers that are also known as **mule ears** and **shirt tail pies**. But there are nuances: Half moons can be made with almost any fruit; mule ears are usually filled with sun-dried peaches; and shirt tail pies are filled with dried apples.

Hicker nuts: Colloquial for wild hickory nuts in southern Appalachia.

Hoecakes: Campfire corn breads; in days past, simple cornmeal mush (cornmeal, water, salt) was shaped into patties, laid on the blade of a hoe, and propped near an open fire to bake.

Jambalaya: You might call this a rich Creole-Cajun pilau. But rice is merely the beginning. In addition to sausage, shrimp, crawfish, chicken, turkey, or other meat—not to mention onions, garlic, tomatoes, bell peppers, and a carload of heady seasonings—jambalayas usually contain ham. Some etymologists believe that its name comes from *jamón*, the Spanish word for ham. Food historian Karen Hess *(The Carolina Rice Kitchen)* dismisses this, however, citing several early jambalaya recipes that contain no ham. She further suggests that jambalaya derives from the Provençal *jambalaia, jabalaia,* and *jambaraia* defined by Frédéric Mistral in the late nineteenth century as an Arab word. Hess suspects that Arabs may have introduced jambalaya-like dishes to the South of France during their occupation there or perhaps, she adds, it may have been Sephardic Jews, who also settled in Provence before and during the Middle Ages. Whatever its origin, jambalaya is fusion cooking at its best: the flavors of the Near East, Africa, France, and Spain bubbling in a single pot. In his *Dictionary of American Food and Drink*, John Mariani offers yet another explanation for the recipe's name. It seems that when a gentleman stopped by a New Orleans inn late one night, the cupboard was bare. Undaunted, the innkeeper told his chef, Jean, to rustle up a little something—*balayez*, in the local patois, according to Mariani. Pleased with his odds-and-ends dinner, the guest gave it a name: *Jean Balayez*. Which over time became *jambalaya*. Apocryphal or not, it's a charming story. (See recipe, page 126.)

Jimmy: A male blue crab. The tips of its claws are bright blue; the female's are as red as fingernail polish.

Kentucky wonder beans: A popular variety of **pole beans** (see page 396) characterized by its plumpness and almost nutlike flavor. In size and taste, they're more like Italian green beans than conventional snap beans.

Lady peas: The most delicate **southernpea** (see page 398); the peas (actually beans) are small, pearly, and devoid of "eyes." Lady peas are also sometimes called cream peas.

Lard: The snowy, creamy rendered fat of hogs; the Southerner's shortening of choice. Nothing makes flakier biscuits or pie crusts and for many Cajuns, it is the only fat to use in a roux. Another plus: Lard adds subtle meaty flavor.

Leather britches beans (also called **shuck beans**): Green beans that have been dried until shriveled and leathery. In the old days, fresh beans were threaded onto string and hung in the attic to dry, a method of preserving learned from the Cherokee, it's said. Today the beans are more often "dried" in a dehydrator. Leather britches beans should be reconstituted in water before they're cooked.

Lighten or light bread: Yeast bread, especially yeast-raised corn bread. Here's a recipe for Old-Fashioned Corn Light Bread from Mrs. W. A. McGlamery of Clay County, North Carolina, just as it appears in *From North Carolina Kitchens: Favorite Recipes Old and New* (an uncopyrighted volume of recipes compiled fifty years ago by the state's Home Demonstration Club women): "One quart water in a pot, let come to a boil; add one teaspoon salt, stir in cornmeal to make a thick mush. Add enough cold water to make it lukewarm, stir in meal to make a thick batter, cover and set by fire to keep warm; let rise twice and stir down; have oven hot; when it rises third time, put in oven and bake quickly." The bread generates its own yeast.

Liver mush (also called **liver pudding**): A baked loaf made of ground boiled pork liver, cornmeal, sage, salt, and black pepper—a southern breakfast specialty. Before being served, it's sliced and fried in bacon drippings or butter. (See Heirloom Recipe, page 109.)

Loppered milk: Clabber.

Loquats: Also called Japanese plums, these sunny little fruits are ones that I will forever associate with Charleston, South Carolina; they seem to grow everywhere there. Depending upon variety, they can be as sweet as cane syrup or fairly sour. During their all-too-brief early spring season, loquats are made into pies, boiled into preserves, or eaten out of hand. Unfortunately, they are too fragile to ship.

Love Feast buns: Large round buns made from a rich yeast dough that in many versions contains mashed potatoes. According to Elizabeth Hedgecock Sparks, who was for many years the food editor of the *Journal-Sentinel* in Winston-Salem, North Carolina, Moravian Love Feasts are held on Christmas, New Year's, Easter, and other days of significance to the church. At the Home Moravian Church in Winston-Salem, Love Feast buns are accompanied by coffee (with cream and sugar). In *North Carolina and Old Salem Cookery*, Sparks, herself a Moravian, writes, "The idea behind the simple meal is that those who break bread together are united in the fellowship the way a family is." (See recipe, page 267.)

Marsh hen: The Lowcountry word for the clapper rail. A shy bird that hides among the reeds and salt grasses, it is difficult to spot. Still, persistent hunters bag it in season and claim to like its fishy taste.

Maypops (also called **mountain apricots** or **field apricots**): Passion fruits. One of the things we kids loved to do was stomp on the lime-green, lime-size passion fruits that grew in the red clay gullies of our edge-of-Raleigh neighborhood. They popped like firecrackers and, given their name, must have begun appearing sometime in May, although it seems to me that these tangled vines bore fruit all summer long. I remember the flesh inside being frosty-white; I guess you could say pithy. My father, a botanist, explained to my older brother and me that these were passion fruits—a delicacy in many parts of the world. I couldn't imagine eating a maypop; of course the ones we squashed with such glee were immature. I didn't taste mature passion fruits until many years later. When I was on assignment on the island of Madeira, I was served a passion-fruit dessert. Jacques Pépin, who happened to be on the island at the same time with his wife, Gloria, called it "Portuguese Jell-O."

We all liked the local passion-fruit firewater much better. To me, passion-fruit flowers are incredibly delicate and beautiful. Measuring about two inches across, they are fringed in a starburst of purples, mauves, and whites. And their centers—fleshy and pale green or gold, if I'm remembering correctly after all these years—are said to resemble Christ's crown of thorns. Hence the name "passion fruit." According to Joseph E. Dabney (*Smokehouse Ham, Spoon Bread, and Scuppernong Wine*), passion fruits are best after the first frost. Prized throughout the Smokies, they are gathered and turned into puddings and preserves. Dabney adds that "the Amerindians, including the Cherokee, made a delicious drink of the fruit."

Mess o' greens: A big pot of collards, turnip greens, poke sallet, or other popular southern green cooked ("overcooked," my Yankee mother always said) in water with a piece of side meat or streaky. The greens are usually served in little bowls with plenty of pot likker (the leftover cooking water) and a corn bread of some kind to sop it up.

Mirliton: A type of squash popular in the Deep South (see page 68).

Mississippi mud: There are Mississippi mud pies and Mississippi mud cakes, both of them chocolate, both of them as dark and gooey as a Mississippi River mud bank, and both of them of fairly recent origin. I'd never heard of them until the mid 1970s. Even Mississippi-born-and-bred *New York Times* food editor Craig Claiborne wasn't aware of them until after he'd moved north. I once ate a frozen Mississippi mud pie in Charleston, South Carolina, that was a bit different: a crushed Oreo crust mounded with chocolate ice cream mounded with whipped cream drizzled with chocolate syrup and strewn with curls of semisweet chocolate. While traveling about Mississippi, I've come across Mississippi mud cakes steamed in preserving jars. They look messy, but to chocoholics like me they are glorious! I shudder to think of the calories.

Mountain apricots: See **Maypops.**

Mountain dew: Better known as **moonshine** or **white lightning**, this is bootlegged corn liquor. During Prohibition, bootleggers worked overtime in the mountains of North Carolina, Tennessee, Virginia, and West Virginia, hence the name "mountain dew." A "revenuer" (government agent) once told me that a sure way to tell a bootlegger was to look at the back end of his car. If the body was "jacked"—riding several feet above the rear wheels—the owner was a bootlegger. Of course if the car *looked* jacked, the trunk was empty and no arrest could be made. On the other hand, if the trunk was full, the car looked normal. That was the point. I saw a lot of jacked cars when I worked as an assistant home demonstration agent in Iredell County, North Carolina. In fact, when I was to visit a poor family in the north end of the county, I was told to tell them exactly what time I'd arrive. "Don't be early," my boss warned me. "And don't be late 'cause they'll come out shooting." I knew what that meant: I might be mistaken for a "revenuer." That wasn't my first encounter with a bootlegger, however. A friend of ours bought a farm near Raleigh and, to his astonishment, discovered a still operating in its nether reaches. The dead giveaway: a stream turned rusty yellow by the still's runoff. My brother and I were shown the stream one day and, though I couldn't have been more than ten, I'll never forget the Day-Glo brilliance of that water.

Mudbug: Crayfish or **crawfish** (see page 392).

Mudcat: Catfish.

Muffaletta: The New Orleans equivalent of the hero sandwich. Created in 1906 by owner Salvatore Lupo at the Central Grocery, it consists of a small but sturdy round loaf mounded with thinly sliced cheese, mortadella, and salami plus a ladling of pickled olives or olive salad. According to John Mariani in *The Dictionary of American Food and Drink*, *muffaletta*, translated from the Sicilian dialect, means "a round loaf of bread baked so that the center is hollow" and can be stuffed.

Mule ears: Fried turnovers filled with dried peaches, popular in the Smokies and Carolina hill country. They are also called **half moons** (see page 394).

Owendaw: See **Awendaw.**

Oyster plant: Salsify, a favorite southern vegetable, particularly among the antebellum planter aristocracy. In early southern cookbooks, the recipe that appears over and over again is Scalloped Oyster Plant, parboiled, creamed, strewn with buttered crumbs, and baked until bubbling and brown. (See recipe, page 208).

Peach leather: Fresh peach purée boiled with sugar until the consistency of jam, spread thin on a marble slab or large flat plate, and dried in the sun for several days until leathery. Some Southerners roll the peach leather into a cone at this point and munch it like taffy. But there's a more elegant finish: Dust the peach leather with confectioners' sugar, roll it up jelly-roll style, and slice into rounds at ½- to 1-inch intervals. Then it's back into the sun for two to three more days. Stored in an airtight container, peach leather keeps for weeks.

Philpy: A rice bread popular in the South Carolina Lowcountry from Colonial times up through the nineteenth century. It is rarely made today.

Pilau: Southern for rice pilaf; in the Lowcountry dialect, it's **purloo.**

Pinder, pindar: What some old-timers call peanuts, especially those who grow them. In his *Garden Book*, Thomas Jefferson called them "peendars" and wrote of planting them at Monticello.

Plantation soup: A more elegant term for **Pot likker** (see page 397).

Poke: A sack, usually a brown paper grocery bag. Southerners like to say that they'd never "buy a pig in a poke," meaning they want to have a good look at something before they lay down any hard cash.

Poke sallet: Pokeweed leaves. When young and tender, they are edible. Most Southerners boil them just as they would turnip greens or collards—with a piece of side meat.

Pole beans: Green beans "on steroids." Actually they're about 1½ times the size of regular green beans and must be staked on poles, hence their name. For growin' and eatin' most Southerners would agree that Kentucky Wonder Beans are the best.

Pompey's head: A large, domed, highly seasoned meatloaf once popular down south. There's a recipe for it in *Mrs. Hill's Southern Practical Cookery and Receipt Book* (1872). As for the unusual name, southern culinary historian-cookbook author Damon Lee Fowler writes in the book's glossary that it may have come from the "ancient Roman statesman Pompeius," whose unusually broad head the meatloaf was said to resemble.

Portulaca (also called **Purslane**): A fleshy salad green popular long ago among southern cooks that's being rediscovered by trendy chefs. I've seen lush beds of it in eastern North Carolina, also farther south in the Lowcountry. But I've had no luck growing it in my Chapel Hill garden; perhaps winters here are too harsh. Still, I keep an eye peeled for portulaca at my farmer's market. It reminds me of the Italian *puntarella*.

Pot likker: Vegetable cooking water, particularly that left over from cooking collards, turnip greens, or green beans. It's sopped up with corn bread.

Pulled pork: North Carolina barbecue, especially eastern style, for which the whole hog is pit-roasted over hickory coals until so tender the meat can be pulled from the bone. The classic sauce consists mainly of oil, vinegar, and cayenne pepper.

Pully bone: The chicken wishbone; children pull it to see who gets the longer piece—and a secret wish.

Purloo: A colloquial word, especially in the Lowcountry, for **pilau** or **pilaf**. (See Turkey Purloo, page 144.)

Purslane: See **portulaca**.

Ramps: Wild leeks. Ramp festivals erupt in spring and summer across the Smokies and Blue Ridge.

Ratafia: A cordial made by steeping berries or other fruits in brandy. Old Charleston ratafias call for soaking peach kernels in brandy and adding orange flower water for flavor.

Receipt: The preferred southern word for *recipe*, especially in Tidewater Virginia and the South Carolina Lowcountry. It may derive from *recette*, the French word for *recipe*. Many French Huguenots settled in the Lowcountry.

Red and white: Popular New Orleans phrase for red beans and rice. (See recipe, page 175.)

Rock (also called **rockfish**): What Outer Bankers and others living on the South's other barrier islands call striped bass. (See Rock Muddle recipe, page 57.)

Roux: The fat-and-flour paste used to thicken gumbos and scores of other Cajun and Creole dishes. There is blonde roux for delicate gravies and sauces and a rusty brown roux for more robust recipes. Miss Tootie Guirard, a lively Cajun cook I profiled for *Family Circle* some years ago, told me, "You must work the roux very slowly in a very heavy pot for at least half an hour until it turns a rich rusty brown. Any time I see a recipe that says to cook the roux five minutes, I know it's no good."

Sallet: Salad greens (usually a mixture) or the salad made from them. Some Southerners also call turnip greens "turnip sallet."

Sally (or **she-crab**): A sexually immature female blue crab, easily ID'd by its scarlet claw tips and triangular apron (belly).

Salt pork: Freshly butchered cuts of pork, laid down in crocks with saltpeter or salt. Before refrigeration, this was one way meat could be preserved. Today, salt pork is not readily available—and the salt pork I've found is fat, not lean.

Salt-rising bread: Ruth Current, for years the state leader of the North Carolina Extension Service's home demonstration clubs, introduced me to salt-rising bread. Born and brought up on a farm in Rowan County, Miss Current made this special bread every Christmas to give to friends and colleagues and I was lucky enough to be a beneficiary. The taste and texture of salt-rising bread are unlike any other. It's not as sour as sourdough, not as sweet as yeast bread. And its chewiness? Slightly less than that of an English muffin. (See Heirloom Recipe, page 268.)

Samp: An old-fashioned word for cornmeal mush, derived, it's said, from the Algonquin word *nasaump*. In Colonial days and even later, Southerners breakfasted on samp with milk or butter, dined on samp and gravy, and even made a dessert of it by adding molasses or sweet sorghum.

Shine: Moonshine.

Short'nin' bread: A song I heard a lot when I was growing up down south—long before such things were "politically incorrect"—was "Mammy's little baby loves short'nin,' short'nin,' Mammy's little baby loves short'nin' bread." Some believe it's the southern equivalent of Scottish shortbread, an easy three-ingredient recipe: butter, sugar (often light brown instead of granulated), and flour, although sometimes cornstarch replaces part of the flour to make the shortbread more tender.

Shuck beans: Another name for **leather britches beans** (see page 394).

Side meat: The same as **fatback** (see page 393).

'Simmon: Country colloquial for wild persimmon.

Skip-in Jenny: What Charlestonians call leftover Hoppin' John.

Snow biscuits: Yeast-raised biscuits. They're rolled, cut into rounds, pricked with a fork, and baked in a hot oven straightaway—no rising period. Served hot with homemade jam or jelly, they sometimes substitute for dessert.

Sook: A sexually mature female blue crab, easily distinguished from the male because the tips of its claws are red, not blue. A sook can also be recognized by its bell-shaped apron (belly); the male's is phallic.

Sorghum molasses (also called sweet **sorghum**): Southern farmers, particularly those of Appalachia, grow a grain called sorghum to feed their livestock. They also press juice from the ripe seed clusters and boil it down until thick, syrupy, and the color of amber. This is sorghum molasses, mellower than sugarcane molasses and a popular sweetener. In the Blue Ridge and Smokies, sweet sorghum is ladled over breakfast biscuits. (See Sources, page 401.)

Sour mash: To many Southerners, sour mash means the ultra-smooth, charcoal-filtered corn whiskeys of Tennessee, with Jack Daniel's being the epitome of them all. But in truth, most bourbons are "sour mash" whiskeys, meaning that one day's spent mash (a mix of grain, yeast, water, and sugar or molasses) is used to jump-start the next day's fermentation. (See Jack Daniel's Tennessee Whiskey, page 23, also Bourbon, page 342.)

Sourwood honey: A beloved Appalachian honey—delicate, pale as straw, and not overly sweet—produced from the nectar of sourwood blossoms. (See Sources, page 401.)

Souse meat: A congealed loaf of ground pickled pork (usually the head and trotters) well seasoned with vinegar, salt, sage, and black pepper. It was always made with great care (each family using its own recipe), ladled into crocks, heavily weighted, and stored in the coldest part of the house. Considered a delicacy, it's great in a sandwich, delicious sliced and eaten cold or breaded and fried. In the old days, souse meat was one of the by-products of the annual fall or winter hog killing. (See Heirloom Recipe, page 93.)

Southern house wine: Sweet tea.

Southernpea (also called **cowpea, field pea,** and **black-eyed pea**). The nomenclature of the beans so dear to Southerners (for these are beans) boggles because they go by different names in different parts of the South. One cook's cowpea, for example, is another cook's crowder pea. To clarify things, cookbook author Elizabeth Schneider, in *Vegetables from Amaranth to Zucchini*, tracked down Blair Buckley, an authority at Louisiana State University's Calhoun Research Center. Here's how he groups the southernpeas—from delicate to assertive: (1) cream or lady pea, (2) pinkeye purple hull (variously mottled pods ranging in color from green to burgundy with rose-eyed green or dusty tan peas), (3) black-eyed pea (yellow-green pods packed with black-eyed tan or pale green peas), (4) crowder pea (greenish-grayish pods so crammed with peas they're misshapen). Shelling southernpeas is labor-intensive, but most farmer's markets, thank goodness, now sell them already shucked. Moreover, some of these peas—black-eyes, in particular—are available frozen and/or dried.

Sowbelly: The same as **fatback** (see page 393).

Spat: A baby oyster.

Sponge crab: An egg-laden female blue crab. She carries her eggs—a spongy mass—on her belly. In the Chesapeake, females move to the intensely salty waters of the lower bay to spawn, even into the Atlantic.

Stack cake: A homespun hill-country dessert that consists of five, six, or even more wafer-thin, Frisbee-size shortbread or cookie rounds sandwiched together with a dried apple filling. Some cooks spike the filling with bourbon or Tennessee whiskey; some don't. (See recipe, page 286.)

Stone-ground meal: Cornmeal ground the old-fashioned way: between stones. Some southern mills still sluice water onto giant wooden water wheels that set the grindstones in motion, which explains why it is also sometimes known as water-ground meal. One of the best places to see an early water-powered mill is at Cades Cove, Tennessee, in the Great Smoky Mountains National Park. (See Sources, page 401.)

Streaky: Pork fat (or fatback) with a streak of lean. Often cooked along with collards, creecy greens, kale, turnip greens, poke sallet, or green beans, it adds delicate meat flavor and eliminates the need for butter.

Sunchoke: Jerusalem artichoke.

Sweet milk: Fresh milk as opposed to buttermilk (or sour milk).

Sweet sorghum: See **sorghum molasses.**

Sweet tea: The presweetened iced tea both southern home cooks and restaurants serve. Today some restaurants also offer the option of "unsweet tea." In country or small-town restaurants, glasses are continually refilled at no extra charge.

Swimpy: Colloquial for "shrimp," especially along the Gulf Coast and in the Georgia–South Carolina Lowcountry.

Syllabub: A frothy milk punch spiked with bourbon or rum introduced to the South by the English gentry who settled there. In the old days, cows were milked directly into the mix and that created the froth.

Tasso: Cold-smoked, cured, pickled pork or beef. Richly spiced, often peppery, and traditionally used to season gumbos, jambalayas, and other Cajun and Creole dishes, tasso has found new favor among innovative chefs elsewhere about the South who slip it into everything from "nouvelle Hoppin' John" to Brunswick stews their grandmothers would never recognize.

Tassies: Bite-size tarts served mainly at teas, open houses, and receptions. Most popular flavors? Pecan (as in pecan pie) and lemon (as in lemon chess pie).

Tupelo honey: A rare honey made from the nectar of tupelo gum blossoms. These trees grow mainly in Florida and along the Gulf Coast. (See Sources, page 401.)

Vegetable pear: Another name for **mirliton** (see page 395).

Virginia ambrosia: Brunswick Stew. (See recipe, page 127.)

Water-ground meal: See **stone-ground meal.**

White lightning: Bootlegged whiskey. Also called **moonshine** (or **shine**) and **mountain dew.**

Winter cress: See **creecy greens.**

Zephyrinas ("Zeffies"): I must confess that in all my years of living in the South, I've yet to meet a zephyrina, let alone taste one. Fortunately, when I was researching the subject, two fellow Southerners, good friends and colleagues, were there to enlighten me: James Villas, who grew up in Charlotte, North Carolina, and Damon Lee Fowler of Savannah. Jim tells me that zephyrinas are wispy-thin crackers made of biscuit (usually beaten biscuit) dough, a Charleston specialty. "I remember as a child eating them there spread with pimento cheese at the wonderful old Henry's restaurant . . . I think Mother and Daddy used to love them at Henry's also with she-crab soup." He adds that his grandmother would make "extra biscuit dough just to pound it out thin with a rolling pin for zephyrinas—or zeffies." Jim includes a recipe for them in his engaging cookbook, *Biscuit Bliss* (2003), giving credit where credit is due. "Bill Neal writes about [zephyrinas] in his book, *Biscuits, Spoonbread, and Sweet Potato Pie*," Jim says. "I include the recipe in my biscuit book with an acknowledgment to Bill." Damon Lee Fowler tells me that zephyrinas, or rather crisp, flat wafers much like them, were a Savannah specialty as well. They differ, he explains, "only in detail and were traditionally served with turtle soup." While on the zephyrinas hunt, Damon turned up a recipe for them in Sarah Rutledge's *Carolina Housewife* (1847). And there they are in the "Breads, Cakes, Etc." chapter of this predominately Lowcountry collection of receipts, calling for a pint of flour, "a small spoonful of butter," and "sufficient water to make a dough that may be kneaded, and some salt." Rutledge directs the reader to roll the dough "not thicker, if possible, than a sheet of paper," to cut into rounds with a saucer, to prick with a fork, and to bake "in an oven moderately warm. They are baked instantaneously." I should think so.

Sources

For Most Things Southern

boiledpeanuts.com. Everything from boiled peanuts and benne wafers to MoonPies, sorghum molasses, cane syrup, and stone-ground grits plus canned Brunswick stew, creecy greens, poke sallet, and she-crab soup.

southernseason.com. Grits and grains, parchment-thin Moravian cookies (ginger, sugar, lemon, black walnut), cheese straws hot and mild, wild honeys, barbecue sauces, pickles, and relishes (including the beloved Jerusalem artichoke pickle relish).

thevirginiacompany.com. Peanuts every which way, cheeses, cheese biscuits, crab cakes, Smithfield hams (even ham biscuits), smoked bacon and sausage links, fruit butters and spiced peaches, cookies and candies as well as some of the Old Dominion's best wines.

Heat-and-Eat Barbecue, Brunswick Stew, and Other Savory Classics

barbarajeans.com. Crab cakes large, medium, and mini—all lump crabmeat, no fillers. *Southern Living* magazine calls them "the best." Also she-crab soup.

carolinacurlytailbbq.com. Smoky, sweet-sour, hand-picked Eastern North Carolina barbecue by the pound and homemade Carolina Brunswick stew by the quart.

chesapeakebaygourmet.com. Maryland-style crab cakes, crab imperial, crab-stuffed mushrooms or shrimp, tomato-based Maryland crab soup, and more.

virginiatraditions.com. Barbecued ribs, breaded oysters, crab cakes, Virginia Brunswick stew, and so forth.

Bakeware

bakerscatalogue.com. Pan shapes and sizes not often available in retail stores.

cooksdream.com. Hard to find 7- and 8-inch tube (angel food cake) pans plus a variety of decorative pans both large and small.

Cakes and Pies, Cookies, and Candies

byrdcookiecompany.com. Headquarters for benne wafers, butter thins, Key lime coolers, peach cookies, and more. A Savannah tradition since 1924.

cajunpecanhouse.com. Mardi Gras king cakes, Cajun fruitcakes, pecan pies, and butter-roasted pecans plus sugared, cinnamon, or praliné pecans.

cakesbyjane.com. Moist, feathery, from-scratch pound cakes baked in some half dozen flavors (almond, Key lime, lemon, orange, pumpkin [November only], vanilla).

fudgeman.com. The world's only saltwater fudge: smooth, creamy, addictive.

gethsemanifarms.org. Kentucky bourbon fruitcake and fudges (chocolate bourbon and butter-walnut bourbon).

hanescookies.com. Making gingery, super-thin Moravian cookies for more than 75 years, the Hanes family still hand-rolls, hand-cuts, and hand-packs each and every one.

mscheesestraws.com. Cheese straws sweet and savory, also Mississippi Mud Puppies® (oatmeal-pecan cookies chock-full of chocolate chips).

oldsalem.org. Paper-thin Moravian cookies (ginger, sugar, lemon, black walnut) plus Winkler Bakery mixes for Moravian Love Feast buns, sugar cake, gingerbread, and sweet potato muffins. Located on Old Salem's Main Street, the 200-year-old Winkler Bakery still bakes its breads and cookies in wood-fired brick ovens.

sosupreme.com. Long on nuts and short on candied fruits, these Scott family fruitcakes win scores of "best I ever ates" and are shipped all over the world. Also, homemade peanut brittle, butter pecan crunch, chocolate-covered pecans, and more.

sunnylandfarms.com. Nut barks, brittles, clusters, and pralines.

thebestcake.com. Now available by mail, the perfect pound cake made with pure butter, eggs, sugar, and flour. This cake won "best in show" at the North Carolina State Fair.

Canning and Pickling Supplies

bakerscatalogue.com. A source for the powdered ascorbic acid and citric acid (sour salt) used to keep apples, peaches, pears, and other foods from darkening when canned or frozen.

canningpantry.com. Headquarters for pressure canners, water-bath canners, meat grinders, juicers, dehydrators, and a variety of other food conservation essentials.

goodmans.net. A large inventory of canning equipment and accessories.

homecanningsupply.com. Everything for the home canner: apple peelers, bean slicers, jelly jars, pickling crocks, pressure canners, and steam canners.

polsteins.com. Jars large and small, jar lifters, wide-mouth canning funnels, liquid and powdered pectin, even electric tomato squeezers.

mrswages.com. Pickling lime, pickling salt, and an anti-browning agent plus a variety of pectins and pickling mixes.

Cheeses

bedfordcheese.com. Aged, additive-free Cheddars.

gethsemanifarms.org. Making cheese since the 1940s, these Kentucky monks offer three different Trappist cheeses: mild, aged, and hickory-smoked.

Coffees

martinezfinecoffees.com. Outstanding estate coffees from Central and South America, Kenya, Hawaii, Jamaica (where the Martinez family has roots), and elsewhere. Personally selected beans, "the pick of the crop" roasted on the day of purchase or shipment.

Condiments, Sauces, and Seasonings

thencstore.com. Bone Suckin' barbecue sauces hot and mild (voted "America's best" by *Food & Wine* magazine) plus Bone Suckin' mustard, salsa, rib rub, and hot pepper sauce.

tonychachere.com. Gumbo filé, Cajun and Creole seasoning blends, marinades, gravy and batter mixes.

Fish and Shellfish
Blue crabs:

ilovecrabs.com. Hard- and soft-shell blue crabs, also jumbo Gulf Coast shrimp.

lintonsseafood.com. One-of-a-kind Maryland blue crabs from Crisfield on Chesapeake Bay. Also soft-shells in season, lump crabmeat, crab balls, crab soups, and chowders. A good source, too, for Chesapeake oysters and clams.

virginiatraditions.com. Jumbo soft-shell crabs.

Stone crabs:

Stone crabs are prized for their large claws and the sweet, firm-but-tender meat they contain. The season for fresh stone crabs? Mid-October through mid-May.

beststonecrabs.com. Colossal stone crab claws packed and shipped.

freshchoiceseafood.com. Stone crab claws in four sizes: medium, large, jumbo, and colossal.

freshfloridastonecrab.com. Cooked stone crab claws as well as fresh in a variety of sizes.

ozonacrabco.com. A group of independent fishermen who concentrate on the Gulf's prize catch: stone crabs. Founded nearly 100 years ago, the company is based near Tarpon Springs where, it's said, stone crab claws are the biggest and best.

twinmarketplace.com. Right-off-the-boat stone crab claws overnighted to you plus a well-worth-ordering mustard-based stone crab sauce.

Catfish:

Kajun Catfish. No website. Purveyor of wild, freshly caught catfish. Phone: (504) 758-7454.

Des Allemands Out Law Katfish. No website. Another source for wild catfish. Phone: (985) 758-7454.

Crawfish:

lacrawfish.com. This family-owned business in Natchitoches, Louisiana, guarantees that the crawfish shipped to your door will arrive live and kicking. They also pack and ship jumbo Gulf shrimp.

cajuncrawfish.com. Shrimp, live crawfish, and a variety of other Cajun foods.

Flour, Cornmeal, Grits, and Other Grains

ansonmills.com. Organic, stone-ground cornmeal and grits milled in small batches; they're praised for their fresh corn flavor. Also headquarters for the precious Carolina Gold rice.

hoppinjohns.com. Stone-ground grits (the coarsest grind), cornmeal, and corn flour.

J. T. Pollard Milling Co. No website; phone: 1-334-588-3391. Edna Lewis and Scott Peacock consider its stone-ground cornmeal the South's best.

Logan Turnpike Mills. No website; phone: 1-800-844-7487. *Atlanta Cuisine* calls its water-ground grits "the best in the nation." Logan also grinds cornmeal and flour.

marthawhite.com. An old Tennessee company relocated to Minnesota, Martha White still mills the soft-wheat flours southern bakers prize. Many southern supermarkets still stock Martha White flours, cornmeals, and mixes but if unavailable, they can be ordered online.

oldmillofguilford.com. From an eighteenth-century water-powered mill: yellow or white cornmeal and grits, unbleached plain or self-rising flour, high-gluten flour, rye flour, buckwheat flour, and more.

whitelily.com. Miller of the South's beloved soft (low-gluten) flours (all-purpose and self-rising), essential for feathery cakes, flaky biscuits, and pastries. Other products: unbleached bread and self-rising flours; biscuit, brownie, cornmeal, muffin, and pancake mixes.

Fruits and Vegetables

Creecy greens (wild cress of the mustard family):

Available in 14.5-ounce cans from InTown General Mercantile in Aberdeen, North Carolina. **www.eintown .com/ourstore.**

Key limes:

Some high-end southern groceries carry fresh Key limes in season (fall and early winter) as does the Whole Foods chain of stores.

Key lime juice:

floridajuice.com. Key lime juice by the case in small (1-pint), medium (1-quart), and large (1-gallon) bottles.

keylimejuice.com. What began as a Key West cottage industry more than thirty years ago (backyard Key limes squeezed into beer bottles) has become the wholly professional Nellie & Joe's Famous Lime Juice. For home cooks there are 16-ounce (1-pint) bottles; for food service industries there are 55-gallon drums.

williams-sonoma.com. Key lime juice in handy 12-ounce bottles.

Vidalia onions:

byronplantation.com. Spring and fall harvest Vidalias, baby Vidalias, plus Vidalia relishes, vinaigrettes, and other products.

manningfarms.com. Fresh Vidalias as well as cookbooks and assorted products.

vidaliasfinest.com. Jumbo Vidalias from the L. G. Herndon, Jr., Farms shipped in 10- or 40-pound boxes from May through September.

robisonfarms@cybersouth.com. Two sizes of Vidalias—3-inch-or-larger Jumbos and 1¾- to 2¾-inch Mediums—shipped in season.

vidaliaarea.com/pdfs/OnionGrowersList. For a complete list of Vidalia Onion growers and handlers.

Ramps (wild leeks):

earthy.com. Fresh ramps, available only from late March through June.

Wild Persimmon Purée:

dillmanfarm.com. Just what you need for persimmon bread and pudding.

Hams, Bacon, Sausages, and Other Meats

Benton's Smoky Mountain Country Hams. No website; phone: 1-423-442-5003. Sugar-cured or hickory-smoked hams and bacons, also American prosciutto.

cajunspecialtymeats.com. Purveyors of a variety of Cajun products, among them the classic tasso, andouille, and boudin as well as heat-and-eat turducken (duck-and-chicken-stuffed turkey) and crawfish étouffée–stuffed chicken.

comeaux.com. An excellent source for tasso; recommended by Slow Food USA.

ncsmokehouse.com. Headquarters for tasso, andouille, boudin, and other Cajun sausages.

newsomscountryham.com. Fine-fleshed hams aged from a 200-year-old curing process. Also available: smoked bacon and sausages, aged prosciutto hams.

smithfieldcollection.com. The famous Smithfield hams as well as Virginia country hams.

smithfield-companies.com. Smithfield hams, honey-cured hams, roasted ham, smoked ham, Virginia country ham, even ring-necked pheasant.

smithfieldhams.com. Smithfield hams featured in *The New York Times*, also ham and turkey combos and bacon and cheese biscuits.

smokymtnbbq@skybest.com. Nitrite-free country hams made the same way for nearly 100 years. Ingredients: Ham, salt, brown sugar, fresh mountain air, and time.

thevirginiacompany.com. Honey-glazed Edwards hams and Smithfield hams plus smokehouse samplers from Smithfield.

virginiatraditions.com. The famous hickory-smoked Edwards Virginia hams (cooked or uncooked, bone-in or -out, whole, halves, or slices); bacons (sugar-cured, hickory-smoked, or nitrite-free), and sausages (smoked or fresh, links or patties).

Jams and Jellies, Pickles and Preserves

bedfordcheese.com. Wine jellies, hot pepper-pecan jelly, lemon curd.

sosupreme.com. Everything from blackberry jelly to peach marmalade to hot red pepper jelly. Wonderful mustards, too, plus a stellar tomato relish.

Soft Drinks

Cheerwine. Cherry-flavored soda from Salisbury, North Carolina. Available from **boiledpeanuts.com.**

Royal Crown Cola. Southerners suffering withdrawal symptoms because they can't find their favorite southern cola can order it from **boiledpeanuts.com.**

Sun Drop. Another popular southern soda available from **boiledpeanuts.com**.

Farm and Orchard Nuts

ab-nc.com. Home-style southern peanuts: blister-roasted, raw redskins, raw blanched peanuts, chocolate-dipped, and spicy, smoky Wingnuts®.

auntrubyspeanuts.com. Peanuts (the plump, sweet Virginias): salted in-the-shell, honey-roasted, raw shelled (even shelled and blanched), country-style, chocolate clusters.

byronplantation.com. Mammoth pecans in the shell or out plus pecan candies.

natchitochespecans.com. Pecans sugared, pecans spiced from a 400-acre Louisiana orchard.

thencstore.com. Toasted, wine-marinated peanuts (chardonnay or merlot), also mocha nuts, a margarita mix, and Fire Dancer jalapeño peanuts.

pearsonfarm.com. U.S. Grade #1 fancy pecans: pieces or halves, plain, roasted and salted, spiced, or chocolate-dipped.

pnuts.net. Blister-fried peanuts, spiced or chocolate-coated peanuts.

priesters.com. Gloriously fresh pecans, in the shell or out, roasted or raw plus various candied pecans. Priester's has been shelling and packing the South's finest pecans since 1935.

sunnylandfarms.com. Not just Georgia pecans; that means almonds, Brazil nuts, cashews, English walnuts, hazelnuts, macadamias, peanuts, pistachios, and hard-to-find black walnuts.

werenuts.com. Truly fresh pecans large and small, plain and fancy, plus almonds, black walnuts, Brazil nuts, cashews, and macadamias.

Wild Hickory Nuts

It takes about four hours to extract one pound of "meat" from wild hickory nuts, which explains why the shelled are so expensive. Still, if you've ever tried to do the job yourself, you will happily pay top dollar.

pinenut.com/hickory-nuts.htm. Five-pound boxes of ready-to-shell hickory nuts.

rayshickorynuts.com. Shelled hickory nuts by the pound; there's a one-pound minimum.

wildpantry.com. Shelled hickory nuts in one-pound bags.

Pottery

There are hundreds of fine potteries scattered about the South, but not all of them offer a good variety of *functional* cookware and/or tableware. These do:

bulldogpottery.com. Bruce Gholson's one-of-a-kind glazed vases, salad bowls, and other serving pieces plus Samantha Henneke's whimsical ceramic tiles.

cadyclayworks.com. Contemporary tableware, much of it with layered glazes—blue/green, orange/brown, etc. Also lidded stoneware casseroles.

chickenbridgepottery.com. Rusty Sieck's jugs and mugs, platters, bowls, and serving pieces are colorful, contemporary, and ever-changing.

gailpittman.com. Arguably Mississippi's most popular artist, Gail Pittman hand-decorates tableware in colorful designs, from the geometric to the floral.

Hickory Hill Pottery. No website; phone: 1-910-464-3166. Daniel Marley's utilitarian glazed earthenware and stoneware (pie plates, angel food cake "pans," casseroles, spoon holders, pitchers, pour bowls). Also tableware in classic shapes and simple glazes (blues, yellows, browns, white; some spatterware).

jugtownware.com. Classic country tableware and cookware: casseroles, pie plates, pour bowls, soup tureens glazed in blues, grays, bronzy greens ("frogskin"), mustardy yellows, rusts, and brown ("tobacco spit").

peterspottery.net. The four Woods brothers turn out plates, bowls, pitchers, and platters with unique "marbleized" glazes (mostly blues, rusts, and greens).

siglindascarpa.com. Unglazed, terra-cotta–colored stoneware roasters, casseroles, fish poachers, bean pots, and paella "pans" that can be used both in the oven and on the stovetop. Also glazed pitchers, teapots, platters, serving pieces.

westmoorepottery.com. Reproductions of seventeenth-, eighteenth-, and nineteenth-century redware, greenware, and salt-glazed stoneware including some Moravian plates and platters of intricate design. Also here: the candlesticks, goblets, bowls, and decanters of Virginia glassblowers John Pierce and Dave Byerly. These, too, are reproductions, in this case, of early European designs.

Syrups, Honeys, and Molasses

Cane syrup:

steensyrup.com. Aromatic pure sugarcane syrup; good for baking, for glazing hams and meat loaves, and as an all around sweetener.

Sorghum molasses (sweet sorghum):

newsomscountryham.com.

smokiesstore.org. Jars of the Smoky Mountains favorite made the age-old way.

springhillmerchant.com. North Carolina sorghum in 20-ounce Mason jars.

Sourwood honey:

Appalachian "gold," a varietal mountain honey with a buttery caramel flavor. Perfect for biscuits, perfect for baking. Because of the sourwood's intensely fragrant, cascading white blossoms, some mountain folk call it "the lily-of-the-valley tree."

exclusiveconcepts.com. Sourwood honey in one-pound jars. Also tupelo honey.

fourseasonstreasures.com. Sourwood honey with comb in 44-ounce jars.

mtnhoney.com. Honey in the bottle or honey in the comb. Also beeswax candles and frozen bee pollen.

sourwoodhoney.com. Beekeeper Chuck Norton's raw sourwood honey ("the most flavorful you can buy") in jars small, medium, and large.

Tupelo honey:

The Deep South favorite that's gained considerable cachet ever since it appeared in the movie *Ulee's Gold* (1997). The most expensive of southern varietal honeys, tupelo honey is made from the snowy blossoms of the white tupelo gum, which bloom in April and May in the Apalachicola, Choctahatchee, and Ochlockonee river valleys of northwest Florida. Top-quality pure tupelo honey is gold with glints of green. It is smooth and sweet and thanks to its high levulose content, it will never crystallize.

armsteadsporch.com. Slim 20-ounce fluted bottles of tupelo honey from the Savannah Bee Company.

floridatupelohoney.com. Unadulterated raw tupelo honey from the Smiley Apiaries, unfiltered and unheated.

dutchgoldhoney.com. One-pound jars of pure tupelo honey.

lltupelohoney.com. Jars and jugs from 12 ounces to 2½ gallons.

Wild unprocessed honey:

newsomgcountryham.com

Wines

thevirginiacompany.com. Carefully selected wines from Virginia's best vineyards.

Bibliography

Allison-Lewis, Linda. *Kentucky's Best*. Lexington: The University Press of Kentucky, 1998.

The American Heritage Cookbook and Illustrated History of American Eating and Drinking. New York: American Heritage Publishing, 1964.

Anderson, Jean. *The American Century Cookbook*. New York: Clarkson Potter, 1997.

———. *The Grass Roots Cookbook*. New York: Times Books, 1977.

———. *Recipes from America's Restored Villages*. New York: Doubleday, 1975.

Apple, R. W., Jr. *Apple's America*. New York: North Point Press, 2005.

Arnett, Earl, Robert J. Brugger, and Edward C. Papenfuse. *Maryland: A New Guide to the Old Line State*. 2nd ed. Baltimore and London: The Johns Hopkins University Press, 1999.

Auburn Entertains. Compiled by Helen Baggett, Jeanne Blackwell, and Lucy Littleton. Nashville: Rutledge Hill Press, 1983.

Barker, Ben, and Karen Barker. *Not Afraid of Flavor: Recipes from Magnolia Grill*. Chapel Hill: University of North Carolina Press, 2000.

Barker, Karen. *Sweet Stuff: Karen Barker's American Desserts*. Chapel Hill: University of North Carolina Press, 2004.

Bartram, William. *Travels of William Bartram*. Facsimile edition of the original printed in Philadelphia in 1791, edited by Mark Van Doren. New York: Dover Publications, undated.

Beard, James. *James Beard's American Cookery*. Boston: Little, Brown, 1972.

Beaumont Inn Special Recipes. Compiled by Mary Elizabeth Dedman and Thomas Curry Dedman, Jr. Louisville, KY: Allegra Print & Imaging, 1983.

Best of the Best from Louisiana: Selected Recipes from Louisiana's Favorite Cookbooks. Edited by Gwen McKee and Barbara Moseley. Baton Rouge, LA: Quail Ridge Press, 1984.

Bethabara Moravian Cook Book. 7th ed. Compiled by the Women's Fellowship, Bethabara Moravian Church, Winston-Salem, NC, 1981.

The Black Family Reunion Cookbook: Recipes and Food Memories. Compiled by the National Council of Negro Women. New York: Fireside, 1993.

Botkin, B. A. *A Treasury of American Folklore*. New York: Crown, 1944.

Brazile, Donna L. *Cooking with Grease: Stirring the Pots in American Politics*. New York: Simon and Schuster, 2004.

Brown, Dale, and the editors of Time-Life Books. *American Cooking*. New York: Time-Life Books, 1968.

Brown, Marion. *The Southern Cook Book*. Chapel Hill: University of North Carolina Press, 1951.

———. *Marion Brown's Southern Cook Book*. New ed. Chapel Hill: University of North Carolina Press, 1968.

Bryan, Lettice. *The Kentucky Housewife* (1839). Facsimile of the first edition with a new introduction by Bill Neal. Columbia: University of South Carolina Press, 1991.

Butter 'n' Love Recipes. Produced by the Crossnore Presbyterian Church, Crossnore, NC. Pleasanton, KS: Fundcraft Publishing, 1982.

Cabbage Patch Famous Kentucky Recipes. Compiled by the Cabbage Patch Circle, Louisville, KY, 1952.

Cane River Cuisine. Published by The Service League of Natchitoches, Louisiana, Inc. Memphis: Wimmer, 1974.

Cannon, Poppy, and Patricia Brooks. *The Presidents' Cookbook: Practical Recipes from George Washington to the Present*. New York: Funk & Wagnalls, 1968.

The Carolina Collection. Published by The Junior League of Fayetteville, Inc. Fayetteville, NC, 1978.

Celebrations on the Bayou. Published by The Junior League of Monroe, Inc. Monroe, LA: Cotton Bayou Publications, 1989.

Charleston Receipts. Published by The Junior League of Charleston, Inc. Charleston, SC: Walker, Evans & Cogswell Company, 1950.

Charleston Receipts Repeats. Published by The Junior League of Charleston, Inc. Charleston, SC: Walker, Evans & Cogswell Company, 1986.

Charleston Recollections and Receipts: Rose P. Ravenel's Cookbook. Edited by Elizabeth Ravenel Harrigan. Columbia: University of South Carolina Press, 1989.

The Charlotte Cookbook. Published by The Junior League of Charlotte, Inc., Charlotte, NC, 1971.

Church Mouse Cook Book. Compiled by the women of St. Paul's Episcopal Church, Ivy, VA, 1964.

Claiborne, Craig. *Craig Claiborne's Southern Cooking*. New York: Times Books, 1987.

———. *Craig Claiborne's The New York Times Food Encyclopedia*. New York: Times Books, 1985.

Collin, Rima, and Richard Collin. *The New Orleans Cookbook*. New York: Alfred A. Knopf, 1979.

Colquitt, Harriet Ross. *The Savannah Cook Book*. Introduction by Ogden Nash. New York: J. J. Little and Ives, 1933.

Come On In! Recipes from The Junior League of Jackson, Mississippi. Published by The Junior League of Jackson, Inc. Printed in Japan, 1991.

Conroy, Pat. *The Pat Conroy Cookbook: Recipes of My Life*. Recipes developed by Suzanne Williamson Pollak. New York: Nan A. Talese (Doubleday), 2004.

Cook Book. Compiled by the W.S.C.S. Methodist Church of Tate, GA, 1953.

A Cook's Tour of Athens. Compiled by The Junior Assembly of Athens, Georgia, 1963.

The Cooking Book. Published by The Junior League of Louisville, Inc. Jeffersontown, KY: Reynolds-Foley, 1978.

Cooking with Sunshine. Sunkist Kitchens, Sunkist Growers, Inc. B. J. Doerfling, recipe coordinator. New York: Atheneum, 1986.

The Cotton Country Collection. Published by The Junior League of Monroe, Inc., Monroe, LA, 1972.

Council, Mildred. *Mama Dip's Family Cookbook*. Chapel Hill: University of North Carolina Press, 2005.

———. *Mama Dip's Kitchen*. Chapel Hill: University of North Carolina Press, 1999.

Coyle, L. Patrick. *The World Encyclopedia of Food*. New York: Facts On File, 1982.

Dabney, Joseph E. *Smokehouse Ham, Spoon Bread, and Scuppernong Wine: The Folklore and Art of Southern Appalachian Cooking*. Nashville: Cumberland House, 1998.

Darden, Norma Jean, and Carole Darden. *Spoonbread and Strawberry Wine*. Garden City, NY: Doubleday, 1978.

Davidson, Alan. *The Oxford Companion to Food*. Oxford and New York: Oxford University Press, 1999.

DeBolt, Margaret Wayt, with Emma Rylander Law and Carter Olive. *Georgia Entertains*. Nashville: Rutledge Hill Press, 1983.

DeMers, John. *Arnaud's Creole Cookbook*. New York: Simon and Schuster, 1988.

Dining at Monticello in Good Taste and Abundance. Edited and with recipes by Damon Lee Fowler. Chapel Hill: University of North Carolina Press, 2005.

Doar, David. *Rice and Rice Planting in the South Carolina Low Country*. Edited by E. Milby Burton. Charleston, SC: 1936.

DuBose, Sybil. *The Pastors' Wives Cookbook*. Memphis, TN: Wimmer Brothers Books, 1978.

Dull, Mrs. S. R. *Southern Cooking*. 1928. Revised ed. New York: Grosset & Dunlap, 1968.

Dyer, Ceil. *The Carter Family Favorites Cookbook*. New York: Delacorte Press/Eleanor Friede, 1976.

Edge, John T. *A Gracious Plenty: Recipes and Reflections from the American South*. New York: HP Books, 2002.

———. *Fried Chicken: An American Story*. New York: Putnam Publishing Group, 2004.

———. *Southern Belly: The Ultimate Food Lover's Guide to the South*. Atlanta: Hill Street Press, 2002.

Egerton, John. *Southern Food: At Home, on the Road, in History*. New York: Alfred A.Knopf, 1987.

The Farmington Cookbook. A fund-raiser published to benefit Farmington, an 1810 Federal-style Kentucky home designed by Thomas Jefferson. Louisville, KY: Courier-Journal Lithographing, 1968.

Favorite Recipes of the Lower Cape Fear. Published by the Ministering Circle, Wilmington, NC. Revised ed., 1980.

Feibleman, Peter S., and the editors of Time-Life Books. *American Cooking: Creole and Acadian*. New York: Time-Life Books, 1971.

Flexner, Marion. *Out of Kentucky Kitchens*. New York: American Legacy Press, 1949.

Follett, Richard. *The Sugar Masters: Planters and Slaves in Louisiana's Cane World, 1820–1860*. Baton Rouge: Louisiana State University Press, 2005.

Folse, John D. *The Encyclopedia of Cajun and Creole Cuisine*. Gonzales, LA: Chef John Folse & Company Publishing, 2004.

Food Editors' Hometown Favorites Cookbook. Edited by Barbara Gibbs Ostmann and Jane Baker for The Food Editors and Writers Association, Inc. Maplewood, NJ: Hammond, 1984.

Foods that Rate at NC State. Compiled by the State College Woman's Club of the North Carolina State College of Agriculture and Engineering: Raleigh, 1948.

Footsteps in the Kitchen: Heritage and Contemporary Recipes from the Pencsak, Mumford, Gibson, and Reed Extended Families. Compiled and edited by Nancy Mumford Pencsak in association with Chef Marion Gibson. Dallas: Nancy Mumford Pencsak, 2003.

Fowler, Damon Lee. *Damon Lee Fowler's New Southern Baking: Classic Flavors for Today's Cooks*. New York: Simon and Schuster, 2005.

———. *Damon Lee Fowler's New Southern Kitchen: Traditional Flavors for Contemporary Cooks*. New York: Simon and Schuster, 2002.

Fox, Minnie C. *The Blue Grass Cook Book*, 1904. Facsimile of the first edition with a new introduction by Toni Tipton-Martin. Lexington: University of Kentucky Press, 2005.

From North Carolina Kitchens: Favorite Recipes Old and New. Compiled by the North Carolina Federation of Home Demonstration Clubs. Raleigh: North Carolina State College Press, 1953.

From the Heart of Our Kitchen: Cooking with the Bread Lady and Friends. Compiled by the Kathryn F. Rhodes Liver Transplant Committee. Raleigh, NC: Marblehead Printing and Publishing Co., 1997.

Fullinwider, Rowena J., James A. Crutchfield, and Winette Sparkman Jeffery. *Celebrate Virginia! Cookbook*. Nashville: Cool Springs Press, 2002.

Full Moon, High Tide: Tastes and Traditions of the Lowcountry. Compiled by the Beaufort (SC) Academy. Memphis: Wimmer Cookbooks, 2001.

Furrh, Mary Leigh, and Jo Barksdale. *Great Desserts of the South*. Gretna, LA: Pelican Publishing Company, 1988.

Fussell, Betty. *Crazy for Corn*. New York: HarperPerennial, 1995.

———. *I Hear America Cooking*. New York: Viking, 1986.

———. *The Story of Corn*. New York: Alfred A. Knopf, 1992.

Gantt, Jesse Edward, Jr., and Veronica Davis Gerald. *The Ultimate Gullah Cookbook*. Beaufort, SC: Sands Publishing Company, 2003.

Garner, Bob. *North Carolina Barbecue*. Winston-Salem, NC: John F. Blair, Publisher, 1996.

Gasparilla Cookbook: Favorite Florida West Coast Recipes. Compiled by The Junior League of Tampa, Inc., 1961.

Good Recipes by Athens' Housewives. Compiled by Circle 6 of Athens, GA, 1916–1917.

Gracious Goodness! Compiled by The Junior League of Macon, Georgia, Inc. Memphis: Wimmer, 1981.

Great Baking Begins with White Lily Flour. Produced by the White Lily Foods Company, Knoxville, TN. Des Moines: Meredith Publishing, 1982.

Guste, Roy F., Jr. *Antoine's Since 1840 Cookbook.* New York: W. W. Norton, 1980.

———. *The Restaurants of New Orleans.* New York: W. W. Norton, 1982.

Hanley, Rosemary, and Peter Hanley. *America's Best Recipes: State Fair Blue Ribbon Winners.* Boston: Little, Brown, 1983.

Harris, Jessica B. *The Africa Cookbook.* New York: Simon and Schuster, 1998.

———. *Beyond Gumbo: Creole Fusion Food from the Atlantic Rim.* New York: Simon and Schuster, 2003.

———. *Iron Pots & Wooden Spoons: Africa's Gifts to New World Cooking.* Fireside edition. New York: Simon and Schuster, 1999.

———. *The Welcome Table: African-American Heritage Cooking.* New York: Simon and Schuster, 1996.

Hartley, Dorothy. *Food in England.* London: MacDonald & Company, 1954.

Hays, Constance L. *The Real Thing: Truth and Power at the Coca-Cola Company.* New York: Random House, 2004.

Hearn, Lafcadio. *Lafcadio Hearn's Creole Cook Book.* Facsimile edition with added drawings and writings made during Hearn's stay in New Orleans from 1877 to 1887. Gretna, LA: Pelican Publishing Company, 1990.

Heritage Corn Meal Cookery. Compiled by York Kiker for the North Carolina Department of Agriculture, Markets Division; published by the North Carolina Corn Millers Association. Raleigh: Litho Industries, Inc., 1970.

Heritage Recipes. Compiled by the Haywood County Extension Homemakers. Waynesville, NC: 1971.

Hess, John L., and Karen Hess. *The Taste of America.* New York: Viking/Grossman, 1977.

Hess, Karen. *The Carolina Rice Kitchen: The African Connection.* Featuring in facsimile: *Carolina Rice Cook Book* (1901). Mrs. Samuel G. Stoney. Columbia: University of South Carolina Press, 1992.

Hewitt, Jean. *The New York Times Southern Heritage Cookbook.* New York: G. P. Putnam's Sons, 1972.

Hibben, Sheila. *The National Cookbook.* New York: Harper & Brothers, 1932.

Hill, Albert F. *Economy Botany.* New York: McGraw-Hill, 1952.

Hill, Annabella P. *Mrs. Hill's Southern Practical Cookery and Receipt Book.* 1872. Facsimile edition with observations and explanations by Damon Lee Fowler. Columbia, SC: University of South Carolina Press, 1995.

Hooker, Richard J. *A History: Food and Drink in America.* Indianapolis/New York: Bobbs-Merrill, 1981.

Horry, Harriott Pinckney. *A Colonial Plantation Cookbook: The Receipt Book of Harriott Pinckney Horry.* 1770. Facsimile edition edited by Richard J. Hooker. Columbia, SC: University of South Carolina Press, 1984.

Jim Graham's Farm Family Cookbook for City Folks. Published by the Office of College Advancement, College of Agriculture and Life Sciences, North Carolina State University. Raleigh, NC: 2002.

Jones, Evan. *American Food: The Gastronomic Story.* New York: E. P. Dutton, 1975.

Key West Cook Book. Published by The Key West Woman's Club. Key West, 1949.

Kimball, Marie. *Thomas Jefferson's Cook Book.* Charlottesville: University of Virginia, 1993.

Kremer, Elizabeth C. *We Make You Kindly Welcome: Recipes from the Trustees' House Daily Fare, Pleasant Hill, Kentucky.* Harrodsburg: Pleasant Hill Press, 1970.

———. *Welcome Back to Pleasant Hill: More Recipes from the Trustees' House, Pleasant Hill, Kentucky.* Harrodsburg: Pleasant Hill Press, 1977.

Kronsberg, Jane. *Charleston: People, Places, Food.* Charleston: Wyrick & Company, 1997.

Land, Mary. *Louisiana Cookery.* Jackson: University of Mississippi Press, 2005.

Landon, Luann. *Dinner at Miss Lady's.* Chapel Hill, NC: Algonquin Books, 1999.

Lewis, Edna. *The Taste of Country Cooking.* New York: Alfred A. Knopf, 1976.

Lewis, Edna, and Scott Peacock. *The Gift of Southern Cooking.* New York: Alfred A. Knopf, 2003.

Louisiana, A Guide to the State. New revised ed., Harry Hansen, ed., American Guide Series, originally compiled by the Federal Writers' Program of the Work Projects Administration of the State of Louisiana. New York: Hastings House, 1971.

Lovegren, Sylvia. *Fashionable Food*. New York: Macmillan, 1995.

Lundy, Ronni. *Butter Beans to Blackberries: Recipes from the Southern Garden*. New York: North Point Press, 1999.

———. *Shuck Beans, Stack Cakes, and Honest Fried Chicken: The Heart and Soul of Southern Country Kitchens*. New York: Atlantic Monthly Press, 1991.

Mariani, John F. *The Dictionary of American Food and Drink*. Completely revised and updated edition. New York: Hearst Books, 1994.

———. *America Eats Out: An Illustrated History of Restaurants, Taverns, Coffee Shops, Speakeasies, and Other Establishments that Have Fed Us for 350 Years*. New York: William Morrow, 1991.

Martha Washington's Booke of Cookery and Booke of Sweetmeats. Transcribed by Karen Hess. New York: Columbia University Press, 1995.

Martha White's Southern Sampler. Produced by Martha White Foods, Inc. Nashville: Rutledge Hill Press, 1989.

Maryland's Way: The Hammond-Harwood House Cook Book. Annapolis: The Hammond-Harwood House Association, 1963.

Masters, Colonel Michael Edward. *Hospitality– Kentucky Style*. Bardstown, KY: Equine Writer's Press, 2000.

McClane, A. J. *The Encyclopedia of Fish Cookery*. New York: Holt, Rinehart and Winston, 1977.

Mead, Anne. *Please Kiss the Cook*. New York: Self-published, 1964.

More Gems from Many Kitchens. Compiled by The Garden Club of Georgia, Athens, GA: 1971.

Natchez: Authentic Antebellum Recipes of the Old South, 1790-1865. Compiled by Southland Graphics. Kingsport, TN: 1987.

Neal, Bill. *Bill Neal's Southern Cooking*. Chapel Hill: University of North Carolina Press, 1985.

———. *Biscuits, Spoonbread, and Sweet Potato Pie*. New York: Alfred A. Knopf, 1990.

Neal, Bill, and David Perry. *Good Old Grits Cookbook*. New York: Workman, 1991.

Neal, Moreton. *Remembering Bill Neal: Favorite Recipes from a Life in Cooking*. Chapel Hill: University of North Carolina Press, 2004.

The North Carolina Guide. Edited by Blackwell P. Robinson. Chapel Hill: University of North Carolina Press, 1955.

Of Pots and Pipkins: Recipes from The Junior League of Roanoke Valley, Virginia, Inc. Roanoke: Stone Printing Company, 1971.

Osteen, Louis. *Louis Osteen's Charleston Cuisine: Recipes from a Lowcountry Chef*. Chapel Hill, NC: Algonquin Books, 1999.

Paddleford, Clementine. *How America Eats*. New York: Charles Scribner's Sons, 1960.

Paths of Sunshine Cookbook. Published by the Florida Federation of Garden Clubs, Inc. Memphis: Wimmer, 1988.

Patteson, Charles. *Charles Patteson's Kentucky Cooking*. New York: Harper & Row, 1988.

Pendergrast, Mark. *For God, Country & Coca-Cola*. 2nd ed., revised and expanded. New York: Basic Books, 2000.

Peterson, James. *Fish & Shellfish*. New York: William Morrow, 1996.

The Picayune's Creole Cook Book, Sesquicentennial ed. Edited by Marcelle Bienvenu. New Orleans: *The Times-Picayune*, 1987.

Pinckney, Eliza Lucas. *The Letterbook of Eliza Lucas Pinckney, 1739–1762*. Edited, with a new introduction, by Elise Pinckney. Columbia: The University of South Carolina Press, 1997.

Pinderhughes, John. *Family of the Spirit Cookbook: Recipes and Reminiscences from African-American Kitchens*. New York: Simon and Schuster, 1990.

Pinson, Maxine, and Malyssa Pinson. *Lowcountry Delights*. Savannah, GA: SSD, Inc., 2002.

The Plantation Cookbook. By the Junior League of New Orleans. Garden City, NY: Doubleday & Company, 1972.

Plantation Country. Published by the Women's Service League of St. Francisville, Louisiana. Baton Rouge: Land and Land Printers, 1981.

Prudhomme, Paul. *Chef Paul Prudhomme's Louisiana Kitchen*. New York: William Morrow, 1984.

Putting on the Grits. Published by The Junior League of Columbia, South Carolina, Inc. Columbia: State Printing Company, 1985.

Randolph, Mary. The Virginia House-wife. 1824. Facsimile of the first edition with additional material from the 1825 and 1828 editions; historical notes and commentaries by Karen Hess. Columbia: University of South Carolina Press, 1984.

Rawlings, Marjorie Kinnan. Cross Creek Cookery. New York: C. Scribner's Sons, 1942.

———. Cross Creek. New York: C. Scribner's Sons, 1942.

River Road Recipes. Produced by The Junior League of Baton Rouge, Inc, Baton Rouge, LA. Memphis: Wimmer Cookbooks, 1959.

River Road Recipes II: A Second Helping. Produced by The Junior League of Baton Rouge, Inc, Baton Rouge, LA. Memphis: Wimmer Cookbooks, 1976.

Roanoke Island Cook Book. Compiled by Members and Friends of the Manteo Woman's Club. Manteo, NC: Times Printing Company, undated.

Robinson, Sallie Ann. Gullah Home Cooking the Daufuskie Way: Smokin' Joe Butter Beans, Ol' 'Fuskie Fried Crab Rice, Sticky-Bush Blackberry Dumpling, and Other Sea Island Favorites. Foreword by Pat Conroy. Chapel Hill: University of North Carolina Press, 2003.

Root, Waverley. Food. New York: Simon and Schuster, 1980.

Root, Waverley, and Richard de Rochemont. Eating in America. New York: William Morrow, 1976.

Rudisill, Marie. Sook's Cookbook: Memories and Traditional Recipes from the Deep South. Atlanta: Longstreet Press, 1989.

———. Fruitcake: Memories of Truman Capote & Sook. Athens, GA: Hill Street Press, 2000.

Rutledge, Sarah. The Carolina Housewife. 1847. Facsimile edition with a new introduction by Anna Wells Rutledge. Columbia: University of South Carolina Press, 1979.

Sanders, Dori. Dori Sanders' Country Cooking: Recipes and Stories from the Family Farm Stand. Chapel Hill, NC: Algonquin Books, 1995.

Savannah Style. Published by The Junior League of Savannah, Inc. Memphis: Wimmer, undated.

Schneider, Elizabeth. Uncommon Fruits & Vegetables: A Commonsense Guide. New York: Harper & Row, 1986.

———. Vegetables from Amaranth to Zucchini. New York: William Morrow, 2001.

Sea Island Seasons. Published by Beaufort County (SC) Open Land Trust. Memphis: Wimmer Cookbooks, 1980.

Shields, John. The Chesapeake Bay Cookbook. Berkeley, CA: Aris Books, 1990.

Simmons, Marie. Rice: The Amazing Grain. New York: Henry Holt, 1991.

Smalls, Alexander, with Hettie Jones. Grace the Table: Stories and Recipes from My Southern Revival. Foreword by Wynton Marsalis. New York: HarperCollins, 1997.

Smith, Andrew. The Tomato in America: Early History, Culture and Cookery. Columbia: University of South Carolina Press, 1994.

Smith, Bill. Seasoned in the South: Recipes from Crook's Corner and from Home. Chapel Hill, NC: Algonquin Books, 2005.

The South Carolina Cook Book. Revised ed. Collected and edited by the South Carolina Extension Homemakers Council and the Clemson Extension Home Economics Staff. Columbia: University of South Carolina Press, 1953.

South Carolina: The WPA Guide to the Palmetto State. 1988 edition. Compiled by the Workers of the Writers' Program of the Work Projects Administration in the State of South Carolina with a new introduction and two new appendices by Walter B. Edgar. Columbia: University of South Carolina Press, 1988.

Southern Foodways Alliance. Cornbread Nation 1: The Best of Southern Food Writing. Edited by John Egerton. Chapel Hill: University of North Carolina Press, 2002.

———. Cornbread Nation 2: The United States of Barbecue; The Best of Southern Food Writing. Edited by Lolis Eric Elie. Chapel Hill: University of North Carolina Press, 2004.

———. Cornbread Nation 3: Foods of the Mountain South: The Best of Southern Food Writing. Edited by Ronni Lundy. Chapel Hill: University of North Carolina Press, 2005.

The Southern Junior League Cookbook. Edited by Ann Seranne. New York: David McKay, 1977.

Sparks, Elizabeth Hedgecock (Beth Tartan). *North Carolina and Old Salem Cookery*. 4th ed. Charlotte, NC: The Dowd Press, Inc., 1969.

Stern, Jane, and Michael Stern. *American Gourmet*. New York: HarperCollins, 1991.

———. *Real American Food*. New York: Alfred A. Knopf, 1986.

———. *Roadfood*. New York: Random House, 1977.

———. *Square Meals*. New York: Alfred A. Knopf, 1984.

———. *A Taste of America*. Kansas City/New York: Andrews and McMeel, 1988.

Stitt, Frank. *Frank Stitt's Southern Table: Recipes and Gracious Traditions from Highlands Bar and Grill*. New York: Artisan, 2004.

Strickland, Sharon A., and Rosemary A. Newman. *Southern Ladies Know How To Cook It*. Savannah: Self-published, 1998.

Sturtevant's Notes on Edible Plants. Edited by U. P. Hedrick. Albany: J. B. Lyon Co., 1919.

Sturges, Lena E. *Southern Living: Our Best Recipes*. Birmingham, AL: Oxmoor House, 1970.

Taylor, John Martin. *Hoppin' John's Lowcountry Cooking*. New York: Bantam Books, 1992.

Taylor, Joyce. *Mariner's Menu: 30 Years of Fresh Seafood Ideas*. Chapel Hill: University of North Carolina Press, 2003.

Terry, Elizabeth, with Alexis Terry. *Savannah Seasons: Food and Stories from Elizabeth on 37th*. New York: Doubleday, 1996.

300 Years of Carolina Cooking. Tricentennial edition. Published by The Junior League of Greenville, Inc. Greenville, SC: 1970.

Thorne, John, with Matt Lewis Thorne. *Serious Pig: An American Cook in Search of His Roots*. New York: Farrar, Straus & Giroux, 1996.

Thorne, John. *Simple Cooking*. New York: Viking Penguin, 1987.

Toast to Tidewater: Celebrating Virginia's Finest Food & Beverages. Published by The Junior League of Norfolk-Virginia Beach, Inc. Norfolk: Teagle and Little, Inc., 2004.

Trager, James. *Foodbook*. New York: Grossman, 1970.

———. *The Food Chronology*. New York: Henry Holt, 1995.

Two Hundred Years of Charleston Cooking. Recipes gathered by Blanche S. Rhett; edited by Lettie Gay; facsimile of original 1930 edition. Columbia, SC: University of South Carolina Press, 1976.

Very Virginia. Compiled by The Junior League of Hampton Roads, Inc. Memphis: Starr-Toof, 1995.

Villas, James. *Biscuit Bliss*. Boston: Harvard Common Press, 2003.

———. *James Villas' Country Cooking*. Boston, Toronto: Little, Brown and Company, 1988.

Villas, James, with Martha Pearl Villas. *My Mother's Southern Desserts*. New York: William Morrow, 1998.

———. *My Mother's Southern Kitchen: Recipes and Reminiscences*. New York: Macmillan, 1994.

Vintage Vicksburg. Compiled by the Junior Auxiliary of Vicksburg, Mississippi. Memphis: Wimmer, 1985.

Virginia Cookery Past and Present. Compiled by the Woman's Auxiliary of Olivet Episcopal Church, Franconia, Virginia: 1957.

Voltz, Jeanne A. *The Flavor of the South: Delicacies and Staples of Southern Cuisine*. New York: Doubleday & Company, 1977.

Voltz, Jeanne, and Caroline Stuart. *The Florida Cookbook: From Gulf Coast Gumbo to Key Lime Pie*. New York: Alfred A. Knopf, 1993.

Walter, Eugene, and the editors of Time-Life Books. *American Cooking: Southern Style*. New York: Time-Life Books, 1971.

Ward, Artemas. *The Encyclopedia of Food*. New York: Artemas Ward, 1923.

Warner, William W. *Beautiful Swimmers: Watermen, Crabs and the Chesapeake Bay*. Boston: Atlantic Monthly Press by Little, Brown and Company, 1976.

The Williamsburg Art of Cookery or Accomplish'd Gentlewoman's Companion: Being a Collection of Upwards of Five Hundred of the Most Ancient & Approv'd Recipes in Virginia Cookery. Edited by Helen Bullock. Williamsburg: The Colonial Williamsburg Foundation, 1985.

The Williamsburg Cookbook. Originally compiled and adapted by Letha Booth; updated and enlarged by the staff of Colonial Williamsburg with commentary by Joan Parry Dutton. Williamsburg: The Colonial Williamsburg Foundation, 1975.

The World Atlas of Food. Jane Grigson, contributing editor. London: Mitchell Beazley Publishers, and New York: Simon and Schuster, 1974.

The WPA Guide to Florida: The Federal Writers' Project Guide to 1930s Florida. 1984 ed. Compiled by the Workers of the Writers' Program of the Work Projects Administration in the State of Florida with a new introduction by John I. McCollum. New York: Pantheon Books, 1984.

Zimmer, Anne Carter. *The Robert E. Lee Family Cooking and Housekeeping Book*. Chapel Hill: University of North Carolina Press, 1997.

Index